TO HONOR
THESE MEN

MERCER
UNIVERSITY PRESS

Endowed by
TOM WATSON BROWN
and
THE WATSON-BROWN FOUNDATION, INC.

TO HONOR
THESE MEN

A HISTORY OF THE PHILLIPS GEORGIA
LEGION INFANTRY BATTALION

RICHARD M. COFFMAN

and

KURT D. GRAHAM

MERCER UNIVERSITY PRESS

MACON, GEORGIA

MERCER

MUP/H733

© 2007 Mercer University Press
1400 Coleman Avenue
Macon, Georgia 31207

First Edition.

Library of Congress Cataloging-in-Publication Data

Coffman, Richard M.
To honor these men:
a history of the Phillips Georgia Legion InfantryBattalion
Richard M. Coffman and Kurt D. Graham–1st ed.
p. cm.
Includes bibliographical references and index.
ISBN-13: 978-0-88146-060-5 | ISBN-10: 0-88146-060-5
(hardback: alk. paper)
1. Confederate States of America. Army. Phillips Legion. Infantry Battalion.
2. United States–History–Civil War, 1861-1865–Regimental histories.
3. United States–History–Civil War, 1861-1865–Campaigns.
4. Georgia–History–Civil War, 1861-1865–Regimental histories.
I. Graham, Kurt D. II. Title.
E559.5.P44C64 2007
973.7'42–dc22

2007039610

This book is dedicated to the memory of my Georgia ancestors who fought in the most calamitous war in American history. They include my great-great grandfather John Fielding Milhollin and his brothers-in-law, Alfred Newton Dodgen, John Calvin Dodgen, and William M. Dodgen. My great-great grandmother, Lucinda Eveline Dodgen Milhollin, also fought bravely on the home front. She was a tiny woman, just over 5 feet tall. After enduring the burning of her home in Cassville, Georgia, by the 5th Ohio Volunteer Cavalry, she confronted one of this unit's officers the next morning when he tried to lure her into accompanying him back to Ohio. She stood her ground and told him in Victorian parlance what to do with his offer, then collected her six children and youngest sister Jane, moved in with the next-door neighbors, raised her family, and died in 1914 at 82 years of age at her home in Cassville.

Richard M. Coffman

For my grandfather, Griffith Smith Graham, who encouraged me to read and opened my eyes to the world.

Kurt D. Graham

Contents

Preface

As far back as I can remember, a faded copy of a nineteenth-century ambrotype was the centerpiece of my home in Dayton, Ohio. My mother, an antiques dealer for over forty years, had positioned the old photograph in a place of honor on the mantelpiece above our fireplace. Hazel, my mother, always reminded me that my great-great grandfather, Captain John Fielding Milhollin, the subject of the photograph, was watching me. Like many of these early images, the bearded soldier stood stiffly at attention in his cadet gray uniform, saber in hand with blade over his right shoulder and full-fluted army pistol in his belt. His facial expression suggested no nonsense, sternness I had never known in my young life. My great-great grandfather had been the commander of Company B of the Phillips Georgia Legion Cavalry Battalion. He was killed on 10 November 1863 while leading a scout near Brandy Station, Virginia.

I was only mildly curious about all this in my early adolescence and somewhat unnerved that someone who had been dead for nearly a century and a half might be observing my every move, evaluating me. Shortly after this warning, my parents enrolled me in the oldest private military school in the country, Kentucky Military Institute, where I spent my high school years. Time passed, along with my college years at Ohio State University. The cold war was getting hotter every day and I decided to attend Officer Training School in the United States Air Force, become an officer, and serve my country. After my Vietnam tour, I was assigned to the faculty of the United States Air Force Academy. A friend in the history department insisted I read the book *Killer Angels* by Michael Shaara. Reading this fascinating novel was the first benchmark that led me to a writing project on the Legion that lasted for over a decade. Who was my great-great grandfather? Where did he live? How was he killed? The research for the answers to these questions further piqued my fascination. I learned that Grandfather was a Confederate officer in a Georgia Legion. This was confusing. I knew about Roman legions but had no idea why legions, or small field armies, existed during the Civil War. I discovered that a "true" Civil War legion was intended to be a small field army consisting of all three combat arms: infantry, cavalry, and artillery, somewhat like a modern regimental combat team.

Amazingly enough I discovered that nothing had ever been written in the form of journal articles or books on the Phillips Georgia Legion. This was probably the reason Grandfather had glared at me, perhaps telling me—"You do it. If you don't, nobody will." I began collecting period photographs, copies of period letters I found from networking with Civil War scholars and buffs and my own elderly family members, diaries, newspaper articles, memoirs, and reminiscences—anything I could find that had a connection to the legion. I met many generous and kind people at places such as Dahlonega, Georgia. One sweet lady with a delightful sense of humor told me about her Legion grandfather but informed me I couldn't have copies of his letters because they were in a trunk that had a snake in it. (In spite of the snake, I managed to get copies of them later.)

Grandfather's three brothers-in-law were Phillips Legion soldiers. One was with him when he was hit by grapeshot and died after suffering through the night at Brandy Station. Grandfather's brother-in-law John Dodgen, a Company B soldier, attended the premier opening in Atlanta of the clas*sic* film *Gone with the Wind*. John lived with my mother and her father in South Georgia just before the First World War. He shared stories of his war experiences with my mother, who shared them with me.

While stationed with the Air Force Reserve Officers Training Corps detachment at Rutgers University, I befriended the military historian Dr. Richard H. Kohn and studied under him in a military history writing course. My literary skills improved and I produced an article for the *Civil War Times Illustrated* on the Phillips Georgia Legion. My friendship with Dick Kohn, which has endured through the years, was the second benchmark that led to this book. In truth, Dick, if it had not been for your friendship and encouragement as well as your harsh critiques, this book would never have come to fruition.

The letters and the diaries told me what these men had been through. Their experience seemed to be to be far more than they could possibly bear. How did they do it? How did they find the courage to go on after hearing the moaning of the wounded and dying all night at Marye's Heights, and seeing the thousands of dead Union soldiers on the field the next morning? We tried to trace combat and personal experiences of the Phillips Legion troops and bring them to life, having them speak in their own words. These young men (and a few old ones) came from fifteen North Georgia counties, most located in the northern part of the state. The letters told us that they bonded closely with each other as soldiers always do. These bonds maintained them through the worst fighting in Maryland, Pennsylvania, Tennessee, western Virginia, and Virginia. Men like Jesse McDonald, Daniel B. Sanford, and Tom Mitchell yearned for home. The memories of the backbreaking farm work they had endured while growing up drifted to thoughts of Sunday dinners and the price of corn. They pleaded with family and friends for clothing, anything to cover the holes in their ragged uniforms, and blankets to keep them warm. Jesse McDonald professed abounding love for his wife Sally. Some, deeply religious, left their future in the hands of God.

My work started with a magazine article and grew into this book. My wife and I drove countless miles visiting battlefields, university libraries, and Civil War shows searching for clues, anything that would help us tell these men's lives. I was extremely fortunate to find my coauthor and friend Kurt Graham. I have him to thank for the accuracy of all sixteen chapters. He is literally a walking encyclopedia of the Civil War. I do not believe this project would have come together if it had not been for Kurt. He did far more than any coauthor could or would. Kurt has memorized the Legion's troop movements and battlefield locations for all of the battles in which they participated. Working with Kurt was a great pleasure. We also want to thank Richard Reeves for sharing his in-depth research and for permission to use the image of his Legion ancestor. Lieutenant Colonel Frederick V. Malmstrom saved the day on more than one occasion. Several distinguished historians gave freely of their time. Kurt and I are indebted to Frank A. O'Reilly, Robert Krick, Mac Wyckoff, Kent McCoury, and Keith Bohannon. We would also like to thank the following fine people for their help with research as well as their encouragement: David and CeCe Gandy, Brigadier General John H. Napier, Dr. Ann Bailey, Henry Howell, Dr. Donald Hopkins, Jane A. Benson, Greg White, Steve Stotelmyer, Jimmy Anderson, Colonel Joseph Alexander, Libby Buchanan, Wilena B. Branch, Steven Catlett, Ione Crow, Richard B. Domingos, Bobby Horton, Ann Kadham, Howard M. Madaus, Laura Beardsley, James Chandler Peterson, Mary Carolyn Mitton, Barbara and Don Penn, Fritz Rauschenberg, Dr.

Gerald A. Smith, Martha Tripod, David Vaughn, and Dr. Stephen Wise. In addition, numerous decendents of Legion soldiers contributed a great deal of information concerning their ancestors. Many libraries and historical societies opened their doors for us, for which we are very grateful. They include: the United States Army Military History Institute, Atlanta History Center, Georgia Historical Society, Georgia Genealogical Society, Cobb County Library's Georgia Room, University of Georgia's Hargrett Library, Georgia Archives, Alabama Department of Archives and History, Cedartown Library, Chattanooga-Hamilton Library, Clayton Library, Central Georgia Genealogical Society, Dalton Historical Society, Robert W. Woodruff Library of Emory University, James A. Rogers Library of Francis Marion University, Florence County Library, Greene County Library, Ida Hilton Public Library, R. T. Jones Memorial Library, Laurens County Library, Magnus Library, Macon Historical Society, McClung Historical Collection, Monroe-Walton County Library, Norris Library, Newnan-Coweta Historical Society, Richard J. Reardon of the Central Library Local History Department in Los Angeles, California, Rockmart Library, Ringgold Library, East Tennessee Historical Society, City of Houston Public Library, and Washington Library. Special thanks to the best researchers I have ever known: Deborah Petite, Amanda Cook, and Charlotte Ray. I will be forever grateful for the unflagging encouragement I received from my wife Scintilla and my children, Kevin, Rachel, Christopher, and Rebecca. No man is more blessed than I am for the wonderful wife and children that have been granted to me. Thanks also to all those I may not have mentioned but who helped us in this endeavor. They were "Legion."

Pvt. Robert Hammond Baker enlisted in Co. B at age 18 in June 1861.
He was wounded through both thighs and in the head at Chancellorsville
in May 1863. Deemed unfit for field service, he was reassigned to the
Quartermaster's Dept in Charleston, S.C.

Cpl. Augustus "Gus" Franklin Boyd enlisted in Co. E at age 16 in June 1861.
He transferred to the 52nd Georgia Infantry in March 1862 as Sgt Major.
Elected Captain of Co. B, he was killed at the battle of Champions Hill, Mississippi
on May 16, 1863

Pvt. Virgil V. Brown enlisted in Co. D in June 1861. Already wounded once at Gettysburg, he was wounded again at Cold Harbor in June 1864. Furloughed home to recover, he was captured by Federals and executed as a spy.

Robert Pinkney Burnett enlisted in Co. A at age 29 in June 1861. This photo shows him in the distinctive navy blue uniform worn by Co. A in 1861. Burnett served through the war until being captured April 6, 1865 at Sailors Creek, VA.

Lt. Alexander Smith Erwin enlisted in Co. C at age 17 in June 1861. Severely wounded in the right arm near Chattanooga on September 24, 1863, Erwin spent the rest of the war as a recruiting/conscript officer in Georgia. Ending the war as Captain of Co. C, Erwin became the recipient of Confederate Cross of Honor # 1.

Fourteen-year old GMI Cadet **Coatesworth C. Hamilton** trained Legion soldiers at Camp McDonald in 1861 before going north to Virginia as an aide to his brother, Captain Joseph Hamilton. He died from typhoid on the retreat from western Virginia in November 1861.

Lt. Colonel Joseph E. Hamilton shown as a 20-year old student at Wofford College in 1859 and as Lt. Colonel commanding the Legion infantry in 1864. Hamilton was wounded three times during the war but survived to become an educator in southern California. These pictures clearly illustrate the effects of four years of war..

Lt. Henry Johnson McCormick (at left) enlisted in Co. O at age 23 in May 1862. Later that same month near Pocataligo, S.C. his left ankle was shattered by the accidental discharge of one of his men's muskets. Following amputation, McCormick would spend the rest of the war in Georgia serving as a recruiting/conscript officer.

Lt. William Rhadamanthus Montgomery enlisted in Co. L at age 23 in April 1862 as 1st Sergeant. Promoted to 1st Lieutenant in the 3rd Georgia Sharpshooter Battalion in April 1863, he left a valuable diary and letter collection.

Lt. American Ford Johnson transferred into Co. L from the 10th Alabama infantry as a Sergeant in early 1863. His older brother, James, was the Captain of Co. L. Promoted to Lieutenant after being wounded at Gettysburg, he was severely wounded in front of Fort Sanders at Knoxville TN in November 1863 and retired from the service.

Capt James M. Johnson enlisted as Captain of Co. L in April 1862.
Wounded at South Mountain and Fredericksburg, he was killed storming Fort
Sanders at Knoxville in November 1863. He lies in an unmarked grave in the
Knoxville City Cemetery.

Lt. Abraham "Ham" Jones enlisted in Co. D at age 34 in June 1861.
Younger brother of Lt. Colonel Seaborn Jones. "Ham" would be killed at Fox's
Gap on South Mountain September 14, 1862.

Capt Leroy Napier, founded Napier Artillery, later known
as Macon Light Artillery

Pvt. Jesse Monroe Pendley enlisted in Co. C at age 25 in March 1862. Pendley
sports a rare McElroy "lasso knife" and model 1855 rifle with sword bayonet.
Wounded at Gettysburg, Pendley survived the war and lived until 1909 in Alabama.

Colonel William M. Phillips founded his Legion in 1861 and led it until forced to resign in February 1863 due to the effects of typhoid fever. Phillips was prominent in postwar Georgia politics and built a railroad through north Georgia. He died in 1908 and is buried in the Marietta City Cemetery.

Pvt. Mark Reeves enlisted in Co. M at age 27 in April 1862. Although in poor health throughout the war, he remained with his company and fought in all of its battles. He survived the war and lived to be 83 years old.

Captain Daniel Benjamin Sanford enlisted in Co. A as a Private in June 1861. Promoted to Lieutenant in December 1861, Sanford would rise to Captain in May 1864. Severely wounded April 6, 1865 at Sailors Creek, VA, he survived the war. Sanford was prominent in the Milledgeville, GA community after the war and passed away at age 73 in 1910.

Surgeon William Francis Shine, a Florida native, became the Legion's surgeon in July 1863. He became the surgeon for Wofford's brigade in July 1864 and served in that capacity until war's end. After the war he practiced medicine at St. Augustine, FL until dying there at age 75 in 1910.

Chaplain George Gilman Smith went to war with the Legion in 1861.
A prolific writer of Methodist church history, Smith left a wonderful account
of his wartime experiences until he was shot in the neck and crippled
at South Mountain in September 1862.

Pvt. Samuel Hunter Scott enlisted in Co. O at age 25 in May 1862. Scott served
with the Legion until returning home during the autumn of 1863 and joining the
1st Georgia Cavalry (an Army of Tennessee unit). Sam served out the war with the
cavalry and rose to the rank of Lieutenant.

Cpl. John William Turner Hutcheson enlisted in Co. E at age 21 in July 1861. Promoted to Corporal in 1862, Hutcheson was severely wounded in the leg at Second Manassas August 30, 1862. Promoted to Sergeant in 1863, he was wounded again at Chancellorsville. After having his finger shot off at Spotsylvania in May 1864, he went home on wounded furlough and never returned.

Pvt. John Williams (Johann Wilhelm) was born in Bavaria in 1844 before moving to New York City with his parents in 1845. Now using the name John Williams, he was working for his uncle in Greene County GA when war broke out in 1861. Joining Co. A, he served faithfully through the entire war without injury. After the surrender, he returned to New York City, married, raised a large family and passed away in 1921.

Pvt. Light Heckleman Wilmoth enlisted in Co. M at age 19 in April 1862. He transferred to Co. L in 1863 to join his two older brothers. He fought throughout the war without injury until furloughed home in January 1865. Light died in 1886 at age 42 and is buried in the Marietta City Cemetery just a short distance from Colonel Phillips.

Pvt. John Pleasant Bryan enlisted in Co. M at age 21 in April 1862. Bryan had already served with the 7th Georgia infantry in 1861 and suffered a wound at the battle of First Manassas. Captured in the assault on Fort Sanders at Knoxville in November 1863, he would languish in prison at Camp Chase, Ohio until, in failing health, he agreed to take the Oath of Allegiance to get out in June 1864.

J Fletcher Lowrey enlisted as the 2nd Lt of Co L in March 1862. He would rise to company Captain before being mortslly wounded by shellfire at Sailors Creek April 6.1865. This photo is his 1861 wedding photo. We believe that it shows him in his Marietta Volunteer Fire Dept uniform.

Seventeen year old **Joseph Tarplay Lowrey** joined the 7th Georgia Infantry in 1861 and transferred to his older brother Fletcher's Legion Co L in August 1862. Joe survived the war. This early war photo shows him in his 7th Georgia uniform.

Eighteen year old **John Miller Erwin** enlisted in Co C in June 1861.
He served through the war until captured at Sailors Creek April 6, 1865.
Miller Erwin would die in a lumbering accident near Sharon, Tn. in 1898.

Chapter 1[1]

Setting the Stage
"Who the hell is Joe Brown?"

For one brief moment, Georgia was a sovereign, independent republic. The governor was faced with a difficult decision on how to deal with the Federal presence in his state. Otherwise he would risk the citizens taking the law into their own hands. Governor Joseph E. Brown had prepared himself; it was not his nature to shy away from controversy or stressful decisions. So it was that he and his aides, Colonel Henry R. Jackson and Colonel William M. Phillips, rode to Augusta in early January 1861 to seize the Federal arsenal on behalf of the new Republic of Georgia.[2]

Just five days earlier the state of Georgia became the fifth state to secede from the Union. Although war had not yet been declared, preparations were evident everywhere in the South. The election of Abraham Lincoln and the consolidation of Federal troops at Fort Sumter created rumors of war and incited a cry for removal of what was considered to be a foreign, potentially hostile enemy. Fort Pulaski in Savannah had been seized a few weeks before and now Brown, Phillips,

---

[1] Chapters 1–6 include materials pertinent to both the infantry and cavalry battalions since both served together during the time these chapters cover. For all practical purposes the end of the South Carolina assignment marked the separation of the infantry and cavalry battalions. From this period on, they served in dedicated infantry and cavalry brigades. The separation became official with the issue of Army of Northern Virginia Special Order No. 104 on 14 April 1863.

[2] Earlier in the month the people of Savannah feared that the Federal presence along the Georgia coast might close the main seaport of Georgia. The menace was similar to the threat posed at Charleston by Federal control of Ft. Sumter. On the Georgia coast there were two United States forts, Jackson and Pulaski near Savannah. Ft. Pulaski was situated at the mouth of the Savannah River on a major railroad line. Gov. Brown, having been advised of the situation at Savannah, and of the probability that Pulaski and Jackson would be seized by the people if he failed to act, visited the city. After consulting the citizens he took the step of ordering an immediate occupation, which was accomplished on 3 January 1861. See Henry H. Fielder, *A Sketch of the Life and Times and Speeches of Joseph E. Brown* (Springfield: Press of Springfield, 1883) 178–81.

and Jackson demanded that Captain Arnold Elzey, commanding the 2d Artillery, United States Army, abandon the arsenal at Augusta and withdraw his eighty troops from the state.[3]

At first Captain Elzey rejected the demands but reconsidered his situation when Lieutenant Colonel Alfred Cumming readied 800 Augusta militiamen to support Governor Brown. Elzey had received a communication earlier from the United States Secretary of War directing him to avoid any act of desperation and, if withdrawal became necessary, to do so with honor. Armed with these instructions and grossly outnumbered, Elzey asked to meet in conference with Governor Brown, who was joined by Colonel H. R. Jackson, Colonel William M. Phillips, and other dignitaries.

The men promptly negotiated terms for an honorable withdrawal. The Georgia delegation gave Elzey, a personal friend of many of the assembled dignitaries, assurances of their personal esteem. They raised their glasses as Colonel Jackson offered his heartfelt and memorable sentiment: "The flag of stars and stripes, may it never be disgraced, while it floats over a true Southern patriot." The group then expressed their hopes for a solution to the current difficulties without resorting to hostilities. They realized the gravity of the situation but did not quite grasp the peril that lay before them.[4]

---

[3] J. Boifeullet, "Unveiling of the Phillips Monument at Marietta," *Atlanta Journal*, 16 May 1931, 4. On 19 January 1861 the Georgia Secession Convention rescinded the 1788 action that ratified the Constitution of the United States. In early January 1861, Gov. Brown wrote Alexander Hamilton asking where Georgia might find the original document by which it ratified and accepted the Constitution, presumably to withdraw any physical evidence of ratification. Hamilton replied on 25 January. On 2 February, Brown thanked Hamilton for his response and acknowledged Hamilton's views regarding political relations between the North and South as truly patriotic, but in Brown's opinion the time for settlement was irretrievably past. Whether a reconstruction of the old Union could ever be effected time alone would show, although Brown regarded that prospect as very distant. "There was a time when the people of the South cherished the old Union, but their attachment for it has been growing weaker and weaker for several years; and now, I must say, has become almost extinct." "Joseph E. Brown to Alexander Hamilton," Governor's Letter Book, 1 January 1847–23 April 1861, Georgia Department of Archives and History, Morrow GA.

[4] At 10 o'clock Gov. Brown, with Gens. Williams and Harris and his staff, Col. H. R. Jackson, Col. William M. Phillips, Lt. Col. M. C. Fulton, Lt. C. V. Walker, and Lt. Col. Henry Cleveland, rode to the arsenal, where the terms of the surrender were agreed upon. Col. Henry Walker, who had attended West Point with Elzey, also participated. I. Avery,

On 24 January 1861, after a thirty-three-gun salute, one for each star on the old flag, the stars and stripes was lowered and the Lone Star flag of Georgia floated over the arsenal.[5] A battery of artillery, 20,000 muskets, and a large quantity of munitions came into Georgia's possession. Within a few months Captain Elzey resigned his commission in the United States Army and entered Confederate service, ultimately achieving the rank of major general.[6]

Many Georgians harbored strong sentiment against secession prior to November 1860. The election of Abraham Lincoln by a purely regional vote gave rise to fears that the Union had fallen under the sway of a party antagonistic to the South. Secessionists capitalized on these fears and soon the politics and emotions of the times released a flood of disunion sentiment. But even many of those who favored disunion maintained hope that hostility could still be averted. Many others felt strongly that if it came to war, the conflict would be short-lived. Nonetheless, Georgia had to be ready.[7]

The Georgia state militia stood in general neglect before Governor Joe Brown's 1857 election. The militia had few division, brigade, regimental, battalion, or company officers and no rolls of men eligible for military duty. Georgia's constitution named the governor commander in chief of a nonexistent army and navy. Concern for the condition of the state's preparedness and impending dangers prompted Governor Brown, on 7 November 1860, to recommend that the legislature call a convention of the people to decide the question of secession and appropriate the sum of $1,000,000 as a military fund for the ensuing year. The legislators responded immediately, appropriating the requested funds "for the protection of the rights and preservation of

---

The History of the State of Georgia from 1850 to 1881 (New York: Brown & Derby, 1881) 161–64; J. Boifeullet, "Unveiling of the Phillips Monument at Marietta," *Atlanta Journal*, 16 May 1931, 4.

[5] The new flag consisted of a red star against a white background. L. Kennett, *Marching Through Georgia: The Story of Soldiers and Civilians during Sherman's Campaign* (New York: Harper Perennial, 1995) 20.

[6] C. Evans, ed., *Maryland and West Virginia*, vol. 2 of *Confederate Military History* (Harrisburg PA: Confederate Publishing Co., 1899).

[7] Lincoln was not on the ballot in the 1860 election. Although radical candidate John C. Breckenridge received a plurality of votes, the two Unionist candidates Stephen A. Douglas and John Bell received a combined total that exceeded Breckenridge's total.

the liberties of the people of Georgia." The agreement created an office of adjutant general authorizing the governor to accept 10,000 troops.[8]

In mid-March 1861 Governor Brown began raising the troops authorized by the legislation. He contemplated the creation of two divisions, appointing Colonel Henry R. Jackson major general of the First Division and Colonel William H. T. Walker major general of the Second Division. Brown divided the state into four sections, intending to raise one brigade of volunteers in each section. Only one division was found to be practicable. It was tendered to Jackson but he declined in favor of Colonel William H. T. Walker, late of the United States Army. Colonel Paul J. Semmes was offered command of the division's 2d Brigade and Colonel William M. Phillips was assigned the 4th Brigade. Both were to be named state brigadier generals. Impatient to get into active duty as soon as possible, Walker and Semmes resigned before they organized their respective commands and left for service under the Confederate government.[9] William Phillips, Brown's upcountry friend and a young man of thirty-five years, accepted the position as brigadier general of the 4th Brigade.[10]

---

[8] "Governor Brown's Address to the Georgia Legislature, November 7, 1860," in *Life and Times and Speeches of Joseph E. Brown*, 162–69; *An Act to Provide for the Common Defense of the State of Georgia*, Georgia Law 54, 1860, vol. 1, p. 49, Georgia Department of Archives and History.

[9] Avery, *State of Georgia*, 186; S. Temple, *The First Hundred Years, A Short History of Cobb County, in Georgia* (Atlanta: Walter W. Brown Publishing Co., 1935) 235–36; "Message from Governor Brown to the Georgia Legislature, November, 1861," in *Confederate Military History*, ed. Evans, 6:53–55.

[10] Phillips was appointed brigadier general on 8 March 1861, pursuant to *An Act to Provide for the Public Defense and for Other Purposes*, Georgia Law 55, 1860, vol. 1, p. 50, Georgia Department of Archives and History. His brigade was denominated the Fourth by General Order No. 2, issued by the Georgia adjutant general's office on 16 January 1861. This also directed recruitment from the Cherokee, Blue Ridge, Western, and Tallapoosa judicial circuits. The organization included two regiments of infantry, one battalion of riflemen, one battalion of cavalry, and one battalion of artillery. Henry Wayne, "To William Phillips," 8 March 1861, Adjutants Letter Book, 18 February 1861–25 April 1861, 2:163, RG 22-1-34, LOC 3340-09, Georgia Department of Archives and History, Morrow GA; Rev. George Gilman Smith, "General William Phillips," *Atlanta* (GA) *Journal*, 15 June 1907, p. 7. On 28 March 1861, Brig. Gen. Phillips received instructions to report to Maj. Gen. W. H. T. Walker of the Irish Division of Volunteers in accordance with *An Act to Provide for the Public Defense and for Other Purposes*, Georgia Law 55. Henry Wayne, "To William Phillips," 28 March 1861, Adjutant General's Letter Book, 18 February 1861–25 April 1861, 2:419.

Phillips and Brown had been close friends since their days in the Blue Ridge Judicial Circuit. William M. Phillips was solicitor general for the circuit and Joseph E. Brown was judge. Phillips had helped secure Brown's nomination for governor. His involvement carried on the Phillips family's long tradition of political activism. William's father had served in the state house of representatives and the senate from 1838 to 1856, as did William and his two brothers at various points throughout their careers.[11] William was born 8 July 1824, the eldest of three sons of Doctor George DuVal and Elizabeth Patton Phillips. At the time of his birth, William's parents resided in Asheville, North Carolina, a town founded by his maternal grandfather. Dr. Phillips served as a physician in South Carolina during the War of 1812 and had lived there before moving back to Asheville. By the time William was six years old, the family moved to Clarkesville, Habersham County, Georgia. There he spent his boyhood, later attending Franklin College, the predecessor of the University of Georgia. By 1850 William had settled in Marietta, Georgia, where he studied law in the office of Charles James McDonald, a former governor of Georgia. In 1859 Phillips helped found the Marietta Paper Mill, later burned by Sherman's troops as was the Phillips's home. Phillips also helped charter the Polk Slate Quarry Railroad that was planned to connect with the Western and Atlantic at Marietta and run through Cobb, Paulding, and Polk counties to the Alabama state line.[12]

In June 1857 the delegates of the state Democratic convention deadlocked, preventing the selection of a candidate from among the slate of gubernatorial candidates. After a lengthy session and repeated ballots, all of the candidates fell by the wayside. Phillips was appointed to a committee of twenty-four to propose a compromise nominee and present him to the convention. Phillips, then solicitor general of the Blue Ridge circuit, knew Joseph E. Brown, then a young judge on the same circuit. Because the convention could not agree on any of the

---

[11] Betty Hargis Peardon, "General William Phillips Family of Cobb County," *Georgia Genealogical Society Quarterly Journal* 5/3 (September 1995): 93–97. Williams's brother, Charles D. Phillips, an attorney, served as colonel in the 52nd Georgia Regiment and his brother, Dr. James Patton Phillips, served as major in the Confederate army.

[12] Smith, "General William Phillips," 7; Peardon, "General William Phillips' Family," 93–97; Temple, *First Hundred Years*, 152, 153–4, 410.

prominent men nominated, the young man from Cobb County startled the body by proposing the judge as a compromise candidate. Phillips not only suggested Brown's name to the committee but also seconded the nomination before the full convention. Judge Joe Brown was such an unfamiliar name to the conventioneers that Robert Toombs reacted to the news by exclaiming, "Who in the hell is Joe Brown?" In a display of solidarity, however, Brown received the nomination by acclamation.[13] Brown learned of his nomination while shaving on a hot summer afternoon after cutting wheat near Canton in Cherokee County.

Brown was born in Pickens District, South Carolina, in 1821. While he was a youth his father moved the family to Union County in mountainous North Georgia. The elder Brown was a farmer of limited means. At age nineteen, and with only a rudimentary education, young Joe Brown set out for Dr. Waddell's academy in South Carolina where he proved to be an excellent student. He borrowed money to study law at Yale, returning to Georgia in 1846. Despite the Yale degree, Brown remained unsophisticated in manner and bearing. He tried teaching, opened a law practice in Cherokee County, served as state legislator from 1849 to1850, and in 1855 became a circuit judge. He worked hard and held to his course with an iron will. He displayed no flamboyance and little discernible emotion. He never used alcohol or tobacco, uttered a profane oath, or related an obscene or vulgar anecdote. Many Georgians of modest station considered Joe Brown to be one of them, one of the common folk, even though he became a wealthy man through wise land and mineral investments.[14]

Exhibiting a "no nonsense" manner, the new governor immediately went to work in the administration of the state government. He went to war against the state's bankers who had suspended specie payments in the aftermath of the Panic of 1857. He tightened up the state administration and increased the revenues of the state's Western and Atlantic Railroad. His proslavery stance put him in good stead with the small but powerful planter population, and he convinced the larger

---

[13] Smith, "General William Phillips," 7; Kennett, *Marching Through Georgia*, 15–19; Fielder, *Joseph E. Brown*, 69–70.

[14] Kennett, *Marching Through Georgia*, 15–19; Fielder, *Joseph E. Brown*, 69–70; F. Garrett, *Atlanta and Environs, A Chronicle of Its People and Events*, 3 vols. (Athens: University of Georgia Press, 1954) 2:423.

population of non-slaveholders that leaving the Union was essential to their interests.

Brown provided strong leadership in the crisis over secession, a step he personally favored. He was a jealous guardian of the sovereignty of the State of Georgia and a devotee of states' rights even to the point of jeopardizing the common cause. Throughout the war Brown insisted upon strict construction of the Confederate Constitution, a policy that frequently brought him into conflict with President Jefferson Davis. Governor Brown, with Alexander H. Stephens, vice president of the Confederate States, his half-brother Linton, Robert Toombs, and others, led the way in opposing Confederate policies and was especially critical of Jefferson Davis.[15] Brown's policy battles were so frequent and public that, at times, he gave the impression that he considered the Confederate administration a hostile power. At one point the controversy between Governor Brown and the president escalated to the point that it gave rise to reports in the North that Georgia was about to secede from the Confederacy.[16] Thomas Reade Rootes Cobb wrote that Davis held Brown in great contempt as the only man in the seven states who persistently thwarted him in every endeavor to carry out the policy of the government.[17]

Conflict between the two men was inevitable. Brown was self-willed, argumentative, and jealous of his prerogatives. Jefferson Davis was a "born controversialist." Brown maintained rigid views of Georgia sovereignty and states' rights throughout the war. Although Davis had a strong attachment to the states' rights doctrine, he was enough of a practical statesman to know that strength lay in unity of purpose and action. During the upcoming conflict, the Confederacy must be a consolidated nation and not an aggregate of sovereign states. The fullest embodiment of this nationalism lay in the Confederate army, whose very existence was a departure from states' rights. For the South to be successful, the state governors could not be commanders-in-chief of

---

[15] Kennett, *Marching Through Georgia*, 15–19.

[16] *New York Herald*, 3 August 1861, in *The Southern Confederacy* (Atlanta GA), September 1861, n.p.; Temple, *First Hundred Years*, 541.

[17] Lynda L. Crist and Mary S. Dix, eds., *The Papers of Jefferson Davis*, 11 vols. (4 more projected) (1861; repr., Baton Rouge: Louisiana State University Press, 1992) 7:147.

their own armies. But this was exactly the power Joe Brown intended to exercise.[18]

When the Provisional Congress passed the act of 28 February 1861, authorizing the president to assume control of military operations in the Confederate states, the first major confrontation occurred. Brown considered his right to keep troops to be the *sine qua non* of his state's sovereignty; consequently, he considered states' rights in terms of state troops. Georgia's state constitution made the governor commander in chief of the army and navy of Georgia and the militia thereof. As chief executive of a state that even the Confederate Constitution described as being of a "sovereign and independent character," he felt it was his responsibility and right to protect his state when the Richmond government could not or would not do so.[19]

The initial flashpoint came in March 1861, when Secretary of War Leroy P. Walker made the first call to Georgia for troops to counter threats at Pensacola, Florida. Brown contended that the troops should be sent as fully organized regiments in order that he might commission the officers before the troops left the state. He believed that if the men were sent as independent companies, the president would organize them into regiments and appoint the officers himself. Although Walker urged haste, Brown did not send the volunteers until after the firing on Fort Sumter. This seemingly small action set a collision course for Brown and the Confederate government over the right to organize troops and appoint officers.

Over the following year, Brown attempted to confer military titles on a great number of Georgians by forming as many skeleton regiments as possible. He sought to appoint all officers through the rank of colonel, and in the early months he even attempted to appoint general officers. Brown also tried to please the masses of his constituents by insisting, whenever possible, that the state's soldiers be allowed to elect their company-grade officers rather than accept commanders appointed by the Confederacy.[20]

---

[18] W. Bragg, *Joe Brown's Army: The Georgia State Line, 1862–1865* (Macon GA: Mercer University Press, 1987) 2–3; T. Bryan, *The History of the State of Georgia from 1850 to 1881* (New York: Brown & Derby 1881) 48–49; T. Bryan, *Confederate Georgia* (Athens: University of Georgia Press, 1953) 80–85.

[19] Ibid.

[20] Ibid.

Brown's friend, William Phillips, was about to become the center of a battle between the governor and the president over who had the power to organize military units, control their use, and appoint their field grade officers. The Phillips Georgia Legion was about to be born from the unhappy marriage between these two leaders of the fledgling Confederacy.

Chapter 2

Born in Anger

*"...tell the girls they must not put too much dependence
on what a soldier says."*

As the nation stood poised for war in early 1861, firebrand rhetoric
became commonplace and drowned out rational, calm discussion.
Dramatic standoffs played out at Fort Sumter in Charleston Harbor and
Fort Pickens in Pensacola Harbor. Confederate forces held Union
garrisons under siege at both forts and the deadly tension threatened to
erupt into full-scale war at any time.

The first spark ignited on 12 April when secessionist gunners
opened up on Fort Sumter. A lopsided artillery duel followed for two
days until Union Major Robert Anderson finally surrendered. *The
Southern Confederacy* trumpeted the news in uppercase headlines: "War!
At Last. Bombardment of Fort Sumter Commenced!"[1]

The city of Savannah, Georgia, a major port, stood only a short
distance down the coast from Charleston. The presence of Federal
troops along the coast, easy access to ports by Federal fleets, as well as
the bombardment of Fort Sumter convinced Governor Brown that
Savannah was in danger of attack. In accordance with his perceived
duties as Georgia's commander in chief, Brown took action. He ordered
Militia General William Phillips to organize his 4th Brigade and create a
camp of instruction for officers and orderly sergeants of the brigade. The
officers would drill and immerse themselves in military tactics in order
to train their own companies later.[2]

---

[1] No author, "War! At Last. Bombardment of Fort Sumter Commenced!" *The
Southern Confederacy* (Atlanta GA), 13 April 1861, n.p.

[2] William Phillips, "To Joseph E. Brown, April 1, 1861," in Incoming
Correspondence to Governor Joseph E. Brown, 1861, Georgia Department of Archives
and History, Morrow GA, RG 1-1-5, LOC 3335-08.

Brown and Phillips had been preparing for war for some time. Phillips actively raised volunteer companies across the state in late 1860 and early 1861. Both spoke out, supporting delegates to the Secession Convention who would vote in favor of Georgia's departure from the Union. Phillips railed against delegates who advocated compromise with the Unionists, claiming they were too soft. Phillips wrote to Brown that he was studying military tactics harder than he ever studied law. Brown had plans for this militia officer who participated in the seizure of the Augusta arsenal, supported the governor in his first election, and was now raising troops for Georgia.[3]

The 4th Brigade became the first brigade raised by the state of Georgia. Phillips selected the old Smyrna Camp Meeting Ground located 4 miles south of Marietta for the camp of instruction, naming it "Camp Brown." Sufficient companies were tendered to Phillips within five days to provide a pool of over 10,000 soldiers.[4] Brigade organization was nearly complete by 15 April 1861. Colonel William Tatum Wofford would command one heavy infantry regiment and Colonel William W. Boyd the other. Three more units completed the brigade; a cavalry battalion under Major William W. Rich, an artillery battalion under Captain Marcellus A. Stovall, and a light infantry rifle battalion under Lieutenant Colonel Seaborn Jones, Jr.[5]

The cadets of the Georgia Military Institute in Marietta conducted training under the supervision of Francis W. Capers, the school's superintendent.[6] The cadets worked hard to train their older, inexperienced charges. The majority of the men were untrained in drill or tactics and unaccustomed to the regimentation and discipline required in a military organization. They adjusted well with only minor problems to be expected with volunteer soldiers, and they were lighthearted in

---

[3] Ibid., 3 January 1861.

[4] Editorial correspondence, *Rome* (GA) *Weekly Courier*, 19 April 1861, citing the *Marietta* (GA) *Advocate*, 15 April 1861 n.p.; W. Bragg, *Joe Brown's Army: The Georgia State Line, 1862–1865* (Macon GA: Mercer University Press, 1987) ix–x.

[5] Editorial correspondence, *Rome* (GA) *Weekly Courier,* 10 May 1861, n.p. The 4th Brigade of Georgia Volunteers was comprised of two regiments and three battalions, one each of cavalry, rifle, and artillery.

[6] Keith Bohannon, "Cadets, Drillmasters, Draft Dodgers and Soldiers: The Georgia Military Institute During the Civil War," *Georgia Historical Quarterly* 79 (Spring 1995): 5–29.

spirit and attitude. Their humor, repartee, music, and songs eased the boredom on and off duty.[7]

The presence of the green soldiers and their strange, exciting military activities never ceased to fascinate the locals. They visited the camp daily, often trekking long distances from outlying settlements and villages. Although such a large concentration of troops drained the countryside of fresh provisions such as beef, poultry, eggs, and butter, the locals did not seem to mind. Ladies, filled with curiosity, often rode out to watch the troops drill. Some created a sumptuous dinner for the soldiers, who had not tasted genuine home cooking for nearly ten days.[8]

General Phillips addressed his officers on the first day of camp, telling the men that Governor Brown had ordered the camp of instruction to prepare the company officers of the brigade for leadership positions in active service. Phillips made it clear that he believed the command would be called to active duty as soon as it was sufficiently drilled. Further, the 4th Brigade was no "Home Guard" but was to be organized to serve the Confederate states, whether in Georgia or elsewhere, wherever they might be needed.[9]

A large, fine-looking, approachable man, Phillips cared deeply for his soldiers and they reciprocated with affection and trust. In spite of a lack of military training, he had no shortage of leadership skills. More than one correspondent described how much beloved he was to all and how his general orders and instruction infused the right spirit into the men under his command.[10] This kind of laudatory praise was often echoed throughout William Phillips's life as a soldier, businessman, and citizen.

Unfortunately, the opposite proved to be true of Governor Brown. He appeared in camp on the evening of 29 April 1861 and spoke at a reception honoring his arrival. After supper, the soldiers asked for more words from the governor, who delivered a speech both ill-timed and inappropriate. The 4th Brigade would defend Georgia. The state might be invaded and he feared it would be. The 4th Brigade, this corps, was to

---

[7] Editorial correspondence, *Rome* (GA) *Weekly Courier*, 27 April 1861, n.p.

[8] S. Temple, *The First Hundred Years: A Short History of Cobb County in Georgia* (Atlanta: Walter W. Brown Publishing Co., 1935) 238. Editorial correspondence, *Rome* (GA) *Weekly Courier*, 10 May 1861, n.p.

[9] Editorial correspondence, *Rome* (GA) *Weekly Courier*, 3 May 1861, n.p.

[10] Ibid., 17 May 1861.

be the "Home Guard." Further, while he presumed every man was eager for the fight, discretion was at least as noble a virtue as valor. Inasmuch as the men were not sufficiently skilled in the science of war to make their efforts correspond with the spirit of their intentions, Brown planned to keep the brigade at home until it was well disciplined, or until there should be a reasonable apprehension of an invasion of the state. He went on to say that he might send other companies, younger and less disciplined, into immediate service but that the honor of the state was at stake in this organization. He would strive to get the brigade into action as a whole, but if that should be impractical they should go as regiments or battalions, or finally as companies. In each case they should go with their officers and in the most extended organization possible.[11]

These remarks, at odds with General Phillips's previous oration, did not go over well, creating grumbling and dissension throughout the encampment. The irate officers prepared a petition for change in his policy, asking that Brown send to earliest service the oldest and best-disciplined companies. In an attempt to quell the unrest, Brown spoke again the next morning and modified his position. He told the men that all would get into service as soon as they could reasonably desire it, in Georgia or elsewhere in the Confederate states. He reiterated that some might be called upon to exercise the cardinal virtue of patience, but this would be to their own and the state's advantage. Brown's words offered some reconciliation but masked his actual intent to retain rigid control over the organization and deployment of the brigade.[12] This incident foreshadowed the coming controversy between Brown and Confederate authorities over control of the brigade.

Phillips wrote to the governor soon after Brown's inflammatory speech, insisting that he understand that it would be impossible to hold the brigade together unless they were received into Confederate service. Some of the officers were concerned that the men in their companies would seek to leave the brigade for Confederate service as individual companies or with other organizations. Phillips conveyed the officers' request that the governor provide a written reply so they could have it published in hopes of holding their companies together. Finally, Phillips informed Brown that he planned to extend the camp of instruction for

[11] Ibid., 10 May 1861.
[12] Ibid.

one more week. Although the officers were improving rapidly, they would not be qualified at the end of two weeks to instruct their companies properly.[13]

Phillips extended the instructional period to end 9 May 1861. Tents were struck after reveille that Thursday morning and some 200 officers returned to their respective companies prepared for the work at hand. Colonel Seaborn Jones, Jr., ordered the rifle battalion into camp near Cartersville the following week of 15 May 1861. Others went into camp shortly thereafter.[14] Trouble continued to reverberate from the governor's speech at Camp Brown. The McDonald Guards disbanded and many other companies were restless. Phillips offered to resign if, in the governor's opinion, it would help resolve the controversy. Phillips wrote Brown that a great clamor had arisen against him, created by impatient soldiers as well as politicians who wanted to displace the governor. Phillips was willing to support Brown and fight for his defense of states' rights, but if there was no possibility of the Brigade seeing service as a brigade, he wished to resign. Phillips insisted that he wanted to do his duty—"First to Georgia and then to the Confederacy." If the governor needed or wanted his service, then Phillips was ready as a private in the ranks or as a brigadier general.[15]

Less than a month later the governor responded by calling the brigade into camp. Federal activity at Harpers Ferry, skirmishes in western Virginia, and concerns over a possible invasion along the Georgia coast prompted Brown to call "his" army to duty. Brown ordered Phillips to organize a camp of instruction for the brigade and hold the troops in readiness for immediate action should an emergency require it. On 11 June 1861 Phillips began organizing Camp McDonald at Big Shanty, 7 miles north of Marietta near Kennesaw Mountain. He named the camp in honor of his law tutor and mentor, former governor Charles J. McDonald.[16] Undaunted, Brown managed to deepen the resentful mood prevalent at the new camp by spending much of his time there. While claiming that he wanted to spent time outdoors to improve

---

[13] Phillips, "To Joseph E. Brown," n.d., in *Incoming Correspondence*, n.p.

[14] Editorial correspondence, *Rome* (GA) *Weekly Courier*, 17 May 1861, n.p. *Augusta* (GA) *Daily Chronicle & Sentinel*, 12 May 1861, p. 2.

[15] Phillips, "To Joseph E. Brown, May 20, 1861," in *Incoming Correspondence*, n.p.

[16] Charles James McDonald was governor of Georgia from 1839 to 1843.

health, he undoubtedly saw this brigade, created by state legislation, as his progeny.

On 12 June 1861 the governor addressed the 4th Brigade at Camp McDonald to explain the terms upon which the companies composing the brigade would be received and mustered into service. The troops, assembled in front of General Phillips's headquarters, listened attentively while the governor explained that that they would train for sixty days unless they were needed sooner. The men would receive half pay while encamped for drill. Still evasive, Brown said he would decide whether or not to tender the brigade into Confederate service when their instruction was completed. He reminded them that the 4th Brigade had initially tendered its service to the state. However, while the officers were assembled at Camp Brown, they expressed a unanimous desire to enter active service of the Confederacy. Since President Davis had stated that no troops would be received for less than three-year enlistments, it would be impossible for the governor to comply with the wishes of the 4th Brigade unless their tender was changed to meet the president's requirements. In order to prepare for potential Confederate service and honor the views of the majority of the brigade, Brown was changing the term of enlistment to "for the war" rather than twelve months. Brown went on to say that any soldier who was unwilling to comply with these terms was at liberty to leave with honor by 9:00 A.M. the following day.[17]

About 500 men expressed dissatisfaction with the terms of enlistment and withdrew. Some returned the next day after sleeping on the matter. Brown expressed no concern over the withdrawals since many additional companies were applying for admission to the brigade. Phillips believed that over thirty companies were knocking at his door.[18]

During that evening and night the encampment was in an uproar, some considering the governor's remarks as dictatorial and delivered in a repulsive and defiant style. In a letter to his brother, Benjamin Franklin Sitton described the anger and resentment felt by the soldiers. "We expected to go into the service of the Confederate states, but in this we were mistaken. We find ourselves in the service of the State of Georgia

---

[17] Editorial correspondence, *Rome* (GA) *Weekly Courier*, 21 May 1861, n.p. Joseph E. Brown, "To Jefferson Davis," in Governor's Letter Book, 1 January 1847–23 April 1861, RG 1-1-1, LOC 3341-10, Georgia Department of Archives and History, Morrow GA.

[18] Editorial correspondence, *Rome* (GA) *Weekly Courier,* 21 June 1861, n.p.

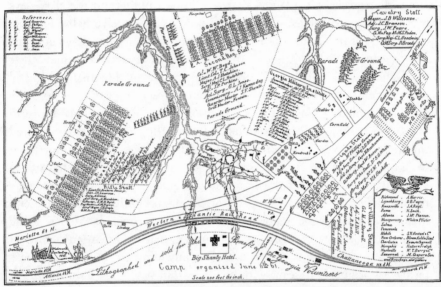

CAMP McDONALD

A School of Instruction for the 4th Brigade Georgia Volunteers.

His Excellency Governor Joseph E. Brown, Commander in Chief.

The Georgia Military Institute was organized at Marietta, Georgia, in 1851, by Colonel A. V. Brumby; chartered at the session of the General Assembly in the winter of 1851-1852, and modeled after the U.S. Military Academy at West Point. During the war between the states CAMP McDONALD was established, including the Georgia Military Institute grounds and extending to Big Shanty (now called Kennesaw). Here recruits for the Confederate Army were drilled by the cadets and new regiments organized.

During the campaign from Dalton to the sea in 1864 the Georgia Military Institute cadets served with great credit. Camp McDonald was destroyed by Sherman and the school was never revived.   *Joseph Tyrone Derry.*

on half pay. And this I assure you does not take so very well, and I do not know how the people of Lumpkin will like it as they have gone to considerable expense to fix us up to serve during the war."[19] The press reported the governor's speech as having nearly broken up the brigade.

On Wednesday evening Colonel Wofford addressed his 1st Regiment, appealing to the men to be quiet and promising them that he would go to Atlanta the next morning to see the governor and prevail upon him to modify the orders. During Wofford's absence, General Phillips appeared in front of the headquarters of the 1st Regiment. The sergeant major ordered the regiment to fall into line but not one soldier obeyed. One company had already left the regiment and two others seemed likely to follow. Colonel Wofford returned Thursday evening and delivered an eloquent and patriotic address, appealing to the men to stand firm with him. He announced that the arrangements were not as satisfactory as he would have desired, but the best way for the regiment to get into service was through the brigade and that was the only way to obtain arms. Nearly all who heard the speech agreed to be mustered into service. General Phillips arrived and delivered a short but impressive address. The general confessed that he too had been misled. He had understood that the brigade was to have been received for twelve months and that he, as well as the other officers and men of the brigade, had been deceived as to the terms of enlistment.[20] Some disgruntled companies did choose to depart the brigade but others quickly filled their places. In the five-company rifle battalion, the Campbell Rifles and the Cass Rifles would be replaced by the Greene Rifles and the Blue Ridge Rifles. In the four-company cavalry battalion, the Walton Guards and the Cherokee Cavalry would be replaced by the Governor's Horse Guards and the Johnson Rangers. Other company replacements and reorganizations would take place in the two heavy infantry regiments. Finally, the crisis passed and the soldiers went back to training, anxious to fight the Yankees.

Although these men were accustomed to rough life, they still found camp life stressful. The great majority of Georgians resided in the

[19] Benjamin Franklin Sitton to Brother, 11 July 1861, Boyd-Sitton Letters, Lumpkin County Library, Madeline K. Anthony Collection, series 3, box 2, folders 11, 12, 13; no author, "Much Between Gov. Brown and the Cherokee Volunteers—A Brigade Nearly Broken Up," *Augusta* (GA) *Daily Chronicle & Sentinel*, 23 June 1861, p. 2.

[20] "Much Between Gov. Brown," *Augusta* (GA) *Daily Chronicle & Sentinel*, p. 2.

countryside. Only one of Georgia's 136 counties had over 30,000 inhabitants. The population was young, fueled by young marriages and large families. Settlements and the countryside abounded with youths in their late teens and early twenties who had become accustomed to hard work in field and forest. One member of one of the new rifle companies, Augustus Franklin Boyd, wrote to his sister: "We have plenty to eat and good tents. We drill four hours a day. I am messing with J. Reese…three of us cooks at a time.[21]

Benjamin Sitton had just reached camp on the evening of 18 July 1861. He had made a very uncomfortable march from Dahlonega, baking in the mid-summer sun with the men of the Blue Ridge Rifles. Sore, blistered feet caused misery with every step. On arrival in camp they confronted a scourge of wildly contagious diseases such as mumps and measles. Also the misery of home*sick*ness was universal and the troops grumbled endlessly.[22]

Crammed together in camp with thousands of other men, away from any civilizing influences such as home and family, sometimes led to vices. While the Sabbath was generally observed on Sunday with preaching and singing, some of the more pious troops felt that Camp McDonald was a place of wickedness. Many men used prolific profanity as did others who professed religion at home where they never used foul language. Gambling was common and strong drink created its problems. Liquor contributed to a near-violent incident on the Fourth of July. The fracas started with the Jackson Guards of the 2d Regiment, better known as the Irish Company. These Sons of Erin had acquired a supply of drink and fighting broke out. The company guard tried to halt the row but most of the company resisted, armed themselves, and prepared to fight. The entire regiment was called to arms and it appeared there might be an actual armed battle. After an uneasy few moments peace was restored. Fortunately no one was seriously injured, but had the men been supplied with cartridges, some would have undoubtedly been killed.[23]

---

[21] August Franklin Boyd to Sister, 14 July 1861, Boyd-Sitton Letters.

[22] L. Kennett, *Marching Through Georgia: The Story of Soldiers and Civilians during Sherman's Campaign* (New York: Harper Perennial, 1995) 19; Benjamin Franklin Sitton to Brother, 11 July 1861, Boyd-Sitton Letters; correspondence, "A Private," *Central Georgian*, 24 July 1861, p. 2.

[23] Correspondence, "A Private."

A. J. "Jack" Reese, who also arrived with the Blue Ridge Rifles, received some sage advice from his aunt to avoid these vices and celebrate the Sabbath. She had heard of some of the problems in camp. Her heart ached at having to give up those who were so near and dear to go to battle with a merciless foe. For this vice to be placed before them day and night was too much to bear. "Where men are allowed to gamble, curse and swear and do many other things…how can they think the Lord will give them the victory?" She admonished Jack to "never touch a card or drink a drop of spirits or use any bad language."[24]

The Georgia Military Institute cadets continued to drill the men for 4 hours each day, hardening them to camp life. In some cases, gray-haired men were drilled by boys in their early teens. One of the cadet drillmasters, fifteen-year-old Coatesworth Hamilton, was the brother of Captain Joseph Hamilton of the Blue Ridge Rifles. On Sundays the men were free to stroll about visiting other companies while the camp band provided entertainment. Food was good and plentiful as the state provided meat, bread, coffee, sugar, and spices. The men furnished butter, eggs, and vegetables at their own expense if such foodstuffs could be found.[25]

While the men trained, a heated political and philosophical debate erupted between Governor Brown and President Davis. The issues centered on control of the 4th Brigade and the potential appointment of General Phillips as a Confederate general. The crux of the controversy stemmed from events that occurred while Georgia was still an independent republic. In February 1861, the Provisional Congress passed acts authorizing the president to accept companies, battalions, and regiments into Confederate service as well as authority to assume control of military operations in the Confederate states. President Davis therefore insisted that he had no authority by law to accept larger organizations such as brigades.[26]

---

[24] N. Wimpy to Andrew Jackson Reese, 3 August 1861, Rees/Reese Collection, Lumpkin County Library, Madeline K. Anthony Collection, series 3, box 23, folder 5.

[25] No author, "General Phillips Brigade in Camp at Big Shanty," *Southern Confederacy* (Atlanta GA), 2 July 1861; Benjamin Franklin Sitton to Brother, 3 May 1861, Boyd-Sitton Letters.

[26] E. B. Long and Barbara Long, *The Civil War Day by Day* (New York: Da Capo Press, 1971) 209–10; no author, "Act of Confederate Congress," 28 February 1861, in US War Department, comp., *The War of Rebellion: A Compilation of the Official Records of*

When Secretary of War Leroy P. Walker requisitioned 2,000 men for service in the Confederate states, Brown responded on 1 March 1861 by stating that the Georgia convention had instructed him to raise two regiments that could be turned over to the common government. Before taking any further action to raise the troops, Governor Brown sought to clarify an issue regarding his authority as commander in chief of state forces relative to the president's authority. He had appointed officers for the two regiments and desired to know whether the Confederate government would accept the regiments with all the officers appointed by the governor. He argued that he could not, in justice to the privates, tender the regiments unless they were received with the officers who enlisted them from civil life with the understanding that they would serve under those officers. Brown and Walker exchanged a flurry of dispatches in an attempt to negotiate an agreement. By 27 April 1861 the issue had evolved into a question of whether or not the Confederacy would receive volunteers by division or brigade. Walker responded that the organization of brigades belonged to the president under the sixth section of the Act to Provide for Public Defense. On 7 May 1861, Walker informed Brown that no more troops would be received for any other term than the war.[27]

Brown had informed Davis on 7 June 1861 that he had ordered General Phillips's full brigade into camp of instruction. On 18 June 1861 Brown telegraphed Davis that Phillips's brigade was in camp and the state would arm and equip the brigade. Brown used the communiqué to make clear his expectation that the men would have the privilege of electing their field officers.[28] In another communiqué on 18 June 1861, the secretary of war stated that if a regiment was organized before being mustered into service, the regiment could elect its field officers. If, however, they were mustered into service as companies or before electing regimental officers, the president would appoint the field

---

the Union and Confederate Armies, 128 vols. (Washington DC: Government Printing Office, 1880–1901) ser. 4, vol. 1, p. 117.

[27] Joseph E. Brown to "L. P. Walker," 1 January 1847–23 April 1861, in Governor's Letter Book, 796.

[28] Jefferson Davis telegram "To Joseph E. Brown," 6 June 1861, in Governor's Letter Book, 44; Joseph E. Brown telegram "To Jefferson Davis," 18 June 1861, in Governor's Letter Book, 58; A. Candler, comp., *The Confederate Records of the State of Georgia, 1861–1865*, 6 vols. (Atlanta: State Printer, 1909) 2:96.

officers. Secretary Walker's reference to the powers of the president of the Confederate States to appoint officers of regiments touched a nerve in Governor Brown. He believed the state of Georgia alone had that right. Brown immediately protested and the conflict began to escalate.[29]

By the end of June, Governor Brown appeared ready to test the authority of the president to appoint officers. He had decided that the hot, humid climate would serve to deter any invaders along coastal Georgia during August, September, and October. On 28 June 1861 Brown offered the 4th Brigade to President Davis with the provision that it be sent back to Georgia if needed for coastal defense.[30] He presented the president two heavy infantry regiments armed with US model 1842 muskets, a light infantry rifle battalion consisting of five companies armed with US model 1857 rifles, four companies of artillery, and a four-company battalion of cavalry armed with state-of-the-art Sharps carbines. He reflected, "A finer body of men I have nowhere seen and a more orderly camp can nowhere be found. The officers are exceedingly attentive, and the men are improving rapidly in all of the exercises of the soldier." The governor reminded the president that the brigade was organized for state defense by the Georgia Legislature. He explained that he had ordered the brigade into camp for two months on rations and half pay and had imposed the further condition that he would, if he chose to do so, tender them to the Confederate government for the war. Some companies had left the encampment rather than submit to those terms, but their places were promptly filled by other companies.[31]

In the event the president accepted the brigade, the governor stated that General Phillips would be pleased to have the president suggest some army officer who would be a suitable adjutant, whom the governor would promptly appoint. General Phillips had mentioned Major Elzey, a

---

[29] L. Walker telegram "To Joseph E. Brown," 18 June 1861 in Governor's Letter Book, 58; *Confederate Records*, comp. Candler, 2:96–97.

[30] Joseph E. Brown to Alexander H. Stephens, 25 June 1861, in Governor's Letter Book; U. Phillips, ed., *The Correspondence of Robert Toombs, Alexander H. Stephens and Howell Cobb* (New York: Da Capo Press, 1970) 571; Joseph E. Brown "To Jefferson Davis," 28 June 1861, extracted from *The Papers of Jefferson Davis*, 11 vols. (4 more projected), ed. Lynda I. Crist and Mary S. Dix (1861; repr., Baton Rouge: Louisiana State University Press, 1992) 7:216.

[31] Joseph E. Brown "To Jefferson Davis," 28 June 1861, in Governor's Letter Book, 63–4.

personal friend, as a possibility. Elzey was the former US commander of the Augusta Arsenal that had been seized by Brown and Phillips earlier in the year. The general would also be pleased to have other proper staff officers assigned to him. Brown further suggested that the brigade might be used in East Tennessee to keep the peace and intercept arms being sent to Union sympathizers.[32]

Three days later, Davis replied to Brown's offer by directing him to prepare the two heavy infantry regiments for movement. Brown's reaction was abrupt: he had not offered two regiments. He had offered a brigade composed of two regiments and three battalions. If the president wanted to take any, he must take the whole brigade.[33]

Brown now made a bold move. On 30 June 1861, Secretary Walker submitted another requisition for 3,000 men to be mustered into service by companies and used as a reserve force. These men would be placed into camps of instruction established by the state. The president would appoint officers to command the companies as well as the field and staff officers. On 6 July 1861, Brown renewed his protest, continuing to object to the president's presumed authority under the Confederate States constitution to appoint field and staff officers. Rather than appear obstinate by withholding the troops, Brown used a novel tactic. He agreed to furnish the men but insisted that he could not provision them within his limited resources. He had only sufficient resources to equip regiments organized by the State of Georgia and permitted to enter the service with field officers appointed by state authority. Once again, would the president like to have the previously offered "State's brigade, thoroughly armed and equipped?"[34]

On 8 July 1861 Brown sweetened the pot. After the requisition of the 3,000 men, Secretary Walker made an additional requisition for two regiments. Brown interpreted this as an attempt to break up the brigade and requisition the troops by regiments. Brown's response was firm: if the object involved taking from the brigade the two regiments and to

---

[32] Ibid.

[33] Jefferson Davis telegram "To Joseph E. Brown," 1 July 1861, in Governor's Letter Book, 67; Joseph E. Brown telegram "To Jefferson Davis," 2 June 1861, in Governor's Letter Book, 67.

[34] "Official Correspondence of Governor Joseph E. Brown, 1860–1865, Inclusive," in *Confederate Records*, comp. Candler, 3:110; see Brown's reply of 6 July 1861, in Governor's Letter Book, 69.

reject the three battalions and the commanding officer, he respectfully declined to comply with the requisition. Instead, he would collect all such companies in the state as have arms and organize them into two regiments to fill the requisition. Further, if the Confederate government agreed to receive the brigade as is, armed and equipped, with General Phillips in command, Brown would then agree that the president would appoint all staff officers except one confidential aide. If there were any question about the government's ability to receive a full brigade, they could receive the individual regiments and battalions with Phillips in command of all of them. Brown agreed to fully arm and equip the brigade at any cost of labor or expense, even if he had to pay by his own personal means. Within ten days from the date of acceptance of his proposition, Brown would furnish two other regiments in addition to the brigade.[35]

Brown sought to use the influence of other powerful Confederate leaders while negotiating directly with President Davis and Secretary Walker. He appealed to Secretary of State Robert Toombs and Vice President Alexander H. Stephens. In a letter to Stephens, Brown stated:

> I have tendered the brigade to the President fully armed and equipped, but he has not yet thought proper to accept the tender. He wishes the two regiments, but does not seem to take all together. General Phillips is willing that the President appoint his entire staff except one confidential aide. I appeal to you to assist me in getting the brigade into service as a brigade. If the President does not accept a brigade, he can accept its parts and appoint Phillips its commander and thus receive the whole. Phillips is very popular with his officers and men and is very rigid in his discipline. If they are ordered to the field without him, there will be great dissatisfaction, and I think it would be very bad treatment of him. May I appeal to you to give this

---

[35] "Joseph E. Brown, 1860–1865, Inclusive," in *Confederate Records*, comp. Candler, 2:108–110. At the same time that Davis was refusing Brown's request for a commission for Phillips, he was commissioning several state generals under Governor Isham Harris of Tennessee when Harris's state army was transferred to the Confederacy; Thomas Connelly, *Army of the Heartland: The Army of Tennessee, 1861–1862* (Baton Rouge: Louisiana State University Press, 1967) 32, 37; Joseph E. Brown "To L. P. Walker," 8 July 1861, in Governor's Letter Book, 71–72.

matter your special attention and get the President to have them and the brigade, which is equivalent to five armed regiments tendered at once, and I do not think the President should take them under state organization.[36]

In another such letter to Toombs Brown offered future favors for help in getting an appointment for Phillips: "Phillips and his friends are your friends, and he is competent. We appeal to you to have this matter set right. I rely on you and will try to accommodate you in turn when in my power. Please look into it at once as my proposition is equivalent to a tender of five regiments armed and equipped."[37]

Governor Brown received little support from those he assumed to be his allies. Stephens replied on 11 July 1861 that the law authorized only acceptance of companies, squadrons, battalions, and regiments and placed responsibility for appointment of generals on the Confederate government. Certainly the governor would not ask as a condition of furnishing troops that he should select officers to be appointed by the president.[38]

Davis telegraphed Brown that the law provided no authority to the president to receive a brigade but devolved upon the president the responsibility for selecting generals for all troops incorporated into the Army of the Confederate States. The president then appealed to Brown. The country needed all the armed troops that could be furnished. He repeated his request for the two regiments or any others the state could send. Brown, unrelenting, responded the same day that he did not feel authorized by state statute to disband the brigade. If the Act of Congress stood in the way, the president could accept the brigade as a whole by commissioning the general now in command.[39]

The game was near checkmate for Brown. Every proposal to the president had been rebuffed and Stephens had declined to help. Toombs did not help either, simply urging Brown to send every regiment

---

[36] Phillips, ed., *Correspondence*, 571–3; Joseph E. Brown "To Robert Toombs," 8 July 1861, in Governor's Letter Book, 73.

[37] Ibid.

[38] Extracted from *The Papers of Jefferson Davis*, ed. Crist and Dix, 7:237.

[39] Jefferson Davis telegram "To Joseph E. Brown," 11 July 1861, in Governor's Letter Book, 74; Joseph E. Brown telegram "To Jefferson Davis," 11 July 1861, in Governor's Letter Book, 74.

possible and leave the question of appointments for the future. Public opinion also battered the governor.[40]

Secretary Walker was also losing interest in the squabbling. He was heavily pressed to create an army. On 12 July 1861, Walker telegrammed Brown: "The crisis of our fate may depend on your action. For the sake of our cause and the country I beseech you to send them, without standing upon the point of the brigade organization. The President has no power to accept a brigade. If you refuse, you will regret it. It is not necessary that I should say more."[41] Brown held firm, again reiterating his position on 14 July 1861 that he did not feel authorized by state statute to disband the brigade. The president could accept it as a whole by commissioning the general now in command.

Davis decided to bring the impasse to an end. On 15 July 1861, he stated firmly that he could not appoint William Phillips to command the brigade. These messages served only to reinforce Brown's stubborn attitude. Now in a state of high dudgeon, he wrote to Secretary Walker:

> After you learned from my letter the component parts of the State Brigade, you made requisition on me, which reached me ten days since, for two armed regiments, which are no part of Georgia's equal quota; probably with a view to disband the brigade. You now demand the two regiments of the brigade as indispensable to success. The brigade which I am training at State's expense under an act of her legislature consists of two regiments and three battalions. The battalions are as good men and as well armed as the two regiments. If the regiments are indispensable to our success, why are not the three armed battalions needed? I have tendered all together. If armed men are indispensable to success, I offer you 2,500 together in place of 1,500, and beg you, for the sake of our common cause, to accept them. If it is desired to an act of justice to the state, the President can obviate all legal difficulties in the way of accepting them in a moment by commissioning the general in command.[42]

---

[40] Robert Toombs telegram "To Joseph E. Brown," 12 July 1861, in Governor's Letter Book, 74.

[41] *Confederate Records*, comp. Candler, 2:116.

[42] William Henry Talbot Walker telegram "To Jefferson Davis," 15 July 1861, acknowledges a telegram from Davis in the governor's absence (Walker was secretary to

Not one to give up easily, Brown wrote to Georgia Congressman Thomas R. R. Cobb, who had just formed the Cobb Legion. He asked Cobb to unite with former governor Howell Cobb and Alexander Stephens to work for the brigade as Brown had worked for Cobb's Legion in supporting its organization and equipping it with arms. Cobb responded on 3 August 1861: former governor Cobb and Mr. Stephens had exhausted every effort and failed. Two days later, Brown threw in the towel.[43]

Brown had no choice. The Confederate government vigorously opposed him and had the law on its side. His "friends," Stephens, Toombs, and the Cobb brothers, had been unable to help and he was beginning to be pummeled by the press. Furthermore, the gubernatorial elections loomed on the horizon, scheduled to take place in September 1861. On 1 August 1861, Brown wrote to Davis: "In view of the emergency I am obliged to yield the brigade organization, as I am determined to send the troops to the field. I consolidate the rifle battalion and cavalry and form a legion, which General Phillips will command as colonel."[44]

It was not over yet. Brown asked for approval to attach the artillery battalion of five companies armed with muskets and half a battery of brass pieces to the legion, and he requested three more guns to complete at least one battery. Davis thanked Brown for his decision and directed him to send the troops to Lynchburg, Virginia, where they would receive further orders. The two heavy infantry regiments left as separate organizations, leaving the rifle, cavalry, and artillery battalions to form a legion. The 1st Regiment under Colonel William T. Wofford departed on 3 and 4 August 1861 and the 2d Regiment under Colonel William W. Boyd followed two days later. These regiments would go on to become the 18th and the 19th Georgia Infantry Regiments.

Davis had checkmated Brown. Although Davis agreed to provide the guns to complete a single artillery battery, he wrote that "it was not

---

Brown). *Papers of Jefferson Davis*, ed. Crist and Dix, 7:244; *Confederate Records*, comp. Candler, 3:116–17.

[43] W. McCash, *Thomas R.. R. Cobb, The Making of a Southern Nationalist* (Macon: Mercer University Press, 1983); Joseph E. Brown telegram "To T. R. R. Cobb," 27 July 1861, in Governor's Letter Book, 78.

[44] *Confederate Records*, comp. Candler, 2:119–20.

well to organize artillery with infantry, as in the service of large armies they must soon be separated." Davis did offer to provide more guns for additional batteries or accept the artillery battalion as infantry. In that case he would attach the company with the half-battery and send it as an artillery company. Davis agreed to accept the artillery battalion as infantry minus the one company but suggested increasing the companies to regiment size as preferable to the battalion organization.[45]

As things turned out, Colonel Phillips's Legion would be made up of the now six-company rifle battalion and the four-company cavalry battalion. The last-minute increase in the size of the rifle battalion resulted when an all-Irish company from the Macon area was added. Dubbed the Lochrane Guards after noted Irish-born jurist Oliver Lochrane, these native-born sons of Ireland would be the only unit in the rifle battalion not armed with rifles. At this distance in time it is not possible to say whether this was due to a lack of rifles or the period bias against the Irish.

Davis was the clear winner of the Brown-Davis debates. He had thwarted Brown's plan to form a state-controlled brigade and made it clear that only the president had the authority to appoint general officers. Davis allowed Brown to form the Phillips Legion as an equivalent to a regiment, but Davis gained control over the legion by virtue of his authority to place regiments within larger organizational structures. Davis denied Brown's request to create a self-contained unit of infantry, cavalry, and artillery that could act independently. Finally, Davis denied Brown's attempt to increase the size of the legion by adding the artillery battalion as infantry.[46]

The 4th Brigade had seen its day. A grand review marked its end. People from the upper part of the state crowded into the tiny community of Big Shanty, coming by the Western and Atlantic Railroad, wagons, carriages, and oxcarts. The camp authorities added an extra train from Rome with tickets offered at half price to accommodate all of

---

[45] Joseph E. Brown telegram "To Jefferson Davis," 1 August 1861, in Governor's Letter Book, 79.

[46] Jefferson Davis telegram "To Joseph E. Brown," 3 August 1861, in Governor's Letter Book, 79; Joseph E. Brown telegram "To Jefferson Davis," 5 August 1861, in Governor's Letter Book; Jefferson Davis telegram "To Joseph E. Brown," 6 August 1861, in Governor's Letter Book; *Confederate Records*, comp. Candler, 2:120; no author, "Gen. Phillips Brigade," *Augusta* (GA) *Daily Chronicle & Sentinel*, 4 August 1861, p. 1.

the citizens attending the review. At 2 o'clock in the afternoon two regiments and three battalions formed in line and more than 2,000 troops passed in review before Governor Brown. The crowd was thrilled. Maneuvers by skirmishers followed by a cavalry charge on the line of infantry brought the cheering crowd to its feet. Spirits were high. At the conclusion of the day's activities Governor Brown tuned in to the happy feelings with a rousing speech. The military events at Camp McDonald came to a close for the last time as the soldiers departed for the front.

Jack Reese was anxious over the long trek to Virginia. He was attentive to his aunt's advice in one of many letters he wrote during the conflict: "You stated in your last letter that now was a good time to work on the sympathies of the young men. I hope my sympathies have not bin [*sic*] worked on so far at least not so far but I can still say that my heart is my own. You must tell the girls that they must not put too much dependence in what a soldier says. If you advise me not to make matrimonial engagement till the war is over I will do it."[47] A child of compromise, the Phillips Legion was born in anger and confusion. The young men who made up the legion marched off to war in ignorance of the horrors to come. They could not have imagined the hellish experiences that lay ahead.

---

[47] Andrew Jackson Reese to Nancy W. Wimpy, 6 August 1861, Rees/Reese Collection, Lumpkin County Library, Madeline K. Anthony Collection, series 3, box 23, folder 5.

Chapter 3

Orders for the Front

*If Virginia can secede from the United States why cannot West
Virginia secede from Virginia?*

While marching with the Phillips Georgia Legion troops to join General
John Buchanan Floyd's forces in the mountains of western Virginia, Jack
Reese's feet were causing him agonies. He had purchased a new pair of
shoes in Lynchburg and they were not yet broken in. None of the legion
troops had toughened up to the never-ending marching. Their blistered
feet and the stiff leather casings reminded them of their lack of marching
experience with every step they took. Jack decided he could never make
the 90-mile trek from Jackson River to Lewisburg and desperately
sought a ride. Any means of transport other than his own feet would do.
Providence smiled on Reese as a supply wagon appeared on the scene,
but first he had to do some fast talking. "Come up with a wagon that was
empty. It was stoped. I commenced getting in. The wagner commenced
cussing me. Swore I should not ride. Said he wold pull me out. I kept
talking good to him. Told him I was the best friend he had. Was going
to fight for him. He swore it was not so. Said ever man fooled himself in
this country. It would done you good to have heard us talking but we got
to ride to Lewisburg. He had one man to drive & live in wagon."[1]

Colonel Phillips arrived at Lynchburg with the main body of his
command in early August 1861. The remainder of the legion reached
camp by September.[2] Lynchburg, Virginia, a prominent tobacco market,

---

[1] Andrew Jackson Reese to Nancy W. Wimpy, 27 September 1861, Rees/Reese
Collection, Lumpkin County Library, Madeline K. Anthony Collection, series 3, box 23,
folder 5.

[2] Alexander Stephens to Jefferson Davis, 17 August 1861, in *The Papers of Jefferson
Davis*, 11 vols. (4 more projected), ed. Lynda L. Crist and Mary S. Dix (1861; repr.,
Baton Rouge: Louisiana State University Press, 1992) 7:287; no author, "Act of
Confederate Congress," 28 February 1861, in US War Department, comp., *The War of
Rebellion: A Compilation of the Official Records of the Union and Confederate* Armies,

was built on a bluff opposite the James River. The population of the city was around 15,000. It was surrounded by rolling hills and commanded a view of the cloud-capped summits of the Blue Ridge Mountains both to the north and west. The city itself was seedy, sidewalks narrow and uninviting for the occasional strollers. The Confederacy operated a staging area and camp of instruction for Southern troops on their way to the front. Hundreds of troops had arrived from throughout the Confederacy, and many of them were making last-minute preparations for war. The soldiers of Phillips Legion trained hard in drill and tactics while awaiting orders.

The legion was encamped at a fairground just 2 miles outside of the city. The citizenry was friendly and helped ease the discomforts of camp life and the dreariness of the town. Jack Reese described his feelings about the locals: "The ladies have been the redemption of Lynchburg in our estimation; their frequent acts of hospitality, and an occasional banquet bestowed in return for courtesy shown them, inspire the boys with the highest admiration for the fair Virginia lasses."[3] Young women appeared in crowds to see the troops at dress parade. Wearing their best uniforms and having a grand time, the men were on their best behavior. War was still in the future. They were all certain it would end in a few short months with little bloodshed.

Until now many of the legion soldiers had not traveled more than a few miles from their family farms, and the trip north to Lynchburg had been a great adventure. Their itinerary had taken them through Dalton, Knoxville, and Bristol. Arriving at Bristol they switched to the Virginia and Tennessee Railroad for the final leg of the journey. A crowd had assembled at Dalton to bid the legion goodbye. When they began their departure the voices of the adoring crowd blended into one thunderous roar. The many admirers maintained their clapping and shouting along the road until the sky darkened in the late afternoon. Nearly every house along the way sported a Confederate flag. Young ladies threw bouquets with patriotic notes attached while others lobbed fruits and treats. The soldiers were delighted.

128 vols. (Washington DC: Government Printing Office, 1880–1901). *OR*, ser.1, vol. 51, pt. 2, supplemental serial no. 108, p. 234.

[3] Andrew Jackson Reese to Nancy W. Wimpy, 27 September 1861.

The men rode in stock cars but spirits were high. They enjoyed themselves, lowing like cattle, squealing like pigs, and braying like mules, calling for corn and fodder. It was warm during the day and pleasantly cool at night. Only a heavy shower briefly dampened their spirits before arriving at Knoxville.[4]

Now moving through eastern Tennessee, they found themselves stuck in the drafty cars from noon until 7:00 A.M., and their happy state darkened. The weather now turned dismal and damp. The closer they came to their next destination, the locals seemed to be less interested in them. Strong Union sentiment was the reason. They were often denied even drinking water.

The men of the legion remained in Lynchburg through the warm days of August and early September 1861. Colonel Phillips was busy outfitting and drilling his troops. All were eager to join the fray. The *Augusta Daily Chronicle & Sentinel* echoed their feelings, reporting that the feud between Brown and Davis was impeding the movement of the legion's 1,000 men to western Virginia where they were sorely needed. The paper added that "The President was anxious to obtain the brigade for service in western Virginia, where Garnett's command had met with a recent disaster for want of support—and had these Georgians been there, the Laurel Hill retreat would never have occurred."[5]

Frustrated, Colonel Phillips set out to seek help from a fellow Georgian, Vice President Alexander Stephens, in order to obtain necessary supplies as well as orders for his legion. Stephens had been an antisecessionist and was largely ignored by President Davis and other members of the Confederate administration. Somewhat isolated, Stephens would come to oppose most of Davis's wartime policies.

Phillips sent one of his most reliable associates, Legion Chaplain George G. Smith, with several letters. Smith had been most effective during the early organization of the legion. He had amassed an astonishing quantity of supplies from counties supportive of the legion and the Confederacy. He was an articulate and persuasive spokesman. Smith visited Stephens and his brother Linton at the vice president's

---

[4] No author, "Virginia Correspondence. In Camp near Lynchburg, Va.," *Columbus* (GA) *Daily Times,* 3 September 1861.

[5] No author, "The Fourth Georgia Brigade—Something the People Ought to Know," *Augusta* (GA) *Daily Chronicle & Sentinel,* 2 August 1861, p. 3.

home in Richmond. Stephens's face was so heavily lined and darkened that he appeared to be much older than he actually was. He suffered from a variety of physical ailments; Reverend Smith described him as "a little, ugly, dried-up man." Smith did, however, find Stephens to be considerate and urbane. Stephens read the letters carefully and offered a considered but blunt response:

> Mr. Smith, I have no influence with this administration and I don't think I can do anything for you."
> "But, Mr. Stephens..."
> "There is no use to argue this matter, Mr. Chaplain, the facts are as I state them."
> "I did not intend to argue, Mr. Stephens, I merely wished to make a statement."
> "Ah, Mr. Smith, you are no lawyer, or you would know a statement is an argument."

Stephens did help. He arranged an appointment for Chaplain Smith with the quartermaster general and the assistant secretary of war, Judah P. Benjamin, whom Smith often referred to as the bravest man in the cabinet. His pleas for help had accomplished little but Smith found some satisfaction when he returned to Lynchburg and discovered that the legion had been ordered to the Army of Western Virginia under the command of General Robert E. Lee.[6] Local newspapers noted that the legion received the news with great enthusiasm and joy. Calls for clothing and blankets were printed in papers in the surrounding areas as well as in letters written home.[7] Winter was looming and the mountains of western Virginia were cold—colder than the Georgia boys had ever experienced.

Jack Reese and his comrades now marched to Lewisburg and to war. After a brief respite from the political storm during its entry into Confederate service, the Phillips Legion now marched into another controversy in western Virginia. The coming campaign would prove to

---

[6] Rev. George Gilman Smith, "Reminiscences," n.d., unpublished manuscript, Microfilm Library, drawer 283, box 40, Georgia Department of Archives and History, Morrow GA.

[7] S. Temple, *The First Hundred Years: A Short History of Cobb County, In Georgia* (Atlanta: Walter W. Brown Publishing Co., 1935) 246.

be poorly conceived and planned and the Legion was to be at the center of it. The combat would be confined to small skirmishes, and the maneuvering in the western counties of Virginia yielded little advantage to either side. This campaign would provide much-needed lessons in maintaining coherent organization and dealing with political interference in officer appointments. Experience in dealing with feuds among local commanders as well as logistical problems in feeding and transporting large bodies of troops in remote regions of the country would toughen and mature Confederate commanders.

In 1861 Virginia was one of the largest states in the Union. It extended from the Atlantic Ocean westward to the Ohio River and 300 miles north from North Carolina to Pennsylvania. The Allegheny Mountains cut through the middle of the state. These mountains would play a vital part in funneling military actions into certain areas. Geographical, cultural, and ideological characteristics of eastern and western Virginia were radically different. Eastern Virginia was a region of plantations, aristocratic exclusiveness, a large slave population, and profitable agriculture. Western Virginia was inhabited by German and Scots-Irish settlers, who were independent hunters, farmers, lumbermen, miners, and small manufacturers. Small subsistence farms dotted the landscape. The social structure tended to be egalitarian in the west and aristocratic in the east with its regimented plantation systems. Separated by mountains from the rest of Virginia, the residents of the western counties, especially those located in the northwest, had more in common with Ohio and Pennsylvania. Secessionism was rampant in the east and unionism equally so in the west.

Within days after Virginia voted for the ordinance of secession, the citizens of the towns and more populous counties of western Virginia were grumbling, talking among themselves about the formation of a new state.[8] The *Wheeling Intelligencer*, the only newspaper in Virginia to support Lincoln's 1860 run for president, posed the question: "If Virginia can secede from the United States, why cannot West Virginia secede from Virginia?"[9] Mass meetings were held throughout the region

---

[8] Horace Greely, *The American Conflict: A History of the Great Rebellion in the United States of America, 1860–1865*, 2 vols. (Hartford: O. D. Case and V. W. Sherwood, 1866) 1:518.

[9] Stanley Cohen, *The Civil War in West Virginia* (Charleston WV: Pictorial Histories Publishing Company, 1976) 7.

to denounce the action taken in Richmond. A call for a general convention of disaffected counties went out immediately. The First Wheeling Convention met on 13 May 1861. It laid the foundation for what was to become the State of West Virginia.[10] North and South began the struggle for the hearts and minds of the citizenry of Western Virginia.[11] Perhaps the primary fight was actually for this strategic corridor between North and South.

---

[10] Clayton R. Newell, *Lee vs. McClellan* (Washington DC: Regnery Publishing Co., 1996) 184.

[11] *OR*, ser. 1, vol. 2, p. 2.

Chapter 4

Sewell Mountain

*"After seeing after the sick as well as I could I rode on to Little
Sewell where our army was encamped. I found it in camp on the
summit of Little Sewell. I think your Aunts Home is only a few
miles from where we were encamped. We could see the tents of
Rosencrantz army on the mountains beyond."*

Reverend George Gilman Smith of the Phillips Georgia Legion must
have been awed by the sight of several thousand Yankee tents on the
distant mountains. He had traveled many miles in mud up to his horse's
knees and was in a dreary mood. Passing a makeshift hospital filled with
sick soldiers probably did nothing to improve his state of mind. Meeting
General Robert E. Lee mounted on Traveler helped cheer him.[1]

The legion troops were now part of a force that sought to deny
Federal access to the Shenandoah Valley. As the most important
strategic feature of the Old Dominion it could be used by either side as a
clear line of transport and communications running southwest from
Maryland into Tennessee. To the west the rugged Allegheny Mountains
helped impede any Federal forces operating from Ohio and must be
held. If the Federals overran the western mountains the valley would
soon be invaded and the North would be able to gain access to central
Virginia through the many gaps that carved up the Blue Ridge
Mountains.

Confederate troops had to control the western counties in order to
defend the valley. This mountainous region of western Virginia was
comprised of enormous forests between the Ohio River on the west and
the Shenandoah Valley on the east. Canyon-like valleys cut by fast-
flowing rapids slashed the landscape, making easterly movements

---

[1] Rev. George Gilman Smith, "Reminiscences," n.d., unpublished manuscript,
Microfilm Library, drawer 283, box 40, Georgia Department of Archives and History,
Morrow GA.

extremely difficult. Few good roads existed in this area, nor did any rail lines run through the mountains. The Rebel troops had to control this primitive transportation network.

Virginia Governor John Letcher had appointed Robert E. Lee as commander in chief of Virginia's state militia following Lee's resignation from the United States Army in April 1861. In May Lee became a general in the Confederate service. Initially he planned to position five regiments in the western counties but manpower proved to be a serious problem as did confused command responsibilities. After several setbacks for the Southern forces, Lee took the field and arrived at Huntersville on 6 August 1861.[2]

One major mistake on the part of Confederate authorities involved President Jefferson Davis. Without consulting General Lee, he requested that John B. Floyd raise a brigade of "mountain riflemen with their own tried weapons." Davis compounded the error by commissioning former Virginia governor Henry Wise as a Confederate brigadier general, authorizing him to recruit a legion of men from western Virginia.[3] A bitter confrontation between the two resulted in a state of acrimony that would have disastrous consequences for the Southern cause. For the second time in 1861, the Phillips legion troops found themselves caught between two competing egotistical men who would frustrate planning and inhibit military efficiency. Generals Floyd and Wise would quarrel and snipe at each other throughout the western Virginia campaign. By August 1861 Floyd finally managed to assume command of all forces of the Army of the Kanawha but a disgruntled Wise often ignored or refused to obey Floyd's orders. The feuding became so virulent that General Lee shifted his headquarters to the Sewell Mountain sector on 21 September in an attempt to bring the situation under control. On 25 September, shortly after Lee's arrival, Wise received orders to report to Richmond.[4]

---

[2] Robert Howison, "History of the War," in *Southern Literary Messenger* 38/1 (January 1864), David L. Phillips, *War Diaries: The 1861 Kanawha Valley Campaigns* (Leesburg: Gauley Mount Press, 1990) 49.

[3] US War Department, comp., *The War of Rebellion: A Compilation of the Official Records of the Union and Confederate* Armies, 128 vols. (Washington DC: Government Printing Office, 1880–1901) ser. 1, vol. 2, p. 838; *OR*, ser. 1, vol. 51, pt. 2, supplemental serial no. 108, p. 102.

[4] *OR*, ser. 1, vol. 5, pp. 148–49.

By mid-September General Wise had stationed his troops on Big Sewell Mountain, where he held the high ground. A 15,000-man Federal force under General William Rosecrans occupied a ridge about a mile to the west. Only a few minor skirmishes occurred from 15 to 30 September 1861. Lee expected an attack at any moment and urged General Floyd to bring his army forward from Meadow Bluff as quickly as possible. With a united force, Lee was confident his 12,000 entrenched soldiers could repel any Federal attack.

While Lee prepared for battle on Sewell Mountain, the Phillips legion departed Lynchburg, Virginia, on Monday, 23 September. They traveled first by train and then on foot to Lewisburg to join Floyd. Officers rode in passenger cars, enlisted troops in freight cars, and horses in stock cars. The train rattled through a mile-long tunnel on its trek through the mountains. The legion soldiers were amazed at the sight of the primitive western Virginia vista. They stopped for the night at Staunton, where they kindled fires and slept on the grass. Excitement animated the soldiers as their train plunged deeper into the mountain wilderness. At Millboro the authorities added an engine to push cars up a steep grade. The country became increasingly less civilized as the legion reached Jackson River, a supply depot supporting Confederate troops. From here the men were only 50 miles from their destination at Lewisburg.

Men and horses set out through rain and muddy slime. The horses showered the troops constantly with splattered mud while they slogged through fields to avoid the churned up roadway. The wagons lagged behind and the soldiers had to sleep in the pouring rain without tents. Some of the more resourceful troops placed poles over forked limbs and covered them with rail then covered the rails with oilcloths, enabling them to build fires for warmth and cooking. Morale remained high despite the trying conditions. The troops were confident in their soldierly abilities and proud of their officers. William D. Harris of cavalry Company C wrote his wife: "You all need not think our officers are too big-headed, for they will stand by us in all trials. Colonel Phillips does even take and give up his horse to the boys on foot, roll up his pants and wade in the mud and water and tote the *sick* on his back. This he did yesterday and day before. You need not doubt them. They are all the best set of officers in the war times."[5] The men passed through Callaghan, a well-known hostelry, 6 miles from Covington with the Jackson River winding around the picturesque town then pushed on over the mountains to a narrow gap, their chatter accompanied by more grumbling over the rough terrain. Some of the troops had never seen anything higher than a gopher hill. Arriving at White Sulphur Springs, most of the troops camped for the night while an advance party went on to Lewisburg. White Sulphur Springs was a resort surrounded by mountains on all sides with a sumptuous (for the times) hotel and several cottages. Now used as a hospital, the resort was showing signs of neglect but still retained an air of grandeur. The remaining legion soldiers continued their march the next morning, making slow progress because of muddy roads. They finally reached Lewisburg on 27 September and made camp. *Sick* men beset by all manner of disease and fatigue were scattered from the Jackson River to Lewisburg.

On the same evening, Colonel Phillips received a dispatch from General Floyd directing him to proceed to Meadow Bluff the next day to march with Floyd to Sewell Mountain. More *sick* men remained behind while the legion trudged ahead to Meadow Bluff.[6] General Floyd notified Lee on 28 September that he expected the arrival of the advance guard of the legion, which consisted of 400 of the riflemen and 100 of the cavalry, along with General William W. Loring's 2,000 men.[7] (The legion infantry and cavalry battalions operated as a unit at this time.) Floyd confirmed the arrival of the legion on the following day at 5:00 P.M. Private William H. Dobbins of infantry Company C found time to write to his father. After telling of their journey from Lynchburg he discussed attrition:

> Some of our company and also from other companies gave out on the road, exhausted with fatigue. The majority of them however were those who had just recovered from the mumps and measles. James Lowery came with us as far as the railroad extended but not feeling strong enough to attempt the journey,

---

[5] William D. Harris to Wife, 29 September 1861, Microfilm Library, drawer 283, roll 28, Georgia Department of Archives and History, Morrow GA.

[6] Smith, "Reminiscences."

[7] *OR*, ser. 1, pt. 2, supplemental serial no. 108 pp. 321, 324.

concluded to remain there. Bob Chitwood and one other stopped at the same place. Jim Chitwood was left behind twenty five miles from Lynchburg by going too far from the train and we have since heard that he returned to the hospital in L. Jim looks very badly but I have no idea that there is anything more than the blues was the matter with him. He has become tired of camp life and wants to go home. Hughs was left in Lynchburg but I think he was quite well. We also left half a dozen or more at the White Sulphur Springs, Bill Nichols included in the number.[8]

There would be little opportunity for rest as Floyd ordered his force forward to join Wise's men at Sewell Mountain. Floyd directed the following to decamp the next morning at 6:00 A.M.: the 36th, 50th, and 51st Virginia regiments of Volunteers, a section of Lieutenant John H. Guy's battery, First Lieutenant Warren Adam's section of artillery, the brigade under General Samuel R. Anderson, the brigade of militia under General Augustus A. Chapman, cavalry under command of Major Henry B. Davidson, and the Phillips Georgia Legion under command of Colonel Phillips. They were to take up line of march toward Sewell Mountain and report to General Lee on arrival.[9]

With the addition of General Loring, the reinforcements from the Phillips Georgia Legion, and the 20th Mississippi Regiment, Lee's numbers nearly equaled Rosecrans's. Rosecrans had been falsely informed that he would face only feeble resistance on the march to Lewisburg. Leading the Federal advance, General Henry W. Benham pushed his men over rutted roads through drenching rains. When he reached the summit of Big Sewell Mountain, he was shocked to find a Southern army in strong entrenchments. Both armies were ready to fight at Sewell Mountain. The green recruits of the legion struggled up to high ground to view the tents of Rosecrans's army. Some of the men looked through a spyglass to get a glimpse of the enemy. They watched the Federals on horseback and others huddled in small groups.[10] While

---

[8] William D. Dobbins to Dear Pa, 2 October 1861, Special Collections, microfilm call no. 322, Robert W. Woodruff Library, Emory University, Atlanta GA.

[9] *OR*, ser. 1, vol. 51, pt. 2, supplemental serial no. 108, p. 325.

[10] John A. Barry to Dear Sister, 7 October 1861, Barry Papers accession no. 3015, Southern Historical Collection, University of North Carolina Library, Chapel Hill NC.

the infantry waited for an attack, they amused themselves by ribbing the cavalry pickets, shouting that the cavalry was doing nothing more than scaring up bears for the infantry to fight while the Yankees got away. John A. Barry of infantry Company B described a "sheep hunt" in a letter to his sister: "We were drawn out in line of battle day before yesterday behind our breast works on account of firing of guns outside supposed to be pickets some of which came running in on the opposite side. Our company was sent out to know the cause. After going about half a mile we met a squad of our men that were sent out foraging with about eleven sheep on their backs which they had shot causing the whole army to fall into line. A pretty good joke...."[11]

The weather on Sewell Mountain amounted to eleven days' worth of gale-force winds and rain. Pickets did fire at each other nearly every day with little effect. Private Dobbins described the death of a Confederate colonel in a letter to his father: "Their pickets killed one of our Colonels a short time since, who went out with a part of his regiment. He was drunk when he went out and took only six companies, the rest refusing to follow him, while intoxicated. He tied himself to his horse which ran into camp with his body after he was shot...we are in daily expectation of a fight but know not whether we will attack them or wait for them to attack us."[12] On Sunday morning, 6 October, the legion soldiers awoke to find old "Rosey" gone. His tents had disappeared, or so it seemed. In fact, General Rosecrans had decided to withdraw to Gauley Bridge. The weather was rapidly deteriorating and the Gauley River had flooded, making resupply nearly impossible. Rosecrans decided to move his army to Gauley Bridge to procure stores from steamboats. The Northern army departed on the evening of 5 October under cover of darkness and mountain mists. By the next morning they had struggled over only 4 miles of washed-out roads. Lee ordered immediate pursuit by the cavalry, but it went for naught. The legion cavalry advanced down an old road that had been constructed before the turnpike. They moved cautiously until they were in full sight of the retreating Federals and charged. A timely volley from the rear guard did little damage but persuaded the cavalrymen to turn back. Southern infantry had just started out from camp when they met their own returning cavalry. Lee

---

[11] Ibid.
[12] William Dobbins to Dear Pa, 2 October 1861.

decided to call it a day. The Federals had departed Big Sewell but the reason was not at all clear. Chaplain Smith pondered the matter, observing: "There seemed to be a great army of them, but they have vamoosed, and after all our marching and all the mud, we did not fire a gun except at some sheep."[13] The Sewell Mountain standoff ended with hardly a whimper. Winter was rapidly approaching and Lee was left to decide on his next move.

---

[13] Smith, "Reminiscences."

Chapter 5

The Rag End of Hell

"The Yankees are the scariest set of fellows in the world."

Rosecrans's Federal army had retreated back to Hawk's Nest and Gauley Bridge at the head of the Kanawha River over nearly impassable roads. Oncoming winter, washed-out roads, and the Federal retreat convinced General Lee that the season for active campaigning was rapidly drawing to a close. Jefferson Davis urged Lee to return to Richmond. General Wise reported to Richmond on 28 September 1861. His legion would follow him at a later date to North Carolina, where they had been reassigned.[1]

General Floyd, however, wanted another opportunity to attack the Federals. He planned to assault Rosecrans before winter weather ended the mountain campaign. In the same spirit, Lee directed Floyd to quickly prepare his brigade to operate on the south side of the Kanawha.[2] Lee planned for Floyd to move to the head of the Kanawha Valley and disrupt Federal communications while Lee pressed Rosecrans by way of the James River and Kanawha Turnpike. General Loring's men and the Wise Legion were to be retained on Sewell Mountain for a short time to secure the road while Floyd marched his troops to the Kanawha via Green Sulphur Springs, Raleigh Court House, and Fayetteville.[3] On 12 October 1861, Floyd's army embarked on its roundabout journey to the Kanawha Valley with the Phillips Legion at the head of the column.[4]

---

[1] US War Department, comp., *The War of Rebellion: A Compilation of the Official Records of the Union and Confederate* Armies, 128 vols. (Washington DC: Government Printing Office, 1880–1901) ser. 1, vol. 51, pt. 2, supplemental serial no. 108, p. 269. Special Order No. 272 directed the Wise Legion under Col. Lucius Davis to duty in the Department of Hemrico. *OR*, ser. 1, vol. 51, supplemental serial no. 108, p. 426.

[2] *OR*, ser. 1, vol. 51, pt. 2, suppl. 108, p. 335.

[3] *OR*, ser. 1, vol. 51, pt. 2, pp. 337–38.

[4] This excludes the North Carolina regiment and the 50th Virginia regiment, the latter of which had been nearly decimated by illness, as well as the Wise Legion that Floyd

Following a difficult trek over poor mountain roads, the Confederates passed through Green Sulphur Springs then crossed the New River in jury-rigged boats. They marched on to Raleigh Court House, then to Fayette County and the Red Sulphur Turnpike. Strategically important to Floyd's plans, this turnpike provided access to the Kanawha's south bank. Floyd's army arrived at Raleigh Court House Saturday evening of 19 October.

Jack Reese heard a rumor that the Federals were just 25 miles ahead at Fayetteville and that Floyd planned to push ahead and attack on the following morning. Reese was exhilarated but apprehensive: "The Yankees are the scariest set of fellows in the world...they run and keep out of our reach so we cannot get to show them much less cut them with our big knives but, we will soon run them on the other side of the Ohio or in it. Only if they keep on running there is no telling where they will stop, but just let them run, I don't care. I had just as soon they would run as to stay and let me kill them...you know I am dangerous...what a pity I haven't got somebody to hold me."[5] The troops were tired, poorly clothed for the cold, wet climate, and short on food. After seven weeks in the mountains the legion soldiers were miserable. Sergeant Elisha J. Humphries of legion rear guard cavalry Company A penned a short note on the subject, exclaiming, "Western Virginia is not worth fighting for...it is the rag end of hell...it is nothing but mountains."[6]

---

determined to be in such a state of insubordination and so poorly disciplined as to be unfit for military purposes. For orders given for the march issued 11 October 1861, see *OR*, ser. 1, vol. 51, pt. 2, supplemental serial no. 108, pp. 341–42: "This army will march tomorrow morning at 6 o'clock in the following order: First, Phillips Legion; second, Second Brigade under Col. Tompkins; third, First Brigade under Col. Heth; the artillery; Fifth, baggage wagons belonging to Gen. Floyd's headquarters; Sixth, ammunition wagons, ordnance; Seventh, hospital wagons; Eighth, regimental baggage wagons; Ninth; supply train. A detail of one officer and twenty-five men will be made from the First Brigade as rear guard. Commanders of regiments will pay particular attention to keeping their men in ranks, and to allow no one to go into houses, or take or destroy property along the road. By Order of Brig. Gen. Floyd: H. B. DAVIDSON, Maj. and Acting Assistant Adjutant Gen."

[5] Andrew Jackson Reese to Archibald G. Wimpy, 20 October 1861, in Rees/Reese Collection, Lumpkin County Library, Madeline K. Anthony Collection, series 3, box 23, folder 5.

[6] Elisha J. Humphries to Wife, 19 October 1861, in Jeanne Humphries Collection, microfilm, drawer 238, roll 29, Georgia Department of Archives and History.

Endless rains turned the roads into quagmires. The teamsters needed six horses to haul a load that usually required but two. Mounted riders could not move any faster than a man could walk. At one point, Floyd was compelled to cut a new road 4 miles long. His resolute brigade pushed on despite the obstacles. After ten days of hard marching, the command reached Fayetteville around noon of 21 October. Without halting they continued on to the junction of Millers Ferry Road and the Raleigh Turnpike, 3 miles from Fayetteville. Federal pickets were posted just ahead and the command halted while Colonel Phillips chased the Federals down the Millers Ferry Road with seventy dismounted legion cavalrymen. The Federal pickets reached the ferry and crossed over to join their main force. A brisk firefight erupted between the legion troopers on the south bank and Federal infantry on the opposite side. Jack Reese wrote home: "...the first day we arrived our cavalry had a fight with them at the ferry and we learned since from a prisoner that they killed 27 men and a Lieutenant Colonel. Two of our men were wounded but slightly only. Col. Phillips was in the thickest of the fight."[7] Chaplain Smith reported on his own participation in the fighting: "I soon heard the crack of the rifles and knew a skirmish was going on. Skirmishers take all the protection they can secure and I took refuge behind a log. I saw a Yankee about a thousand yards away and I fired at him. I know I did not hit him for I saw him run, but a better marksman than I was among the Blue Coats shot at me and struck the log behind which I was lying about opposite to where I was."[8] The Federals were positioned on the north bank of the New and Kanawha Rivers in a line stretching from Miller's Ferry through Hawk's Nest to their headquarters at Gauley Bridge. Steamboats laden with supplies navigated the Kanawha to a point 6 miles east of the main Federal base. A road ran along the river's north side and all supplies for the Federals at Gauley Bridge had to move on this road.[9] This single track was the key to holding the headwaters of the Kanawha Valley. Federal fortifications along this road confirmed its significance.

---

[7] Reese to Mrs. Nancy Wimpy, 30 October 18, in Rees/Reese Collection.

[8] Rev. George Gilman Smith, *The Boy in Gray: A Story of the War* (Macon: Macon Publishing Company, 1894) 95–96.

[9] Robert Howison, "History of the War," *Southern Literary Messenger* 38/1 (January 1864).

After the fighting ended that evening Floyd established his camp at the Dickerson Farm near the junction of the Raleigh and Millers Ferry Roads. The legion was ordered to picket the woods opposite Hawk's Nest along the New River.[10] By 28 October, Floyd had shifted 4,000 of his troops, including the legion, to an advanced camp at nearby Cotton Hill. Cotton Hill was a moderately steep, wooded mountain lying in the river bend directly south of the junction of the Gauley and New Rivers, which join to form the Great Kanawha. The river was 500 yards wide at this point, pooled behind a 22-foot-high rock ledge called Kanawha Falls that extended across the riverbed. Cotton Hill dominated Gauley Bridge from across the Kanawha River and provided a strong strategic advantage, with the right flank protected by the cliffs of the New River and Piney Gorge for some 40 miles. Floyd pleaded with the Confederate War Department for much-needed reinforcements to retake the Kanawha Valley. He intended to seize the river and roads downstream from the Federals at Gauley Bridge, trapping the Federals between Floyd's army and Lee's forces at Sewell Mountain.[11] When Floyd had departed Big Sewell, the general plan called for Lee to attack Rosecrans while Floyd blocked the Federal line of retreat down the Kanawha.

Floyd urged Lee to move his army forward and attack according to the original plan.[12] Unfortunately, Lee's situation at Sewell Mountain had significantly deteriorated. The weather worsened by the day and the supply system was at a standstill. A steady stream of men were taken to hospitals in the rear with a variety of deadly illnesses. Many of them died. Also, General Loring's force was urgently needed at Cheat Mountain where the Federals were threatening to attack. On 20 October Lee informed Floyd that Loring's force was departing and that the Wise Legion, in poor condition, was to pull back to Meadow Bluff.[13] Lee finally realized that conditions would not allow him to take the offensive. He would leave Meadow Bluff on 29 October and return to Richmond. Frustrated, Floyd wrote to President Davis that he feared the campaign would end without result and all the forces assembled around Sewell

---

[10] Rev. George Gilman Smith, "Reminiscences," n.d., unpublished manuscript, Microfilm Library, drawer 283, box 40, Georgia Department of Archives and History, Morrow GA.

[11] *OR*, ser. 1, vol. 5, pp. 917–18.

[12] Ibid., pp. 924–25.

[13] Ibid., pp. 908–909.

Mountain would be of no profit to the war. Floyd's small army had to guard five important ferries. This divided his force, preventing him from making an attack along against an imposing enemy force. Floyd now pressed for authority to establish winter quarters, aiming to harass the Federals across the river. [14] Thirty-three-year-old Lieutenant Abraham "Ham" Jones of legion infantry Company D described the situation to his brother:

> I wrote you last from Sewell Mountain just after the bloody [Federals]…retreated from that place and since then we have been marching over the roughest country & the worst roads mortal man ever saw, some of us making our own roads as we marched. It does appear to me that this is the worst managed army that ever was. Some days marching through the rain then stoping on fine marching days and consequently we had and shall have a great many of our own men *sick*. We have lost some. We have now fit for service only four hundred men in the Legion and if we continue on in the same way will soon have none. Wm. Wood of Cedar Town died at New River on Thursday (16th) of this month—Typhoid Fever. A. O. Barton at Meadow Bluff a week before that of pneumonia. They are the only ones in our company who have died to my knowledge. Bill Knight and John Dodd have over taken us at last and have gotten about well again. We are sometimes tolerably hard…for something to eat & pretty hard living at that—no sugar & coffee. Bred & meat scarce—beef-beef-beef is the cry. We are here again in sight of the Yankees camped on the opposite side of the river for several miles—supposed to be from ten to fifteen thousands strong & we have not more than 3,000 men fit for service (only Gen. Floyd's command). What he expects to accomplish here with so small a force against such odds I don't know. He is planting his cannon on the hills by the river at different points for the purpose of giving them a few rounds as there is no chance for a fight with small arms unless they attempt to cross the river to get at us—which I don't think they

---

[14] No author, "From Western Virginia," *Augusta* (GA) *Daily Chronicle & Sentinel*, 2 November 1861, p. 1; *OR*, ser. 1, vol. 5, p. 900.

will do unless they go higher up or lower down-with a view of intercepting our supplies from Newbern on the Va & East Tenn R. Road. Our cavalry had a brush with them across the river the first evening they got here—they dismounted & got amongst the rocks & fired at them with their carbines—it is reported our boys killed 29 & amongst them one Col who was cursing his men at the time for being cowardly. Four of our boys received slight wounds & are getting on finely now.[15]

Early on 1 November, Floyd began cannonading from the heights of Cotton Hill opposite Gauley Bridge and below Kanawha Falls opposite Montgomery's Ferry. Floyd's gun crews had wrestled their guns into position through several miles of broken, wooded hills. This unexpected attack confused Rosecrans but he recovered and ordered a battery of three mountain howitzers to take position and respond to the fire. Shells screamed back and forth until nightfall. The long-range artillery duel lasted for seven days with minimal damage to either side. The Confederate fire halted Union ferry traffic and closed the north bank supply road during the daylight hours until the Federals brought up six Parrott rifled guns on 7 November and forced Floyd's gunners to retreat. High waters kept the Federals from crossing in force but heavy skirmishing continued as the Federals worked to dislodge the Rebels.[16] Private Dobbins of Company C related a close call in a letter to his father:

> I was detailed with some others of our company to go and guard Jackson's battery which has been firing upon the camps of the enemy from an imminence on this side of the river. The battery has not effected a great deal of damage (with the exception of killing six or seven men) which is owing to our having employed smoothbore guns. On that morning I was there the place of one of the smoothbore guns was supplied by a six pound rifle piece which I think will do much greater execution. We fired the rifle cannon four times to get the range and then

---

[15] Abraham "Ham" Jones to Dear Bob, 28 October 1861, private collection of Mr. and Mrs. David Harlan, Atlanta GA.

[16] *OR*, ser. 1, vol. 5, p. 285–88.

ceased on account of having no cartridges. The enemy returned fire promptly but did no damage. One of their shells exploded in about two steps of me and sent its contents whistled by my ears, but, fortunately, and I must say almost miraculously, none of them touched me. I think it would have killed one of our cavalrymen had he not been sitting on the ground, as the shell flew over his head as it burst. I found a piece of the shell after the explosion which I intended to keep but lost it in some way or another.[17]

Rosecrans had received word of the Confederate plans to move against him on both sides of the river but scouts informed him early in November that most of the Southern force had departed from Sewell Mountain. Now free to operate against Floyd's isolated force, Rosecrans made plans to encircle and capture Floyd's 4,000 troops.[18]

On 4 November, Colonel Phillips and several subordinate commanders advised Floyd that it was impractical to attempt to hold Cotton Hill and other positions occupied by the Rebels any longer that season. They recommended that the command march to Newbern, Dublin, or some other point near the railroad.[19] Floyd rejected their advice, stating that he had communicated with the Confederate War Department about winter quarters and would await those orders as he anticipated a site other than Newbern.[20]

Rosecrans now set his trap to catch Floyd. Cotton Hill's position persuaded Rosecrans that by crossing the New River above and the Kanawha River below the Confederate position, Floyd could be cut off and captured. On 6 November, Union Brigadier General Henry W. Benham crossed the Kanawha at Loup Creek with 3,000 men and moved his command several miles up the Creek. He was directed to march quickly, when so ordered, to get behind Floyd and cut off his escape route to the south. Union Brigadier General Robert C. Schenck was to cooperate by crossing his force over the New River at Townsend's Ferry

---

[17] William Dobbins to Father, 9 November 1861, Special Collections, microfilm call no. 322, Robert W. Woodruff Library, Emory University, Atlanta GA

[18] *OR*, ser. 1, vol. 51, pt. 2, supplemental serial no. 108, pp. 252–58.

[19] *OR*, ser. 1, vol. 51, pt. 2, supplemental serial no. 108, pp. 287–88.

[20] Ibid.

then push west and link up with Benham.[21] Rosecrans would hold the Confederates at the river by attacking with a small force up Cotton Hill.

"Ham" Jones located his unit in a letter to his brother: "Camp Dickerson South Side of New River Opposite the Mouth of Gauley—4 miles from Cotton Hill. 7 miles west of Fayetteville Fayette County Western Va. Nov. 8/61." He continued:

> I have been this particular in the heading of my letter because Pa complains that he cannot trace us on the map—all of those places are put down on the map of Va which is the only one we have in camp—but you can find the junction of New & Gauley on any map—we are about a mile from the New River about 8 miles above the junction of New & Gauley—Cotton Hill is directly opposite the junction on the south side of New— we have artillery planted on several bluffs for 7 miles up & down the river extending from the mouth of Gauley up the New River—the enemy have camps all along the bluffs—suppose to be about 6,000 men—according to what a prisoner told us—there was 12 redgments of Rozencrantzs force—we have only about 3,500 men fit for service.[22]

Around this time, Colonel Phillips was stricken with the typhoid fever that was sweeping through the army. General Floyd asked Chaplain George Smith to find an ambulance and evacuate the colonel to Raleigh Court House.[23]

On 10 November, General Cox detached Colonel Charles A. DeVilliers and 200 men from the Eleventh Ohio to cross the New River by ferry just above the mouth of the Gauley River. The Federals ran into the Rebels and drove Floyd's troops from the hill frontage and beyond Blake's Farm. Quickly reinforced, the Confederates pushed DeVilliers back to the woods near Blake's Farm, where he remained until evening. An additional six companies from the 2d Kentucky joined DeVilliers that

---

[21] Smith, *Boy in Gray*, 96.

[22] Abraham "Ham" Jones to Dear Brother, 8 November 1861, private collection of Mr. and Mrs. David Harlan, Atlanta GA.

[23] Smith, "Reminiscences," 43.

evening, drove the Rebels from the hills in front of New River, and occupied the ridge.

Renewing the action the next morning, Colonel DeVilliers attacked with the 11th Ohio and 2d Kentucky foot soldiers and pushed Floyd from the heights of Cotton Hill. Floyd's men retreated 3 miles back toward Dickerson's Farm to established breastworks. The edgy Confederates worked to strengthen the barricades in a heavy rain and waited to see what would happen next.

Rosecrans informed General Benham that Union forces had captured Cotton Hill. He directed the general to march to Cassidy's Mill and prepare for a decisive movement on the Confederate flank or rear on Fayette Road. On 12 November Benham' s troops were marching for the rear of the Rebel position when a civilian appeared in camp and alerted Floyd of the Federal approach. Moments later another mounted civilian appeared, informing Floyd that the Federals had been seen crossing at Bowyer's Ferry in the early morning of 10 November.[24] An alarmed Floyd realized that he was in danger of being surrounded. To buy time, he sent a detachment of Virginians under Colonel Henry Heth to delay the Federal flanking column. Benham's men advanced up the Laurel Creek ravine and stumbled into Heth's ambush. A sharp skirmish ensued with two killed on each side. Benham ordered his troops to retreat a short distance and camp.[25] The Confederates began a full retreat at nightfall. Because of a shortage of wagons they torched many tents, uniforms, and blankets and dumped food supplies on the ground to keep the enemy from capturing them.[26] The cavalry battalion of the legion and Colonel John McCausland's mountain battalion formed a rear guard. After the infantry departed, the legion's cavalry followed, fully expecting to make contact with the Federals on the road. They managed to pass safely out of the trap thanks to General Benham, who halted his troops just 2 miles from the road to await reinforcements.[27] General Rosecrans would eventually call for Benham to be court-martialed for allowing Floyd's army to escape.

---

[24] Smith, *Boy in Gray*, 98

[25] *OR*, ser. 1, vol. 5, pp. 283–84.

[26] Frank Moore, *Rebellion Record*, 6 vols. (New York: G. P. Putnam, 1861–1871) 2:388.

[27] Smith, *Boy in Gray*, 98–99.

Unbeknownst to Floyd, several regiments were on their way to reinforce him. A dispatch from the secretary of war dated 15 November 1861 noted that three regiments and two rifled 12-pound guns were en route. President Davis felt certain this would enable Floyd to hold Cotton Hill. The secretary also stated that he hoped Floyd would not feel compelled to abandon Cotton Hill until he forced the enemy to desert their camp at the junction of the Gauley and Kanawha.[28] It was too late for Floyd to hold Cotton Hill or any other place in Fayette County, his withdrawal ending Southern activity in this area for the remainder of 1861. True to form, Georgia Governor Joseph E. Brown asked the secretary of war to return the legion, which, he stated, was trained and armed at state expense for the protection of Savannah. The secretary promptly denied his request.[29] Though furious with Benham for failing to intercept Floyd's retreat, Rosecrans permitted him to pursue Floyd, who fell back as rapidly as possible, marching about 12 miles before halting for the night. At 4:00 A.M. the next morning, the march resumed with the troops covering almost 20 miles before encamping at McCoy's Mill. Benham caught up with the rear guard on the third day just as Floyd was departing the mill. Not realizing Benham's men were so close, the Confederates were caught by surprise. Colonel George Croghan, Floyd's cavalry commander, was killed leading twenty-five of his lancers in a charge to blunt the pursuit. Floyd quickly moved the bulk of his force to the south, leaving two regiments of infantry and the legion cavalry to delay the Federals. The Rebels checked the Federal attack and held Benham's men long enough for Floyd to get away.[30]

Floyd's troops were reduced by illness by this time, numbering less than 3,200 effectives. Benham's force totaled around 4,500 and might have overtaken Floyd, but Benham received word that a large force of Southern cavalry was somewhere in his rear. Heavy rain fell and a winter storm threatened. Receiving orders from General Schenck to return to Fayetteville, the miserable Ohioans retraced their steps.[31] Floyd had escaped once more but the operation was successful in dislodging the

---

[28] *OR*, ser. 1, vol. 5, p. 955.

[29] Allen D. Candler, ed., *The Confederate Records of the State of Georgia, 1860–1865*, 6 vols. (Georgia: State Printer, 1909) 142–43.

[30] Smith, *Boy in Gray*, 99.

[31] Howison, "History of the War," 68; *OR*, ser. 1, vol. 5, p. 258.

Confederates and driving them away from that area of the country. Floyd continued the march for the next two days to Raleigh Court House. Rain fell continually and the roads turned to quagmires, causing terrible suffering. After resting several days just south of Raleigh Court House, Floyd's troops resumed their march to Peterstown on the present-day West Virginia and Virginia border.[32] Still suffering from typhoid fever, Colonel Phillips joined the retreat in an ambulance. One of the Phillips Legion soldiers encountered General Floyd during the retreat. Ambling along, whistling, this carefree spirit was confronted by the general. Ethelred E. Rainey of cavalry Company D recorded Floyd's exchange with the unknown legion trooper in his diary: "Floyd was on top he walked up to the Georgian and asked him if he knew how to salute an officer. 'Well I used to did at Lunchburg [*sic*] but I most forgot how since I've been up here.' 'Do you know who you are talking to' said Floyd. 'Well yes I believe I do. You look just like the old fellow I saw the other day running from Cotton Hill on a mule.' We all made the mountains sing with laughter at this."[33]

Special Order No. 254 arrived at Peterstown on 4 December 1861. It directed Floyd to take post at Newbern on the Virginia and Tennessee Railroad and await further orders.[34] Confederate authorities arrived at Newbern to inspect Floyd's command and determine its fitness for future operations. George Deas, assistant inspector general, submitted his report to Richmond on 14 December. The Phillips Legion with six companies of infantry and four of cavalry were included in the inspection. Deas reported that the troops had suffered great hardships during the active campaigning in western Virginia and were suffering the aftereffects of the many diseases that had swept through the ranks. He believed the brigade was improving and with rest would soon be able to engage in any service required. To Deas's critical eye the Georgians appeared as raw, undisciplined troops. Instruction was entirely wanting. Indeed, the men had had little opportunity to receive proper instruction because they had been constantly engaged in active operations since

---

[32] Thomas J. Riddle, "Reminiscences of Floyd's Operations in West Virginia in 1861," in *Southern Historical Society Papers*, 52 vols. (New York: Charles Scribner's Sons, 1883) 11:92–98.

[33] Diary of Ethelred Rainey, 25 November 1861 entry, Hargrett Rare Book and Manuscript Library, MS 1152, University of Georgia, Athens GA.

[34] *OR*, ser. 1, vol. 5, pp. 980–81.

September. Deas concluded that these troops had gone through a campaign that would do credit to any force and that they had suffered the hardship without complaint. Deas also recommended that the brigade not be moved far for the winter but he did recommend that the 13th Georgia Regiment, the Phillips Legion, and the 20th Mississippi Regiment should be ordered to a milder climate. He believed that the severe winters of western Virginia would be fatal to these men from the Deep South.[35]

On 16 December, Floyd was notified that he was not to establish winter quarters, as his troops were needed to counter active Federal threats in other areas. The Phillips Legion, the 20th Mississippi, the 13th Georgia, and Major George C. Waddill's battalion would be sent to South Carolina, where General Lee now commanded the coastal defenses. The remaining troops under Floyd's command were to move to Bowling Green, Kentucky, to reinforce General Albert Sydney Johnston. Special Order No. 268 directed the Phillips Legion and the Twentieth Mississippi to Coosawhatchie, South Carolina.[36] Confederate authorities ordered the troop movement with the proviso that the legion cavalry battalion's horses could be rested and follow at a later date. The year closed with no organized Confederate forces in western Virginia except in the northeast. Rosecrans had 40,000 Federal soldiers in the state, organized into three military districts. General Floyd would embarrass himself in Tennessee at Fort Donelson by fleeing its surrender and was relieved from command in March 1863. General Lee's performance in the western mountains offered little to enhance his reputation, but President Davis continued to demonstrate great respect for Lee's judgment and capabilities. Time would prove Davis's trust to have been well-placed.

Sergeant Humphries of the Phillips Legion cavalry summed up the thoughts of the men when he wrote to his wife in late November from Peterstown: "If I do ever get away from here I never want to see this part of the world again. The fellows of our Legion have died up here considerably since we have been in Virginia. We had four corpses on hand at one time last Sunday. We have not had any to die in our company yet though we have got over twenty *sick* at this time scattered

---

[35] Ibid., pp. 995–96.
[36] Ibid., pp. 1000–1001.

through the country around here."[37] General Floyd expressed a similar opinion: "It cost us more men, sick and dead than the Battle of Manassas."[38] Thirty legion soldiers died from disease during the campaign. Another twenty-four men's final muster roll entries, dated 31 October or 1 November 1861, end with notations showing "present" or "sick." Many of these men might have perished in the rugged mountains as they have never been located in any postwar census or pension records. In addition, many soldiers who survived the variety of diseases were so disabled that they were discharged from the service.[39] It was an elated group of soldiers who piled into the cars of the Virginia and East Tennessee Railroad in late December to begin their journey to South Carolina. The nightmare of the mountains was behind them, and the sunny South lay ahead.

---

[37] Elisha J. Humphries to wife, 28 November 1861, microfilm, drawer 283, roll 29, Georgia Department of Archives and History.

[38] Gen. John B. Floyd to Secretary of War, 16 October 1861, in *OR*, ser. 1, vol. 5, p. 900.

[39] Compiled Service Records, National Archives micropublication, M266, rolls 592–600, Georgia Department of Archives and History, Morrow GA.

Chapter 6

Mussceeters, Gallinippers, and Flies

*"The other day I caught a shark two feet long, and carelessly put
my fingers in his mouth to pull out the hook, and he caught me!"*

Lieutenant John "Jack" L. Dodds of Company D must have recuperated
from the misery he suffered in western Virginia in early January 1862
when he wrote to his friend Bob from Hardeeville:

> After a long period of absence I have concluded to drop you
> a few lines asking you down to this happy land of Canan [*sic*].
> When I contrast the climate with north West Va I feel like I
> have been transported from hell to paradise, for if there be a hell
> on this earth it must be in Va and the road there is very easy
> found & to prevent you or any of my friends from going there I
> will tell you the way. Take the Rail Road & proceed to
> Lynchburg & thence to Stanton & there to Jackson River &
> there pack your nap sack & leave the balance of your baggage in
> the old stable that stands on the bank of the river, then take a
> haver sack & fill it with hard crackers & boiled beef without salt.
> Pack it all on your back & proceed in the direction of Cotton
> Hill mostly through the woods and after marching seventy miles
> you come to what they call in that land a pike, but before
> reaching there you come to what is called fiddlers green on
> pinch of [sulfur{?}]...creek where several of the Devil's
> emissaries live. They will encourage you on as fast as possible.
> Well after you reach the pike you take the right end of it &
> proceed on to cotton hill, then take your stand on the margin of
> the hills west side which over looks the Gauley River & on the
> oposit [*sic*] bank you can see the old Deamon and all of his
> emissaries. By the way I learn that one of his agents has got
> down in to the Ga Legislator & spoke flewently [*sic*] of the

congenial climate of his Happy Land & the good conditions of
the Soldiers in that region. When you see him again I want you
to ask him what he has been eating god dam him.[1]

The warm Atlantic breeze of coastal South Carolina stood in sharp
contrast to the cold and rugged mountains of western Virginia. The area
was hot, dotted with sand hills and marshland. This was the oldest
settled part of the state. The French had arrived here over 300 years
earlier and the British been permanently established for the past 200
years.

Located south of Charleston, Bluffton was one of many small
hamlets that served as summer homes for the wealthy citizenry. It was a
quaint little village surrounded by live oaks and pines on a bluff above
the May River. The islands along the coast were famous for producing
excellent long-staple cotton and the rice plantations on the mainland
were well situated on freshwater rivers. The sea was generous, providing
the legion soldiers with a rich harvest of fish and oysters. The marsh and
wiregrass of the pinewoods furnished pasturage for cattle while the rice
and corn produced on every plantation provided plentiful grain.
Steamers arrived every three weeks on their way from Charleston to
Savannah, providing the planters contact with the broader world. For
generations these people on the coast and sea islands had lived in great
luxury. Their lives had been untroubled—until the fall of Port Royal.
With the Federal Navy's capture of this port the residents of the region
were thrown into panic. They fled to the interior of Georgia and South
Carolina, abandoning nearly all their worldly goods. Libraries of books,
carved mahogany chairs, bureaus, and ornate sofas remained behind to
accommodate the troops. Only a few old men stayed on and there were
no ladies closer than Hardeeville, 20 miles distant.[2]

Georgia Governor Joseph E. Brown had been obsessed with the
vulnerability of the Southeastern coast since the beginning of the war.
The Federals had blockaded the coastal areas but quickly learned that
their blockade was ineffective due to a lack of support bases along the

---

[1] John "Jack" Luther Dodds to Friend Bob Jones from Hardeeville, 11 January 1862,
private collection of Mr. and Mrs. David Harlan, Atlanta GA.

[2] Rev. George Gilman Smith, *The Boy in Gray: A Story of the War* (Macon: Macon
Publishing Company, 1894) 1894, 110–15.

coast. If the Union controlled selected ports along the Confederacy's coastline, their use as supply, refitting, and refueling depots would enable a more efficient blockading operation. Thus was born a plan for combined army-navy expeditions to capture key Southern harbors. Port Royal was selected as the best site on the Georgia and South Carolina coast.[3] The harbor at Port Royal offered the Union Navy safe and ample anchorage. It also afforded adequate camp space for the army of Brigadier General Thomas W. Sherman, who was in charge of the combined expedition. The capture of Port Royal on 7 November 1861 provided the United States fleet and army an excellent permanent base of operations against the entire Southeast coast. Although Sherman commanded less than 15,000 men, it was readily apparent that Union landings could easily be accomplished within a few miles of strategic bridges on the Charleston and Savannah Railroad. The village of Bluffton, easily reached by gunboats, offered a good landing site and base of operations against the railroad at Hardeeville, only 4 miles from the Savannah River and 15 miles from Savannah itself.[4]

On the day after the fall of Port Royal, General Robert E. Lee arrived to take command of the Department of South Carolina and Georgia. It was quickly evident that the rivers and sea islands could not be defended with the troops at his command. The Federal Navy commanded access to the vast network of sounds, rivers, and creeks that infiltrated the Carolina and Georgia coasts. Union infantry could land under cover of gunboats whenever they chose. Scarcely a day passed that a demonstration was not made at some point, making it necessary to maintain troops at the ready.[5] Lee prepared for the inevitable, concentrating his meager force at strategic points. He established his headquarters at Coosawhatchie about 10 miles south of Pocataligo and divided his line of defense into five military districts. Lee assigned responsibility for the fifth district, covering the area from Port Royal to the Savannah River, to Brigadier General Thomas Fenwick Drayton,

---

[3] D. Ammen, "DuPont and the Port Royal Expedition," in vol. 1 of *Battles and Leaders of the Civil War*, 4 vols., ed. Robert U. Johnson and Glarence C. Buel (New York: De Vinne Press, 1884) 671–91.

[4] C. Evans, *Confederate Military History*, 7 vols. (Atlanta: Confederate Publishing Co., 1899) 5:35.

[5] C. Dowdy, *The Wartime Papers of Robert E. Lee* (Boston: Little Brown, 1961) 108–109.

who was headquartered at Hardeeville.[6] One of Lee's key priorities was protection of the 100-mile-long Charleston and Savannah Railroad. Lacking the manpower to defend the entire length of the railroad, he assembled troops at likely points of attack beyond the range of gunboats. Cavalry patrolled the coast to keep the Union ships some distance from the shore. Lee planned to use the railroads to move infantry reinforcements to any threatened points along the coast.

Governor Brown had continued to harangue Confederate authorities for the return of "his" army to Georgia. Citing the threat to Savannah, on 11 November he demanded that Confederate Secretary of War Judah Benjamin return the old Fourth State Brigade to his control, contending that all these troops had been trained and armed at state expense. Secretary Benjamin refused, observing that it would be suicidal to remove the troops while they were actively engaged in the western Virginia campaign.[7] The situation changed in December when it became evident that the western Virginia campaign had ended and the legion received orders to join General Lee in South Carolina. However, just as Phillips's Georgians prepared to leave Dublin, Virginia, they received startling news. Floyd stunned the legion with an announcement that their destination would be Kentucky, not South Carolina, and they would remain under his command. In the absence of Colonel Phillips, who had returned to Georgia to recuperate from typhoid, Lieutenant Colonel Seaborn Jones telegraphed the secretary of war, who immediately cleared the confusion. The legion was to report to Lee in South Carolina. Greatly relieved, the infantry battalion hurriedly boarded the trains and departed Dublin. They passed through Petersburg, Virginia, on 4 January 1862, reaching Hardeeville, South Carolina, a day later.

The cavalry battalion did not arrive in South Carolina until the end of January. In early December 1861, cavalry troopers had started for Carter County, Tennessee, to take up winter quarters and rest their horses. The troopers rode through Virginia into Tennessee and camped at Elizabethton. Major John B. Willcoxon, the cavalry commander,

---

[6] Evans, *Confederate Military History*, 5:38; Dowdy, *Robert E. Lee*, 117.
[7] Charles P. Byrd, vol. 2 of *Confederate Records of the State of Georgia, 1860–1865*, 6 vols. (Atlanta: State Printer, 1909); OR, Vol. 6, 315. Benjamin's response of 12 November 1861 is found in Byrd, *Confederate Records*, 2:142–43.

wrote to General Lee describing the wretched state of his horses. The animals had suffered from inadequate forage in western Virginia and had been further stressed by the 180-mile march to Tennessee. Willcoxon requested permission to camp in Georgia for four to five weeks to rest the horses and obtain replacements. Lee granted the request and in late January 1862 the legion horsemen arrived at Hardeeville.[8] Hardeeville was station number 9 on the Charleston and Savannah Railroad. The village consisted of a scattered collection of summer homes. The Phillips Legion was assigned to Brigadier General Thomas F. Drayton. An 1828 West Point graduate, Drayton had served in the United States Army for eight years before resigning to become a planter. For several years before the war, Drayton served as the president of the Charleston & Savannah Railroad. Drayton's command was initially headquartered at Hardeeville and then moved to Bluffton. The Phillips Legion companies were detailed in groups along the railway line in order to protect it from Federal troops on the nearby sea islands. Many of the company officers and men found comfortable quarters in the numerous abandoned homes. The unsheltered misery of the western Virginia campaign was behind them, and there could be no better place for them to rest and replenish their thinned ranks.[9]

Life on the South Carolina coast became a routine of drill and picket duty. Videttes stood their posts along the rivers on 2-hour watches. They kept careful watch for enemy gunboats and exchanged occasional fire with enemy pickets across the river with little effect.[10] Rumors of Union activity occasionally broke the tedium. On 4 February 1862, Lee ordered General Drayton to advance a company to establish an observation post on the approaches to the Savannah River. Lee hoped Drayton's men could intercept Federal reconnoitering parties reported to be in the area. Drayton selected Company E, the Blue Ridge Rifles of

---

[8] No author, "Phillips Legion Cavalry Arrives Atlanta, Awaiting Transport to S.C.," *Atlanta Southern Confederacy*, 12 January 1862, p. 3; Maj. John B. Willcoxon, commander of Phillips Legion cavalry battalion, dispatch to Maj. Gen. Lee, C.S.A., commander of Confederate state forces in South Carolina and Georgia, 23 December 1861, Eleanor S. Brockenbrough Library, Museum of the Confederacy, Richmond VA.

[9] Smith, *Boy in Gray*, 111–12; Rev. George Gilman Smith, "Reminiscences," n.d., unpublished manuscript, Microfilm Library, drawer 283, box 40, Georgia Department of Archives and History, Morrow GA.

[10] Smith, *Boy in Gray*, 113.

the legion's infantry battalion. On 5 February the company marched down the coast some 4 to 5 miles and built breastworks. As matters developed, the only real action was the daily firing of big guns aimed at a deserted fort at Red Bluff.[11]

While assisting the cavalry in patrolling the South May River 20 miles east of Hardeeville, soldiers from Company A, the Greene Rifles of the Phillips Legion's infantry battalion, sighted Federal gunboats. Lieutenant Daniel B. Sanford wrote to his sister on 28 February, detailing Company A's assignment on the South May River:

> I believe you are aware of our company being detached from the Battalion and sent to this point to assist a cavalry company in picket duty. We have a distance of ten miles to guard on this and New River. We can see Yankee boats from all our posts but none have attempted to land or come nearer than one mile since we have been here. They burnt up some very valuable houses and plantations before we came here. This is the most desolate looking country you ever saw. Fine houses and furniture left without any one to take care of it. I have to go by one house when I visit the pickets about ten miles from camp where there is a fine piano. I always go in and play a tune but I can't enjoy it for the Yankees can land any where at high tide and I feel uneasy for fear that they will slip up & catch me. This is the most pleasant camp we have ever had. It is delightful to be here by ourselves. We have plenty of oysters and take boat rides whenever we feel like it. I have a horse furnished me when my day comes to visit the pickets. Tell Lieut. Fuller and Sergt. Johnson if you see them that they are missing all the fun. The Yankee boats have all disappeared except three or four. I expect they are going to make an attack either on Savannah or Charleston. We will hear their big guns tomorrow. I reckon this is a favorable time for them. The tide is higher at this season

---

[11] Dowdy, *Robert E. Lee*, 109; no author, "Special Correspondences from the South Carolina Coast," *Atlanta Southern Confederacy*, 21 February 1861, n.p.

than any other during the whole year. It rises ten or fifteen feet here.[12]

On 13 March Lieutenant Sanford and his Greene Rifles moved to a new camp 2 1/2 miles from Bluffton. Sanford was not impressed with their new location, writing to his sister that it was

> one of the gloomiest locations that your imagination could possibly picture. Just imagine piney woods, swamps, long moss and the palmetto so thick that you can't walk through it. Snakes in the greatest variety and a country where no one ever did or ever can live and you have a faint idea of our situation. And that is not the worst. We are fifteen miles in front of the whole of Drayton's army with the exception of 3 cavalry companys who are 2 1/2 miles in our rear and Yankees by the thousands just two miles in our front and on each side.[13]

The Federals almost surrounded the Greene Rifles, who feared being cut off and captured. Sanford expressed his fear of being captured, telling his sister, "I don't expect anything when I lie down at night but to wake up and find myself a prisoner in the hands of the yanks for they can cut us off from a half dozen different ways. Why we are stationed here, I can not imagine for we are not strong enough to make any kind of a stand against the enemy if they should land with much force, which they will certainly do if they land at all."[14]

Sanford's fears were realized just four days later, on 20 March, when four of his men were captured on picket duty in support of the cavalry battalion. They represented the only combat losses for the legion during the time spent in South Carolina. The captives were Privates James O. Belk, James O. Wright, James T. Scott, and Leonidas S. Youngblood. Later paroled and exchanged, these four men returned to duty with the legion at Richmond in August 1862. On 20 March the infantry battalion's Company E, the Blue Ridge Rifles, had force-

---

[12] Daniel B. Sanford to Sister, 28 February 1861, private collection of Mr. Sanford Penticost, Atlanta GA.

[13] Daniel B. Sanford to Sister, 16 March 1862, private collection of Mr. Sanford Penticost.

[14] Ibid.

marched to reinforce the Greene Rifles but the Federals had departed by the time they arrived. On this same day Major Willcoxon of the legion's cavalry battalion reported that the enemy had landed a regiment at Buckingham and another at Hunting Island with a battery of artillery and were advancing toward Bluffton. Willcoxon sent twenty men each from Captain Charles DuBignon's and Captain William W. Rich's cavalry companies to intercept the enemy at Hunting Island. He dispatched Captain William B. C. Puckett's Company C to Seabrook Church to support the pickets. DuBignon and Rich's companies were soon engaged at the edge of Bluffton but were not able to advance. Willcoxon ordered his troopers to fall back to the opposite side of the town. They dismounted at Pope's Place and advanced on foot. Soon finding his men in danger of being cut off from their horses, Willcoxon directed them to remount and retreat to the end of Mr. Crowell's lane in order to better shelter the horses. Here they made preparations to resist any further enemy advance. Lieutenant John F. Milhollin of cavalry Company B and five men remained behind to keep watch and report any enemy movement. Two days later Milhollin reported that the enemy had retired from Bluffton. He was ordered to follow them and report on their movement but no further engagement took place. [15]

During this campaign Lieutenant Milhollin described in a letter to his wife a confrontation with Federal steamers:

> I am in common health by no means good—I was on duty to day being officer of the day, hence I had another [illegible]...for several miles along the beach during which time I again saw quite a number of Yankee steamers, some of which ran in gun shot of us, that is cannon shot, at one time I suspected they were fixing to give me and the pickets a broad side but she turned her course and ran off to join a part of the blockading

---

[15] Maj. John B. Willcoxon dispatch to Gen. Drayton, 20 March 1862, US War Department, comp., *The War of Rebellion: A Compilation of the Official Records of the Union and Confederate* Armies, 128 vols. (Washington DC: Government Printing Office, 1880–1901) ser. 1, vol. 6, pp. 103–104; Maj. Willcoxon report to Lt. Col. Seaborn Jones Jr., 23 March 1862, *OR*, ser. 1, vol. 6, p. 106; Maj. Willcoxon dispatch to Col. William Phillips, 24 March 1862, Eleanor S. Brockenbrough Library, notified Phillips that four pickets belonging to the Greene Rifles were missing near Bluffton and were feared captured.

fleet…just a while the steamer hove into view, one of our pickets shot a Yankee on a little sail boat and she at once tucked and skimmed away. There were no cannons on her and she came in speaking distance of the pickets.[16]

The tedium of duty in South Carolina soon caused the soldiers to become restless as well as home*sick*. Sergeant Jack Reese of legion infantry battalion Company E complained: "We have seen more service and less fighting than any set of men in the service."[17] The inevitable daily drills continued. The men had time on their hands when not on picket duty and could come and go as they pleased as long as they were present for drill and roll call. They devoured the daily papers to stay updated on the war and showed equal enthusiasm for mail from home. Some of the bored soldiers arranged to have their wives or other family members visit them in camp. Napping was also a popular pastime. The Georgians loved to boat and fish. Many caught fish, crabs, and oysters by the score, and they were amazed at the variety of fish. Nothing like this existed in North Georgia. Chaplain Smith described the stingray as "an awful fellow, with a diabolical look, long tail, and awful barb, which he wears just coming out of his back. This barb he sends into his victim, and it holds him like a fishhook." The reverend related his painful encounter with a sea creature: "The other day I caught a shark two feet long, and carelessly put my fingers into his mouth to pull out the hook, and he caught me! I was caught for sure; but the Sergeant came to my rescue, and pried the shark's jaws open. He had bitten through my finger nail."[18]

The young soldiers continued to experience new adventures. While on picket duty one night, a few of the men heard an odd splashing noise. It was dark with little moonlight to illuminate their area. Terrified, they fired their carbines at the supposed enemy, mounted their horses, and dashed back to camp. The bugler sounded "saddles" and in short order the cavalry raced to the scene. They found neither Yanks nor gunboats, just a school of porpoises rolling over and over, enjoying themselves.[19]

---

[16] Lt. John F. Milhollin to Dear Ev, undated, private collection of Richard M. Coffman, Huntersville NC.

[17] Andrew Jackson Reese to Aunt, 2 March 1862, Rees/Reese Collection, Lumpkin County Library, Madeline K. Anthony Collection, series 3, box 23, folder 5.

[18] Smith, "Reminiscences," 46.

[19] Ibid.

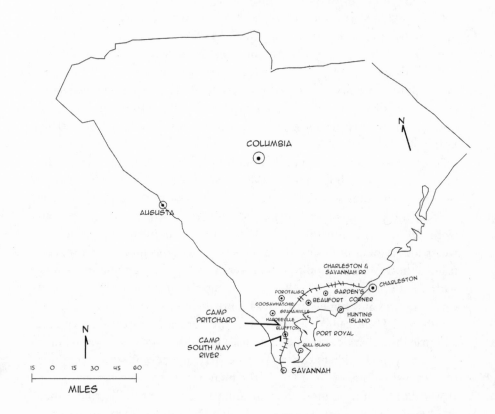

The South Carolina Interlude, January 1862–July 25, 1862

Some of the men found the alligators fascinating, and a few of the braver troops dragged a 7-footer into camp. The local swamps were supposed to be full of gators and around the campfires considerable discussion went on about swamp critters. Snakes also slithered throughout the piney woods and swamps. In the camp area the men killed at least one rattlesnake per day.[20]

Chaplain Smith recounted an encounter with an intruder while sharing a tent with Colonel Phillips. One morning after a sound night's sleep he was awakened by his body servant, Sam, who said to him: "See here, Parson, what I found under your pillow! It was a red snake."[21] The soldiers of Company E, the Blue Ridge Rifles, built two tree swings for entertainment. They occupied the swings from morning until late evening. Unfortunately some of the men got carried away swinging and severely injured themselves. Jack Reese admitted that he might fall and break his arm, as that was the only way he might obtain a furlough. Reese had hoped the war would end by spring 1862. The warmer climate had reinvigorated him and he thought often of the fairer sex and settling down. If they would just let him go home he might have some fun with the girls: "Or at least I think I would. I have not been in the company of any girls of consequence since I left home and would not know how to behave myself if I had to get in the company of some of the girls in old Dahlonega. I will be 21 years old day after tomorrow and then look out for the squalls and hide out the gals for I am coming home to marry. You ought to see my mustache and goatee. I have a nice set of whiskers which make me look fine I imagine."[22] While the legion was settling into its new routine, political maneuvering was underway back in Atlanta and Marietta. The smoldering Brown-Davis feud heated up again when Governor Brown renewed his campaign to gain Colonel Phillips a promotion to brigadier general. Phillips had written to Governor Brown on 25 February 1862, informing him that Colonel Thomas R. R. Cobb had obtained approval to enlarge his legion. Phillips asked why the same privilege should not be afforded him. He believed

---

[20] Ibid.

[21] Ibid.

[22] Andrew Jackson Reese to Aunt, 31 March 1862, Rees/Reese Collection.

that only intercession by Brown and Vice President Alexander Stephens would gain the approval for an increase of his legion.[23]

Davis responded to Brown on 27 April: he was unable to accede to the request. His denial was not for lack of desire but because the law did not permit him to comply with Brown's request. He stated further that Brown was misinformed on the subject of Colonel Cobb's legion. He had not been authorized to increase his command to 5,000 men. As soon as ten companies of infantry were combined under one command, the law knew no other organization for them than a regiment. Hence all legions were restricted to a number of infantry companies less than ten and to a proportionate number of cavalry and artillery companies, generally about four or five companies of cavalry and one or two batteries of artillery. Davis steadfastly refused to augment any legion beyond a colonel's command. In fact, Cobb had indeed requested an increase in strength and believed Davis had given his consent, probably in part a result of the growing animosity between Brown and Davis. Cobb was furious when he learned that Davis had changed his mind. He enlisted the aid of friends in an attempt to sway Davis, but to no avail. Eventually given the choice of commanding a regiment of infantry or cavalry or a modestly expanded legion, Cobb chose the latter.[24]

In mid-March Colonel Phillips visited his legion. He delivered the news that the regiments Brown had wanted to attach to the legion, which had been training at Camp McDonald, would not be joining them. He had, however, received approval to add several additional companies of infantry and cavalry. The men were elated to see their commander again after his long illness. They gathered round to serenade the colonel, who responded with a stirring speech. Reese confided to his aunt that the boys liked Phillips better than Lieutenant Colonel Jones, but he observed that Phillips still did not look well. Reese added that Phillips had returned to Marietta to muster in the new companies.[25]

---

[23] Col. William Phillips to Gov. Joseph E. Brown, 25 February 1862, Incoming Correspondence to Gov. Brown, record group 1–1–5, no. 93–1219A, box 43, Georgia Department of Archives and History, Morrow GA.

[24] From *The Papers of Jefferson Davis*, 11 vols. (4 more projected), ed. Lynda I. Crist and Mary S. Dix (1861; repr., Baton Rouge: Louisiana State University Press, 1992), 8:112, 135.

[25] Andrew Jackson Reese to Mrs. Nancy Wimpy, 21 March 1862, Rees/Reese Collection.

During the early months of 1862, some company officers had returned to Georgia to recruit replacements for the men lost in 1861. By March 1862, the officers had enlisted more than 100 new recruits into the existing companies.[26] Phillips was granted approval to expand his legion in the same proportion as Cobb's legion, and he worked hard in March and April to recruit five new companies.[27]

Three new infantry and two cavalry companies were added by the end of May, the companies arriving in South Carolina throughout April and May.[28] The arrival of the new men changed the veterans' routine. Their duties now expanded to include the training of these new soldiers. As was always the case, many of the new recruits soon fell ill as they were exposed to the trials of living in camps; six would succumb to their ailments. Even veteran members of the legion had not yet fully developed immunities to the plethora of diseases that roamed the camps. Eleven of them also died during the time spent on the coast.[29]

On 29 May 1862, Colonel William S. Walker, commanding the Confederate forces of the Third Military District of South Carolina, received reliable intelligence that the Federals had landed at Port Royal. They were said to be advancing to cut off the Charleston and Savannah Railroad about 40 miles north of Bluffton at Pocotaligo. The Phillips Legion boarded a train for Pocotaligo to reinforce Walker's troops. Walker's Rebels collided with the enemy's advance guard, dismounted, and opened fire with shotguns at a distance of around 40 yards. Walker's small force of seventy-six men held their position for over three hours until the Federals succeeded in flanking the Confederates forcing Walker to retire, re-supply ammunition, and await reinforcements.

---

[26] Gen. Drayton dispatch to Maj. T. A. Washington, A.A.G., to Gen. Pemberton, 7 March 1862, Eleanor S. Brockenbrough Library.

[27] Gen. Drayton dispatch to Maj. J. R. Waddy, A.A.G., to Gen. Pendleton, 26 May 1862, Eleanor S. Brockenbrough Library.

[28] The new infantry companies were: (1) Company L, Blackwell Volunteers, Cobb County, Cpt. James M. Johnson; (2) Company M, Denmead Volunteers, Cobb County, Cpt. James F. McCleskey; and (3) Company O, Marietta Guards, Cobb and Bartow Counties, Cpt. Thomas K. Sproull. The new cavalry companies were: (1) Company N, Bibb Cavalry, Bibb County, Cpt. Samuel S. Dunlap; and (2) Company P, Coweta, Henry, Carroll and Newton Counties, Cpt. Wesley W. Thomas.

[29] Compiled Service Records, National Archives micropublication, M266, rolls 592–600, Georgia Department of Archives and History, Morrow GA.

Learning the Federal troops were withdrawing for unknown reasons, Walker pursued until 10:00 A.M. when he ran into the Federal rear guard. The Yankees had halted at Garden's Corner. Walker prepared for a 12-mile march that would have placed his soldiers in the rear of the Unionists but canceled the plan because his troops were both exhausted and outnumbered by the Federals. Learning that the Phillips Legion was at Pocotaligo, he decided to attack the following morning. Now reinforced by the legion, Walker tracked the Federals for over 19 miles to the Port Royal Ferry, where he discovered that the enemy had crossed during the night. Without a fight, the legion soldiers returned to Camp Pritchard, about 2 miles from the New River Bridge.[30] Although the legion did not engage the enemy in this affair, they did suffer a casualty. A soldier in Company L accidentally discharged his .69-calibre musket and the blast hit his lieutenant, Henry J. McCormick, in the left ankle. The devastation done by the large buck and ball load shattered the unlucky Lieutenant's ankle and his foot had to be amputated. McCormick would spend the rest of the war in Georgia serving as a recruiter and conscription officer.[31]

New cavalry recruit Private John T. Swan, of Company P, believed that the likelihood of a significant battle was small but noted the continuous shelling of Confederate pickets by the Federals. During early June 1862 Swan heard shelling from his camp on the South May River near Bluffton, 15 miles from Hardeeville and about 6 miles from Foot Point. He also reported hearing Yankee drums beating on Savage and Bull Islands. Swan described to his wife the misery of the South Carolina biting insects: "We have plenty of mussceeters, gallinippers [large mosquitoes or crane flies] & flies. They can bite me through my pants. There is none at camps but they are down on the River where we stand picket."[32]

---

[30] US War Department, comp., *The War of Rebellion: A Compilation of the Official Records of the Union and Confederate* Armies, 128 vols. (Washington DC: Government Printing Office, 1880–1901) ser. 1, vol. 14, pp. 24–27.

[31] Compiled Service Records and Pension Application Records, National Archives micropublication, M266, roll 597, Georgia Department of Archives and History, Morrow GA.

[32] John T. Swan to Dear Wife, 20 June 1862, Microfilm Library, drawer 283, box 40, Georgia Department of Archives and History.

During this time Lieutenant Abraham "Ham" Jones, of infantry Company D, expressed the legion's discontent. Writing to his brother, Jones related that:

> I fear our Legion is going to the devil in disgrace as fast as it can. It is just as I told you last winter. Phillips is not fit for Col he has no discipline & since Seab (Lt. Col. Seabom Jones) left he is beginning to show it very plain. The men see it & say THE OFFICER of the Legion is gone & those who do not know it now will soon find it out. They say what the Legion was [,] was owing to Seab [;] what it will be [,] Phillips will get the credit for it. I would to God & so does the Capt—wish our company was out of it before it is disgraced. He looks & acts more like a candidate for some office than Col of a Legion. He boot licks all that will allow him to do so & those who will not allow it does not remember when he makes his honorable dictates such as court martials and committees. He is nothing but a puff, self conceited brogadacio & no dependence in anything that he says. Major Willcoxon has resigned & starts home tomorrow. I don't know the reasons but suppose he does not like the treatment he has received. It won't be long before many others will do the same if they can—but enough of him for this time.[33]

General Lee had returned to Richmond in March to serve as military advisor to the president, and rumors began to circulate that the legion would also soon depart for Chattanooga, Richmond, Atlanta, or Rome. Lt. Sanford expected the legion to move any day, probably in direct support of Charleston or Savannah, both of which were threatened. He discounted the rumors about Chattanooga, saying that he thought the forces on the coast were too small to deplete. He fully expected "hot work" before many more weeks. As with many rumors, the speculation about a move to Chattanooga had some basis in fact. On 2 May Davis had asked if Brown could spare a brigade from the Georgia

---

[33] Abraham Jones to Dear Bob, 17 June 1862, private collection of Mr. and Mrs. David Harlan, Atlanta GA. Both Lt. Col. Seaborn Jones and Maj. John B. Willcoxon resigned and returned home in late June citing health problems. The senior company captain, Robert T. "Tom" Cook, assumed command of the infantry battalion upon Lt. Col. Jones's resignation.

coast to serve at Chattanooga. Brown replied that if troops were to be ordered to Chattanooga, the Phillips Legion should be included since many of them were from North Georgia and would fight hard to defend their homes.

On 17 July 1862 the legion received orders to strike tents and board a train. Major General John C. Pemberton directed General Drayton to proceed to Richmond where he would command a brigade consisting of the Phillips Legion, Colonel James E. Slaughter's 51st Georgia Regiment, Colonel William R. Manning's 50th Georgia Regiment, Colonel William D. DeSaussure's 15th South Carolina Regiment, and Lieutenant Colonel George S. James's 3rd South Carolina Battalion. The Phillips Legion's infantry battalion and Colonel Manning's 50th Georgia Regiment departed from Savannah and Branchville and went by way of Augusta.[34] The legion's cavalry battalion would follow at a later date. Because more than one train was required, the first group arrived in Augusta on Sunday morning, 20 July. The second group followed a few days later. Camped on the west side of town, they took advantage of a two-day layover to see the sights and visit family and friends. They anticipated tough times ahead but believed it could not be more difficult than their experience in western Virginia with General Floyd. Jack Reese speculated that they would reinforce Stonewall Jackson.[35] The legion infantry arrived in Richmond on the evening of 29 July. Drayton's men would soon see the active campaigning they had wished for during their interlude on the coast.

---

[34] *OR*, ser. 1, vol. 14, p. 537; *OR* ser. 1, vol. 2, pt. 3, p. 644.
[35] Andrew Jackson Reese to Mrs. Nancy Wimpy, 30 July 1862, Rees/Reese Collection.

Chapter 7

A Village Called Manassas

"When I felt something fall on my breast just over my pack it fell
as gently as if it had been laid by a child's hand."

John A. Barry of Company A and Jack Reese of Company E were of similar minds during late July 1862, although Reese was more concerned about his stomach. They were on the move by rail from Hardeeville, South Carolina, to Virginia, where they would face their first serious combat on the old battlefield of Manassas. Arriving in Columbia, South Carolina, by way of Augusta, Georgia, Reese fell ill for several days before recuperating and continuing his journey north. The local ladies greeted Barry with smiles and fruitcakes when the legion arrived in Columbia, South Carolina. Jack Reese caught up to the legion at Columbia and they continued on to Raleigh, North Carolina, finally reaching their destination at Richmond, Virginia, on Tuesday 29 July. Reese thought they were heading to Virginia to join "Old Stonewall," not knowing where Jackson was but sure he was in the right place to confound the enemy.

Prices for food and sundries were extremely high in the Virginia capital at this time. Frustrated, Reese described the exorbitant prices: "No one knows where old Stonewall is. Some say he is in the Vallie. Some say he is in the rear of McClelland [*sic*] but no doubt he is in the right place. Let him be...where him is. I have saw no one that I know as yet. Ever thing is very high $1.00 for a meals victuals. $1.00 a piece for chickens & ever thing to eat in proportion. Shoes from six to twenty dollars. Hats we could of have got at $25 cts when I left home have to pay eight to ten dollars for now."[1] Blockaded ports caused inflated prices for all imported goods throughout the South at this time. Men who were

---

[1] Andrew J. Reese to Aunt, July 1862, Rees/Reese Collection, Lumpkin County Library, Madeline K. Anthony Collection, series 3, box 23, folder 5.

accustomed to farming their fields were now in uniform, pushing prices for farm goods even higher.

Camped near the Fairgrounds in Richmond, the two soldiers knew they would be moving out in the next few days. John Barry closed a letter home with a request for a pair of pants. He wanted them sent right away, as "such things are very high here."[2] Lee had succeeded in halting McClellan's army on the outskirts of Richmond during the Seven Days Campaign. McClellan's battered troops withdrew down the James River to Harrison's Landing, where they remained until shortly before the battle of Second Manassas. As Lee's army rested and recuperated from the severe fighting, another Union threat appeared in Central Virginia—Major General John Pope's army. On 17 July 1862 the Phillips Legion's infantry battalion had received orders to head to Virginia from South Carolina to bolster Lee's army. The cavalry battalion would follow, but at a slower pace. As part of General Thomas F. Drayton's mixed Georgia, South Carolina brigade, they would join Major General James "Old Pete" Longstreet's wing of the Army of Northern Virginia. The legion troops would once again be under overall command of General Robert E. Lee. The Seven Days Battles were over and Confederate troops covered the hills around Richmond in every direction, ready to counter any threat from McClellan. The men knew something big was in the wind and were ready for action.[3]

Whatever the something big was, it was not at Richmond but well north of the capital where a brand new Federal army was forming. General "Stonewall" Jackson had defeated three separate Union armies during the Shenandoah Valley campaign. President Lincoln decided to unify all armies in Virginia not directly reporting to McClellan. He looked to the west for fresh, aggressive leadership for the new 50,000-man Army of Virginia and found it in the guise of forty-year-old Major General John Pope. The president would come to regret his decision.[4] Pope would prove to be arrogant and abrasive, irritating not only his superiors but his supporters and troops as well. Pope and McClellan did

---

[2] John Barry to Dear Sister from Raleigh NC, 27 July 1862, Barry Papers accession no. 3015, Southern Historical Collection, University of North Carolina Library, Chapel Hill NC.

[3] John J. Hennessy, *Return to Bull Run: The Campaign and Battle of Second Manassas* (New York: Simon & Schuster, 1993) 21–24.

[4] Ibid., 3–10.

not work together effectively and soon became estranged. In addition, Pope issued proclamations announcing that he would wage war on civilians as well as soldiers. An angry Lee dispatched Jackson's wing of the army north to defeat Pope before reinforcements from McClellan could reach him. In a letter dated 29 July 1862, Lee stated clearly: "I want Pope suppressed."[5] Pope's strategy was clear. He would lure the Confederate forces from around Richmond by shifting south along the east side of the Blue Ridge Mountains, threatening the town of Charlottesville and the Virginia Central Railroad. If successful, McClellan, at Harrison's Landing, would march his enormous army to attack Richmond while Pope would fall back to protect the northern capital or settle into the Shenandoah Valley.

On 2 August, the Phillips Legion troops marched east for about 10 miles from Richmond to Chaffin's Farm, opposite Drewry's Bluff on the James River. The men were busy building breastworks on 4 August just a mile east of their camp. The following day found the legion infantrymen in line of battle just a mile and a half east of their camp in response to a Federal probe from Malvern Hill. On 13 August, the Legion Georgians folded their tents around 11:00 P.M. and marched on toward Richmond, arriving at the rail depot at 2:00 A.M. They boarded the Virginia Central Railroad 4 hours later, arrived at the Gordonsville at 1:00 P.M., marched 4 miles south, and camped in an open field without tents. The legion commander, Colonel William M. Phillips, suffered a typhoid fever relapse at Gordonsville and was forced to leave the legion. Completely prostrated, he was moved to a Lynchburg hospital under the care of Dr. Reed of Savannah, Georgia, and Dr. Tennant of Marietta. Phillips did not respond to treatment, and he returned to Marietta in October. He would return to Richmond in December 1862, but his condition remained poor. In January 1863 he resigned his commission and returned to Georgia. The legion lost its beloved commander. He briefly commanded a state militia cavalry battalion later in 1863 but was stricken with a vision ailment, causing him to lose his sight in one eye. He would serve five terms in the postwar Georgia legislature and

---

[5] Gary Gallagher, ed., *Fighting for the Confederacy: The Personal Recollections of General Edward Porter Alexander* (Chapel Hill: University of North Carolina Press, 1989); Robert K. Krick, *Stonewall Jackson at Cedar Mountain* (Chapel Hill: University of North Carolina Press, 1990) 7; Hennessy, *Bull Run*, 25–26; Bevin Alexander, *Robert E. Lee's Civil War* (Holbrook MA: Adams Media Corporation, 1998) 41–58.

promote railroad construction in the northern part of the state. He lived
to be 84 and died in 1908.[6]

The legion remained camped near Gordonsville without their tents
and on short rations until marching for Orange Court House on the
evening of 18 August. They arrived 4 miles east of Orange Court House
and made camp at 5:00 P.M. on the 19th. Taking up the march again on
the 20th, the legion crossed the Rapidan River at Raccoon Ford and
camped 8 miles from Stevensburg. Chaplain Smith jotted his experience
in his diary:

> We marched all night long and just about the dawn we
> reached Racoons [*sic*] Ford. There was neither bridge nor boats
> and no time to undress and so we boldly walked into the waves
> and reached the other side. We were at Racoon Ford to join
> Jackson who was coming down the valley and we expected to
> have Burnside moved from Fredericksburg and attack us but he
> was afraid to do it and so Jackson left us and we began our march
> toward Manassas where we expected to meet Pope who had
> superseded Burnside. I tried to march on foot with the men and
> did so without breaking down.[7]

By Thursday, 21 August, the legion infantrymen must have sensed
an approaching fight. Assigned to the rear guard, diarist Thomas M.
Mitchell could hear the rumble of cannon, and Chaplain Smith could
almost smell the acrid odor of cannonading. Smith's diary revealed his
feelings: "We had our first smell of gunpowder from the artillery when
we reached the Rappahannock River. The wagons had come and we had
our rations given out but we had no cooking vessels."[8] Ignoring the
distant fire, the resourceful Smith improvised his cooking utensils from
otherwise useless materials:

---

[6] William Phillips, "Personal Account Written by William Phillips," unpublished
manuscript, Smyrna Historical Society, Smyrna GA. Also see Robert Manson Myers,
Children of Pride: A True Story of Georgia and the Civil War (New Haven: Yale
University Press, 1972) 1643.

[7] Rev. George Gilman Smith, "Reminiscences," n.d., unpublished manuscript,
Microfilm Library, drawer 283, box 40, Georgia Department of Archives and History,
Morrow GA.

[8] Ibid.

I had my flour & Bacon but no Spider nor frying pan and no cook. I got my breakfast however. I took a pan a soldier had and mixed my flour with water. I made a bed of coals in a little excavation. I put my dough on an improvised grid iron only there was no iron about it and I then put my Bacon on a stick and held it to the fire. I held the dripping bacon over my cooking bread and I made a very savory compound. I have eaten more elegant meals but none I enjoyed more. We got in camp the cooks came up and the cooking utensils and so I resigned my place as Chief Cook and only resumed it once afterward.[9]

While stationed on the Rappahannock around this time, Smith witnessed a sad sight that he dutifully recorded in his diary: "It was while we were on the Rappahannock that I saw a poor Federal soldier hung as a spy. I did not see him hung but I saw him as he hung suspended from the tree. He was the first man I had seen in all my campaign who had fallen victim to the wars decree. He had been not only convicted as a spy but as a murderer for he had killed the poor boy he had robbed of his papers which were maps of the river fords."[10] Lieutenant Alex Smith Erwin of Company C witnessed the execution, noting that the Federal soldier had killed one of General Jackson's couriers before taking his papers and maps.[11]

On Saturday, 23 August, at 3:00 A.M. the legion infantry had marched 3 miles east and halted near the north bank of the Rappahannock to support Confederate artillery at Beverly's Ford. Some of the soldiers were lying down behind trees when they heard the shriek of shells and the cracking of trees followed by an explosion. Chaplain Smith was called upon to pray for a mortally wounded Legion soldier: "Our guns replied, and it was a lively time. I heard someone cry out, 'Where is the Chaplain??' I answered, and he said: 'There is a man dying and he wants you to pray for him.' Sure enough, I found poor McAfee

---

[9] Ibid.

[10] Ibid.

[11] Lt. Alexander Smith Erwin to Willie from Camp between Leesburg and Winchester, 14 September 1862, quoted in Alexander Smith Erwin, "Camp Between Leesburg and Winchester, Sept. 14, 1862," *Athens* (GA) *Watchman*, 1 October 1862, p. 2.

with both legs torn off by a shell. I prayed for him and in a little while the end came.'"[12] One of the first legion casualties of the campaign, Private Franklin Alexander McAfee, was the younger brother of fellow Company E soldier William Hamilton McAfee. Just 22 years old, Frank was from Lumpkin County, Georgia.[13]

By Sunday, 24 August, General Robert E. Lee was tired and frustrated. His men had chased Union General John Pope relentlessly in spite of constant delays caused by rain and logistical problems. On this day General Thomas J. Jackson locked in an artillery duel with Pope's troops at Waterloo Bridge and White Sulphur Springs. After dueling with Federal General Irvin McDowell at Beverly's Ford and Rappahannock Station a day earlier, General James Longstreet crossed the Hazel River at Welford's Ford and pushed on to Jeffersonton, a crossroads several miles west of White Sulfur Springs. Lee's chances for defeating Pope were diminishing. Some of McClellan's troops were starting to reach Pope, marching up the Rappahannock from Fredericksburg. More were heading south from Alexandria. Lee seemed to be stalemated.

Major General J. E. B. Stuart's cavalry had performed a successful raid around Pope's right flank on 22 August, hoping to burn a key bridge on the Orange and Alexandria Railroad. Stuart reached the railroad without serious opposition but heavy rains prevented him from burning the bridge. He did, however, capture Pope's dispatch book containing marching orders, troop strengths, and the plans for the juncture of McClellan's men with his own. This raid gave Lee the valuable knowledge that Pope's right flank was open to exploitation. Conferring with Jackson, Lee agreed that Stonewall would make a broad flanking movement around Pope's right through Thoroughfare Gap in the Bull Run Mountains. This would allow him to strike Pope's supply base on the Orange and Alexandria Railroad at Manassas Junction. Pope would be forced to pull back from his line along the Rappahannock, giving Lee the choice of throwing Longstreet on Pope's rear or following in the footsteps of Jackson's flank march. Lee thus adopted a flexible strategy of maneuver, avoiding a potentially costly frontal assault. If Pope's supply

---

[12] Smith, "Reminiscences."
[13] Ibid.

line was cut, the Federals would be forced to retreat.[14] The plan's major risk factor involved the separation of the two wings of Lee's army. Jackson and Longstreet would be separated not only by distance but by the mass of the Bull Run Mountains. If the Northerners were able to close Thoroughfare Gap after Jackson passed through, the two wings of the army would be severed.

Lee remained with Longstreet's wing as Old Pete pushed ahead to Waterloo Bridge to relieve A. P. Hill so that Hill could join Jackson's march. At 6:00 A.M. on Sunday, 24 August, the legion marched off. Thomas M. Mitchell described the early morning march, the river crossings, and his empty stomach: "Marched at Six A. M. Have to wade several creeks half-thigh deep, pass Jeffersonville at Five P. M. Considerable cannonading on our right. Camp near Jeffersonville with our rations."[15] The next day, Tuesday, 25 August, Drayton's brigade took position at Waterloo Bridge on the north fork of the Rappahannock River. The legion arrived at 7:00 A.M. They stayed under cover for most of the afternoon as General David R. Jones sent other troops from Drayton's brigade to engage the enemy across the river. The legion held its position near the bridge that evening.[16]

Pope had neglected his rear defenses, leaving only three companies of infantry at Bristoe Station and three infantry companies, a battery of artillery, and a regiment of cavalry at Manassas Junction. On 26 August, Jackson marched unmolested from Salem, then successfully passed through Thoroughfare Gap where he met Confederate cavalry. Together they reached Bristoe Station at sunset.[17] After derailing a train, Jackson night-marched the van of his army up the railroad to Pope's huge supply base at Manassas Junction. The lead elements of Jackson's force surprised and captured the small Federal garrison there, rupturing Pope's supply line. Jackson's exhausted men could not resist the cornucopia laid before them, rampaging through the mountains of food and supplies.

---

[14] Alexander, *Lee's Civil War*, 41–58.

[15] Diary of Thomas M. Mitchell, 24 August 1862 entry, private collection of Mr. R. D. Thomas, Chattanooga TN.

[16] *OR*, ser. 1, vol. 12, pt. 2, p. 579.

[17] Edward Porter Alexander, *Fighting for the Confederacy* (Chapel Hill: University of North Carolina Press, 1989) 130–31.

Meanwhile, back on the Rappahannock, Longstreet continued to hold Pope's attention by pounding the Federal positions with artillery. Lee ruminated over Longstreet's movement. The answer came when Pope received a telegram late on 26 August notifying him that Confederates had cut the railroad behind him. Realizing that his right had been turned, he issued orders directing his army to fall back toward Manassas Junction and Centreville. He believed he could take advantage of the divided Southern force and catch an isolated Jackson before Longstreet could reach him. Meanwhile, Longstreet received orders to follow Jackson's route through the mountains to join him. Legion diarist Thomas M. Mitchell described the march: "nine A. M. march down to the Bridge, the enemy having disappeared part of the Legion left for picket, was relieved at Twelve. We pass through Amissville, have to wade the River, Camp at Eleven...eleven miles South west from Salem.[18]

Jackson's position was precarious on the morning of 27 August. His three divisions were separated from Lee. Meanwhile Pope had moved between Jackson and the Confederate main body still west of the Bull Run Mountains in the vicinity of White Plains.[19] He had two choices. He could retrace his steps through Gainesville (now occupied by Union General Irvin McDowell) or he could mass his army in a strong defensive position north of Manassas Junction and wait for Lee and Longstreet to join him. Shortly before midnight on 27 August, Jackson's troops torched the supplies at Manassas Junction. General William B. Taliaferro's division then set off by way of New Market-Sudley Springs Road across the Warrenton Turnpike. At daylight on 28 August the division bivouacked near Groveton by Sudley Mills just north of the 1861 Manassas battlefield. Around 1:00 A.M. General A. P. Hill started out from Manassas Junction, crossed Bull Run, and, due to confused orders, marched to Centreville. Confederate General Richard S. Ewell followed Hill at daylight, heading for Centreville. When Jackson discovered that Hill and Ewell had not followed Taliaferro, he sent staff officers out to find the two wayward divisions, which were quickly redirected into position north of Groveton. The position selected was an

---

[18] Thomas M. Mitchell, diary, 27 August 1862 entry.

[19] Ibid., 56–57; Douglas Southall Freeman, *Lee's Lieutenants: A Study in Command*, 3 vols. (New York: Charles Scribner's Sons, 1942–1944) vol. 1, 100-101. Gen. Clement Anselm Evans, *Confederate Military History*, 18 vols. (Atlanta: Confederate Publishing Co., 1899) 6:97–8.

unfinished railroad bed on a low ridgeline north of and roughly paralleling the Warrenton Turnpike. Taliaferro's men had formed on the western end of the position and now Ewell's troops fell into line on his left, with Hill's division completing the eastern end of the strong position.[20] Generals McDowell and Pope were laboring under the assumption that Jackson was retreating, and they were surprised when they did not find him at Manassas Junction or on the roads to the northwest.[21]

While Pope fumbled around searching for Stonewall Jackson, the men of the Phillips Legion's infantry battalion ambled along parallel to the railway through Culpeper, Fauquier, and Prince William counties on their way to Manassas Junction. The hot, dry weather and dust stung the men's eyes and caused continual hacking and coughing. The terrain along the Bull Run Mountains had been rugged, but marching proved easier in Culpeper and Fauquier. The men reached Thoroughfare Gap early in the afternoon of 28 August. The Gap was watered by Occoquan Creek, with an average width of around 80 yards. Basaltic rock faces rose vertically from 100 to 200 feet with random sprigs of wild ivy pushing through the fissures.

The Rebels prepared to traverse the Gap but ran into Federal pickets and artillery fire that temporarily halted them. As the column halted, Chaplain Smith observed General Lee for the first time since the legion's return to Virginia. Lee had aged, his beard and hair gone gray. The chaplain also had an unnerving experience here:

> We were lined up in a rail way cut at Thoroughfare Gap. Here the rail way runs through a gap in the mountains. The Federals had been hovering near us and there was an occasional artillery fire but there was not engagement. They were in some force near Thoroughfare Gap and an artillery duel was going on between their guns and ours. Our men were lying in this rail road excavation and the guns were being fired over their heads. When I felt something fall on my breast just over my pack it fell

---

[20] Hennessy, *Bull Run,* 122–23; James Longstreet, *From Manassas to Appomattox* (New York: Da Capo Press, 1992) 171; John Pope, "The Second Battle of Bull Run," in *The Struggle Intensifies,* vol. 2 of *Battles and Leaders of the Civil War,* ed. Robert U. Johnson and Clarence C. Buel (New York: De Vinne Press, 1888) 449–94.

[21] Ibid.

as gently as if it had been laid by a child's hand. It was a piece of shell which had burst on the mountain. I gave it to a lady living near by where I got my supper and in whose barn I think I slept that night.[22]

General Drayton prepared his men for a charge against the Federal batteries on the left while other Southern troops attacked through the Gap. The Federals withdrew before this charge made it through the Gap. The legion did not get into the fighting this day.[23]

On Friday, 29 August, Jackson's wing was stretched out in a long northeast-southwest line along the unfinished railroad bed north of the Warrenton Turnpike. Pope had finally found Jackson late on the afternoon of 28 August when Jackson pounced on King's division of McDowell's corps as they marched east on the Warrenton Turnpike. After a savage battle across the fields of Brawner's farm, both sides disengaged as darkness fell. Pope now knew Jackson's location and marshaled his forces to attack at dawn. Pope proceeded to pound away at Jackson's position and was oblivious to Longstreet's late morning arrival from the west on the Warrenton Turnpike. Jackson was hard-pressed and Lee urged Longstreet to attack Pope's exposed left flank. Around the same time, Longstreet discovered Union General Fitz John Porter's V Corps coming up Manassas-Gainesville Road from the south. Porter's action threatened Longstreet's right flank. Old Pete convinced Lee that he should deal with Porter before launching an attack on Pope. Longstreet sent out a scouting force that included the Phillips Legion as part of Drayton's brigade. Confused by Longstreet's appearance on his front, Porter had difficulty deciding whether to push forward and engage or backtrack and loop around to the east to rejoin Pope. While trying to decide his next move, Porter ordered several batteries forward to shell the Southerners in his front. The legion had been thrown forward as skirmishers and incoming Federal artillery rounds soon found their mark. Companies A and E were hit hard. Thomas Stanley of Company A and Daniel Simmermon of Company E were killed. James Billingslea and Adial Florence of Company A and Corporal William J. T. Hutcheson of Company E were all severely wounded. Billingslea and

---

[22] Smith, "Reminiscences," 82.

[23] *OR*, ser. 1, vol. 12, pt. 2, pp. 580–82.

Florence each lost an arm and would sit out the rest of the war back home in Georgia.[24]

Later in the afternoon, Lee proposed to attack and Longstreet demurred again because of the late hour. Instead, Longstreet insisted on a reconnaissance in force and Lee agreed. If scouts could find a weak spot everything would be arranged for a daylight attack. The reconnaissance ran into heavy opposition and the Confederates withdrew from their advanced positions after dark. Judging from the long line of campfires above Bull Run that night, Lee knew that the Federals were not falling back. Longstreet reported that Generals Hood and Wilcox both advised against an early attack, and Lee once again agreed to delay the assault. Longstreet shifted General David R. Jones's division—which included Toombs's, Anderson's, and Drayton's brigades—forward and to the right of General James L. Kemper's division. Forbidden to speak above a whisper, the legion troops lay all night on their arms. The next morning, discovering that Porter's troops were no longer in their front, the legion marched out into an open field and formed line of battle. Positioned to guard the extreme right and out of range of shells, they had no way of knowing what was taking place.[25]

General Pope had deluded himself into thinking that a Confederate retreat would take place on the following morning, 30 August, and headed out to pursue Jackson. Fitz John Porter had retreated during the previous night, but Longstreet was still worried over Porter's intentions. He held Drayton's brigade in position while he readied the rest of his command for an attack. The legion with Drayton's brigade saw no action but could hear a major battle raging to their north and east. After massive and repeated attacks on Jackson were beaten back, Lee and Longstreet agreed the time had come for Longstreet to hit Pope's weakened left flank. Longstreet's troops rolled forward and smashed into the Federals, forcing them back. Union resistance stiffened at Chinn Ridge, and General Jones's division was ordered into the fray. The result was a fierce fight and the Federals were driven back to Sudley Road. As the battle raged, Jones, realizing there was no Federal presence on the

---

[24] Compiled Service Records, National Archives micropublication, M266, rolls 593–95, 599, Georgia Department of Archives and History, Morrow GA; Lt. Erwin to Willie, 14 September 1862.

[25] George Francis Robert Henderson, *Stonewall Jackson and the American Civil War* (1898; repr., New York: Konecky & Konecky, 1993) 167.

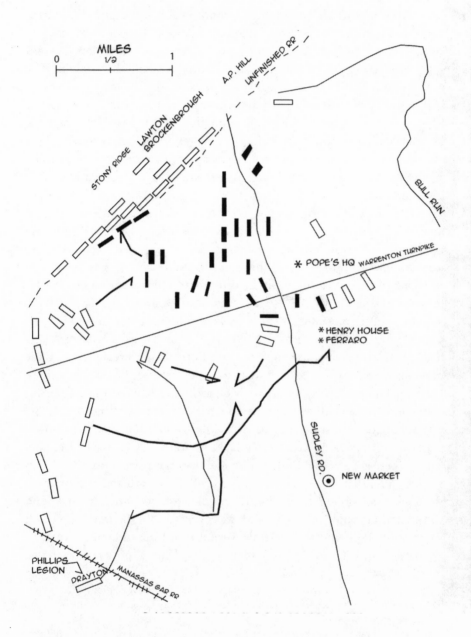

Longstreet attacks the Federal left, August 30, 1862.

flank, sent word for Drayton's command to join the division on Chinn Ridge. Chaplain Smith wrote about the call to action and the confusion caused by the color of Confederate uniforms:

> Our soldiers had uniforms of different colors, and one company had black jackets. They had been sent out to picket. About four o'clock in the afternoon an Aid came running to General Drayton and said: "General, if you would share in the glory of the victory, bring your brigade at once, as rapidly as possible, to the field." The order came, "MARCH! Double Quick!" The Aid said, "General, you needn't blow your men, but come as rapidly as you can." We were just on the edge of the battlefield when the command was given: "Halt! Right—about face! March!" and we went back. General Rosser, or some other cavalry commander, saw our company which we had left on pickets, coming out of the woods and supposing they were Federals, told General Drayton, and he took the responsibility to withdraw his brigade. We discovered the mistake too late to take the ground we were to occupy in time to do the work General Lee had expected us to do.[26]

Drayton began to backtrack to examine Rosser's information but left the legion near Chinn Ridge. By the time the legion troops arrived on Chinn Ridge, General Jones's other brigades and General R. H. Anderson's division were fighting the Federals dug in at Sudley Road. As the legion charged across Chinn Ridge's open fields, they were swept by artillery fire from north of the Warrenton Pike and sustained a number of casualties. One of these was Private James Newton "Newt" Greene of Company O. His nephew, Marcus L. Greene, wrote to his mother: "My feeling was awful—I saw him start to fall and saw him strike the ground & stopped & looked at him. He never moved hand nor foot. We had three more men wounded & [I] saw all of them by the time they struck the ground."[27]

---

[26] Smith, "Reminiscences," 83.

[27] Marcus L. Greene to mother, 4 October 1863, private collection of Mrs. S. Harden, Jasper GA.

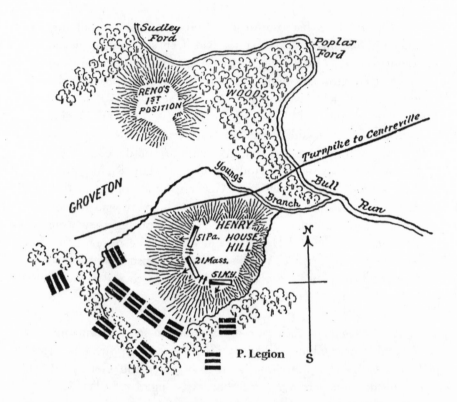

Legion approaches left flank of Ferrero's Brigade on Henry Hill at dusk
but does not attack, August 30, 1862.

The legion troops tried desperately to get into the fight, but had difficulty maneuvering around other Confederate units fighting in the woods to their front. Eventually they made their way far enough to the right past the flank of the southern line and began to move eastward. The Federals finally abandoned Sudley Road as darkness began to fall. Confederate units involved in dislodging these Federals had taken heavy losses and paused to regroup. As the Yankees fell back across Henry Hill, a single IX Corps brigade under General Edward Ferrero accompanied by a battery of guns went into position there as a rear guard. The Phillips Legion troops inched east along a wooded ravine north of Henry Hill when, in the gathering darkness, they noticed troops on the hill. The legion's sergeant major walked out of the woods and inquired as to their identity. Federal troops replied that they were units from New York, Pennsylvania, and Massachusetts. The sergeant sidled slowly back into the woods, barely avoiding a deadly encounter. Now in full darkness, the legion bedded down for the night. The legion and the 15th South Carolina were the only unit in Drayton's brigade to take significant casualties. The other three units did not see action as they countermarched to verify General Rosser's incorrect report of a Federal flanking movement. Lieutenant Alex Erwin, a keen observer of events, reported:

> We, after some delay, found a point lower down on the right, where we had no troops, and with our Regiment alone (Drayton, for some cause, not sending up the other Regiments of the Brigade to support us) marched up on a whole Brigade of Yankees supporting a battery. Our Sergeant Major asked what regiments they were and they told him some N.Y., Mass and Penn. regiments. He replied, "All right." It was nearly dark and we would probably have been used up pretty badly if they had known we were enemies. We, without any confusion, marched quietly past them under a shower of balls from other parts of the field and stopped just out of sight of them in the woods. If we had been supported by the rest of the Brigade we could have driven their Brigade off and probably taken their battery—Drayton's conduct is severely criticized by all who know anything of the officer. We were in a tight place certainly, but Providentially got out of it without much loss…it was about

9 o'clock when the firing ceased. We remained on the field all night, and the next morning early I walked over the scene of the conflict. Never will I forget the sight I saw that day. Strewn in thick profusion—in every position—wounded in every place—the dead and dying lay...the fight lasted from about 2 until 8 that night and was, without doubt, a glorious decisive victory for us. The enemy's army was completely broken up and disorganized and fled to the fortifications around Washington.[28]

The legion infantrymen were now full-blooded combatants. General Robert E. Lee now made a fateful decision. He would invade the North and carry the action north of the Potomac River.

---

[28] Lt. Erwin to Willie, 14 September 1862.

Chapter 8

Maryland, My Maryland

"Parson, we've been whipped, the regiment is retreating."

Second Lieutenant Alex Erwin's feet were killing him! This Company C officer had endured many long, hard marches over the several weeks leading up to the great Southern victory at Second Manassas. The nineteen-year-old reported that the blistered condition of his feet required him to ride in a regimental wagon from the Manassas battlefield to Leesburg, Virginia.[1] Erwin was greatly relieved when he learned that General Longstreet had issued an order that "all the barefooted, weak and inefficient troops of each regiment be left behind with the baggage in charge of an officer." He was that officer. The 150 soldiers left behind with young Lieutenant Erwin indicated the worn condition of the Phillips Legion's infantry.[2]

On 5 September 1862 Longstreet's command headed northeast for a camp near White's Ford on the Potomac River.[3] General Robert E. Lee had decided that the time was "propitious" to carry the war northward. The Northern army was thought to be cowering in the Washington defenses after its defeat at Second Manassas. Authorities reasoned that the Southern army could shift the hard hand of war out of Virginia, drawing Federal attention away from Richmond. Some thought had also been given to the liberation of Maryland, a border state with many ties to the South. Repressive Federal actions had coerced the state into remaining in the Union. Finally, Lee held hope that a Southern victory north of the Potomac would lead to foreign

---

[1] Alexander Smith Erwin, in "Camp Between Leesburg and Winchester, Sept. 14, 1862," *Athens* (GA) *Watchman*, 1 October 1862, p. 2.

[2] Ibid.

[3] Diary of J. Edings, Manuscript Division, Library of Congress, Washington DC, Papers of Edward Willis, box 4, MMC 318, 5 September entry.

intervention and a negotiated peace, providing the South with its independence.

The 360-man legion infantry battalion, commanded by Lieutenant Colonel Robert T. Cook, broke camp early on 6 September and crossed into Maryland around 8:00 A.M.[4] The long columns of Confederate infantry fording the Potomac were dirty, tattered, and unshaven but this did not seem to dampen their spirits. With flags waving and bands blaring "Maryland, My Maryland," the soldiers shouted and joked in their excitement. Many stripped off their pants and drawers and assaulted the Old Line State in "nature's uniforms."[5] They continued the march north to Three Springs near Buckeystown,[6] camping there that evening with their brigade and division. The pace was an easy one as Stonewall Jackson's wing of the army marched ahead of them and the Federals remained a distant threat well to the south. The next day would bring a leisurely 4-mile march to Monocacy Junction,[7] where the men spent the rest of Sunday resting, swimming, and washing clothes in the muddy waters of the Monocacy River. On Monday they crossed the Monocacy and camped on the outskirts of Frederick.[8] The illnesses that had plagued the Southern army in Virginia continued to wreak havoc in Maryland. The legion chaplain, George Smith, recalled: "many of our men were *sick*, many were ragged and barefooted, and our army was not half the size of the Army with which we had left the field of Second Manassas."[9]

An examination of the deaths that occurred during and just after the August and September campaigns revealed a high incidence of typhoid and chronic dysentery. This is not surprising considering the numerous comments in period letters and diaries indicating the difficulty of finding clean drinking water in quantities sufficient to supply a large army. Further problems existed with the availability of food and clothing.

---

[4] Ibid.

[5] J. Harsh, *Taken at the Flood, Robert E. Lee and Confederate Strategy in the Maryland Campaign of 1862* (Kent OH: Kent State University Press. 1999) 103.

[6] Ibid.

[7] Ibid,. 111.

[8] J. Edings, diary, 8 September entry.

[9] Rev. George Gilman Smith, "Reminiscences," n.d., unpublished manuscript, Microfilm Library, drawer 283, box 40, Georgia Department of Archives and History, Morrow GA.

During the first few weeks of August, orders had been issued requiring the troops to place knapsacks, tents, extra blankets, and clothing in storage to enable them to proceed in "light marching order." The baggage left behind remained in various locales between Richmond and the Rapidan River, not to be recovered until late October or early November.[10] The hard marches leading up to Second Manassas had left many troops shoeless and, although some of these men were permitted to remain in Virginia by virtue of General Longstreet's 3 September order, many other dedicated souls crossed into Maryland wearing ill-fitting or badly worn footgear. Many of the soldiers started the August campaign with little or no spare clothing and, by the time they reached Frederick, Maryland, their garments were mostly tattered rags. One observer described them as "these bundles of rags, these cough-racked, diseased and starved men." Another stated, "O, they are so dirty! I don't think the Potomac River could wash them clean; and ragged! There is not a scarecrow in the cornfields that would not scorn to exchange clothes with them; and so tattered! There isn't a decently dressed soldier in the entire army."[11]

The supply of food was inconsistent among various parts of Lee's army. Many of the men of Jackson's wing had been well supplied from Federal stores captured at Manassas Junction just prior to the battle of Second Manassas. These more fortunate troops were probably better fed when they moved into Maryland, as they were in the van of the army. Longstreet's men, following in their wake, would find little more than "roasting ears" of corn and green apples impressed from Maryland farmers by the Confederate Commissary Department. Meanwhile only a trickle of food was reaching the Confederate army from the South. General Lee had notified President Davis on 5 September that he was shifting his supply line westward to the Shenandoah Valley, the recently recaptured town of Winchester serving as his supply base. Since Federal garrisons at Martinsburg and Harpers Ferry prevented supplies from Winchester from reaching the army in Maryland, Lee knew he must

---

[10] K. Bohannon, "Dirty, Ragged and Ill–Provided For, Confederate Logistical Problems in the 1862 Maryland Campaign," in G. Gallagher, ed., *The Antietam Campaign* (Chapel Hill: University of North Carolina Press, 1999) 108.

[11] J. Schildt, *Roads to Antietam* (Shippenburg PA: White Mane Publishing Co., Burd Street Press, 1997) 38.

subsist his troops on the Maryland countryside until these obstacles were removed.[12]

Henry E. Young, who had been General Drayton's assistant adjutant general before Second Manassas, revealed the conditions endured by the men of the brigade in a letter penned to his uncle on 29 September: "Half clad and without tents, they would suffer intensely from the cold. One simple fact I know will surprise you. So restricted are the men in every means of cleanliness—even officers, Generals and all, sometimes do not see clean clothes for two weeks together and so often are they cut off from their knapsacks—marching only with "three days rations and one blanket"—that it has ceased to be a reproach for the private to be 'lousy.' How our men endure it is almost past belief; and when the officers abuse them for their dirt, for taking green apples and corn when the gov't neither feeds them decently nor pays them their wages (many haven't been paid for 6–8–10 months)—I confess my sympathies are generally with them and I cannot feel but what an immense debt of gratitude the country owes them; and only wonder how they manage to keep up any self-respect whatever."[13]

While the men of the legion rested at Frederick, Robert E. Lee and his wing commanders were planning the army's next moves. Lee had thought that the Federal garrisons at Martinsburg and Harpers Ferry would abandon these positions to avoid being isolated and captured when his army shifted into Maryland. When this did not occur, it became painfully apparent that further movement north would be inadvisable with a large Federal force sitting squarely astride the Southern line of communication and supply. The Confederate response to this situation was detailed in Special Order No. 191, issued 9 September 1862. It called for the army to split into various detachments to carry out the encirclement and capture of the Federal garrisons at Martinsburg and Harpers Ferry, thereby eliminating these threats to the rear of Lee's forces. Dividing the army north of the Potomac carried some risk as Stuart's cavalry reported the pursuit of McClellan's army from the south. It seemed likely the Southerners could easily capture the two isolated garrisons and reunite before McClellan put any serious

---

[12] Bohannon, "Dirty, Ragged," 108.

[13] H. Young to My Dear Uncle, 29 September 1862, R. Gourdin Papers, collection 27, box 2, item 2, Woodruff Library, Emory University, Atlanta GA.

pressure on them. Marching orders appeared and the legion tramped through Frederick at 3:00 P.M. on 10 September, following in the steps of Jackson's men who had headed west early that morning. Too *sick* to be moved, four Legion soldiers, Sergeant W. S. Bell and Privates William Jones, William Fahey, and Joseph Stancell, did not march with their comrades and were left behind.[14]

Just prior to Second Manassas, General Drayton had a falling out with his assistant adjutant general, Henry Young, and was now accompanied by his newly appointed replacement, Captain J. Evans Edings.[15] Edings noted in his diary that they marched until 1:00 A.M. on 11 September and made camp at Middletown, just east of South Mountain, which loomed ahead in the darkness.[16] They remained at Middletown that day while traffic cleared on the roads ahead of them, as Edings noted their next march to have commenced at 8:00 A.M. on 12 September. The original plan had called for Longstreet and the two divisions still with him to bivouac in the vicinity of Boonsboro, just west of South Mountain. Rumors of Federal forces approaching from the north caused Lee to order Longstreet to march 10 miles north to Hagerstown, Maryland, to block this approach.[17] The legion made the march in good order and went into camp several miles south of Hagerstown at 2:30 P.M. on 12 September.[18] When no additional marching orders were issued for the next day, the Legion soldiers settled into the camp routine they anticipated would last several days. As Chaplain George Smith observed, "we were expecting quite a time of repose."[19]

The chaplain was quite surprised to be roused on the morning of 14 September by an order to march back toward Boonsboro. Still there was no great sense of alarm, as Smith noted: "I had not the remotest dream

---

[14] Compiled Service Records, National Archives micropublication, M266, rolls 592, 594, 596, 599, Georgia Department of Archives and History, Morrow GA.

[15] H. Young to My Dear Uncle Henry, 24 September 1862, R. Gourdin Papers, collection 27, box 2, item 1.

[16] J. Edings, diary, 11 September entry.

[17] US War Department, comp., *The War of Rebellion: A Compilation of the Official Records of the Union and Confederate* Armies, 128 vols. (Washington DC: Government Printing Office, 1880–1901) ser. 1, vol. 19, pt. 1, p. 145.

[18] J. Edings, diary, 12 September entry.

[19] G. Smith, "Campfire Sketches & Battlefield Echoes," in Will C. King, *A Fighting Chaplain* (Springfield MA: 1886) 147–49.

of any hot work, nor do I think any of us had, for we had no idea that the Army of the Potomac could be reorganized and mobilized so soon. We thought the assault upon our lines was merely a feint of cavalry."[20] Major General David R. Jones's division marched first, with the brigades of Brigadier General George T. "Tige" Anderson and Brigadier General Thomas F. Drayton leading the way. The steady attrition continued. Private Ephraim Sellars of Company C, who had fallen ill, would be left behind at Hagerstown. He would pass away that afternoon while his comrades fought for their lives on South Mountain.[21]

What the chaplain and the legion soldiers could not have known was that on the evening of the 13 September Lee had received dispatches from both Brigadier General Daniel Harvey Hill and Major General James Ewell Brown Stuart disclosing that McClellan's large army was moving west into the Middletown Valley, just east of South Mountain, at an uncharacteristically rapid pace. Later, just after midnight, Lee received a second dispatch from Stuart. It revealed that McClellan had somehow come into possession of a copy of Special Order No. 191 detailing the campaign against Harpers Ferry.[22] Lee quickly realized that the success of the Harpers Ferry operation and, indeed, the safety of his entire army depended on preventing McClellan from crossing South Mountain to interpose his army between Jackson and Lee. Orders were issued and Lee and Longstreet led the two divisions south to the assistance of General D. H. Hill's division, which was guarding the key passes through South Mountain just east of Boonsboro.[23]

Early on the morning of 14 September, McClellan had ordered the Federal I and IX Corps forward to probe the South Mountain passes. Major General Jesse Reno, commanding the IX Corps, ordered the Kanawha Division to shift south and seize a key pass over South Mountain where Old Sharpsburg Road passed through Fox's Gap. Control of this location, slightly less than a mile south from the main pass at Turner's Gap, would permit the Federals to flank any

---

[20] Ibid.

[21] Compiled Service Records, M266, roll 599.

[22] J. Harsh, *Sounding the Shallows: A Confederate Companion for the Maryland Campaign of 1862* (Kent OH: Kent State University Press, 2000) 7, sec. G.

[23] *OR*, ser. 1, vol. 19, pt. 1, p. 146.

Southerners guarding the passage of National Road over the mountain at Turner's Gap.[24]

On the evening of 13 September, D. H. Hill had posted Colonel Alfred Colquitt's Georgia brigade at Turner's Gap and left his other four brigades in the valley to the west, expecting no significant Federal movements for several days. Later that evening Colquitt advised Hill of increased Federal activity. Hill ordered Brigadier General Samuel Garland's North Carolina brigade to arrive at the top of the mountain early on the morning of 14 September.[25]

When Hill and Garland arrived at Turner's Gap, the sunrise presented them with an astonishing sight. The valley floor to their east had become a writhing carpet of blue-clad soldiers. Hill quickly ordered Garland to march his 1,000-man brigade a mile to the south to guard the pass at Fox's Gap[26] while Colquitt's Georgians continued to cover Turner's Gap. Hill also sent orders back to have his remaining brigades move up to the passes and sent word to Longstreet and Lee that he was in serious trouble and needed reinforcements. Longstreet promptly marched most of his troops south from Hagerstown toward Boonsboro.[27]

The Phillips Legion with Drayton's command and "Tige" Anderson's brigade, located south of Hagerstown, were in the van of Longstreet's march. The two brigades moved rapidly down through Boonsboro and on up the winding mountain road to Turner's Gap.[28] As they arrived around 2:00 P.M., D. H. Hill breathed a sigh of relief and guided them south to Fox's Gap where an earlier disaster had unfolded. Attacked by two Federal brigades of 4,000 troops, Garland's 1,000 North Carolinians had been overwhelmed and pushed west out of the gap and off the mountain. Garland had been killed early in the fight. Only a gutsy holding action by two of Brigadier General George B. Anderson's regiments and a few survivors from Garland's command kept the Federals from moving north from Fox's Gap to capture Turner's Gap. While the Federals pulled back into the forest south of Fox's Gap to regroup for another attack, the remainder of G. B. Anderson's brigade

---

[24] *OR*, ser. 1, vol. 19, pt. 1, p. 48, 49.

[25] G. Grattan, Paper in *Southern Historical Society Papers.*

[26] Ibid.

[27] *OR*, ser. 1, vol. 19, pt. 1, p. 839.

[28] Ibid., pp. 885, 886.

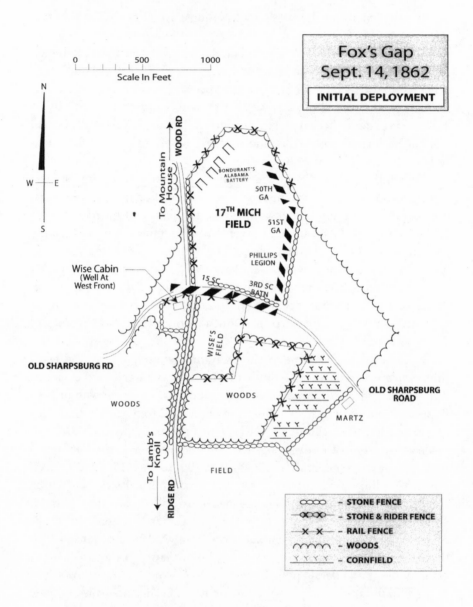

Deployment of Forces at Fox's Gap, approximately 3:00 P.M. to 4:00 P.M.
(Copyright 2000, Society of Descendents of Frederick Fox)

and Brigadier General Roswell S. Ripley's brigade arrived late in the morning. For the moment, the situation stabilized.[29]

With the arrival of "Tige" Anderson's and Drayton's 1,900 men, Hill felt he had enough troops at Fox's Gap to mount a counterattack. He would attempt to sweep the Federals back from the gap and down the mountain to the east.[30] As Hill and the various brigade commanders discussed the battle plan, the legion's soldiers filed into position behind a stone wall facing east. This wall stood just north of Old Sharpsburg Road and around 100 hundred yards below the crest of the mountain to their rear. The 50th and 51st Georgia Regiments were in line to the legion's left; the 15th South Carolina Regiment and the 3rd South Carolina Battalion were formed at a 90-degree angle to their right in Old Sharpsburg Road, looking south over a 4-acre field adjoining the south side of the road. Captain James W. Bondurant's four-gun Alabama battery was posted in the field well behind the legion, lobbing shells over them into the woods to the southeast. No Federals were visible but everyone knew they were there, at the southern and eastern sides of the field south of the road, just out of sight beyond the trees.[31]

Hill's plan called for Drayton's brigade, located at Fox's Gap, to serve as the pivot for a left-wheeling assault of four brigades that would start from Old Sharpsburg Road on the west side of the mountain.[32] As the other three brigades (G. B. Anderson's, Ripley's, and G. T. Anderson's) filed off down Old Sharpsburg Road to the west, Drayton shifted the Phillips Legion into Old Sharpsburg Road to join the 3rd South Carolina Battalion and most of the 15th South Carolina in an attack southward across the 4-acre field. The legion soldiers completed their redeployment and charged south with the two South Carolina units at 4:00 P.M.[33] As the charge began, Drayton redeployed the 51st and 50th into Old Sharpsburg Road as a reserve. This move would open up

---

[29] Ibid., p. 1020.

[30] Ibid.

[31] Smith, "Reminiscences," 54; William O. Fleming to *Savannah Republican*, 11 October 1862, in W. Fleming, "The Expedition into Maryland, Interesting Incidents & C.," *Savannah* (GA) *Republican*, 11 October 1862, p. 1.

[32] *OR*, ser. 1, vol. 19, pt. 1, pp. 1021–22.

[33] Smith, "Reminiscences," 54.

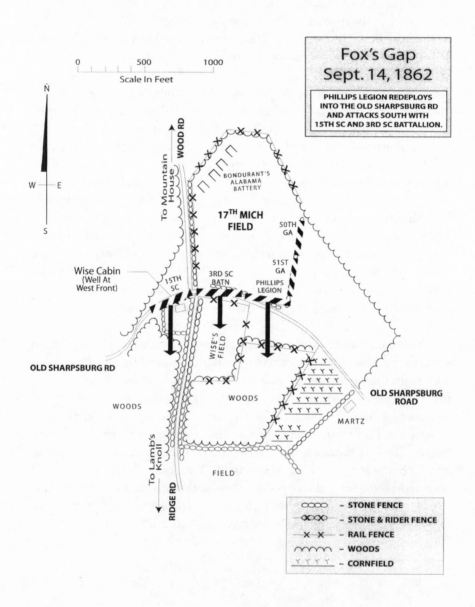

Attack South of Old Sharpsburg Road by Phillips Legion,
3rd South Carolina Battalion and 15th South Carolina,
approximately 4:00 P.M. to 4:15 P.M.
(Copyright 2000, Society of Descendents of Frederick Fox)

Drayton's left (eastern) flank with subsequent fatal results.[34] The legion, on the left of the attack force, entered the woods east of the field while the South Carolinians moved south across the open field. The legion infantrymen ran into trouble immediately, encountering large numbers of Union troops to their left front. The Federals, it turns out, were about to launch their own assault just as the legion entered the woods. Masses of bluecoats soon pushed the Georgia troops northwest out of the woods into the 4-acre field. Other Federals south of the field now opened up and drove the South Carolinians back. To compound the problems, G. T. Anderson's brigade had shifted too far down the road to the west, opening up a 300-hundred yard gap between Drayton's right and Anderson's left.[35] More Federals poured into this opening, surrounding the Georgia soldiers and the South Carolinians on three sides. Meanwhile, the three Confederate brigades that were to have attacked with Drayton had become lost, entangled in the dense forest on the west side of the mountain, and played no further part in the present action.[36] Chaplain Smith described how it all happened:

> Soon an order came to change front. We were looking eastward and were to go into the turnpike [Old Sharpsburg Road] and look southward. We entered the pike, crossed it and entered a wood. As we did, I found the enemy were in our front. As I reached the regiment I heard Cook, my Lt. Colonel cry out, "For God's sake, don't fire, we are friends." I saw a body of our own men about to fire on us thinking we were Federals. I ran back to check them and was pointing out the position of the troops when I looked up the road we had abandoned [Old Sharpsburg Road], and saw a body of Federals moving behind us. I saw their line of battle was moving upon the stone fence we had left, but it struck me from the way they moved that they did not know it was abandoned. I ran to the General [Drayton] and told him about it. He ran up to the fence and said something about charging, but there was nobody [available] to charge. A

---

[34] P. McGlashan to *Savannah Republican*, 16 October 1862, "The Fiftieth Georgia Regiment in Virginia and Maryland," in *Savannah Republican*, 16 October 1862.

[35] *OR*, ser. 1, vol. 19, pt. 1, pp. 908–909.

[36] Ibid., p. 1021.

Colonel Gist [Major William M. Gist, Fifteenth South Carolina] was in command of the rear guard. I thought it was the Fifteenth South Carolina. I told him the status. He told me he had only a [small] rear guard. I suggested we make a feint until our troops could be withdrawn. I do not know what he did. I soon saw the Federals were on our right, so we had them in front, on the left, on the right and there was a little gap left.[37]

At this juncture, Smith, seeing Federals circling from the east and west, decided he had better run back to his unit in the field to the south and warn them that they were being surrounded. Smith continued:

The firing was now fierce, but I felt my regiment must be brought out of that pocket at all hazards and I started to warn it, when I found it retreating. Poor Ellis [Private Ellis E. Williams, Company D, KIA] a Welchman, had run the Gauntlet and given them warning and the regiment was now retreating in a broken and confused manner. One of the boys, Gus Tomlinson, in tears said, "Parson, We've been whipped. The regiment is retreating." "And none too soon, either, said I for we are surrounded on all sides but one."

Immediately afterward a minie ball struck Chaplain Smith in the neck and ranged downward, exiting near his spine, paralyzing his arm for life.[38]

At this point, the Federals who had circled around the eastern flank attacked the 50th and 51st Georgia Regiments from behind. Attacked from front and rear, these troops suffered enormous casualties and were soon fleeing to the northwest.[39] The Fifteenth South Carolina retreated in fairly good order and the Phillips Legion followed, just barely escaping the closing Federal trap. The commander of the 3d South Carolina Battalion, Lieutenant Colonel George James, held his unit in position on Ridge Road between two stone walls and stubbornly resisted

---

[37] Smith, "Reminiscences," 54.

[38] G. Smith, "Campfire Sketches & Battlefield Echoes," 147–49.

[39] Fleming to *Savannah Republican*, 11 October 1862; McGlashan to *Savannah Republican*, 16 October 1862.

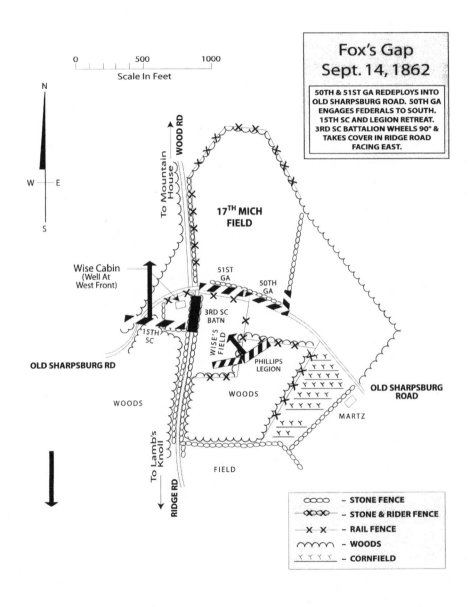

**Fox's Gap
Sept. 14, 1862**

50TH & 51ST GA REDEPLOYS INTO
OLD SHARPSBURG ROAD. 50TH GA
ENGAGES FEDERALS TO SOUTH.
15TH SC AND LEGION RETREAT.
3RD SC BATTALION WHEELS 90° &
TAKES COVER IN RIDGE ROAD
FACING EAST.

Phillips Legion and 15th South Carolina retreat.
3rd South Carolina Battalion wheels 90 degrees into Ridge Road,
approximately 4:15 P.M. to 4:45 P.M.
(Copyright 2000, Society of Descendents of Frederick Fox)

the Yankees, now pouring fire into his men from all directions. James and his second-in-command Major Rice were shot down, and their entire unit was nearly annihilated, with only two dozen men escaping death or wounds and capture.[40]

The legion had endured its first major combat action and suffered terribly. Thirty men lay dead on the field and another thirty-seven were wounded. Some, like Chaplain Smith as well as William Bannister, Sr. and W. H. Sauls (Company M men, both of whom lost an arm), were wounded so badly that they never returned to the army. The Federals marched forty-five off the mountain to prison at Fort Delaware. The legion lost 40 percent of the men it took into this fight.[41] So severely wounded that he was expected to die, Major Sandy Barclay survived due to attentive care provided by several sympathetic Maryland women. He would not rejoin the legion until May 1863, becoming its Lieutenant Colonel after Tom Cook's death at Fredericksburg, but the severe after-effects of his wounds would force him to resign at the end of 1863.[42] First Lieutenant Abraham "Ham" Jones of Company D, younger brother of Lieutenant Colonel Seaborn Jones who had resigned in July, was shot dead. He had written his older brother Bob on 6 September: "if they keep up this heavy, hard service, I will resign and come home until next Spring and then go into the cavalry or gorilla [sic] service so that I won't be in such a large body of troops. A man has to live like a hog where there is so many troops. I had rather be a private in a gorilla [sic] company than an officer when there is such a large force and where there is so little discipline."[43]

Among the other officers, Captain Oliver Daniel (Company A) was wounded; Second Lieutenant John W. Duggan (Company F) and First Lieutenant William O. Watson (Company O) were killed; and Lieutenant Michael Walsh (Company F) was captured.[44] Young William H. Dobbins, who had left his classes at Emory University to join Company C, was listed as wounded and missing. His father, John, began

---

[40] C. Calhoun, *Liberty Dethroned* (Greenwood SC: n.p., 1903); A. Dickert, *History of Kershaw's Brigade* (Washington DC: Elbert H. Aull Co., 1899) 173.

[41] Compiled Service Records, M266, rolls 592–600.

[42] Obituary for Barclay, 6 June 1872, in *Darien Georgia Times*.

[43] A. Jones to Augustus Jones, 6 September 1862, private collection of Mr. and Mrs. David Harlan, Atlanta GA.

[44] Compiled Service Records, M266, rolls 593, 594, 600.

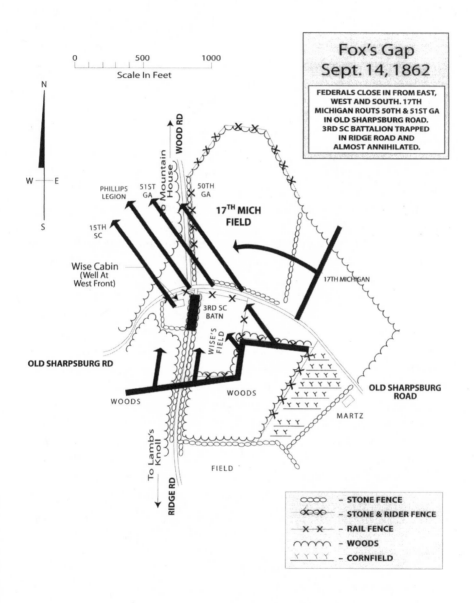

Confederate forces overwhelmed by Federals,
approximately 4:45 P.M. to 5:15 P.M.

(Copyright 2000, Society of Descendents of Frederick Fox)

a frantic letter-writing campaign to try to determine his whereabouts. After gaining hope from an account that his son had been captured, he finally learned in December from Lieutenant Alex Erwin that William had been shot in the chest during the attack and almost certainly died shortly thereafter.[45] Drayton's brigade was decimated, losing 626 men. While redeploying into the Old Sharpsburg Road, the 50th Georgia suffered enormous casualties, losing 181 of 225 men.[46]

At day's end Northern forces held the high ground to the north of Turner's Gap as well as Fox's Gap. Another Federal assault that afternoon had overrun the Confederate defenders at Crampton's Gap, 6 miles to the south. Battered, and facing renewed Federal assaults in the morning, Lee ordered Hill and Longstreet to retreat west to Sharpsburg, Maryland. Harpers Ferry fell to Stonewall Jackson on 15 September, and Lee was able to reconsolidate most of his army at Sharpsburg on the 16th. McClellan followed cautiously and launched an attack early on the morning of 17 September.

After savage fighting on the north and center of the field, the Federal IX Corps attacked a thin line of Confederate defenders on a ridge southeast of town in the late afternoon. Drayton's command, including the legion infantry, was part of this meager defense located behind a fence with Kemper's tiny Virginia brigade to their right. The Southern defenders at this point numbered no more than 800 muskets. The ground to their front was open and rolling, and it must have been an unnerving sight to watch some 9,000 Yankee troops roll inexorably toward them in the line of battle. Drayton's men had faced these same Federal attackers three days earlier at Fox's Gap. Resisting fiercely, the Rebels mowed down oncoming Federals of Colonel Harrison Fairchild's New York brigade directly in their front while other Federal brigades pressed in on their flanks. The level of Confederate resistance can be derived from the nearly 50 percent casualties sustained by Fairchild's command. Fairchild's men finally closed in on Drayton's and Kemper's men. The action briefly degenerated into a melee of bayonets and clubbed muskets before most of the two small brigades collapsed and

---

[45] A. Erwin to John S. Dobbins, 28 December 1862, John S. Dobbins Papers, Special Collections Department, collection MSS322, roll 1 (of 2), Woodruff Library, Emory University, Atlanta GA.

[46] Compiled Service Records, M266, rolls 505–10.

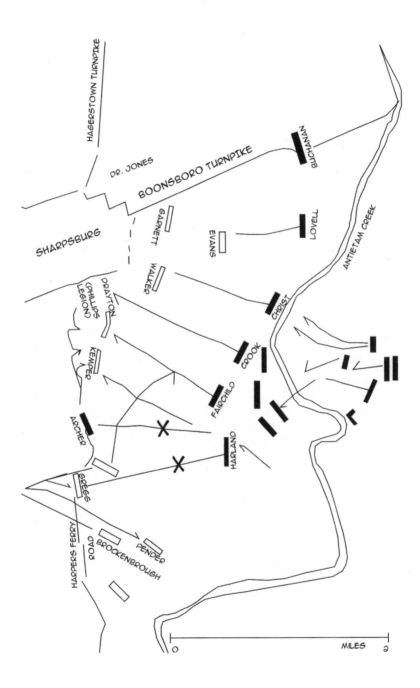

Drayton with Phillips Legion and Kemper's Brigades attacked
by Federal IX Corps, Sharpsburg, September 17, 1862.

fled back into Sharpsburg in disarray. The 15th South Carolina managed to maintain a semblance of order and formed a rear guard to screen the fleeing Confederates, which caused the Federals to pause to regroup before pressing on into town.[47] Disaster now stared Robert E. Lee squarely in the face. With no reserves and the Federal IX Corps positioned to cut the Army of Northern Virginia off from its single ford back to Virginia, two nearly simultaneous events would save the day.

General Robert Toombs's 2d and 20th Georgia Regiments had held up the IX Corps advance during the morning at what would thereafter be known as "Burnside's Bridge" over Antietam Creek. The general was joined by his newly arrived 15th and 17th Georgia Regiments in an area behind Drayton's position. Rallying the survivors of the 2d and 20th Georgia, he launched an attack to recapture a battery of Southern guns that had been positioned to Kemper's right. At the same moment, the head of General A. P. Hill's relief column from Harpers Ferry arrived just south of Toombs and attacked on his right. The sudden appearance of Southerners charging out of the corn on the Federal left flank caused an inexperienced Northern brigade to disintegrate. The attack rolled up the Northern flank and soon the entire IX Corps retreated back to the bluffs just west of Antietam Creek.[48]

That evening the remnants of Drayton's brigade reoccupied the position they had held earlier and officers counted heads. One-hundred-fifteen of the five-hundred men who had received Fairchild's attack had been killed or wounded.[49] Thirty-five of these casualties were from the Phillips Legion. Private Joseph C. Barry (Company B), who had been wounded on 23 August at Beverly's Ford in Virginia, had just caught up with his company on 16 September. During the attack he had been shot in the leg and, while trying to tend to his wound, was shot in the head and killed instantly. His comrades tenderly wrapped him in a blanket and buried him on the field. In addition, Corporal John T. Mapp, age twenty-three (Company A); Elijah F. Reed (Company B); William J. Johnston, age twenty-two (Company C); William D. Zachary, age nineteen (Company C); Irishman Cornelius McGinley (Company F); and Alfred G. Arwood (Company O) were all killed. Alfred's wife

---

[47] *OR*, ser. 1, vol. 19, pt. 1, pp. 886–87.
[48] Ibid.
[49] Compiled Service Records, M266, rolls 592–600.

Lucinda, back in Cobb County, filed a death claim to obtain Alfred's back pay and allowances. She would perish from typhoid the following year, orphaning an infant daughter. Private Zachary's father James would retrieve his son's body and bury him in the family's plot at Townville, South Carolina. Irish-born John Kelly (Company F) was left behind severely wounded and died in a Federal hospital on 23 September. William H. Hendrix was shot through the leg. Evacuated to Richmond, he would die there in November from the effects of his wound. Today he lies in Richmond's Oakwood Cemetery. William H. H. Branch (Company A) would lose and arm and be discharged from service on 15 October. He would spend the rest of the war as a drillmaster, training new recruits. Sixteen-year-old Lorenzo Dow Wright (Company A) was also wounded. He recovered from his wound and joined the 3d Georgia Sharpshooter Battalion in 1863, learning the deadly craft of the sniper/scout. He survived the war and lived to a ripe old age. Sergeant Charles E. Clyde (Company C) was wounded but recovered to march to Gettysburg, where on 2 July 1863 he would be fatally wounded. James H. Sauls (Company L) lost his leg and would spend the remainder of the war disabled in Cobb County. Sixteen-year-old Sergeant James B. Young (Company L) was also wounded. Ironically, on 10 September an order had been issued in Richmond discharging him from service by reason of being underage. Privates William B. Dobbs and J. P. Robertson both suffered hand wounds that were severe enough to result in their discharge from service.

Lee and McClellan faced off against each other on 18 September 1862 but neither side attacked. Lee used the time to shuttle his wagons and wounded back across the Potomac then led his battered army back to Virginia that evening. The hard marches, disease, exhaustion, and vicious combat left the legion infantry with only 100 effective soldiers. Stragglers, *sick*, wounded, and broken-down men, were scattered across Maryland. The small band of battered survivors who staggered over Blackford's Ford (also known as Boteler's Ford near Shepherdstown) were relieved to be alive and in good spirits on their return to Virginia. By year's end their elation would be tempered by the next savage confrontation with the hated Yankees at Fredericksburg.

Chapter 9

Behind the Stone Wall at Fredericksburg

*"I have been in many engagements before but I never saw in
my life such a slaughter."*

"...yea, the wall of Babylon shall fall."

After the savage combat at South Mountain and Sharpsburg, General
Robert E. Lee withdrew his battered army to the Shenandoah Valley to
refit and rest his exhausted troops. Lee kept a watchful eye on the Army
of the Potomac by posting Longstreet at Winchester and Jackson at
Bunker Hill while Stuart's cavalry covered the approaches from the
north and east and watched the Potomac fords from Williamsport to
Harpers Ferry. Lee also seized the opportunity to destroy railroads, thus
hindering any plans the Federals might have to invade and occupy the
Shenandoah Valley.

The Confederate War Department appointed seven lieutenant
generals, including Longstreet and Jackson, and established the two-
corps system that Lee had cautiously tested after the Seven Days
campaign. By this time, Lee had developed firmness in dealing with his
senior officers. He relieved the legion's brigade commander, General
Thomas F. Drayton. Drayton had been an embarrassment from the time
the army had left Richmond. He was tardy in bringing his brigade to the
support of General Jones at Second Manassas. This same brigade of
Georgia and South Carolina soldiers was battered at South Mountain
and again at Sharpsburg. Command and control were lost and casualties
were high. Although some of Drayton's officers and men suggested that
alcohol was a factor, its role in Drayton's dismal performance has never
been firmly established. Regarded as incompetent, Drayton was relieved
and eventually reassigned to non-combat duty in the west. The Phillips
Legion infantry was transferred to Brigadier General Thomas R. R.
Cobb's Georgia brigade in Major General Lafayette McLaws's division.

Much like their experience under the incompetent General Floyd in western Virginia, the Phillips Legion again escaped service under an ineffective commander.[1]

The legion infantry, now commanded by Colonel Robert T. Cook, had recuperated from the disasters of the Maryland campaign for a few short weeks but still needed supplies and equipment. Jack Reese griped from camp on Martinsburg Road, near Winchester, that the men were in dire need of clothing and were still waiting for the supply trains carrying their knapsacks to catch up with them. Some of the men had no shoes or blankets. A contemplative Reese confided to his aunt: "I would be glad to see this war come to a close. I have had enough of fighting to do me but there is more to do yet I suppose."[2] Reese was right. In less than a month the brigade received orders to cook two days' rations and prepare to march. Commanders then received orders on 30 October, and the brigade marched the following morning. Crossing the Shenandoah River, they passed through Front Royal on 1 November and Sperryville on 3 November as General Longstreet kept pace with General George B. McClellan's movements.[3]

McClellan hoped to use this respite to guard Washington as well as equipping and reorganizing his Army of the Potomac. Lincoln was

---

[1] Drayton's official removal and the reassignment of the Phillips Georgia Legion to Cobb's Brigade did not take place until the end of November, at which time the legion was preparing for battle at Fredericksburg. Drayton, however, effectively ceased to be a brigade commander following Sharpsburg. See US War Department, comp., *The War of Rebellion: A Compilation of the Official Records of the Union and Confederate* Armies, 128 vols. (Washington DC: Government Printing Office, 1880–1901) ser. 1, vol. 21, pp. 1029, 1030, 1033. In addition, Alexander S. Erwin, Company C, Phillips Georgia Legion, wrote the *Southern Watchman* (Athens GA) after Second Manassas, stating that "Drayton's conduct is severely criticized by all who know anything of the officer" *Southern Watchman* [Athens GA], 1 October 1862). Similarly, Andrew J. Reese wrote to his uncle: "It is said that our brigade is bursted up & that Gen. Drayton has been assigned to another post. I only hope it is true but fear it is not. From all I can hear Gen. Drayton does not stand very high in the estimations of other generals nor among the officers of the brigade & c." (Andrew Jackson Reese to Uncle, 28 November 1862, Rees/Reese Collection, Lumpkin County Library, Madeline K. Anthony Collection, series 3, box 23, folder 5).

[2] Andrew Jackson Reese to Aunt, 9 October 1862, Rees/Reese Collection; Andrew J. Reese to Uncle, November 1862, Rees/Reese Collection.

[3] Diary of Thomas M. Mitchell, October 1862–May 1864, private collection of Mr. R. D. Thomas, Chattanooga TN.

especially impatient for McClellan to take advantage of the autumn weather and resume the offensive. He directed General-in-Chief Henry Halleck to push McClellan to give battle and drive the Confederates farther south. By late October 1862, McClellan was beginning to move. The Confederates destroyed anything and everything necessary to impede the Federal advance. The legion took part in this effort as part of a raid to tear up the Baltimore and Ohio Railroad near Harpers Ferry on 22 October. They created raging fires, heated the rails over them, and bent the tracks so they could not be reused. The Rebels also destroyed all railroad shops and foundries in Martinsburg.

McClellan intended to move quickly to gain the rear of the Confederates. He hoped to strike between Culpeper Court House and Little Washington to split the Southern army or force them back as far as Gordonsville. This would place McClellan's army in position to advance upon Richmond by way of Fredericksburg or move directly to the peninsula. It was not to be as Lincoln had finally lost patience with his slow-moving general. On the night of 7 November he received an order by a special courier relieving him of command and instructing him to turn over the army to Major General Ambrose E. Burnside.

Burnside had achieved several military successes, including complex multi-service operations on the North Carolina coast. He had accepted his appointment as the new commander of the Army of the Potomac not through any ambition of his own. He feared that if he did not accept, Lincoln would instead appoint his arch-rival General Joseph Hooker. Burnside's predecessor McClellan was reputed to have remarked that Burnside lacked command ability for any unit larger than a regiment.[4] Curiously enough, the good-natured Burnside agreed with him. At the time McClellan was relieved, orders had already been dispatched for the planned movements to begin on 9 November. Shortly thereafter, Burnside submitted an alternative plan to Henry Halleck for a diversion toward Culpeper or Gordonsville while moving rapidly to Fredericksburg in order to place his army between Lee and Richmond. Threatening Richmond was fine with Lincoln, but the president demanded that Burnside keep his army in position to protect the national capital at all times. Burnside was convinced his plan would meet

---

[4] James Longstreet, *From Manassas to Appomattox* (New York: Da Capo Press, 1992) 292.

the needs of both goals. The shortest and most reliable route to Richmond involved proceeding directly from Fredericksburg south to the Confederate capital. By following the Fredericksburg line, the Federal army would be between the Confederate army and Washington.[5] The Confederates were anticipating just such a Federal movement in the vicinity of Culpeper Court House and were surveying points of possible concentration in order to meet that move. Although Halleck disagreed with Burnside's plan, Lincoln reluctantly consented provided Burnside moved rapidly.[6]

Burnside had 127,574 men in his three "Grand Divisions." Major General Edwin V. Sumner commanded the Right Grand Division. At daylight on the morning of 15 November, Sumner started down the north bank of the Rappahannock River, reaching Falmouth just opposite Fredericksburg two days later. The success of Burnside's plan depended on his immediate occupation of Fredericksburg. Once there he planned to organize his wagon trains, loading them with a minimum of twelve days' supplies, and then make a rapid march on Richmond.

Upon learning of the Federal change of command, Robert E. Lee was uncertain of Burnside's intentions. Would Burnside turn down the Rappahannock River toward Fredericksburg? Playing the odds, Lee sent a battery of artillery with an infantry regiment to reinforce the small Confederate outpost at Fredericksburg. On 18 November, Lee directed McLaws's division to proceed from Culpeper to Fredericksburg and sent Ransom's division to the North Anna River. Lee considered both as possible arenas of battle. The following day, Lee directed Longstreet's remaining divisions to follow. More than 6,400 of Longstreet's troops set out shoeless in the freezing November cold.[7]

---

[5] *OR*, ser. 1, vol. 19, pt. 2, pp. 552–54. Lee originally preferred to make a stand along the North Anna River, where the Ground allowed for a counterattack. Although Jackson argued for keeping with the original plan, Lee decided to defend Fredericksburg because Burnside acted so slowly. Jackson believed the Confederates could win at Fredericksburg with its excellent defensive topography, but after the Union assault the Confederates would have no space to swing around Burnside and break apart his army. Federal artillery on the higher Stafford Heights would serve to deny any move against the Union flank (Longstreet, *Manassas to Appomattox*, 292–93).

[6] Ibid.

[7] Ibid.

The Phillips Legion infantry was well positioned near Culpeper to move quickly to Fredericksburg, and by 19 November they were just 8 miles away. The following day they camped south of town in a cold, driving rain. That evening legion troops drew picket duty near town along the Rappahannock River.[8] Burnside desperately needed pontoon trains to shift his troops across the Rappahannock. General Halleck had promised their arrival in a timely manner but unfortunately, and perhaps fatally, the pontoons did not arrive until 25 November—eight days after Sumner reached the river. Hoping to maintain the element of surprise, Sumner had recommended that Burnside move a portion of his force across the Rappahannock without waiting for the pontoons. Burnside rejected Sumner's plan, reasoning that it would be impractical to cross large bodies of troops without pontoons and insisting that it would be dangerous to attempt such a crossing even in small groups. This decision was a fatal mistake. The small Confederate garrison at Fredericksburg would have offered little opposition, and the delay permitted Lee to position a significant portion of his army in and behind the city.

Burnside now faced a formidable force across the river. Longstreet was situated firmly on the heights behind the town by 19 November, days before Burnside's tardy pontoons arrived. Burnside still had some advantage in that only a portion of Lee's army confronted him. The larger Army of the Potomac might have interposed itself between Longstreet's 1st and Jackson's 2nd corps of the Army of Northern Virginia since Jackson was still in the vicinity of Orange Court House, nearly 40 miles west of Fredericksburg. Burnside concluded that his plan for rapid movement had collapsed because of the missing pontoons and the expanding enemy force on the other side of the river. Clearly he had lost the element of surprise and what little advantage he might have enjoyed. Rather than make an immediate direct assault, Burnside began massing supplies during the last days of November and the first days of December in preparation to attack Lee. Lee was no less busy on the other side of the river strengthening his line along the range of hills behind the town. The Confederate army now occupied Fredericksburg itself as well as a ridge extending from above the Falmouth Ford to Massaponax Creek, 5 miles below the town. The hills on the Confederate side were lower than Stafford Heights, which was crowned

---

[8] Thomas M. Mitchell, diary, 20 November entry.

by massed Federal artillery on the north side of the river. Lee accordingly directed the construction of earthworks along the crest of the hills behind the town.

The narrow Rappahannock at Fredericksburg presented opportunities for the Federals to lay pontoon bridges secure from the fire of the Confederate artillery. Union guns on Stafford Heights dominated the entire plain of Fredericksburg, preventing significant opposition to bridge construction or river passage without exposing Rebel troops to destructive artillery fire. Lee in turn selected his position to resist the Federal advance after they had crossed. He left only a small force at the river to harass the Federal movement.

Noting the Yankee cannons on Stafford Heights and the Confederate cannons placed to return fire, Jack Reese of the legion infantry doubted that much fighting would occur at the river: "The Yankees have their cannons planted to shell the town & we have ours planted so as to shell them. How long things will remain in the present attitude is hard to tell. I do not think there will be much fighting just at this time. I think we will fall back so as to let the enemy cross the river & get out where we can get a fair chance at them."[9] Future events would prove that Reese was right on the mark.

Burnside's incompetence became clearer as he piled mistake upon deadly mistake. Little could be expected from an offensive at this time of year, largely because of the cold, wet days of winter and muddy roads. One might speculate that somehow, on some level, Burnside was aware of his precarious situation, but because of political pressures, he pressed on anyway. Any plan to attack the 78,000 Confederates under Longstreet and Jackson (who had now joined Lee at Fredericksburg) in well-fortified positions of their own choosing was an enterprise that would tax the abilities of the most able commanders on either side. Lee was solidly deployed in a line nearly 8 miles long. His left flank, held by Longstreet's I Corps, ran along commanding terrain towering over the open plains immediately west of the city. Anderson's division rested upon the Rappahannock River while the divisions of McLaws, Pickett, and Hood extended to the right of Anderson and joined the left of Jackson's corps downriver. Ransom's division supported the batteries on

---

[9] A. J. Reese to Uncle, 28 November 1862; and A. J. Reese to Uncle, Rees/Reese Collection.

Marye's Heights and Willis's Hill, backing up McLaws's troops. The right wing of the army, Jackson's II Corps, was deployed south and west of Fredericksburg. General Lee must have been pleased with his good fortune. His positions seemed impregnable, and he doubted Burnside would be foolish enough to assault him directly at Fredericksburg, believing that any attempt to cross the river would be somewhere below the city. Lee ordered Jackson to place his men along the Richmond, Fredericksburg, and Potomac Railroad where he could easily support Longstreet or confront any advance farther down the Rappahannock.[10]

Burnside had spent a month examining numerous crossing sites only to find each of them rife with problems. He had planned to cross at Skinkers Neck but Jackson's arrival on 3 December scuttled the plan because Skinkers was no longer on the southern flank but at the center of Jackson's line. Earlier, Burnside had planned to seize some point on the Confederate line near Massaponax Creek and split the Confederate forces on the Rappahannock River by driving around Longstreet's right and seizing Hamilton's Crossing. Burnside abandoned the proposed crossing at Skinkers Neck and instead decided to throw two bridges across the river opposite the upper part of town, one near the lower part and one a mile or so below the town. Questioned about this decision by authorities following the battle, Burnside explained that he changed his plan because he had discovered that Lee had stationed a large force downriver. This force weakened the Confederate defenses in front of Fredericksburg in anticipation of a crossing at Skinkers Neck. He hoped to cross the river rapidly near the town and separate the Confederate troops from their cohorts downriver.

Burnside prepared his Grand Divisions to move early on 11 December. He ordered the bridges to be placed within the next 2 to 3 hours.[11] Confederates posted along the waterfront heard the construction activity, but a heavy mist shrouded the river and prevented any sightings of the enemy. When the mist finally lifted, sharpshooters of Brigadier General William Barksdale's Mississippi brigade opened fire on the bridge workers. The Federals made three futile attempts to complete the upper bridge but accurate musket fire stopped them.

---

[10] D. Freeman, *R. E. Lee, A Biography*, 4 vols. (New York: Charles Scribner's Sons, 1934) 2:438.

[11] *OR*, ser. 1, vol. 21, pp. 87, 88, 840, 841.

Burnside's soldiers managed to complete the lower bridges but Burnside refused to permit any crossing until all bridges were completed. Lee must have been absolutely certain that Burnside intended to attack directly through Fredericksburg.[12] When Lincoln replaced McClellan with Burnside, Lee was reputed to have remarked: "I fear they may continue to make these changes till they find someone I don't understand." Burnside would not be this individual! If anyone understood Burnside, it was Lee.

Burnside realized that the Confederate sharpshooters must be driven from the riverfront in order to finish construction of the upper bridges. Following a round of intensive shelling, a group of Federal volunteers piled into several pontoon boats and rushed across the river. Once ashore they drove back the Mississippians who later withdrew under cover of darkness. Federals were now over the river but the planned assault had been delayed by one more day. The deadly work of Barksdale's sharpshooters had afforded Jackson enough time to start shifting his divisions to support the Confederate forces in Fredericksburg.

On that same evening, General Cobb placed his brigade under arms and marched in the numbing cold to relieve General Barksdale's brigade at the foot of Marye's Heights. The two brigades met at Telegraph Road, just along a sunken portion of the road running parallel to the river at the base of Marye's Heights. The 18th and 24th Georgia Regiments and the Phillips Legion took position behind a stone retaining wall that ran 480 yards along the sunken road. The legion formed on the left, the 24th Georgia in the center, and the 18th Georgia on the right, covering the entire front of the hill. The brigade's other units, the Cobb Legion and the 16th Georgia, had been decimated at Crampton's Gap in September and were held in reserve during this action. Cobb's men arrayed themselves along the wall while General Ransom moved the 24th North Carolina Regiment to extend the left. They joined Cobb's line where the Habersham Volunteers, Company C of the legion, were located, just beyond the protection of the stone retaining wall where Telegraph Road passed through it. Over 2,000 Confederates waited behind the wall for the attack while the remainder of Ransom's division was held in reserve just to the rear of Marye's

---

[12] Freeman, *R. E. Lee, A Biography*, 2:438.

Heights. McLaws's other brigades were stationed from Cobb's right to Lee's Hill then south to connect to Pickett's division.[13]

McLaws had Cobb's troops dig a ditch along the inside of the stone retaining wall, deep enough for men to stand in and fire at oncoming Federals from behind the shoulder-high position, while at the same time minimizing their own exposure. The legion troops went to work digging their part of the trench while that part of Company C not shielded by the wall hastily scratched out shallow rifle pits. Lee had avoided placing too many earthworks on the hills for fear of convincing Burnside that the position was impregnable, deciding to rely more on the natural protection offered by the sloping hills. This was an excellent defensive position, and Longstreet was confident that no Federals would come within effective range of his infantry positions at Marye's Heights. The position in the sunken road turned out to be so effective, so well hidden from view of the Federals, that survivors later commented that they never knew any Rebels were there until they opened fire.[14]

Next morning as legion Company B, the Dalton Guards, suffered picket duty in front of the stone wall, Burnside began shuffling the Right Grand Division into the city by the upper bridges and the Left Grand Division by the bridges below Deep Run (south-southwest of modern-day Route 64 intersects Ridgefield Parkway). Lee and Longstreet were increasingly sure that Burnside intended to strike at Marye's Heights and Prospect Hill. Longstreet and Jackson were well positioned at both sites. The men of the legion lay behind the stone wall on freezing ground, waiting for the coming attack with orders not to fire until the enemy reached a plank fence 60 yards from the stone wall.[15] Unbeknownst to

---

[13] *OR*, ser. 1, vol. 21, pp. 579, 580.

[14] Report of 24th Georgia, 20 December 1862, in *OR*, ser. 1, vol. 21, pp. 607–608.

[15] Gen. McLaws reported on the battle on the night of 11 December 1862; see *OR*, ser. 1, vol. 21, pp. 578–83; see also report of Lt. Col. Elbert Bland, commanding the 7th South Carolina, in *OR*, vol. 21, pp. 597–98, and Kershaw's report, pp. 588–91: "Marye's Hill, covered with our batteries, falls off abruptly toward Fredericksburg to a stone wall, which forms a terrace on the side of the hill and the outer margin of the Telegraph road which winds along the foot of the hill. The road is about 25 feet wide, and is faced by a stone wall about 4 feet high on the city side. The road having been cut out of the hill, this last wall in many places is not visible above the surface of the ground. I found, on my arrival, that Cobb's Brigade, Col. McMillan commanding, occupied our entire front, and my troops could only get into position by doubling on them. This was accordingly done,

them, their orphan artillery unit, the Macon Light Artillery, was in direct artillery support and fired many effective rounds on their behalf.[16]

On the morning of the following day, 13 December 1862, an impenetrable mist hid the two armies. The mist blinded Cobb's troops beyond a distance of 60 to 80 yards from the stone wall as General Sumner prepared to assault the heights at the rear of the town.

The first of many assaults got underway when Major General William Franklin threw two divisions at Jackson's Prospect Hill position. Effective counter-battery fire enabled the Federals to reach a marshy gap in Jackson's front but their leading divisions received no support and Jackson closed the breach. Confusing orders from Burnside led Franklin to make no further effort and retire with severe casualties.

Simultaneously, Longstreet's troops began the grim business of slaughtering wave after wave of Federals staggering uphill into the hail of lead at Marye's Heights, 1/2 mile west of the city. When the battle opened on the Confederates' left around 10:00 A.M., Sumner had positioned several divisions in the town anticipating attack orders. A few hundred yards from town a 15-foot-wide canal spillway called a millrace was crossed by three bridges. Just beyond the sluiceway the area sloped slightly, giving the Federals good cover to deploy into line. Unfortunately, once the Unionists crested the slight rise they were exposed for the 400 yards to the Confederate lines. Only a small bank about halfway to the Confederate position allowed the men to flatten themselves with minimal cover.[17]

Brigadier General Nathan Kimball's Union brigade of Brigadier General William H. French's division were the first Northern troops to challenge the Confederates at Marye's Heights. A cloud of skirmishers moved to clear the way, driving in the legion Company B pickets from the skirmish line. Sergeant William Rhadamanthus Montgomery, a veteran of several battles, would write later to his Aunt Frank: "it would have made your blood run cold to have seen their great numbers coming

---

and the formation along most of the line during the engagement was consequently four deep."

[16] See Appendix A, "The Macon Light Artillery."

[17] M. Church, "The Hills of Habersham," 61, in *Reminiscences of E. H. Sutton, 24th Georgia,* 13 December 1862; Stephen Dent, "With Cobb's Brigade at Fredericksburg," *Confederate Veteran* 22/11 (November 1914): 500–501.

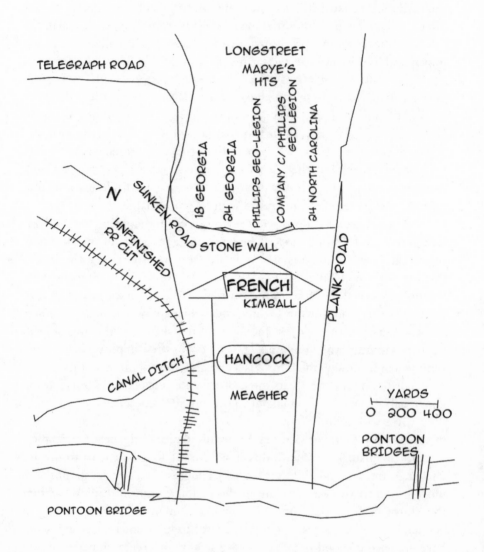

Phillips Georgia Legion behind the stone wall at Fredericksburg.

over to oppose our little handful."[18] Kimball's veterans led the way through the battered town of Fredericksburg, across the millrace, and uphill to death by the muzzle blasts of the Confederate defenders. Their mission was to plunge ahead and take the Confederate batteries on the crest of Marye's Heights. The Federal troops were forced to feel their way across the plank bridges and remove fences blocking their advance. As Kimball's men began their advance they were met with grape and canister from the Washington Artillery, whose guns were trained on the open field along Cobb's front. Those who survived the artillery barrage and approached the stone wall were shocked when Cobb's men appeared to rise from out of the ground and blast them with a solid sheet of fire. The Rebels had held their fire until the Federals were right on top of them and General Cobb shouted, "Get ready, boys, here they come!" and gave the order to rise and fire. The next act in this ghastly drama was part of a predictable pattern as the Yankees struggled bravely toward the heights: Confederate troops suddenly appeared; commanders shouted over the din of wounded and dying men and roaring artillery fire; thousands of rifles and cannons belched a deafening roar and Kimball's brigade was shredded. Surviving Federals dropped to the ground, trying desperately to find some kind of cover, load, and return fire. Kimball and several of his regimental commanders were wounded. The assault, lasting approximately 20 minutes, produced 520 casualties, over one-fourth of Kimball's total strength.[19] The surviving Federals broke for the rear.

Southern cheers had scarcely abated when the Confederates saw another column advancing, then another, and another—an endless sea of blue moving inexorably forward, struggling to position themselves to support their mates and being cut down like wheat before a scythe.

---

[18] William R. Montgomery to Aunt Frank from Camp near Fredericksburg VA, 17 December 1862, in G. F. Montgomery Jr., ed., *Georgia Sharpshooter: The Civil War Diary and Letters of William Rhadamanthus Montgomery* (Macon GA: Mercer University Press, 1997) 76–78.

[19] Quoted in "Burnside's Campaign—Fredericksburg," in *Harper's Pictorial History of the Great Rebellion*, ed. A. H. Guernsey and H. M. Alden (1866; repr. New York: Fairfax Press, [1996?]) 414; 13 December 1862 extract from diary of Thomas M. Mitchell, handwritten copyright written on the abstract, in the private collection of Mr. R. D. Thomas, Chattanooga TN; Montgomery to Aunt Frank, 17 December 1862.

General Cobb went down, mortally wounded after the first assault had been beaten back. How he was wounded is not at all clear. Considered a definitive source on the death of Cobb, David Preston, in his article "The Glorious Light Went Out Forever," suggests Cobb was killed by a shell.[20] Period accounts vary, identifying the cause as a bullet or a shell fragment and locating Cobb in various positions at the time he was wounded. Another source places the onus on a disgruntled Phillips Legion soldier. The 21 March 1901 edition of the *Marietta Journal* set off a firestorm of controversy with an article titled "Who Killed General Cobb?"[21] The article stated that, according to an unnamed Cobb County veteran of the Phillips Legion Infantry Battalion, a legion soldier named "Sam" had intentionally shot and killed General Cobb at Fredericksburg. According to this account, Cobb had confronted the unnamed veteran and Sam during a march when they dropped out of ranks to fill their canteens from a small creek. A heated exchange took place between Sam and the general when Cobb demanded they get back in the ranks, threatening to shoot Sam if he did not. Sam told Cobb to go ahead and shoot him; Cobb relented and rode away. Sam shouted after the general that he would kill him at the first opportunity. Shortly after allegedly shooting Cobb during the battle of Fredericksburg, Sam was himself mortally wounded. The unnamed veteran went on to relate how he had visited Sam after he was wounded and confirmed that Sam had indeed shot Cobb. This article produced angry rebuttals from various parties, which were published in the *Atlanta Journal* over the following months. It is interesting to note that these various "eyewitness" accounts do *not* agree on how General Cobb was mortally wounded. Some state he was struck by a shell's explosion while others indicate that he was shot by a rifle ball.

Two accounts place Cobb between 15 and 45 feet in front of the lines behind a house on Telegraph Road. This house marked the right flank of the sector manned by the Phillips Legion troops. Of possibly greater interest is the fact that one of the veterans who wrote to the Atlanta paper to refute the Marietta article confirmed that the canteen

---

[20] David Preston, "The Glorious Light Went Out Forever," in vol. 4, no. 4 of *Civil War Regiments: A Journal of the American Civil War* (Mason City IA: Savas Publishing Co., 1995).

[21] No author, "Who Killed General Cobb?" *Marietta* (GA) *Journal*, 21 March 1901, p. 2.

incident actually took place. He went on to state that General Cobb's reason for taking action at the creek involved possible poisoning or tainting of the water. One can only wonder why, if this were the case, the general did not simply tell the soldiers this rather than threaten to shoot them. It is even possible that Cobb specifically referred to this incident in a letter to his wife dated 24 October 1862. He wrote that two days earlier his troops had marched to the railroad just below Duffield Station and torn up the tracks. He further recounted: "General Drayton, who was also along [with his brigade containing the Phillips Legion] allowed full scope to straggling from his brigade and this caused me great trouble." The authors have also been able to identify "Sam." He was Private Samuel Drake of legion infantry Company M, who hailed from precisely the same place in Cobb County, Georgia, as the veteran who in 1901 gave the story to the Marietta paper. Samuel Drake, a twenty-eight-year-old farmer from the Lost Mountain district of Cobb County, was wounded in the shoulder at Fredericksburg on 13 December and died 24 December 1862 at Richmond's General Hospital No. 4. He is buried at Hollywood Cemetery in Richmond under the name "S. Drink." Obviously, at this distance in time, this must remain just another of history's mysteries, but the authors felt it useful to present the facts. One question that troubled us is why the old legion veteran would come forward in 1901 to relate such a story if it were not true. It is hard to believe that he could have anticipated it would bring him any great acclaim, as Cobb had, by then, become an icon of the Lost Cause.

Colonel Robert McMillan of the 24th Georgia immediately took brigade command. The veteran Sergeant Montgomery, in line with his legion compatriots behind the stone wall, observed: "The whole time of our engagement our brave & gallant Gen Cobb was encouraging on his men until a shot from the enemy's cannon gave him his mortal wound. He was on the right of our Co. only a few feet from me when wounded. Payson Ardis being one of our litter bearers ran to him & I shall never forget his last look as they laid him on the litter to bear him from the field. His last words were 'I am only wounded Boys, hold your ground like brave men.'"[22] Despite Payson Ardis's and the doctor's best efforts, Cobb soon expired from loss of blood.

The Phillips Legion suffered a great loss when its popular commander, Lieutenant Colonel Robert T. "Tom" Cook, was shot through the head during the initial attack and died immediately. Captain James S. Johnson of Company L, who had just rejoined the legion after recovering from his Maryland campaign wounds, stepped in and was immediately wounded in the foot. Lieutenant Julius A. Peek of Company D took over and was soon wounded in the neck. First Lieutenant John S. Norris , the senior officer then present, assumed command.[23] As the fighting intensified, the legion began to run low on ammunition. McMillan called up the 16th Georgia of Colonel Goode Bryan to assist and, shortly thereafter, Brigadier General Joseph B. Kershaw's South Carolina brigade arrived on McLaws's orders. The 2nd South Carolina fell in behind the Phillips Legion, the 8th South Carolina behind others in Cobb's brigade, all bringing fresh ammunition with them. Ransom advanced his 25th North Carolina to provide additional support. All of these reinforcements could not have been more timely. Sergeant Montgomery had begun to fear that without ammunition Cobb's brigade would have to charge bayonets. He breathed a sigh of relief when he saw help on its way: "the old 2nd S. C. Vols coming…I felt good, for we had shot away 70 rounds of cartridges and the Yankees were still coming."[24]

The ranks of the Confederates were four or five men deep, the rear files loading and passing muskets to the front ranks, the men firing a solid blast of lead. Color Sergeant Peyton W. Fuller, the legion's impetuous young color bearer, waved his flag like a matador's cape from behind the wall all afternoon. On three occasions Federal sharpshooters

---

[22] *OR*, ser. 1, vol. 21, pp. 555, 564, 570, 580, 608, 624–26; D. S. Freeman, *Lee's Lieutenants: A Study in Command*, 3 vols. (New York: Charles Scribner's Sons, 1942–1944) 2:361–62; *The Tide Shifts*, vol. 3 of *Battles and Leaders of the Civil War*, ed, Robert U. Johnson and C. Buel, 4 vols. (New York: De Vinne Press, 1888) 94. "The litter bearers brought him down the road by us and when they came to our company (Company C, 24th Georgia) the fire was so heavy that they laid him down and sheltered themselves under the wall for a while. When the lull came they went on with him to the hospital" (Mary L. Church, *The Hills of Habersham* [Clarksville GA: Mary Church, 1962] 74) in reminiscences of E. H. Hutton, 24th Georgia, 13 December 1862.

[23] Longstreet, *Manassas to Appomattox*, 313; Joseph H. Alexander, "Defending Marye's Heights," *Military History Quarterly* 9/3 (Spring 1997): 86–96.

[24] Montgomery to Aunt Frank, 17 December 1862.

shot the flagstaff from his hands. Finally, the staff beyond repair, he nailed the tattered colors to a board, then stood up to wave the awkward flag defiantly high overhead. Fuller was met with a grazing shot to the forehead that knocked him and his flag into the muddy road. Only slightly chastened, he continued to wave the colors but more carefully from behind the stone wall. By day's end, the flag had been punctured by fifty-eight bullets.[25]

Of all the innumerable suicidal assaults, perhaps the most memorable was that of Brigadier General Thomas F. Meagher's "Irish Brigade." Known for hard drinking, fierce fighting, and proud display of the Irish green, these troops seemed to have no counterpart on either side when it came to raw courage. Prior to their assault, Meagher sent orderlies bearing bunches of green boxwood to each of his officers, and each man was given a green sprig to wear on his uniform. The green flag of Meagher's brigade and the green sprigs, emblems of Erin, would surely encourage the dogged fighting Irish and spread terror among the Confederate ranks.[26] The Irish Brigade filed off the city wharf at the extreme end of Fredericksburg and rested in place next to a cotton mill that spewed acrid smoke from a fire set earlier that morning by an artillery round. Meagher's men waited impatiently for the order to move out as shells from Confederate artillery burst in every street of the battered town. Standing amidst the incoming artillery was more terrifying than facing the enemy directly. The Irishmen watched as the wounded were carried from the battlefield, providing a hellish preview of their coming role in the battle. The general himself appeared and shouted the order to advance with fixed bayonets.

The brigade marched up the streets in the general direction of Marye's Heights. They walked directly into an artillery barrage as the Confederates observed the enemy movement and opened a furious fire, killing and wounding many of the oncoming Irishmen. The brigade marched on relentlessly amid the rain of fire until they arrived at the other end of town, where they halted under cover of the frame buildings to regroup and prepare for the charge. Urging the men to hold steady, the officers ordered the troops to "double quick." The brigade turned a

---

[25] Alexander, "Defending Marye's Heights," 86–96.

[26] William McCarter, Kevin O'Brien, eds., "My Life in the Irish Brigade" (Campbell CA: Savas Publishing Co., 1996) 167.

corner near the end of town and reached the base of a hill as Federal artillery fire from Stafford's Heights provided cover for the advance. Confederate artillery fire increased in turn. Upon arriving at the base of the hill, winded from the double-quick march, the men halted to rest, sheltered from the fire by the slight rise of the hill. Here they were forced to break ranks to cross the millrace, some 4 or 5 yards wide, stumbling across narrow plank bridges or wading through the shallow water. Those who successfully crossed the water now had to navigate a shallow depression covered with Union dead and wounded until they reached the Fredericksburg and Richmond Railroad, where they found cover.

The brigade reformed and was then ordered to advance. The gutsy Irishmen screamed in Gaelic and pressed on until they reached the top of the hill and some level ground 200 yards from the Confederate line, behind the stone wall. They were staggered by a blast of musketry but recovered and pushed on. As they came within 50 yards of the wall, Cobb's brigade arose from its concealment to pour volley after volley into the Irishmen, cutting them down and halting any further advance.[27]

Colonel McMillan, himself a transplanted Irishman, joined the fray when Meagher's troops began their ascent of the hill. McMillan joined with Captain Patrick McGovern of the Lochrane Guards, the legion's own Irish company, to hurl Gaelic battle cries and obscenities back at their Irish counterparts.[28] "Thus, Greek met Greek" was trumpeted by a prominent Southern newspaper.[29] Despite its bravery, Meagher's Irish Brigade met the same fate as all other Federal attackers vainly attempting to breach the stone wall, and they were thrown back by the overwhelming Confederate firepower.

Some legion troops suffered from a problem more vexing than the advancing Federals as South Carolinians behind the legion, higher up the hill, were not shooting high enough for their musket balls to pass over their comrades below. Private James Springer Wood of Company D, the Polk Rifles, described their frustration: "I think our greatest loss was caused by the guns of our own men stationed on the hill to our rear...Gus Tomlinson went twice and Lucius Stone once on the hill and

---

[27] Ibid., 178.
[28] Alexander, "Defending Marye's Heights," 94.
[29] Ibid.

told them they were killing our own men at the foot of the hill. Friendly fire may have caused nearly as many casualties as enemy fire.[30]

The Phillips Georgia Legion and sister units behind the stone wall withstood fourteen charges and repulsed each one, resulting in horrendous Union losses. William R. Montgomery observed: "I have been in many engagements before but I never saw in my life such a slaughter."[31]

Burnside, seemingly out of touch with reality, demanded more suicidal assaults. Early evening's darkness brought an end to the massacre. The Union army had suffered a crushing defeat; it was disorganized and demoralized. Although Burnside was determined to attack again the next day, his subordinates finally dissuaded him. All the next day Federal wounded lay in freezing agony on the slope while Burnside dithered. Finally, on 15 December, he sent a flag of truce to retrieve the wounded and bury the dead, many of whom had been stripped of clothing and equipment by the ragged Southern soldiers. The scene must have been nightmarish—Federal surgeons and litter bearers struggling to identify and treat the wounded, mingling with shivering Confederates seeking clothing and arms; mangled bodies and body parts scattered over the battlefield; men from both sides in shock. Dante could not have portrayed it any better. By this time any sense of ghoulishness must have abated. Surely it was better for soldiers to take whatever they needed from those who no longer had any need for anything but proper burials. One Confederate stooped to strip a pair of shoes from the feet of what he thought to be a Federal corpse when the soldier "woke up." The startled Confederate put the shoe back on the ground, saying, "Beg pardon, Sir, I thought you had gone above."[32]

That evening, Brigadier General Paul Semmes relieved Cobb's brigade against the wishes of Colonel McMillan, the acting commander. McMillan objected to relinquishing such a position of honor.[33] Lee's

---

[30] In reminiscences of J. S. Wood, Co. D, Phillips Legion, Microfilm Library, Georgia Department of Archives and History, drawer 283, box 40. Adjutant Byrd reported that "several [companies] suffered from the fire of two South Carolina regiments who were behind us, higher up the hill, and did not shoot high enough for the balls to pass over" (*Augusta Daily Constitutionalist*, 27 December 1862, p. 2).

[31] Montgomery to Aunt Frank, 17 December 1862.

[32] Dent, "With Cobb's Brigade," 501.

[33] *OR*, ser. 1, vol. 21, p. 581.

generals urged him to pursue the beaten Union army but Lee declined, not wanting to lose the advantage of the position. In view of the magnitude of Burnside's preparations and strength of numbers, Lee was not convinced that he would limit himself to one attempt. As the fog melted on 16 December, pickets reported that the Federal force had retired across the river and removed their pontoon bridges. Wasting no time, Confederate troops immediately reoccupied the shattered remains of Fredericksburg, the once-lovely city now a smoking ruin. Hardly a house remained that had not been torn to pieces by shell and shot or burned to ashes.

The Phillips Legion infantry went into winter camp with the Army of Northern Virginia. They passed a bleak Christmas in makeshift shelters south of the devastated city of Fredericksburg. The cost in dead and wounded was enormous. The Federals had suffered casualties of over 13,000 killed and wounded. Confederate losses were less severe at about 5,000. The Phillips Legion lost seventy-two men, including their commander Lt. Colonel Robert T. Cook. Modern author Colonel Joseph Alexander provides an excellent description of the legion's immense firepower. "The Phillips Legion, accomplished marksmen occupying premier firing positions along at least half of the sunken road from start to finish, contributed the major share of the slaughter. The sheer weight of lead and volume of fire delivered by the Legion alone is difficult to imagine: 400 riflemen, each shooting an average of 60 buck and ball cartridges, equates to 24,000 rounds fired at troops advancing upright across an open field in broad daylight at a distance rarely greater than 200 yards."[34]

The Phillips Legion's losses were thirteen killed, fifty-nine wounded (ten of whom would later expire from their wounds). Slightly different and more detailed casualty figures appear in the *Official Records of the Union and Confederate Armies*: one officer killed (Lieutenant Colonel Robert T. Cook), twelve enlisted men killed, six officers wounded, and forty-nine enlisted men wounded for a total of sixty-eight men.[35]

Company C, the Habersham Volunteers, which had been positioned on the legion's left flank and largely beyond the protection of

---

[34] Alexander, "Defending Marye's Heights," 95.
[35] *OR*, ser. 1, vol. 21, p. 584.

the stone wall, suffered the greatest loss. In a letter dated 28 December, Lieutenant Alex Erwin commented: "Our company suffered terribly the other day in the battle of Fredericksburg. Our brigade being more actively engaged than any other. In our company alone we lost seven killed—one mortally wounded and twenty-one wounded not mortally."[36] One odd casualty was Private Phillip Jefferson "Jeff" Perry of Company C. A postwar history of Company C, written by an unidentified veteran of the unit, provides details of casualties the company suffered during the war. In detailing casualties for Fredericksburg, the veteran stated: "and here is where the brave and loyal Jeff Perry was killed by an officer of his own company." No mention of this incident is found elsewhere, and the nature of the comment would lead one to believe that Perry was not trying to shirk his duty. If one considers the massed lines of soldiers manning the wall, it is possible that a friendly-fire accident took place and it was thought best not to be mentioned elsewhere.[37]

In addition to the severe battle losses, the Phillips Legion also suffered heavily from disease during the period between the end of the Maryland campaign and the Fredericksburg fight. The stress of the Maryland campaign manifested itself in the deaths of twenty-six additional men, largely from typhoid fever. Some died in Richmond hospitals while others died at Winchester, Lynchburg, Charlottesville, Warrenton, and Staunton. One unfortunate, Private George Reid of Company A, died in a barn near Fairfax.[38]

Curiously, Longstreet stated that, before the battle, the stone wall was not thought a very important element. The Confederate leadership assumed that the assault would come at Lee's Hill and the Federals would try to turn the sunken road and the plateau where Marye's mansion stands. Instead, a signal victory had been achieved at Marye's Heights.

---

[36] Alex S. Erwin to J. S. Dobbins, 28 December 1862, Manuscript Collection #86, Cobb-Erwin Collection, box 3, folder 13, Hargrett Library, University of Georgia, Athens.

[37] "War Between the States, History of Col. Phillips Legion Infantry," *Tri-County Advertiser* (Clarkesville GA), centennial ed., 5 July 1979, 18.

[38] Compiled Service Records of Phillips Georgia Legion, National Archives micropublication M266, roll 598, Georgia Department of Archives and History, Morrow GA.

Nature herself provided an omen of things to come: the aurora borealis illuminated the northern sky over the martyred city of Fredericksburg in pulsating blood-red color. Perhaps this was a warning to the exhausted Confederates that yet another savage battle awaited them at a crossroads and country tavern, just down the road, called Chancellorsville.[39]

---

[39] Alice Rains Trulock, *In the Hands of Providence: Joshua L. Chamberlain and the American Civil War* (Chapel Hill: University of North Carolina Press, 1992) 100. Chamberlain described the sight as "An Aurora Borealis, marvelous in beauty. Fiery lances and banners of blood, and flame, columns of pearly light, garlands and wreaths of gold-all pointing and beckoning upward. Befitting scene!"

Chapter 10

All Quiet on the Rappahannock
at this Time

*"We drove down the road & got into the fight again about 4
miles above Fredericksburg, Drove them across the river with
heavy loss taking a good many prisoners, leaving the ground
strewn with dead & dying."*

On Saturday, 10 January 1863, the soldiers of the Phillips Legion
infantry battalion were on the move again. On this day they moved their
camp 4 miles down Telegraph Road to an area with more wood for
cooking and warmth. Morale was generally high as the result of the
major role they played in the battle of Fredericksburg. They didn't know
where the next confrontation with Burnside's men might occur, but they
were confident and ready to whip the Yankees again. By 24 January they
learned that Burnside had made another major blunder while trying to
redeem himself for the Fredericksburg slaughter. This was the infamous
"Mud March."[1]

On the face of it, General Burnside's planning seemed plausible. He
regarded the move as an "auspicious moment to strike a great and mortal

---

[1] US War Department, comp., *The War of Rebellion: A Compilation of the Official
Records of the Union and Confederate* Armies, 128 vols. (Washington DC: Government
Printing Office, 1880–1901) ser. 1, vol. 21, p. 755. Lee wrote to Secretary of War James
A. Seddon on 29 January 1863, stating that despite signs of Federal planning for an
advance, no attempt had been made. All indications pointed to a massing of the Federal
army in the vicinity of Hartwood Church. Pontoon trains were expected to move into
place along the river while Gen. Slocum's command advanced toward the Confederate
positions at Banks and the United States Mine Fords. However, on the evening of 20
January, rain began falling and continued for two days. A second storm began on 27
January, leaving 6 inches of snow. Lee did not know whether the storms frustrated
Burnside's advance, but no attempt was made to cross the Rappahannock. Report from
Lee to Seddon, 29 January 1863. Also see diary of Thomas M. Mitchell, 10 January
entry, private collection of Mr. R. D. Thomas, Chattanooga TN.

blow to the rebellion, and to gain that decisive victory which is due to the country."[2] As matters unfolded, Burnside's determination to make one more attempt to dislodge the Rebels at Fredericksburg was far from auspicious.

Convinced he could flank Lee out of Fredericksburg, Burnside pushed his army rapidly up the Rappahannock River toward United States Ford 10 miles above Fredericksburg. On 20 January, nature intervened as torrential rains turned the roads into bogs. The Federals found themselves struggling through rivers of mud so deep that shoes were sucked off the men's feet. Artillery and supply wagons were mired beyond hope for successful extraction and were abandoned. The Rebels taunted the Federals by erecting a humiliating sign on the riverbank declaring "Burnside's Army Stuck in the Mud," and one even more provocative that was scrawled "This Way to Richmond." Burnside finally surrendered to nature's dictate, abandoned the movement, and ordered his soldiers back to their camps across from Fredericksburg. General Burnside felt he was not entirely to blame for his failures and pressed President Lincoln for the removal of Generals Joseph Hooker, William B. Franklin, and William F. ("Baldy") Smith. Lincoln took a dim view of all this and relieved Burnside, on 26 January 1863 naming General Joseph Hooker the new commander of the Federal Army.[3] Legion diarist Thomas Mitchell penned an entry on 22 January noting that they were preparing to build quarters to make themselves comfortable. On 28 January he reported the condition of their encampment: "Wednesday the 28th. Snow to the depth of Ten or Twelve inches."[4]

Lee wasted no time on his side of the Rappahannock River, mulling over the question of how best to use his smaller army to oppose Hooker's far larger one. The answer to this question would result in Lee's finest hour. While planning the coming battle and insuring that his troops were rested and refitted, Lee and his generals were considering two possible movements. The first involved crossing the upper fords of the Rappahannock; the second a shift to southeast

---

[2] Shelby Foote, *The Civil War: A Narrative*, Fredericksburg to Meridian, vol. 2/3 (New York: Random House, 1963) 2:129–30.

[3] *OR*, ser. 1, vol. 21, pp. 1004–1005.

[4] Thomas M. Mitchell, diary, 22 and 28 January entries.

Virginia where the Federal IX Corps had materialized. On 18 February, Lee ordered General Longstreet to move south of Richmond with Hood's and Pickett's divisions to confront the Federals operating from Suffolk. Lee reasoned this would permit these two divisions to protect the agricultural bounty of that area as well as subsist themselves upon it. Generals Lafayette McLaws and Richard H. Anderson's divisions of Longstreet's I Corps would remain at Fredericksburg with Jackson's II Corps.[5]

Stonewall Jackson's corps formed Lee's right, which extended along the river below Fredericksburg from Hamilton's Crossing to Port Royal. McLaws and Anderson formed the left. To Jackson's left, McLaws's 8,000 men extended the line across the hills behind Fredericksburg. On the extreme left, two of Anderson's brigades commanded by Brigadier General Carnot Posey and Brigadier General William Mahone guarded the United States Ford while Brigadier General Cadmus Wilcox's brigade covered Banks Ford.

The legion infantry was assigned to McLaws's division, General William T. Wofford's brigade. Wofford had assumed command of the brigade in January, replacing the fallen T. R. R. Cobb. Young Major Joseph Hamilton commanded the legion's infantry battalion in the absence of Lt. Colonel Sandy Barclay, who was still recovering from wounds.[6]

While standing picket duty, blue and gray soldiers often struck up conversations with each other to pass the time and often to trade for tobacco, coffee, and newspapers. In a letter to his uncle, Jack Reese described these subversive activities that came to characterize much of the quiet times for the remainder of the war: "They [Yankee pickets] seemed to have a disposition to chat with us but our orders forbade us. I fixed them up a paper on a piece of plank & the wind being favorable sent it over to them. Also stated on the paper who it was from & for them to send me one in return. They fixed one up but the wind was against them & it did not come over."[7]

---

[5] *OR*, ser. 1, vol. 18, pp. 883, 884.

[6] *OR*, ser. 1, vol. 21, p. 1100. Wofford commanded the 18th Georgia until his promotion in January 1863 to brigade command.

[7] Andrew Jackson Reese to Uncle, 23 March 1863, Rees/Reese Collection, Lumpkin County Library, Madeline K. Anthony Collection, series 3, box 23, folder 5.

Sergeant Reese was a solid performer and well respected by the enlisted men of his company. While away in Georgia on recruiting duty, he had been elected second lieutenant of Company E, the Blue Ridge Rifles. Arriving back in camp on 23 March, he wrote to his friend Gus Boyd to relay the good news. He also mentioned that he would have married while in Georgia but thought it best to postpone the matter until after the war. He probably realized that the war would not be short and there was no certainty of his survival.[8]

The legion infantry and cavalry battalions officially parted company around this time. Army of Northern Virginia Special Order No. 104, dated 14 April 1863, stated: "By authority of the Hon. Secretary of War, the Infantry and Cavalry of Phillips Ga. Legion are separated and will each constitute a distinct organization and will be raised to a regiment as soon as possible."[9]

The infantry and cavalry battalions had received extra companies, but neither reached the ten-company requirement for full regimental status. Both battalions retained their identity as "Phillips Legion." The legion's infantry officers did make an attempt to obtain regimental status. In a letter to Samuel Cooper dated 18 April 1863, thirty-three of the legion's infantry officers pointed out that the Phillips Legion had been split into two battalions of infantry and cavalry, respectively, and that efforts were underway to add a tenth company. There is no record of any response from Cooper but one might speculate that had their request been granted, the legion's infantry battalion might have become just another numbered infantry regiment.[10]

Officers seldom briefed their soldiers on military plans—or waited until the last moment to do so. Not surprisingly, half-truths and downright distortions were usually the order of the day. A rumor that General Longstreet had been killed in a skirmish was expressed with dread by W. R. Montgomery in an April 1863 letter to his aunt: "Am

---

[8] Reese to Aunt, 23 March 1863, Rees/Reese Collection.

[9] Army of Northern Virginia Special Order No. 104, 23 March 1863, National Archives micropublication, M921, roll 2.

[10] Phillips Georgia Legion officers to Samuel Cooper, 18 April 1863, National Archives micropublication, M474, roll 77, frame 78.

indeed sorry to hear it and do not want to believe it, for he is one of our gallant officers and who knows but few equals and no superiors."[11]

Although this rumor turned out to be false, some humor drifting through camp was nearer the truth: "The Yankies say that we have a new Gen in command of our army & say his name is General Starvation & I think for once they are about right, for we only get 4 ounces of bacon & one small pound of flour & sometimes a little salt."[12] General Hooker labored to improve the morale of his troops. He abolished Burnside's cumbersome Grand Divisions and reorganized his army into seven infantry corps, placing the Union cavalry into a consolidated corps for the first time since the war's onset. By mid-April he was prepared to move his 130,000-man army across the Rappahannock River to attack Lee's 63,000 veterans. He would turn Lee's flank, forcing the wily Southerner to give battle or retreat toward Richmond.

Hooker planned to strike in a pincer movement, forcing Lee to abandon the Fredericksburg entrenchments. Major General John Sedgwick's half of the army, the I, III, and VI Corps, would march down the Rappahannock below Fredericksburg. The remaining half, made up of the V, XI, and XII Corps under Hooker himself, would cross upstream at Kelly's Ford then head south, cross the Rapidan River, and consolidate at Chancellorsville. Each of these two wings of the Federal army nearly equaled Lee's entire command. The Federal cavalry would open the campaign by heading south toward Richmond, severing Lee's supply line and creating confusion in the Confederate's rear. A portion of the II Corps would remain in full view of the Confederates across from Fredericksburg; the rest of the corps would march northwest along the Rappahannock to Banks Ford and United States Ford. Hooker hoped to deceive Lee by leading him to believe that the Federals were crossing the nearer fords, following the route of Burnside's earlier Mud March.[13]

The plan seemed promising. Much of the Union army would remain open to Lee's view at Fredericksburg while other troops shifted to the southeast. The entire vista was visible to the Confederates and

---

[11] George Montgomery, Jr., ed., *Georgia Sharpshooter: The Civil War Diary and Letters of William Rhadamanthus Montgomery* (Macon GA: Mercer University Press, 1997) 79.

[12] Ibid.

[13] *OR*, ser. 1, vol. 25, pt. 2, p. 199.

would suggest an attack on or below Fredericksburg. Simultaneously Hooker would march troops northwest, then south into the rear of Lee's army. Both wings of the infantry would then close on Lee and crush him as he retreated. If the Southerners attempted to retreat south, the cavalry would be well positioned to attack them. Lee's army would be surrounded and face annihilation or surrender.

Rapid movement and surprise were the keys to Hooker's plan. Unlike some of his predecessors he took great pains to insure secrecy, not even informing his own generals of the complete plan. The Federals began stirring on 21 April as small bodies of Union infantry appeared at Kelly's Ford and the Rappahannock railroad bridge to hold these crossings for the larger force to come. The men of the legion were alerted as described by Sgt. Montgomery: "We received orders the other night to cook rations & be ready to move at a moment's notice. I thought the time had arrived when we would commence our long and tiresome marches but for once we did not have to leave. But I am looking every day for orders to leave & when we begin our marches Heaven only knows when & where we will stop."[14]

On 26 April 1863, Hooker ordered his right wing to begin the movement. Two days later, the V, XI, and XII Corps were concentrated around Kelly's Ford, ready to cross the Rapidan. To confuse Lee and distract his attention from Northern operations, Sedgwick's three corps threw pontoon bridges across the Rappahannock below Fredericksburg on the night of 28 April and crossed the river the following morning. Their objective was to keep Lee at Fredericksburg or take the city if Lee moved his forces toward Chancellorsville. Sedgwick was to hold the core of Lee's army at Fredericksburg long enough for Hooker to loop around from the west and squeeze Lee between the two Federal forces. A dense fog screened Sedgwick's troops, who were crossing the Rappahannock at Deep Run and then massing out of view under the steep banks of the river. On the following morning, 29 April, General Jackson's outposts engaged Sedgwick below Deep Run. Diarist Thomas M. Mitchell described what appeared to be a major attack in the making:

Wednesday the 29th. Cannonading commenced this morning at Five O'clock. Long roll at Six A.M., form a line of

---

[14] *Georgia Sharpshooter*, ed. Montgomery, 79–82.

Battle below Fredericksburg near where we was camped last December. At Five P.M. marched down to the Breast works just west of Deep Run Creek, worked on the Breast works until Eleven O'clock P.M. The Yankees having crossed the river this morning at Seven O'clock about Four miles south of Fredericksburg just below the mouth of Deep Run Creek. There was considerable cannonading through the day but very little Infantry fighting. Nothing more than skirmishing with the enemy's pickets.[15]

As happened during the previous December, the pontoon bridges across the Rappahannock at Fredericksburg were effectively protected from direct Confederate artillery fire by the depth of the riverbed. Meanwhile Federal batteries on the opposite heights completely commanded the wide plain between the Rebel lines and the river. Lee had selected positions on the heights behind the city to resist the Federal advance once they crossed the river. He was certain that this approach would be the most expedient as he would be able to avoid heavy losses in trying to prevent the crossing. Around 6:30 P.M., McLaws received orders to pull his troops out of Fredericksburg, leave his sharpshooters, and take positions on the heights in back of the town, as was done in December, extending his right to Deep Run. Legion troops settled into their positions around 11:00 P.M.[16]

While the Confederates stood guard against an expected attack at Fredericksburg, Lee received word that several corps of Union infantry and cavalry had moved from Kelly's Ford toward Ely's and Germanna Fords on the Rapidan River. The routes they had taken after crossing the Rapidan converged near the Chancellorsville House where several roads led to the rear of Lee's position at Fredericksburg. Lee ordered Brigadier General Richard H. Anderson, whose three brigades were guarding fords northwest of Fredericksburg, to form his troops into a right angle with the Rappahannock to cover the Rebel left and hold Chancellorsville.[17]

---

[15] Thomas M. Mitchell, diary, 29 April 1863 entry.

[16] R. E. Lee dispatch to Lafayette McLaws, 29 April 1863, in *OR*, ser. 1, vol. 25, pt. 2, p. 759.

[17] *OR*, ser. 1, vol. 25, pt. 1, pp. 796, 1046; also see the 30 April 1863 diary entries of Marcus Lafayette Greene and Thomas M. Mitchell.

Anderson was on his way at 9:00 P.M., riding in a drenching rain and arriving at Chancellorsville around midnight. Two of Anderson's brigades under Generals William Mahone and Carnot Posey had arrived before him, having withdrawn from the United States Ford as Hooker advanced. Anderson also learned that the Federals had crossed the Rapidan at Ely's and Germanna Fords and were heading toward him in full strength. Upon hearing this news, Anderson decided to fall back early on the morning of 30 April to the intersection of the Old Mine and Plank Roads near Tabernacle Church and prepare entrenchments. Mahone was positioned on the Orange Turnpike with Posey on the Orange Plank Road. McLaws was directed to prepare his troops to move the next day in case they were needed to support Anderson.[18]

At mid-afternoon, 30 April, Hooker reunited his right wing at the road junction near Chancellorsville and established his headquarters at the Chancellor House. By holding Chancellorsville, Hooker controlled the direction of Lee's withdrawal if the general decided not to stand and fight. Chancellorsville, located a few miles west of Fredericksburg and 50 miles north of Richmond, was not a village but a country home that had served as an inn before the war. It consisted of a single residence adjacent to a dense, tangled scrub forest known as the "Wilderness."[19] When Hooker arrived at the Chancellor mansion he was welcomed coldly by the owner, Mrs. Fannie Chancellor, one son, and six teenage daughters. All these plus a few Fredericksburg refugees and neighbors totaled sixteen individuals, the females often referred to by Hooker and his entourage as "You Rebel women." The Federal officers quickly hustled the Chancellors, neighbors, and refugees into a back room of the house.[20]

The Wilderness's military significance was in part its centrality; many roads diverged from it connecting it with every part of Virginia. Three roads led to Fredericksburg. The Orange Plank Road and the Orange Turnpike united at Tabernacle Church, providing a direct route

---

[18] *OR*, ser. 1, vol. 25, pt. 1, pp. 795–96, 849; pt. 2, p. 759.

[19] Alfred Pleasonton, "The Successes and Failures of Chancellorsville," in *The Tide Shifts*, vol. 3 of *Battles and Leaders of the Civil War*, ed. Robert U. Johnson and Clarence C. Buel (New York: De Vinne Press, 1888) 172; R. Happel, "The Chancellors of Chancellorsville," *Virginia Magazine* 71/3 (July 1863): 259–77; C. M. Smith, "In the Wilderness," *Confederate Veteran* 29/16 (June 1921): 212–15.

[20] Ibid.

to Fredericksburg, and River Road passed along Banks Ford. Various other roads and trails of military importance radiated out from Chancellorsville.

The Wilderness was no place for defensive operations, lacking commanding positions for artillery. The country was far more advantageous as a staging point for an attacking army. It was here that Hooker concentrated his 50,000 troops, with 18,000 more under General *Sic*kles nearby. General Sedgwick's 40,000 troops threatened Lee's right below Fredericksburg. Simultaneously, 13,000 Federal cavalry were moving to threaten the Confederate railways.

Until now the Federals had encountered little or no opposition. Moreover, they were in position to press eastward, break clear of the Wilderness, and take control of Banks Ford downstream, significantly shortening the distance between their two wings. By that evening Hooker had succeeded in placing half of his army, itself larger than Lee's entire army, in Lee's rear. Lee was completely unaware of the magnitude of the problem he faced. Yet, declining the initiative, Hooker directed his army to halt at Chancellorsville to await the arrival of *Sic*kles's III Corps, which was on its way from Fredericksburg. Some of Hooker's officers argued that shifting the Federal army just a few miles east into open country where their artillery could be effective would sustain momentum and catch Lee napping before he could reposition his army to meet the threat. Hooker was poised to strike but, in declining to wait until the next day, gave Lee just enough time to regroup.[21]

Lee did not comprehend Hooker's intentions clearly enough to warrant decisive action until Thursday night. Stuart's cavalry continued to gather vital intelligence and retard the Federal cavalry's advance. Stuart had been able to glean intelligence from prisoners confirming that Hooker's V, XI, and XII Corps were at Chancellorsville. In receipt of this intelligence on the morning of 30 April, Lee realized that Hooker intended to turn the Confederate left and had divided his forces. He now knew that Hooker's crossing at Fredericksburg was only a ruse, and it explained why the Federals had crossed the river but failed to attack. It was clear that the larger force reported by Stuart to the west was his real

---

[21] Alfred Pleasonton, "The Successes and Failures of Chancellorsville," in *Battles and Leaders*, ed. Johnson and Buel, 3:172.

threat.[22] Thomas Mitchell described the activities of the legion infantrymen back at Fredericksburg: "Thursday, April the 30th, 1863. Was called up to the Breast Works at Four O'clock this morning. At Eleven A.M. I was with a detail to cut down trees off the Banks of Deep Run. Cannonading commenced this P.M. at Six O'clock between our Batteries near Hamilton's Cross Roads and the Enemy's on the opposite side of the River."[23]

Lee acted immediately, sending detailed instructions to Anderson near Chancellorsville to prepare his line for additional troops and directing McLaws to go to Anderson's support. At 1:00 A.M. the legion infantry was marching west on Plank Road in the direction of Chancellorsville. Their brigade, with Semmes's and Kershaw's brigades, were to reinforce General Anderson at Tabernacle Church. "Stonewall" Jackson was also on the road to Tabernacle Church accompanied by the divisions of Generals Robert E. Rodes, Raleigh E. Colston, and A. P. Hill. Major General Jubal A. Early's division and General William Barksdale's brigade of McLaws's division remained at Fredericksburg to man the defenses. The morning of 1 May found the men of the Phillips Legion digging earthworks alongside Malone's Virginians just north of Zoar Church on the turnpike 10 miles from Fredericksburg.

They were ready to fight. General Jackson soon arrived and decided to carry the fight to the Federals. Throwing down picks and shovels, McLaws's three brigades marched forward behind Mahone's brigade to confront Federals ahead on the Orange Turnpike. Quickly encountering Federal cavalry, Mahone's skirmishers pushed them back until they reached a line of Federal infantry behind Mott's Run. This force was George Sykes's V Corps division containing two brigades of vaunted US regulars. Mahone deployed astride the turnpike while Wofford's brigade went into position in the forest to the right. Semmes's brigade deployed to Mahone's left. Both sides brought up artillery, and a hot duel ensued. As the fighting developed, Kershaw's brigade went on line to Semmes's left, and Perry's brigade extended Wofford's line to cover the approaches from US Ford. Meanwhile, several miles to the south,

---

[22] Special Order No. 120, 30 April 1863, in *OR*, ser. 1, vol. 26, pt. 1, p. 762; Report of Maj. Gen. Lafayette McLaws, 10 May 1863, in *OR*, ser. 1, vol. 25, pt. 1, p. 824; *OR*, ser. 1, vol. 25, pt. 2, p. 761; Andrew J. Reese to Uncle, 8 May 1863, Rees/Reese Collection.

[23] Thomas M. Mitchell, diary, 30 April entry.

Posey's and Wright's brigades were pressing west on Plank Road with Jackson's men not far behind. The legion would spend the day working through the woods north of the turnpike in an attempt to turn the Federal's left flank while Jackson's troops, pressing north from Plank Road, threatened the opposite flank. Late in the afternoon, Hooker ordered his men to disengage and fall back to their Chancellorsville defenses.[24] Thomas Mitchell described the day's action:

> Friday, May the 1st, 1863. At one A.M., left the Breast Works and marched on Plank Road towards Chancellorsville to reinforce Gen. Anderson. The Yankees having crossed the River above Fredericksburg at the United States Ford with heavy force, we arrived on the field about Ten A.M., formed a line of Battle on right of road about Three miles above Selma [sic] Church, cannonading on the left at one P.M. and heavy infantry fighting on the left, nothing more than skirmishing in our front, near Sun down we advanced about Two miles, the enemy falling back as we advance.[25]

Lieutenant Jack Reese, who had been left at Fredericksburg in charge of a group of sharpshooters, described the brigade's departure and his detachment's scramble to catch up on 1 May:

> I was put in charge of a Co. of sharpshooters in the morning & was put in advance of the Brigade. About 10 O'clock at night the Brigade received orders to move immediately up the river...had all night & reached the battlefield the morning of the first of May. There was plenty hard fighting throughout the day, drove the enemy back about 1 1/2 miles through pine & cedar thickets swamps & c I was ordered to join the Legion to day with the men I had in charge started about 12 O'clock but didn't find them to day. Stayed by the roadside at night.[26]

---

[24] John Bigelow Jr., *The Campaign of Chancellorsville* (New Haven: Yale University Press, 1910) maps 12, 13, and 14.

[25] Thomas M. Mitchell, diary, 1 May 1863 entry.

[26] Andrew Jackson Reese to Uncle, 8 May 1863, Rees/Reese Collection.

Marcus Greene of Company O described the day's action: "Friday 1st of May 1863 lying in line of battle 10 miles from F.B. [Fredericksburg]. Started F.B. last night at 1 O'clock. 9 O'clock A.M. we left Earley's Division at F.B. fighting commenced this evening. Our Legion was not engaged but was under fire. Sergt. J. M. Smith slightly wounded. we saw them fighting very plain. 11 yankee pickets come over and give up."[27]

Hooker was taken aback by the day's action. His plan called for Lee to retreat, not advance and attack, but Lee wasn't cooperating. His V Corps probe down the turnpike had been stopped and almost surrounded, while the XII Corps advance on Plank Road had run into the fearsome Stonewall Jackson. Nonetheless, he felt that his plan was still unfolding as expected. He had his army over the rivers in good order and had maneuvered Lee out of his Fredericksburg entrenchments. It was even possible that Lee, emboldened by this day's action, would attack him in a strongly fortified position. Hooker met with his corps commanders that evening and made it clear, despite some protest, that they would entrench and await Lee's attack. Federal pioneers and soldiers immediately went to work to fortify their positions. The Federal line was impressive. Starting with Meade's V Corps at Scott's Dam on the Rappahannock, it ran southwest along Mineral Spring Road to connect to two divisions of Couch's II Corps at the intersection of Ely's Ford Road. The II Corps works ran south, crossing the turnpike just east of Chancellorsville, and connected to Slocum's XII Corps at Plank Road. Slocum's men were entrenched in an arc that looped south of Fairview and ended back on Plank Road 3/4 of a mile to the west. Oliver Howard's XI Corps was stretched out along Orange Plank Road to the west, ending at a point some 2 1/2 miles west of Chancellorsville. A gap that existed between Slocum and Howard was filled during the night by the arrival of David Birney's division of the III Corps, which deployed across the north side of an elevated clearing at Hazel Grove.[28] Hooker expressed concern that Howard's XI Corps line ended "in the air" to the west and suggested it be swung back to the north to protect the western flank better. Howard argued that a withdrawal would demoralize his men and promised to augment his line with breastworks and abatis.[29]

---

[27] Marcus L. Greene, diary, 1 May 1863 entry.

[28] Bigelow, *Campaign of Chancellorsville*, map 16.

[29] *OR*, ser. 1, vol. 25, pt. 2, p. 334.

Howard even went so far as to send back a III Corps brigade and battery that had come to assist him. Although the terrain was not optimal for the use of artillery, positions had been found for the incorporation of thirty-one batteries into the defenses. By the morning of 2 May, Hooker would have 72,000 troops in line to meet Lee's best efforts.

Confederate officers had reported stubborn opposition on both roads leading to Chancellorsville. The Federals were preparing to make a strong stand. Jackson alerted his troops to hold in place for the night and went to meet with Lee. McLaws's men bivouaced along a low ridge about 1 mile east of Chancellorsville. Pickets were posted, and the men, exhausted by a night and day of marching and fighting, were quickly asleep on their arms. On the morning of 2 May the Confederate line of battle in front of Chancellorsville ran at right angles to Plank Road, extending on the right to Old Mine Road and to the left in the general direction of Catherine Furnace.[30]

Lee must have been uneasy. Things had gone well so far, but why had Hooker given up the initiative to the outnumbered Confederates? Still pondering this question, Lee and Jackson met under a grove of trees along Plank Road on the evening of 1 May. After weighing their options, they concluded that attacking was their only practical course of action. Reconnaissance had revealed that an attack on the Federal left was impracticable due to the strength of the position, dense woods, and protection afforded by a flank anchored on the Rappahannock.

General Stuart rode in and joined the counsel with startling news. General Fitzhugh Lee had discovered the open flank of Howard's XI Corps on Orange Plank Road. After examining maps and interrogating some of the locals, a route was laid out that would bring a southern flanking force out on Plank Road to the west of the open Federal flank. Lee asked Jackson what force he would utilize in the flank attack, and Jackson responded that he would take his entire corps. Lee realized this would leave him with only seven brigades of infantry under Anderson and McLaws to distract Hooker's massive army while Jackson made the

---

[30] Bigelow, *Campaign of Chancellorsville*, map 16.

long march to the west. After a short pause, Lee nodded and said, "Well, go ahead."[31]

With Rodes's division in the lead, followed by Colston and Hill, Jackson's troops got underway by 8:00 A.M. on the morning of 2 May. Lee went about drawing Hooker's attention, directing McLaws and Anderson to engage the Federals at an early hour with strong skirmish lines. Their challenge was to occupy the Federals without disclosing their relative weakness or bringing on a Federal attack. It would be a long day.

It had already been a restless night for the legion. Marcus Greene jotted in his diary: "was up nearly all night the pickets was fighting at intervals all night."[32] General Wofford had his troops moving early in the morning as both Mitchell and Greene noted a 6:30 A.M. move to the west to connect to Mahone's right flank. Greene also indicated that cannon fire opened at this early hour.[33]

At around 10:00 A.M., III Corps Federals at Hazel Grove spotted the rear of Jackson's flanking column near Catherine's Furnace and opened with artillery. The Federals assumed Lee's army was retreating south, and Hooker gave the III Corps his approval to harass the column. A small but hot action ensued, the Federals were beaten back, and Jackson's column continued its march. The Federals had not observed Jackson's turn to the west and continued to think a Confederate retreat was in the works. Fitzhugh Lee provided Jackson with updated intelligence. The Federal flank rested along the old turnpike, and the bluecoats were unprepared to receive an attack. If Jackson would launch his attack here, just west of Dowdall's Tavern, he would find the Federal troops lolling around, smoking, playing cards, and eating. Oliver Howard had done little to fulfill his promise to strengthen his line. Hooker was so convinced Lee was retreating that he sent word to Sedgewick back at Falmouth to throw his entire force across the Rappahannock, capture Fredericksburg, and pursue the "fleeing" Confederates. Jackson's men pressed on to the west.

---

[31] Hotchkiss to G. F. R. Henderson, 1897; J. P. Smith to Hotchkiss, 16 April 1897, both in Hotchkiss Papers, Library of Congress, B. T. Lacy narrative, Southern Historical Society Collection, University of North Carolina.

[32] M. L Greene, diary, 2 May 1863 entry.

[33] Ibid.; T. M. Mitchell, diary, 2 May 1863 entry.

While Jackson's soldiers marched, McLaws's and Anderson's men worked hard to provide the Federals on their front with the image of a Southern attack in the making. Strong Southern skirmish lines dueled with the Federals, and artillery maintained a steady bombardment. Wofford's men shifted out of the woods north of Plank Road in the early afternoon and took position in the open, supporting a Southern battery that was dueling with its Union counterparts. This was a daunting assignment since they could do little more than hug the ground as Federal shells screamed in and exploded. Corporal William Ruede of Company L was struck and killed by a shell around 3:00 P.M. Privates Henry Channell and Stephen McGinnis of Company O were wounded.[34]

At 5:15 P.M., Jackson was in position and unleashed his attack on the unsuspecting Federals. Three waves of gray veterans rolled forward up the turnpike with Rodes's division in front and Colston's and A. P. Hill's troops right behind. The plan worked beautifully. Even the wildlife panicked as turkey, deer, and rabbits rushed through the Federal encampment while the Northerners fell back in disarray. Position after position was captured as well as guns of all types. The Federal troops could not be rallied and fled east to escape the howling Confederates. The tangled Wilderness only made things worse.[35] Sergeant Montgomery told it well: "Came upon the Yanks Friday, Drove them before us like sheep until Saturday they made a stand. Our Division [Gen. McLaws] held them in until old 'Stone Wall' & Gen. A. P. Hill would go round and take them in the rear which they accomplished nicely."[36]

As the muttering and flashing of battle rolled toward Lee from the west, he advanced his troops in order to fix the attention of the Federals and prevent Hooker from withdrawing troops to reinforce Howard. The Confederates brushed the Federal skirmishers aside and pushed up to their entrenchments. McLaws advanced his entire line in an attempt to force the Federals to engage them in intense firefights without bringing

---

[34] M. L Greene, diary, 2 May 1863 entry. Channell disappears from all military records after Chancellorsville. Since he could not be found after the war, it is assumed that he died from his wounds.

[35] Shelby Foote, *The Civil War, A Narrative, Fredericksburg to Meridian*, vol. 2 (of 3) (New York: Random House, 1963) 291–94.

[36] *Georgia Sharpshooter*, ed. Montgomery, 83.

on a full-scale battle. Wofford led a charge of his brigade's sharpshooter battalion followed by the remainder of the brigade. Montgomery described this newly formed unit: "Gen Wofford had 50 men detailed from each Regt in the brigade to form a battalion of Sharp Shooters. Bill Anderson is recommended for Capt., myself for first Lieut & two others for 2nd & 3rd Lts. We are to camp to ourselves & are known as the 1st Geo 'sharpshooters' but have no commissions yet. Payson Ardis is recommended as 1st Lt. in the Co next to ours."[37]

Though the Confederate War Department had not yet formally approved this new battalion, it went into action at Chancellorsville as a discrete organization providing its own unique skirmishing function. One company was comprised of soldiers from the Phillips Legion, including Sergeant Montgomery who served as its acting first lieutenant. He told of their fight on Saturday evening: "We are always in front of the brigade, about 300 to 400 yards., to clear out the way & I tell you we done it too, to perfection. You ought to hear Gen Wofford praise us. Saturday evening our little Battalion charged the Yankies breast work, our whole brigade behind it, charged three times but the fire was hot from the enemy. We had to fall back. Our loss was quite heavy."[38]

A number of those who had recently transferred to the sharpshooter battalion became casualties on this day and the next. Young Peyton Fuller, the legion's courageous color bearer at Fredericksburg who acted as second lieutenant, was shot in the head and died instantly. Private Leonidas Youngblood was also killed, and eight others were wounded.[39] Legion casualties were lighter as they were not as closely engaged as the sharpshooter battalion. With darkness coming on and Federal resistance stiff, McLaws directed Wofford to withdraw his brigade. When darkness fell, Lee ordered McLaws to shift back to his original line.

Several miles west, Jackson's attack finally lost its momentum after driving Howard's demoralized XI Corps 2 miles eastward. Jackson was everywhere at once, eager to finalize the victory. He rode along the lines, shouting orders and exhorting his exhausted soldiers to press forward. After dark, with his men getting ready for a night attack, Jackson rode

---

[37] Ibid., 84.

[38] Ibid.

[39] Frederick C. Fuller, casualty list published in *Atlanta Southern Confederacy*, 19 May 1863, p. 1.

out in front of his lines to reconnoiter. As his small party rode back toward the Southern line, tragedy struck. Jittery North Carolina troops mistook Jackson's party for Union cavalry and opened fire, severely wounding the general. Jackson died eight days later of pneumonia at Guiney's Station. George W. Fenn, in a letter to his brother Newton Fenn, both of legion infantry Company C, wrote: "we lost old Stonewall Jackson, he got his arm shot off and he was struck with the numony [*sic*] fever and did not live but a short time."[40] Jackson's flank attack was spectacular, but his death left Lee with a yawning gap in the command structure.

Command fell to General A. P.Hill, but Hill was wounded just moments after Jackson. Senior division commander Robert Rodes then assumed temporary command, quickly decided that the troops were not in condition to resume operations, and began preparing for a morning attack. Although he was a cavalry officer, next in line to command the corps was General J. E. B. Stuart, who replaced Rodes. Directed earlier to seize the road to Ely's Ford, Stuart rushed back and found Rodes's and Colston's divisions reforming on the open road near Dowdall's Tavern.[41] General Stuart also dismissed the possibility of a night attack and decided to await daylight to mount further action. The Rebel troops rested on their arms in line of battle that night. Lee directed Stuart to take decisive action at dawn to drive the Federals out of Chancellorsville.[42]

Hooker had taken a pounding on 2 May, but he still held the advantage at Chancellorsville. I Corps provided reinforcements during the night, and III Corps had moved back from Catherine's Furnace to reoccupy Hazel Grove. These movements divided the Confederates into separate wings controlled by Stuart and Lee. With a more aggressive attitude, Hooker might have defeated each wing in turn. The victory might also have been clinched if Sedgwick had pressed forward from Fredericksburg and attacked Lee's rear.

At the close of day on 2 May, Generals Ambrose R. Wright and Carnot Posey of Anderson's division were positioned on the left facing

---

[40] George Washington Fenn to Newton Jasper Fenn, undated, Georgia Department of Archives and History, Microfilm Library, drawer 283, box 25.

[41] *OR*, ser. 1, vol. 25, pt. 1, pp. 942, 943.

[42] *OR*, ser. 1, vol. 25, pt. 2, p. 769.

west toward Catherine's Furnace at least 1/2 mile beyond the rest of Lee's command. Mahone was on McLaws's left facing north. Kershaw, Semmes, and Wofford of McLaws's division continued the line across the turnpike and Plank Road running east-northeast and facing toward Chancellorsville. Perry marched to the left flank near Catherine's Furnace during the night.[43] Stuart, now in command of the II Corps, faced Hooker from the west. General Robert E. Lee was prepared to deliver the coup de grace to Hooker at Chancellorsville.

Around 11:00 P.M., the legion troops could hear cannonading on their left so heavy it seemed like a volcanic explosion. Diarist Thomas Mitchell wrote that it seemed "as if the very hills were blowing up, received no orders, go to sleep again."[44]

The fighting began again in earnest the following morning, as they were called into the line of battle at sunrise on 3 May. William R. Montgomery described the sharpshooter battalion's resumption of their attacks on the Northern lines: "Soon Sunday morning the Gen sent us in again. We charged again under the most deadly fire. Got within a few feet of the works, but it was fixed with brush that we could not climb then & had to fall back Our loss was again more. Lost our Col Patten. P.Ardis Co lost Capt& 2nd Lt (not killed but badly wounded). Our Co lost 2nd Lt & one man killed dead & 8 badly wounded. Other companies lost in proportion."[45]

At first light Lee directed Stuart to advance his command as quickly as possible up Orange Plank Road to join McLaws and Anderson. Stuart promptly ordered three brigades from A. P. Hill's division to the south of Plank Road, inclining the group to the east toward Hazel Grove. The Rebels were in luck as Hooker had ordered General Sickles to abandon Hazel Grove at dawn to consolidate his defenses around Chancellorsville. Stuart's troops battled the III Corps rear guard but soon had Hazel Grove under their control. This high ground proved to be a superb platform for Confederate artillery to bombard Union troops and batteries at nearby Fairview. Shouting at his troops to remember Jackson, Stuart pushed the exhausted soldiers onward. By 9:30 A.M. they

---

[43] Bigelow, *Campaign of Chancellorsville*, map 22.

[44] T. M. Mitchell, diary, 3 May 1863 entry.

[45] *Georgia Sharpshooter*, ed. Montgomery, 84.

had broken the Federal hold on Fairview in vicious fighting with high casualties on both sides.

Now occurred one of the key events of fate that decide the outcome of battles. Porter Alexander had learned that the Chancellor house was Hooker's headquarters and had a couple of his men, stationed at Hazel Grove, firing long-range rifled guns at the home. Hooker, directing troops to threatened points, happened to be on the front porch leaning with one hand against a tall wooden column when a round ordered by Alexander shattered it. Struck violently along one side of his body by a section of the column, Hooker fell senseless and was unconscious for twenty minutes. Showing the classic symptoms of a brain concussion, Hooker revived but did not seem capable of clear thought. After vomiting, he staggered away from the Chancellor house to a nearby tent, where he gathered his senses enough to summon his senior commander, II Corps Major General Darius Couch. Around 11:00 A.M., he managed to raise himself to a sitting position and turn command over to Couch, directing him to withdraw the army to a new defensive position north of Chancellorsville. News of Hooker's wounds flowed like a tidal wave through the Union high command.[46] With calls for support coming in from Fairview and no one in effective command, this "lost hour" was all Lee and Stuart needed to turn the tide in their favor.

Simultaneously, Lee had advanced McLaws and Anderson from the south and east of Hooker's position to unite with Stuart. About 8:00 A.M., Semmes moved his troops forward in support of Kershaw, who was advancing to link up with troops on his left who were driving the Federals. The advance continued until all brigades had reached the turnpike near the brick house about 11:00 A.M. On the right, Wofford's brigade with the Phillips Legion infantry charged the Federal breastworks. Exhibiting reckless bravery, Wofford led his troops in the first charge on the Federal entrenchments. They fell back only in the face of a withering close-range fire from the Federals.

Around 10:00 A.M., Wofford led the way again and the breastworks were taken. He then organized a portion of his brigade to shift across a small valley between his position and Chancellorsville to trap some of the escaping Federal troops. He and his men pressed forward, capturing ordinance, stores, and an entire Federal regiment and part of another.

---

[46] Darius Couch in *Battles and Leaders*, 3, 167.

Montgomery related the action: "When we fell back Sunday morning we only fell back under a hill only a few yards. About 12 o'clock we thought it a good time to charge again. So at them we went like so many wild Indians. Fired only two or three rounds when they showed a white flag. We all rushed forward and found that about 800 or 900 men had surrendered to only a small Batt of Sharp Shooters (one whole regt 27th Connecticut and many more). We sent them to the rear and pushed forward."[47]

Kershaw and Semmes were now to bear left toward Anderson, sweep around the plains of Chancellorsville, then march along Plank Road in order to join Wofford's left. Couch began the withdrawal of Union forces to a new defensive position between Hunting Run and Mineral Spring Run. Lee now had complete possession of Chancellorsville.

At Fredericksburg, Early bided his time as his troops faced Sedgwick's. There had been some confusion on 2 May when a discretionary order permitting Early to withdraw toward Lee was misinterpreted as a peremptory order. Early had put most of his troops on the road to Chancellorsville, leaving only two brigades to cover the town when the mistake was discovered. Early quickly countermarched his men back into the Fredericksburg entrenchments on the evening of 2 May before Sedgewick could take advantage of the opening.[48]

That same evening, Hooker had directed Sedgwick and Gibbon to move through Fredericksburg, destroy Early, march toward Chancellorsville, and attack Lee's rear. Seemingly unaware of the power of the six corps with him at Chancellorsville, Hooker was convinced that his fate depended on Sedgwick attacking Lee's rear. Approaching from the east, Sedgwick could squeeze Lee against Couch at Chancellorsville. Then the Federals would be free to deal with Jackson's II Corps before the two Confederate wings reunited. Hooker reasoned that Lee had depleted his forces at Fredericksburg to provide the large attack force that had shattered the XI Corps the previous evening. He was positive

---

[47] *Georgia Sharpshooter*, ed. Montgomery, 84.
[48] *OR*, ser. 1, vol. 25, pt. 1, pp. 800, 801.

Sedgwick would have no difficulty proceeding directly through Fredericksburg to reach Lee's rear.[49]

General Early had assumed the main attack would come on the right and posted most of his division below Fredericksburg near Deep Run. This left General Barksdale's Mississippi brigade to cover the entire Marye's Heights and Lee's Hill sector. He did have support on his left in the form of Harry Hay's brigade of Louisianans. At 9:00 A.M. on 3 May, Sedgewick began his attack against Barksdale's two regiments posted behind the infamous stone wall at the foot of Marye's Heights. Two assaults against the position were repulsed, but a third penetrated the thin line of defenders. The Mississippians fled up and over the hill behind them with the Federals in pursuit.[50]

An article in the *Atlanta Southern Confederate* penned by a member of Wofford's brigade described the fighting at the Stone Wall: "...the enemy, under Genl. Sedgwick, crossed at Fredericksburg and those below town marched up, and a force variously estimated at from 15,000 to 25,000 strong attacked Gen'l Barksdale's Mississippi brigade and captured the stone fence rendered immortal by our brigade on the 13th day of December, 1862 and captured six pieces of the celebrated Washington Artillery. This they did with overwhelming numbers being able to attack in front and both flanks at once."[51]

Surprised by the attack to his north, Early retreated, shifting his division to a point 2 miles down Telegraph Road to cover the railroad to Richmond. Hay's Louisiana brigade moved cross-country to rejoin Early. Barksdale rallied his command and fell in with Early's troops. Unfortunately, this left Plank Road to Chancellorsville (and Lee's rear) wide open, but providence smiled on Lee at this juncture. Cadmus Wilcox's Alabama brigade was guarding Banks Ford when the fighting broke out at Fredericksburg. Marching to the sound of the guns, Wilcox headed down River Road to support Barksdale. Arriving too late to fight at Marye's Heights, he quickly realized that he could best contribute by delaying Sedgwick's advance to Chancellorsville. He utilized hit-and-run, harassing attacks from ridge to ridge along Plank Road before

---

[49] *OR*, ser. 1, vol. 25, pt. 1, pp. 350, 558, 559; *OR*, ser. 1, vol. 25, pt. 2, pp. 359, 365.

[50] *OR*, ser 1, vol. 25, pt. 1, pp. 839, 840.

[51] J. R. Parrott, correspondence from Wofford's brigade, *Atlanta Southern Confederacy*, 19 May 1863, p. 1.

digging in on good defensive ground at Salem Church. As Early's command fell back to the south, Wilcox held his brigade between Sedgwick and Lee.[52]

Lee was apprised of these developments and concluded that he must continue to press Hooker but also deal with this new threat to his rear. To the amazement of his troops as well as historians for decades to come, Lee further divided his army, detaching a portion of it to join Early. Lee immediately decided to send Mahone's and Kershaw's brigades to join Wilcox. McLaws was to follow with the remainder of his division, leaving Lee with some 37,000 men to discourage Hooker from taking the offensive.[53]

Providence seemed to intervene once more on behalf of the Confederates when Sedgwick decided to delay his march from Fredericksburg in order to allow fresh troops to move up and lead the advance. As a result, he did not get underway until around 3:00 P.M. Wilcox then slowed the Federal advance several more hours with delaying tactics just west of Marye's Heights before dropping back to the ridge near Salem Church. Wilcox took position across Plank Road and waited for reinforcements from Lee.

McLaws directed troops into line as soon as they came up. First, Mahone's Virginians to Wilcox's left and Kershaw's South Carolinians to his right. Semmes's Georgians arrived, and McLaws shifted Mahone further left and placed Semmes between Wilcox and Mahone. Wofford's men completed the line, taking position on the right flank adjacent to Kershaw. The Confederates were still settling into position as Sedgwick opened with artillery at about 5:00 P.M. Anticipating light resistance, Sedgwick's infantry struck the center along Wilcox's position and the left center defended by Semmes's troops. After some initial Federal success, Wilcox counterattacked, charging the Union infantry with the aid of two of Semmes's regiments and driving the Federals back to their artillery near the tollgate. McLaws strengthened his left by shifting the Cobb and Phillips legions into line between Semmes and Mahone. Wofford's troops on the right were only lightly engaged, but the legion

---

[52] *OR*, ser. 1, vol. 25, pt. 1, pp. 854–59.

[53] M. L. Greene, diary, 3 May 1863 entry; McLaws took about 7,000 men with him to Salem Church. *OR*, ser. 1, vol. 25, pt. 1, pp. 801, 826, 851.

suffered a few casualties in their new position.[54] As darkness drew near, firing ceased on both sides. McLaws bivouacked his command with the troops sleeping on their arms in line of battle.[55]

The ever-aggressive Lee now saw an opportunity to destroy Sedgewick's isolated force and sent a note to Early telling him that if the Federals were attacking McLaws, Early must come up on their left flank and unite with McLaws to destroy Sedgwick. Lee sent the same message to McLaws, but by the time it was delivered fighting had ceased for the night.[56]

McLaws received a note from Early late that night. Early suggested that he concentrate his forces in the morning to drive the Federals from the heights at Fredericksburg and cut Sedgwick's connection with the troops remaining in the area rather than attacking his flank as Lee had suggested. After retaking the heights behind Fredericksburg, Early intended to march west to envelop Sedgwick. McLaws sent this note to Lee near midnight. Lee approved the plan and enjoined McLaws to press the Federals to prevent them from concentrating on Early. On the morning of 4 May, Early easily carried the heights and sent word to McLaws describing his success at Fredericksburg, informing him that he was ready to join forces against Sedgwick. McLaws replied that he would advance provided that Early attacked first. McLaws had become cautious and called on General Lee for reinforcements. Two of Anderson's brigades (Mahone and Early) were already facing Sedgwick and Lee agreed to send Anderson's remaining three brigades (Wright, Perry, and Posey). McLaws became insistent that he could not attack until these brigades arrived. Anderson finally arrived with the first of his brigades at 11:00 A.M., but his final brigade did not arrive until 1:00 P.M. Lee fumed at the delay and became progressively angrier as the day wore on. McLaws was not even fully aware of the location of Sedgwick lines, and more time was expended in detemining that he had taken up a horseshoe-shaped position with both flanks on the Rappahannock enclosing Banks Ford. The top of the salient crossed Plank Road at the tollgate and ran almost 2 miles eastward before recrossing the road again to run northward to Taylor's Hill on the river. More time was consumed

---

[54] T. M. Mitchell, diary, 4 May 1863 entry.
[55] Ibid.; M. L. Greene, diary, 4 May 1863 entry.
[56] *OR*, ser. 1, vol. 25, pt. 2, pp. 769, 770.

in getting Anderson's brigades into attack position south of Plank Road. McLaws seemed convinced that his force was too small to make a successful frontal assault and awaited sounds of Early's attack before taking action.[57]

Time was ticking away. Hooker remained quiet in his own salient north of Chancellorsville, but this situation could not be counted on to last forever. By late in the afternoon, an angry Lee wanted action.[58] He took the reins himself and rode to Early's sector near Lee's Hill at Fredericksburg to discuss what might be done. Early proposed to advance his troops and turn the Federals' left flank while Anderson's brigades and McLaws's two rightmost brigades attacked the top of the salient near Plank Road. Lee approved and instructed McLaws to launch Kershaw and Wofford once firing was heard on the right. The remainder of McLaws's troops would hold his front until Anderson and Early drove Sedgwick's lines toward him, and then he would attack to the north.[59]

Signal guns fired at 5:30 P.M., and Early and Anderson advanced. They initially met with success but encountered strong resistance and were pushed back. Along McLaws's front, Kershaw's and part of Wofford's brigade pushed their way through thickets to Plank Road as night began to fall on the battlefield. Darkness did not deter Lee. Around 10:00 P.M., Lee notified McLaws that he wanted the Federals pushed over the river that night. Sedgwick must be smashed. If he were permitted to remain undisturbed during the night, he would be able to entrench and give battle the following day. This would delay Lee's plan to reconcentrate his army at Chancellorsville. Lee's concern over Hooker taking the offensive was given new weight by reports from Stuart that Federal vehicles were on the move just beyond Chancellorsville. In fact, Sedgwick was withdrawing.[60]

Racket from men and wagons suggested the Federals were crossing pontoon bridges. Wofford's brigade advanced as far as River Road, continually engaging the enemy. A member of Wofford's brigade wrote

---

[57] McLaws report, *OR*, ser. 1, vol. 25, pt. 1, pp. 827, 828.

[58] Freeman concluded that McLaws made no forward movement until 6:00 P.M. that evening. There was no account for McLaws's long delay in advancing. Freeman, *Lee's Lieutenants*, 2:631.

[59] McLaws report, *OR*, ser. 1, vol. 25, pt. 1, pp. 802, 828.

[60] *OR*, ser. 1, vol. 25, pt. 1, pp. 795, 802, 828, 840, 860.

a description of this strange evening that appeared in the 19 May 1863 *Atlanta Southern Confederacy*:

On Monday about 3 o'clock it was understood that we had the enemy in a semicircle resting on the river above and below the ford. It was further understood that the attack would be made on the right which would be the signal for a general advance of all our forces. Hours passed, the evening was passing, and the chances for the escape of the circumscribed for were increasing, but no advance was made. Gen Wofford was chafing like a furious charger, so much was he impressed with the idea the enemy should be attacked at once, and so anxious was he to rush upon the cowards now at bay. But no order came until about 6 o'clock in the evening when Gen Wofford received orders to move forward and take position on the plank road—the position then held by the enemy. This splendid brigade of tried veterans marched up with buoyant spirits to the attack, but the enemy gave way and the General, observing some evidence of disorder in his lines, ordered a charge which was responded to with a rush and such yells as only victorious Georgians can give, and the enemy fled. Coming to a house we captured about 30 prisoners, among them a Lt. Colonel and several other officers. Learning from an old citizen at the house that the flight of the Yankees was an utter rout, the General took the citizen as a guide and pressed on in the charge through a terrible pine and cedar thicket so dense that a single individual could not pass through it in daylight without difficulty, until twelve at night, until we had got within half a mile of the enemy's pontoons on the river where his frightened hordes were crossing. We got nearly a mile in front of all other troops, when our own batteries were playing immediately in our front. Here the General sent back requesting our gunners not to fire on us as we were friends. So great was the flight of the Yankees and so anxious to get "to hum" that they threw away guns, bayonets, knapsacks, coats, hats, breeches, socks, shirts, drawers and almost anything a man eats, wears or uses, and they were so thick in places that scarcely could we ride over them. Our poor soldiers have more stuff that the cowards left than they can carry. Every man has some trophy won from the vandals.[61]

Wofford halted for the night within 1/2 mile of the river and put out pickets. McLaws sent a startling report. The Federals had thrown away their arms and fled across the river.[62]

W. R. Montgomery described the frenzied combat and pursuit:

> At the signal forward we all moved at once. The Yankees fought well at first, but when they found we were on three sides of them they made for the river. We still moved forward—pressing them at every point until one o'clock at night—capturing many prisoners. Sharpshooters made a charge in a pine thicket—not knowing anybody was in it—dark as Egypt—fired a volley & you ought to have heard the Yanks beg for quarter—took a Lt Col & about half a Regt.[63]

Sedgwick hoped for support from Hooker, who had promised to assist when he heard the sound of guns. Unfortunately for Sedgwick, Hooker had decided to abandon his own salient north of Chancellorsville. Sedgwick was on his own and barely got his troops across the river without being trapped.

At daybreak, 5 May, McLaws appeared on horseback at Kershaw's and Wofford's positions. McLaws received information from scouts that confirmed the Federals' river crossing. Lee, frustrated by Sedgwick escape, witnessed the close of the fight and began the process of reforming his troops in the area around Chancellorsville to deal with Hooker. Lee ordered Early to proceed to Fredericksburg while McLaws and Anderson marched to Chancellorsville. Wofford's brigade and the legion infantrymen were left at Banks Ford to prevent Union cavalry attacks along Lee's right flank.[64] Marcus Greene of Company O recounts his version: "Tuesday 5th. We are on picket at bankers ford. The yanks retreated last night the last fighting was done last night at 12

---

[61] J. R. Parrott, correspondence from Wofford's brigade, *Atlanta Southern Confederacy*, 19 May 1863, p. 1.

[62] *OR*, ser. 1, vol. 25, pt. 1, p. 828.

[63] *Georgia Sharpshooter*, ed. Montgomery, 85.

[64] McLaws Report, 10 May 1863, *OR*, ser. 1, vol. 25, pt. 1, p. 824.

o'clock it is now 3 in the afternoon. We give Hooker a complete whipping."[65]

Lee was forced to postpone an assault against Hooker until the following morning because of the lateness of the hour and an impending rainstorm. On the morning of 6 May, as Lee was preparing to order the advance, General Pender arrived at a gallop at Lee's headquarters at Fairview Cemetery. Pender informed his commander that the reports he had received from his scouts were reliable. Hooker was gone! Under cover of heavy rain the previous night, concealed by his formidable entrenchments and unbroken forest in the area of the United States Ford, Hooker had withdrawn his army on pontoon bridges over the Rappahannock. He had left behind his dead and wounded, so Marcus Greene did some pickpocketing: "Wednesday 6th, on picket at Banks ford it is raining. I got some thing out of yankee's pocket last Monday at Salem Church. I taken a pocket knife and looking glass out of one's pocket, a nice needle case out of another. $10,000 in greenbacks out of another, a ladies ambrotype another and taken a gold ring off one's finger."[66]

The vicious combat at Chancellorsville was over. The Phillips Legion had taken moderate losses in comparison to many other Southern regiments. Casualty lists in the *Central Georgian* for 20 May 1863 and the *Athens Southern Banner* as well as the Compiled Service Records list three killed, one mortally wounded, twenty-nine wounded, and one desertion. These totals include the legion troops that had just been transferred to the new sharpshooter battalion. Three officers were struck down. Acting Second Lieutenant Payton W. Fuller was killed. Fuller had been the legion's color sergeant before moving to the new sharpshooter battalion and was killed before his officer's promotion could be confirmed. Also wounded were Second Lieutenant James Patton Phillips, brother of Colonel William M. Phillips, and Second Lieutenant Joseph W. Barrett.[67]

Jack Reese survived the battle and lived to write many more letters to friends and family members describing his combat experiences,

---

[65] M. L. Greene, diary, 5 May 1863 entry.

[66] Ibid.; 6 May 1863 entry.

[67] Jack Rook Jr., "HQ McLaws Division Hospital," *Sandersville Central Georgian*, 20 May 1863, p. 2; Frederick C. Fuller, "Casualties in Phillips Legion," *Athens Southern Watchman*, 20 May 1863, p. 2.

fatigue, sorrows, and homesickness. In a letter to a friend from camp near Fredericksburg, dated 25 May 1863, he summed up the end of the battle: "Friend Gus. You must keep your eyes...as some of the Yankie sharpshooters shootes right at persons. I received yours yesturday of the 12th. I was glad to hear from you to hear you was well & c. I have nothing of interest to write you at present. All quiet on the Rappahannock at this time. How long it will remain so I cannot tell."[68]

A bemused Jack Reese contemplated the failure of yet another commander of the Army of the Potomac and pondered to no one in particular, "Poor old Joe. I wonder who they will put in command next."[69]

---

[68] Andrew Jackson Reese to Friend Gus, 25 May 1863, Rees/Reese Collection. Ironically, his friend Gus would never receive this letter. Captain Augustus "Gus" Boyd (formerly of Phillips Legion Co. E) had been killed at the Battle of Champions Hill in Mississippi on 16 May 1863.

[69] Andrew Jackson Reese to unknown recipient, 5 May 1863, Rees/Reese Collection.

Chapter 11

How Long the Time Has Appeared

"I hope that I will never be called upon to invade again while this war lasts, the trip to Pennsylvania has been a most awful shock upon this Army, one from which I fear it will take a long time to recover."

On Sunday, 10 May 1863, a beautiful spring day, Thomas Mitchell was feeling good. At a church service he had thanked God for his survival and for the great victory over the Northern forces at the battle of Chancellorsville. Unfortunately, the tranquility of the day was disrupted when Mitchell and the legion troops received orders to prepare rations and be ready the following morning to move back to their old winter encampments. A heavier mood settled on Mitchell when he arrived at the old camp. All the chimneys they had so painstakingly cobbled together were torn to pieces and littered the campground.[1]

Rumors fluttered through the camp like spring butterflies. The French were going to intervene, forcing Lincoln to make peace. It all turned out to be a forlorn hope that existed only in the soldiers' wishful thinking. Worse carnage was yet to come.

While the armies regrouped around Fredericksburg, Lincoln was thinking about replacing General Joseph Hooker. His mediocre leadership had cost the Federal army over 17,000 casualties at Chancellorsville. Corps commanders under Hooker were in a rebellious state and experienced troops were leaving at the end of their two-year enlistments. Lincoln offered the command to Major General John Reynolds, but Reynolds rejected the offer. He wanted freedom from

---

[1] Diary of Thomas M. Mitchell, 10 May 1863 entry, private collection of Mr. R. D. Thomas, Chattanooga TN.

Washington's interference, and this was something Lincoln was not prepared to grant. Hooker was retained for the time being.[2]

General Robert E. Lee was disappointed with the victory at Chancellorsville. His army had not pressed the Federals and lost another opportunity to destroy the Army of the Potomac. Once the opposing armies were back on the Rappahannock River, the rough terrain complicated any attack on Federal positions without risking enormous casualties. Lee decided to concentrate on countering Hooker's next move as well as feeding and supplying his battered army. He convinced President Davis of the need to return several detached divisions to him and considered a replacement for Stonewall Jackson. Lee knew he had to break out of the Fredericksburg area. Not to do so would be to invite another Federal turning movement, perhaps a thrust at Richmond by water if he remained in place on the Rappahannock. Lee would now seriously considered an invasion of the North. Such a move would enable him to transfer the war to the North, providing his men with Northern food and supplies.[3]

Lee replaced Jackson with two commanders and eliminated the unwieldy two-corps structure, replacing it with a three-corps organization. Longstreet retained I Corps, R. S. Ewell assumed command of II Corps, and A. P. Hill directed the new III Corps.[4]

Lieutenant Colonel Elihu "Sandy" Barclay, just recovered from his South Mountain wounds, commanded the Phillips Legion infantry. The legion's infantry battalion was still assigned to General William T. Wofford's brigade, General McLaws's division of the I Corps. I Corps included the brigades of Generals Joseph B. Kershaw, William Barksdale, Paul J. Semmes, and Wofford.[5]

Lee had his army ready to invade Pennsylvania by Wednesday, 3 June 1863. Richmond was out of immediate danger and Hooker's troops

---

[2] E. Coddington, *The Gettysburg Campaign: A Study in Command* (1968; repr., Dayton: Morningside Bookshop, 1979) 35.

[3] US War Department, comp., *The War of Rebellion: A Compilation of the Official Records of the Union and Confederate* Armies, 128 vols. (Washington DC: Government Printing Office, 1880–1901) ser. 1, vol. 25, pt. 2, pp. 713–14.

[4] Clifford Dowdey and Louis H. Manarin, *The Wartime Papers of R. E. Lee* (New York: Bramhall House, 1989) no. 445, pp. 487–89.

[5] Douglas S. Freeman, *R. E. Lee, A Biography*, 4 vols. (New York: Charles Scribner's Sons, 1934) 2:403, 3:15.

along the Rappahannock were quiet. That evening the legion soldiers assembled their camp gear, muskets, cartridges, and tents and headed out toward their unknown destination. They marched 8 miles to a point just south of Chancellorsville and camped on the battleground of early May. Lieutenant Marcus Greene jotted in his diary:

> Thursday 4th—Stopped by the road side we started from Camp F.B. last night at 8 o'clock, marched eight miles stopped and slept the balance of the night (on the Old Chancellorsville Battleground) got up the next morning and the dead Yankees was lying all round us that was killed May 1st but we paid no attention to them, but we taken [sic] the plank road toward Culpeper, 6 o'clock, now camp at Racoon [sic] Ford on Rapidan River. Marched 22 miles today. My feet are badly blistered. We marched through the Chancellorsville Battleground today. Saw dead men and horses lying by the road side for about six miles and the woods had burnt over lots of them"[6]

Tom Mitchell took the time to note the legion's location on Saturday, 6 June: "Leave camps at Seven A.M., cross the Rhapidann [sic] River at Raccoon ford, march within two miles of Culpeper turn to the East gap through Stevensburg and Camp." [7]

By 8 June, Longstreet and Ewell assembled near Culpeper Court House. Hooker was mystified as his sources provided conflicting information. Surely Lee would not withdraw from Fredericksburg and leave Richmond unprotected. He telegraphed Washington for guidance, since his previous instructions called for protecting Washington and Harpers Ferry. If he attacked Lee's rear, the head of the Southern army could cross the Potomac and threaten the capital. Lee knew that Hooker was probably aware of his intentions and might disrupt his plans by moving on Richmond. He decided to send Ewell into the Shenandoah Valley to attack the Federal garrison there, leaving I Corps near Culpeper to force Lincoln to pull the Army of the Potomac back to defend Washington. Mitchell reported Union activity near his camp on 9 June: "Cannonading commenced this morning at Six O'clock in the

---

[6] Marcus L. Greene, diary, 4 June entry.
[7] Thomas M. Mitchell, diary, 6 June entry.

direction of Kelleys [*sic*] Ford on the Rhapahannock [*sic*] River. We formed a line of battle East of Culpeper about Two miles. The Enemy crossed the River at Kelly's ford but was driven back by our Cavalry. We pitched our Tents near where we formed the line of battle."[8] Two days later, legion companies F, L, M, and O traded their smoothbore muskets for rifles captured from the Federals at Chancellorsville.[9] The legion infantry was now completely armed with rifles.

On 13 June, the Georgians received orders to advance with the I Corps along the eastern slope of the Blue Ridge Mountains. Three days earlier, General Ewell's corps was in the Shenandoah Valley headed for a collision with the Federal garrison at Winchester commanded by Major General Robert H. Milroy. Milroy had dismissed reports of any Confederate activity in the valley, laboring under the assumption that Lee's army was still in place around Fredericksburg. On 14 June, Ewell's forces attacked. Milroy, stunned, attempted to beat a retreat the following day, but Ewell had sealed off the escape routes. Ewell captured nearly half of Milroy's division, but Milroy himself managed to slip away.[10]

Still uncertain of Lee's intentions, Hooker was on the move from his position on the Rappahannock River, attempting to keep his troops between the Confederates in the valley and the Federal capital. Hooker continued to badger Lincoln for approval to move on Richmond. Lincoln denied Hooker's request and instructed him to follow on Lee's flank, fighting him at every opportunity.[11]

On 16 June, Lee directed Longstreet to move to Front Royal with Hood's division in the advance, followed by McLaws and three brigades of Pickett's division. I Corps went by the Winchester Road as far as Gaines Crossroads where it turned off to Rock's Ford. They crossed Hedgeman's River, followed Edgeworth and Barbee's Crossroads, and arrived at Markham. If all went according to plan, Longstreet could then

---

[8] Ibid., 9 June entry.

[9] *OR*, ser. 1, vol. 27, pt. 1, pp. 30, 31, 34, 38–39; also see Ordinance Return of Cobb's Brigade, 26 December 1862, from the ordinance officer Edward Taliaferro, Compiled Service Records of CSA officers and staff, Nara micropublication, RG 109, M331, roll 241. The legion had three types of cartridges: .54-, .57-, and .69-caliber.

[10] *OR*, ser. 1, vol. 27, pt. 3, p. 128; *OR*, ser. 1, vol. 27, pt. 2, pp. 305–306; Douglas S. Freeman, *Lee's Lieutenants*, 3 vols. (New York: Charles Scribner's Sons, 1971) 2:714.

[11] *OR*, ser. 1, vol. 27, pt. 1, pp. 34, 44–47.

march into the valley by way of Paris or Manassas Gap Road. Longstreet was to prevent Hooker from sending troops into the valley through the many gaps in the Blue Ridge Mountains. He would act on his own, threatening the Federal right flank to keep the Unionists away from the Potomac.[12]

The Phillips Legion had departed from Culpeper Courthouse on 15 June, crossed the Hazel River the following day, then rested and camped at Woodville. On 17 June the Georgia soldiers marched along the south slope of the Blue Ridge Mountains, passed Gaines Crossroads, and camped about 3 miles from Little Washington. The extreme heat produced numerous sunstroke victims. Some died but most simply plodded along, stumbling through clouds of suffocating dust kicked up by the thousands of men and animals, their eyes stinging and tearing. The ambulances could not handle all the sunstroke cases.[13]

From Gaines Crossroads, Longstreet's wagons rattled along by way of Front Royal into the Shenandoah Valley while the troops marched through several mountain gaps. On Friday, 19 June, Mitchell reported the legion's movements: "Marched at Seven A.M. pass Piedmont Pass at south foot of Blue Ridge Mountain. Cross the mountain at Ashby Gap, camp at western foot of the mountain areas near the Shenandoah River."[14]

McLaws was posted at Ashby Gap, Hood's division at Snicker's Gap and Pickett's division guarded all points between the three units. The legion was miserable. The men slept in a blinding rainstorm, consuming their rations without cooking utensils because their supply wagons had taken a route that delayed their arrival. On 19 June, Marcus Green was among the miserables: "We lay in an old field last night, had no tents, it rained all night. We marched about 12 miles yesterday and camped at Pedemont [sic] Depot on the road from Winchester to Manassas. We have not marched through but one trenchhole today. Lieut Bowie was taken sick yesterday. He was taken suddenly. We issued rations in the rain and had nothing to cook in."[15]

---

[12] *OR*, ser. 1, vol. 27, pt. 2, pp. 357, 358.

[13] Thomas M. Mitchell, diary, 17, 18 June entries.

[14] Ibid., 19 June entry.

[15] Marcus L. Greene, diary, 19 June 1863 entry.

By 20 June, McLaws had moved his troops out of the gaps and started fording the heavily swollen Shenandoah River. Hooker was worried. Lee had crossed the Potomac? Was this a raid or an invasion? Where was Lee going? On 21 June, a courier dashed pell-mell into McLaws's camp with orders to re-cross the river and rush back to Ashby's Gap to meet a Federal probe. At 4:00 P.M. Wofford's brigade accompanied McLaws's division back across the river toward Ashby's Gap while Thomas Mitchell and a detachment of legion infantry remained behind to build breastworks. Mitchell noted: "The Brigade passed us going to meet the Enemy on East side of the Mountain."[16]

McLaws placed his troops in the line of battle at the crest of the gap. The men spent a miserable night suffering in the biting wind, huddled together in soaked clothing. Officers allowed no fires so close to the enemy. The next morning a few of the Georgians picked wild strawberries for breakfast. Wofford's troops were positioned across the eastern slope of the mountain toward Upperville, just a few miles from the gap. The enemy had camped there for the night, but on sighting Wofford's troops the Unionists withdrew toward Middleburg, allowing the brigade to rejoin the division. Around 4:00 P.M. McLaws's division crossed the Shenandoah for the third time and continued their march north. It was 7:00 by the time the legion soldiers crossed the river. Mitchell had rejoined his company but now remained behind to bury the dead: "Monday the 22d. I crossed the River this morning to go to the Brigade. Find them in line of Battle about two miles East of Paris. At Four P.M. the Brigade moved back toward the River. I am left behind to help bury the dead. Stay all night at a house near by."[17]

By this time Ewell's corps had advanced into Pennsylvania and Lee felt it vital to bring the other corps within supporting distance. On 23 June Longstreet would march by way of Berryville, Martinsburg, and Williamsport into Maryland. A. P. Hill's corps had moved ahead of I Corps as planned; the time had arrived for Longstreet to follow into Pennsylvania. At dawn the following day, the command pushed ahead. Pickett's division, the Reserve Artillery battalions, and Hood and McLaws's divisions were on the road. On 25 June, Pickett's division and

---

[16] Thomas M. Mitchell, diary, 21 June 1863 entry.
[17] Ibid., 22 June 1863 entry.

the battalions of the Reserve Artillery crossed the Potomac. Hood and McLaws's divisions followed the next day.[18]

The legion trudged along with Longstreet's corps through Berryville and Smithfield, crossed the Potomac in the rain at Williamsport on 26 June, and camped near Hagerstown. The next day they plodded on through Greencastle, Pennsylvania, and camped at Marion, where they found brandy, chicken, butter, and bread. On 28 June they passed through Chambersburg. Lee's three corps had deployed in an arc stretching across lower Pennsylvania with Longstreet and Hill near Chambersburg. Two of Ewell's divisions, under Major Generals Robert Rodes and Edward "Allegheny" Johnson, had halted at Carlisle, 30 miles to the northeast. Ewell's third division under Jubal Early had marched to York, intending to break the railroad between Baltimore and Harrisburg and seize the bridge over the Susquehanna at Wrightsville.[19]

Hooker now knew that Lee's objective was Pennsylvania and began moving his troops across the Potomac. The Phillips Legion soldiers were in the dark at least as much as the enemy general. They had no idea why the army was marching or where it was heading. Some thought Maryland was the goal, but after the third crossing of the Shenandoah they finally learned their destination. Marcus Greene wrote in his diary: "We will take up line of march in a few moments. We are going to Gettisburg."[20] At some point in the march northward, legion commanding officer Lieutenant Colonel E. S. "Sandy" Barclay realized that the lingering effects of his 1862 wounds were worse than he had thought and turned over command to young Major Joseph Hamilton. Hamilton would lead the legion at Gettysburg.

General Lee now learned that Hooker had been replaced by General George Gordon Meade and Lee developed a plan to outwit the new Federal commander. He would concentrate his forces to engage and defeat individual parts of Meade's army as it advanced. Orders went out to the corps commanders and Southern forces began marching toward Cashtown at the eastern foot of South Mountain. On 29 June, General

---

[18] *OR*, ser. 1, vol. 27, pt. 2, pp. 307, 358; *OR*, ser. 1, vol. 51, pt. 2, p. 726.

[19] Thomas M. Mitchell, diary, 23–28 June 1863 entries; *OR*, ser. 1, vol. 27, pt. 2, p. 316; Marcus L. Greene, diary, 22–23 June 1863 entries.

[20] Marcus L. Greene, diary, 24 June 1863 entry.

A. P. Hill directed General Harry Heth to move his division from Fayetteville to Cashtown. In turn, Heth ordered General J. Johnston Pettigrew to proceed with his brigade to Gettysburg to capture supplies but not engage the Federals. The venture failed when Pettigrew sighted Federal cavalry near Gettysburg and returned empty-handed.[21]

Absent his cavalry commander General J. E. B. Stuart, Lee did not realize that Meade's army was not far from Gettysburg. Lee believed he would have time to concentrate his troops. In fact, Meade was already approaching Gettysburg in force.

Lee and Hill were not greatly concerned about Pettigrew's brush with the Federal cavalry. Their information indicated that Meade's troops were still well to the south. What Lee did not realize was that Meade had a good idea of the location of Lee's army. Meade had pushed Brigadier General John Buford's cavalry division toward Gettysburg while hurrying his infantry corps forward in forced marches.[22]

On 30 June, the legion soldiers were still in the dark about their destination as they marched with Longstreet to a gap in South Mountain 3 miles beyond Fayetteville. Upon arrival at the gap, McLaws ordered Wofford's brigade to Caledonia, where the legion took up picket duty around Graffenburg Springs and Thaddeus Stevens's recently destroyed ironworks. A few hours later the legion troops were back on the road, marching to Greenwood, 17 miles west of Gettysburg. While camped there, McLaws was ordered to march to Gettysburg the following day.[23]

The next morning McLaws's division was held up at Greenwood as Johnson's III Corps division and its supply trains clogged the road. McLaws finally got his division on the road at 4:00 P.M. The legion served as rear guard for I Corps and remained in camp until 8:00 P.M. Lieutenant Marcus Greene reported signs of the upcoming battle: "Wednesday, July the 1st. Heared [sic] Cannonading in front today. There are many troops passing to the front along the Pike Road...leave

---

[21] *OR*, ser. 1, vol. 25, pt. 2, p. 637; Maj. Gen. Henry Heth, "Causes of Lee's Defeat at Gettysburg," in *Southern Historica Papers*, 52 vols. (Richmond: Virginia Historical Society, 1877) 4:157.

[22] *OR*, ser. 1, vol. 27, pt. 1, pp. 68–69, 70; *OR*, ser. 1, vol. 27, pt. 3, pp. 416–17; J. Biddle, "General Meade at Gettysburg," in *Annals of the War*, ed. Alexander K. McClure (New Jersey: Blue and Grey Press, 1966) 205.

[23] Thomas M. Mitchell, diary, 27–29 June 1863; Marcus L. Greene, diary, 27–30 June 1863 entries.

camp at Eight P.M. pass Cashtown two miles and Camp. See many wounded men comeing [*sic*] from the front to night."[24]

McLaws continued his march and around midnight camped 3 miles west of Gettysburg at Marsh Creek. Earlier in the day Heth had again tried to appropriate supplies in Gettysburg, this time initiating a major fight. It began as a minor skirmish west of town and escalated into a major fight, igniting the Battle of Gettysburg.[25]

Overall the first days' fight had gone well for the Confederates. Both sides had poured arriving troops into the vicious action until the timely arrival of Ewell's corps from the north and northeast finally broke the Union position, resulting in the disorderly retreat of the Federal 1st and XI Corps to the ridge south of town. Casualties had been heavy on both sides but Lee held the field while Longstreet's fresh I Corps was on the way. At 5:00 P.M. Longstreet arrived and conferred with Lee, urging him to disengage and swing behind the Federals' left flank. Lee disagreed, fearing he might be cut off from his lines of supply and communication running southwest down the Cumberland Valley. Lee would confer with his generals late into the night, but 2 July would dawn without his having formulated a detailed plan of attack.[26]

At dawn, Meade's forces were laid out south of town in a fishhook-shaped line—the tip at Culp's Hill, the hook curved around Cemetery Hill, the shank along Cemetery Ridge, and the eye at the Round Tops. Lee positioned his troops around the outer perimeter of the hook. Ewell covered the north, A. P. Hill the center, and Longstreet the south. The Federals had the advantage of defending interior lines.

Mitchell's diary entry for the day reported the legion troops up early and on their way to battle: "Thursday the 2nd. Leave Camps at Seven A.M. Move to within Two miles of Gettysburg and formed a line of Battle, we advanced on the Enemy who after a hard fought Battle, fell back Two miles to a range of Hills [Round Tops], firing continued until after night."[27]

Around 8:30 A.M., McLaws's division, which included Wofford's brigade and the Phillips Legion infantry, arrived west of town. While

---

[24] Marcus Greene to Parents, 1 July 1863 entry.

[25] *OR*, ser. 1, vol. 27, pt. 2, pp. 316–17; *OR*, ser. 1, vol. 27, pt. 3, pp. 418, 420, 458.

[26] Longstreet, "Lee in Pennsylvania," in *Annals of the War*, ed. McClure, 422.

[27] Thomas M. Mitchell, diary, 2 July 1863 entry.

McLaws awaited further orders, Kershaw's brigade, which was at the head of the column, rested near the Hoss House.[28]

Reconnaissance information came in during the morning, indicating that the Round Tops on the Federal left were unoccupied. This convinced Lee that his best attack option was an *en echelon* assault on this end of the Union position. By 11:00 A.M. Lee had decided that Longstreet's corps would initiate the attack. McLaws was to anchor his left on Emmittsburg Road at the Peach Orchard in line of battle facing northeast toward Cemetery Hill. Hood's division would attack on McLaws's right. After Longstreet's attack reached full force, A. P. Hill's divisions would continue the attack to the north. Ewell would demonstrate strongly on the Federal right to hold these troops in place. With good planning and a little luck, Longstreet would surprise the Federal left and rout them from Cemetery Ridge and Cemetery Hill.[29]

Longstreet convinced General Lee to allow him to wait for the arrival of Law's Alabama brigade before beginning the march to the south. They arrived at noon and Longstreet's two divisions moved out. Unfortunately, the route had not been properly reconnoitered, and when it became obvious that they would be seen by the Federals on Little Round Top, the entire column had to be counter-marched. Hood and McLaws's divisions became entangled, taking precious time to get them sorted out and then finding a new route to the attack's jump-off point on Warfield Ridge. Longstreet had been told there would be nothing in his immediate front when he reached Warfield Ridge, and he had passed this expectation along to his subordinates. One can only imagine their consternation when the lead brigades broke into open ground around 3:00 P.M. to find the Peach Orchard to their left front swarming with Union soldiers and artillery. McLaws deployed his brigades before deciding what to do next while Hood's brigades moved off to the right. Kershaw's South Carolina brigade drew artillery fire and went into position behind a stone wall that ran through a field adjoining Biesecker's Woods. Paul Semmes's Georgians went into line behind and slightly left of Kershaw with their right in Biesecker's Woods. William

---

[28] Brig. Gen. Joseph B. Kershaw to John Bachelder, in *The Bachelder Papers*, 3 vols., ed. David L. and Audrey J. Ladd (Dayton: Morningside House, 1994) 1:452.

[29] Maj. Gen. Lafayette McLaws, "Gettysburg Revisited, The Opportunity Missed—The Planning for the 2nd Day," in *Southern Historical Society Papers*, 1879, 68–69.

Barksdale's Mississippians formed on the left of Millerstown Road in front of Pitzer's Woods, behind a stone wall some 600 yards from Emmittsburg Road. Wofford moved up 150 yards behind Barksdale in Pitzer's Woods on the reverse slope of Warfield Ridge. He deployed his regiments with the Phillips Legion on the extreme left, followed by (left to right) Cobb's Legion, the 24th Georgia, the 18th Georgia, and the 16th Georgia. The 3d Georgia Sharpshooter Battalion deployed in front of the brigade as skirmishers.[30]

After several heated exchanges with McLaws, Longstreet finally realized that a significant Union force was in his front, and he consulted with General Lee to modify the attack plan. These Union troops belonged to Major General Dan Sickles's III Corps. Deployed in a large salient with its apex at the Peach Orchard, they had moved forward without Meade's authorization and now found themselves in a highly vulnerable position. Hood would now lead off from the right and engage the Federals, who were spread out thinly from the Round Tops through the Devils Den and on into Rose's Woods. Once Hood became fully engaged, McLaws would attack the Peach Orchard and Rose Farm. With Confederates massing in front, Meade saw that he could not withdraw *Si*ckles's men and rushed to throw additional units into the coming fray. Orders went out to shift V Corps and elements of II Corps to Sickles's support. The Confederate attack began around 3:45 P.M. with an artillery barrage. Shrapnel and wood splinters showered the legion infantry as they waited in the woods behind General William Barksdale's line but caused little harm to them because their brigade had deployed on the reverse slope of Warfield Ridge. As Hood's division, then two of McLaws's brigades engaged the enemy, the attack degenerated into a series of close-range firefights that saw the action seesaw back and forth. By late afternoon, as the sun settled in the west, the Confederate advance stalled and Longstreet decided to send in Barksdale and Wofford. Shortly before 6:00 P.M. Barksdale's troops charged straight for Sherfy's Peach Orchard to silence the batteries that had pounded them for several hours. The onrushing Mississippians overran the Federals in the Peach Orchard then veered north to enfilade

---

[30] Gerald J. Smith, *One of the Most Daring of Men: The Life of Confederate General William Tatum Wofford* (Murfreesboro TN: Southern Heritage Press, 1997) 81; also see L., "Wofford's Georgia Brigade," in *Richmond* (VA) *Enquirer*, 5 August 1863, p. 2.

other Federal units along Emmittsburg Road. Wofford, coming up behind Barksdale, moved straight ahead through the Peach Orchard with his left on Wheatfield Road. His presence greatly inspired his men.[31]

As the Georgians came abreast of Kershaw's stalled Carolinians, a member of the brigade observed: "General Wofford, calmly brave as ever, throughout, riding up, assured them that the Georgians, instead of the enemy, were on their left; they rallied and, joining his brigade, all moved rapidly on after the fleeing foe."[32] The legion troops were in line astride Wheatfield Road as the attack pressed on toward the Wheatfield.[33]

The sight of Wofford's Georgians tramping straight at them in parade ground order unnerved the tired Federal brigades commanded by Colonel William Tilton and Brigadier General Samuel Zook. Positioned in the woods on Stony Hill at the west end of the Wheatfield, the Federals retreated northwest to the edge of Trostle's Woods. They then turned to fire on Wofford's oncoming troops. Staggered momentarily, Wofford's men pressed on and the demoralized Federals fled eastward.

Bursting from the woods on Stony Hill, the right of Wofford's line halted and volleyed into the right flank of Union Colonel Jacob Sweitzer's isolated V Corps brigade at the south end of the Wheatfield. As Sweitzer scrambled to rotate his two right flank regiments to meet this fire, the Cobb and Phillips legions wheeled right and went for Sweitzer's flank and rear.[34]

The 4th Michigan on Sweitzer's right flank found themselves nearly surrounded as Kershaw pressed from the southwest, Wofford's Georgians poured over Stony Hill in their front, and the two Georgia legions swept in from the north. The 4th Michigan had been ordered by its colonel, Harrison Jeffords, to pivot 90 degrees to face Stony Hill.

---

[31] L., "Wofford's Georgia Brigade," Richmond Enquirer, 5 August 1863, 2.

[32] Ibid.

[33] J. Coxe, "The Battle of Gettysburg," Confederate Veteran 21/8 (September 1913): 435.

[34] W. Youngblood, "Unwritten History of the Gettysburg Campaign," in Southern Historical Society Papers, 38:315; OR, ser. 1, vol. 27, pt. 2, pp. 610–13; "The Great Battle of Gettysburg," L. McLaws, Southern Historical Papers, 7:73; W. T. Wofford to Major J. M. Goggin, 14 August 1863, National Archives micropublication, M474, roll 71, letter 902-L-1863.

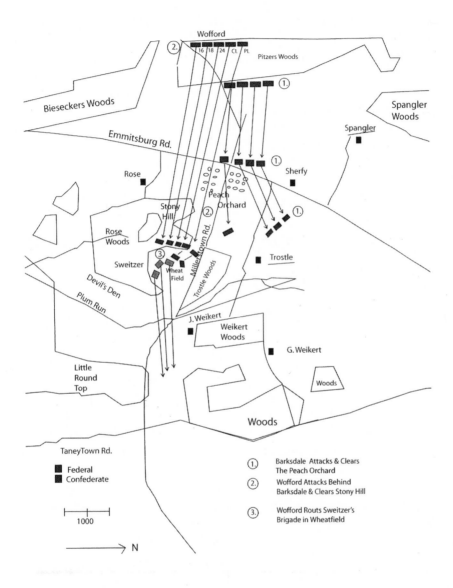

Wofford's Brigade routs Sweitzer's Brigade at Wheatfield.

While this movement was in progress, the 4th Michigan became mixed with the onrushing Confederates and the action degenerated into a hand-to-hand brawl. The 4th Michigan's color bearer was either wounded or simply abandoned the regimental color. Jeffords watched as a Confederate grabbed the flag and shouted for help from Major R. Watson Seage and Lieutenant Michael Vreeland. All three made a dash to recover the flag and Jeffords grabbed its staff. Seage struck the Rebel but other Southerners now surrounded the three officers. A bayonet thrust mortally wounded Jeffords while Seage and Vreeland were both shot, beaten, and stabbed. The flag was torn to shreds in the fight.[35] Sweitzer's brigade evaporated, the routed survivors fleeing eastward for Cemetery Ridge.

A letter from Brigadier General William Tatum Wofford to Division Headquarters, dated 14 August 1863, describes a July 2nd incident involving Private Thomas Jolly of the Phillips legion. After describing the circumstances of the capture of a Federal color by Cobb's legion (known to be that of the Eleventh Regular United States Infantry), Wofford continued:

> I enclose a note from Major Hamilton commanding Phillips Legion, in which he states that the colors captured by his command have been sent to Governor Brown of Georgia. The incidents relating to the capture are as follows: two stands of colors were captured, one of them by Private Alfred Norris of Co. E, which he carried to the rear and delivered to a Lt. who claimed to be of Barksdale's Brigade and who was wounded and sent to the hospital carrying the flag with him, which was supposed to still be in his possession. The other stand was captured by Private E. I. Smith of Co. E and was also carried to the rear and handed to a Lt. of Fraser's Battery, but was returned when the battle was over and has now been sent to the Governor of Georgia. Private Thomas Jolly was bayoneted and killed with a stand of colors in his hands. His death was bravely avenged by Private McGovern of Co. F, Private Blanton of Co. B and Private Austin of Co. L. The two former each bayoneting

---

[35] Henry S. Seage to Bachelder, September 23, 1884, in *Bachelder Papers*, 2:1070; *OR*, ser. 1, vol. 27, pt. 1, pp. 603, 611–12.

a man, the latter taking from the belt of the enemy's colorbearer his pistol, killing him and two others. In this hand to hand fight the colors of the gallant Jolly were lost by the men who strove bravely to obtain them, though supposed to be in the hands of some other regiment.[36]

The similarities of the Seage and Hamilton accounts of the fight for the flag, and the fact that in both accounts the flag was not captured, prompts one to reason that Jeffords of the 4th Michigan may have collided with Rebels from the Phillips Legion. Wofford's account of Jolly's death sounds a great deal like the fight for the 4th Michigan's flag. This fight is memorialized in Don Troiani's painting "Saving the Flag." Private Jolly had enlisted in Company B of the legion infantry in June 1861. He actually survived his harrowing experience and was captured by the Federals when McLaws's men retreated from the Wheatfield. After the battle he was declared dead by his comrades. His wife, Eliza, filed a death claim in September 1863, not knowing of his survival and subsequent May 1864 parole and exchange from Point Lookout Prison. He was furloughed home to Dalton, Georgia, which by the time he reached it in June was behind Federal lines. Eliza was astonished to see him alive. Soon, he and Eliza became involved in a plot to derail a Federal supply train on the Western and Atlantic Railroad. Tom was captured and sentenced to spend the rest of the war at Camp Chase, Ohio. He was released on 2 May 1865 and would later become Dalton's town marshal. He lived thirty more years, dying in 1893 in Alabama.[37]

Union resistance was fading as Brigadier General John C. Caldwell's II Corps division began to retreat out of the Wheatfield. Caldwell requested Brigadier General Romeyn Ayres's Division of United States Regulars, from the V Corps, to connect with his left. Ayres wheeled Colonel Sidney Burbank's brigade left to the south edge of the Wheatfield. Before a connection could be made, Caldwell's troops fell back in confusion under a heavy crossfire as Wofford's Confederates arrived on their right flank and other Confederates attacked from the Rose Woods. As Caldwell's men retreated, the euphoric Georgians rolled up Burbank's regulars. Colonel Hannibal Day's brigade of

---

[36] Wofford to Goggin, 14 August 1863.
[37] Compiled Service Records, National Archives micropublication, M266, roll 596.

regulars now covered the disordered Federal retreat across Plum Run Valley, taking heavy losses. By 7:15 P.M., the Confederates had broken through the Federal defenses.

Wofford's brigade fought Federal troops from the II, III, and V Corps on Stony Hill and the Wheatfield, the troops battering each other in fierce unrelenting fights. Wofford's men succeeded in intimidating the battle-wearied Federals, forcing their withdrawal and giving a shot in the arm to Kershaw's and Semmes's troops. Wofford pressed the flank and rear of the retreating Federals, loading and firing in good order. The tattered Rebels, in all colors and types of garb, fought like lions. J. S. Wood of Company D was in the middle of it all: "We went into them with our bayonets and clubbed them with our guns. It was here that I went after the flag, and after shooting one man, and clubbing five others, I was in the act of reaching for the flag when a fellow named Smith jumped in ahead of me and grabbed it. I came very near clubbing him, but he put up such a pitiful mouth about having a family of small children that he wanted to see so bad, I let him have it so he could get a furlough."[38]

By now the Confederates had become disorganized but small groups aggressively pursued the Federals, who fled up and over Cemetery Ridge. Wofford's brigade now spotted Captain Charles Walcott's six-gun artillery battery, which was posted north of Wheatfield Road along J. Weikert's Farm lane, and attacked. With no infantry support and a wave of screaming Georgians bearing down on them, the Federal gunners beat a hasty retreat.

Wofford's troops advanced past the captured guns about 50 yards to the protection of a stone wall and eyed the slopes of Little Round Top to their right front. Captain Frank Tibbs's First Ohio Federal battery was on the northwest slope, peppering the attacking Rebels with canister. Accounts suggest that some of Wofford's men did not stop at the wall but, flushed with victory, continued their attack forward up the slope. Attacking around and over the huge boulders with canister pouring into them, the attack broke up and the Southerners took cover wherever they could find shelter.

---

[38] J. S. Wood, "Reminiscences," Microfilm Library, drawer 283, box 4, Georgia Department of Archives and History, Morrow GA.

Brigadier General Samuel W. Crawford's 3d Division of V Corps now launched a counterattack from Cemetery Ridge. The Federals of Colonel William McCandless's First Brigade formed in two lines, fired a volley, and charged down the hill. By this time, with dark shrouding the battlefield, the exhausted Rebels approaching Little Round Top were running out of steam. The surprise Federal assault simply overran many who had reached advanced positions on the slopes of Little Round Top. Longstreet ordered the Rebels to break off the attack. Benning, Anderson, Kershaw, and Semmes withdrew but Wofford, at the stone wall, resisted Longstreet's order, insisting that his Georgians had driven the Federals from the field. McLaws directed Wofford to reform his brigade across Wheatfield Road near the northern extension of Stony Hill. Longstreet was better informed than Wofford on this day. He knew the enemy were massing their force in his front, the Rebel troops were too fatigued to mount a new attack, and the light was fading. His two divisions had been reduced by at least 4,000 killed and wounded. They faced Cemetery Ridge and Little Round Top in a single line, without any support on the left, against over 20,000 Federals. To attack would have been madness.

The Federals were also exhausted and not inclined to continue the fight into the night. While the Rebels regrouped at the western end of Rose Wheatfield, the Northerners halted at the eastern end of Trostle's Woods. It had been quite a fight for Longstreet's troops. Wofford's brigade alone was credited with killing, wounding, and capturing more enemy troops than he had in his entire command. He brought off three Federal flags, captured by the infantry of Cobb's and the Phillips Georgia legions, and passed so many prisoners to the rear that at one time he feared the enemy had launched an attack on his rear.[39]

The following morning of 3 July, Wofford placed the 3d Georgia Sharpshooters in the woods on Stony Hill where they engaged a Federal skirmish line. The musket fire roared so loud that Wofford, anticipating a Federal attack, shifted his entire brigade forward, forming it on the right of the sharpshooters. Wofford remained in position throughout the

---

[39] No author, "The Great Battle of Gettysburg," *Charleston* (SC) *Mercury*, July 23, 1863, p. 1.

day as Major General George Pickett's troops made their valiant but
failed charge—one history has memorialized as "Pickett's Charge."[40]

General Robert E. Lee's battered Army of Northern Virginia spent
the next ten days in an agonizing retreat to Virginia. On 6 July 1863, the
head of Lee's column crossed into Maryland near Meadowsburg Pass
and camped around Hagerstown. On this date, Jack Reese's Aunt Frank
noted the passage of time: "2 years to day since your Co. left for Camp
McDonald. How long the time has appeared to those at home. I expect
the time has passed as slow with you."[41]

The Rebels had skirmished with the Federals on several occasions
and they were now in the defensive line along the river from
Williamsport to Falling Waters, anticipating an attack. The legion had
worked on breastworks all night and formed into line of battle at 4:00
P.M. on 11 July, participating in a light skirmish. They dropped back a
half mile that evening and dug in. They were in action again on Sunday
with Mitchell noting: "Sunday the 12th. Some skirmishing throughout
the day. The enemy does not show much disposition to advance."[42]
General Meade finally abandoned his efforts to follow and destroy Lee's
army when the Southern troops slipped back across the Potomac into
Virginia on 14 July.

Suffering from illness, Company A's Lieutenant Daniel B. Sanford,
who had taken refuge in a private residence, caught up with his legion
compatriots outside Culpeper. On his way, Sanford was nearly captured
when a Federal cavalry unit passed several miles to the rear of
Longstreet's corps. They passed within 200 yards of Sanford, who hid in
a thicket until a Confederate brigade arrived and scattered the Federals.
Upon reaching the legion, Sanford wrote to his sister, expressing his
despair over the course of the war: "I hope that I never will be called
upon to invade again while this war lasts, the trip to Pennsylvania has
been a most awful shock upon this Army, one from which I fear it will
take a long time to recover. Our Army seems to be depressed. The

[40] Longstreet, "Lee in Pennsylvania," in *Annals of the War*, ed. McClure, 414,
429–30; W. Taylor, *Four Years with General Lee* (Indiana: Indiana University Press,
1996) 1031.

[41] Andrew J. Reese to Aunt, 6 July 1863, Rees/Reese Collection, Lumpkin County
Library, Madeline K. Anthony Collection, series 3, box 23, folder 5.

[42] Thomas M. Mitchell, diary, 11, 12 July 1863 entries.

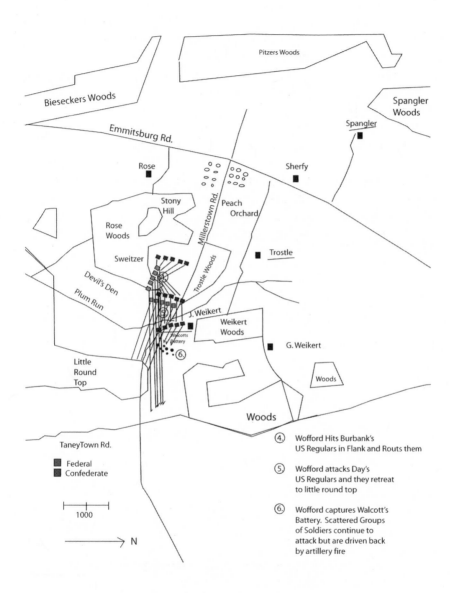

Pitzers Woods

Bieseckers Woods

Spangler Woods

Emmitsburg Rd.

Spangler

Rose

Sherfy

Stony Hill

Peach Orchard

Millerstown Rd.

Rose Woods

Sweitzer

Trostle Woods

Trostle

Devil's Den

Plum Run

J. Weikert

Weikert Woods

Walcott's Battery

G. Weikert

Little Round Top

Woods

TaneyTown Rd.

Woods

■ Federal
■ Confederate

1000

⟶ N

④ Wofford Hits Burbank's US Regulars in Flank and Routs them

⑤ Wofford attacks Day's US Regulars and they retreat to little round top

⑥ Wofford captures Walcott's Battery. Scattered Groups of Soldiers continue to attack but are driven back by artillery fire

Wofford's brigade routs US Regulars and charges Little Round Top.

reverses in the West have had a bad effect. I can't imagine where this Army is going but I think we will take up our same old line on the Rappahannock."[43] The legion suffered six killed, forty-four wounded (two mortally), and forty-two captured in its single agonizing day of combat at Gettysburg.[44]

The legion's performance on the second day of the battle was nothing short of spectacular. In the last of Longstreet's brigades to attack, they went in fast and hard at a critical point in the action. Their gallant charge routed several Federal brigades, temporarily captured a battery, and advanced almost a mile and a half. General Longstreet summed it up well, boasting that the afternoon's action had been the "best three hours fighting ever done by any troops on any battlefield."[45]

---

[43] D. Sanford to Sister, 25 July 1863, private collection of Mr. Sanford Penticost, Atlanta GA.

[44] Compiled Service Records, M266, rolls 592–600.

[45] "Lee in Pennsylvania," from *Annals of the War*, ed. A. K. McClure, 424.

Chapter 12

From the River of Death to the
Fortress at Knoxville

*"And the high fortifications of his walls he will bring down,
lay low, and cast to the ground, even to the dust."*
(Isaiah 25:12)

*"They all ran out, but when they found that we could not get
over it they came back and threw all the picks, shovels and
hand grenades they had over on us."*

The battered Gettysburg veterans of the Phillips Georgia Legion were on their way to assist General Bragg's Army of the Tennessee was opposing Union General William S. Rosecrans. The move from Virginia to Tennessee promised to be a logistical nightmare. Major Frederick Sims, a Southerner who knew the differing gauges for each rail line, the deplorable condition of the trains, and lack of replacement parts as well as an extreme shortage of qualified mechanics, solved all of these problems. On 2 September 1863, Union Major General Ambrose Burnside had taken Knoxville and cut the Virginia and Tennessee Railroad. As a result, the two divisions of Longstreet's I Corps being sent west were required to proceed in a wide arc through the Carolinas to reach Bragg's army in north Georgia.

Sims's genius and tenacity proved to be indispensable. By 8 September 1863, troops and equipment were on the move.[1] The legion brought up the rear, not boarding the cars of the Virginia Central Railroad at Hanover Junction until 11 September. Diarist Tom Mitchell described their fits and starts: "Tuesday 8th. Leave camp at Four A.M. Cross South Anna River at Davenport's Bridge. Come to the Va. Central

---

[1] J. Bowers, *Chickamauga & Chattanooga: The Battles that Doomed the Confederacy* (New York: Harper Collins Publishers, 1994) 52–53.

RR at Beaver Dam Station. Camp at Anderson Siding three miles north of Hanover Junction."[2]

By Friday, 11 September, the legion troops had boarded cars in the early morning and departed by 11:00 A.M., arriving in Richmond around 1:00 P.M; departed at 9:00 P.M., and arrived at Petersburg around 11:00 P.M. Even by nineteenth-century standards, the next few days would prove to be a miserable ride; but the soldiers were glad to be on the move.[3]

The troops climbed aboard an array of cars—passenger, baggage, mail, box, platform. Horses were shoved and pulled up ramps into boxcars. Guns and caissons came creaking and groaning aboard flatcars. The ancient wobbly cars and engines snaked through pristine countryside in late glorious summer, going about 10 miles an hour, the rails groaning and complaining.[4]

The next stop, on Sunday, 13 September, was Weldon, North Carolina, and from there to Wilmington, arriving at 9:00 A.M. on the 14th. The troops were pelted with rain as they crossed the Cape Fear River by steamboat. Once across they embarked on yet another railroad for Florence, South Carolina.[5]

On 15 September the legion soldiers arrived at Florence, then moved on to Charleston, arriving there the next day at 1:00 P.M. Next destination was Savannah, Georgia, with an immediate departure and arrival at Savannah at 8:00 A.M. on the 17th. Heading west, they clattered across Georgia and arrived in Atlanta at 7:00 P.M. on the 18th. Many of the legion's troops were from counties just north of Atlanta and had not seen their families in well over a year. The temptation was just too great. The troops pulled out of Atlanta on a northbound W&ARR troop train at 8:00 A.M. on the 19th. As the slow-moving train rolled across the Chattahoochee River into Cobb County, men began to drop off the cars and head for their homes. Lt. Marcus Green of Company O noted in his diary entry for the 20th that "nearly all of the Legion jumped off the cars and went." He went on to say that he remained at his

[2] Diary of Thomas M. Mitchell, 8 September 1863 entry, private collection of Mr. R. D. Thomas, Chattanooga TN.

[3] Ibid.

[4] G. Seymour, *Divided Loyalties: Fort Sanders and the Civil War in East Tennessee* (Knoxville: East Tennessee Historical Society, 1982) 90.

[5] Thomas M. Mitchell, diary, 13, 14, 15 September entries.

home in Cobb County until the 25th when he left to rejoin the legion near Chattanooga. Diarist Tom Mitchell of Company B observed that the train stopped at Dalton on the evening of the 19th. Dalton was the home of Company B and Mitchell got to see his father and brother for three hours before the train continued on to Ringgold, arriving there at 11:00 P.M. Those troops that had not taken off for home caught a few hours sleep before marching west at 8:00 A.M. on the 20th. They could hear the roar of cannon fire in their front, and surmised that a major battle was in progress somewhere up ahead. They did not make it to the front that day and went into camp 5 miles west of Ringgold without seeing action. On Monday 21 September, they proceeded north through the grizzly remains of the battle that had just been fought and camped north of Chickamauga Creek. They now realized that they had just missed the brutal two-day Battle of Chickamauga (translates as "river of death" in the Cherokee language[6]), but would soon join in some of the deadly skirmishing that followed on the next few days after the battle as the Federals were pushed back into Chattanooga. Most of the AWOL troops of the legion would rejoin their unit within the next few days. They were to rejoin General Longstreet's I Corps, most of whom had arrived the previous day and had participated in the significant but costly victory for the Confederacy.

Longstreet's arrival on 19 September was not auspicious. Despite Yankee General Rosecrans's reluctance to believe it, Old Pete had indeed arrived at Catoosa Station near Ringgold, and he was not happy. General Bragg had forgotten his manners. No one was on hand to meet Longstreet to guide him and his staff to Bragg's headquarters. He converted his ire and nervous energy to good use, riding across the countryside until he finally located Bragg around 11:00 P.M. for a conference. The atmosphere was electric with Longstreet's barely suppressed wrath. Hovering over a crude map, the two men discussed the military situation. Longstreet noted the various roads and streams between Lookout Mountain, the Chickamauga River, and the Confederate positions. Severe skirmishing had occurred sporadically earlier that day. At first light the next morning, the second day of battle

---

[6] J. Korn, *The Fight for Chattanooga: Chickamauga to Missionary Ridge* (Alexandria: Time-Life Books, 1985) 43; J. Arnold, *Chickamauga 1863: The River of Death* (Oxford UK: Osprey Publishing Company, 1992).

began in earnest. Bragg assigned command of the army's Left Wing of Hood and Hindman's divisions to Longstreet, as well as some troops from Brigadier General Bushrod Johnson's division and some artillery battalions. The strategy was clear: Bragg would smash the Federal left and cut them off from Chattanooga. He would bottle up Rosecrans and destroy him. General Polk's right wing would initiate the attack and Longstreet would follow with an attack en echelon. The attack was to be in echelon. The division on the extreme right would take the lead and the others would follow.

At daybreak, 20 September, the battle took shape. During the night, Union and Confederate commanders had repositioned their troops in order to improve defensive positions. Rosecrans now committed a major error. He misunderstood the actual locations of his troops and gave orders that resulted in the creation of a gap in his lines. Longstreet's troops roared through the gap and routed Sheridan's and Davis's divisions, driving the Federal right wing north. Believing his entire army was defeated, Rosecrans and his generals retreated north to Chattanooga. Meanwhile, Major General George Thomas, with two brigades from General Gordon Granger, managed to hold their positions on the left, preventing a complete rout of the Union army. Running low on ammunition, Thomas withdrew to Rossville Gap at dark. Bragg followed slowly, eventually seizing Missionary Ridge and holding the town of Chattanooga in a state of siege. Avenues of approach were blocked, resulting in near starvation for the Federals until the "Cracker Line" was finally opened in October. Although a victory for the Rebels, Chickamauga cost the South higher losses than those suffered by the Union forces.[7]

Legion surgeon, Dr. Shine, reported on the aftermath of the battle: "We marched on until dark [toward Chattanooga], when we went into camp for the night. I slept in a little cabin on the road side with several other officers. Soon after going into camp the prisoners began to pass to the rear and we saw about 1500 or 2000 pass in our squad. This was very encouraging to us, the report is-that the Yankees are flying before us; and that we have killed and captured a great many, though our loss is

---

[7] Bowers, *Chickamauga & Chattanooga*, 161.

said to be very heavy."[8] The next day, while resting on the Chickamauga battlefield, Dr. Shine recorded a grisly scene: "On the 'Battle Field' I saw the bodies of 3 men who it seemed had taken refuge in a little house. I suppose they were wounded & helpless, that had been burned to a crisp by the house being set on fire, by a shell. We judge them to be Yankees, from some pieces of clothing near by."[9]

Except for major discomfort and achy muscles from their train ride from Virginia, the Phillips Legion infantrymen had been relatively unscathed—until 24 September. With McLaws's division, they were ordered to pursue the Federals on 22 September. Union General George Thomas had been ordered to establish a defense at Rossville Gap in Missionary Ridge. Fearing his position was weak and might easily be flanked, he requested permission from General Rosecrans to withdraw into the defenses being thrown up around Chattanooga. There, on 24 September, the legion soldiers ran into Thomas's fortified position in the valley between Missionary Ridge and Lookout Mountain. Company E, in the lead, lost two killed and five wounded (two mortally). Lieutenant Alexander Erwin of Company C was also badly wounded and disabled for the remainder of the war.[10]

1 November 1863 marked the departure of the legion's popular brigade commander William Wofford. The pressures of leadership under the worst of conditions had degraded his physical and mental health—he had led the brigade in two major campaigns as well as the battles of Chancellorsville and Gettysburg. When he received news of the death of his young daughter, the pain was more than he could bear. He was granted a furlough and left for home on 1 November. He would not return to his brigade until 10 January 1864. He was temporarily replaced by the commander of the 18th Georgia Infantry Regiment, Colonel Solon Z. Ruff.[11]

---

[8] Diary of William Francis Shine, 20 September 1863 entry, North Carolina State Archives, Archives and Records section, Private Manuscripts Collection, call no. PC 589, Raleigh.

[9] Ibid., 21 September entry.

[10] Compiled Service Records, National Archives micropublication, M266, roll 592–600.

[11] Gerald J. Smith, *One of the Most Daring of Men: The Life of Confederate General William Tatum Wofford* (Murfreesboro TN: Southern Heritage Press, 1997) 99.

By 4 November, the legion soldiers had shifted their positions several times, suffering from torrential rains and disease but fortunately little combat. John Barry of Company B was starved, but in a letter to his sister made light of his rumbling stomach: "I received your last letter yesterday. Was sorry to hear that Ma was suffering so much. Hope she will soon get over it. I will have to let you know that I am complaining again with my same old complaint. Guess I will get used to it after a while. Think it may be like the Dutchman's horse getting used to living without food. About the time he got used to it he went up a spout."[12]

On 4 November Longstreet's corps was officially detached from Bragg's army and ordered to move to Knoxville in an attempt to eliminate a small Federal army there. The following day, Thursday, 5 November, the men marched to the Cleveland and Chattanooga Railroad and boarded the cars at Tyner's Station. Mitchell described the accommodations as "the filthiest place I was ever in."[13] They arrived at Sweetwater and camped a mile east of town. By 14 November they had nearly reached their destination at Loudon. The next day they crossed a pontoon bridge just below Loudon and camped near Lenoir Station on Huff Ferry Road.[14] Most if not all of Longstreet's troops probably were unaware that they were in a race with General Burnside's retreating Northerners. The goal was a nondescript village known as Campbell's Station (known today as Farragut). The village had been established in 1787 as a frontier fort, named after Colonel David Campbell. In later days it became a trading post and travelers' rest.[15]

Burnside was determined to reach the village first and retreat unmolested to Knoxville. Longstreet intended to beat him there and block his way to Knoxville, forcing him to fight outside of his earthworks. Bluecoats and graybacks sloshed along in the drizzling rain, but Burnside got there first with Longstreet only minutes behind. Longstreet organized his troops for an attempted double envelopment but with little effect; Burnside continued toward Knoxville. Mitchell was aware of the fighting but, being in the rear, the legion soldiers were not

---

[12] John Barry to Dear Sister, 4 November 1863, Southern Historical Collection, accession #3015, Wilson Library, University of North Carolina, Chapel Hill.

[13] Thomas M. Mitchell, diary, 5 November entry.

[14] Ibid., 15 November entry.

[15] L. Deaderick, ed. *Heart of the Valley: A History of Knoxville, Tennessee* (Knoxville: East Tennessee Historical Society, 1976) 185.

actively involved: "Monday 16th. Our Front Guard have been skirmishing with the Enemy more or less all day, we formed a line of Battle near Loveville. Considerable cannonading. Enemy fall back slowly and we advance, camp on Battlefield."[16]

The Rebels closed on Knoxville the next day, coming within 3 to 4 miles of the city. They spent the entire day of 17 November establishing their lines in an arc west and north around Knoxville. As they did so, Federal General William P. Sanders advanced his 700-man cavalry brigade to a hill on Kingston Road just west of Knoxville where they took cover behind barricades of fence rails. General Joseph Kershaw's South Carolina brigade ran into the Federals while advancing and the fight was on. Some of the Federals were armed with the Spencer repeating rifle, and the South Carolinians were held in check until dark when the Southerners retreated and went into camp. On the following day, Sanders held his advanced position to buy the Federals additional time to complete Knoxville's fortifications. Kershaw's men came on again at dawn and Sanders's men pushed them back again. At noon, frustrated by the delay, Longstreet ordered Colonel E. P. Alexander's 24-pound howitzers to pour artillery fire into the barricades. After 2 hours of pounding, Longstreet ordered another infantry assault. When it seemed the attack was failing, Captain Stephen Winthrop, an Englishman serving with Alexander's artillery, jumped on his horse and charged the barricades. Miraculously reaching the Federal line, Winthrop and was shot through the collarbone but was carried off the field and survived.[17] Inspired by Winthrop's impromptu charge, the South Carolinians leaped to their feet and charged to the summit, screaming their piercing battle cry. As they over came the defenses and took the position, Sanders, who had been brilliant in its defense, was mortally wounded. His retreating men carried him back to Knoxville, where he would linger until the morning of 19 September. Five days later a grateful General Burnside issued an order renaming Fort Loudon, at the northwest corner of the Union fortifications, Fort Sanders.[18] This

---

[16] Thomas M. Mitchell, diary, 16 November entry.

[17] Edward Albert Pollard, *Southern History of the War: The Third Year of the War* (New York: Charles B. Richardson, 1865) 142–43.

[18] *OR*, ser. 1, vol. 31, pt. 3, p. 241.

fort would soon bear ominous meaning to the history of the Phillips Legion.

While the legion soldiers prepared to attack Knoxville, General Ulysses S. Grant (who had relieved Rosecrans at Chattanooga) began to move to break the siege of Chattanooga. On 23 November 1863, Federal troops under General Joseph Hooker battled their way up 1,100-foot-tall Lookout Mountain; early the next day the 8th Kentucky raised the Stars and Stripes on the crest.[19] The Confederate defenders retreated east across Lookout Valley and joined their comrades on Missionary Ridge east of Chattanooga.

On Missionary Ridge, the situation seemed favorable for the Confederate commander General Braxton Bragg on 25 November. He possessed a strong position with his right composed of fourteen brigades of General William Hardee's corps. Rebel General John C. Breckenridge's nine brigades covered just over 2 miles opposite Grant's center. Three parallel lines of entrenchments had been prepared but were only partially completed—one line on the base of the ridge and another halfway up the slope. A third was on the crest itself. On 24 November, Grant ordered Sherman to attack the north end of the Southern line at dawn, and Hooker was to continue his advance to Rossville Gap and find and attack Bragg's left flank. Sherman's objective was Tunnel Hill, and his troops were on the move at first light. Numbers favored the Federals: Sherman had six divisions with over 26,000 men to attack 10,000 troops under Rebel Generals Patrick Cleburne and Carter Stevenson. Fortunately for the Southerners, the hilly terrain was cut by creeks and ravines that helped even the odds. Grant was shrewd enough not to assault the Southern center and waited for favorable results on the flanks. Sherman's efforts were disappointing. Although taking some high ground, his soldiers did not take Tunnel Hill itself. Hooker was delayed on the Federal right rebuilding a bridge and removing other obstructions. He was not in position to attack until the afternoon when he would threaten Bragg's left flank. The fight for Tunnel Hill began in full force by late morning as attacks swept back and forth. By early afternoon, Hooker had commenced his attack on the Confederate left, forcing the Confederates to withdraw. With Sherman

---

[19] Mark M. Boatner III, *Civil War Dictionary*, rev. ed. (New York: David McKay Company, Inc., 1988) 145.

stalled on the left, Grant realized he must take additional steps to refocus the Confederates' attention on their center. Grant ordered George Thomas to take the Rebel rifle pits at the foot of Missionary Ridge and await further orders. What happened next was amazing.

Bragg had divided his forces, sending half of each regiment into the rifle pits at the base of the ridge while stationing the rest on the crest itself. If attacked, the men in the rifle pits were to fire one volley and withdraw up the hill. Somewhere in the recent past Confederate engineers had made errors that would help to doom the Confederate defense. The unfinished breastworks atop the ridge had been situated incorrectly. They had been built on the geographic crest, which was the highest elevation, while they should have been positioned further forward on the military crest where they would have commanded maximum fields of fire down the forward slope.

Untion General George Thomas's troops were to advance when they heard six cannon reports. They did so without hesitation and were greeted by withering Confederate fire that thinned their ranks. The Federals pressed on and the Confederates scurried to the breastworks on the crest. The Northerners in the abandoned Confederate trenches at the foot of the ridge were now taking heavy fire from the ridge. Unwilling to retreat or remain where they were and be slaughtered, clusters of men began to move forward up the slope. Grant was apoplectic, believing that he had lost control of the battle, and demanded to know who had ordered the troops up the slope. More troops began to join the spontaneous uphill movement, scrambling as best they could to the top of the ridge. With Hooker now rolling up Bragg's left and Federals pouring over their works in front, the Rebels panicked, fleeing off the ridge to the east. Rebel General Patrick Cleburne held off Sherman on the north as dark fell and firing finally died out all along the line. With Cleburne providing a rear guard, Bragg withdrew south toward Dalton, Georgia. Chattanooga was lost to the Confederates. The door to Georgia was wide open and Sherman would proceed to drive through it toward Atlanta in 1864.

The legion infantry at Knoxville was unaware of the calamity that had struck the Southerners at Missionary Ridge. Diarist Mitchell documented its activities: "Tuesday the 24th. Nothing but skirmishing since Friday. Built Breast works west of the Rail Road, yesterday near

College Hill."[20] "Thursday 26th. Moved over near the Breast-works to be in supporting distance of our skirmishers."[21] Saturday, 28 November, found Wofford's brigade massed in a declivity just northwest of Union Fort Sanders. 29 November 1863 would provide a bitter footnote to the Chattanooga campaign: on this day the climactic battle of Fort Sanders would end the siege of Knoxville.

Longstreet had no intention of delaying his planned attack on Knoxville for any reason. General Lafayette McLaws had written Longstreet, pleading with him to wait until the results of the Chattanooga battle were in. Was Bragg defeated? Longstreet should be certain one way of the other. If defeated, they could not return to Chattanooga and rejoin Bragg's forces there. If both Bragg and Longstreet were defeated, would they be in a condition to make the long march back to Virginia? The enemy may well have cut their communications, preventing Bragg from reinforcing them.

General Micah Jenkins also tried to warn Longstreet of problems with the assault on Fort Sanders. The operation would be risky because the fort's outer ditch could be far deeper than Longstreet believed. Scaling ladders and fascines (bundles of sticks for filling ditches) would be needed. Longstreet responded, informing them both that the ditch was only 2 to 3 feet deep. Further, observers had seen an enemy soldier walk across the parapet and over the ditch. The attack would proceed as ordered. Finally, he would not desert General Bragg in his time of need. Old Pete would learn shortly that appearances are often deceiving.[22]

Knoxville's defenses were too strong for Longstreet to establish a regular siege of the town but he tried hard to do so. Longstreet's quasi-siege lasted from 18 November to 4 December. An unusual feature of the siege involved the numbers of attackers and defenders: they were approximately equal. Union General Orlando M. Poe, reputed to have been an outstanding engineer, was the architect of the Federal defenses around Knoxville. Seventeen forts and batteries formed a quadrilateral around the city. After extensive scouting and consultations with Bragg's chief engineer, Longstreet had determined to focus his attack on Fort

---

[20] Thomas M. Mitchell, diary, 24 November entry.

[21] Ibid., 26 November entry.

[22] H. Barrow, "Private James R. Barrow and Company B Cobb's Legion Infantry," (Dalton GA: privately published, 1996) 146–47. Also see Seymour, *Divided Loyalties*, 187–88.

Sanders, which was situated in the northwest portion of the defenses. The sides of the fort measured 114 yards on the south front, 95 yards on the west front, 125 yards on the north front, and 85 yards on the east front. On the west of the Union defenses, the Rebels faced a line that ran north to Fort Sanders. There, the line turned to the east across the rear of the city. Guns and muskets covered open fields that had been flooded by two creeks flowing into the Holston River. The Federal line then turned south and ran to the river. Rebel artillerist and general Edward Porter Alexander considered the most opportune area of the Federal defenses for attack to be Fort Sanders, on the northwest corner. The architectural profile of the fort was classic: moat, embankment, and parapet. The northwest bastion, a prominent salient, was built on a hill that dropped off sharply to the northwest. The fort was commanded by twenty-four-year-old Federal Lieutenant Samuel Benjamin. Benjamin had at his disposal four 20-pound Parrotts and six 12-pound Napoleons as well as two 3-inch rifles. The gunners had four types of projectiles to fire at attackers: for long-range, solid shot, explosive shell, or spherical case. "Canister," a kind of tin can of small iron or lead balls, was available for close-quarters use against assaulting troops. The enterprising Lt. Benjamin supplemented his cannon by preparing a supply of shells converted to grenades that could be lit and tossed over the walls. Beneath the brow of the hill on which the fort was situated, a large attacking force would be able to approach to within 120 yards without being seen or fired upon from either the fort or enemy troops in adjacent rifle pits.[23]

The attack began around 6:00 A.M. on Sunday, 29 November. Alexander knew that the Rebel brigades were in battle formation by the report of a signal gun fired from near the Armstrong House. Confederate sharpshooters blasted the parapet while artillery fire exploded over the beleaguered fort and any supporting entrenchments. Although the Confederate fire lit up the black sky, no one in the fort fired back. Alexander was irritated to the extreme because Longstreet had ordered him to cease fire after a very short bombardment.

The Phillips Legion troops were crouched in position northwest of the fort where they had spent most of a long, cold night without fires.

---

[23] Shelby Foote, *The Civil War: A Narrative*, Fredericksburg to Meridian, vol. 2/3 (New York: Random House, 1963) 2:864.

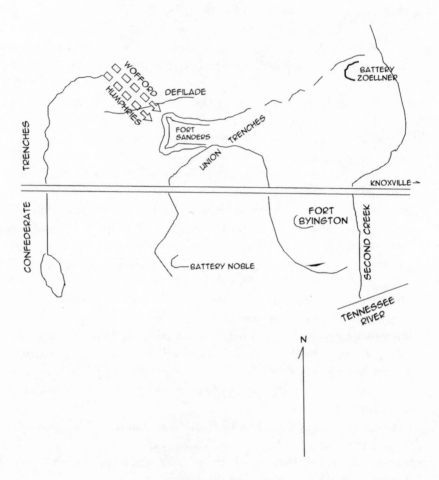

Attack on Fort Sanders, Knoxville, Tennessee, 29 November 1863.

Supporting troops moved up. Mitchell reported his experience at this time: "Sunday the 29th. Legion was called from the breastwork last night. while our lines advanced, we returned to Camps this morning at Three O'clock, and at Five A.M. we formed a line of Battle just on the West side of Fort Sanders, charged the Fort about Six. A.M., the Legion first, several regiments follow us."[24]

Sharpshooters kept up a continual fire on the fort whose garrison totaled over 500 men. The legion troops under command of Lieutenant Colonel Joseph Hamilton led the way with fixed bayonets. They were followed by the 16th, 18th, and 24th Georgia Infantry Regiments, and by Cobb's legion. Both Wofford's and Humphrey's brigades were aligned in regimental columns. When the fort was captured Kershaw was to advance on the right while Jenkins came in on the left. It was a good plan but one doomed to failure.[25]

The columns moved rapidly across ground studded with tree stumps interlaced with telegraph wire. The front lines stumbled over these obstructions but men chopped away the wire with axes and pushed on beyond this temporary annoyance. The ditch at the base of the fort was another matter. Instead of the presumed 3- to 4-foot depth, it turned out to be 8 feet deep and 8 to 12 feet wide. Due to Longstreet's insistence that they would not be needed, no fascines or ladders were available. Worse yet, the Federals had poured water onto the fort's walls, which froze in the bitter cold temperature; this made it nearly impossible for the attackers to find handholds to climb up the sides without scaling ladders. A few of the troops rammed bayonets into the wall, used them as grips, and managed to reach the top of the parapet but were either captured or shot almost immediately. Shelby Foote described one color bearer as being grabbed by the neck and snatched from sight, flopping like a hooked fish being landed.[26] To make matters worse, Lt. Benjamin began lobbing his jury-rigged grenades over the wall. This set off a panic in the ditch as men scrambled to escape the sputtering shells.[27] Ironically, Longstreet would decide to courtmartial McLaws for failing

---

[24] Thomas M. Mitchell, diary, 29 November entry.
[25] Seymour, *Divided Loyalties*, 152.
[26] Foote, *Civil War*, 2:864.
[27] Seymour, *Divided Loyalties*, 198.

to provide ladders, but the War Department saw through this attempted diversion of blame and exonerated McLaws in 1864.[28]

Blood spattered the men attempting to scale the walls and puddled on the floor of the ditch. The attack had failed. The enormity of the defeat is best summed up by the casualty figures. While the Confederate suffered a loss of 813 men in the attack, the Northerners lost only 5 killed and 8 wounded. Mitchell summed up the failed effort: "Charged the Fort about six A.M., the Legion first, several regiments follow us, was not able to got over the Fort on account of a deep ditch in front, we retreated from the Fort with a heavy loss. I was not hurt but got very bloody, return to camp about 3 P.M., a flag of truce having been raised so as to take care of the dead and wounded."[29] B. F. Red, of Company C of the legion infantry, had this to say about his misfortune in the assault on the fort:

> After we left Chattanooga we went to Knoxville, where we charged Fort Sanders; but no one went over that fort except Adjutant Cummings, of the 16th Georgia Regiment. An old Federal soldier here says he saw Cummings knocked in the head with an ax. There is another old solder living in Arkansas who says he was in that fort when we charged it. They all ran out, but when they found we could not get over it they came back and threw all the picks, shovels and hand grenades they had over on us. They had poured water on the edge of the fort and it ran down and froze.[30]

Dr. Shine reported on the dead and wounded as well as the work of surgeons:

> Nov. 29th—Sunday. Our Division charged on the Yankee Fort in front of Knoxville, this morning at daylight, but were unable to take it in consequence of the depth of the ditches, and fell into the hands of the enemy. In the evening we exchanged

---

[28] *OR*, ser. 1, vol. 31, pt. 1, pp. 505–506.

[29] Thomas M. Mitchell, diary, 29 November entry.

[30] B. Red, "McLaws' Division at Chickamauga," *Confederate Veteran* 21/12 (December 1913): 585.

wounded with the enemy under a flag of truce (We had several of their wounded who we had taken since we left Loudon). We did not get through operating on the wounded at the Hospital until about 9:00 P.M. The weather was very cold and disagreeable.[31]

Ivy F. Thompson of Company D detailed the experience of his capture at Fort Sanders:

> On the morning of the 29th November, 1863, we assaulted Fort Sanders, but failed to take it. We made the charge just at daylight and the men went up with the determination to take the fortifications if possible. But the work was too strong, it being 27 feet from the bottom of the ditch to the top of the Fort. Our men (or as many of them as could do so) had to fall back. I was among the captured…. We were confined in the jail at Knoxville until the 15th of December. We were crowded together in the jail so much that there was not room for all to lie down at the same time. And it seemed that the Federals had lost that magnanimity which once characterized them. For they did not give us more than half enough to eat. Indeed they barely gave us enough to keep us alive.[32]

Thompson's treatment did not improve. He and some other prisoners were moved north to a military prison by way of Louisville, Kentucky. They arrived there at the end of the month, having subsisted solely on parched corn and a little water. They left Louisville a short time later and proceeded on to the Rock Island (Illinois) Military Prison, arriving there on 6 January 1864. Starvation rations continued. Thompson remained a prisoner at Rock Island until 21 June 1865, when he was released. His misery was over but his anger would remain.[33]

Lieutentant Marcus Green of Company O detailed the complete action in a letter penned to his parents on 30 November.

---

[31] William Francis Shine, diary, 29 November entry.

[32] Diary of Ivy Thompson, in *Phillips Georgia Legion, Confederate Reminiscences and Letters 1861–1865*, 22 vols. (Atlanta: Georgia Division United Daughters of the Confederacy, 1998) 8:155.

[33] Ibid., 156.

We was ordered into line night before last about Eight
Oclock to support the 24th Ga Regt while it attacked the
(Federal) picket line & drove it in & dug rifle pits. It took them
till 3 oclock next morning. We had to ly there without any fire.
We built some fires but the Enemy Shot at us. We had to put
them out & lie close to the ground to keep from getting killed.
We nearly frozed. At 3 oclock we got orders to go to Camps but
we had to be back there into line by 5 to assault the Enemys
works. So we was back at 5 oclock & formed into Columns of
Regiments & our Legion was put in front to Charge the Yankee
fort. So just at daylight we was ordered to forward. So here we
went through the pine tops & brush of evry kind the enemy had
cut to keep us from charging them. So we Charged up to the
fort but we couldn't clime over the top of the fort & the balance
of our Brigade & other Brigades come to our support but we all
couldn't take the fort because we couldn't get into it. They
would shoot every man down that did get on top of it. So we had
to fall back. Col S Z Ruff Commanding Brigade was killed.
Major Hamilton got his arm broke. Capt Johnson killed. Lieut
Bowie flesh wound to the thigh. George Channel killed. Wash
Eubanks killed. Tom White lost a leg. Ford Johnson severely
wounded. (Hiram) Harrison severely wounded in head by
canister ball & two of our comp missing. I don't know whether
they are killed or wounded. Many other wounded. Capt Lemons
18th Ga killed. Bill Stanley [rest of line illegible]. Walter
Manning Co C Phillips Legion who is a Lieut lost a leg & the
Dr thinks he will die. The Yankees had wires all around the fort
to throw us as we come up & they used Hand Grinades on us
that is things like bom shells only they throw them over the fort
with their hands. Our color bearer planted our Colors about
halfway up the side of the fort. I tell you if we could have got
over it we would have don it. Ours, Hemphreys [Barksdales Old
Brigade], Briants [Simmes Old Brigade] and Anderson or old
Tigs Brigades are the ones that charged. All got to it & fought
some time but had to fall back which we done in a hurry I tell
you. But thank God by doing some of the fastest running a man
ever did I got out safe. But it was a close place. I did think &

now know that Longstreet acted very foolish to charge that hill. But [illegible] his way it taken lots of good men. [Illegible] gave him the name he has got. I don't think he is [illegible] General.[34]

The assault on Fort Sanders over, Longstreet and Burnside arranged for the care of the dead and wounded. Burnside chivalrously allowed the Rebels use of his wagons and facilities. Grant sent a message of congratulations to Burnside, purposely allowing the message to fall into the hands of the Confederates. The message also stated that Sherman was on his way toward Maryville and Knoxville. Old Pete called off the siege and made plans to move toward Virginia. By 4 December, Longstreet's men were headed east.[35]

The Phillips Legion had suffered dearly at Fort Sanders. On 29 November, twelve men had been killed, six mortally wounded, twenty wounded, and forty-nine captured. Five of the captured men would later die in prison. Captain James Johnson of Company L was killed; Lieutenant Colonel Joseph Hamilton was shot in the arm; and Lieutenant George Manning of Company C was wounded, lost an arm, and was captured. Lieutenant Gus Tomlinson of Company D and Lieutenant Richard Deignan of Company F were captured; Lieutenant American Ford Johnson (brother of Captain James Johnson) of Company L was severely wounded and captured; Lieutenant Robert McCown of Company L was hit in the neck; and Lieutenant Theophilus Bowie of Company O was also wounded. Six men of Company F, the Irish Company, were captured, later switched sides, and enlisted in the United States Army as "Galvanized Yankees." They ended the war fighting Indians in the west. Colonel Solon Z. Ruff, the acting brigade commander, was killed in the ditch, and Lieutenant Colonel N. L. Hutchins replaced him.[36]

Longstreet began preparing his troops for the long trek back to Virginia. They would spend a long, cold, hungry winter in the

---

[34] M. L. Greene to father and mother, 30 November 1863, private collection of Mrs. S. Harden, Jasper GA.

[35] G. Seymour, *Divided Loyalties*, 164. Also see S. Woodworth, *Six Armies in Tennessee: The Chickamauga and Chattanooga Campaign* (Lincoln: University of Nebraska Press, 1998) 211.

[36] Compiled Service Records, M266, rolls 592–600.

mountains of East Tennessee before returning to General Lee's army. The blood and suffering would continue.

Chapter 13

The Burning Bush to Spotsylvania

*"The boys raised the old rebel yell and went on them like a
duck on a June bug."*

With the disastrous Knoxville campaign almost over, on 2 December 1863 the men of the Phillips Georgia Legion's infantry battalion were moving their camp about a half-mile away from the city of Knoxville. Just days earlier on 29 November, they had taken a pounding at Fort Sanders. They now headed northeast toward Virginia, where Longstreet intended to reunite with Lee and the Army of Northern Virginia. On the night of 3 December, legion soldier and diarist Tom Mitchell found himself on picket duty in a pouring rain. The following day, he documented the legion's march north on Bristol Road: "Friday, 4th. Legion was relieved at Seven P.M. Marched to camps and formed with the Brigade. Marched to north of Knoxville on Bristol Road, seven miles and camp. Enemy said to be coming in our rear from Loudon."[1]

The legion continued its long, tedious march, Mitchell faithfully recording each major event. The men camped near Blaines Crossroads on 5 December and on the following day arrived at camp southwest of Rutledge. They passed by Bean's Stage Station and Rocky Springs, camping on 8 December near Moorsburg. By Wednesday, the following day, they had marched some 6 miles toward Rogersville and camped again, resting their sore feet and preparing to meet the pursuing Federals. They were not long in coming, arriving 14 December 1863 at an old stagecoach stop and fortified station named after a long-forgotten character named William Bean. Bean's Station was located at the intersection of two main stage routes and was the site of a hotel that boasted the largest tavern between Washington City and New Orleans.

---

[1] Diary of Thomas M. Mitchell, 4 December 1863 entry, private collection of Mr. R. D. Thomas, Chattanooga TN.

Although the Phillips Legion was not engaged, the men were ready. Mitchell recorded this minor episode: "Monday 14th, Marched at Seven A.M. pass Moorsburg and Rocky Springs, skirmishing in Front. Formed a line of Battle near Bean's Station. There was heavy Cannonading and skirmishing. Brigade was not engaged. Camp west of Beans Station on Road leading to Clinch Gap."[2]

The Federals, under the command of Major General John G. Parke, had been pursuing Longstreet's troops as they marched toward Rogersville. Parke was wise enough to pursue but keep his distance. He sent Brigadier General J. M. Shackleford, with 4,000 cavalry and infantry, to search for the Confederates. By 13 December, Shackleford approached Bean's Station. Longstreet was ready, determined to entrap the Federals in the mountain gap on the road to Tazewell and then capture Bean's Station.

In a letter to General Samuel Cooper at Richmond, Longstreet reported:

> Your dispatch of the 14th is received. On the 14th instant I made an effort to intercept the enemy at this point. We were unsuccessful owing to bad roads and a rise in the Holston, which delayed our column of the cavalry some twelve hours. The enemy have escaped in the direction of Knoxville. We captured sixty-eight of his wagons, about forty loaded with sugar and coffee and other stores. We had a sharp skirmish at this place, losing about 200 men, chiefly from Johnson's division. I regret to report General Gracie as having received a severe flesh wound. We shall be obliged to suspend active operations for want of shoes and clothing.[3]

The effort failed. The Federals had taken position inside the three-story hotel and managed to withstand the Confederate assaults. This small confrontation petered out when the Federals withdrew from Bean's Station and retreated to Blain's Crossroads. Heavy rains as well as

---

[2] Ibid., 14 December 1863.
[3] *OR*, ser. 1, vol. 31, pt. 3, pp. 817, 818.

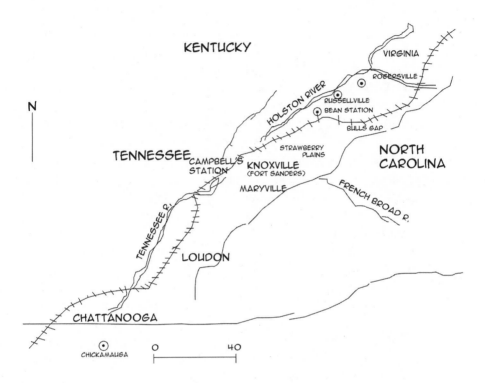

Phillips Legion with Longstreet in East Tennessee, 1863–1864.

snow and sleet now proved formidable enemies. Roads were mired, the thick mud sucked shoes off the troops' feet, and a general state of misery set in. Although Longstreet's I Corps remained in east Tennessee until late April 1864, for all practical purposes the battle at Bean's Station marked the end of the Knoxville campaign. On the following day, Mitchell noted the end of this skirmish: "Tuesday 15th Enemy having fallen back last night we marched north of Clinch Gap road and camp."[4]

On 20 December, the legion marched south to a position near Long's Ferry on the Holston River and camped. By 23 December they had crossed the East Tennessee and Georgia Railroad near Russellville and began preparing an encampment for winter quarters. Wednesday, 23 December, found the troops building chimneys for their tents. They remained there until Thursday, 30 December 1863, when they were sent out as guards for the brigade's wagon train on a foraging expedition. They covered quite a bit of territory that day, camping near Parrottsville. They had completed their mission by 4 January 1864 and escorted the wagons back to camp at Russellville.[5] Longstreet remained determined to capture Knoxville, requesting reinforcements from Richmond. These were denied but Longstreet held his army in place and continued to lobby for an attack on Knoxville. From Strawberry Plains, Tennessee, on 31 December 1863, Federal General Parke reported the results of a reconnaissance to Major General E. E. Potter:

> General: I have just received reports of reconnaissance up the Rutledge road. The party went 4 1/2 miles beyond Bean's Station. Here they found a rebel hospital with a number of wounded, too badly hurt to be moved. They took 4 prisoners—part of the hospital attendants. They learned that Jones's command was at Mooresburg, and Vaughn's, 2 miles in the rear of Mooresburg. The enemy's pickets were about a mile beyond, as reported by citizens. Citizens reported that the main body of the enemy was at Rogersville and Morristown, but could not specify what troops were at these points. The party that went up the river road met a small party of rebels at Turley's

---

[4] Thomas M. Mitchell, diary, 15 December 1863.
[5] Ibid., 4 January 1864.

Mill, and were fired upon by parties from the south side of the Holston, all important points of which are guarded from Turley's Mill up to Noe's or Marshall Ferry, where, it is reported, the enemy has one regiment, with artillery, and rifle-pits.[6]

That Rebel hospital Parke mentioned was probably the one set up by surgeons J. B. Clifton and William F. Shine, as recorded in the men's journal. Dr. Shine served as the surgeon for the Phillips Legion Infantry Battalion and, later, the brigade. He noted in his journal: "Went to Bean's Station, a distance of about 1/4 of a mile from camp, and established a hospital in the large brick house which is there. We found several dead Yankees who were killed in the house by our artillery a day or two ago when we had the fight."[7]

January through March 1864 involved continual movement for the legion troops. On Friday, 15 January, the men departed their encampment and headed west in the general direction of Morristown, where they camped. Three days later they returned to their Russellville camp. On 28 January they were again ordered west to meet another Federal probe and reached a point 5 miles west of Dandridge on the 29th. Next morning they heard artillery fire in the distance but observed no Federals. That evening they fell back to Dandridge and made camp. The threat having passed, on 31 January they marched back to their camp at Russellville. After a brief respite, on 10 February they again headed west, camping the next evening at New Market Station on the East Tennessee and Virginia Railroad. Monday, 22 February, found them marching east back through their old camp at Russellville to Bull's Gap; by month's end they were camped at Greenville. After spending two weeks at Greenville they were ordered back north to the railroad near Bull's Gap, arriving there on 15 March. Five days later they were once more back in camp at Greenville. On 28 March they began the move that would eventually return them to Virginia. They reached Bristol, Tennessee, on the final day of March and made camp.[8]

---

[6] *OR*, ser. 1, vol. 31, pt. 1, p. 664.

[7] Diary of William Francis Shine and J. Clifton, 16 December 1863, North Carolina State Archives, Archives and Records section, Private Manuscripts Collection, call no. PC 589, Raleigh.

[8] Thomas M. Mitchell, diary, 15 January–31 March 1864 entries.

Despite the brief respite from fighting, the troops were not without troubles. In a letter to his sister dated 5 April 1864 at Bristol, Lt. Daniel B. Sanford of Company A reported an ugly incident that involved a few members of the legion's infantry battalion:

> We had a rather disgraceful and sad affair in our brigade last Saturday night. Our rations have been and are extremely short; meat about one day in seven, and a party of some four or five hundred concluded they would charge the commissary department at Bristol and procure a supply. The provost guard ordered them to disperse but they heeded not the order upon which the guard fired on them, killing four, one being a First Lieutenant and wounding twelve others, some mortally. I regret that such an outrage should have occurred in the brigade. The men were hungry I have no doubt but they had a sufficiency of bread to keep them from starving or even suffering much. There was none of our company in this outrage and but eight or ten of the Legion concerned in it. All of the aggressors are now under arrest and some of them are handcuffed. Such affairs as this does much to encourage the Yankees for it is impossible to keep it from them in a Union country like this. They think we are starving when such reports reach them but to be candid, I think myself, supplies for the army is becoming a very serious matter but as for me I am willing to live on roots and acorns if we can only achieve our independence.[9]

Wednesday, 13 April 1864, was a banner day for the men of the Phillips Legion. They boarded the cars in Bristol at 5:00 A.M. and rested their feet until their arrival the next day at Lynchburg, Virginia. There they changed cars, arriving at Charlottesville around 7:00 P.M. They camped here until Sunday, 17 April, departing at 7:00 A.M., crossing the Roxana River near Charlottesville and the Orange and Alexandria Railroad at station number 20, before finally camping at nearby Grace Church. The following day the legion troops decamped at 6:00 A.M.,

---

[9] Daniel Benjamin Sanford to Sister, 5 April 1864, Bristol TN, private collection of Mr. Sanford Penticost, Atlanta.

crossed the Orange and Alexandria Railroad again at station number 19, passed through Mechanicsville, and camped just south of Gordonsville.

On Friday, 19 April, General Robert E. Lee reviewed the entire division (now under the command of General Joseph B. Kershaw). All of Longstreet's I Corps was on the field. On Wednesday, 4 May, they were on their way to do battle in the Wilderness. They decamped at 4:00 A.M. and around 9:00 P.M. crossed the Virginia Central Railroad just south of Milton Siding Camp near Ellis's Mill.

Thursday, 5 May, found the legion troops on the march at 3:00 A.M. Covering 16 miles on poor back-country roads, they camped at Richard's Shop about 8 miles west of Spotsylvania Court House. They could hear the ominous sound of cannonading in their front.[10] The legion, with Longstreet's I Corps, did not arrive on the scene until the following day, 6 May 1864. Mitchell briefly described the second day's fighting: "Friday 6th Leave Camp about 1 a.m. Arrived on the Wilderness Battle Field at 6 a.m. found the Enemy driving Our Troops back in confusion, Our Division drawn in line and Charge the Enemy driving the Enemy back at every Point. Brigade engaged Several times during the day. The Enemy has been driven back all along the Line to day."[11]

Friday, 4 May 1864, marked the first day of Lieutenant General Ulysses S. Grant's Overland Campaign.[12] Grant, newly arrived from the western theatre and promoted to lieutenant general in command of all Union armies, was to face General Robert E. Lee's Army of Northern Virginia in unrelenting combat that would bring horrendous casualties to both sides. The first major confrontation took place in a 17-square-mile area of Virginia real estate known as the "Wilderness," an area overgrown with vines, stunted trees, and creepers. The place was a dreary wasteland long known by Native Americans for its productive hunting. During the earliest days of white American settlement the pines and oaks had been destroyed to provide fuel for iron ore smelting. As time passed, a second level of growth—scrub trees, dense undergrowth, and thorny bush—replaced the old forest. It was enough to create the

---

[10] Thomas M. Mitchell, diary, 4–5 May 1864 entries.

[11] Ibid., 6 May 1864 entry.

[12] E. Steere, *The Wilderness Campaign* (Harrisburg PA: Stackpole Co., 1960) 1.

worst imaginable environment for the fight Grant and Meade hoped to avoid.[13]

On 4 May 1864, General Gouverneur Warren's V Corps was the first of the Army of the Potomac's corps to cross the Rapidan River at Germanna Ford. Warren's leadership ability had been questioned for his failure to carry through with Meade's orders to attack the powerful Confederate breastworks at Mine Run during the fall of 1863; this time he was determined to turn in an excellent performance. The VI Corps was next across the river. Commanded by Major General John Sedgwick, Grant had utmost confidence in this corps' leadership. Major General Winfield Scott Hancock crossed his II Corps at Ely's Ford, just 6 miles east of Germanna. This corps would take a terrible beating in the coming days. Grant had one more ace in the hole: Major General Ambrose E. Burnside's IX Corps. Burnside's men would initially remain behind to keep an eye on the Orange and Alexandria Railroad, from Manassas Junction south to Rappahannock Station.

Although outnumbered nearly two to one, Lee was ready. He had predicted Grant's crossing at Germanna Ford on his right and had the advantage of operating on interior lines. Lee had three corps and trusted his corps commanders: Lieutenant General Richard S. Ewell commanded II Corps, Major General Ambrose Powell Hill, III Corps, and Lee's "old war horse," Lieutenant General James Longstreet, I Corps. Lee's cavalry was in good hands. General James Ewell Brown Stuart had been and would continue to provide good service as Lee's "eyes and ears."

After his Rapidan crossing, Grant had to pause in the Wilderness to wait for his enormous supply train to catch up with the army. This was just what Lee had hoped for, and he put his infantry on the march immediately. Ewell would march on the Old Turnpike toward Chancellorsville; Hill would move parallel to Ewell along Orange Plank Road and both generals would engage the enemy. Simultaneously, Longstreet would move around the enemy's left flank on Catharpin Road.[14]

---

[13] Douglas S. Freeman, *Lee's Lieutenants*, 3 vols. (New York: Charles Scribner's Sons, 1944) 3:346–47.

[14] Gerald J. Smith, *One of the Most Daring of Men* (Murfreesboro TN: Southern Press, 1997) 107–110.

At this time the Phillips Legion troops were guarding I Corps' large wagon train. They probably itched to join the fighting but would be delayed with Longstreet until the next day, 6 May 1864. The legion and their brigade commander, General William Tatum Wofford, who had resumed command in January, would shine on this day. Remaining alert to unfolding events, Wofford learned that Hill had smashed head on into the Federal enemy and had been battered badly in the process. By day's end on 5 May, Hill's troops were scattered in a roughly perpendicular pattern to Plank Road, just west of the Brock Road intersection, while Lee was nearby at the Widow Tapp farm.

Longstreet knew he would have to reinforce Hill immediately. This would require I Corps to cease its flanking movement on Catharpin Road then turn left and strike Plank Road near Parker's Store. At 1:00 A.M. on 6 May, Wofford received orders to move his brigade.[15] The legion got underway at 2:00 A.M. due to their position as rear guard. The day of 6 May 1864 proved to be one of the most difficult days for commanders and troops on both sides. Extreme confusion, poorly timed attacks, and lack of coordination were the order of the day. To compound the stress of combat, muzzle flashes ignited fires in the dry brush and wounded soldiers were burned to death in spite of efforts to save them. The legion with Kershaw's division approached Plank Road only to be deafened by the roaring of artillery just ahead. General Hancock had launched a major attack on Hill's corps at 5:00 A.M. Heth and Wilcox divisions tried desperately to hold their ground but finally began to crumble.[16] Longstreet, who had become lost while looking for a shortcut, pushed Fields and Kershaw's divisions forward at double time. Fields's soldiers jogged to the left of Plank Road. Kershaw's men moved on the right. Sighting Tapp Farm ahead, Longstreet's troops threaded their way through disorganized elements of Hill's corps. It was around 6:00 A.M.[17]

---

[15] Ibid.

[16] Memoirs of Henry Heth II, in *Civil War History* (Kent OH: Kent State University Press, 1962) 300–26.

[17] Smith, *Most Daring of Men*, 109.

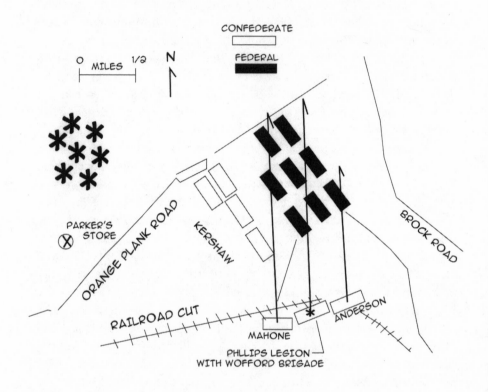

Phillips Georgia Legion in flank action, noon, 6 May 1864.

A. J. McWhirter described Wofford's brigade's experience in the Wilderness. McWhirter was a member of the 3d Georgia Sharpshooter Battalion (see Appendix). (Some of the legion's best troops had been assigned to this elite unit's Company F.) McWhirter wrote:

At the Wilderness five Yankees were taken prisoners with empty guns on the morning of 6 May 1864, as Wofford's Georgia brigade was returning from Tennessee to Virginia. The brigade was composed of the Eighteenth, Twenty-fourth and Sixteenth, Phillips and Cobb's Georgia Legions, Third Georgia Sharpshooters. The brigade came to the Wilderness on the Plank Road at double-quick time, where A. P. Hill had been fighting the day before. There was heavy skirmishing going on, the battalion was in front by the right flank, rear resting on the Plank Road, remainder of brigade went by the left flank, rear brigade, resting on battalion.[18]

Confederate III Corps was near collapse. Many of Hill's troops were streaming to the rear, flowing past Poague's artillery battalion positioned in the Tapp farm field. While Lee and others attempted to rally the demoralized men, Poague's gunners opened on the pursuing Federals. Hancock must be stopped. As Lee contemplated impending disaster, a brigade of Texans and Arkansans came into view. They were the leading edge of Longstreet's corps and were anxious to get into the fight. Caught up in the moment, Lee tried to lead the Westerners forward himself. The troops refused to advance in spite of Lee's desire to lead them until he would agree to move to the rear. Lee acquiesced and Field and Kershaw's divisions slammed into the Federals, driving them back several hundred yards east of the farm. The time was now around 8:00 A.M. Longstreet was the man of the hour. His countercharge had saved the day for the Army of Northern Virginia by halting the Federal advance and forcing back the enemy troops, often in hand-to-hand fighting. His leadership resulted in the recovery of the ground from which Hill had been driven earlier that morning. General Wofford had a

---

[18] A. J. McWhirter, "Gen. Wofford's Brigade in the Wilderness," *Atlanta Journal*, 21 September 1901, p. 2.

close call that would prove to be a dire omen for Longstreet: "A minie ball struck him in the breast, penetrated his overcoat, glanced upon a button and dropped into the lining of his vest...."[19] The fight was not over yet. Wofford's brigade was positioned on the far right and he allowed his troops some well-deserved rest following their morning attack. The 3ʳᵈ Georgia Sharpshooters were sent to scout the area, and there they discovered a valuable topographical feature. McWhirter explained: "We advanced a short distance, occasionally shooting, then we halted. The enemy was going by the left flank and that threw the battalion in the rear of brigade. We marched about two miles and came to an old railroad. The rails had never been laid. We went down this road for some distance, halted and fronted to the left and were ordered to forward...."[20]

Longstreet was probably informed of the railroad cut by both Wofford and his chief engineer, Major General Martin L. Smith. Longstreet knew that the unfinished railroad led past Hancock's left flank. Armed with this new information, Wofford proposed a bold plan to Kershaw and Longstreet. He would move his brigade east along the railroad bed and hit the Federals in the flank. Longstreet gave his assent but decided to expand the proposition by including G. T. Anderson and Mahone's brigades as well. Longstreet sent his chief of staff, Colonel Moxley Sorrell, to coordinate the attack. Other brigades would press the enemy in front after the flankers began to drive the Federals back.[21] Just a half-mile from Brock Road, the attack force wheeled left and deployed with Mahone on the left, Wofford in the center, and Anderson on the right. A. J. McWhirter of the 3d Georgia Sharpshooters recorded his memories of the next stage:

> The brigade struck the enemy on the flank and broke their line. Captain Strickland was in command of battalion. I said to him: "I see their line of battle; they are lying down." Captain Strickland gave the command to charge at the very top of his voice. The boys raised the old rebel yell and went on them like a duck on a June bug. Some few of them fired, and a good many of

---

[19] Smith, *Most Daring of Men*, 109.
[20] McWhirter, "Wofford's Brigade," p. 2.
[21] Smith, *Most Daring of Men*, 113–15.

them ran, throwing down their guns as they went; some lay flat on the ground.... The Yankees had another line of temporary works, and they made another stand. The Johnnies made no halt at all, and the enemy fled before them as they had done a short time before. There was one who would not surrender. His gun was empty, and he stood just in front of J. W. Kirk, whose gun was likewise empty, though Kirk had some advantage in loading. Both of them were doing their best to load quickly—it was a race of life and death. When Kirk, who was the first to load, fired on the Yankee, they were standing not more than five feet apart. The ramrod and ball went clear through his adversary's body, making a hole as big as a man's fist.[22]

The Phillips Legion troops were soon heavily engaged. They pushed the surprised enemy hard all the way to Brock Road, coming close to severing the Federal line. Even so, they had hurt the enemy badly. Around this time, disaster occurred. Riding forward on Plank Road at the head of fresh troops who would press the attack on the Federals, General Longstreet was accidentally shot by troops of Mahone's brigade. Severely wounded, "Old Pete" would remain out of action for many months. Several other officers were also killed or wounded. Popular South Carolina general Micah Jenkins was shot in the head and died the next day. Like Stonewall Jackson a year earlier, and in roughly the same area, Longstreet and his entourage had been shot accidentally by their own troops.[23]

By 4:00 P.M. the fighting had become disorganized, partly as a result of Longstreet's wounding. While Lee worked to organize a new attack, Hancock was able to rally his troops and entrench along Brock Road. Before being wounded, Longstreet had directed Wofford to shift his brigade back to the far right in hopes of repeating the success of his earlier flank attack. Lee attacked Hancock's position around 5:00 P.M. and the entrenched Federals cut the Confederates to pieces. The woods were on fire, as were the log breastworks on Brock Road. The stench of smoke and the acrid odor of burnt black powder, as well as the

---

[22] McWhirter, "Wofford's Brigade," p. 2.
[23] Gordon C. Rhea, *The Battle of the Wilderness, May 5–6, 1864* (Baton Rouge: Louisiana State University Press, 1994) 370–72.

screaming of wounded soldiers crying for help, some burning to death, was a scene of nightmarish proportions. Unsupported on the far right, Wofford disengaged, put out pickets, and rested his troops. This day of horror had finally ended.[24] In his field diary, Colonel Sorrell described his feelings: "The attack resulted in no decided success, the enemy not being dislodged, night coming on the long days struggle is closed—the most wearisome, severe and exciting battle in which I have yet participated...."[25]

The race for Spotsylvania Courthouse began a short time later, although neither Lee nor Grant was fully aware of the contest. Like a bulldog, Grant would not release his grip. He would pursue Lee no matter what the risk or the cost in casualties. The tiny crossroads at Spotsylvania Court House was to be the next scene for some of the most ferocious combat of the Civil War. The men of the Phillips Legion would likely remember 12 May 1864 for the rest of their lives.

The morning of 7 May 1864 was eerie. The Wilderness was shrouded by fog and smoke, beset by an unearthly calm that was particularly unnerving following the roar of the recent days' battle. Grant had decided to move his troops southeast to Spotsylvania Court House. Once settled there, he would be in control of the most direct route to Richmond. Lee would have to attack or block Grant in order to protect the Confederate capital. Grant decided that General Warren's V Corps would set out on Brock Road after darkness and begin the 10-mile march to Spotsylvania. Lee was not fooled. He suspected that his enemy might make such a move. Lee had his engineers prepare a cut through the heavily forested area to connect his right flank to a road leading to Spotsylvania. Major General Richard H. Anderson, now commanding the I Corps after Longstreet's wounding, would push his troops on the Confederate right flank by way of the cut toward Spotsylvania. Generals Ewell and Hill would follow Anderson.

The Federal march went poorly. The bluecoats were exhausted and choking from the swirling dust. The road was clogged with wagons and ambulances full of Federal wounded. By the time Meade arrived with Warren's troops at Todd's Tavern, just 5 miles from Spotsylvania, he

---

[24] Ibid.
[25] Moxley Sorrell, *Recollections of a Confederate Staff Officer* (Jackson TN: McCowat-Mercer, 1958) 44.

was astonished and furious to find his way blocked by Sheridan's cavalry under Brigadier General Wesley Merritt. Meade did not know there had been a cavalry fight. Merritt had driven Major General Fitzhugh Lee's division down Brock Road, where the Confederate cavalry held. Strangely, Sheridan had ordered Merritt to move back toward the tavern, allowing Fitz Lee to strengthen his position. Merritt was ordered to sweep the Rebels off the road but made little headway. Warren sent General Robinson's infantry to attack the Southerners and drive them away from their defenses. Lee's cavalry retired down the road, grudgingly yielding ground until falling into line on a low ridge known as Laurel Hill.

The situation for the Southern cavalry was fast becoming desperate. Pressed from the front by Warren's infantry, the men found that General James Wilson's Union cavalry division had slipped in behind them at Spotsylvania Court House. General J. E. B. Stuart called upon General Anderson to come up as rapidly as possible. Anderson quickly pushed Kershaw's division forward; Colonel John W. Henagan and General Benjamin Humphries's brigades deployed at Laurel Hill while Bryan and Wofford's Georgians drove on Wilson at the Court House. The Southerners made it to the field just in time to drive back Warren's attack. Meade rushed more troops forward but it was too late. The 17,000 Rebel soldiers of Ewell's corps were now settling in on Anderson's right. By the time darkness fell, the fighting had stopped. Lee had won the race to Spotsylvania, and the Federals were blocked.[26]

Legion Company B's Tom Mitchell described the day's experience: "Monday the 9th Marched all night last night to near Spotsylvania C. H. the enemy tried to flank our right while charging our front."[27] The legion arrived at Spotsylvania Court House on the morning of 9 May. A newspaper report recounted Wofford's movements:

> In the meantime, a brigade of the enemy's cavalry had passed entirely around the right of our forces, and occupied Spotsylvania Court House in the rear of Gen. Fitz Lee's division, Gen. Wofford was selected to dislodge this force. He at

---

[26] Time-Life Books, ed., *Voices of the Civil War: The Wilderness* (Alexandria VA: Time-Life Books, 1988) 86.

[27] Thomas M. Mitchell, diary, 8 May 1864 entry.

once determined to make an effort to capture the entire party. His brigade was moved rapidly in a circuitous route to the rear of the court house, being completely hidden from the enemy's view by the dense forest in the vicinity.[28]

Wofford was unsuccessful. He led his men through a heavily wooded area without attracting enemy attention and deployed his troops. At this very moment part of Field's division, unaware of Wofford's plan, appeared at the court house and advanced directly on the Federals. The bluecoats caught on immediately and retreated out of the trap. The only other major action on this day occurred around 3:00 P.M., when Warren's V Corps attacked the Rebels at Laurel Hill. Warren's troops were thrown back and badly mauled.[29] Wofford's brigade was placed in reserve for the next four days. Dr. Shine had established his infirmary on 6 May near Parker's Store on Plank Road where he and Dr. Clifton had received and cared for the wounded. On Sunday, 8 May, they reestablished the infirmary a few miles from Spotsylvania Court House. Shine noted, "The firing has been very slow until the afternoon, when it seemed to be a general engagement, though mostly artillery."[30]

General Robert E. Lee was an excellent engineer. He determined to protect the northern stretch of the Confederate lines around Spotsylvania Court House by building field fortifications and entrenchments. Unfortunately, he had to build along previously established lines and cope with dense woods. To the east of Anderson's I Corps, Johnson and Rode's divisions of Ewell's corps were positioned in a thumb-shaped salient projecting north about a mile with sides sloping southeast and southwest. Ewell believed the salient to be a good artillery position. This projecting bulge became known by the Rebel soldiers as the Mule Shoe. Lee put the troops to work building 3 miles of semicircular works with flanks on good defensive ground. The graycoats were short of tools, so they proceeded to scoop out the soil with flattened canteens, tin cups, sharp sticks, and even their hands. Others cut down trees in their front and built defensive abatis.

---

[28] *Atlanta Southern Confederacy*, 15 June 1864.
[29] Smith, *Most Daring of Men*, 116.
[30] Shine-Clifton diary, 9 May entry.

On 10 May 1864, Grant launched II, V, and VI Corps elements against Laurel Hill and the west side of the salient. The brunt of II and V Corps' attacks hit Fields's division of Anderson's corps and was stopped cold. Kershaw's division, posted east of Fields in the area between Laurel Hill and Ewell's salient, was not heavily engaged. For once the legion would "catch a break." A hand-picked group of VI Corps regiments under Colonel Emory Upton attacked Ewell's line on the western side of the salient. They succeeded in punching through the southern line but failed when reinforcements did not arrive on time. A sad note for the legion was the day's loss of Captain Fred Fuller of Company A. Connecticut-born Fuller had been in the war from the start. Before the war he had been a successful attorney and editor of the local paper in Greene County.

On 11 May the skies opened with a continuous, cold rain, drenching the miserable troops on both sides. General Grant remained determined. He wrote Washington that he would "fight it out on this line if it takes all summer."[31]

At dawn on 12 May, Grant sent Hancock's crack II Corps crashing over the top of the salient. They overran the top part of the Mule Shoe and captured most of General Edward Johnson's division. Lee counterattacked with numerous brigades and halted the enemy advance, pushing them back toward the captured upper portion of the salient. Ramseur and Wofford were sent in to assist in plugging the gap on the western side of the salient. The legion plunged into the fight wholeheartedly. Wofford's troops joined with Rode's brigades in the hand-to-hand fighting. Another downpour, lasting until 2:00 A.M., added to the mud and misery. The fighting was horrendous. In many places the forces were fighting from opposite sides of the same earthworks, only feet apart. Corpses lay in piles and the wounded drowned in waterlogged trenches. The combatants would later describe this action as Hell on Earth, and the tip of the salient would ever-after be known as the "Bloody Angle."

Dr. Shine observed: "Still it continues to rain. Last night about 11 o'clock, we received orders to be ready to move at a moment's notice, but did not move. The fighting commenced by day light this morning, and continued all day with the greatest severity. All agree that the fight

---

[31] *OR*, ser. 1, vol. 36, pt. 2, p. 627.

to day has been the most desperate fight of the war. The fight continued all night without the slightest cessation, and until about sun rise this morning. It is still raining and the roads are in a very bad condition."[32] Following 12 May, the legion remained with Wofford's troops in the Spotsylvania entrenchments. Private Mitchell described the scene: "Sunday May 15th Two miles north west of Spotsylvania C. H. We have been under fire of the enemy every day more or less since the 6th instant. We have met the enemy in all his movements he has been charging our works with very heavy loss to them."[33]

Phillips Legion casualties from 6–16 May added up to fourteen killed and sixty-three wounded. Four of the wounded would die shortly after the battle. Much of the detailed information for legion casualties was gleaned from period newspaper accounts, which do not indicate where soldiers fell. Roughly 60 percent of their losses occurred on 6 May in the Wilderness; the bulk of the remaining casualties were suffered on 12 May at Spotsylvania during the counterattack up the west leg of the Mule Shoe.[34] Many of the 12 May casualties were likely incurred in a poorly advised charge out of the west side of the salient at 4:00 P.M. Lieutenant R. J. Wilson of Cobb's Legion wrote of this attack:

The battle raged with great fury till about 4 o'clock P.M. When it was thought the enemy had left our front, our Brigade was ordered forward over our fortifications, which order was promptly executed. The missiles of death were flying thick and fast. We had at that time advanced, I suppose, a distance of about one hundred yards in front of our works when it was discovered that the enemy was in too strong force for us and we were ordered to fall back."[35]

General Grant would continue to maneuver around the Confederation position at Spotsylvania, stubbornly seeking an opening

---

[32] Shine-Clifton diary, 13 May entry.

[33] Thomas M. Mitchell, diary, 15 May 1864 entry.

[34] Compiled Service Records, National Archives micropublication, M266, rolls 592–600, Georgia Department of Archives and History, Morrow GA; J. T. Hackett, "Casualties—Wofford's Brigade," *Richmond* (VA) *Enquirer*, 2 July 1864, p. 2.

[35] R. J. Wilson to Mr. John White, 23 May 1864, repr. in Lt. R. J. Wilson, obituary, *Athens* (GA) *Southern Watchman*, 13 July 1864, p. 3.

for another assault. On 14 May he shifted II and VI Corps from the north end of his line for an attack on Lee's right flank, but the skies opened and the assault had to be postponed. Lee, alerted by this movement, shifted Anderson's corps from their Laurel Hill entrenchments on his left flank to the far right of his line between Massaponax Church Road and the Po River. On the evening of the following day, the legion marched south to a camp in a pine grove near the Po River. Stymied, Grant positioned II and VI Corps back around to his right and attacked Ewell's men, who on the morning of 18 May were entrenched across the base of the old Mule Shoe salient. Diarist Mitchell noted that the Phillips Legion marched back north as support. However, Ewell's troops easily repelled the Federal attack and the legion returned to its camp near the Po that same evening.[36]

Receiving what appeared to be reliable intelligence from his cavalry, General Lee attempted to slip around Grant's northern flank in order to cut his supply line back to Fredericksburg. Ewell's corps was selected for the attack and moved out of their trenches on 19 May. The men of the Phillips Legion, along with the rest of Kershaw's division, were sent to occupy the position across the base of the Mule Shoe while Ewell marched north. Ewell's assault was poorly executed and his men were driven back. The legion returned to its pine grove camp near the Po River.

Grant finally realized the truth: Lee had stalemated him at Spotsylvania. He began moving his army east and south late on 20 May in another attempt to get around Lee's right flank. Lee countered immediately, as he always seemed to sense his opponent's next moves, and started his army south on the next day.

The opening phase of Grant's Overland Campaign had ended. Like two angry bulls, Grant and Lee would meet again—first on the banks and surrounds of the North Anna River and then at a place oddly named Cold Harbor. Both blue and gray soldiers would quickly learn there was nothing cold about it.

---

[36] Thomas M. Mitchell, diary, 18 May 1864 entry.

Chapter 14

The Inverted "V" to Cold Harbor

*"I have escaped so far without being hit and I hope I will get
through this Campaign safe though the Minnie Balls have
whistled around my head and the bursting shells have thrown
dirt all over me."*

In spite of his fatigue after an all-night march, Thomas Mitchell did not forget to scribble in his diary on 22 and 25 May 1864. Many of his entries reflect his railroad experience with the Memphis and Charleston Railroad in Huntsville, Alabama, before he enlisted in the Phillips Legion in 1862. He had uncommon knowledge of Southern railroads and often noted their locations when marching with the legion. Early Sunday morning, 22 May 1864, he was exhausted but alert enough to jot down a few lines before arriving near Hanover Junction just below the North Anna River. His friends must have noticed his hangdog appearance. He had just learned that General Joseph Johnston had fallen back from Dalton, Georgia, leaving his family behind enemy lines: "Sunday 22nd left Pine Grove Camp last night and marched until day light, rest three hours then march again. Cross South Anna River [Mitchell meant the North Anna River] on a Bridge just above where the Richmond and Fredericksburg R.R. [Richmond, Fredericksburg, and Potomac Railroad] crosses it. Camp just on south side of river, it being about three miles from Hanover Junction."[1]

By 22 May 1864, the battle for Spotsylvania Court House was over but Grant remained as determined as ever to continue pushing Lee south, regardless of the cost. The loss in lives had been high for both sides but Grant knew he could replace his fallen soldiers, whereas Lee was reaching the end of his human assets. If the war continued with equal losses for the Union and the Confederacy, the South was doomed

---

[1] Diary of Thomas M. Mitchell, 22 and 25 May 1863 entries, private collection of Mr. R. D. Thomas, Chattanooga TN.

to defeat. Grant was not about to change his strategy. He would continue to attack Lee until the Army of Northern Virginia finally collapsed.[2] Grant hoped Lee would make some error Grant could turn to his advantage. In fact, Lee almost made just such an error. Sure that Grant was headed further east to cross the Pamunkey River, Lee rested his troops below the North Anna River and issued no orders for his troops to entrench the river line. Henagan's South Carolina brigade, stationed in a small fort on the north side of Chesterfield Bridge, was the only force guarding the river.[3]

The Union army was on the move on the night of 23 May 1864, arriving at Mount Carmel that evening. Meade was ordered to move his troops from their position at Mount Carmel Church at 5:00 A.M. and cross the North Anna River if the Confederates had done so. Hancock's II Corps readied itself march to Chesterfield Bridge upstream from the Fredericksburg and Richmond Railroad across the North Anna. Burnside's IX Corps was to head to Ox Ford, upstream from Hancock. Warren's V Corps was marching further upriver to Jericho Mills, some 4 miles from Chesterfield Bridge. VI Corps would then march behind Warren. By early afternoon, Warren had reached Jericho Mills and the Federals were surprised to see no Rebels dug in on the south bank. Warren pushed Sweitzer's brigade of Griffin's division across the river to hold the crossing. The entire corps then made its way across on a newly laid pontoon bridge. The Federals formed line of battle just half a mile from the river bank, with Crawford's division on the left, Griffin's in the center, and Cutler's coming up to form on the right. A. P. Hill reacted by moving Cadmus Wilcox's division up from Anderson's Station on the Virginia Central Railroad in an attempt to drive the Federals back across the river. Unfortunately, Hill did not realize he was facing the entire V Corps. Union General Lysander Cutler's division had been the last to cross the North Anna River and was not yet in position to receive the attack. His troops fell back with Rebels on their tail. The Southerners ran into Federal artillery and were forced to withdraw to the Virginia

---

[2] Gordon C. Rhea, *To the North Anna River* (Baton Rouge: Louisiana State University Press, 2000) 155–57; US War Department, comp., *The War of Rebellion: A Compilation of the Official Records of the Union and Confederate Armies*, 128 vols. (Washington DC: Government Printing Office, 1880–1901) ser. 1, vol. 36, pt. 2, pp. 206, 207.

[3] Rhea, *To the North Anna River*, 288.

Central Railroad. Skirmishing continued for the remainder of the day but ended when VI Corps arrived on the scene at Jericho Mills.[4]

Hancock formed his corps on the heights a mile north of the North Anna River, with his left under General John Gibbon abutting the Richmond, Fredericksburg, and Potomac Railroad and his right under General David Birney west of Telegraph Road. Birney was confident he could take the bridge and talked his superiors into allowing the attempt. Two brigades from his division attacked at 6:30 P.M. and overran Henagan's brigade north of Chesterfield Bridge, driving the South Carolinians to the south bank. The Confederates were able to maintain control of the south end of the bridge; they tried to burn it but all efforts failed. Further downstream Gibbon prepared to charge across the railroad bridge but alert Southern troops anticipated the attack and burned the bridge. On arrival at Ox Ford, a mile west of Telegraph Road, Burnside found the Rebels so strongly entrenched on the south bank of the North Anna that he abandoned any notion of attacking the heavily fortified position.[5]

That evening Lee held a conference to decide his next move. The North Anna line had been breached and the Union V Corps had a strong lodgement on the south bank, threatening Lee's left flank. It seemed that retreat was in order but Lee was reluctant to give up the key rail link at Hanover Junction. Lee's chief engineer proposed that position be taken on high ground running southwest from Ox Ford to Little River and another line to the east running from Ox Ford to the railroad just north of Hanover Junction. The position would take the form of an inverted V, giving Lee the advantage of interior lines. With the point resting on the river at Ox Ford, the position also offered the possibility that Grant might split his force to operate separately against the eastern and western legs. Lee liked the possibilities of the plan and ordered it done. Hill's corps would man the western leg, Anderson's I Corps would hold the upper part of the eastern leg, and Ewell's troops would guard the lower part of the same leg above and east of Hanover

---

[4] Ibid., 304–17.
[5] Ibid., 300–303.

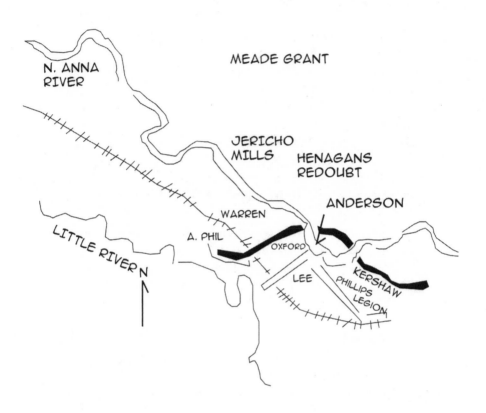

Phillips Legion on right side of inverted V.

Junction.[6] The Phillips Legion would be posted in woods on the upper eastern leg of the V formation, about a half-mile below Ox Ford.

All information coming in to Grant and Meade suggested that the Rebels were in retreat to the South Anna, and orders were issued for pursuit. Hancock would advance down the railroad and Telegraph Road toward Hanover Junction. Burnside would cross at Ox Ford and operate on Hancock's right. Warren and Wright would come down from Jericho Mills on the far right. It soon became apparent that not all the Confederates were in headlong retreat. Hancock's troops crossing at Chesterfield Bridge came under heavy artillery fire from Southern guns at the tip of the V formation just east of Ox Ford. The Federals were able to cross but it was a harrowing experience. Burnside, at Ox Ford, faced Southerners dug in atop high bluffs with artillery support. An attack appeared to be suicidal. Burnside found another ford upstream at Quarles Mill and recommended a flanking movement. He would send one division east to cross Chesterfield Bridge and another west to cross at Quarles Mill. The two divisions would then march west and east and pinch off the troublesome Confederates at Ox Ford. Convinced Burnside faced only a rearguard contingent, Grant approved and ordered the corps on the eastern and western flanks to continue pressing south while Burnside eliminated the stubborn pocket of resistance at Ox Ford. Grant was falling into Lee's trap.

Burnside's pincer movement quickly ran into fierce resistance from both legs of the Southern formation. Potter's division attacking west from Chesterfield Bridge ran into a hail of fire, dropped back, and dug in. The lead brigade of Crittenden's division crossed upstream at Quarles Mill. Led by "politician turned general" James H. Ledlie, it advanced without waiting for support and attacked Mahone's strongly entrenched division. The result was predictable. Ledlie's men tumbled back in disarray, having suffered 220 casualties.[7]

The Confederate battle line was a dream come true for any military engineer. In order to reinforce his left or right, Grant would have to pull troops back across the North Anna River, march past the rear of

---

[6] Noah Andre Trudeau, *Bloody Roads South: The Wilderness to Cold Harbor* (Boston: Little, Brown and Company, 1989) 241–43.

[7] Rhea, *To the North Anna River*, 338–39.

Burnside's corps at Ox Ford, and cross the North Anna again. His army was neatly sliced into three parts. He could not break the point of the V formation at Ox Ford. Further, he could not put all of his troops into action at any time without crossing the river twice. General Lee, on the other hand, had excellent interior lines and could easily move troops and supplies back and forth, up and down, as needed. By 24 May, Lee the master tactician was ready—but he was also extremely ill, prostrated with a severe case of dysentery and exhausted from two weeks without rest. He was further crippled because Generals Hill and Ewell were also near total collapse, Ewell also from dysentery and Hill from an unspecified disorder. General Anderson's lack of command experience at corps level added to Lee's woes.[8]

The window of opportunity for Anderson and Ewell to pounce on Hancock's isolated Federals now began to close. The ever-reliable Hancock had been pushing his troops south and sent one of Gibbon's brigades to probe the Rebel position. Union General Thomas Smyth's troops ran head-on into Ewell and Anderson's corps, drawing Gibbon's entire division into a fierce fight near the Doswell plantation. Gibbon's troops made some headway until Grimes's brigade halted Gibbon's men, using bayonets to force the Federals back. Drenched by rainstorms, the thoroughly miserable soldiers on both sides ended combat operations around midnight. It rapidly became apparent to Grant that he was facing a determined, well-entrenched foe. It began to dawn on the stubborn Midwesterner that Lee's entire army might be positioned between the wings of his army.

The Phillips Legion troops, located in a heavily wooded area on the right leg of the V formation, were not attacked and did not engage in the fighting on 23 and 24 May. Mitchell's diary entry suggested that they remained in place: "Tuesday the 24th, we formed our Brigade line last night just above Wagon Road Bridge. The Enemy having gained possession of the Bridge yesterday, was some Fighting to day on our right and left. None in our Front." [9]

On the night of 25 May, Grant decided to pull his troops back to the north side of the river in preparation for another movement around Lee's right. Lee anticipated this move and began preparing his army for

---

[8] Trudeau, *Bloody Roads South*, 241–43.
[9] Thomas M. Mitchell, diary, 24 May 1864.

another march. The Federals skillfully disengaged on 27 May and moved off to the east.

Mitchell notes that the Federals did not attack the legion on Thursday, 26 May, but the troops could hear cannonading and were aware of some skirmishing. On the following day, Mitchell states that the enemy troops had retired the previous night from the bridge, and the legion soldiers marched south along the railroad to Ashland, where they turned east and camped after a 6-mile march.[10]

Lieutenant Jesse M. McDonald of infantry Company E wrote his wife, describing the 27 May legion casualties at Hanover Junction, where his company had skirmished with enemy troops. The Company E soldiers ran into Hancock's rear guard as he was shifting his and part of Burnside's corps east across the North Anna:

> Today we are in camps for the first time in some days but I don't know how long we will remain here. While I am writing I can hear the Cannon fireing [sic] in front which is a token of hard times to the soldiers. This leaves me & the boys all well what of them that did not get wounded. In my last letter I gave you names of the wounded up to that time. Since then Company "E" got into a skirmish with the yanks at Hanover's Junction in which Sergt Forrest, Riley & James Blackwell got wounded. Forrest and Riley was seriously wounded. James Blackwell received a painful wound in the leg but not serious. The company lost ten men wounded since the fight began. Fortunately none have been killed so far.[11]

The legion "caught a break" in this fight. These three casualties were the only ones inflicted during the North Anna engagement and all three men would survive the war. Wounded Company E soldier Riley (H. W. Riley Jr.), mentioned by McDonald, was a son of the infamous Harrison W. Riley (1804–1874) of Dahlonega, Georgia. Riley Sr. styled himself a general although he never served in either the Confederate or the Georgia State forces. Purportedly the wealthiest man in White and

---

[10] Ibid., 26–27 May 1864.

[11] Jesse McDonald to Wife, 30 May 1864, private collection of Ms. Ione Crow, Chattanooga TN.

Lumpkin counties, he was reputed to have left a buried treasure that is still being sought today. Although he never married, he is also believed to have fathered over 100 children by both slave and white women. Our research in the 1880 US census located H. William Riley, Jr. in Bexar, Texas. His age matches that of Company E's Riley and his birthplace is shown as Georgia. The census-taker identified Riley as "mulatto." Was he a black Confederate soldier—possibly the offspring of Riley Sr. and one of his slaves?[12]

27 May 1864 found Grant's army marching down the north bank of the North Anna River. He was headed toward Hanovertown, where he planned to turn southwest, cross the Pamunkey River, and, barring any serious objections on the part of Lee's troops, insert his army between Lee and Richmond.

Hard marching and cavalry sparring occupied the next two days as Lee again managed to position his army between Grant and Richmond. On 29 May the Phillips Legion was part of Lee's defensive position behind Totopotomoy Creek near Pole Green Church, about 3 miles northeast of Mechanicsville. Lieutenant Jesse McDonald wrote his wife Sallie: "We are camped near the old Mechanicsville Battle Field. Grant's Army is down below here on the Pamunkey River. I expect we will run up against the yanks some of these days. If we do have to fight them again I hope we will fight them in our Breastworks."[13]

Grant's infantry pressed on to Totopotomoy Creek, arriving on the evening of 29 May. Lee's troops were positioned on the opposite bank with three corps in line of battle. Lee, wanting to prevent Grant from shifting further southeast, ordered General Early to probe the Federal left. Anderson's corps, including the legion, shifted into Early's earthworks as Early moved out on 30 May to attack the Federals near Bethesda Church. The assault was poorly managed and repulsed. The Federal path further south lay open and Sheridan's cavalry was already on the move.[14]

---

[12] Jimmy Anderson, *The Life and Times of Gen. Harrison W. Riley*, in *North Georgia Journal of History*, 4 vols. (Alpharetta GA: Legacy Communications, Inc., 1989) 1:166.
[13] Jesse McDonald to Wife, 30 May 1864, Crow collection.
[14] E. B. Furgurson, *Not War but Murder: Cold Harbor* (New York: Alfred A. Knopf, 2000) 67–71.

To make matters worse, Lee had received word that Federal reinforcements from the Army of the James were on their way to Grant. Lee appealed to Richmond for help, and he soon received the welcome news that General Robert F. Hoke's 7,000-man division was on its way north by rail to reinforce him. Lee directed Hoke to march his men to Cold Harbor.

Both commanders now seemed to have similar thoughts, recognizing the importance of the road intersection at Old Cold Harbor. Federal cavalry had moved on Cold Harbor on 31 May and routed a mixed force of Confederate infantry and cavalry. The Southern force retreated a mile west to a low ridge and dug in. Lee had already dispatched Anderson's I Corps to join Hoke's division at Cold Harbor to secure the crossroads, but the fighting had ended before they arrived.[15]

Before marching south to Cold Harbor on the 31st, the legion took two casualties from artillery fire while in line near Pole Green Church. Lieutenant Jack Reese's younger brother Benton had recently joined Company E; Corporal Noah White's younger brother Frank had just enlisted in the same company. Lieutenant Reese wrote a short message informing his aunt of the tragedy: "I have nothing good to write. White [Frank] of our company was killed about two hours ago and poor Benton was wounded in the left leg, below the knee. The doctor is now amputating it, the bone being broken. I am so sorry."[16]

Cold Harbor was oddly named. It was not near water, so it certainly was not a harbor. Perhaps the name had something to do with cold meals being served at a shack-like tavern in a nearby grove of trees. A traveler could lodge there but not get a hot meal. The five-road intersection was another matter. One road ran east to White House Landing, another northwest to Bethesda Church. These two of the five roads connected Grant to his supply base, allowing him to easily extend his left flank.[17]

Lee placed Hoke under Anderson's command. Their combined 21,000-man force should be enough to counter the Federal pressure. Anderson wanted to find out what was in his front and planned a two-

---

[15] Ibid., 81–82.

[16] A. J. Reese to Aunt, 31 May 1864, Rees/Reese Collection, Lumpkin County Library, Madeline K. Anthony Collection, series 3, box 23, folder 5.

[17] Gregory Jaynes, *The Killing Ground: Wilderness to Cold Harbor* (Alexandria VA: Time-Life Books, 1986) 150–51.

pronged reconnaissance in force for the morning of 1 June. Anderson began to move at dawn with the understanding that Hoke would also move forward on his right. Kershaw's division led Anderson's advance, with Kershaw's old brigade under Colonel Lawrence Keitt taking the lead. Anderson was confident he could handle Sheridan's cavalry and any other Federal troops on hand. Keitt was new to the Virginia army, having just led his large 20th South Carolina Regiment north from Charleston. The 20th had served in the Charleston defenses and had "seen the elephant" but lacked field combat experience. Without throwing out skirmishers, the rashly brave Keitt charged Sheridan's dismounted cavalry line on horseback with his men right behind him screaming the rebel yell. Unfortunately, he chose to charge across an open field where Federals occupied woods on his flank and to his front. Sheridan's cavalry were armed with repeating carbines and backed by horse artillery. In short order Keitt was shot off of his horse by massed, converging volley fire; his troops went to pieces, literally trying to burrow into the ground to escape the rain of fire. For some unexplained reason, Hoke did not bother to advance his troops. Bryan's brigade had supported the attack but had not gotten far enough into the action to sustain heavy casualties. Kershaw's division fell back and entrenched on a low ridge between Old and New Cold Harbor, with Hoke's division straddling the road connecting the two hamlets and Kershaw to his left. At the point where Kershaw's right met Hoke's left, a ravine bisected the ridge. This depression lay in a thicket of pines jutting well out in front of the line with swampy ground and a stream running through the gully.[18]

Wofford's brigade held the right of Kershaw's position with Brigadier General Thomas L. Clingman's brigade of Hoke's division about 100 yards away on the other side of the ravine. This left a gap of sizable proportion that portended trouble. Hoke placed Brigadier General Johnson Hagood's brigade in the woods between and in front of Wofford and Clingman's lines to seal the gap. Wofford's men began digging in immediately, cutting trees and brush to form defensive abatis. All afternoon the Southern troops watched as steady streams of Federal infantry arrived and moved into position. These troops consisted of the 30,000 men in six divisions of VI and XVIII Corps. Late in the

---

[18] Gerald J. Smith, *One of the Most Daring of Men* (Murfreesboro TN: Southern Heritage Press, 1997) 119, 120.

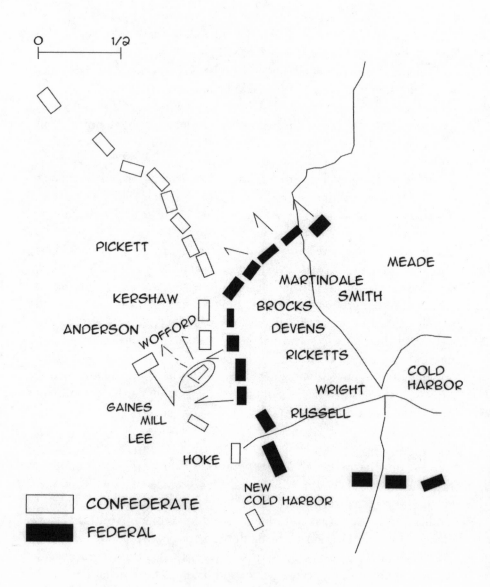

Phillips Legion with Wofford at Cold Harbor, 1 June 1864.

afternoon, the Federal line had extended so far south that it overlapped the right end of Hoke's division. Hoke reacted by pulling Hagood's brigade out of the wooded gap between Wofford and Clingman, sending it south to cover his right flank. Unfortunately, he did so without bothering to tell Wofford or Kershaw to his left.[19]

At 6:00 P.M. four Federal divisions attacked Kershaw and Hoke's divisions. Although outnumbered two to one, the Confederates had the advantage of good cover and shot apart the Federal advance. Drake's brigade of Deven's XVIII Corps division charged Wofford's position and reached the works before being repulsed. Now Barton's brigade of this same division moved up, maintaining strong pressure on the Georgians' front. Wofford's troops suddenly began to fall back. Brigadier General James Ricketts's troops of the 3rd Division of the VI Corps had appeared on Wofford's right flank and rear, having penetrated the open gap between Clingman and Wofford. The assault from both front and flank forced the collapse of Wofford's line and the Georgians scrambled rearwards as fast as they could run. The Phillips Legion on the left of the brigade was the last to flee, but the shock of being hit from the rear was too great and they also gave way. A number of Georgians were trapped and forced to surrender. This was a rough day for Wofford's Georgia boys, but the battle was far from over.[20]

With night quickly approaching, Confederate commanders rushed in reinforcements to seal off the half-mile-wide breach in their line. Kershaw sent the 2nd South Carolina Regiment and 3rd South Carolina Battalion from his old brigade and a single smoothbore cannon to attack the Federals. Striking the 112th and 48th New York Regiments in Wofford's old trenches, the Carolinians overwhelmed the New Yorkers and drove them back into the woods. On the other side of the breach, Hoke sent troops from Colquitt's Georgia brigade to attack the Federals on that side. Vicious fighting continued into the night as Kershaw brought additional troops in from his left, forming a new horseshoe-shaped defensive line around the breakthrough. Wofford rallied his men and placed them to the left rear of their original position, to the right of

---

[19] Gordon C. Rhea, *Cold Harbor: Grant and Lee, May 26–June 3, 1864* (Baton Rouge: LSU Press, 2002) 232.

[20] Ibid., 248–50.

Bryan's brigade. The Confederate line now formed an inward bulge surrounding the swampy, wooded ravine.[21]

The day had been nightmarish for both sides. The Federals had lost 2,200 men and had little to show for this except the (now sealed-off) breakthrough. Meanwhile the Confederates had lost 1,800 troops (500 of these in Wofford's brigade). The Phillips Legion suffered three men killed, thirteen wounded (one mortally), and twenty captured. Seven of the captured men would later die at the infamous Elmira prison. One poor soul, G. C. Smalley, did not even make it to prison. He was killed in a train wreck at Shohola, Pennsylvania, while being transported to Elmira.[22]

Grant decided to mount an even larger attack on 2 June. He ordered Hancock's 25,000-man II Corps to march to Cold Harbor. The next day, unfamiliar roads, heat, and blowing dust delayed the movement of Hancock's men. By mid-afternoon, Grant realized that preparations for an attack would not be completed until too late in the day and postponed the assault until 3 May. This delay worked to Southern advantage, as Lee was also shifting units south to face the rising Union threat. Grant's delayed attack gave Lee the opportunity to insure the arriving units were well placed and strongly entrenched. Thomas Mitchell noted an uneventful day for the legion: "Thursday June 2, 1864 Was much skirmishing and cannonading in our front to day. Nothing important occurred."[23] The Southerners made good use of the extra day, building a new fortified line to cover the ravine where the breakthrough had been made the day before. When completed on the evening of 2 May, they had created a masterful trap for any attacking Federals who might choose this approach again.[24]

On the evening of 2 May, Wofford's brigade was pulled back into the newly constructed works. Then, just before dawn on 3 May, they were moved out of the line and into a reserve position. Immediately after making this move, the Federals attacked. Mitchell wrote in his diary: "Friday 3rd Last night at this Point we straitened [sic] our line. This A.M. we was relieved to go to the rear and just after wards the Enemy

---

[21] Ibid., 264–65; Thomas M. Mitchell, diary, 1 June 1864 entry.

[22] Ibid., 266–68; Compiled Service Records, National Archives micropublication, M266, roll 599, Georgia Department of Archives and History, Morrow GA.

[23] Thomas M. Mitchell, diary, 2 June 1864 entry.

[24] Smith, *Most Daring of Men*, 124–126.

Charged our works. We reinforced the line just to the Left of the old position. Nothing but skirmishing after we get there. At night we go to the rear to rest."[25]

True to form, Grant launched his attack before dawn, at 4:30 A.M. on 3 May. Meade respected Lee's engineering skill, expecting to confront a complex and effective set of entrenchments. Brigadier General Gilman Marston's brigade and John H. Martindale's divisions of XVIII Corps would attack through the gap. The Rebel defenses were not visible because of the trees in the ravine, but Brooks and Martindale were told that the Rebel defenses would be weak.[26]

While Grant's massive assault utilized three corps and 50,000 troops across a wide front, we will focus on the action at the ravine. The Rebels held their fire to allow as many Federals as possible to move into the crossfire of musketry and artillery that had been prepared for them. When the Confederates opened up, the hapless Federals were torn to pieces by well-aimed rifle fire and canister rounds. The slaughter was so pronounced that it prompted General Evander Law to comment: "It was not war; it was murder."[27] The legion troops, in line behind Tige Anderson's Georgians, busied themselves loading muskets, passing them and ammunition forward. Succeeding attacks also failed and the survivors either dug into whatever cover was available or fell back into the trees of the ravine. It was all over in an hour. Kershaw sent a message to Anderson stating: "We are sustaining little loss. Damaging the enemy seriously. If they keep this game up long, we will have them."[28] The legion moved back into the works after the major Federal attacks had ended; there they engaged in skirmishing with pockets of isolated Federals as well as those in the tree line 200 yards away. The only legion casualty that day was its commander, twenty-five-year-old Lieutenant Colonel Joseph Hamilton, who was severely wounded in the neck. This was Hamilton's third wound of the war, but he would recover and rejoin the command in January 1865. Grant called off the attacks around noon,

---

[25] Thomas M. Mitchell, diary, 3 June 1864 entry.

[26] Smith, *Most Daring of Men*, 124–26.

[27] Evander Law, "From the Wilderness to Cold Harbor," in *Retreat with Honor*, ed. R. Johnson and C. Buel (New York: De Vinne Press, 1887) 4:141.

[28] Kershaw to Sorrel, 7:50 A.M., 3 June 1864, Edward Porter Alexander papers, Southern Historical Society collection, CB #3926, box 2, Wilson Library, Manuscripts Department, University of North Carolina, Chapel Hill.

leaving massive numbers of dead and dying Federals all along the front. The morning's attacks cost Grant 3,500 casualties while the defending Confederates suffered only 700.[29] Cold Harbor was a bloody victory for the Confederates, who stared at the horrific battlefield in utter disbelief.

The armies faced off for the next ten days, until the Confederates awoke on 13 June to find the Federals gone from their front. Grant had stolen a march on Lee, shifting to the peninsula below Petersburg and threatening the Confederate capital. Lee quickly pursued and the legion was on the road that same day. Mitchell scribbled in his diary: "There has been nothing but skirmishing and cannonading since we came to this line. Last night the Enemy retired from our Front. We crossed the Chickahominy River near Gains Farm and marched south ward and camped on the Fraziers Farm Battle-field. Can hear cannonading in our front."[30]

By 18 June 1864, the legion troops with Wofford's brigade were settled in the Petersburg defenses. The Overland Campaign was history. The war would degenerate into a grinding siege outside the major rail center at Petersburg, a few miles south of Richmond. The Phillips Legion, however, would not end its war here. In just a few months, they would march north to a beautiful valley they had visited before.

---

[29] Rhea, *Cold Harbor*, 362.
[30] Thomas M. Mitchell, diary, 13 June 1864 entry.

Chapter 15

From the Cockade City to
Cedar Creek and Back

*"It has often bin said that the darkest time is just before the
day. I think that everything looks gloomy now but still ever
thing may work out right yet."*

For the Phillips Legion infantrymen hunkered down in the trenches
around Petersburg, there seemed no end in sight to the cycle of blood
and boredom. Still, they had hope. During the spring of 1864, Lee's
Army of Northern Virginia and Grant's Army of the Potomac had
battered each other from one blood-soaked battlefield to another, only
to end up deadlocked before the city of Petersburg. Some soldiers on
both sides had thought that maybe, just maybe, if Lincoln were defeated
in November 1864, the peace democrats under McClellan would end it
all and they could go home. It was a forlorn hope and some probably
knew it—but they would soldier on.

By mid-June 1864, the four corps of the Army of the Potomac had
pulled out from their positions at Cold Harbor. Grant was determined
to move the war to a position south of the James River and hoped to
capture the key rail center at Petersburg before Lee realized what was
happening. The Federals crossed the Chickahominy and marched hard
for the James River. Near Windmill Point on the James, Federal
engineers laid a 2,200-foot-long pontoon bridge in just half a day. By 16
June, the Federals were on the south bank of the river close to
Petersburg. Grant's plan had worked perfectly. This time Grant was one
up on Lee, as Petersburg was only lightly defended by a handful of
militia and a few regular troops. The main assault would be made by
General W. F. Smiths' XVIII Corps. Smith's 15,000-man corps arrived
in front of Petersburg and deployed around noon. The massive
Confederate fortifications seemed to intimidate Smith, and he spent

most of the afternoon trying to figure out what he was up against. Receiving a dispatch from Grant that Hancock's II Corps was marching his way, Smith sent a message to Hancock requesting his participation in a night attack on the Confederate works. Grants also ordered Hancock to move to Smith's support as rapidly as possible. Hancock got his men moving toward Smith and sent a message at 5:00 P.M. that he was on his way. Smith finally got his attack underway at 7:00 P.M. and overran a stretch of Southern works without great effort or loss. Now, Smith's nerve seemed to fade with the daylight and he called off further attacks. Hancock's men arrived and relieved Smith's men in the captured works.

The following day, Confederate General Pierre G. T. Beauregard fell back to his final defensive line and moved troops from the Howlett Line at Bermuda Hundred. Placing them to guard the key approaches to Petersburg, he effectively blocked any action by Hancock. Disjointed Federal attacks occurred on the 16th and 17th, but Beauregard successfully juggled his small force and prevented a breakthrough. Lee finally realized that the bulk of the Federal army was south of the James and began shifting his troops to Petersburg. Beauregard had held the hesitant Federals and the siege Lee dreaded was on.[1]

The Phillips Legion, now commanded by Major John S. Norris in the absence of wounded Lieutenant Colonel Hamilton, was on the move with Kershaw's division. Kershaw's lead unit arrived in Petersburg around 7:30 A.M. on 18 June. Legion diarist Mitchell related their movement: "Saturday 18th Marched at Four A.M. Pass through Petersburg and form a line in the City Breast Works it being nearly South of Town. At night we was relieved and go in reserve near the City Water Works. Has been Skirmishing in our front all day."[2]

That morning found two of Lee's divisions settling in behind Beauregard's battered troops, who were so pleased to see relief coming their way that some cheered and openly wept. The legion with the rest of Kershaw's division relieved Bushrod Johnson's brigade while Field's division held the right. Beauregard now had 20,000 combat-ready soldiers, but Grant had almost 70,000 troops on hand.

---

[1] Noah Andre Trudeau, *The Last Citadel, June-April 1865* (Boston: Little, Brown and Company, 1991) 29–55.

[2] Diary of Thomas M. Mitchell, 18 June 1864 entry, private collection of Mr. R. D. Thomas, Chattanooga TN.

Petersburg, a vital port that received goods of all sorts from all over the world, was situated on the south bank of the Appomattox River. A small town of just over 18,000 souls, progressive and wealthy—Petersburg was a major hub of water and rail systems that linked the James River, Chesapeake Bay, Atlantic Ocean, and inland points south and west. Underscoring its strategic importance were the five railroads that converged from all directions. Shipments of military supplies and provisions arrived in Petersburg on rail lines from the south and west. They were then consolidated and sent north to Richmond for the Southern armies.

This quaint old town was called the "Cockade City" because of the rosette-like insignia American troops from the area had worn on the sides of their caps during the War of 1812.[3] Lee knew Petersburg must be held. Petersburg and Richmond were like Siamese twins: if one died, the other was doomed. In 1862 Captain Charles H. Dimmock, a Confederate engineer, had overseen the construction of a massive defensive line south and east of the city. His "Dimmock" line, over 10 miles in length, provided a dizzying assortment of trenches, forts, redans, and batteries that shielded the city. Shelby Foote described them as being

> ten miles in length, a half oval tied at its ends to the Appomattox River above and below the town, and contained in all some 55 redans, square forts bristling with batteries and connected by six-foot breastworks, twenty feet thick at the base and rimmed by a continuous ditch, another six feet deep and fifteen wide. In front of this dusty moat, trees had been felled, their branches sharpened and interlaced to discourage attackers, and on beyond a line of rifle pits for skirmishers, who could fall back through narrow gaps in the abatis. The ground had been cleared for half a mile to afford the defenders unobstructed fields of fire that would have to be crossed naked to whatever lead might fly, by whatever moved against them.[4]

---

[3] Trudeau, *Last Citadel*, 6.

[4] Shelby Foote, *Red River to Appotomattox*, in *The Civil War: A Narrative*, 3 vols. (New York: Random House, 1974) 3:430.

For the past two years the Dimmock line had been under reconstruction and improvement. If not impregnable, it must have seemed so—not only to the Rebel troops peering over the parapets but to the first Union soldiers preparing to attack it.[5]

The Union II, V, IX, and XVIII corps attacked on 18 June in a final attempt to smash through into Petersburg but were thrown back with heavy loss. Legion surgeon Shine described the situation that day: "There has been quite a severe fight going on all day, but ceased, to a considerable degree, about 5 O'clock P.M. Gen. Beauregard fought the Enemy yesterday and day before. Several women and children are said to have been wounded by the shells thrown in the city yesterday, and one Negro woman was killed...the enemy captured a portion of our works yesterday, but we are said to have re-captured them today."[6]

Grant and Meade grudgingly realized they had lost the opportunity for a quick victory and settled down to the work of mounting a siege.

Captain Daniel B. Sanford of Company A found time to write a letter to his sister on 21 June 1864 in which he related the misery the soldiers experienced daily in the Petersburg trenches.

I expect you think me very negligent about writing; but do not think for a moment that my silence is intentional for I think of home and loved ones nearly all the time; but circumstances are such that I cannot write oftener. I am in a state of suspense from morning til night and from night til morning and indeed I am in no spirit for writing. We are now living in and around the suburbs of this distressed city where the shells are constantly flying over us not knowing at what moment we may have to face the missiles of death coming thick and fast, to reinforce some part of our lines where the attack may be heaviest. I had much rather be on the front lines than in reserve. There is no safer place, hardly a day but some one is killed in our brigade...the enemy are hovered around the east side of this city in mighty force. They have made repeated assaults on our works but have been repulsed and they are now showing spite by throwing shell into the city. How long this siege will last I have not the

---

[5] Ibid., 6.
[6] Ibid.

remotest idea. This is the forty-eighth day since this fight commenced. Will the Yankees grow weary of this struggle? I am almost completely worn out. I have not seen a day in three months that I could say that I was well. I have not changed my clothes since the first of this month. I cannot give you a more correct idea of my style of life now, than to compare it with that of the hog. We lay in the dirt, very seldom wash our faces, have the itch, full of soldier bugs [alias lice]. Can you imagine a more wretched condition?[7]

Diarist Mitchell reported the legion "on the line" on 24 June, but they were inexplicably relieved and sent to the rear. The legion soldiers were back in the "ditches" on 29 June. First Sergeant John Newton Davis of Company E would take his third wound of the war on 30 June and would not return to the legion before the surrender.[8] Mitchell reported on 1 July that they were marched south to prevent a raid on one of the key railroads: "Legion was relieved last night off the line and returned to the same camp in the rear and this A.M. about Three O'clock we started on the march went down the W & P R R [Petersburg & Weldon Railroad] about six miles as the enemy was making some move on our Right. In the evening we returned to Petersburg to same camp."[9] As Lieutenant Sanford observed, the area behind the lines was no safer than the trenches themselves. Lieutenant W. R. Montgomery of the sharpshooter battalion jotted an example of these hazards in his diary on 3 July 1864: "Duff [George D.] Rice was wounded night before last while asleep in camp and died this morning at 3 o'clock. Was buried today. I wrote to his Ma."[10]

In a letter to his aunt, Jack Reese expressed sadness over the 14 July desertion of five men from his company: "I am sorry to state that five of the boys deserted a few nights ago. Two of them were verry poore soldiers. H. Davis & M.H. Grizzle. But Mos...& the two Norrises were good soldiers. Johnson's [sic] falling back has a tendency to discourage

[7] D. B. Sanford to sister, 21 June 1864.

[8] Compiled Service Records, National Archives micropublication, M266, roll 593, Georgia Department of Archives and History, Morrow GA.

[9] T. M. Mitchell, diary, 24, 29 June and 1 July 1864 entries.

[10] W. R. Montgomery, diary, 3 July 1864 entry, from *Georgia Sharpshooter*, 54.

the troops from our section of Georgia. A good many of them think the country will be overrun and never recovered by our troops."[11]

On 23 July the legion left their camp, crossed the James River above Drewry's Bluff, and camped at Chaffin's Farm.[12] Lee's intelligence indicated increased Federal activity at Deep Bottom, and he shifted Kershaw's division across the James to meet the threat. Grant planned to move forces across the James in hopes of drawing Lee's attention away from Petersburg, where Union General Burnside was preparing to detonate a huge explosion under the Confederate lines. On the night of 26-27 July, Hancock's II Corps and two divisions of Sheridan's cavalry crossed to the north side of the James River on a pontoon bridge at Deep Bottom.

Hancock's task was to turn the Confederate positions at New Market Heights and Fussell's Mill by attacking in the early morning hours of 27 July near Bailey's Creek. Lee saw this coming and reinforced his defenses. Hancock looked over the terrain and Confederate positions and decided to postpone the attack. Hoping to find a way around the Southern left, Grant ordered Sheridan's cavalry to probe Confederate strength on the Darbytown and Charles City roads on the morning of the 28th. Sheridan's troopers promptly ran into three brigades of Confederate infantry and a hot fight ensued. Two hundred Southerners were captured, but the Federals were halted and pushed back. The legion kept on the move during this time as Lee moved his men around to counter Federal thrusts. The evening of 26 June found them in line in the road near New Market Hill where they were shelled by Federal gunboats. No one was wounded, but Private Ezekiel L. Mason of Company M was captured. They moved north to a position near Frazier's Farm on the morning of the 28th, but were not engaged. That evening they marched south on Darbytown Road and took position near Fussell's Mill. No casualties were sustained, but another Company M soldier was captured. Private William M. Kemp was shipped off to Elmira prison, where he would die of pneumonia in February 1865.[13] Lee continued to bring up reinforcements, and Grant, realizing he had

---

[11] A. J. Reese to Aunt, 20 July 1864, Rees/Reese Collection, Lumpkin County Library, Madeline K. Anthony Collection, series 3, box 23, folder 5.

[12] T. M. Mitchell, diary, 23 July 1864 entry.

[13] Ibid., 26 and 28 July 1864; Compiled Service Records, M266, rolls 596, 597.

accomplished his goal of diverting Southern strength away from Petersburg, began shifting his men back across the James. By day's end on the 29th, the Federals completed their transit of the river, leaving a strong garrison at Deep Bottom. The legion pulled out on 31 July, moving to a camp between Richmond and Petersburg 3 miles north of the Appomattox River. On the evening of Saturday 6 August, they moved to Chester Station on the Richmond and Petersburg Railroad and camped.[14]

Next morning they boarded rail cars and headed north to Gordonsville. The legion troops were part of an expeditionary force Lee sent to General Early in the Shenandoah Valley to shore up his strength. This force was commanded by R. H. Anderson and included Kershaw's infantry division, Cutshaw's artillery battalion, and Fitzhugh Lee's cavalry division.

Early's corps had been sent north to the Shenandoah Valley in late June in an attempt to threaten Washington and draw Federal troops away from Richmond. Early was initially successful, routing a Federal force at the Monocacy River and driving all the way to the Washington defenses before VI Corps troops dispatched from Petersburg arrived to save the day. Early retreated north on 12 July but remained a threat. Grant determined to eliminate this threat and sent Major General Phil Sheridan north with the mission of destroying Early's army and the agricultural production of the Shenandoah Valley. Sheridan would lead an army of three corps supported by three cavalry divisions. Early prepared to defend the valley and petitioned General Lee for reinforcements.

Sheridan simultaneously moved his 50,000-man army south via Berryville in hopes of cutting the Valley Turnpike. Lee had determined that Federal troops were leaving the Richmond Petersburg area and decided to send reinforcements to Early. The question now was whether Anderson's force could reach Early before Sheridan could crush him.

The legion departed Gordonsville on Monday, 8 August 1864 around 4:00 A.M. on the Orange and Alexandria Railroad. Piling off the cars at Mitchell's Station near Cedar Mountain, they camped 8 miles from Culpepper Court House. On 12 August, the troops left camp early in the morning, passed through Culpepper, and camped at Hazel River.

---

[14] T. M. Mitchell, diary, 31 July and 6 August 1864 entries.

Saturday, 13 August found them on the march, crossing Hazel River and the north fork of the Rappahannock River. Later that day they passed through Gaines Crossroads and camped at Flint Hill. By Tuesday, 14 August, the legion with Wofford's brigade was camped on the south side of the Shenandoah River near Front Royal.[15]

Around noon on 16 August, Wofford was sent to the north side of the river to dislodge dismounted Union cavalry from an eminence called Guard Hill. After clearing the hill, Wofford led the 16th and 24th Georgia, Cobb's Legion, and the sharpshooter battalion in an attack to drive back Federal reinforcements. Confederate cavalry posted to guard Wofford's flank retreated, allowing Federal cavalry to flank his force and capture 300 men. Wofford's horse was shot from under him, but, while he took a bad fall, he was able to escape capture. Cutshaw's artillery on Guard Hill shelled the Federals, forcing them to withdraw to Cedarville.[16] The Phillips Legion troops were not involved in this affair, but fourteen legion soldiers who had transferred to the sharpshooter battalion were captured. Two of these, James W. Elliott and Sergeant Willoughby Waters, later died at the infamous Elmira prison.[17]

This new presence of Southern troops at Front Royal worried Sheridan. With Early's army in front of him and this new force of unknown size on his flank, he decided to retreat to a better defensive position at Halltown northeast of Winchester. Early ordered Anderson to head directly to Winchester. Early's troops hounded the Federals relentlessly through 20 August until Sheridan arrived at Halltown.

The legion was at the rear of the column as the wagon guard as Anderson's force moved on Winchester. Arriving there on the 18th, the legion was sent 2 miles east to stand picket duty. They were relieved and camped back at Winchester on the evening of the 19th. By the 25th, they were in the front lines facing the Federals about 1 mile east of Charlestown. Skirmishing and sporadic cannon fire marked the day.[18]

On 27 August, Early faced the reality of Sheridan's larger, entrenched force and concentrated his army at Bunker Hill. Sheridan followed, and by month's end the two armies were back in roughly the

---

[15] Ibid., 8–16 August 1864 entries.

[16] Gerald J. Smith, *One of the Most Daring of Men* (Murfreesboro TN: Southern Heritage Press, 1997) 129–30.

[17] Compiled Service Records, M266, rolls 594, 600.

[18] Mitchell, diary, 17–27 August 1864 entries.

same locations they had occupied on 10 August. With the Opequon River between them and both sides unwilling to venture an attack, the front settled into an uneasy stalemate for the next few weeks.

Jack Reese reported on conditions near Winchester in a letter to his uncle:

> Dear Uncle. I received your letter of the 22nd Augt a few days since I take the pleasant time to answer it. I have nothing of interest to write to you at present. We are encamped near Winchester now & have bin for several days past but we had had a right smart of fighting or skirmishing with the Yankies since we came here in the Valley. Our troops up here are doing very well. Plenty to eat & I believe we can whip the Yankies any time they get ready to fight us. But notwithstanding all that the Georgians are dissatisfied with the way things are going in Georgia and I must confess that it looks dark in that quarter to me. Altho things may change. But now that Sherman is in Atlanta it is my opinion that he will winter there. Altho I hope not. If he does ever thing in upper & middle part of the state will as they boys say be gone up. It has often bin said that the darkest time is just before the day. I think that ever thing looks gloomy now but still ever thing may work out right yet.[19]

The legion was active during this quiet period. They remained close to Winchester but shifted about performing picket duty on various roads leading into town.[20]

In early September, Sheridan's scouts learned that Kershaw's division and Cutshaw's artillery battalion would soon return to Petersburg. With Sheridan seemingly stalled on the defensive, Lee had better uses for Anderson's force. The reality of the matter was that Richard Anderson had grown tired of dealing with the crotchety Early and wanted to return to Richmond. It is likely that Anderson would have been willing to leave Kershaw's division with Early, but Early did not ask for them. Anderson put his force on the road early on Thursday, 15 September 1864, departing from Winchester and marching southwest

---

[19] A. J. Reese to Uncle, 9 September 1864, Rees/Reese Collection.
[20] T. M. Mitchell, diary, 1–14 September 1864 entries.

up the Pike. By 18 September, they had crossed the Blue Ridge and were camped 2 miles east of Woodville in the Virginia Piedmont.[21] Early and Anderson's inability to get along had produced a grievous mistake. Sheridan had simply been waiting for Anderson to depart before assuming the offensive.

Early was badly mistaken in his belief that Sheridan was timid, as the events of 19 September 1864 around Winchester would prove. The Battle of Third Winchester (or Opequon) was one of the most viciously contested actions in the Shenandoah and marked the turning point in the fight for control of the valley. Early had scattered four of his divisions while raiding the Baltimore and Ohio Railroad at Martinsburg. On the 19th, Sheridan's VI and XIX Corps crossed Opequon Creek and headed toward Winchester on the Berryville Pike. Early managed to delay the Federal advance long enough to mass his troops to meet the main Federal assault. The outnumbered Confederates fought well for several hours, and casualties were heavy. Around 3:00 P.M., as Crook's VIII Corps occupied the Confederate left, Averill's and Merritt's cavalry divisions charged astride the Valley Pike and shattered the Rebel left flank, compelling Early to order a retreat. With Federal cavalry seemingly everywhere, the retreat quickly disintegrated into a rout with Southern troops scrambling back through Winchester in a desperate attempt to escape their pursuers. Southern officers rallied enough men to throw together a rear guard position several miles south of Winchester, halting Northern pursuit as darkness fell. The day's fight cost Sheridan 5,000 casualties and Early just over 3,000. Later that evening when roll calls were taken, both sides were surely stunned at the number of losses.[22]

Later that night, the Confederates withdrew up the Valley Pike to Fisher's Hill south of Strasburg, arriving there around daylight. The last groups of Confederate soldiers filtered into the lines around noon. The position was formidable, but Early had only 10,000 troops to man a 4-mile line between the North Fork of the Shenandoah River and Little North Mountain. Spreading his infantry across the stronger terrain on

---

[21] Ibid., 15–18 September 1864.

[22] Jeffry D. Wert, *From Winchester to Cedar Creek* (Mechanicsburg PA: Stackpole Books, 1997) 71–97.

the right and center, he inexplicably placed his cavalry on his weaker left. Early was ready to fight again by 22 September 1864.

Sheridan's 35,000-man army had promptly followed Early up the valley on 20 September. On the 21st, the Federal commanders surveyed the imposing Southern position and discussed the best way to attack. General Crook proposed to take his two divisions around the Confederate left and attack it from Little North Mountain. When Crook attacked, the remaining Federal troops would attack from the front and roll up Early's line from west to east. Around 4:00 P.M. Crook's screaming men charged off the wooded mountain and slammed into the startled Rebel cavalry. The plan worked perfectly. As the cavalry fled to the rear, the assault rolled down the Southern line with additional Union troops attacking up the face of the hill. The demoralized Rebel defense collapsed, and the army retreated to Rockfish Gap near Waynesboro in great disarray. The collapse had occurred so quickly that casualties were relatively light. Early lost 1,200 men (most of whom were captured), and the Federals suffered fewer than 500 losses.[23]

Early reported his defeat to General Robert E. Lee on the afternoon of 23 September 1864: "Late yesterday the enemy attacked my position at Fisher's Hill and succeeded in driving back the left of my infantry line, when the whole of the troops gave way in a panic and could not be rallied. This resulted in a loss of twelve pieces of artillery, though my loss in men is not large. I am falling back to New Market, and shall endeavor to check the enemy if he advances, Kershaw's division had better be sent to my aid, through Swift Run Gap, at once."[24]

Kershaw had his men on the road early on the 24th and joined what was left of Early's army at Brown's Gap (located near present-day Elkton and Harrisonburg) on the morning of the 26th. The twelve guns of Cutshaw's battalion arrived with Kershaw. General Wofford did not return to the valley with his brigade due to injuries suffered when his horse fell on him during the Guard Hill fight in August. He had remained with his brigade through September while it was shuttled eastward to Gordonsville with Kershaw's division, but felt unable to lead it in the coming campaign. Wofford received medical leave in October

[23] Ibid., 117–29.
[24] *OR*, ser. 1, vol. 43, pt. 2, p. 878.

and went back to Georgia, never to return to active command of the brigade.[25]

Although prodded by Grant to take Charlottesville and advance toward Richmond, Sheridan decided this was too risky and embarked on an alternate course of action. Regarding Early's small force as no more than a nuisance, Sheridan decided to destroy the agricultural resources of the valley before marching out the way he had come. On 26 September, the Federals commenced a campaign of total destruction, burning barns, mills, and any buildings construed to be of aid to the Southern war effort. Livestock was confiscated or slaughtered. For the next ten days, pillars of smoke cast a pall over the valley, and there was little Early's small force could do to prevent it.

Sheridan began his retrograde movement down the valley on 6 October. As the column moved along the Valley Pike, Federal cavalry ranged widely to both sides, continuing the destruction. Early followed, ordering his cavalry under Colonel Thomas Rosser to harass the Federal cavalry. By 8 October, Rosser had moved 20 miles ahead of Early's main body and was in close proximity to the Federal cavalry at Tom's Brook. Annoyed by Rosser's hit-and-run tactics, Sheridan determined to turn on the Southern cavalry and eliminate them. The resulting attack on 9 October by an overwhelming Union cavalry force shattered Rosser's troopers and sent them reeling in all directions. Absolutely certain now that Early posed no further threat, the Federals resumed their trek up the valley. While Crook's Corps and the XIX Corps camped behind Cedar Creek, the VI Corps marched on to Front Royal with Powell's cavalry division. Convinced their work was done, the Federals began to plan their departure from the valley.[26]

On Sunday, 6 October 1864, the legion troops passed through Mount Crawford and camped 2 miles south of Harrisonburg. By the 13th they had marched through New Market, Mount Jackson, Woodstock, Fisher's Hill, and Strasburg, where they formed a line of battle a mile from town and heard firing in their front. The noise arose from a small fight that occurred at Cedar Creek when Early bombarded the Federals across the water to see how they would react. The Federals sent Thoburn's division across the creek, and a hot fight ensued until

---

[25] Smith, *Most Daring of Men*, 130.
[26] Wert, *From Winchester to Cedar Creek*, 161–66.

Confederate reinforcements forced Thoburn's men to retreat. This probing attack had the unfortunate effect of causing Sheridan to recall Wright's VI Corps from Front Royal. That evening, the legion and the rest of Early's army marched back to the foot of Fisher's Hill. On the next morning they took position in the old breastworks on the hill.[27]

Early now saw an opportunity to ambush Sheridan's army. Reconnaissance showed the Federal force camped between Cedar Creek and the North Fork of the Shenandoah River. The corps alignment was somewhat disjointed and invited attack. The plan called for three II Corps divisions under General John B. Gordon to cross the North Fork of the Shenandoah River and attack the main Union force from the east. Meanwhile, Kershaw's division would strike across Cedar Creek and annihilate Thoburn's division of Crook's VIII Corps, posted well in advance of the main Federal positions. Wharton's division with the artillery would attack directly down the Valley Pike. If all went as planned, Thoburn's division would be captured or destroyed while the main Federal force would be caught between Wharton's force coming down the pike and Gordon's divisions attacking from the east. Jubal Early hoped 19 October would be a day of redemption for his battered and oft-defeated command.

The Battle of Cedar Creek began before dawn in a landscape shrouded by impenetrable fog. At 3:30 A.M., the divisions of Gordon, Pegram, and Ramseur had arrived at the Shenandoah River fords. By 4:30 A.M., Kershaw had crossed Cedar Creek while Gordon's divisions had crossed the Shenandoah and surprised the Federal pickets. Kershaw's four brigades deployed with Wofford's brigade on the right and attacked Thoburn at 5:00 A.M. Moments later, Ramseur's, Pegram's, and Gordon's divisions attacked Crook's second division under Rutherford B. Hayes. Crook's VIII Corps disintegrated and fled north in utter confusion.

---

[27] T. M. Mitchell, diary, 7–14 October 1864 entries.

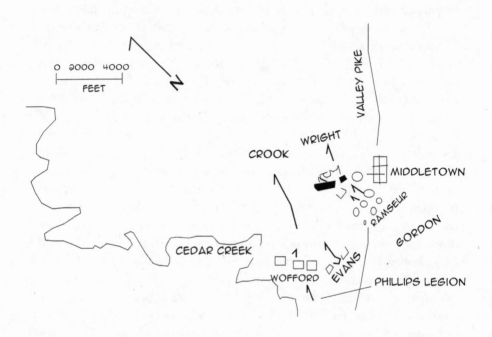

Morning attack of Confederates at Cedar Creek, October 19, 1864

The thick fog so reduced visibility that the legion with Wofford's brigade had marched past the left flank of Thoburn's shattered command and kept going until finally coming to the camps of Hayes's division, which Gordon's men had already overrun. Faced with a cornucopia of Federal supplies, it seems likely that the ragged, hungry soldiers made the most of the opportunity to plunder the camps. With Pegram and Ramseur already fighting the XIX Corps ahead of them, the Georgians settled in and waited for orders.[28]

Crook's VIII Corps and the Emory's XIX Corps were both routed and pushed back on VI Corps. Early was delighted, believing he had achieved a signal victory. As Early celebrated, his men began to run into a stiffening Federal defense as the now alert VI Corps was prepared for attack, holding a ridgeline just west of Middletown. The Confederates hammered away at the VI Corps position until, flanked by Southern troops in Middletown, the Northerners withdrew to a new position astride the Valley Pike about 3/4 mile north of town.

The legion had been ordered to the northern outskirts of Middletown, where it joined Pegram's and Wharton's divisions in a face-off against a force of 7,500 Union cavalry that had begun arriving shortly before 10:00 A.M.[29] The legion would remain in this position, with Wofford's brigade detached from Kershaw's division, as the day went on.

With the arrival of the Union cavalry north of Middletown and the retreat of VI Corps to their new position, the Confederate attack began to run out of steam. Many troops had dropped out of ranks to plunder captured Federal camps, and others were simply too exhausted to go on. Although he ordered a probe of the Federal position at 1:00 P.M., Early made it clear that the attack should not be pressed if the Federals were found to be too strong. He was also concerned by the large Union cavalry concentration east of the Pike. The Union horsemen had so far been held in check by Wofford's and Wharton's men but were shelling them heavily and had mounted several charges. One of the Federal shells landed squarely in the middle of legion Company C, killing Sergeant John. H. Bellah, Private James D. Kistleburg, Private Jesse N. Lambert,

---

[28] Wert, *From Winchester to Cedar Creek*, 211.
[29] Ibid., 215.

and Sergeant William S. Manning.[30] It appeared that Early was reaching the conclusion that his army had done enough on this day.

Sheridan was in Winchester that morning after returning from Washington where he had attended a strategy meeting with Grant. Mounting his horse, Rienzi, he raced to the field, arriving around 10:30 A.M. Sheridan's return inspired his men, and he busied himself reorganizing them for a counterattack that commenced around 4:00 P.M. Early's forces west of the Pike were routed and driven back. As the Federal advance neared Middletown, Early ordered Wofford's and Wharton's commands to fall back and cover the retreat. The demoralized army fled to Fisher's Hill with many continuing to Strasburg while others fell into line in the Fisher's Hill breastworks. The exhausted Federals were content to have pushed the Rebels back and called it a day.

Tom Mitchell wrote of the day's harrowing experiences in his diary: "Wednesday 19th. Left camp about one a.m. pass Strawsburg [Strasburg] crossed Cedar Run, below the Pike and attacted [sic] the Enemy taking him by surprise drove him about eight miles [near Middletown] late in the P.M. The enemy turned our Left putting our men to complete rout. I was on vidette at the Time and was cut off from the army and run for dear life, crossed the Shenandoah River at Bartlets Stations. Camped on the Side of the mountain South East of Strawsburg."[31] Mitchell found his way back to the legion the next day after crossing a mountain to Fort Valley. There he found "a large portion of my regiment in the mountains. Camp[ed] near Caroline Furnace."[32]

The Confederates withdrew the following day to New Market. Their stunning victory had turned into a humiliating defeat. Sheridan lost 5,665 men and Early 2,910. The Confederate losses included 25 guns, ambulances, ammunition wagons, most of the baggage, and forage wagons.[33]

---

[30] Compiled Service Records, M266, rolls 592-600; G. O. Megarity to father, 29 October 1864, MS 075, AC 71-416, Georgia Department of Archives and History, Morrow GA.

[31] T. M. Mitchell, diary, 19 October 1864 entry.

[32] Ibid., 20 October 1864.

[33] Wert, From Winchester to Cedar Creek, 246.

By Monday, 24 October 1864, the legion was on picket duty on Winchester Pike about 3 miles from New Market. They continued their odyssey on the roads through places already well known to them: Mount Jackson, Edinburg, Woodstock, Strasburg, Middletown, New Town, Fisher's Hill, and back and forth to some of them—an awkward dance punctuated by the ominous noise of cannonading, the misery of rotten weather, and the pain of sore feet, hunger, and exhaustion.[34]

Once again, Sheridan considered Early's decimated army to be of little consequence and began planning to shift his army out of the burned valley. Lee reached the same conclusion and began withdrawing forces from Early's command. Kershaw's division went first, departing for Richmond on 18 November. Mitchell jotted in his diary: "This morning about Four Oclock we got aboard the cars at Waynesboro. Arrived in Richmond about Three P.M. Camp about Two and a half miles from Richmond on the Williamsburg Pike."[35]

They had left the valley for good. On 23 November, the legion was marched northeast for 2 miles to a line of breastworks on the north side of the York River Railroad. They built quarters there on a line parallel to the works until the evening of 7 December, when they marched 6 miles south to reinforce General Hoke's position on the left of Fort Gillmore (Gilmer). This proved to be a false alarm, and the legion returned to their camp late on the 8th. On the 19th, Wofford's brigade had moved about 1 mile southwest of Darbytown Road and relieved Kirkland's brigade of Hoke's division.[36] Hoke's troops had been dispatched by rail to Wilmington, North Carolina, to counter a Federal attempt to capture that port.

In January, Lieutenant Colonel Joseph Hamilton rejoined the legion following a long recuperation from his severe Cold Harbor wound. The brigade also got a new commander, Brigadier General Dudley DuBose. General Wofford had been reassigned to North Georgia at the request of Governor Brown. DuBose, a veteran Army of Northern Virginia officer and Georgian, had been acting as the commanding officer of Benning's brigade when the call came to take over Wofford's command.

---

[34] T. M. Mitchell, diary, 24 October–13 November 1864 entries.
[35] Ibid., 18 November 1864 entry.
[36] Ibid., 23 November–19 December 1864 entries.

Diarist Mitchell left for home on furlough on Saturday, 21 January 1865 and would not return until Tuesday, 21 February. Mitchell's diary entries provide an interesting example of how difficult it was for a Georgian in the Army of Northern Virginia to take leave in early 1865:

Saturday 21st I having received a Furlough for Twenty Four days [to go to Dalton Georgia] I left camps this morning went to Richmond got transportation and left on the cars at eleven a.m. for Danville.Arrived in Richmond about [4] p.m.

Sunday 22nd This a.m. I arrived in Danville. In evening I departed for Greensboro

Monday 23rd Arrived early this morning in Greensboro and at Ten a.m. left for Charlotte North Carolina

Tuesday 24th This a.m. I arrived in Charlotte and left this evening passing Columbia South Carolina for Augusta Georgia

Wednesday 25th Arrived in Augusta this evening at Six Oclock

Thursday 26th Stayed today in Augusta with friends

Friday 27th Left Augusta this a.m. on Georgia R.R. Stop at Madison with friends

Saturday 28th Today I ride on the cars as far as Social Circle it being as far as cars are running Stay near Yellow River

Tuesday February 7th 1865 I left home last night to return to my command in Virginia. To night I am stoping about Five miles south of Calhoun [GA]

Wednesday 8th Stoping to night in Cartersville [GA] with friends

Thursday 9th Stoping tonight in Marietta

Friday the 10th Learned to day in Atlanta that the Enemy have cut the Rail Road near Branchville. Stoping to night in Decatur [GA]

Saturday the 11th Stop to night near Conyers

Sunday 12th Arrived at Social Circle about Five P.M. and found the cars just ready to start for Rutledge. Stay all night there with Friends

Monday 13th Left Rutledge on cars about Eight a.m. arrived at Washington [GA] about Five P.M. I leave the R R here and will have to go around Shermans army to get to my command at Richmond. Stay all night one mile and a half from Washington

Tuesday 14th Started early this a.m. cross the Savannah River just below the mouth of Broad River. Stay all night about Three miles east of the River.

Wednesday February 15th 1865 To Night I am at Abbeville South Carolina

Thursday 16th This morning I left Abbeville on the Cars, arrived at Allsteen at Four P.M. I learned that the Enemy is near Columbia. Left Allsteen on Foot a gain. Go about Three (3) miles and stop for the night

Friday 17th All day I have heard Cannonading towards Columbia. Arrived at Winnsboro at Three P.M. and find the cars ready to start for Charlotte.

Sunday 19th Arrived at Charlotte this a.m. and departed at 6 P.M.

Monday 20th Arrived at Danville this Evening and departed at Eleven P.M.

Tuesday 21st Arrived in Richmond about Four P.M. Walked out to the command about Six miles East of Richmond and one mile north side of Fort Gillmore (Gilmer). I have been gone just one month. Have walked nearly Four hundred miles and stayed at home Four days.[37]

Captain Dan Sanford of Company A wrote his mother and sister in February, pondering the reasons for the war and the apparent hopelessness of their situation:

Could it not have been avoided? I think it would had our rulers exercised a moderate degree of discression but I will not discuss the errors of the poweres that be here, for I fear I would not enliten you much at least you know where these "honorable" men have erred as well as I do. It is all left with this Army now. We have got to fight the whole Yankee nation they are closing in upon us from every side the soldiers here are much distressed in spirits and a great many are deserting to the Yankees, but the

---

[37] Ibid., diary, 21 January–21 February 1865 entries.

G.R.'s [Greene Rifles] still maintain their honor yet, and are as hopeful as could be expected under the circumstances; We are entirely deprived of hope. I think a man will hope until the last moment however doubtful our prospects appear. Congress has decided against putting the Negroes in the Army. A very unwise decision I think, I believe if the Negroes had been put in the Army this war would soon end but how? I cannot say; but I know this, let the war go on or stop now, the institution of slavery is dead: the main issue in this contest and why not settle it by negotiation? It is a discouraging thought to think there is such a few of us to fight this issue out, when the result is so uncertain. Grant's demonstrations indicate active work here at any moment. He will try to form a junction with Sherman. I don't know what will become of us.[38]

Sanford was correct in his statement of the fidelity of Company A. During the entire war, only one soldier deserted from the Greene Rifles. Desertion rates rose in the legion in 1865 but were still low compared to many other units from the Deep South. Three men deserted in January, four in February, and sixteen in March when the situation began to appear hopeless. The Federals had also contrived to make desertion more attractive to Southern soldiers with a proclamation that Rebels who gave up and took the Oath of Allegiance to the Union would not be sent to prison.[39]

On Friday, 3 March 1865 the legion troops moved south and occupied the works between New Market Road and Fort Gillmore (Gilmer). As the Federals held the only nearby wooded area, legion members suffered from the cold because of scarcity of firewood.[40]

An ailing Daniel Sanford wrote to his family on 13 March: "I have suffered for two weeks past with neuralgia and going on picket last Saturday has made me worse. We have so few officers present that I hate to miss my time on picket and I have been doing duty when I was not able. The boys here are in very low spirits, a great many deserting to the

---

[38] D. B. Sanford to Mother and Sister, 24 February 1865.
[39] Compiled Service Records, M266, rolls 592–600.
[40] T. M. Mitchell, diary, 3 March 1865.

Yankees. I think if I could get well and sound I would not be depressed in spirits much."[41]

A much more optimistic Jack Reese wrote his aunt on 27 March: "I confess that it will be a good while before peace is near but I see nothing to discourage us if we are true to ourselves and country and if we are ever subjugated our own people will be the cause of it. There are too many playing out that ought to be at the front. There will be some pretty hard fighting this summer but I don't think that it will be as sevear as last summer although there is no telling. I have not been in a fight in some days but I expect we will make up for lost time some of these days."[42]

Young Lieutenant Reese's optimism would soon prove to be ill founded. On 29 March 1864, Grant launched a large force in another attempt to swing around Lee's right flank and pry him out of the Petersburg defenses. Lee reacted quickly, sending Pickett's division and cavalry to the west. By the end of the day on 30 March, the Southerners appeared to be holding their own and were digging in at Five Forks. Grant had suffered 2,300 casualties while Lee had lost about 1,700. This would change on 1 April when Sheridan's cavalry and the V Corps overran and shattered Pickett's division at Five Forks.[43] The legion troops remained in their trenches east of Richmond while this disaster occurred. Grant planned a massive follow-up assault for the next day. The end was near.

Hope for the tired men of Phillips Georgia Legion must have been on the wane. Nonetheless, they still maintained an almost mystical belief in the power of their revered chief, General Robert E. Lee. They would soldier on and see what the morrow would bring.

---

[41] D. B. Sanford to Mother and Sisters, 13 March 1865.

[42] A. J. Reese to Aunt, 27 March 1865.

[43] John Horn, *The Petersburg Campaign* (Conshohocken PA, Combined Publishing, 1993) 219–47.

Chapter 16

Going Down of the Sun

"Fought till we were surrounded & compeled to surrender."

When General Robert E. Lee learned of the death of General Ambrose Powell Hill, he could only say tearfully, "He is at rest now, and we are the ones left to suffer."[1] By early April 1865, Lee could have been bemoaning the fate of the entire Confederacy. He knew what was coming but hoped to delay the inevitable for a short time in order to link up with General Joseph E. Johnston in North Carolina. On 2 April 1865, a massive Federal offensive had broken through Southern lines in several places; the offensive came close to capturing Lee at his headquarters. Lee's army would have to evacuate Petersburg and retreat north across the Appomattox River. He held until nightfall to give his army the chance to slip away after dark. He sent a telegram to Secretary of War John C. Breckinridge advising that preparations must be made to evacuate Richmond that night. Lee then went to work planning the withdrawal in spite of President Davis's dispatch complaining of the loss of valuables.[2]

Lee's challenges were daunting. He had to locate pieces of an army that were scattered around Petersburg and Richmond, then funnel them all to an assembly point at the small town of Amelia Court House, Virginia, about 35 miles west of Petersburg. Some of the Confederate units would have to cross the Appomattox River twice and the viability of three important bridges was suspect. No plan would work unless the Federals were prevented from entering Petersburg that day. Lee hoped

---

[1] Shelby Foote, *The Civil War, A Narrative*, Red River to Appomattox, vol. 3/3 (New York: Random House, 1974) 3:880.

[2] G. Walsh, *Damage Them All You Can: Robert E. Lee's Army of Northern Virginia* (New York: Forge, A Tom Doherty Associates Book, 2002) 417–19; Foote, *Civil War*, 3:884.

to follow the line of the Richmond and Danville Railroad to combine with General Joseph E. Johnston's Army of Tennessee, which had been opposing Sherman in North Carolina. After joining forces they would assume the offensive against Sherman.

Rebel troops fought tenaciously in defending Battery Whitworth and Fort Gregg; they paid dearly to buy desperately needed time. While Lee's forces struggled north across the Appomattox toward Richmond, the capital was undergoing its own agonies. The Confederates in Richmond torched warehouses to keep the contents from falling into Federal hands. All civil authorities abandoned the capital; what remained was a mob of army deserters, convicts who had broken out of the penitentiary, and local prostitutes. Police and firefighters were helpless to stop the rampage. Casks of liquor were emptied into the gutters. The remaining human debris scooped up the liquor in any available container or actually cupped their hands and drank it from the street.[3] Kershaw's division had been left in the Richmond defenses when the rest of Longstreet's I Corps had marched south to address the threat at Petersburg. Kershaw assigned two battalions in an attempt to stop the looting but they met with little success. On 3 April 1865, James Lewis Barton of Company D recorded his impression of the conditions in Richmond: "Sunday 2nd went to Church returned at 2 P.M. Ate dinner & went down on the right of the line Forts Gilmore [Gilmer] & Gregg. Recd orders about 6 o'clock to get ready to move & was up all night. Monday 3rd left the trenches at 3 passed through Richmond just at day light the Government stores all thrown open & the women fighting over the commissary the whisky flowing in the streets marched 23 miles camped for the night."[4]

In later years old soldiers expressed disagreement as to which soldiers and/or whose command had been the last to depart Richmond that April. In an April 1909 letter to the *Confederate Veteran*, Daniel B. Sanford, captain of the Greene Rifles, Company A, Phillips Legion, believed the legion could rightfully claim the honor:

---

[3] Ibid.

[4] Diary of James L. Barton, 3 April 1865 entry, Civil War Miscellany-Personal Papers, Microfilm Library, drawer 283, roll 17, Georgia Department of Archives and History, Morrow GA.

There seems to be some dispute as to what soldiers or commands of soldiers was the last to leave Richmond on the morning of 3 April 1865. My recollection is that Phillip's Georgia Legion Infantry were the rear guard and the last soldiers to leave that city on that day. When this command crossed the bridge over the James River, the bridge [Mayo Bridge] was on fire in many places on each side, and we had to run with all our might and shinney from side to side of the bridge to keep from being burned to death. No other soldiers could have crossed this bridge after we did. This command left camp near Drury's Bluff about twelve o'clock Sunday night, 2 April 1865, and reached Richmond a little after daylight Monday morning.[5]

After assembling his scattered forces, General Robert E. Lee marched the Petersburg forces west toward Bevil's and Goode's Bridges over the Appomattox. Nearing Bevil Bridge, scouts reported back to Lee that the bridge's approaches were flooded and the column would have to turn north toward Goode's Bridge. Further north on the Appomattox, Ewell's force from Richmond (including the legion with Kershaw) arrived at Genito Bridge to find that the pontoons needed for filling in the approaches had not been laid. Detouring downstream, they managed to cross on the Danville and Richmond Railroad bridge. Troops continued to pour across Goode's Bridge, and by day's end on 4 April, the Petersburg army was reunited at Amelia Court House.[6]

The tired, hungry troops arrived to receive a crushing disappointment. Lee had ordered a trainload of rations sent out from Richmond, but when the rail cars were opened they were discovered to be full of ammunition. Lee issued a proclamation appealing to local citizens to share whatever food they could with his men and also allowed foraging parties to scour the countryside. This foraging cost a day's march and produced little in the way of food; meanwhile the Federals were closing in rapidly behind the Confederates.[7] Lee ordered 200,000

---

[5] Daniel Benjamin Sanford, "Last Confederate Command to Leave Richmond," in *Confederate Veteran* vol. 20 (April 1909): 337.

[6] Chris M. Calkins, *The Appomattox Campaign* (Conshohocken PA: Chris Calkins, 1997) 75–76.

[7] Ibid., 75, 85.

rations to be sent by rail from Danville to Burkeville Junction. Then, on 5 April at 1:00 P.M., he sent his troops southwest down the railroad toward Burkeville Junction. Ewell's force from Richmond (including the legion with Kershaw) was just entering Amelia Court House as Lee moved out and it would not follow until later in the day. What Lee did not realize was that General Phil Sheridan had blocked the railroad at Jetersville between Lee and Burkeville Junction. On the evening of 4 April, Union V Corps soldiers were digging in astride the railroad.

Lee's cavalry discovered the Federals at Jetersville. After satisfying himself that they were there in force, Lee shifted his destination to Farmville. Farmville, located 23 miles west on the South Side Railroad, was known to have 80,000 rations on hand.[8] Embarking on a night march north of the Federal left flank, the army would cross Flat Creek, pass by Amelia Springs and the crossroads at Deatonville, then struggle through a marshy area cut through by Little Sailor's Creek. Along the way Lee's scouts intercepted a Federal dispatch stating that General Grant was at Jetersville and Federal infantry at Burkeville. His southern route blocked, Lee decided to fall back across the Appomattox River at Farmville and the High Bridge 4 miles east. Burning the bridges to delay Federal pursuit, he headed west in search of an opening to turn south or, failing that, head for Lynchburg.[9]

Longstreet's I and III Corps led the column, followed by Anderson's small corps, then Ewell's corps of Richmond garrison troops (including the legion with Kershaw), then a wagon train, and finally Gordon's II Corps as rear guard. Disaster struck at 11:00 A.M. on 6 April, when Crook's Union cavalry struck the line of march at Holt's Corner just before reaching Little Sailor's Creek. Anderson deployed to meet the threat while Mahone marched ahead, opening a 2-mile gap. Anderson quickly chased Crook's troopers away but the damage had been done. As Anderson's men reached Marshall's Crossroads, 1 mile beyond Sailor's Creek, they discovered that General George Custer's Union cavalry division had slid into the gap, blocking their path. Learning of Anderson's predicament, Ewell, next in line, decided to send

---

[8] Ibid., 91–92.

[9] Christopher Calkins, *Lee's Retreat: A History and Field Guide* (Richmond VA: Page One Inc., 2000); Christopher Calkins, *From Petersburg to Appomattox , 2–9 April 1865* (Farmville VA: Farmville Herald Publishing Co., 1983) 15–16.

his artillery and wagon train north on Jamestown Road. His infantry, led by Kershaw's division, continued west across Little Sailor's Creek and took position on high ground overlooking the stream. Gordon's rear guard, unaware of all this and pressed by Union Major General A. A. Humphreys's II Corps, followed the wagon train up Jamestown Road.[10] As Ewell and Anderson met to decide their next move, two Federal VI Corps divisions arrived near the Hillsman House across the creek from Ewell's troops while two more Union cavalry divisions went on line to Custer's left. Ewell and Anderson were now deployed almost back to back with strong Federal forces ahead of Anderson and behind Ewell. To make matters even worse, twenty guns of the VI Corps artillery dropped trail near the Hillsman House and began shelling Ewell's troops. Since Ewell's own artillery had been sent north with the wagon train, the Southerners could only stand and take the punishment. The Phillips Legion was located with DuBose's Georgia brigade on the far right of Ewell's line with the rest of Kershaw's division. Custis Lee's division of Richmond defense troops and the Naval battalion held the line to Kershaw's left. Sailor's Creek was downhill about 300 yards to the east and the Federal guns were about 800 yards away.[11]

Captain Fletcher Lowrey of legion Company L had been very lucky up to this point in the war. Enlisting in the company as a second lieutenant when it was mustered in April 1862, he had risen to captain in November 1863 when Captain James M. Johnson was killed in the attack on Fort Sanders. In a war that cost most line officers several wounds, Fletcher had come through the war's major battles without a scratch. Records indicate that he also had managed to avoid the plethora of diseases that plagued the armies. Given a thirty-day leave in February, Fletcher returned to Georgia to see his parents, wife Sallie, and two-year-old daughter Addie, all of whom had fled south from Marietta when it was overrun by Sherman in 1864. Somehow managing to return to his company in late March, he led Company L on the flight from Richmond. He was standing next to Sergeant James L. Wylie on the ridge above Sailor's Creek when a Federal shell struck him in the leg.

---

[10] Calkins, *Appomattox Campaign*, 105–107.
[11] Ibid., 108

The impact was so severe that the nearly severed limb spun around in a circle, striking Sergeant Wylie's arm and breaking it.[12]

At 6:00 P.M., after a half-hour bombardment, 7,000 Federal infantry advanced in line of battle to the creek, where they ran into Southern skirmishers. Pressing across the flooded creek with some difficulty, the VI Corps soldiers dressed their lines and attacked.[13]

Ewell's men surprised the attackers, rising and pouring a deadly volley into them that caused panic and confusion among some units. Caught up in the spirit of the moment, a group of Custis Lee's troops counterattacked and chased the wavering Federals back to the creek; there Union artillery met the overzealous Southerners with blasts of canister, driving them back to their lines. The bluecoats regrouped and charged again, reaching the Confederate line by sheer weight of numbers. As the two sides came together, the fighting went hand to hand until the Confederates, realizing they were overwhelmed, began to surrender. Small groups of troops drifted back into the woods in an attempt to escape. Lieutenant Colonel Joseph Hamilton, commander of the Phillips Legion, led one group of 200 men through the woods only to run into Custer's cavalry on the opposite side. The Confederates repelled several attacks but, realizing they were surrounded, Hamilton called an officers' conference to decide their next move. The officers determined to let a captured Federal colonel rejoin Federal forces to negotiate the Confederates' surrender. The colonel soon returned with Major Andrew Glover of the 2nd New York cavalry, who accepted their surrender. That evening, Major Glover invited Hamilton and Captain Gober of the 3rd Georgia Sharpshooter Battalion to have tea with him. Later that night Glover would return to the captured Confederate officers, who were being held under guard in a pen and confiscated all their valuables.[14] Some 3,400 of Ewell's command became prisoners while 1,450 were able to slip away through the woods. One of the captives, James Lewis Barton of Company D, noted the day's events: "Thursday 6th Saw cousin Lewis until about 12 o'clock Battle & charged

---

[12] Compiled Service Records, National Archives micropublication, M266, roll 596; James L. Wylie, veteran's pension application, Cobb County Library, Georgia Room, microfilm ref. G.973.7458-pen, roll GCP-99.

[13] Calkins, *Appomattox Campaign*, 108–111.

[14] "How a Confederate Captain and Color Bearer Cheated the Enemy of Them," *Savannah* (GA) *Morning News*, 6 November 1888.

the Yankee cavalry & drove them off, moved to the right & formed new line on the face of a hill 3 pieces of artillery playing on us the heaviest fire I was ever under till we were surrounded & compeled [*sic*] to surrender."[15] "Black Thursday" marked the end of diarist Thomas M. Mitchell's service: "I was captured by the enemy to day. So far I have been treated with respect."[16]

The Confederates fared no better at the other two overlapping battles. Anderson's fight to the west at Marshall's Crossroads against three Union cavalry divisions resulted in the capture of 2,600 more Confederates while Gordon's rear guard action to the north cost another 1,700 men. Altogether the three battles at Sailor's Creek culminated in a disaster for the Southerners, with losses of over 7,700 men, eight generals, fifteen guns, and hundreds of wagons.[17] The Federals suffered 1,148 casualties.

During this time Longstreet's troops were engaged in skirmishing while guarding Rice's Depot several miles to the west. Lee, worried about the rear of his column, rode back with Mahone's division toward Sailor's Creek. Arriving above the valley of Big Sailor's Creek, he observed a disorganized mob of gray soldiers streaming west. Shocked, Lee blurted, "My God! Has the army been dissolved?"[18]

Compiled service records reveal that around two dozen of the Phillips Legion soldiers at Sailor's Creek managed to slip away to Appomattox. Ironically, they were immediately paroled and released after the final surrender. Those legion troops who were captured at Sailor's Creek would spend the next few months in Federal prisons. The majority of the legion troops who would surrender at Appomattox were staff and support soldiers who had been on the move with the wagon train along another road.

The end was near. That same night, 6 April 1865, Lee decided to stake everything on one final effort. Gordon's corps crossed High Bridge over the Appomattox River early the next day and headed down the railroad to Farmville. Mahone's rear guard division moved across, then torched the bridge. Due to some confusion in orders, the wagon bridge

---

[15] James L. Barton, diary, 6 April 1865 entry.

[16] Thomas M. Mitchell Diary, 6 April 1865 entry, private collection of Mr. R. D. Thomas, Chattanooga TN.

[17] Calkins, *Appomattox Campaign*, 111–14.

[18] Ibid., 115.

adjacent to the railroad bridge was not promptly set afire and pursuing Federals doused the flames before the bridge was badly damaged. Mahone headed northwest on the road to Cumberland Church with the Federals close behind. General Lee had led Longstreet's infantrymen and nephew Fitzhugh Lee's cavalry north to Farmville, arriving on the morning of 7 April. There the starving men were issued rations of bread and meat. They ate as quickly as possible, but even this brief respite would be denied some of them when the crack of carbine fire was heard to the east. Federal cavalry was nearing the town. The remaining rations were sent westward in boxcars. The Southern troops hoped to catch up to these rations at Appomattox Station, 30 miles to the west.[19]

With the approach of the Federals, Longstreet's troops in Farmville crossed to the north side of the Appomattox River and General E. P. Alexander fired the bridges. Farmville was in Federal hands by 1:30 P.M., when Lee discovered that the Union army was over the river at High Bridge. Suppressing his rage at this unwelcome news, Lee rode out to check the threat. He found that his men had successfully held off the Union II Corps in a fight at Cumberland Church, 4 miles north of Farmville. While at Cumberland Church, Lee received a letter from Grant asking him to surrender and save the expenditure of any more lives. Lee handed the note to Longstreet, who scanned it and handed it back with the terse comment, "Not yet."[20]

To stay ahead of Grant, Lee ordered yet another night march and at 11:00 P.M. his army set off to the west. This would be their third consecutive night march and many men were approaching complete exhaustion. The bulk of the surviving Phillips Legion representing its staff and logistical support had already headed west with the wagon train earlier in the day, but a handful of men who had escaped the fiasco at Sailor's Creek were still with Longstreet. Lee planned to reach Appomattox Station on the railroad before the Federals, issue rations, then head west to Campbell Court House, where he could move south toward Danville. At mid-afternoon on 8 April, Lee's men halted just northeast of Appomattox Court House. They looked forward to obtaining additional rations from supply trains that had been sent from

---

[19] C. M. Calkins, *Thirty-six Hours before Appomattox* (Farmville VA: Farmville Herald Publishing Co., 1980) n.p.

[20] Calkins, *Appomattox Campaign*, 131–35.

Lynchburg to Appomattox Station. Soon the cry arose, "Yankees! Sheridan! The cavalry are coming; they are at the station and coming up the hill!"[21] Federal cavalry had indeed reached the station, capturing the three heavily laden supply trains awaiting Lee. By nightfall Lee's troops could see the glimmer of Federal campfires ahead. Federal cavalry had blocked the routes both south and west. The overriding question now was whether Federal infantry lay beyond the cavalry.

Consulting with his generals, Lee decided on another attempt to reach the railroad and fight his way out of the trap. On the morning of 9 April 1865, General Gordon, aided by cavalry, assaulted the Federal cavalry blocking the road. Gordon initially made good progress but this ended when the Union cavalry drew back, revealing a solid line of blue infantry. Around 8:30 A.M. Lee received word from Gordon that his command had been fought to a frazzle and he could not go forward without Longstreet's help. Longstreet was not available, however, having formed a line behind Lee to fend off the approaching Union II and VI Corps. The Army of the James was in front while the V Corps with Sheridan's cavalry lay just southeast.[22] The demise of the Army of Northern Virginia waited patiently like an unwanted guest. Lee's words said it all: "There is nothing left for me to do but to go and see General Grant, and I would rather die a thousand deaths."

On 9 April 1865, at the Wilbur McLean House in Appomattox Court House, Virginia, General Robert E. Lee surrendered the Army of Northern Virginia. Grant's terms were generous: officers could keep their sidearms; enlisted men could keep their horses and mules for planting and plowing in the spring. Over 25,000 rations were provided to Lee's starving troops. Captive James Lewis Barton recorded his experience during these final days: "Friday 7th marched to Burksville Junction camped for the night, drew 4 crackers. Saturday 8th marched 12 miles drew beef no salt parched corn for bread. Sunday 9th marched 14 miles without Bread & meat. Monday 10th lay over, drew rations, raining all day."[23]

On Friday, 14 April, Barton found himself headed to prison at Point Lookout, Maryland: "Passed Fortress Monroe just at daylight, go

---

[21] Ibid., 154.

[22] Ibid., 164–85.

[23] James L. Barton, diary, 7–10 April 1865.

to Point Lookout at 6 P.M., given our names & was searched, take all our Bed clothing except one blanket. Saturday, 15th got in a tent with 7 other men. Sunday, 16th had inspection, got a tent of my own & while putting it up my attention was attracted by a big laugh across the street which was caused by a man wearing a Barrel Shirt for stealing rations."[24]

Barton and the pitiful remnants of the Phillips Legion scattered through several Federal prisons would take the Oath of Allegiance and head home over the next few months. Some legion soldiers had languished in prisons for many months, some since Gettysburg. Legion casualties from the fighting at Sailor's Creek and other skirmishing at this time, so close to the end, must have been unbearable. Two soldiers captured at Sailor's Creek died from causes other than combat. John H. Elrod of Company C died while on the way home after being released from Point Lookout on 4 June 1865. Henry A. Robins of Company B died on 15 July at Newport News from typhoid and exhaustion. Merida Brown of Company E, wounded at Sailor's Creek and hospitalized at Washington DC, until his death on 25 April, bears the rare distinction of being the only Phillips Legion soldier buried at Arlington National Cemetery.[25]

Captain Daniel B. Sanford of Company A was seriously wounded at Sailor's Creek, his left leg shattered by a minie ball. In the awful confusion, everything seemed to be going to pieces and there was no time to tend to the wounded. Sanford lay where he fell, surrounded by the dead and dying. He would have succumbed to his injuries had not a passing Union soldier seen his distress and sympathetically given him a canteen and a raw codfish. He sustained himself with these rations until he was finally discovered and taken to a hospital in Washington DC.[26]

According to the Federal surgeons who patched him up, Company M Captain Samuel Young Harris's wounds consisted of "flesh, scalp and left index finger." In a situation almost identical to that of Fletcher Lowrey, he had enlisted with the company in April 1862 and by 1863 had risen to command Company M. Also coming through the war free of wounds or major illness, he had furloughed home in February 1865 to marry his sweetheart. Like Lowrey, he somehow managed to return to

---

[24] Ibid., 14 April 1865.
[25] Compiled Service Records, M266, rolls 592, 594, 598.
[26] *Confederate Veteran*, 20 (1912): 337; Compiled Service Records, M266, roll 599.

his company in late March. In a bitterly ironic twist of fate, on 9 April Captain Sam Harris was killed by a stray bullet at Burkeville. Sam rests today in the small Confederate Cemetery at Burkeville, Virginia.[27]

And what became of Fletcher Lowrey? In a letter to his brother dated 12 May 1866, Fletcher's father, Reverend Basil Lowrey, wrote:

> I have some sad news to give you in regard to my family. Our Dear Fletcher fell in Battle three days before Lee's surrender. He had one leg torn off by a shell about 5 minutes before his whole command was captured. He was a Captain in Wofford's Brigade Longstreet's Corps. He has left a wife & one little daughter; you cannot imagine the amount of trouble it brought to us; his mother came very near to dying from it. It threw her into convulsions and spasms & she had them occasionally for 2 months after we got the news. We first heard he was a prisoner unhurt, until the soldiers began to return from northern prisons & we began to look for our Dear Fletcher. When the sad news came to us like a peal of thunder in a clear sky that poor Fletcher was gone; he fell into the hands of the yankeys. They carried him to their hospital & let him lay until the fourth day before they attempted to amputate the limb or do anything with it, and in that time he had lost so much blood that he was not able to bear it and he died upon the table. But we had the joyful news that he expressed himself as being prepared for his change. I saw a Captain who told me he talked with him on the subject the day after he was wounded.[28]

Federal medical records indicate that twenty-six-year-old Fletcher died on 8 April 1865 at the Burkeville General Hospital.

The Phillips Legion Infantry Battalion surrendered ninety-three men at Appomattox:

---

[27] Mattie Harris Lyon, *My Memories of the War Between the States: Confederate Reminiscences and Letters 1861–1865*, 13 vols. (Atlanta: Georgia Division, United Daughters of the Confederacy, 1996) vol. II, 84-85; Compiled Service Records, M266, roll 595.

[28] Rev. Basil Lowrey to Brother, 17 May 1866, private collection of Mrs. Nancy Brown, Leesburg GA.

Company A: one corporal, sixteen privates

Company B: three sergeants, thirteen privates (twelve of these men are listed under a nonexistent Company I but all were in Company B; probably an administrative error made by the Federals)

Company I: (all in Company B; probably an administrative error)

Company C: two sergeants, six privates

Company D: ten privates

Company E: Second Lieutenant J. G. Burt, two sergeants, five privates

Company F: None, although two men from Company F appear on Company A's parole list

Company L: two sergeants, four privates

Company M: Second Lieutenant B. J. Hamby, one sergeant, fifteen privates

Company O: one corporal, seven privates

Assistant surgeons S. W. Field and G. M. Willis

First Lieutenant A. J. "Jack" Reese of Company E commanded the legion at the time of surrender

Major Samuel M. H. Byrd, Quartermaster, and First Lieutenant J. A. Peek, Assistant Quartermaster, surrendered with the brigade staff.

Nineteen-year-old Lorenzo Dow Wright, originally of the Phillips Legion, had transferred to the 3rd Georgia Sharpshooter Battalion in 1863 and surrendered with that unit. He was the only former legion soldier still with the sharpshooters.[29]

Diarist Thomas M. Mitchell was paroled on Friday, 14 April. After a long and arduous trek south, he "crossed the Conestoga River at Chilton. Arrived at home (my Fathers) about eleven a.m. and find the family all in good health."[30]

---

[29] R. A. Brock, *The Appomattox Roster* (New York: Antiquarian Press, 1962) 175–76.

[30] Thomas M. Mitchell, diary, 3 May 1865.

Afterword

Remembering Appomattox

In early December 2003, we received a letter from Ms. Mary Carolyn Mitton in which she told us everything she knew about her ancestor Colonel Edgar Fearn Moseley. Killed at Petersburg late in the war, Moseley had been a Confederate artillery officer whose command at one time included the "Macon Light Artillery." She went on to describe her great-grandmother's experience as a little girl living at the family home known as "Wheatland." Wheatland was located just 18 miles from Appomattox at the time of the Confederate surrender. We have read many letters in the course of preparing this book for publication, but a few lines from this one resonated with our thoughts and feelings at the time. It read:

> As news of the surrender spread, she asked her father, Dr. Wm. Moseley, if she could walk down to the road, present day Virginia Rt. 56, to see the soldiers, the C.S.A. This was a 1/2 mile walk down a dirt lane to the dirt road. She recalled many things about them...dirty, ragged, bloodied, unshaven, drooping shoulders. The description of the soldiers crying was foremost in her mind when she was in her nineties. This story stayed in my mind too, being born in 1939, because at the age I was when she was telling me this, it hadn't occurred to me that grown men cried.[1]

This bit of family lore has probably come down through the generations in various forms, the story having been told dozens of times to dozens of people, but somehow it still rings true. We wondered if any of the Phillips Georgia Legion soldiers had headed home by this same back road, or perhaps a similar route. We wondered how they felt after the surrender. Were they anxious to leave? Did they want to get home in

---

[1] Mrs. Mary C. Mitton to Richard M. Coffman, December 2003.

time to prepare for the harvest? Were they burdened with hatred and
sorrow? Our imaginations suggested something like this:

*The Legion soldiers huddled in small groups, staring at each other with
empty eyes, many shaking hands, then turning away to gather whatever few
possessions they owned, and heading out alone, or in twos or threes. Others,
confused, stumbled about, not sure where to go; some had blood-crusted bandages
wound around wounds; some, hands covering their faces, rocked back and forth
on their haunches like old men; others wept openly. Many of these wounded souls
may have saved their tears for the long trek home. All of these tears arose from
the same wellspring and washed their eyes for the same reasons: for the blood
and horror of combat, for the mangled bodies of friends and enemies, for losing
after all the pain, all the hell they'd been through—or maybe simply because
they hadn't wept at all until now. These battered men had given all they had on
earth for the Confederacy and the Legion, but mostly for themselves and their
comrades they knew they'd never see again. They went on, like phantoms,
ghostly figures, evaporating slowly as they moved off down the rutted roads, not
bothering to look behind them. Dust stung their vacant eyes, blending with the
tears and dirt that coated their gaunt faces and beards. They cared deeply for
each other, a few with arms draped casually over the shoulders of the men next
to them. They were going to homes they hadn't seen in years, hoping their loved
ones would still be waiting there.[2]*

Now that we have spent years following our rebel soldiers—reading
the letters, diaries, and reminiscences scribbled on scarce paper,
wondering where they found the grit and stamina to do what they
did—we are certain of one thing: they will always be part of us. In one
sense, these men were not unusual. They were the American soldiers of
the ages. They fought and died just like young soldiers are now fighting
and dying in the Middle East: bravely, feeling the same pain, the same
monotony broken by bursts of terror, knowing what most of us will
never know. We have done our best to honor these men.

---

[2] Written by Richard M. Coffman.

Bibliography

1. Primary Sources

Albergotti, T. C. "Memoir." Hampton's Legion. South Carolina Historical Society Charleston SC.

Bachelder, John. Papers. New Hampshire Historical Society.

Barry, John Alexander. Papers. Phillips Georgia Legion. Southern Historical Collection, University of North Carolina Library.

Barton, James Lewis. Diary. Phillips Georgia Legion. Emory University, Woodruff Library, Atlanta.

Brown, Alexander. Letters. Duke University Library, Durham NC.

Confederate Miscellany. Emory University, Woodruff Library, Atlanta.

Dobbins, William. Letters. Phillips Georgia Legion. Emory University, Woodruff Library, Atlanta.

Drayton, General Thomas F. Papers. Historical Society of Pennsylvania, Philadelphia.

Ells, Charles A. Diary. Macon Light Artillery, 1862. Washington Library, Macon GA.

Greene, Marcus. Diary. Phillips Georgia Legion, Kennesaw Mountain National Military Park, Kennesaw GA.

Heth, Major General Henry. "Causes of Lee's Defeat at Gettysburg." In volume 4 of *Southern Historical Society*. 52 volumes. Richmond: Virginia Historical Society, 1877. Page 157.

Jones, Abraham. Letters. Personal papers of Mr. and Mrs. David Harlan, Atlanta.

Kavanaugh, Mrs. John, Pension Application, Muscogee County, Drawer 275, box 33, Microfilm, GA Dept of Archives and History, Morrow GA.

Kershaw, Joseph. Papers. South Caroliniana Library, University of South Carolina.

"Letters Received by the Confederate Secretary of War 1861–1865." Record group 10785. National Archives, Washington DC.

McLaws, Major General Lafayette. "Gettysburg Revisited, The Opportunity Missed—The Planning for the 2nd Day." In *Southern Historical Society Papers*. 52 volumes. Richmond: Virginia Historical Society, 1877. Pages 68–69.

Milhollin, John F. Correspondence. United States Army Military History Institute, Carlisle Barracks, Carlisle, Pennsylvania.

Mitchell, T. M. Diary. Phillips Georgia Legion. Private collection of Robert D. Thomas, Chattanooga TN.

Phillips, William. "Personal Account Written by William Phillips." Unpublished manuscript. Smyrna Historical Society, Smyrna GA.

Rainey, Ethelred. Diary. 25 November 1861 entry. Manuscript 1152. Hargrett Rare Book and Manuscript Library. University of Georgia, Athens.

Reese, Andrew Jackson. Letters. Phillips Georgia Legion. Rees/Reese Collection. Lumpkin County Library, Madeline K. Anthony Collection, series 3, box 23, folder 5.

Riddle, Thomas J. "Reminiscences of Floyd's Operations in West Virginia in 1861." In volume 11 of *Southern Historical Society Papers*. 52 volumes. New York: Charles Scribner's Sons, 1883. Pages 92–98.

Shockley, William. Letters. 18th Georgia. Duke University Library, Durham NC.

Smith, Reverend George G. "Autobiography." Phillips Georgia Legion. Southern Historical Collection, University of North Carolina Library.

———. "Reminiscences." Unpublished manuscript. Microfilm Library, Georgia Department of Archives and History, Morrow GA, drawer 283, box 40.

Sorrell, Virginia Moxley. Diary. Longstreet's Staff. Eleanor Brockenbrough Library, Museum of the Confederacy, Richmond.

Stephens, Alexander H. Letters. Emory University, Woodruff Library, Atlanta.

Thompson, Ivy F. Diary. In volume 8 of *Phillips Georgia Legion, Confederate Reminiscences and Letters 1861–1865*. 22 volumes. Atlanta: Georgia Division United Daughters of the Confederacy, 1998.

Waring, Frederick. Diary, 1864–1865. Wilson Library, University of North Carolina, Chapel Hill.

Willcoxon, Major John B., commander of Phillips Legion cavalry battalion, dispatch to Major General Lee, C.S.A., commander of Confederate state forces in South Carolina and Georgia, 23 December 1861, Eleanor S. Brockenbrough Library, Museum of the Confederacy, Richmond.

Shine, William Francis, and J. B. Clifton. Diary. Phillips Georgia Legion. North Carolina State Archives, archives and records section, Private Manuscripts Collection, Raleigh. Call number PC 589.

Wofford Family Genealogy File. Georgia Department of Archives and History.

Young, Pierce Manning Butler. Correspondence. Emory University, Woodruff Library, Atlanta. Youngblood, W. "Unwritten History of the Gettysburg Campaign." In volume 38 of *Southern Historical Society Papers*. 52 volumes. Page 315. Richmond VA.

2. Newspapers
Athens Southern Banner
Athens Southern Watchman
Atlanta Constitution
Atlanta Journal
Atlanta Southern Confederacy
Augusta Daily Chronicle & Sentinel
Cassville Pioneer
Central Georgian
Charleston Mercury
Columbus Daily Times
Federal Union
Marietta Advocate
New York Herald
Philadelphia Weekly Press
Philadelphia Weekly Times
Richmond Sentinel

Rome Weekly Courier
Savannah Morning News

3. Official Publications
Acts and Resolutions of the General Assembly of Georgia, 1834–1877.
Army of Northern Virginia. Special Order No. 104. 23 March 1863. National
    Archives micropublication, M921, roll 2.
Candler, A., compiler. *The Confederate Records of the State of Georgia, 1861–1865*. 6
    volumes. Atlanta: State Printer, 1909.
Compiled Service Records of Confederate soldiers who served in organizations from
    the state of Georgia. Phillips Georgia Legion. National Archives
    micropublication. Georgia Department of Archives and History, Morrow GA.
    M266, roll 598.
Compiled Service Records showing service of military units in Confederate
    organizations, Confederate service records of Confederate soldiers in
    organizations from the state of Georgia, Confederate Medical Officers reference
    file. National Archives, Washington DC.
Confederate Pension Records of Georgia 1890-1940. Georgia Department of
    Archives and History, Morrow GA.
Governor's Letter Book, 1 January 1847–23 April 1861. Georgia Department of
    Archives and History, Morrow GA. RG 1-1-1, LOC 3341-10.
Incoming Correspondence to Governor Joseph E. Brown. 1861. Georgia
    Department of Archives and History, Morrow GA.
United States Bureau of the Census, Seventh, Eighth, and Ninth Census records,
    1850–1870. National Archives Building, 700 Pennsylvania Ave, Washington
    DC.
United States War Department, compiler. *The War of Rebellion: A Compilation of the
    Official Records of the Union and Confederate* Armies. 128 vols. Washington DC:
    Government Printing Office, 1880–1901.

4. Other Printed Materials
Alexander, Edward P. "Assault on Fort Sanders." In volume 3 of *Battles and Leaders of
    the Civil War*. 4 volumes. Edited by Robert U. Johnson and Clarence C. Buel.
    New York: De Vinne Press, 1888.
Ammen, D. "DuPont and the Port Royal Expedition." In volume 1 of *Battles and
    Leaders of the Civil War*. 4 volumes. Edited by Robert U. Johnson and Clarence
    C. Buel. New York: De Vinne Press, 1884. Pages 671–91.
Anonymous. "Sharpshooting in Lee's Army." *Confederate Veteran* 31895): 98.
Biddle, J. "General Meade at Gettysburg." In *Annals of the War*. New Jersey: Blue
    and Gray Press, 1966.
Chancellor, Sue. "Recollections of Chancellorsville." *Confederate Veteran* (June 1921):
    214.
Church, Mary. "The Hills of Habersham." In *Reminiscences of E. H. Sutton, 24th
    Georgia*. 13 December 1862.

Couch, Darius. "The Chancellorsville Campaign." In *Battles and Leaders of the Civil War*. Edited by Robert U. Johnson and C. Buel,. 4 volumes. New York: De Vinne Press, 1884-1888.

Coulter, E. M., editor. "From Spotsylvania Court House to Andersonville." *Georgia Historical Quarterly* 41 (June 1957): 528–29.

Coxe, J. "The Battle of Gettysburg." *Confederate Veteran* 21/8 (September 1913): 435.

Davis, Major George B., Leslie J. Perry, and Joseph W. Kirkley. *The Official Military Atlas of the Civil War*. New York: Barnes & Noble Books, 2003.

Dent, Stephen. "With Cobb's Brigade at Fredericksburg." *Confederate Veteran* 22/11 (November 1914): 550–51.

Gaines, Lizzie. "We Begged to Hearts of Stone: The Wartime Journal of Cassville's Lizzie Gaines." *Northwest Georgia Historical & Genealogical Quarterly* 20 (1988): 1–6.

Happel, R. "The Chancellors at Chancellorsville." *Virginia Magazine* 71/3 (July 1863): 259–77.

Heth, Henry. "Memoirs of Henry Heath II." In *Civil War History*. Kent OH: Kent State University Press, 1962. 300–26.

Johnson, Robert U., and Clarence C. Buel, editors. *Battles and Leaders of the Civil War*. New York: De Vinne Press, 1884–1888.

Law, Evander. "From the Wilderness to Cold Harbor." In volume 4 of *Retreat with Honor*, edited by R. Johnson and C. Buel. New York: De Vinne Press, 1887. Pages 118–44.

Longstreet, James. "The Campaign of Gettysburg." *Philadelphia* (PA) *Weekly Times*, 3 November 1877.

———. "Lee in Pennsylvania." In *Annals of the War*, edited by Alexander K. McClure. New Jersey: Blue and Grey Press, 1966.

———. "Lee's Invasion of Pennsylvania." In volume 3 of *Battles and Leaders of the Civil War*. *Battles and Leaders of the Civil War*. 4 volumes. Edited by Robert U. Johnson and Clarence C. Buel. New York: De Vinne Press, 1888. Pages 244–51.

McLaws, LaFayette. "The Battle of Gettysburg." *Philadelphia* (PA) *Weekly Press*, 21 April 1886.

Pleasonton, Alfred. "The Successes and Failures of Chancellorsville." In *The Tide Shifts*, vol. 3 of *Battles and Leaders of the Civil War*, edited by Robert U. Johnson and Clarence C. Buel. New York: De Vinne Press, 1888.

Pope, John. "The Second Battle of Bull Run." In *The Struggle Intensifies*, volume 2 of *Battles and Leaders of the Civil War*, edited by Robert U. Johnson and Clarence C. Buel. 4 volumes. New York: De Vinne Press, 1888. Pages 449–94.

Redd, B. F. "McLaws' Division at Chickamauga." *Confederate Veteran* 21/12 (December 1913): 585.

Sanders, C. C. "Chancellorsville." In *Southern Historical Society Papers* (1921). Pages 166–72. University of North Carolina Library, Broadfoot Publishing, Wilmington, NC, 1991.

Taliaferro, E. "Ordinance Return of Cobb's Brigade." 26 December 1862. Compiled Service Records of CSA officers and staff. Nara micropublication. RG 109, M331, roll 241. Washington DC.

Wood, J. S. "Reminiscences." Microfilm Library. Georgia Department of Archives and History, Morrow GA. Drawer 283, box 4.

5. Books/Primary Sources

Alexander, E. P. *Fighting for the Confederacy: Personal Recollections of General E. Porter Alexander*, edited by Gary Gallagher. Chapel Hill: University of North Carolina Press, 1989.

Andrews, Eliza Frances. *Wartime Journal of a Georgia Girl*, edited by Spencer King, Jr. Macon GA: Ardivan, 1960.

Andrews, W. A. (1st Sergeant, Company M). *Footprints of a Regiment*. Atlanta: Longstreet Press, 1992.

Blackford, W. W. *War Years with Jeb Stuart*. New York: Charles Scribner's Sons, 1945.

Von Borcke, Heros. *Memoirs of the Confederate War for Independence*. New York: Smith, 1938.

Crist, Lynda L., and Mary S. Dix, editors. *The Papers of Jefferson Davis*. Volume 7: 1861. Baton Rouge: Louisiana State University Press, 1992.

Dickert, Augustus. *History of Kershaw's Brigade*. Washington DC: Elbert H. Aull Co., 1899.

Duganne, A. J. H. *The Fighting Quakers*. New York: J. P. Robens, 1866.

Evans, Clement, editor. *Georgia*. Volume 6 of *Confederate Military History*. Atlanta: Confederate Publishing Co., 1889.

Folsom, J. M. *Heroes and Martyrs of Georgia: Georgia's Record in the Revolution of 1861*. Macon GA: Burke and Boykin, 1864.

Longstreet, James. *From Manassas to Appomattox*. 1896; reprint, New York: Da Capo Press, 1992.

Montgomery, George Jr., editor. *Georgia Sharpshooter: The Civil Diary and Letters of William Rhadamanthus Montgomery*. Macon GA: Mercer University Press, 1997.

Myers, Robert Manson. *The Children of Pride: A True Story of Georgia and the Civil War*. New Haven: Yale University Press, 1972.

Owen, William Miller. *In Camp and Battle with the Washington Artillery of New Orleans*. Baton Rouge: Louisiana State University Press, 1885.

Sorrell, Moxley. *Recollections of a Confederate Staff Officer*. Jackson TN: McCowat-Mercer, 1958.

6. Books/Secondary Sources

Alexander, Bevin. *Robert E. Lee's Civil War*. Holbrook MA: Adams Media Corporation, 1998.

Arnold, James R. *Chickamauga 1863: The River of Death*. Oxford UK: Osprey Press, 1992.

Black, Robert C. III. *The Railroads of the Confederacy*. Chapel Hill: University of North Carolina Press, 1998.

Boatner, Mark M. III. *The Civil War Dictionary*. Revised edition. New York: David McKay Company, Inc., 1988.

Bowers, J. *Chickamauga & Chattanooga: The Battles that Doomed the Confederacy*. New York: Harper Collins Publishers, 1994.

Bragg, W. A. *Joe Brown's Army: The Georgia State Line*. Macon GA: Mercer University Press, 1987.

Bryan, T. *Confederate Georgia*. Athens: University of Georgia Press, 1953.

Calkins, Chris. *Lee's Retreat: A History and Field Guide*. Richmond VA: Page One History Publications, 2000.

———. *From Petersburg to Appomattox*. Farmville VA: Farmville Herald, 1983.

———. *Thirty-six Hours before Appomattox*. Farmville VA: Farmville Herald, 1980.

The Battle of Saylor's Creek, April 6, 1865. Farmville VA: Farmville Herald, 1992.

Catton, Bruce. *Bruce Catton's Civil War*. 3 volumes. New York: Fairfax, 1984.

Clayton, Charles Marlow. *Matt W. Ransom, Confederate General From North Carolina*. Jefferson NC: McFarland & Company, Inc., Publishers, 1996.

Coddington, E. *The Gettysburg Campaign: A Study in Command*. 1968; reprint, Dayton: Morningside Bookshop, 1979.

Cohen, Stanley. *The Civil War in West Virginia*. Charleston WV: Pictorial Histories Publishing Company, 1976.

Crute, Joseph H. *Units of the Confederate States Army*. Midlothian VA: Derwent Books, 1987.

Cunningham, H. H. *Doctors in Gray: The Confederate Medical Service*. Baton Rouge: Louisiana State University Press, 1986.

Cunyus, Lucy. *History of Bartow County, Formerly Cass*. Easley SC: Southern Historical Press, 1976.

Deaderick, L. *Heart of the Valley: A History of Knoxville, Tennessee*. Knoxville: East Tennessee Historical Society, 1976.

Dowdey, Clifford, and Louis Manarin, editors. *The Wartime Papers of R. E. Lee*. New York: Bramhall House, 1989.

Eanes, Greg. *Black Day of the Army: April 6, 1865*. Burkeville VA: E & H Publishing Company, Inc., 2001.

Foote, Shelby. *The Civil War: A Narrative*. 3 volumes. New York: Random House, 1963.

Fox, John J. III. *Red Clay to Richmond: Trail of the 35th Georgia Infantry Regiment, C.S.A.*. Winchester VA: Angle Valley Press, 2004.

Freeman, Douglas-Southall. *Lee's Lieutenants*. 3 volumes. New York: Charles Scribner's Sons, 1942-1944.

———. *R. E. Lee, A Biography*. 4 volumes. New York: Charles Scribner's Sons, 1934.

Furguson, Ernest B. *Chancellorsville 1863: The Souls of the Brave*. New York: Alfred A. Knopf, 1992.

Not War But Murder: Cold Harbor. New York: Alfred A. Knopf, 2000.

Greeley, Horace. *The American Conflict: A History of the Great Rebellion in the United States of America, 1860–1865*. 2 volumes. Hartford CT: O. D. Case and V. W. Sherwood, 1866.

Hahn, Steven. *The Roots of Southern Populism: Yeoman Farmers and the Transformation of the Georgia Up-Country*. New York: Oxford, 1983.

Hennessy, John J. *Return To Bull Run: The Campaign of Second Manassas*. New York: Simon & Schuster, 1993.

Hesseltine, William B. *Civil War Prisons: A Study in War Psychology*. New York: Unger, 1964.

Holland, L. M. *Pierce M. B. Young: The Warwick of the South.* Athens: University of Georgia Press, 1964.

Hopkins, Donald A. *The Little Jeff: The Jeff Davis Legion, Cavalry Army of Northern Virginia.* Shippensburg PA: Beidel Printing House, 1999.

Jaynes, Gregory. *The Killing Ground: Wilderness to Cold Harbor.* Alexandria VA: Time-Life Books, 1986.

Kennett, L. *Marching Through Georgia: The Story of Soldiers and Civilians during Sherman's Campaign.* New York: Harper Perennial, 1995.

Kohn, Richard H. *Eagle And Sword.* New York: Free Press, 1975.

Korn, J. *The Fight for Chattanooga: Chickamauga to Missionary Ridge.* Alexandria VA: Time-Life Books, 1985.

Mahr, Theodore C. *The Battle of Cedar Creek: Showdown in the Shenandoah.* Lynchburg VA: H. E. Howard, Inc., 1992.

Mims, Edwin. *Sidney Lanier.* Boston: Houghton-Mifflin, 1905.

Newell, Clayton R. *Lee vs. McClellan.* Washington DC: Regnery Publishing Co., 1996.

O'Reilly, Frank A. *Stonewall Jackson at Fredericksburg: The Battle of Prospect Hill, December 13, 1862.* Baton Rouge: Louisiana State University Press, 1993.

The Fredericksburg Campaign: Winter War on the Rappahannock. Baton Rouge: Louisiana State University Press, 2003.

Pfanz, Harry W. *Gettysburg: The Second Day.* Chapel Hill: University of North Carolina Press, 1987.

Phillips, David L. *War Diaries: The 1861 Kanawha Valley Campaigns.* Leesburg: Gauley Mount Press, 1990.

Pollard, Edward Albert. *Southern History of the War: The Third Year of the War.* New York: Charles B. Richardson, 1865.

Priest, John Michael. *Before Antietam: The Battle for South Mountain.* Shippensburg PA: White Mane Publishing, 1992.

Reese, Timothy J. *High-Water Mark: The 1862 Maryland Campaign in Strategic Perspective.* Baltimore: Butternut and Blue, 2004.

Rhea, Gordon C. *The Battle of the Wilderness, May 5–6, 1864.* Baton Rouge: Louisiana State University Press, 1994.

———. *Cold Harbor: Grant and Lee, May 26–June 3, 1864.* Baton Rouge: Louisiana State University Press, 2002.

———. *To the North Anna River: Grant and Lee.* Baton Rouge: Louisiana State University Press, 2000.

Schiaf, Morris. *The Battle of the Wilderness.* Boston: Houghton Mifflin, 1910.

Sears, Stephen. *Landscape Turned Red: The Battle of Antietam.* New York: Ticknor and Fields, 1983.

Seymour, Digby Gordon. *Divided Loyalties: Fort Sanders and the Civil War in East Tennessee.* Knoxville TN: East Tennessee Historical Society, 1963.

Smedlund, William S. *Camp Fires of Georgia's Troops, 1861–1865.* Kennesaw GA: Kennesaw Mountain Press, 1994.

Smith, David C. *Campaign to Nowhere.* Strawberry Plains TN: Strawberry Plains Press, 1999.

Smith, George G. *The Boy in Gray: A Story of the War.* Macon GA: Macon Publishing Company, 1894.

Smith, Gerald J. *One of the Most Daring of Men: The Life of Confederate General William Tatum Wofford.* Murfreesboro TN: Southern Heritage Press, 1997.

Steere, E. *The Wilderness Campaign.* Harrisburg PA: Stackpole Co., 1960.

Switlik, M. C. *The More Complete Cannoneer.* Monroe MI: Museum & Collector Specialties Company, 1990.

Temple, Sarah. *The First Hundred Years: A Short History of Cobb County, in Georgia.* Atlanta: Walter W. Brown Publishing Co., 1935.

Thomas, Emory M. *The Confederacy as a Revolutionary Experience.* Columbia: University of South Carolina Press, 1971.

Trudeau, Noah Andre. *Bloody Roads South: The Wilderness to Cold Harbor.* Boston: Little, Brown and Company, 1989.

———. *The Last Citadel: June–April, 1865.* Boston: Little, Brown and Company, 1991.

Walsh, G. *Damage Them All You Can: Robert E. Lee's Army of Northern Virginia.* New York: Forge, a Tom Doherty Associates Book, 2002.

Wert, Jeffry D. *From Winchester to Cedar Creek: The Shenandoah Campaign of 1864.* Mechanicsburg PA: Stackpole Books, 1989.

Wiley, Bell Irvin. *Johnny Reb: The Common Soldier of the Confederacy.* New York: Doubleday & Company, Inc., 1943.

Wilkinson, Warren. *Mother May You Never See the Sights I Have Seen: The Fifty-Seventh Massachusetts Veteran Volunteers in the Last Year of the Civil War.* New York: Harper & Row, Publishers, 1990.

Wise, Jennings. *The Long Arm of Lee: Chancellorsville to Appomattox.* Lincoln: University of Nebraska Press, 1991.

7. Thesis

Mahan, J. B. Jr. "A History of Old Cassville 1833–1864." M.A. thesis, University of Georgia, 1950.

8. Articles

Alexander, Joseph H. "Defending Marye's Heights." *Military History Quarterly* 9/3 (Spring 1997): 86–96.

Anderson, Jimmy. *The Life and Times of Gen. Harrison W. Riley.* Volume 1 of *North Georgia Journal of History.* 4 volumes. Alpharetta GA: Legacy Communications, Inc., 1989.

Coffman, Richard M. "A Vital Unit (Phillips Georgia Legion)." *Civil War Times Illustrated* 20 (January 1982): 40–45.

Dodgen, Lily Milhollin. "Grandma's War Memories." *The Bartow* (GA) *Herald.* 9 April 1931.

McWhirter, A. "Gen. Wofford's Brigade in the Wilderness." *Atlanta Journal.* 21 September 1901. Page 2.

O'Brien, Kevin, editor. "The Breath of Hell's Door: Private William McCarter and the Irish Brigade at Fredericksburg." Memoir of William McCarter. In volume

4 of *Civil War Regiments: A Journal of the American Civil War*. Mason City IA: Savas Publishing Co., 1995.

Unit Rosters

Phillips Legion Infantry Battalion Unit Rosters

Field, Staff, and Inspection and Unassigned Soldiers

Commissioned Officers

Barclay, Elihu S. Enlisted 11 June 1861 as cpt. of infantry Co. C, age 29, promoted to maj. 6 July 1862, severely wounded (spine and ankle) and captured 14 September 1862 at Fox's Gap MD, exchanged late 1862, promoted to lt. col. 13 December 1862 but did not return to active duty until 10 May 1863, effects of wound forced him to drop out of Gettysburg campaign, resigned commission 5 August 1863, elected to GA legislature in November 1863, resignation eff 31 December 1863.

Byrd, Samuel Masters Hankins. Enlisted 11 June 1861 as pvt., appointed cpt. and asst. QM 19 July 1861, promoted to maj. and brigade QM 19 February 1864, surrendered at Appomattox 9 April 1865.

Cook, Robert Thomas. Enlisted 11 June 1861 as cpt. of Co. B, promoted to maj. of infantry battalion 1 July 1862, promoted to lt. col. of infantry battalion 1 November 1862, KIA 13 December 1862 at Fredericksburg, buried at Old Hamilton Presbyterian Cemetery at Dalton GA.

Fuller, Frederick Cone. Enlisted 26 June 1861 as 3rd lt. Co. A, age 35, promoted 2nd lt. 2 August 1861, promoted first lt. 18 December 1861, appointed Legion infantry adjutant in November 1862, promoted cpt. of Co. A 1 May 1863, KIA 10 May 1864 at Spotsylvania, had been an attorney, newspaper publisher and mayor of Greensboro (1857–8) before the war, b. in Connecticut 24 May 1825 to Selden and Julia Cone Fuller, married to Julia M. Nickelson 20 June 1860, has a marker at Greensboro City Cemetery but it is not clear whether his remains are there or if this is just a memorial.

Hamilton, Joseph E. Enlisted 9 July 1861 as cpt. of Co. E, stated age as 22 but may have been only 19, WIA (left arm) at Fox's Gap MD 14 September 1862, promoted to maj. 18 December 1862, WIA (right arm) at Knoxville 29 November 1863 per A. J. Reese letter and January 1864 roll, promoted to lt. col. commanding Legion infantry battalion 31 December 1863, WIA (neck) at Cold Harbor 3 June 1864, absent on wounded furlough until January 1865, captured 6 April 1865 at Sailor's Creek and sent to Johnson's Island prison, released 25 July 1865, Oath of Allegiance showed his residence as Social Circle GA, described as being 5' 8" tall with light hair and blue eyes, married Julia A. Stokes 13 January 1864, became a teacher and moved to Los Angeles in 1875, d. 12

June 1907, there is a VA marker for him at the Marietta Confederate Cemetery, Cobb County GA, but he is actually buried at Rosedale Cemetery in Los Angeles CA.

Jones, Seaborn. Enlisted 14 June 1861 as cpt. of infantry Co. D, promoted to lt. col. of infantry battalion June 1861, resigned 3 July 1862 because of poor health, b. 5 October 1825 to John Anselm and Martha Jenkins Jones, d. 13 February 1891 at Rockmart GA, buried Rose Hill Cemetery at Rockmart.

Lawrence, James H. Enlisted June 1861 as adjutant, resigned 12 June 1862.

Mathias, John A. Enlisted 14 June 1861 in Co. D, promoted sgt. maj. 2 August 1861, WIA 14 September 1862 at Fox's Gap MD (foot), promoted 1st lt. And adjutant 12 May 1863, captured 6 April 1865 at Sailors Creek and imprisoned at Johnson's Island until released 26 June 1865 at age 26.

Norris, Andrew M. Enlisted 11 June 1861 in Co. B, appointed legion commissary sgt. 2 August 1861, promoted cpt. and ACS 18 October 1862, transferred to brigade commissary dept. August 1863 when regimental commissaries were consolidated.

Norris, John S. Enlisted 11 June 1861 as 1st lt. of Co. C, age 30, promoted cpt. of Co. C 18 October 1862, promoted to maj. of infantry battalion 31 December 1863, captured at Sailor's Creek and imprisoned at Johnson's Island until released 25 July 1865, oath showed him to be 34 years old, 5' 11" tall with dark hair and blue eyes.

Peek, Julius Algernon. Enlisted 14 June 1861 as 3rd lt. of Co. D, age 23, shown as 2nd lt. on roll dated 31 August 1861, promoted 1st lt. 4 October 1862, WIA at Fredericksburg 13 December 1862 (neck), shown as acting asst. QM on 5 October 1864 roll, surrendered at Appomattox 9 April 1865, b. 4 April 1838, d. 12 July 1924, buried Greenwood Cemetery, Cedartown GA.

Phillips, William Monroe. In early 1861 Governor Joseph Emerson Brown appointed Phillips as commander of the Fourth State Brigade from which the Phillips Legion was derived, Phillips then became colonel of the Phillips Legion until forced to resign in early 1863 due to poor health. Phillips was born in Ashville NC but spent his boyhood in Clarkesville, Habersham County GA, attended Franklin College, the predecessor of the University of Georgia, studied law under Governor Charles James McDonald, he served five terms in the postwar Georgia legislature and promoted railroad construction in the northern part of the state, he lived to age 84 and died in 1908.

Walton, Jr., Robert. Enlisted June 1861 os cpt. and ACS, resigned 4 October 1862.

Non-Commissioned Officers/Enlisted

Bowie, John Middleton. Enlisted 15 March 1864, August 1864 roll showed he was detailed as brigade commissary clerk, no further military record although an Alabama pension application stated that he was in Atlanta at war's end on the staff of General W. T. Wofford, age 14 in 1850 Cobb County census, d. 19 March 1921, son of J. E. and Almedia Bowie, b. in Alabama.

Erwin, Joseph Bryan. Enlisted 11 June 1861, age 20, commissary sgt. on November 1862 roll, transferred to 3rd GA Sharpshooter Battalion in May 1863, surrendered 9 April 1865 at Appomattox, He was b. 15 January 1841, d. 26 April 1916, brother of Alexander S. Erwin, buried in Old Clarksville, Cemetery in Habersham County.

Kincannon, William L. Enlisted 25 June 1861 in Co. B, shown as wagonmaster 1 October 1861, last shown on roll dated 14 January 1864 which showed him as commissary sgt., no further details.

Knight, William C. Enlisted 14 June 1861, appointed QM sgt. 2 August 1861, surrendered at Appomattox 9 April 1865 (listed as QM sgt., Co. E).

Lambert, William R. Enlisted 20 April 1861 in Co. K of the 3rd GA Infantry, transferred (or reenlisted) December 1862 in Co. C of the Phillips Legion infantry battalion, promoted to ordnance sgt. in 1863, captured 5 April 1865 at Amelia Springs VA and imprisoned at Point Lookout until released 29 June 1865, oath showed him to be 5'6" tall with dark hair and hazel eyes.

Lynn, Alexander Walker. Enlisted 11 June 1861 in Co. B, age 21, May/June 1864 roll showed detached as commissary sgt., surrendered at Appomattox 9 April 1865, b. 21 November 1844, d. 14 August 1898, buried at West Hill Cemetery in Whitfield County.

Smith, George Gilman. Served as chaplain for the Georgia Phillips Legion infantry battalion until September 1862, participated in combat as well as conducting religious services, severely wounded in the neck at the Battle of South Mountain, Reverend Smith survived the war and his wounds and became prominent in the Methodist Church in the southeast despite partial paralysis caused by his wound, became a noted author and penned several biographies of men of the cloth as well as several novels, b. 24 December 1836 in Newton (now Rockdale) County, d. in 1913.

Wyly, Levi W. Enlisted 11 June 1861 in Co C as 4th sgt., age 18, roll dated 1 July 1862 listed him as an ordnance sgt., promoted to 2nd lt. 27 July 1863, roll dated 19 January 1864 showed him sick at hospital and later rolls showed him home on sick furlough, Officer roster dated 3 December 1864 stated sick one year, inspection report dated 27 February 1865 stated he was absent sick medical examining board approved.

The following names appeared in the infantry Field, Staff and Inspection file in the National Archives for the Phillips Legion. These were probably unassigned soldiers: Barber, A. W.; Barbour, James R.; Brittingham, O. F.; Brown, Andrew; Bryant, Martin, V. B.; Cannill, Thomas (appears as Thomas J. Channel for Co. O roster); Carroll, William; Clifton, Eldridge; Drummer, Jim; Hames, Gasoway; Heton, L; Huban, Thomas; Hubbard, J. D.; McCord, T. D.; Oliver, M. B.; Olmstead, Willis (also appears in Macon Light Artillery roster); Posley, Washington; Smith, Edward; Thompson, John; Walters, Fred. Although information was sparse, some were deserters, a few were prisoners in various stages of exchange and a few were being discharged for medical reasons. They were probably all assigned to Field, Staff and Inspection on temporary status.

Casualties and Other Losses for Company A
Phillips Legion Infantry Battalion
Company A was formed predominantly from Greene County.

	Company A
Total Enrollment	141
Death/Disease/Accident	10
Discharged/Disability	27
Reenlisted	1
Deserted	3
Captured	43
KIA	11
MWIA	5
WIA	36
Resigned/Substitute	5
Surrendered/Paroled	17
Exchanged	12
AWOL	4
Imprisoned/Rock Island IL	3
Imprisoned/Point Lookout MD	22
Imprisoned/Elmira NY	5
Imprisoned/Johnson's Island OH	1
Imprisoned/Camp Douglas OH	1
Imprisoned/Fort Delaware DE	2
Imprisoned/Newport News VA	2
Transferred Out	12
Transferred In	4
Transferred to Cavalry	1
Transferred to Band	3
Enlisted/No other information available	11

Any one individual may appear in several categories; e.g., he may have been captured, sent to prison and exchanged.

Company A
The Greene Rifles

Akins, Alexander. Enlisted 15 May 1862, WIA (foot) at Chancellorsville May 1863 per casualty list in 19 May 1863 *Atlanta Southern Confederacy*, casualty list in 2 July 1864 *Richmond Enquirer* shows him as KIA between 6 May 1864 and 16 May 1864 indicating he was killed at Wilderness or Spotsylvania, b. in GA 1844 to Thomas and Caroline Akins, brother of Augustus and John T. Akins.

Akins, Augustus. Enlisted 15 May 1862, d. at Richmond GH #19 4 January 1863 from fibris congestion, death claim filed by Thomas Akins, b. about 1842 to Thomas and Caroline Akins, brother of Alexander and John T. Akins.

Akins, John T. Enlisted 1 March 1862, WIA (foot amputated) 3 May 1863 at Chancellorsville, at home disabled rest of the war, b. in GA 19 July 1832 to Thomas and Caroline Akins, d. at Crawfordville GA 19 February 1913, brother of Alexander and Augustus Akins.

Alexander, George D. Enlisted 1 April 1864, captured 19 October 1864 at Cedar Creek and imprisoned at Point Lookout until released 22 June 1865, oath shows him to 5' 6 1/2" tall with brown hair and gray eyes.

Allen, John H. Enlisted 2 August 1861, age 24, left sick at Lynchburg VA 24 September 1861, received a medical discharge 18 December 1861.

Andrews, James A. Enlisted 26 June 1861, age 19, discharged 22 July 1861, son of Matthew and Susan Jones Andrews, older brother of John D. Andrews.

Andrews, John David. Enlisted 1 April 1864, present on roll dated 30 January 1865, not shown as captured at Sailor's Creek or surrendered at Appomattox, paroled at Newton NC 19 April 1865, b. 29 February 1846 to Matthew and Susan Jones Andrews, younger brother of James Andrews, d. 30 May 1921 at Greensboro GA.

Armor, James M. Enlisted 26 June 1861, age 21, last shown present on February 1863 roll, no further military record but genealogical records indicate that he did survive the war, b. 1840 to Reuben B. and Mary S. Armor, brother of William R. Armor.

Armor, James Nelson. Enlisted 15 May 1862, WIA 29 November 1863 at Knoxville per casualty list in 3 February 1864 *Athens Watchman*, last shown present on roll dated 30 January 1865, no further military record but genealogy records indicate he survived the war and d. in Greene County in 1894, b. 29 January 1821.

Armor, William R. Enlisted 15 May 1862, WIA (right hand) 29 November 1863 at Knoxville, retired from service 12 July 1864 due to effects of wound, b. 1835 to Reuben B. and Mary S. Armor, brother of James M. Armor

Bagby, Charles L. Enlisted 2 August 1861, age 19, promoted to cpl. in 1863, promoted to sgt. in early 1864, furloughed home in early 1865, no further military record but pension application shows he survived the war, living in Greene County until his death on 20 February 1911, b. 13 July 1842 to James

H. and Elizabeth Bagby, paroled at Augusta GA 1 May 1865, brother of John H. Bagby.

Bagby, John H. Enlisted 26 June 1861, age 23, promoted cpl. June 1862, promoted sgt. November 1862, KIA 29 November 1863 at Knoxville, death claim filed by widow Sarah R. Bagby, b. about 1838 to James H. and Elizabeth M Bagby, brother of Charles L. Bagby.

Bass, John B. Enlisted 26 June 1861, age 23, captured at Gettysburg July 1863, exchanged September 1863, captured at Cold Harbor 1 June 1864, transferred from Elmira NY prison for exchange 11 October 1864, d. 14 January 1865 at US GH Baltimore from chronic dysentery, buried at Loudon Park National Cemetery in grave B56.

Bass, William Capers. Enlisted 15 May 1862, WIA (shell fragment in left hip) 13 December 1862 at Fredericksburg, captured at Sailor's Creek 5 April 1865 and imprisoned at Point Lookout until exchanged 24 June 1865, oath shows him to have been 5'5" with dark brown hair and hazel eyes, b. in NC 13 January 1831, d. at Macon GA 15 November 1894, buried at Riverside Cemetery in Macon GA.

Belk, James O. Enlisted 26 June 1861, age 23, captured near Savannah GA, 11 April 1862, exchanged 5 August 1862, d. at Winchester VA 6 October 1862, cause of death not stated.

Bickers, William C. Enlisted 26 June 1861, gave age as 23, shown present on every wartime muster roll, surrendered at Appomattox 9 April 1865, b. about 1840 to William and Nancy Bickers.

Billingslea, James F. Enlisted 26 June 1861, age 22, WIA (lost arm) at Second Manassas 29 August 1862, disabled at home remainder of war, b. about 1838 to James and Clementine J. Billingslea.

Boon(e), Alfred H. Enlisted 26 June 1861, age 19, transferred to Macon Light Artillery 15 February 1863, b. about 1842 to Alfred C. and Martha Boone.

Branch, William H. H. Enlisted 26 June 1861, age 21, WIA 17 September 1862 (lost arm) at Sharpsburg MD, discharged from service 15 October 1862, appointed drillmaster with rank of 2nd lt. 15 April 1863, resigned 31 August 1864, b. 16 June 1840 to John and Sarah Branch, d. 11 January 1891, buried at Greensboro GA Cemetery.

Brew, James. Enlisted 26 June 1861, age 18, discharged 22 July 1861.

Brewer, J. P. Enlisted 15 May 1862, present on February 1863 roll, no further military record, 1906 Roster Commission roll states that he transferred to Co. E of the 3rd GA SS Battalion in May 1863 but no record exists for him in this unit.

Brown, John. Enlisted 2 August 1861, age 45, teamster, d. 13 May 1863 at Richmond GH #1, cause of death not stated, buried at Richmond's Hollywood Cemetery, section T, grave 317.

Brown, Walter E. Enlisted 26 June 1861, age 41, discharged 5 October 1862.

Burnett, Robert Pinkney. Enlisted 26 June 1861, age 28, present on all rolls throughout the war, casualty list in 2 July 1864 *Richmond Enquirer* covering period from 6 May 1864 through 16 May 1864 lists him as slightly wounded, captured 6 April 1865 at Sailor's Creek and imprisoned at Point Lookout until released 24 June 1865, oath shows him to be 5'9" tall with grayish hair and blue eyes, b. 1 March 1832 in Cobb County, d. 10 December 1878 at Lonoke AR.

Caldwell, Cullen J. Enlisted 1 March 1862, sick at Richmond's Chimborazo Hospital 16 September 1862 with gonorrhea, furloughed for 40 days 6 November 1862, captured 6 April 1865 at Sailor's Creek and imprisoned at Point Lookout until released 26 June 1865, oath shows him to be 5'7" tall with light brown hair and blue eyes, b. 15 May 1835, d. 22 April 1912, buried at Bairdstown Cemetery in Greene County.

Calvin, Charles. Transferred in from 13th Mississippi 5 June 1864, musician, captured 6 April 1865 at Sailor's Creek and imprisoned at Point Lookout until released 26 June 1865, oath shows him to be 5'7" tall with light brown hair and light hazel eyes.

Carlton, Benjamin F. Enlisted 26 June 1861 as 3rd sgt. age 28, WIA (left hip) 30 August 1862 at 2nd Manassas, shown present on roll dated 30 January 1865, not shown as captured at Sailor's Creek or surrendered at Appomattox, paroled at Newton NC 19 April 1865.

Carlton, Wesley A. Enlisted 26 June 1861, age 23, shown present on roll dated 31 October 1861, transferred to Phillips Legion cavalry battalion Co. B between November 1861 and September 1862 when he is listed on a 6 September 1862 cavalry Co. B roll.

Carson, John L. Enlisted 26 June 1861, age 22, discharged 25 July 1861.

Catchings, R. R. Enlisted 16 June 1862, last shown on June 1862 roll as sick at hospital, document ordering a coffin for him and return of his body to Greensboro was found in the Daniel B. Sanford papers at GCandSU Milledgeville makes it clear that he died from disease in June or early July 1862 at or near Hardeeville SC.

Champion, Charles W. Enlisted 16 May 1862, WIA (foot) 2 July 1863 at Gettysburg per casualty list in 20 July 1863, *Atlanta Southern Confederacy*, surrendered at Appomattox 9 April 1865, b. about 1842 to Jesse Wiley and Louisa Jackson Champion, brother of Henry and James Champion.

Champion, Henry W. Enlisted 26 June 1861, age 27, roll for September/October 1863 dated January 1864 shows him on wounded furlough (date and location when wounded not known but probably Knoxville TN 29 November 1863), roll dated 5 October 1864 still shows him on wounded furlough, rolls dated 14 December 1864 and 30 January 1865 both list him as at home disabled, b. 13 March 1833 in Greene County to Jesse Wiley and Louisa Jackson Champion, brother of Charles and James Champion.

Champion, James David. Enlisted 26 June 1861, gave age as 28, shown as 5th sgt. on
a roll for May/June 1862, 1st sgt. on November 1862 roll, WIA (head) 13
December 1862 at Fredericksburg, present on roll dated 30 January 1865, no
further military record, b. 25 September 1838 in Greene County to Jesse Wiley
and Louisa Jackson Champion, d. 22 September 1912 at Penfield GA, brother
of Charles and Henry Champion.

Cooper, John Edward. Enlisted 26 June 1861, age 41, discharged 4 February 1862, d.
9 October 1898 at Barnesville GA.

Corlew, Martin Van Buren. Enlisted 26 June 1861, age 20, present on all rolls
throughout the war, surrendered 9 April 1865 at Appomattox (listed as M. V.
Corvin), b. about 1841 to Elias and Susan Corlew.

Corry, John Alexander. Enlisted 26 June 1861, gave age as 18, slightly wounded 29
November 1863 at Knoxville, present on all rolls through 30 January 1865, no
further military record, b. 7 May 1845 to William A. and Martha M. Corry, d.
in Taliaferro County GA 28 September 1917, buried Crawfordville Baptist
Church cemetery, brother of William J. Corry.

Corry, William Joshua. Enlisted 15 May 1862, WIA 3 May 1863 at Chancellorsville,
discharged 23 May 1864 (epilepsy), ran lumber train from Bainbridge to
Savannah GA until end of war, b. 3 September 1842 to William A. and Martha
M. Corry, d. 14 July 1893, buried at Bethany Church Cemetery in Greene
County, brother of John A. Corry.

Crabbe, Benjamin R. Enlisted 26 June 1861 as 4th sgt, age 28, promoted 3rd lt. 3
January 1862, resigned 8 August 1862 citing medical problems.

Crawford, James Talbot. Enlisted 25 November 1862, transferred to 3rd GA
Sharpshooter battalion in May 1863, WIA (right thigh) 1 June 1864 at Cold
Harbor, deserted March 1865, took oath of allegiance and sent to Knoxville, b.
18 May 1833 in Greene County to William Hinton and Harriet Crawford, d. 20
November 1919 in Suwanee County FL. brother of Lucious A. Crawford.

Crawford, Lucious A. Enlisted 15 May 1862, last shown on October 1863 roll, a page
from the William H. Crawford family Bible shows his son Lucious A. Crawford
b. 10 March 1841 to him and wife Harriet, d. 16 July 1864, an entry in the book
"Crawford Genealogy" by Lucinda F. Stephens states that Lucious "died on his
way home from the Civil War where he was wounded," brother of James T.
Crawford.

Cunningham,William Henry. Enlisted 26 June 1861, age 19, shown as 3rd cpl. on
November 1862 roll, captured 29 November 1863 at Knoxville, imprisoned at
Rock Island until transferred to Point Lookout for exchange 15 February 1865,
no further record, b. about 1841 to Thomas and Mary Cunningham.

Daniel, Oliver Porter. Enlisted 26 June 1861 as 2nd lt., age 40, promoted to cpt. 18
December 1861, WIA at Fox's Gap MD 14 September 1862, resigned 27 April
1863 citing piles, b. 11 April 1821, d. 6 March 1882, buried at Greensboro City
Cemetery in Greene County.

Davis, B. A. Enlisted 15 May 1862, present on all rolls throughout the war, surrendered 9 April 1865 at Appomattox (listed as D. A. Davis).

Elliott, Benjamin H. Enlisted 15 May 1862, present on all rolls throughout the war, captured 6 April 1865 at Sailor's Creek and imprisoned at Point Lookout until released 26 June 1865, oath shows him to be 5'9" tall with brown hair and light hazel eyes, b. 23 February 1842 to Thomas and Judith Elliott.

Everett, John A. Enlisted 26 June 1861, age 23, last shown present on June 1862 roll, no further record.

Fleetwood, Little Berry. Enlisted 8 April 1863, captured 29 November 1863 at Knoxville TN and imprisoned at Rock Island, b. about 1833, d. 9 August 1864 from dysentery, buried grave #1398 Rock Island Confederate Cemetery.

Florence, Adial S. Enlisted 26 June 1861, age 21, WIA (lost arm) 29 August 1862 at Second Manassas, home disabled for remainder of war, b. 6 May 1842, d. 6 October 1909, buried Westview Cemetery at Monticello in Jasper County.

Fuller, Frederick Cone. Enlisted 26 June 1861 as 3rd lt., age 35, promoted 2nd lt. 2 August 1861, promoted 1st lt. 18 December 1861, appointed Legion infantry adjutant in November 1862, promoted Co. A cpt. 1 May 1863, KIA 10 May 1864 at Spotsylvania, had been an attorney, newspaper publisher and mayor of Greensboro (1857–58) before the war, b. in Connecticut 24 May 1825 to Selden and Julia Cone Fuller, married to Julia M. Nickelson 20 June 1860, he has a marker at Greensboro City Cemetery but it is not clear whether his body is there or if this was just a memorial.

Greenwood, Robert H. Enlisted 26 June 1861, age 42, discharged 23 October 1861.

Gresham, J. H. Enlisted 25 June 1862, shown present on June 1862 roll, no further military record but highly probable he is John Henry Gresham b. 4 June 1844, he is shown enlisting as a sgt. in the 9th GA State Guards Infantry in August 1863, his father Valentine Gresham, was well to do so one can surmise that John ran away to the army in 1862 and was then recovered by his parents before the legion went north in July 1862.

Hall, Isaac R. Enlisted 2 August 1861, age 23, discharged 18 January 1862 because of "fungus in left eye and dimness in right eye."

Hall, James M. Enlisted 2 August 1861, age 17, all rolls after December 1862 show him as absent sick at hospital or absent on sick furlough, there is a surgeon's certificate of disability in his record dated 25 October 1861 but there is no indication that he was discharged, last shown on roll dated 31 January 1865 as absent at hospital but there are no hospital records to support this.

Hall, John Sidney. Enlisted 26 June 1861 as 2nd sgt., age 27, promoted 1st sgt. 12 August 1862, promoted 2nd lt. 14 May 1863, promoted 1st lt. 10 May 1864, captured 6 April 1865 at Sailor's Creek and imprisoned at Johnson's Island until released 18 June 1865, his oath shows him to be 5'11" tall with dark hair and gray eyes, 1880 Greene County census shows him as town marshall in Greensboro GA, b. in Greene County, 18 October 1832 to Elisha Hall and

Elizabeth Reid Hall, d. 10 May 1907 in the Atlanta Soldier's Home, buried at Atlanta's West View Cemetery, grave #143.

Hancock, Augustus C. Enlisted 26 June 1861, age 28, shown as 2nd cpl. on November 1862 roll and as 5th sgt. on October 1863 roll, captured 6 April 1865 at Sailor's Creek and imprisoned at Point Lookout until released 28 June 1865, oath shows him to be 5'8" tall with light hair and blue eyes.

Hargrove, John Thomas. Enlisted 26 June 1861, age 21, transferred to legion band in May 1862, shown present on roll dated 30 January 1865, no further military record but postwar pension application indicates he survived the war.

Hayes, J. B. Not shown on muster rolls, Federal capture record lists him as captured 30 June 1863 at Westminster PA, no Federal prison records.

Hightower, Edward A. Enlisted 7 July 1862, WIA (hip) and captured at Wilderness in May 1864 but no Federal POW or exchange records, present on all wartime rolls, surrendered 9 April 1865 at Appomattox, b. about 1844 to Thomas and Winny Hightower.

Houghton, James Redmon. Enlisted 26 June 1861, age 23, shown as 1st cpl. on roll dated 5 October 1864, captured 6 April 1865 at Sailor's Creek and imprisoned at Point Lookout until released 28 June 1865, oath shows him to be 5'8" tall with dark hair and blue eyes.

Houghton, John H. Enlisted 26 June 1861, age 20, shown sick at home on rolls for last half of 1863 and all of 1864, discharge certificate in record dated 16 December 1864, notes disability as necrosis of the jaw and details him to duty at White Plains, Greene County GA, discharge shows him to be 6' with light hair and blue eyes, b. 13 September 1838 in Greene County.

Howell, Alonzo. Enlisted 1 March 1862, discharged 25 September 1862 at Winchester VA.

Howell, Leonidas W. Record states he enlisted 26 June 1861 but this may be an error because he is not listed on 1861 rolls, 1906 roster commission roll indicates that he was in Co. I of the 8th GA Infantry in late 1861 before transferring into Phillips Legion, Co. A, hospital records for 8th GA show him hospitalized at Richmond in late 1861 and at Charlottesville (with pneumonia) in April and May of 1862, it is probable that he had served out his 12 month term in the 8th and reenlisted in Phillips Legion Co. A in the latter half of 1862, he is first shown in Co. A on a November 1862 roll, February 1863 roll lists him as absent at hospital but there are no hospital records, no further record.

Jackson, Jr., John E. Enlisted 26 June 1861 as G. A. Jackson, age 20, 1862 rolls list him as John E. Jackson, present on February 1863 roll, no further military record but we know he survived the war because he applied for a postwar pension, application states he was discharged in May 1864 because of effects of typhoid and wound received at Drewry's Bluff, 1906 roster commission roll states he was wounded 12 May 1864 at Drewry's Bluff but this is strange because the Phillips Legion was at Spotsylvania on this date, b. 29 October 1842 to John

E. and Martha A. E. Jackson, d. 22 February 1917, buried at Greensboro City
Cemetery.

Jackson, Little Berry. Enlisted 26 June 1861 as 1st lt., age 44, resigned 18 December
1861, later served as 1st lt., 9th GA State Guards Infantry enlisting 4 August
1863, a list of probated wills shows that he d. in 1870.

Jernigan, Albert. H. Enlisted 15 May 1862, 31 December 1862 through
September/October 1863 rolls show him home sick, roll dated 5 October 1864
lists him as wounded in hospital, WIA 6 May 1864 (spine) at Wilderness, roll
dated 31 January 1865 shows him "retired due to spinal wound," b. in Talbot
County 28 January 1840, age 25 when discharged 25 December 1864, discharge
shows him to be 6'1" tall with dark hair and gray eyes.

Jernigan, John R. Enlisted 2 August 1861, age 18, casualty list in 2 July 1864
Richmond Enquirer covering period 6 May 1864 through 16 May 1864 lists him
severely wounded, present on all wartime rolls, WIA (thigh) and captured 6
April 1865, oath shows him to 5'4" tall with dark hair and blue eyes, son of
Albert and Lucy Jernigan.

Johnson, Henry C. Enlisted 26 June 1861 as 1st cpl., age 21, shown as 4th sgt. on
May/June 1862 roll, WIA 17 September 1862 (leg) at Sharpsburg MD, shown as
2nd sgt. on November 1862 roll, promoted Jr. 2nd lt. 15 May 1863, promoted
2nd lt. 10 May 1864, on furlough 27 February 1865, no further record.

King, Albert S. Enlisted 26 June 1861, as 5th sgt., age 22, March/June 1862 roll
shows him transferred to FS and I Band as musician, AWOL as of 30 August
1862, at Culpepper Hospital 29 September 1862 with chronic dysentery,
December 1862 roll shows him home in GA, roll dated 14 January 1864 lists
him sick in hospital, *present* on December 1864 and January 1865 rolls,
surrendered 9 April 1865 at Appomattox.

Kirk, William. Enlisted 25 June 1862, WIA (head) at Fredericksburg 13 December
1862, casualty list in 1 July 1864 *Richmond Enquirer* covering period 6 May 1864
through 16 May 1864 lists him as slightly wounded, captured 1 June 1864 at
Cold Harbor and imprisoned at Point Lookout until exchanged 18 September
1864, furloughed home 24 September 1864, roll dated 31 January 1865 lists him
as absent paroled prisoner, no further record.

Kittle, James W. Enlisted 26 June 1861, age 20, transferred to Cobb's Georgia
Legion 21 December 1862.

Leverett, David N. Enlisted 15 May 1862, captured at Gettysburg 2 July 1863 and
imprisoned at Point Lookout until exchanged 18 September 1864, d. 5 October
1864 at Richmond's Jackson Hospital from dysentery, buried at Hollywood
Cemetery section V grave #500, shown on burial lists as D. M. Levrith, b. about
1841 to Francis M. and Susan Leverett.

Lewis, Edward Lloyd. Enlisted 26 June 1861, age 18, shown as color cpl. on
May/June 1862 roll, discharged December 1862 because of debility caused by
measles, b. 7 August 1843 in Newton County to Miles W. Lewis Sr. and Mary

Ann Thomas Lewis, d. 26 March 1875, buried at Hill-Lewis Family Cemetery
near Siloam in Greene County, older brother of Miles Lewis.

Lewis, Miles Walker (Paddy). Enlisted 1 March 1863, present on all rolls throughout
war, captured 6 April 1865 at Sailor's Creek and imprisoned at Point Lookout
until released 29 June 1865, oath shows him to be 5'8 1/2" tall with brown hair
and dark, hazel eyes, b. 22 January 1845 in Newton County to Miles and Mary
A. T. Lewis, d. 1 January 1892, buried at Hill-Lewis Family Cemetery near
Siloam in Greene County, younger brother of Edward Lewis.

Lindsey, William T. Enlisted 6 June 1861 in Co. C of the 3rd GA Infantry, 43 years
old in 1860 census, discharged in 1862 for being overage, he first appears on a
Phillips Legion, Co. A roll for September/October 1863, prepared in January
1864, so he must have reenlisted sometime during 1863, last shown present on a
roll dated 30 January 1865, no further military record, buried at Penfield
Cemetery in Greene County, no death date shown.

Mapp, Henry Smith. Enlisted 26 June 1861, age 20, WIA 29 November 1863 per
casualty list in 3 February 1864 *Athens Watchman*, roll for September/October
1863 prepared in January 1864 shows him absent on wounded furlough,
captured 6 April 1865 at Sailor's Creek and imprisoned at Point Lookout until
released 29 June 1865, oath shows him to be 5'8" tall with light hair and blue
eyes, b. 15 April 1841 near White Plains GA to James and Mary Wright Mapp,
d. 10 September 1927, buried at White Plains Cemetery, brother of James H.
and John F. Mapp, cousin of John T. Mapp.

Mapp, John Fielding. Enlisted 1 March 1862, shown present on January/February
1863 roll, no further military record, born 3 January 1835 in Greene County to
James and Mary Wright Mapp, entry on Ancestry.com shows that he died 12
March 1863 (no cause or location shown), brother of Henry S. and James H.
Mapp, cousin of John T. Mapp.

Mapp, James Housand. Enlisted 25 June 1862, shown hospitalized and at home sick
throughout the war with hepatitis and rheumatism, last shown home sick on roll
dated 30 January 1865, no further military record, b. 20 November 1836 in
Greene County to James and Mary Wright Mapp, d. 28 February 1900, buried
at White Plains Cemetery, brother of John F. and Henry S. Mapp, cousin of
John T. Mapp.

Mapp, John T. Enlisted 26 June 1861 as 2nd cpl., KIA 17 September 1862 at
Sharpsburg MD, death claim filed by Robert H. Mapp, estate administrator (and
his uncle), final descriptive report shows him to be 5'10" tall with black hair and
gray eyes, b. 17 March 1839 to Littleton and Lucretia McGiboney Mapp, cousin
of John F., James H., and Henry S. Mapp.

Markwalter, Martin. Enlisted 2 August 1861, age 23, March/June 1862 roll (and all
rolls thereafter) show him detailed 1 June 1862 to work at the Richmond
Armory, b. in Prussia, Germany 10 March 1837, d. Greensboro GA 9 April
1912, buried at Greensboro City Cemetery.

Markwalter, William. Enlisted 2 August 1861, age 25, March/April 1862 roll (and all rolls thereafter) show him detailed 1 June 1862 to work at Richmond Armory.

McGiboney, William Robert. Enlisted 26 June 1861, age 18, WIA (hip, chest and shoulder) and captured 19 October 1864 at Cedar Creek and imprisoned at Point Lookout until exchanged 28 March 1865, no further record, b. at White Plains GA 14 May 1845, d. 26 June 1924 at Crawfordville GA.

Miller, Charles H. Enlisted 1 March 1862, roll for September/October 1863 prepared in January 1864 shows him on wounded furlough making it probable that he was wounded at Knoxville, KIA between 6 May 1864 and 16 May 1864 per casualty list in 2 July 1864 *Richmond Enquirer*, b. about 1843 to John and Sarah J. Miller.

Minick, William G. Enlisted 1 April 1864, deserted March 1865 near Petersburg VA, took oath of allegiance and sent to Philadelphia.

Mitchum, James M. Enlisted 26 June 1861, age 16, deserted 23 September 1861 at Lynchburg VA, no further record.

Moore, Robert G. Enlisted 26 June 1861, age 17, transferred to legion band, May 1862, shows home on sick furlough on roll dated 14 January 1864, no further record, b. about 1843 to Greene and Eliza Moore.

Nickelson, Henry Clay. Enlisted 26 June 1861 as 4th cpl., age 18, WIA (shoulder) 2 July 1863 at Gettysburg per casualty list in 20 July 1863 *Atlanta Southern Confederacy*, surrendered 9 April 1865 at Appomattox, b. 8 August 1844 to J. B. and Ann M. Nickelson, d. 10 May 1872, buried at Greensboro City Cemetery.

Oliver, Milus A. Enlisted 16 May 1862, September/October 1863 roll prepared in January 1864 shows him home on wounded furlough making it probable that he was wounded at Knoxville, roll dated 14 December 1864 lists him as at home disabled, b. near Saloam, Greene County GA 4 May 1844 to John G. and May Oliver, d. 25 October 1911, buried in Siloam GA.

O'Neal, Harrison H. Enlisted 15 May 1862, WIA (finger) 2 July 1863 at Gettysburg, present on all rolls, surrendered 9 April 1865 at Appomattox, b. in Greene County GA 19 January 1839 to Wooten and Mary O'Neal, buried at Siloam Cemetery in Greene County (death date unknown), brother of William R. O'Neal.

O'Neal, William R. Enlisted 26 June 1861, age 20, KIA 13 December 1862 at Fredericksburg, b. about 1842 to Wooten and Mary O'Neal, brother of Harrison H. O'Neal.

Osbern, J. 9 April 1865 Appomattox surrender record only, no enlistment record, not on rolls, may have been a late war enlistee or conscript.

Overton, Simon W. Enlisted 26 June 1861, age 18, WIA (right thigh) and captured 29 November 1863, imprisoned at Knoxville and Louisville until released 16 June 1865 at Louisville, his oath shows him to be 5'11" tall with dark hair and hazel eyes, b. in GA in 1844.

Overton, Thomas Jefferson. Enlisted 1 March 1862, detailed to remain at Knoxville
    29 November 1863 to nurse the wounded, sent to Camp Douglas at Chicago 23
    November 1864, released 17 June 1865, oath shows him to be 5'11" tall with
    light hair and gray eyes.

Parker, Richard T. Enlisted 26 June 1861, age 17, records indicate he was appointed
    ensign (a new color bearer position) 20 April 1864, the letter from Lt. Col.
    Hamilton recommending Parker for the appointment states "he has borne our
    colors in every engagement since the battle of Fredericksburg and always
    behaved with the greatest coolness and bravery in action," Camp Winder
    Hospital records show that he was mortally wounded 12 May 1864 at
    Spotsylvania and d. in Richmond 20 May 1864, b. about 1844 to Joseph R. and
    Susan A. Parker.

Parker, Robert Toombs. Enlisted 1 April 1864, roll dated 5 October 1864 lists him
    sick at hospital and later rolls show him at home on sick furlough, records show
    him admitted to Richmond's Jackson Hospital 7 October 1864 suffering from
    chronic dysentery, furloughed home for 60 days 10 November 1864, no further
    record, b. about 1848 to E. S. and Rebecca Parker.

Parrott, John T. "Dock." Enlisted 1 March 1862, KIA 13 December 1862 at
    Fredericksburg VA, probable burial at Fredericksburg Confederate Cemetery
    under marker reading "Ga JTP," b. about 1838 to Curtis and Sarah Parrott.

Perdue, Lomi Crawford. Enlisted 1 March 1862, WIA (contusion of side and wrist)
    13 December 1862 at Fredericksburg VA, home disabled for remainder of war,
    b. in GA 28 August 1841 to Daniel and Mary Finley Perdue, d. January 1911,
    buried at Greensboro City Cemetery, brother of Marquis L. Perdue.

Perdue, Marquis Lafayette. Enlisted 26 June 1861, age 17, captured 29 November
    1863 at Knoxville and imprisoned at Rock Island until released 20 June 1865, his
    oath shows him to be 22, 5'9" tall with auburn hair and blue eyes, brother of L.
    Crawford Perdue.

Phelps, William T. Enlisted 1 April 1864, present on roll dated 30 January 1865, no
    further military record but Florida pension application states that he was
    captured 6 April 1865 and put on a boat to Savannah at Newport News in June
    1865, b. in Elbert County GA, 22 January 1846, d. 17 March 1924 in Alachua
    County FL.

Poore, James A. Enlisted 1 April 1864, captured 6 April 1865 and imprisoned at
    Point Lookout until released 16 June 1865, his oath shows him to be 5'6" tall
    with auburn hair and hazel eyes.

Porter, Horatio W. Enlisted 26 June 1861, age 24, discharged 10 August 1861, son of
    B. F. and D. J. Porter, older brother of William A. Porter.

Porter, William Anthony. Enlisted 26 June 1861, age 21, transferred to Co. E, 3rd
    GA Sharpshooter battalion as 2nd sgt. in May 1863, promoted to 1st sgt. in July
    1863, captured 6 April 1865 at Sailor's Creek and imprisoned at Point Lookout
    until released 17 June 1865, son of B. F. and D. S. Porter, younger brother of

Horatio Porter, buried at Penfield Cemetery in Greene County, no death date
shown.

Purifoy, Robin S. Enlisted 26 June 1861, age 23, captured 18 September 1862 at
Sharpsburg MD, exchanged 17 October 1862, September/October 1863 roll
shows him as 2nd cpl., furloughed home for 60 days from Richmond GH #9 13
September 1864, AWOL on all later rolls, no further record.

Reed, George I. Enlisted 1 March 1862, d. 22 September 1862 in barn four miles
from Fairfax Court House VA from typhoid, death claim filed by widow Mary
E. Reed.

Reynolds, James M. Enlisted 1 March 1862, MWIA 6 May 1864 at Wilderness, d. 21
June 1864 at Lynchburg GH #1 (Burtons Factory Hospital), buried Lynchburg
City Cemetery #7 in 1st line lot 186, b. 27 March 1830, there is a memorial
marker for him at Wright Cemetery in Greene County, uncle of James R.
Reynolds.

Reynolds, James Redden. Enlisted in Co. D, 15th GA Infantry 15 July 1861,
transferred to Co. A Phillips Legion 8 March 1862, WIA (arm) 13 December
1862 at Fredericksburg, WIA and captured 29 November 1863 at Knoxville and
imprisoned at Fort Delaware until exchanged 30 September 1864, surrendered 9
April 1865 at Appomattox (listed as J. B. Renals), nephew of James M. Reynolds,
d. 16 July 1894.

Richards, Titus. Enlisted 26 June 1861, age 20, discharged 30 June 1862, b. 1840, d.
1914, buried at Crawfordville Baptist Church Cemetery in Taliaferro County.

Richards, William A. Enlisted 2 August 1861, age 33, present on all rolls throughout
war, surrendered 9 April 1865 at Appomattox.

Robins, Albert Monroe. Enlisted 15 May 1862, WIA (chest) 17 September 1862 at
Sharpsburg MD, captured 2 July 1863 at Gettysburg and imprisoned at Fort
Delaware until exchanged 31 October 1864, captured 6 April 1865 at Sailor's
Creek and imprisoned at Newport News until released 26 June 1865, oath
shows him to be 5'8" tall with dark hair and gray eyes, b. 17 March 1837 to John
and Elizabeth Robins, d. 17 December 1899, buried at Walker Church
Cemetery in Greene County, brother of James and Seaborn Robins.

Robins, James Richard. Enlisted 26 June 1861, age 20, went home sick in July 1861
and joined Georgia Coastal Service, returned to Co. A, in April 1862, fell ill
again and went home early 1863, present through 1863 but is shown home sick
again on rolls dated 14 December 1864 and 30 January 1865, captured 6 April
1865 at Sailor's Creek and imprisoned at Point Lookout until released 17 June
1865, oath shows him to be 6'1" tall with light hair and dark blue eyes. Became a
doctor in Greene County after the war, b. 23 November 1839 to John and
Elizabeth Robins, d. 27 February 1925, buried at Greensboro City Cemetery,
Greene County GA, brother of Albert and Seaborn Robins.

Robins, Seaborn M. Enlisted 2 August 1861, age 19, his service record ends with a
notation that he was WIA and captured at Gettysburg but there are no Federal

hospital or POW records for him, a reminiscence written in 1920 by his brother James Richard Robins states that "Seaborn was killed by grapeshot through the body at Gettysburg," highly probable that he was mortally wounded at Gettysburg (MWIA) and died on the field, brother of Albert and James Richard Robins.

Robinson, Phillip Baldwin. Enlisted 26 June 1861 as cpt., age 29, resigned 9 October 1861, b. about 1832 to Phillip and Elizabeth Emmanel Robinson, buried at Greensboro City Cemetery, death date not indicated, a list of probated wills indicates he d. in 1874.

Robinson, William A. Enlisted 26 June 1861, age 20, present on 31 October 1861 roll, no further record, b. about 1841 to John P. and Sally Robinson.

Robinson, William E. Enlisted 20 February 1863, shown on wounded furlough 12 June 1864 (probable Cold Harbor casualty), September/October 1864 roll still shows him on wounded furlough, no further record, born about 1836 to Littleberry and Mary Robinson.

Sanford, Daniel Benjamin. Enlisted 26 June 1861, age 22, promoted to 2nd lt. 18 December 1861, promoted to 1st lt. 1 May 1863, promoted to cpt. 10 May 1864, WIA (left thigh and right foot) and captured 6 April 1865 at Sailor's Creek, hospitalized at Washington, DC until released 6 June 1865, b. 11 April 1839 in Greene County to Daniel and Elizabeth Sanford, cousin of T. J. Sanford.

Sanford, Thomas J. Enlisted 26 June 1861, age 19, present on rolls through war, captured 6 April 1865 at Sailor's Creek and imprisoned at Point Lookout until released 19 June 1865, son of Robert and Elizabeth Sanford, cousin of D. B. Sanford.

Scott, James Thomas. Enlisted 26 June 1861 as 3rd cpl., age 21, shown as 4th sgt. on 30 November 1862 roll, WIA (right leg amputated), 2 July 1863 at Gettysburg, at Camp Letterman Hospital in Gettysburg until October 1863 when transferred to Baltimore GH, exchanged 12 November 1865, furloughed home from Richmond's Winder Hospital 28 November 1863, home disabled remainder of war, d. 29 March 1886 at Greensboro GA.

Shannon, William T. Enlisted 26 June 1861 as 1st sgt., age 40, discharged at Frederick MD, 8 September 1862.

Stanley, Thomas. Enlisted 15 May 1862, KIA 29 August 1862 at Second Manassas by artillery fire, death claim filed by estate administrator John A. Cartwright, born about 1835 to unknown father and Leah A. Stanley.

Stewart, Tapley H. Enlisted 25 June 1862, transferred to 3rd GA Sharpshooter battalion in May 1863, captured 16 August 1864 at Front Royal VA, imprisoned at Elmira until exchanged 14 March 1865, no further record, b. 25 August 1844 to Levi A. and Elizabeth Holder Stewart, d. 26 December 1920.

Stovall, R. G. Enlisted 25 June 1862, present on June 1862 roll, no further record.

Wagnon, Eugienius N. Enlisted 26 June 1861, age 18, present on all rolls through
war, captured 6 April 1865 at Sailor's Creek and imprisoned at Point Lookout
until released 22 June 1865, oath shows him to be 5'11 1/2" tall with brown hair
and blue eyes, b. 1844 to Thomas P. and Harriet Crutchfield Wagnon, brother
of Wesley Wagnon.

Wagnon, George H. Enlisted 1 March 1862, absent sick on rolls through February
1863, transferred to 3rd GA Sharpshooter battalion in May 1863 as cpl.,
captured 16 August 1864 at Front Royal VA and imprisoned at Elmira NY until
released 7 July 1865, b. 1837, son of Daniel M. and Martha Swindelle Wagnon,
brother of Pitman Wagnon.

Wagnon, Pitman Monroe. Enlisted 26 June 1861, age 22, transferred to 3rd GA
Sharpshooter battalion in May 1863, WIA 29 November 1863 at Knoxville,
present on 1864 roll, AWOL after December 1864, no further military record,
b. 17 November 1840, d. 28 October 1918 at Tyler TX, son of Daniel M. and
Martha Swindelle Wagnon, brother of George Wagnon.

Wagnon,Wesley F. No enlistment record, not on rolls, casualty list in 2 July 1864
Richmond Enquirer lists a W. F. Wagnon of Co. A as KIA during the period from
6 May 1864 through 16 May 1864, while there is no service record for a W. F.
Wagnon in Phillips Legion, it turns out that another Co. A. soldier Eugenius N.
Wagnon had a brother named Wesley F. Wagnon (age 21 in 1860 census). An
article in the 13 July 1864 *Augusta Daily Chronicle* relates that Wesley had joined
the 6th Alabama infantry in 1861 and served with that unit until wounded at
Seven Pines in 1862. Returning to Alabama, he reenlisted in the 53rd Alabama
Partisan Rangers serving in the western theatre. Wishing to serve with his
younger brother he transferred to legion Co. A on 3 May 1864 and was killed at
the Wilderness or Spotsylvania before he was ever recorded on a muster roll.
Born 1842 to Thomas P. and Harriet Crutchfield Wagnon, brother of Eugenius
Wagnon.

Walker, Joseph B. Enlisted 26 June 1861 as musician, age 26, MWIA 14 September
1862 at Fox's Gap MD, d. 28 September 1862 at Boonsboro, buried 150 yards
northwest of Hoffman barn, disinterred in 1872 and re-buried at Washington
Confederate Cemetery in Hagerstown MD, death claim initially filed by estate
administrator John E. Jackson descriptive list shows him to be 5'11" with black
hair and blue eyes, born Edgefield District SC, another death claim filing shows
estate administrator as James W. Walker.

Ward, Franklin B. Enlisted 26 June 1861 as color cpl., age 19, d. 28 October 1861 at
Raleigh Court House VA, (today's Beckley, WV) of fever, son of R. H. and
Sarah M. Ward.

Ward, Hinton A. Enlisted 11 June 1861, age 27, shown as 5th sgt. on February 1863
roll, shown AWOL on roll dated 5 October 1864 and all rolls thereafter, no
further record.

Wheeler, Alexander H. S. Enlisted 25 July 1864, present on roll dated 30 January 1865, no further military record, b. 20 August 1849 in Newton County, 1916 Florida pension application states he was "struck in the shoulder by a tree blown up by cannon at Fishers Hill VA," dr.'s statement says he suffered a fractured left humerus.

White, William C. Enlisted 15 May 1862, captured 1 June 1864 at Cold Harbor, d. at Elmira NY prison 19 November 1864 from chronic dysentery, buried at Woodlawn Cemetery grave #945 (or #901).

Williams, James E. Enlisted 1 March 1862, d. 3 December 1862 at Knights Factory Hospital, Lynchburg VA of bronchitis, buried at Lynchburg City Cemetery #7 in line 2, lot 100.

Williams, John. Enlisted 26 June 1861, gave age as 19, present on all rolls through war until 30 January 1865, no further military record but his family tells us that he was actually a German immigrant (b. in Bavaria 28 January 1844) named John Wilhelm from New York, he was living with an uncle named Joseph W. Funk in Greene County when the war broke out and joined legion Co. A after serving faithfully through the entire war he returned to New York, married Mary Swick in 1867, raised a large family and lived to a ripe old age, d. 23 November 1921 at St. Marys Hospital in Hoboken, NJ and is buried at Calvary Cemetery in Queens NY.

Williams, William F. Enlisted 1 July 1862 or 9 August 1862, KIA 14 September 1862 at Fox's Gap MD.

Willis, Eugene L. Enlisted 26 June 1861, age 26, at Richmond's Jackson Hospital 14 November 1864 with nephritis/kidney disease, furloughed home 24 December 1864 for 60 days, 31 January 1865 roll lists him absent sick, no further record, born about 1835 to Lowden and Sarah D. Willis.

Wilson, John R. Enlisted 1 September 1862, rolls through 5 October 1864 show him home on sick furlough, present on roll dated 14 December 1864, captured 6 April 1865 at Sailor's Creek and imprisoned at Point Lookout until released 22 June 1865, oath shows him to 5'5" tall with brown hair and gray eyes, b. about 1836.

Winters, J. G. W. Enlisted 15 May 1862, present on rolls through September/October 1863, no further record, b. about 1843 to John and Ellen Winters.

Wood, Edward B. Enlisted 26 June 1861, age 17, 31 October 1861 roll shows him left sick at Lynchburg 28 September 1861, no further record.

Woodham, John E. Enlisted 15 May 1862, captured 19 October 1864 at Cedar Creek and imprisoned at Point Lookout until released 21 June 1865, oath shows him to be 5'10 1/2" tall with dark brown hair and gray eyes, b. 17 July 1835 in Greene County to Garrett and Mary Woodham.

Wright, James Osborne. Enlisted 26 June 1861, gave age as 19, captured near Savannah GA 11 April 1862, exchanged 5 August 1862, captured 16 August

1864 at Front Royal and imprisoned at Elmira NY until Released 21 June 1865, oath shows him to be 6' tall with black hair and gray eyes, b. 23 September 1834 in Greene County.

Wright, Lorenzo Dow. Enlisted 15 May 1862, age 16, WIA 17 September 1862 at Sharpsburg MD, transferred to 3rd GA Sharpshooter battalion in May 1863, surrendered 9 April 1865 at Appomattox, d. 4 January 1922 in Ellis County TX.

Yarbrough, Samuel S. Enlisted 1 August 1861 as musician in Cobb's Legion infantry Co. A, transferred to Phillips Legion during 1863 and joined band, surrendered 9 April 1865 at Appomattox.

Youngblood, Leonidas S. Enlisted 26 June 1861, age 23, transferred to 3rd GA Sharpshooter battalion 1 May 1863, KIA 2 May 1863 at Chancellorsville per casualty list in 15 May 1863 *Atlanta Southern Confederacy.*

Youngblood, Richard J. Enlisted 26 June 1861, age 21, captured 11 April 1862 near Savannah GA, exchanged 5 August 1862, September/October 1863 rolls shows him absent on wounded furlough, casualty list in 2 July 1864 *Richmond Enquirer* covering period of 6 May 1864 through 16 May 1864 lists him as severely wounded, captured 19 October 1864 at Cedar Creek and imprisoned at Point Lookout until released 22 June 1865, oath shows him to be 5'10 1/2" tall with brown hair and hazel eyes.

Zachary, Samuel W. Enlisted 15 May 1862, d. 5 April 1863 at Richmond's Chimborazo Hospital from dysentery, death claim filed by father John Zachary, b. about 1840 to John R. and Penina Zachary.

Casualties and Other Losses for Phillips Legion Infantry Battalion, Company B

Company B was formed predominantly from Whitfield County.
Company B

Total Enrollment	150
Death/Disease/Accident	9
Discharged/Disability	10
Deserted	2
Captured	58
KIA	13
MWIA	4
WIA	47
Surrendered/Paroled	21
Exchanged	20
AWOL	11
Imprisoned/Rock Island IL	7
Imprisoned/Point Lookout MD	8
Imprisoned/Elmira NY	1
Imprisoned/Johnson's Island OH	3
Imprisoned/Camp Douglas IL	1
Imprisoned/Fort Delaware DE	4
Imprisoned/Newport, News VA	16
Imprisoned/Louisville KY	1
Imprisoned/Camp Chase OH	1
Galvanized Yankees	2
Transferred Out	18
Transferred to Cavalry	1
Enlisted/no other information available	15

Note: Any one individual may appear in several categories; e.g., he may have been captured, sent to prison and exchanged.

Phillips Legion Infantry Battalion

Company B
The Dalton Guards

Abraham, August. Enlisted 8 May 1862, WIA (thigh) and captured at Fox's Gap MD, 14 September 1862, exchanged 17 October 1862, captured at Knoxville 3 December 1863 and imprisoned at Rock Island until released 21 May 1865, age at release 24.

Adams, John T. Enlisted 11 June 1861, WIA (head) at Fredericksburg VA 13 December 1862 (head), captured at Sailor's Creek VA 6 April 1865 and imprisoned at Newport News VA until released 25 June 1865.

Alexander, John A. Enlisted 24 June 1861, last shown on November 1861 roll, no further record.

Baker, Robert Hammond. Enlisted 11 June 1861, WIA (both thighs) May 1863 at Chancellorsville per casualty list in 9 May 1863 *Atlanta Southern Confederacy*, 1906 Roster Commission roll states that he was severely wounded at Chancellorsville 3 May 1863 and was detailed to the QM Dept. at Charleston SC as unfit for field service, see ANV SO 225/7 dated 8 September 1863, postwar pension application states he was shot in the head and through both thighs, at Augusta GA at war's end working for Maj. Willis of the QM Dept., b. 14 December 1842 in Whitfield County, d. 11 September 1921, buried at West Hill Cemetery in Whitfield County.

Bard, Henry H. Enlisted 11 June 1861, transferred to Co. F., 3rd GA Sharpshooter battalion in May 1863, listed on rolls as sick in hospital from November 1863–March 1864, no further record but known that he died during the war as his tombstone in the old Hamilton Presbyterian Cemetery in Dalton shows his birth/death dates as 1843–1864, b. in Pennsylvania to James H. and Elizabeth H. Bard.

Barry, Joseph C. Enlisted 1 March 1862, WIA at Beverly's Ford VA 23 August 1862, KIA at Sharpsburg MD 17 September 1862, shot in head and died instantly, brother of John A. Barry, buried on the field where he fell, b. about 1842 in Georgia to C. M. and Elizabeth H. Barry.

Barry, John A. Enlisted 25 July 1861, WIA at Spotsylvania 12 May 1864, letter dated 5 June 1864 from Will Hamilton to John's sister Sallie states that a "cannonball struck him on the right side of the face, inflicting a painful though not severe wound," it turned out to be worse that Hamilton thought as the wound damaged the eye and kept him out of the rest of the war, a letter Barry wrote to his sister 27 December 1864 from an Augusta GA hospital stated that he had been discharged from the hospital and would leave the next day for Richmond to rejoin his company, 1906 Commission roll stated that he lost the sight in his right eye and was retired to the Invalid Corps 14 January 1865, the final entry in his service record showed him captured at Greenville SC 23 May 1865, b. in Georgia 13 March 1840 to C. M. and Elizabeth H. Barry.

Bitting, John Henry. Enlisted 11 June 1861 as 2nd sgt., shown as 1st sgt. on October 1863 roll, surrendered at Appomattox 9 April 1865, brother of Nicholas Bitting, married Mary Eugenia Kelly in 1863 at Lafayette GA, b. 15 April 1835 to John H. and Catherine Frost Bitting at Rural Hill NC, d. 18 September 1881 at Dalton, buried at West Hill Cemetery.

Bitting, Nicholas. Enlisted 28 May 1862, last shown on roll dated 30 January 1865, no further record but survived the war, attended Emory College after the war and became a doctor, married Mary Jane Nichols 1 January 1868 at Dalton, b. 31 March 1845 to John H. and Catherine Frost Bitting at Rural Hill NC, moved to Oklahoma and practiced medicine there until his death 7 May 1904 at Tahlequah, brother of John H. Bitting.

Blanton, George J. Enlisted 11 June 1861, WIA (hand) at Fredericksburg 13 December 1862, captured at Sailor's Creek VA 6 April 1865 and imprisoned at Newport News VA until released 25 June 1865, b. about 1832 to Josiah and Elizabeth Davis Blanton, brother of Jacob Blanton.

Blanton, Jacob A. Enlisted 19 June 1861, WIA (left lung and shoulder) and captured at Fox's Gap MD 14 September 1862, exchanged 17 October 1862, surrendered at Appomattox 9 April 1865, b. 5 November 1829 at Rutherford County NC to Josiah and Elizabeth Davis Blanton.

Bridges, William M. Enlisted 11 June 1861, last shown present on February 1863 roll but 1906 Roster Commission roll states that he was transferred to Co. C, 39th GA Infantry, 10 November 1862, this entry probably should read 10 November 1863 since legion records show that he was paid on 1 September 1863, records for 39th GA, Co. C show him present on the March/April 1864 roll.

Brown, George E. Enlisted 8 May 1862, captured at Sharpsburg (no date given), exchanged 17 October 1862, shown present on February 1863 roll, no further record, son of George R. Brown.

Broyles, Julius J. Enlisted 8 May 1862, no further record but he does turn up in November 1862 as the asst surgeon of the 18th GA Infantry and serves with that unit throughout the war, he had previous medical training so it is likely he transferred over to the 18th to fill this requirement, son of John Taylor and Clorinda Hammond Broyles, b. 18 May 1831, d. in 1898, cousin of Marcellus and Walter Broyles.

Broyles, Marcellus Franklin. Enlisted 4 March 1862, captured at Fox's Gap MD 14 September 1862, exchanged 2 October 1862, captured at Gettysburg 2 July 1863, sent to Chester PA hospital from Fort Delaware 19 July 1863 indicating that he may have been wounded, sent to Point Lookout 4 October 1863, known that he was exchanged in early 1864 because he shows up on a Confederate clothing receipt record with the notation "paroled exchanged prisoner," KIA 6

May 1864 at the Wilderness, brother of Walter Long Broyles, b. 16 July 1837 in Anderson District SC to Maj. Cain and Lucinda Nash Broyles.

Broyles, Walter Long. Enlisted 19 June 1861, d. 13 November 1862 at Crumpton's Factory Hospital, Lynchburg VA of pneumonia, buried in Lynchburg City Cemetery but later removed (name shown in cemetery records as W. L. Boiles), brother of Marcellus Franklin Broyles, b. 25 July 1832 in Greene County GA to Maj. Cain and Lucinda Nash Broyles.

Bryant, William A. Enlisted 16 August 1861, WIA (back) at Fredericksburg 13 December 1862, captured at Knoxville 3 December 1863 and imprisoned at Rock Island, exchanged 2 March 1865, no further record.

Byers, James J. Enlisted 19 June 1861 as 1st sgt., promoted 2nd lt. 6 July 1862, WIA (knee) May 1863 at Chancellorsville per casualty list in 9 May 1863 *Atlanta Southern Confederacy*, promoted 1st lt. 26 May 1863, captured 2 July 1863 at Gettysburg, letter on file from Lt. Col. Joseph Hamilton claims that Byers was a coward who let himself be captured, imprisoned at Johnson's Island until 9 February 1864 when he was transferred to Point Lookout, subsequently transferred to Fort Delaware 25 June 1864, released 12 June 1865.

Callahan, John S. Enlisted 11 June 1861, shown as drummer on 1 May 1862 roll, last shown present on roll dated 31 August 1863, no further military record, postwar pension application states that he went blind in one eye and partially blind in the other from sunstroke and powder burns received at Chancellorsville in May of 1863, b. 6 July 1824 in Greenville SC, d. 8 June 1908 in Whitfield County.

Callahan, W. H. No enlistment date shown, April 1862 roll shows on furlough, no further record.

Carroll, Willis M. Enlisted 11 June 1861, absent sick much of 1862 and 1863, d. 26 December 1864 at Richmond GH #9 of pneumonia.

Carson, John F. Enlisted 11 June 1861, shown present on roll dated 1 November 1861, no further record.

Carter, Nathan. Enlisted 11 June 1861, discharged 20 December 1861.

Carter, Reuben F. Enlisted 11 June 1861, transferred to Phillips Legion cavalry battalion, Co. D, in late 1861 or early 1862.

Carter, Thomas W. Enlisted 11 June 1861, shown present on roll dated 1 November 1861, no further record, high probability that this is an erroneous duplicate entry for William Thomas Carter.

Carter, William Thomas. Enlisted 11 June 1861, detailed to Division Signal Corps 10 October 1862, shown present on May/June 1864 roll, shown on November 1864 clothing receipt roll, no further record, b. 7 July 1842, d. in Texas at age 91, buried at Kendrick Cemetery near Clyde, Texas.

Chapman, Lyman A. Enlisted 2 April 1862, captured at Fox's Gap MD 14 September 1862, exchanged 2 October 1862, WIA (concussion) May 1863 at Chancellorsville per casualty list in 19 May 1863 *Atlanta Southern Confederacy*, WIA (arm) 2 July 1863 at Gettysburg per casualty list in 20 July 1863 *Atlanta*

Southern Confederacy, shown as sgt. maj. on October 1863 roll, captured 6 April
1865 at Sailor's Creek, released at Newport News VA 25 June 1865.

Cline (Klein), Daniel Lufkin. Enlisted 27 June 1861, shown as absent detached
service on 14 January 1864 roll, captured at Graysville GA, 26 November 1863
and imprisoned at Rock Island 13 December 1863, transferred to Camp
Douglas IL, 25 January 1864 and enlisted in US Navy there on 5 February
1864, b. 9 April 1826, d. 18 January 1911, buried at Deep Springs Cemetery in
Whitfield County.

Cook, Robert Thomas. Enlisted 11 June 1861 as cpt., promoted to maj. of infantry
battalion 1 July 1862, promoted to lt. col. of infantry battalion 1 November
1862, KIA 13 December 1862 at Fredericksburg, buried at Old Hamilton
Presbyterian Cemetery in Dalton GA.

Cowan, William. Enlisted 19 June 1861, KIA 14 September 1862 at Fox's Gap MD,
b. in VA about 1832.

Crow, Abram. Enlisted 19 June 1861, MWIA (thigh) 13 December 1862 at
Fredericksburg, d. 8 January 1863, b. 15 April 1841 in Dalton to Thomas and
Mary Cox Crow.

Crow, J. V. Enlisted 1 March 1862, WIA 30 August 1862 at Second Manassas and
disabled for remainder of war.

Currenton, James C. Enlisted 11 June 1861, captured 14 September 1862 at Fox's
Gap MD, exchanged 2 October 1862, d. 25 June 1863 at Hugenot Springs
Hospital from chronic bronchitis, death claim filed by his mother Sabra, b. in
Georgia about 1843 to Anderson and Sabra Currenton.

Davis, Charles C. Enlisted 6 June 1861, teamster, discharged 10 May 1862.

Davis, Frank J. Enlisted 4 March 1862, WIA (thigh) 17 September 1862 at
Sharpsburg MD, WIA (leg) and captured at Gettysburg, no exchange record but
he is shown as present on 1864 rolls, captured 6 April 1865 at Sailor's Creek,
escaped from prison at Newport News VA and walked home, b. 24 November
1842 in Whitfield County GA, d. 5 September 1923 in Texas, buried at East
Mount Cemetery in Greenville, TX, brother of John A. Davis.

Davis, Hardy O. Enlisted 27 July 1861, shown sick on numerous rolls, Danville
Hospital roll shows him there with a gunshot wound 19 November 1863, 1864
rolls show him detailed as a nurse at Danville VA hospital, last shown on
clothing receipt dated 22 December 1864, no further record.

Davis, John A. Enlisted 11 June 1861, d. 16 October 1862 at Brucetown VA of
disease, buried in churchyard at Brucetown seven miles from Winchester,
brother of Frank J. Davis.

Davis, Warren Ransom. Enlisted 8 May 1862, WIA (lost use of right arm), 14
September 1862 at Fox's Gap MD, discharged 1 June 1863, b. 1843, d. 17
March 1896 at Dalton GA, buried at West Hill Cemetery.

Duckett, Eben J. Enlisted 11 June 1861, present throughout war, captured 6 April 1865 at Sailor's Creek and imprisoned at Newport News VA until released 25 June 1865.

Dunn, Samuel. Enlisted 11 June 1861, absent sick throughout war, his 1869 obituary states that he was an officer in the War of 1812 and a Confederate pvt. who had moved to Dalton from Pennsylvania in 1849, his age is stated as 81 indicating he enlisted in Phillips Legion Co. B at the age of 73.

Dye, Jennings. Enlisted 1 October 1863, shown AWOL on roll dated 14 January 1864, no further record.

Dyer, S. M. Enlisted 16 July 1861, discharged 10 November 1861 because of poor health.

Edwards, Adoniza B. "Van." Enlisted 11 June 1861, initials change to AMV on June 1862 roll then change to AMVB on November 1862 roll, transferred to 3rd GA Sharpshooter battalion in May 1863, captured at Front Royal VA 16 August 1864 and imprisoned at Elmira NY until released 27 June 1865, brother of James F. Edwards.

Edwards, James F. Enlisted 11 June 1861, discharged 29 October 1861, letter from R. T. Cook states he was shot in the wrist 18 October 1861 by accidental discharge of his rifle while on picket duty in western VA, discharged by Surgeon Alva Connel, discharge certificate shows him to be 6'2" tall with dark hair and eyes, b. 1 August 1835, d. 8 November 1908 in Gordon County GA, buried at Resaca Cemetery, brother of A. M. "Van" Edwards.

Edwards, John (or Joshua) M. Enlisted 11 June 1861, last shown present on roll dated 14 January 1864, death claim filed by relatives show his date of death as 12 May 1864, location and cause not indicated, casualty list for 6 May 1864 through 16 May 1864 in 2 July 1864 *Richmond Enquirer* lists him as KIA confirming his death at Spotsylvania.

Edwards, William R. Enlisted 11 June 1861, shown present on roll dated 30 January 1865, no further military record, died at Atlanta Confederate Soldier's Home (date unknown), buried at Atlanta's Westview Cemetery grave #108.

Eldridge, Frank M. Enlisted 27 June 1861, KIA at Fredericksburg VA 13 December 1862.

England, Joseph Curtis. Enlisted 19 June 1861, captured at Fox's Gap MD, 14 September 1862, exchanged 2 October 1862, furloughed home from Richmond GH #16, 4 July 1863 to recover from typhoid, transferred to 3d GA Sharpshooter battalion, WIA (left arm) 12 May 1864 at Spotsylvania, captured 6 April 1865 at Sailor's Creek and imprisoned at Point Lookout until released 11 June 1865, b. 28 October 1835 in Burke County NC, d. 21 January 1922, buried at Swamp Creek Baptist Church Cemetery in Whitfield County.

Field, James H. Enlisted 24 June 1861, admitted to hospital 10 July 1864 with gunshot wound to left thigh, captured 6 April 1865 at Sailor's Creek and imprisoned at Newport News VA until released 25 June 1865, brother of William T. Field and asst. surgeon Samuel W. Field.

Field, William T. Enlisted 11 June 1861 as cpl., shown as 4th sgt. on June 1862 roll, detailed as a druggist to Cannon Hospital in Dalton GA 5 November 1862, shown AWOL 6 February 1863, shown detailed as hospital steward 10 August 1864, no further record, brother of James H. Field and asst. surgeon Samuel W. Field.

Fincher, Jesse C. Enlisted 11 June 1861, absent sick on all rolls after 14 January 1864, captured at Jackson Hospital, Richmond 3 April 1865, released 23 May 1865.

Ford, Francis "Frank" Marion. Enlisted 11 June 1861, d. 17 May 1862 of disease at Camp Pritchard SC.

Freeman, J. H. G. Enlisted 11 June 1861, casualty list in 2 July 1864 *Richmond Enquirer* shows him severely wounded between 6 May 1864 and 16 May 1864, captured at Sailor's Creek 6 April 1865 and imprisoned at Newport News VA until released 25 June 1865.

Gambrell, S. V. Enlisted 6 September 1861, discharged for disability, 20 May 1862 at Camp Pritchard SC.

Gambrell, B. Osgood. Enlisted 11 June 1861, appointed musician 1 May 1862, admitted to Richmond GH #16 20 December 1862 with accidental gunshot wound, furloughed home 12 February 1863, shown home on furlough on roll dated 14 January 1864, shown as retired to Invalid Corps 13 April 1864 but then shown present on rolls from March through August 1864, surrendered 9 April 1865 at Appomattox as V. O. Gambrell.

Gambrell, M. Edward. Enlisted 6 September 1861, WIA at Fredericksburg 13 December 1862, shown as 3rd cpl. on 14 January 1864 roll, casualty list in 2 July 1864 *Richmond Enquirer* shows him slightly wounded between 6 May 1864 and 16 May 1864, received clothing in November 1864, no further record.

Gary (Geary), Charles Thomas. Enlisted 16 August 1861, received clothing 31 December 1864, no further military record, postwar pension application states he surrendered at Appomattox, but he is not listed in the paroles, witnesses testify that he was present when they were captured 6 April 1865.

Glover, Darling P. Enlisted 11 June 1861, KIA 14 September 1862 at Fox's Gap MD, death claim filed by adoptive father Darling P. Blaylock of Tilton GA.

Griffin, Thomas W. Enlisted 11 June 1861, transferred to 3rd GA Sharpshooter battalion May 1863, WIA (hand) May 1863 at Chancellorsville, shown at Lynchburg Hospital 18 September 1863, carried on rolls as absent. sick, roll dated 4 December 1864 states discharged on surgeon's certificate.

Hamilton, Thomas. Enlisted 11 June 1861, as 2nd lt., promoted to 1st lt. 1 April 1862, promoted to cpt. 6 July 1862, retired because of poor health 27 February 1865, brother of William Hamilton, b. 12 November 1838 in Roane County, Tennessee to John and Rachel Hamilton, postwar pension application states that he did not see active service after February 1863 because of severe spinal disease, d. 3 October 1900, buried at West Hill Cemetery.

Hamilton, William. Enlisted 11 June 1861 as 3rd sgt., shown as 1st sgt. on May/June 1862 roll, elected Jr. 2nd lt. 18 October 1862, WIA (chest) at Fredericksburg 13 December 1862, promoted to 2nd lt. 26 May 1863, WIA (left arm) 2 July 1863 at Gettysburg, captured 6 April 1865 at Sailor's Creek and imprisoned at Johnson's Island until released 18 June 1865, age at release 24, brother of Thomas Hamilton, died at Atlanta in January 1897.

Hammond, A. H. Enlisted 24 June 1861, absent sick on rolls until June 1862, no further record.

Harden, William Hamilton. Enlisted 8 May 1862 but immediately transferred to Co. A of the 6th GA Cavalry 12 May 1862, later transferred to Co. F, 65th GA Infantry on 30 March 1863.

Hawkins, Benjamin F. Enlisted 16 August 1861, WIA (finger) May 1863 at Chancellorsville per casualty list in 19 May 1863 *Atlanta Southern Confederacy*, final entry on roll dated 14 January 1864 lists him as absent in hospital, no further military record, b. 22 April 1831, d. 9 February 1912, buried Rose Hill Cemetery at Rockmart GA.

Hawkins, James W. Enlisted 6 July 1861, captured 14 September 1862 at Fox's Gap MD, exchanged 2 October 1862, roll dated 14 January 1864 shows him as absent in hospital, no further record.

Headden, Robert Benjamin. Enlisted 6 July 1861, shown as 5th sgt. on May/June 1862 roll and 4th sgt. on roll dated 14 January 1864, WIA at Second Manassas, WIA (right hip) and captured 2 July 1863 at Gettysburg, held at DeCamp Hospital on David's Island in New York Harbor, paroled and exchanged 22 October 1863, surrendered at Appomattox 9 April 1865, became a minister after the war, b. 25 December 1838 at Cassville GA, d. 14 August 1913, buried at Myrtle Hill Cemetery, Rome GA.

Henderson, Shadrack James. Enlisted 24 June 1861, final entry on late 1862 roll shows him as AWOL 14 September 1862, no Federal deserter or POW records, no further military record but it is known that he survived the war as he is located in Nashville TN as an attorney in 1891.

Henton, John H. Enlisted 11 June 1861, surrendered at Appomattox 9 April 1865, (listed as J. H. Hinton), b. in Elbert County GA 21 February 1835, d. in Whitfield County 24 December 1910, buried at Henton Family Cemetery, Riverbend Community, Whitfield County.

Higgins, Oliver Sanford. Enlisted 11 June 1861, appointed musician in battalion's band 1 May 1862, surrendered at Appomattox 9 April 1865, age 78 in 1916 when he filed for a pension in St. Clair County AL, d. 1925.

Hill, Marcus G. "Gus." Enlisted 11 June 1861 as a cpl., shown as 3rd sgt. on May/June 1862 roll, WIA (both thighs) and captured at Sharpsburg MD 17 September 1862, exchanged 17 October 1862, promoted to 2nd lt. 12 June

1863, captured 6 April 1865 at Sailors Creek and imprisoned at Johnson's Island until released 18 June 1865, age at release 29, brother of William D. Hill.

Hill, William D. Enlisted 1 August 1861, captured 29 November 1863 at Knoxville TN and imprisoned at Rock Island until released 20 June 1865, age at release 26, brother of Marcus G. Hill, fatally injured by a train in Dalton August 1898 and died shortly thereafter, buried at Antioch Church Cemetery.

Holland, Ephraim. Enlisted 6 August 1861, age 37, appointed teamster 27 October 1861, shown on sick furlough April/May/June 1862 rolls, turns out he had enlisted in February 1862 as 1st lt. of Co. B of the 36th GA Infantry, served with this unit in the Army of Tennessee until May 1864 when he deserted taking the Oath of Allegiance at Chattanooga 24 May 1864, he had made the statement that he was quitting if Johnston retreated past the Etowah River and did so, then enlisted in the Federal 12th Indiana Artillery (using the name Alexander Holland) as a pvt. on 17 October 1864 and served with that unit until he d. 21 May 1865 of small pox at Nashville TN, his widow received a Federal pension.

Hooper, John W. Enlisted 6 August 1861, WIA (finger amputated) in early May 1864 per casualty list in 2 July 1864 *Richmond Enquirer*, received clothing 10 November 1864, no further record.

Hooper, William J. Enlisted 11 June 1861, last shown on roll dated 14 January 1864 as absent in hospital, no further record.

Howell, James Franklin. Enlisted 13 July 1861, transferred to 3 GA Sharpshooter battalion in May 1863, captured 6 July 1863 at Fairfield PA and imprisoned at Point Lookout until exchanged 18 February 1865, no further record.

Hubbard, W. No enlistment date shown, first shown on roll dated 14 January 1864 as sick at hospital, rolls for March/August 1864 list him as absent prisoner of war but there are no Federal POW records for him, no further record.

Jackson, J. Frank B. Enlisted 11 June 1861 as 1st lt., transferred to 39th Georgia Infantry as lt. col. 12 March 1862.

Jackson, Will W. Enlisted 11 June 1861, transferred to 59th GA Infantry as ordnance sgt. 24 July 1862.

Jolly, Thomas B. Enlisted 11 June 1861, WIA (hand) 13 December 1862 at Fredericksburg, WIA (shot in arm, bayoneted in body) and captured 2 July 1863 at Gettysburg, reported dead by confederates, wife Eliza filed death claim 14 August 1863, imprisoned at Fort Delaware until transferred to Hammond Hospital at Point Lookout 22 October 1863, released from hospital 12 January 1864, exchanged from Point Lookout 3 May 1864 and furloughed home, recaptured 1 July 1864 at Dalton by Sherman's troops (both he, wife Eliza and two other individuals were arrested as spies who had wrecked a Federal supply train per 2 July 1864 telegram from Col. Bernard Laibold commanding Dalton Post to General Stedman at Chattanooga), imprisoned at Louisville until sent to Camp Chase in Ohio 24 October 1864, released 2 May 1865 and sent to New Orleans for exchange, admitted to USGH #2 at Vicksburg with fever 12 May

1865, released 23 May 1865, shown as town marshall of Dalton in 1870 census, age 42, 1880 census still shows him in Dalton and lists him as a disabled veteran, moved to Jefferson County AL and d. there 11 July 1893.

Keith, Chesterfield Marion Enlisted 18 September 1861, WIA (shoulder) 2 July 1863 at Gettysburg per casualty list in 20 July 1863 *Atlanta Southern Confederacy*, shown at Winder Hospital in Richmond on the August 1864, roll for July/August 1864 shows him as on sick furlough, no further military record, b. 12 February 1839 in Murray County GA to Samuel H. and Sarah Douglas Keith, d. 19 January 1909 in Baylor County TX, buried at England Cemetery in Seymour TX.

Kincannon, William L. Enlisted 25 June 1861, shown as wagonmaster 1 October 1861, last shown on roll dated 14 January 1864 which shows him as a commissary sgt., no further record.

Kingsley, Eugene Terrill. Enlisted 25 June 1861, d. 9 October 1861 at Meadow Bluff VA (now WV) from typhoid, b. 8 October 1842 in Anderson District SC to Chester B. and Emmaline Frances Broyles Kingsley, buried at Mt. Olivet Cemetery in Cohutta GA, nephew of Marcellus and Walter Broyles.

Kirby, W. R. Enlisted 1 October 1862, shown AWOL on 14 January 1864 roll, no further record.

Lane, Joseph M. Enlisted 16 August 1861, January 1865 roll shows him at home on furlough of indulgence, deserted at home in March 1865, took Oath and sent north of the Ohio River.

Lewis, F. J. No enlistment date in record and not shown on rolls, shown admitted to Petersburg Hospital with gunshot wound to left leg, furloughed on 15 September 1864, no further record.

Lockard, James R. Enlisted 3 September 1862, captured at Strasburg 22 October 1864 and imprisoned at Point Lookout until exchanged 28 March 1865, no further record.

Lockard, William M. Enlisted 24 June 1861, shown as 1st cpl. on roll dated 14 January 1864, casualty list in 2 July 1864 *Richmond Enquirer* for 6 May 1864 through 16 May 1864 lists him as slightly wounded, promoted 5th sgt. on 31 August 1864, surrendered at Appomattox 9 April 1865, Alabama pension application of widow Maggie A. Lockard states that he d. October 1889 in Jackson County, Alabama.

Lynch, Stephen. Enlisted 6 August 1861, WIA (hand) 2 July 1863 at Gettysburg per casualty list in 20 July 1863 *Atlanta Southern Confederacy*, shown as a deserter on March/April 1864 roll and all rolls thereafter.

Lynch, William. Enlisted 6 August 1861, reported MIA at Fox's Gap MD 14 September 1862 and later declared KIA, death claim filed by mother, Ann R. Lynch.

Lynn (or Linn), Alexander Walker. Enlisted 11 June 1861, gave age as 21, May/June 1864 roll shows detached as commissary sgt., surrendered at Appomattox 9 April 1965, b. 21 November 1844, d. 14 August 1898, buried at West Hill Cemetery.

Lynn (or Linn), L. M. No enlistment record and not shown on rolls, admitted to Charlottesville Hospital 14 August 1863, d. 24 October 1863 from typhoid, buried at University of VA Confederate Cemetery, Charlottesville VA.

Maguire, Thomas. Enlisted 20 October 1863, roll dated 14 January 1864 lists him as "AWOL," no further record.

Malloy, John A. Enlisted 8 May 1862, transferred to 3rd GA Sharpshooter battalion in May 1863, captured at Front Royal 16 August 1864, took Oath in November 1864 and sent to Indiana.

Mayfield, John. Enlisted 11 June 1861, teamster, shown AWOL on 4 January 1864 roll and all rolls thereafter, captured at Fairmount GA 17 May 1864 and imprisoned at Rock Island, enlisted in US Army for frontier service 13 October 1864, his service records indicate that he did not actually enlist in Co. D of the 6th US Volunteer Infantry until 23 March 1865, doing so at Camp Douglas IL, his enlistment shows him to be 25 years old, 5'11 3/4" tall with brown eyes and brown hair, he is shown as detailed to the QM dept. as a teamster and apparently remained at Camp Douglas since he deserted there on 28 November 1865, no further record.

Mercer, John H. Enlisted 27 June 1861, d. at Winchester 3 November 1862 from dysentery, death claim filed by father William A. Mercer, buried Stonewall Cemetery, Winchester grave 889 as J. H. Merrier, b. in Walton County GA 9 May 1838.

Miller, John R. Enlisted in April 1864 as a musician, surrendered 9 April 1865 at Appomattox (listed as J.R.A. Miller), b. 1846 in GA, d. 22 March 1924.

Milton, William O. Enlisted 8 August 1861, musician, surrendered at Appomattox, not shown on rolls prior to September/October 1863 so enlistment date may actually be 8 August 1863.

Mitchell, James H. Enlisted 24 February 1862, KIA 14 September 1862 at Fox's Gap MD, age 18, death claim filed by father Thomas B. Mitchell.

Mitchell, Sr., John F. Enlisted 4 March 1862, not on rolls prior to September/October 1863 so actual enlistment date might be 4 March 1863, surrendered at Appomattox 9 April 1865 (listed as J. T. Mitchell), brother of Wiley P. and Monroe Mitchell, b. 7 September 1817, d. 24 September 1891, buried at Swamp Creek Cemetery in Whitfield County GA.

Mitchell, Jr., John F. Enlisted 24 June 1861 as teamster, captured at Sailor's Creek 6 April 1865 and held at Newport News until released 25 June 1865, b. 3 January 1843 at Springplace GA, brother of Thomas M. Mitchell, son of David W. and Keziah Mitchell.

Mitchell, Monroe. Enlisted 8 May 1862, KIA 14 September 1862 at Fox's Gap MD, age 36, death claim filed by mother Sarah Mitchell, brother of Wiley P. and J. F. Mitchell, Sr.

Mitchell, Thomas M. Enlisted 8 May 1862, captured and paroled 8 April 1865, age 19 in 1860 census, kept a daily diary which details the movements of the Phillips Legion Infantry Battalion throughout the war, brother of John F. Mitchell, Jr., buried at West Hill Cemetery, no date of death shown, son of David W. and Keziah Mitchell.

Mitchell, Washington F. Enlisted 27 July 1861, discharged overage (45) on 16 October 1862 but he must have remained with the legion since Thomas M. Mitchell's diary for 1 June 1863 states "my unkle W. F. Mitchell died today very sudden in his wagon between old and new camp" it appears that he had remained with the legion as a civilian teamster, buried at Fredericksburg Confederate Cemetery as "W. F. Mitchell. Georgia."

Mitchell, Wiley P. Enlisted 24 February 1862, WIA and captured 14 September 1862 at Fox's Gap MD, exchanged 2 October 1862, shown present on January/February 1863 roll, no further military record, postwar pension application states that he was hit in the hip and seriously injured at Fox's Gap so it is probable that he was sent home disabled in early 1863, b. in 1826, d. 14 April 1900, buried in Mitchell Cemetery at Phelps, Whitfield County GA.

Morris, John B. Enlisted 11 June 1861 as 2nd lt., age 35, promoted to 1st lt. 6 July 1862, MWIA (in side) at Chancellorsville 3 May 1863, d. 25 May 1863 at Richmond GH #4, b. in Ireland.

Norris, Andrew M. Enlisted 11 June 1861, appointed Phillips Legion commissary sgt. 2 August 1861, promoted legion cpt./ACS 18 October 1862, transferred in August 1863 to brigade commissary dept. when regimental commissaries were abolished (AIG SO 189/4 dated 10 August 1863).

O'Dell, James A. Enlisted 1 August 1861, discharged 20 February 1862, b. 1841 Murray County GA, nephew of William O'Dell.

O'Dell, James Wesley. Enlisted 29 July 1861, shown AWOL on September/October 1863 roll, deserted and took Oath of Allegiance at Chattanooga 5 March 1864, no further record, b. 1838 in Murray County GA, son of William O'Dell.

O'Dell, William. Enlisted 29 July 1861, present on 31 August 1861 roll, no further military record, b. 14 August 1819 in SC, d. after 1900 in Whitfield County GA, father of James W. O'Dell and uncle of James A. O'Dell.

O'Neill, Robert P. Enlisted 11 June 1861 as 4th sgt., transferred to Co. F, Phillips Legion, as 1st sgt. 10 April 1862, shown as pvt. on January/February 1863 and rolls thereafter, with remnant of Co. F transferred to Co. A late war, surrendered 9 April 1865 at Appomattox as part of Co. A, d. 5 April 1886 at Chattanooga of illness.

Owens, David. Enlisted 27 June 1861, transferred to 3rd GA Sharpshooter battalion in May 1863, deserted 14 December 1863, took Oath of Allegiance 5 January 1864 and sent north of Ohio River.

Pittman, Andrew Jackson. Enlisted 11 June 1861, captured 6 April 1865 at Sailor's Creek and imprisoned at Newport News VA on 14 April 1865, no record of release, postwar Alabama pension application of widow Mary Foster Jackson states he d. in Arkansas 22 September 1889.

Quinn, Charles H. Enlisted 11 June 1861, shown as 1st cpl. on May/June 1862 roll, captured in Maryland in September 1862, paroled 20 September 1862 at Keedysville MD, promoted to sgt. in early 1863, KIA 2 July 1863 at Gettysburg.

Rauschenberg, Carl Franz August. Enlisted 11 June 1861, appointed chief musician 1 May 1862, captured 6 April 1865 at Sailor's Creek and imprisoned at Newport News VA until released 24 June 1865, b. 7 July 1831 in Germany, d. 14 March 1911 in Atlanta.

Reed, Elijah T. Enlisted 11 June 1861, KIA 17 September 1862 at Sharpsburg MD, death claim filed by widow Mary Reed.

Richardson, Benjamin Lewis. Enlisted 8 May 1862, shown wounded (back) at Richmond's Chimborazo Hospital 23 October 1862, surrendered 9 April 1865 at Appomattox (listed as B. L. Rickerson), b. 8 August 1841, d. 1929.

Richardson, David. Enlisted 8 May 1862, transferred to 3rd GA Sharpshooter battalion in May 1863, KIA near Chattanooga, 22 September 1863.

Richardson, Robert H. Enlisted 8 May 1862, WIA (left shoulder) 14 September 1862 at Fox's Gap MD, WIA (left hand) 29 November 1863 at Knoxville, captured 6 April 1865 at Sailor's Creek and imprisoned at Newport News VA, no release date shown, b. 8 March 1843 in Jackson County.

Roberts, David J. Enlisted 6 August 1861, teamster, last shown present on May/June 1864 roll, no further record.

Roberts, Jeremiah L. Enlisted 16 August 1861, captured and paroled at Burkeville VA between 14 and 17 April 1865, b. 2 January 1845, Alabama pension application states that he received a scalp wound at Gettysburg 2 July 1863.

Robins, Henry A. Enlisted 11 June 1861, captured 6 April 1865 at Sailor's Creek, imprisoned at Newport News VA d. 15 July 1865 from typhoid, b. 1843 in Murray County to W. A. and Mary Allred Robins, brother of Samuel and William Robins.

Robins, Samuel H. Enlisted 11 June 1861, WIA 6 May 1864 at the Wilderness, shown at Danville Hospital 23 July 1864 with wound to left knee, captured 6 April 1865 at Sailor's Creek and imprisoned at Newport News VA until released 14 June 1865, service record includes an entry stating that he died at Newport News VA on 15 July 1865 but this is known to be in error since he survived the war and later moved to Johnson County AR in 1872, born 11 April 1840 in Murray County GA to W. A. and Mary Allred Robins, brother of Henry and William Robins.

Robins, William Elias. Enlisted 2 September 1862, surrendered 9 April 1865 at Appomattox, b. 1845 in Murray County to W. A. and Mary Allred Robins, brother of Henry and Samuel Robins.

Russell, Henry L. Enlisted 26 June 1861, captured 14 September 1862 at Fox's Gap MD, exchanged 2 October 1862, surrendered 9 April 1865 at Appomattox (listed as H. S. Russell), b. 28 December 1842 in Chatham County GA, moved to Volusia County FL 14 October 1874.

Samples, John W. Enlisted 24 June 1861, captured 14 September 1862 at Fox's Gap MD, exchanged 2 October 1862, WIA 29 November 1863 at Knoxville per casualty list in 3 February 1864 *Athens Watchman*, shown as 4th cpl. on roll dated 14 January 1864, captured at Sailor's Creek 6 April 1865 and imprisoned at Newport News VA until released 25 June 1865.

Sansom, Thomas J. Enlisted 2 April 1863, captured at Knoxville 29 November 1863, imprisoned at Rock Island IL, enlisted in U. S. Navy and sent to Naval Rendevouz at Camp Douglas, Chicago IL 5 February 1864, no further record.

Shoemaker, Thomas J. Enlisted 11 June 1861, transferred to 3rd GA Sharpshooter battalion May 1863, WIA (right side) at Chancellorsville 3 May 1863, returned to duty 31 July 1863, deserted near Petersburg 22 March 1865.

Simmons, William. Erroneous service record entry (not on muster rolls, hospital death record only), see William P. Summers.

Small, Augustus B. Enlisted 11 June 1861 as 3rd cpl., shown as 2nd cpl. on May/June 1862 roll, detailed for duty at Tunnel Hill Hospital in Georgia late 1862, transferred to ANV staff as courier for General R. E. Lee 12 August 1863.

Stinson, Samuel. Enlisted 8 May 1862, MWIA (back) 13 December 1862 at Fredericksburg, d. 5 January 1863 at Ford's Factory Hospital, Lynchburg, VA from effects of wound and typhoid, buried Lynchburg City Cemetery #9 in 2nd line, lot 79, death claim filed by widow Lucretia.

Stone, Hezekiah K. Enlisted 25 July 1861, captured 6 April 1865 at Sailor's Creek and imprisoned at Newport News VA until released 25 June 1865.

Stone, Richard P. Enlisted 24 June 1861, KIA 14 September 1862 at Fox's Gap MD.

Summers, William P. Enlisted 24 July 1861, d. 1 November 1862 at Winchester VA, cause not stated, buried at Stonewall Cemetery, Winchester VA, gravestone reads "Died Oct 31, 1862 B. 3 March 1842, A Promising and a good soldier, endeared to his Country and his Comrades," death claim filed by father Thomas F. Summers.

Tarver, Ethelred Jordan. Enlisted 24 June 1861, MWIA (shoulder) 29 November 1863 at Knoxville and captured, exchanged through lines and died shortly thereafter, age 27.

Tarver, Robert Martin. Enlisted 8 May 1862, captured 29 November 1863 at Knoxville and imprisoned at Rock Island IL, took Oath 25 October 1864 and volunteered to join U. S. Army for frontier service but was rejected and released from prison, no further military record, b. 9 October 1841, d. 12 March 1918, buried at Dawnville Cemetery in Whitfield County.

Turner, Francis Marion. Enlisted 8 May 1862, captured 14 September 1862 at Fox's Gap MD, exchanged 2 October 1862, WIA (lost finger) May 1863 at Chancellorsville per casualty list in 19 May 1863 *Atlanta Southern Confederacy*, deserted near Petersburg 10 March 1865, took Oath and sent north, b. 1 July 1838, d. 14 June 1906, buried at Richardson Cemetery in Whitfield County.

Varnell, Robert H. Enlisted 27 June 1861, d. 26 December 1862 at Howards Grove Hospital, Richmond from small pox.

Varnell, William E. Enlisted 8 May 1862, WIA (shell fragment, right thigh) 2 July 1863 and captured at Gettysburg, at Chester PA Federal Hospital until sent to Point Lookout MD 2 October 1863, sent to City Point for exchange 16 March 1864, WIA (right hip) at Cold Harbor early June 1864, furloughed home for 40 days 15 July 1864, at Ocmulgee Hospital, Macon GA 7 November 1864, having trouble with old thigh wound, no further record, b. 1844.

Waters, Jesse R. Enlisted 11 June 1861, transferred to 3rd GA Sharpshooter battalion in May 1863, captured at Gettysburg 2 July 1863 and held at Point Lookout MD until escaping 2 May 1864, at Petersburg Hospital 12 June 1864, sent to Raleigh NC 14 June 1864, no further record.

Wells, Lyman P. Enlisted 11 June 1861, transferred to Commissary Staff 50th GA Infantry 1 November 1862.

Wells, Thomas P. Enlisted 16 August 1861, WIA (head) 2 July 1863 at Gettysburg per casualty list in 20 July 1863 *Atlanta Southern Confederacy*, shown as 2nd sgt. on roll dated 14 January 1864, surrendered 9 April 1865 at Appomattox (listed as S. P. Wells).

Whitaker, Philetas. Enlisted 17 May 1864, captured 6 April 1865 at Sailor's Creek and held at Newport News VA until released 25 June 1865.

Whitaker, T. F. Enlisted 11 June 1861, WIA (head) 13 December 1862 at Fredericksburg, surrendered 9 April 1865 at Appomattox.

William, T. F. Enlisted 11 June 1861, promoted to hospital steward Phillips Legion, no further record.

Williams, Cincinnattus C. Enlisted 11 June 1861, last entry states he deserted 14 September 1862, no further record, no Federal POW or deserter records.

Willis, S. Miller. Enlisted 1 March 1862, discharged 26 September 1862.

Wilson, Paschal. Enlisted 11 June 1861, d. 5 October 1861 at Ladies Relief Hospital in Lynchburg VA of pneumonia, buried Lynchburg City Cemetery #3 in 4th line, lot 159.

Worthy, Henry C. Enlisted 8 May 1862, captured at Port Republic 3 October 1864 and held at Point Lookout until released 13 May 1865.

Worthy, William. Enlisted 24 February 1862, WIA (arm) 2 July 1863 at Gettysburg per casualty list in 20 July 1863 *Atlanta Southern Confederacy*, captured 6 April

1865 at Sailor's Creek and held at Newport News VA until released 25 June 1865.

Wright, J. A. Enlisted 12 February 1864, age 19, July/August 1864 roll shows him on wounded furlough, furloughed from Stuart Hospital Richmond 23 August 1864, captured 18 May 1865 at Hartwell GA, b. 12 May 1845 at Cassville GA, d. 1911 and buried at Oakland Cemetery in Rome GA.

Casualties and Other Losses for Phillips Georgia Infantry Battalion, Company C

Company C was formed from Habersham County although numerous recruits from Cobb County were added in early 1862.

Company C

Total Enrollment	170
Death/Disease/Accident	35
Retired to Invalid Corps	2
Discharged/Disability	14
Captured	62
Resigned	1
KIA	25
MWIA	3
WIA	55
Surrendered/Paroled	17
Exchanged	16
Deserted	7
AWOL	15
Imprisoned/Rock Island IL	6
Imprisoned/Hart's Island NY	1
Imprisoned/Point Lookout MD	24
Imprisoned/Elmira NY	7
Imprisoned/Johnson's Island OH	1
Imprisoned/Camp Douglas IL	1
Imprisoned/Fort Delaware DE	6
Galvanized Yankees	1
Transferred In	3
Transferred Out	12
Transferred to Cavalry	2
Sent North to Ohio	3
Enlisted/No other information available	4

Any one individual may appear in several categories; e.g., he may have been captured, sent to prison and exchanged. "Galvanized Yankees" are imprisoned Confederate soldiers who enlisted in a branch of the US Army or Navy during the war.

PHILLIPS GEORGIA LEGION
INFANTRY BATTALION

Company C

The Habersham Volunteers

Alley, James Sanford A. Enlisted 1 March 1862, captured 14 September 1862 at Fox's Gap MD, exchanged 2 October 1862, sick at various hospitals until his death 17 May 1863 at Richmond's Buchanan Hospital from disease, b. 22 October 1827 in GA to William A. and Martha Alley, younger brother of PAC Alley.

Alley, Paul. Augustus Cunningham. Enlisted 1 March 1862, WIA (thigh) 13 December 1862 at Fredericksburg, surrendered 9 April 1865 at Appomattox, b. 28 August 1823 to William and Martha Alley, older brother of J. S. A. Alley.

Ayres, Henry D. Enlisted 11 June 1861, age 40, received medical discharge 22 October 1862, 1906 Roster Commission roll states that he died at home from disease.

Ballew, Noah. Enlisted 25 June 1861, age 18, discharged 1 August 1861.

Barclay, Elihu S. "Sandy." Enlisted 11 June 1861 as cpt., age 29, promoted to maj. 6 July 1862, severely wounded (spine and ankle) and captured 14 September 1862 at Fox's Gap MD, exchanged late 1862, promoted to lt. col. 13 December 1862 but did not return to active duty until 10 May 1863, effects of wound forced him to drop out of Gettysburg campaign, resigned commission 5 August 1863, elected to GA legislature in November 1863, resignation accepted by War Dept. effective 31 December 1863, b. at Clarksville, Habersham County GA 24 May 1832, d. 6 March 1879 at Darien GA, buried there at St. Andrews Cemetery, his older brother William was col. of the 23rd GA Infantry and was KIA 17 September 1862 at Sharpsburg MD, his younger brother Julius was cpt. of Co. G of the 52nd GA Infantry and was KIA 22 July 1864 at the battle of Atlanta.

Barfield, Samuel P. Enlisted 1 March 1862, age 19 in 1860 Cobb County census, captured at Knoxville 29 November 1863 and imprisoned at Rock Island until released 18 June 1865, Oath shows age at release 23, 5'8" tall with brown hair and blue eyes.

Barr, Andrew Milton. Enlisted 11 June 1861, surrendered at Appomattox 9 April 1865 (listed as A. M. Burr) b. 2 March 1842 in GA to Sidney and Eliza Barr, d. 18 February 1924, buried at Level Grove Cemetery near Cornelia GA.

Barrett, James R. Enlisted 11 June 1861, captured 7 July 1863 at Gettysburg, d. 11 February 1864 at Point Lookout from pneumonia, buried at Point Lookout Confederate Cemetery, Scotland MD.

Bellah, John H. Enlisted 25 June 1861, age 20, promoted to sgt. in 1864, WIA (shoulder) 13 December 1862 at Fredericksburg, WIA (face) May 1863 at Chancellorsville per casualty list in 19 May 1863 *Atlanta Southern Confederacy*, KIA at Cedar Creek 19 October 1864 (29 October 1864 letter from G. O.

Megarity states that Bellah, W. S. Manning, J. Lambert and J. Kistleburg were all killed by a single shellburst), b. 19 March 1841 in GA to Rev. Samuel J. and Sarah Patterson Bellah, brother of Richard and Robert Bellah.

Bellah, Richard Watson. Enlisted 1 March 1862, age 18, captured 6 April 1865 at Sailors Creek and imprisoned at Point Lookout until released 24 June 1865, Oath shows him to be 5'3 3/4" tall with brown hair and blue eyes, b. 29 November 1843 in GA to Rev. Samuel J. and Sarah Patterson Bellah, brother of John and Robert Bellah, d. 8 January 1935, buried Mt. Bethel Cemetery Roswell GA.

Bellah, Robert Pollock. Not shown on final roll dated 30 January 1865 so presumed to have enlisted after that date, 13 years old in 1860 census, captured 6 April 1865 at Sailor's Creek and imprisoned at Point Lookout until released 24 June 1865, Oath shows him to be 5' 4 1/4" tall with dark brown hair and blue eyes, b. 15 April 1847 in GA to Rev. Samuel J. and Sarah Patterson Bellah, brother of John and Richard Bellah, d. 2 December 1921 at Columbus GA, buried Linwood Cemetery.

Betterton, Francis Marion. Enlisted 1 March 1862, June 1860 roll shows him home on sick furlough, all later rolls list him as AWOL, b. in GA 1837 to Levi and Elizabeth Betterton.

Boatner, William A. Enlisted 1 March 1862, age 17 in 1860 Cobb County census, WIA May 1863 at Chancellorsville per casualty list in 19 May 1863 *Atlanta Southern Confederacy*, WIA (hand) 2 July 1863 at Gettysburg per casualty list in 20 July 1863 *Atlanta Southern Confederacy*, MWIA 19 October 1864 at Cedar Creek, d. 2 November 1864 at Mt. Jackson Hospital from effects of leg amputation, buried at Our Soldiers Cemetery, Mount Jackson VA, son of Lewis and Matilda Boatner.

Bothwell, J. G. C. Enlisted 25 June 1861, age 46, discharged 29 March 1862.

Bradberry, Lewis J. Enlisted 11 June 1861, age 31, WIA (thigh) 13 December 1862 at Fredericksburg, detailed as shoemaker in February 1863 but in hospital with typhoid until 9 March 1863, shown on sick furlough on roll dated 19 January 1864, AWOL on roll dated 5 October 1864, returned to unit in late 1864 or early 1865 since he was captured at Sailor's Creek and imprisoned at Point Lookout until released 24 June 1865, Oath shows him to be 6'1" tall with dark brown hair and gray eyes, buried at Bethlehem Baptist Church Cemetery in Habersham County, son of Ambrose and Mary Bradberry.

Carpenter, John L. Enlisted 1 March 1862, hospitalized a great deal throughout 1862, 1863 and 1864 with ascites, debility and nephritis, surrendered 9 April 1865 at Appomattox (listed as a sgt.), b. 14 February 1830 in Dekalb County, d. 6 October 1893 in Roswell GA.

Carter, James A. Enlisted 25 June 1861, age 20, transferred to 3rd GA Sharpshooter battalion in May 1863, captured 3 July 1863 at Gettysburg and imprisoned at Fort Delaware until released 16 June 1865, Oath shows him to be 5'11" tall with dark hair and gray eyes, became a policeman in Taccoa GA and was killed in the line of duty 10 May 1892 while trying to stop a bank robbery, son of W. M. Carter, Sr. and brother of W. M. Carter, Jr.

Carter, Jr., William Marion. Enlisted 1 August 1861, age 24, d. 25 October 1861 at Green Sulphur Springs VA (now WV) of typhoid, son of W. M. Carter, Sr. and brother of James Carter.

Carter, Sr., William Madison. Enlisted 25 June 1861 as 2nd cpl., age 51, discharged (overage), 15 October 1862, discharge showed him to be 5'10" tall with dark hair and blue eyes, b. in Rutherford County NC, d. 9 May 1893 at Taccoa GA, buried at Taccoa City Cemetery, father of W. M. Carter, Jr. and James A. Carter.

Cason, P. R. Enlisted 1 March 1862, WIA 17 September 1862 at Sharpsburg MD, WIA (arm) and captured at Gettysburg 2 July 1863 and imprisoned at Fort Delaware until exchanged in February 1865, furloughed home 22 March 1865.

Chitwood, James J. Enlisted 11 June 1861, age 26, shown home on furlough on roll dated 5 October 1864, 1906 Roster Commission Roll stated that he transferred to the cavalry in December 1864, captured at Bentonville NC 21 March 1865 and imprisoned at Harts Island NY until released 15 June 1865, Oath showed him to be 5'10 3/4" tall with light hair and blue eyes, son of John J. and Mary Ann Chitwood, brother of Robert Chitwood.

Chitwood, Robert A. Enlisted 11 June 1861, age 24, captured 6 April 1865 at Sailor's Creek and imprisoned at Point Lookout until released 26 June 1865, Oath showed him to be 5'8" tall with brown hair and blue eyes, b. 26 April 1837 to John J. and Mary Ann Chitwood, brother of James Chitwood, d. 9 February 1904, buried in Old Clarksville Cemetery in Habersham County.

Church, Benjamin Franklin. Enlisted 10 March 1863, captured 1 June 1864 at Cold Harbor and imprisoned at Elmira NY until exchanged 29 October 1864, final roll dated January 1865 listed him as being AWOL, no further military record but genealogical records show that he lived out his life in Habersham County, dying 27 March 1904, buried at Bethlehem Baptist Church Cemetery in Habersham County, born 5 March 1827, had previously enlisted in Co. A of the 2nd GA Infantry 20 April 1861 and was discharged for disability 8 January 1862, a record exists for him in the 2nd GA indicating he was captured and paroled in Augusta GA 8 May 1865.

Clyde, Charles E. Enlisted 11 June 1861, age 19, shown as 4th sgt. on June 1862 roll, WIA 17 September 1862 at Sharpsburg MD, MWIA and captured at Gettysburg 2 July 1863, d. 20 July 1863 at Federal II Corps Hospital four miles southeast of Gettysburg from effects of amputation of right leg, body disinterred 1872 and reburied at Hollywood Cemetery in Richmond VA, son of Thomas M. and Harriett Clyde.

Coker, O. N. Enlisted 1 March 1862, age 18 in 1860 Cobb County census, d. 30 September 1862 at Warrenton VA of intermittent fever, buried in Warrenton Confederate Cemetery, son of A. T. and Mary Coker.

Conger, Benjamin Franklin. Enlisted 1 March 1862, age 31 in 1860 Cobb County census, roll dated 19 January 1864 showed him sick at hospital, later 1864 rolls listed him as absent sick and absent AWOL, detailed to Winder Hospital in Richmond as a nurse 6 May 1864, received clothing 25 November 1864, no further record.

Conger, George Buchanan. Enlisted 1 March 1862, age 27 in 1860 Cobb County census, present on all rolls through January 1865, no further military record but known to have survived the war since he filed for a pension, born in Cobb County in 1833 to Zachariah and Mary Conger.

Conger, Zach. Enlisted 1 March 1862, surrendered at Appomattox 9 April 1865 (listed as Z. Congs).

Crow, John G. Enlisted 1 February 1862, disability discharged 19 April 1862, age 35 at discharge, b. in 1833.

Daniel, Moses N. Enlisted 1 March 1862, age 25, WIA 30 August 1862 at Second Manassas, captured and immediately paroled at Leesburg VA, at Richmond Hospital 19 October 1862 with gunshot wound, returned to duty 23 October 1862, WIA (hand) 2 July 1863 at Gettysburg on casualty list in 20 July 1863 *Atlanta Southern Confederacy*, present on all rolls throughout the war until deserting 19 March 1865 near Petersburg, took Oath of Allegiance and sent to Richmond, Ohio, 1901 Alabama pension application states his age as 64 and also says he was wounded in the arm 1 June 1864 at Cold Harbor and in the left thigh at Petersburg 27 June 1864.

Davis, Tyre Swift. Enlisted 11 June 1861, gave age as 18, promoted to 3rd sgt. in late 1864, captured 6 April 1865 at Sailor's Creek and imprisoned at Point Lookout until released 26 June 1865, Oath shows him to be 5'8" with brown hair and blue eyes, b. 28 December 1844, d. 20 April 1907, buried at Taccoa City Cemetery in Stephens County GA.

Delk, James Jackson. Enlisted 1 March 1862, age 16 in 1860 Cobb County census, captured 6 April 1865 at Sailor's Creek and imprisoned at Point Lookout until released 26 June 1865, Oath shows him to be 5'11 1/4" tall with light hair and blue eyes, b. 4 September 1844 in Cobb County to W. J. and E. T. Delk.

Dobbins, William H. Enlisted 1 August 1861, age 20, KIA 14 September 1862 at Fox's Gap MD, death claim filed by father John S. Dobbins, b. 6 July 1841 in Habersham County.

Dodd, Henry William. Enlisted 11 June 1861, age 23, MWIA 14 September 1862 at Fox's Gap MD, d. 12 November 1862 at Winchester VA, b. 8 April 1839 in Habersham County to William and Abby Dodd.

Donehoo, Barnett W. Enlisted 5 April 1862 in Co. L and transferred to Co. C Phillips Legion, 1 May 1862, age 52 in 1860 Cobb County census, discharged 1

September 1862 because of loss of eyesight, age 54, discharge shows him to be 5'7" with grey hair and hazel eyes, son of Cornelius and Elizabeth Donehoo.

Edgeworth, John. Enlisted 1 March 1862, age 31 in 1860 Cobb County census, present on all rolls throughout war, captured 6 April 1865 at Sailor's Creek and imprisoned at Point Lookout until released 26 June 1865, Oath shows him to be 5' 7 1/2" tall with brown hair and light blue eyes, 1893 Alabama pension application shows his age as 67.

Edwards, George W. Enlisted 25 June 1861, age 26, MWIA (head) 13 December 1862 at Fredericksburg, d. 26 December 1862 at Richmond GH #20, buried at Richmond's Oakwood Cemetery.

Elliott, James W. Enlisted 11 June 1861, age 22, 1906 Roster Commission states he was KIA 2 July 1863 at Gettysburg but this is incorrect, he transferred to the 3rd GA Sharpshooter battalion in May 1863 and was then captured 16 August 1864 at Front Royal VA, briefly imprisoned at Elmira NY where he d. 4 September 1864 from typhoid, son of Samuel and Elizabeth Elliott.

Elliott, Samuel N. Enlisted 1 January 1862, discharged 16 June 1862, overage (54), father of James and William Elliott.

Elliott, William John. Enlisted 1 January 1862, KIA 13 December 1862 at Fredericksburg, death claim filed by father Samuel N. Elliott, son of Samuel and Elizabeth Elliott.

Elrod, John H. Enlisted 11 June 1861, age 20, captured 6 April 1865 at Sailor's Creek and imprisoned at Point Lookout, on a list of sick prisoners released 4 June 1865, 1906 Roster Commission stated that he died on way home after surrender, son of Miriam Elrod.

Elrod, William Thomas. Enlisted 1 March 1862, WIA (lost arm) 30 August 1862 at Second Manassas, at home disabled remainder of war, b. 12 January 1830, d. 4 January 1894, buried at Old Clarksville Cemetery in Habersham County.

Erwin, Alexander Smith. Enlisted 11 June 1861 as 2nd lt., age 18, promoted 1st lt. 16 October 1862, WIA (arm) 24 September 1863 near Chattanooga, detailed to recruiting/conscription duty in GA during 1863 and 1864, promoted to Co. C cpt. 3 December 1863, attempted to return to the company in early 1865 but wound caused him to be retired from service 6 March 1865, married Howell Cobb's daughter, Mary Ann Lamar Cobb after the war and became a judge at Athens GA, recipient of Southern Cross of Honor #1, younger brother of Joseph B. Erwin, b. 19 July 1843 at Clarksville GA to Alexander and Catharine Wales Erwin, d. 6 June 1907 at his home in Athens GA, buried Oconee Cemetery in Athens.

Erwin, John Miller. Enlisted 11 June 1861, age 18, promoted to 3rd cpl. 1 December 1862, admitted Jackson Hospital, with ascites and hernia 5 June 1864, detailed as a nurse there 24 June 1864, furloughed home 26 September 1864 and was back with Legion by November 1864, captured 6 April 1865 at Sailor's Creek and imprisoned at Point Lookout until released 26 June 1865, Oath showed him to be 5'7" tall with light brown hair and dark gray eyes, b. 15 February 1844 in Gordon County GA to William G. and Martha McCrary Erwin, older brother of Sidney Louis Erwin, d. in 1898 from injuries received in a lumbering accident near Sharon TN.

Erwin, Joseph Bryan. Enlisted 11 June 1861, age 20, commissary sgt. on November 1862 roll, transferred to 3rd GA Sharpshooter battalion in May 1863 as QM sgt., surrendered 9 April 1865 at Appomattox, brother of Alexander S. Erwin, b. 15 January 1841 to Alexander and Catharine Wales Erwin, d. 26 April 1916, buried in Old Clarksville Cemetery in Habersham County.

Erwin, Sidney Louis. Enlisted 1 February 1863, captured 6 April 1865 at Sailor's Creek and imprisoned at Point Lookout until released 26 June 1865, 5'6" tall with auburn hair and blue eyes, younger brother of John M. Erwin, died in a gunfight in 1880 at McAlester, Oklahoma.

Evatt, William Robert. Enlisted 11 June 1861, age 20, d. 5 October 1861 at Ladies Relief Hospital, Lynchburg VA, of typhoid, claim filed by mother Emma S. Evatt, buried at Lynchburg City Cemetery #7 in 4th line lot 159.

Fenn, George Washington. Enlisted 6 May 1862 in Co. O, transferred to Co. C 1 July 1862, promoted to 5th sgt. in December 1862, d. 26 February 1865 at Jackson Hospital of chronic dysentery, buried at Richmond's Hollywood Cemetery section W, grave #6, b. 1835 in Clarke County to Thomas A. and Lydia Fenn, brother of Newton and William Fenn.

Fenn, Newton Jasper. Enlisted 1 March 1862, listed as severely wounded in foot 19 October 1864 at Cedar Creek on casualty list in 9 November 1864 *Athens Southern Banner*, shown wounded at hospital on a late 1864 roll, deserted near Petersburg 2 April 1865, look Oath of Allegiance and sent to Richmond, Ohio, b. 1837 in Hall County to Thomas A. and Lydia Fenn, brother of George and William Fenn, d. July 1910 in Fulton County.

Fenn, William P. Enlisted 1 March 1862, KIA 29 November 1863 at Knoxville, death claim filed by widow Susan E. Fenn, b. June 1823 in Hall County to Thomas A. and Lydia Fenn, brother of George and Newton Fenn.

Forrester, William. Enlisted 11 June 1861, age 22, d. 31 October 1861 at Cotton Hill VA (now WV) of typhoid fever, death claim filed by widow Sallie A. Forrester.

Fuller, Alfred D. Enlisted 1 March 1862, WIA (neck, mouth) at Cold Harbor in early June 1864, furloughed home 19 June 1864, present on a late 1864 roll, a medical board record dated 22 February 1865 shows him to be 19 years old, 5'10" tall with light hair and blue eyes and assigns him to light clerical duties because of disability from wounds. Surrendered 9 April 1865 at Appomattox, b. 1845 in GA to John E. and Livonia Jeffers Fuller, brother of Jonathan and Peyton Fuller.

Fuller, Jonathan W. Enlisted November 1864, surrendered 9 April 1865 at Appomattox, b. 5 October 1836 in GA to John E. and Livonia Jeffers Fuller, brother of Alfred and Peyton Fuller.

Fuller, Peyton W. Enlisted 11 June 1861, age 19, promoted color cpl. 1 July 1862, shown as color sgt. 30 November 1862 roll, transferred in late April 1863 to the unit that would officially become 3rd GA Sharpshooter Battalion in June 1863 as 2nd lt. of Co. B, KIA 2 May 1863 at Chancellorsville before his promotion could be confirmed.

Gaines, Edward Presley. Enlisted 1 August 1861, captured 2 June 1864 at Cold Harbor, exchanged 11 October 1864, a late 1864 roll shows him home on parole, later rolls list him as being AWOL, d. 28 February 1881.

Gay, Graniteville L. Enlisted 11 June 1861 as 3rd cpl., discharged 18 October 1862 for being over- age.

Griggs, Junius Augustus. Enlisted 16 June 1864, captured 6 April 1865 at Sailor's Creek and imprisoned at Point Lookout until released 27 June 1865, Oath shows him to be 6'4" tall with red hair and blue eyes, b. 3 February 1834 to Junius and Sarah Griggs, postwar pension application states he was an enrolling officer at Decatur GA until June 1864, d. 19 February 1911.

Guren (or Gerrin), Samuel. Enlisted 25 June 1861, age 36, captured 29 November 1863 at Knoxville and imprisoned at Rock Island until exchanged 2 March 1865, no further record.

Hargroves, J. R. "Jack." Enlisted 1 March 1862, transferred to 7th GA Infantry 11 October 1862, promoted 1st sgt., Co. H 20 November 1862, present on January/February 1863 roll, no further record.

Harkins, Robert T. Enlisted 1 June 1861 as 1st sgt., age 35, discharged 8 March 1863 because of disability.

Harrin, Spencer. Enlisted 25 June 1861, age 25, deserted 14 July 1861, no further record.

Hays, John W. Enlisted 25 June 1861, age 17, transferred to Co. L of Phillips Legion, April 1862, sick a great deal, detailed to Danville Hospital in late 1862, then to Atlanta as a shoemaker in mid-1863, listed AWOL on roll dated 28 January 1865, no further military record, postwar pension application states he was captured and sent to Illinois in September 1864, b. 24 September 1844 in SC, d. 27 August 1919 in Cobb County.

Hayes, Thomas H. First shown on roll dated 5 October 1864 with no enlistment date indicated, captured at Knoxville in early December 1863, d. 6 July 1864 at Rock Island of pneumonia, buried grave #1343, age 14 in 1860 Cobb census, son of John O. and Louisa Hayes..

Heaton, Pinckney "Pink" R. Enlisted 1 March 1862, WIA (lost two fingers) 29 or 30 August 1862 at Second Manassas, discharged from service 9 May 1863, b. 15 May 1836 in SC to Samuel and Malinda Heaton, older brother of Zach Heaton, d. 16 May 1900, buried at Zebulon Baptist Church Cemetery in Stephens County.

Heaton, Zachariah Enlisted 11 June 1861, age 18, WIA 13 December 1862 at Fredericksburg, transferred to 3d GA Sharpshooter battalion in May 1863, records indicate he deserted 30 June 1863 at Caledonia PA, but must have been picked up by Federals since he is next shown at Fort Delaware Prison, joined Co. D, 3rd MD (US) Cavalry in September 1863, enlistment shows him to be 20 years old, 6' tall with blue eyes and brown hair, deserted from this unit 24 December 1863, entry states that he deserted from steamer leaving Baltimore, no further record, b. 1843 in SC to Samuel and Malinda Heaton, brother of Pink Heaton.

Henderson, David W. Enlisted 11 June 1861, age 18, WIA 13 December 1862 at Fredericksburg, WIA (head) and captured 2 June 1864 at Cold Harbor and imprisoned at Elmira NY until released 23 June 1865, Oath shows him to be 5'8" tall with auburn hair and blue eyes, b. 15 February 1842 in GA to Vincent and Margaret R. Henderson.

Hicks, Samuel Washington. Enlisted 11 June 1861, age 20, WIA (concussion) 13 December 1862 at Fredericksburg, captured 3 July 1863 at Gettysburg and held at Point Lookout until exchanged 3 March 1864, captured 6 April 1865 at Sailor's Creek and imprisoned at Point Lookout until released 28 June 1865, Oath shows him to 5'10 1/2" tall with black hair and blue eyes, b. 27 April 1841 in NC to William W. and Cynthia Lamberth Hicks.

Hill, Henry Lumpkin "Lump." Records state he enlisted 29 June 1862 but he is not listed on 1862 and early 1863 rolls, a hospital record shows him furloughed 17 November 1862 from Winder Hospital, Richmond, listed as present on a roll dated 19 January 1864, captured 3 April 1865 at Richmond and imprisoned at Point Lookout until released 28 June 1865, Oath shows him to be 5'4" tall with dark hair and blue eyes, b. 1833 in Habersham County to David and Elizabeth Eaton Hill.

Hockenhull, Charles Henry. Enlisted 11 June 1861, age 25, shown as 2nd sgt. on roll dated 1 July 1862 and 1st sgt. on roll dated 1 December 1862, transferred to Co. A, 11th GA Infantry per entry on 19 January 1864 roll (his father Cpt. and ACS John Hockenhull was the commissary officer for the 11th so the transfer was probably made due to a family connection after the death of his younger brother James at Knoxville), transferred to brigade commissary effective 1 April 1864, surrendered 9 April 1865 at Appomattox, b. 14 October 1834 at Cheshire England to John and Mary Kemp Hockenhull.

Hockenhull, James Fagan. Enlisted 1 March 1862, WIA (arm) 13 December 1862 at Fredericksburg, KIA 29 November 1863 at Knoxville, his father recovered his remains and reinterred him at Salem ME Church at Barrettsville GA, b. 4 December 1842 in GA to John and Mary Kemp Hockenhull.

Hooker, Moses. Enlisted 1 March 1862, age 36 in 1860 Cobb County census, d. 27 September 1862 near Bunker Hill VA, cause not stated but probably typhoid or dysentery, death claim filed by widow Elizabeth A. Hooker.

Howard, John. J. Enlisted 11 June 1861 as 1st cpl., age 27, shown as private on September/October 1862 roll, transferred to 3rd GA Sharpshooter Battalion

May 1863, captured at Gettysburg July 1863, POW at Point Lookout until joining 3rd MD US Cavalry, served with this unit until September 1865.

Hughes, John J. Enlisted 1 August 1861, age 30, transferred to 3rd GA Sharpshooter battalion in May 1863, captured 29 November 1863 at Knoxville but no Federal prison or exchange records so he may have escaped, a 19 January 1864 roll shows him absent sick at hospital, captured at Front Royal 16 August 1864 and imprisoned at Elmira NY until exchanged in October 1864, captured 6 April 1865 at Sailor's Creek and imprisoned at Point Lookout until released 28 June 1865, Oath shows him to be 5'8 1/2" tall with dark hair and eyes.

Hunter, William Jefferson "Jeff." Enlisted 11 June 1861, age 30, shown home sick on rolls from November 1862 through roll dated 19 January 1864, paid $420.71 in back pay and allowances on 20 July 1864 and discharged for disability, b. in NC to Nathan B. and Ann Hunter.

Jackson, Marshall C. Enlisted 1 March 1862, age 21 in 1860 Cobb County census, captured 29 November 1863 at Knoxville and imprisoned at Rock Island until released 18 June 1865, Oath shows him to be 25 years old, 5'8" with light brown hair and blue eyes, b. 1839 in GA to Lewis A. and Mary Jackson, d. 24 February 1913 in Fulton County.

Jackson, Sam. No enlistment date given, only appears on one roll dated 5 October 1864 with notation "Died at hospital 7 July 1864," no cause of death stated, probably a spring, 1864 conscript or enlistee.

Jackson, William. No enlistment date given, only appears on one roll dated 19 January 1864 with notation "KIA 29 November 1863 at Knoxville," probably a fall 1863 conscript or enlistee.

Johnston, John T. Enlisted 1 March 1862, captured 29 November 1863 at Knoxville and imprisoned at Rock Island until exchanged 2 March 1865, no further military record, b. 13 March 1841, d. 8 March 1914 in Cobb County.

Johnston, William J. Enlisted 25 June 1861, age 21, KIA 17 September 1862 at Sharpsburg MD, death claim filed by father William M. Johnston.

Jones, Daniel P. Enlisted 25 June 1861, age 19, promoted 2nd cpl. 1 December 1862, WIA (chest) 13 December 1862 at Fredericksburg, casualty list in 2 July 1864 *Richmond Enquirer* covering period from 6 May 1864 through 16 May 1864 lists him as slightly wounded, captured 19 October 1864 at Cedar Creek and imprisoned at Point Lookout until released 28 June 1865, Oath shows him to be 6' tall with light brown hair and hazel eyes.

Jones, William M. Enlisted 11 June 1861, age 24, at Danville Hospital 17 June 1864 with gunshot wound and typhoid, subsequent rolls show him home on sick furlough then AWOL, no further military record but known to have survived the war because he filed a postwar pension application, pension application states he surrendered at Appomattox but he is not shown on the parole roster, b. 1835 to Richmond and Jane Jones, d. 12 October 1895.

Jones, William P. Enlisted 11 June 1861, age 24, d. 17 December 1861 at Red Sulphur Springs VA (now WV) from typhoid, death claim filed by mother Eliza Jones.

King, George Lumpkin "Lump." Enlisted 1 March 1862, rolls dated 19 January 1864 and 5 October 1864 show him home on sick furlough and later rolls list him as AWOL, captured and paroled 3 May 1865 at Anderson SC, b. 26 January 1845 in Habersham County, d. 24 December 1917, buried in Franklin County GA.

King, Peter. Enlisted 14 September 1863, present on roll dated 19 January 1864, shown home sick on roll dated 5 October 1864 and AWOL on later rolls, medical records show him furloughed home 1 September 1864 suffering from chronic dysentery, captured and paroled 18 May 1865 at Hartwell GA, b. 5 February 1822, d. 24 May 1903 in Cornelia GA, buried at Allens United Methodist Church Cemetery in Douglas County GA.

Kistleburg, William Howard. Enlisted 11 June 1861, age 19, WIA (shoulder) 13 December 1862 at Fredericksburg, transferred to 3rd GA Sharpshooter battalion in May 1863, captured 6 April 1865 at Sailor's Creek and imprisoned at Point Lookout until released 19 June 1865, b. 1842 in GA to Henry and Jinsey Kistleburg, brother of James Kistleburg.

Kistleburg, James D. Enlisted 1 July 1862, WIA (left shoulder) 13 December 1862 at Fredericksburg, KIA 19 October 1864 at Cedar Creek (29 October 1864 letter from G. O. Megarity states that J. H. Bellah, W. S. Manning, J. Lambert and J. Kistleburg were all killed by a single shell burst), b. 1833 in GA to Henry and Jinsey Kistleburg, brother of William Kistleburg.

Kitcham (or Ketchum), Colden C. Enlisted 16 May 1864, captured 6 April 1865 at Sailor's Creek and imprisoned at Point Lookout until released 14 June 1865, Oath shows him to be 5'10" tall with brown hair and gray eyes, b. 1847 in GA to Rev. R. C. and Sarah Ketchum.

Lambert, Jesse N. Enlisted 11 June 1861, age 18, KIA 19 October 1864 at Cedar Creek (29 October 1864 letter from G. O. Megarity states that J. H. Bellah, W. S. Manning, J. Lambert and J. Kistleburg were all killed by a single shell burst), son of Samuel R. and Mary Norris Lambert, brother of William Lambert.

Lambert, William R. Enlisted 20 April 1861 in Co. K of the 3rd GA Infantry, transferred (or reenlisted) December 1862 in Co. C of the Phillips Legion infantry battalion, promoted to ordnance sgt. in 1863, captured 5 April 1865 at Amelia Springs VA and imprisoned at Point Lookout until released 29 June 1865, Oath shows him to be 5'6" tall with dark hair and hazel eyes, b. 1838 in GA to Samuel R. and Mary Norris Lambert, brother of Jesse Lambert.

Little, Lewis J. Enlisted 1 August 1861, age 19, last shown on 31 October 1861 roll sick at Raleigh Court House, there is no legion record for him after this but he reenlisted in Co. I of the 24th GA Infantry at Poplar Springs, Hall County GA on 28 June 1862, he probably received a medical discharge from the Phillips

Legion in late 1861, wounded several times and captured during his service with the 24th and survived the war, b. 2 November 1843.

Little, William. Enlisted 25 June 1861, age 25, teamster, last shown on January 1865 roll home on furlough, captured and paroled at Anderson SC 5 May 1865.

Loudermilk, David Washington. Enlisted 1 July 1862, d. 3 November 1862 at Mt. Jackson VA from pneumonia, death claim filed by widow Caroline Loudermilk, buried at Our Soldiers Cemetery, Mt. Jackson, b. 1837 to Jacob and Mary Washburn Loudermilk, brother of H. E., T. A. and W. C. Loudermilk.

Loudermilk, Henry Ervin. Enlisted 1 March 1862, absent sick through February 1863, WIA and captured 29 November 1863 at Knoxville and imprisoned at Rock Island until released 19 June 1865, Oath shows him to be 24 years old, 5'9" tall with dark brown hair and hazel eyes, b. 12 January 1840 to Jacob and Mary Washburn Loudermilk, d. 2 September 1917, buried at Hazel Creek Baptist Cemetery near Clarksville, brother of D. W., T. A. and W. C. Loudermilk.

Loudermilk, Thomas Asbury. Enlisted 19 March 1862, captured 6 April 1865 at Sailor's Creek and imprisoned at Point Lookout until released 29 June 1865, Oath shows him to be 5'10" tall with brown hair and hazel eyes, b. 1 April 1844 to Jacob and Mary Washburn Loudermilk, d. 20 February 1916, buried at Hazel Creek Baptist Cemetery, brother of D. W., H. E., and W. C. Loudermilk.

Loudermilk, William Cannon. Enlisted 1 July 1862, captured 1 June 1864 at Cold Harbor and imprisoned at Elmira until released 11 July 1865, Oath shows him to be 5'7" tall with auburn hair and gray eyes, b. 16 December 1834 to Jacob and Mary Washburn Loudermilk, d. 1 December 1910, buried at Loudermilk family cemetery near Mt. Airy GA.

Love, David Green. Enlisted 25 June 1861, age 24, present on all rolls through January 1865, this roll lists him home on furlough, no further military record but he filed for Alabama pension stating his age as 71 in 1907, b. in Rabun County GA in March 1836 to William H. and Olive Wheeler Love, d. 22 February 1912 in Fayette County AL, brother of John F. Love.

Love, John F. Enlisted 1 January 1862, WIA (thigh and calf) 13 December 1862 at Fredericksburg, captured 1 June 1864 at Cold Harbor and imprisoned at Elmira until exchanged 20 February 1865, captured 6 April 1865 at Sailor's Creek and imprisoned at Point Lookout until released 29 June 1865, Oath shows him to be 5'8 1/4" tall with auburn hair and blue eyes, born in Habersham County GA in 1840 to William H. and Olive Wheeler Love, brother of David Green Love.

Lowery (Lowrey), James M. Enlisted 1 August 1861, age 28, d. 30 October 1861 at Raleigh Court House VA (today's Beckley, WV) of typhoid pneumonia, death claim filed by father Elisha Lowrey.

Magnis, Lindsey. Enlisted 11 June 1861, age 26, d. 24 October 1861 at Meadow Bluff VA (today's WV) of disease, death claim filed by widow Neatty Magnis.

Manning, Georgia Marion. Enlisted 25 June 1861 as 2nd cpl., age 23, shown as 1st sgt. on July 1862 roll, promoted Jr. 2nd lt. 16 October 1862, WIA (thigh) 13 December 1862 at Fredericksburg, promoted 2nd lt. 11 June 1863, WIA (leg amputated) and captured 29 November 1863 at Knoxville, imprisoned at Fort Delaware until exchanged 28 September 1864, at home disabled remainder of war, b. 25 September 1837, d. 22 November 1892, Buried at Marietta Citizens Cemetery.

Manning, John W. Enlisted in Co. L, 3rd Arkansas Infantry 1 July 1861 at Latonia AR, Promoted 3rd sgt. 1 October 1861, transferred to Phillips Legion Co. C, 1 October 1862, Promoted 2nd sgt. in 1862, transferred to 3rd GA Sharpshooter battalion in May 1863 as 2nd sgt., WIA and captured 2 July 1863 at Gettysburg, exchanged September 1863, shown present on February 1864 roll, retired to Invalid Corps 12 July 1864, b. in GA 1830.

Manning, William S. Enlisted 16 May 1862, shown as 2nd sgt. on January/February 1863 roll, KIA 19 October 1864 at Cedar Creek, (29 October 1864 letter from G. O. Megarity states that J. Bellah, W. S. Manning, J. Lambert, and J. Kistleburg were all killed by a single shell burst), b. 1840 in GA to W. and G. Manning.

McCracken, Joseph W. Enlisted 12 July 1862, WIA (arm) 13 December 1863 at Fredericksburg, captured 2 April 1864 at Russellville TN and imprisoned at Camp Douglas, Chicago IL, d. 9 August 1864 of chronic dysentery, buried at Oak Woods Cemetery, Chicago IL, grave #1258.

McCracken, John V. Enlisted 11 June 1861, age 21, captured at Cold Harbor 1 June 1864 and imprisoned at Elmira until released 16 June 1865, Oath shows him to be 5'6 1/2" tall with auburn hair and blue eyes.

McKinney, James Sidney. Enlisted 11 June 1861, age 19, shown present as 4th cpl. on January/February 1863 roll, no further military record, 1906 Roster Commission roll states that he died in army in 1862, son of Robert and Bernice McKinney.

McKinney, Robert. Enlisted 14 September 1863, WIA during August 1864 and furloughed home 26 August 1864, not on later rolls, captured and paroled 23 May 1865 at Greenville SC, postwar pension application states he was "thrown from train in Va 8/15/1864, broke back, helpless," b. 1 February 1820, d. 11 December 1906, buried at Cool Springs Methodist Cemetery near Clarksville GA, father of J. S. McKinney.

Megarity, Green O. Enlisted 1 March 1862, age 19 on 1860 Cobb County census, WIA (leg) May 1863 at Chancellorsville per casualty list in 19 May 1863 *Atlanta Southern Confederacy*, present on all rolls through war, deserted 29 March 1865 near Petersburg, took Oath of Allegiance and sent to Richmond, Ohio, brother of James A. Megarity.

Megarity, James A. Enlisted 1 March 1862, age 21 in 1860 Cobb County census, present on all rolls through war, deserted 29 March 1865 near Petersburg, took

Oath of Allegiance and sent to Richmond OH, moved to Navarro County TX in 1872 and d. in 1911, brother of Green O. Megarity.

Mills, David F. Enlisted 1 March 1862, roll dated 5 October 1864 shows him home on wounded furlough, casualty list in 2 July 1864 *Richmond Enquirer* covering period from 6 May 1864 through 16 May 1864 lists DF Mills as severely wounded, last shown present on January 1865 roll, no further record, b. 1846 in GA to John P. and Matilda S. Mills.

Mills, Jonas O. Enlisted 1 August 1862, KIA 14 September 1862 at Fox's Gap MD, death claim filed by widow Nancy Mills.

Mills, William H. Enlisted 11 June 1861, age 26, WIA (hand shattered by shell) 30 August 1862 at Second Manassas, transferred to 3rd GA Sharpshooter Battalion as 4th sgt. May 1863, sent to hospital 10 November 1863, AWOL on all further rolls.

Mitchell, John T. Enlisted 1 March 1862, KIA 13 December 1862 at Fredericksburg, age 31 in 1860 Cobb census.

Nichols, William W. Enlisted 11 June 1861, age 20, d. 23 August 1862 in Culpepper County VA, Alex Erwin letter dated 15 September 1862 states that William was left sick at a private home about three miles from Brandy Station, died shortly thereafter and was buried there, b. 28 September 1840 to Andrew J. and Elizabeth Clarke Nichols, death claim filed by father Andrew J. Nichols, body recovered and reinterred at Old Clarksville Cemetery, Habersham County GA.

Norris, John S. Enlisted 11 June 1861, as 1st lt., age 30, promoted cpt. 18 October 1862, promoted to maj. of Infantry battalion 31 December 1863, captured 6 April 1865 at Sailor's Creek and imprisoned at Johnson's Island until released 25 July 1865, Oath shows him to be 34 years old, 5'11" tall with dark hair and blue eyes.

Osborn, Berry A. Enlisted 1 March 1862, age 18, absent sick on all rolls except ones dated 14 November 1862 and 31 August 1863, January 1865 roll shows him AWOL, no further military record, but postwar pension application states he was detailed at the end of the war, b. 25 January 1843 in GA to William and S. J. Osborn.

Payne, John B. Enlisted 11 June 1861 as 3rd lt., age 37, d. 23 October 1861 at Green Sulphur Springs VA, (today's WV) of typhoid.

Pendley, Jesse Monroe. Enlisted 1 March 1862, age 23 in 1860 Cobb County census, WIA 2 July 1863 at Gettysburg, present on January 1865 roll, no further military record but postwar pension application filed in Alabama in 1898 also indicated that he was wounded at Cold Harbor 1 June 1864, b. 24 May 1836 to Reuben and Mary Hisaw Pendley, d. 30 July 1909 in Alabama.

Perry, Phillip Jefferson. Enlisted 1 December 1862, KIA 13 December 1862 at Fredericksburg, death claim filed by widow Mary Ann Perry, a postwar newspaper account detailing the history of Co. C, enigmatically stated (in its discussion of Fredericksburg casualties) "and here is where the brave and loyal Jeff Perry was killed by an officer of his own company."

Phillips, James Patton. Enlisted 18 December 1861 as 2nd lt., WIA (right thigh) 13 December 1862 at Fredericksburg, transferred to 3rd GA Sharpshooter battalion in May 1863 as cpt. and AQM, WIA 3 May 1862 at Chancellorsville, shown in QM function at R. H. Anderson's Corps HQ 5 March 1865, no further military record, b. 17 May 1826 to Dr. George Duval and Mary Patton Phillips, d. 24 May 1918, buried at Phillips family cemetery (Farm Hill) near Clarksville, brother of col. William M. Phillips.

Porter, George W. Enlisted 11 June 1861 as 2nd sgt., age 30, discharged 19 April 1862, discharge shows him to be 5'10" tall with dark hair and blue eyes.

Powers, H. C. Enlisted 1 March 1862, age 17 in 1860 Cobb County census, deserted March 1865 near Petersburg, took Oath of Allegiance and sent to Richmond OH, son of James C. and R. D. Powers, brother of J. J. A. Powers.

Powers, J. J. A. Enlisted 1 August 1861, age 21, captured in Maryland September 1862, paroled at Keedysville MD 20 September 1862, shown present on January/February 1863 roll, not on later rolls, buried at Spotsylvania Confederate Cemetery, date and cause of death unknown but likely that he died from disease between March and August 1863 since he is not listed on the September/October roll (next one after January/February 1863 roll) and does not appear on casualty lists for either Chancellorsville or Gettysburg, son of James C. and R. D. Powers, brother of H. C. Powers.

Pressley, John. Enlisted 1 March 1862, present on all rolls until KIA 1 June 1864 at Cold Harbor.

Pressley, Mike. Enlisted 1 March 1862, roll dated 5 October 1864 showed him home on wounded furlough, casualty list in 2 July 1864 *Richmond Enquirer* covering period from 6 May 1864 to 16 May 1864 listed him as severely wounded, shown AWOL on January 1865 roll, no further military record but postwar pension application stated he went home sick in late 1864 and did not return, b. 1831, d. 1895 in Alabama.

Red, John Benjamin Franklin. Enlisted 11 June 1861, age 19, WIA (knee) 14 September 1862 at Fox's Gap MD, WIA (arm) May 1863 at Chancellorsville per casualty list in 19 May 1863 *Atlanta Southern Confederacy*, shown as 4th cpl. on roll dated 19 January 1864, present on roll dated January 1865, no further military record, b. 8 July 1842 at Henderson NC to Joseph and Elizabeth Red, d. 14 September 1939, buried at Oakland Cemetery in Pulaski County AR.

Reed, J. Posey. Transferred in from 7th GA Infantry 1 August 1862, transferred to Co. M 20 January 1863 then to the cavalry battalion of Phillips Legion 11 February 1863.

Reed, William J. Enlisted 1 March 1862, age 26 in 1860 Cobb County census, d. 4 November 1862 at Winchester VA of disease, son of Joel B. and Mary Chambers Reed.

Richardson, Jesse A. Enlisted 1 August 1861 as 4th cpl., KIA 13 December 1862 at Fredericksburg, death claim filed by father Joseph Richardson, son of Joseph and Mary Richardson, age 10 in 1850 Habersham County census.

Rich, J. Newton. Enlisted 25 June 1861, age 30, WIA (shoulder) 13 December 1862 at Fredericksburg, transferred to 3rd Georgia Sharpshooter battalion 1 May 1863, WIA (knee) 3 May 1863 at Chancellorsville and permanently disabled, b. 31 October 1832, son of Charles and Sarah Taylor Ritch.

Roman, Thomas J. Enlisted 25 June 1861, age 29, KIA 14 September 1862 at Fox's Gap MD, death claim filed by widow Mrs. Caroline Roman.

Roper, Henry C. Enlisted 12 May 1863, WIA (knee) and captured 2 July 1863 at Gettysburg, last shown as furloughed home 18 September 1863 because of Gettysburg wounds, present on roll dated 19 January 1864, casualty list in 2 July 1864 *Richmond Enquirer* showed him KIA between 6 May 1864 and 16 May 1864 indicating his death at either Wilderness or Spotsylvania, son of Jacob and Martha Clardy Roper, age 15 in 1860 Dawson County census.

Sellars, Ephraim. Enlisted 1 March 1862, left sick at Hagerstown MD and estimated to have died there about 14 September 1862, death claim filed by widow, Sarah Sellars.

Sisk, Albert S. Enlisted 1 March 1862, WIA (lost two fingers on left hand) at Second Manassas, January 1865 roll listed him as home on furlough, no further military record but postwar pension application showed he d. 5 October 1915 at Watkinsville GA, b. 10 July 1842 to Singleton and Martha Tatum Sisk, brother of J. C., T. J., W. F., and W. E. Sisk.

Sisk, Gabriel L. Enlisted 19 May 1862, d. 20 November 1862 at CharlottesvIlle VA Hospital from pneumonia, buried at University of Virginia Confederate Cemetery at Charlottesville, b. 1839 to John and Adaline Lovelady Sisk, brother of John F. Sisk.

Sisk, John C. Enlisted 11 June 1861, age 27, present on rolls through the war, last shown present on January 1865 roll, paroled 19 April 1865 at Newton NC, born 1835 to Singleton and Tatum Sisk, brother of A. S., T. J., W. F., and W. E. Sisk.

Sisk, John F. Enlisted 1 March 1862, present on rolls through the war until captured 6 April 1865 at Sailor's Creek, imprisoned at Point Lookout until released 19 June 1865, Oath shows him to be 5'10" tall with dark hair and blue eyes, b. 18 August 1840 to John and Adaline Lovelady Sisk, brother of Gabriel Sisk.

Sisk, Thomas Jefferson. Enlisted 16 March 1863, present on all rolls during the war, surrendered 9 April 1865 at Appomattox, b. 21 April 1827 to Singleton and Martha Tatum Sisk, brother of A. S., J. C., W. F., and W. E. Sisk.

Sisk, Winchester F. Enlisted 16 March 1863, d. 29 April 1864 at home while on furlough, death claim filed by widow Rachel C. Sisk, b. 1833 to Singleton and Martha Tatum Sisk, brother of A. S., J. C., T. J., and W. F. Sisk.

Sisk, William E. Enlisted 1 March 1862, roll dated 5 October 1864 shows him home on wounded furlough, casualty list in 2 July 1864 *Richmond Enquirer* covering the period from 6 May 1864 through 16 May 1864 lists him as severely wounded, listed as AWOL on January 1865 roll, no further military record but a postwar pension application filed by his widow Marcela states he d. 19 June 1916 in Hollingsworth GA, b. 30 October 1837 to Singleton and Martha Tatum Sisk, brother of A. S., J. C., T. J., and W. E. Sisk.

Smalley, G. C. Enlisted 16 March 1863, captured 1 June 1864 at Cold Harbor, d. 15 July 1864 at Shohola PA in train wreck en route to Elmira NY prison.

Smith, Chesley. Enlisted 1 March 1862, d. 22 May 1862 at Camp Pritchard SC from disease, death claim filed by widow Emily Smith, b. 1841 in SC to Tilman and Emily Smith.

Smith, William C. Enlisted 11 June 1861, age 21, d. 23 October 1861 at Green Sulphur Springs VA (today's WV) of typhoid, death claim filed by brother Hugh W. Smith.

Sosebee, Sampson E. Enlisted 18 March 1863, d. 28 April 1863 at Richmond's Chimborazo Hospital #2 of measles, death claim filed by widow Mary K. Sosebee, buried at Richmond's Oakwood Confederate Cemetery as S. Sasher, son of Sampson and Elizabeth Abbott Sosebee, age 36 in 1860 Habersham County census.

Spruell, John Thomas C. Enlisted 1 March 1862, captured 14 September 1862 at Fox's Gap MD, letters indicate he remained behind with mortally wounded William H. Dobbins, exchanged 6 October 1862, d. 14 May 1863 at Richmond's Chimborazo Hospital #2 of typhoid, buried at Richmond's Oakwood Confederate Cemetery as I. T. C. Sprewell, b. 28 November 1842 to Wilson and Elizabeth Austin Spruell, brother of Stephen Spruell.

Spruell, Stephen Manning. Enlisted 25 June 1861, age 22, KIA 13 December 1862 at Fredericksburg, death claim filed by father, Wilson E. Spruell, b. 4 March 1839 to Wilson F. and Elizabeth Austin Spruell, brother of J. T. C. Spruell.

Starnes, J. M. Enlisted 1 March 1862, captured 2 July 1863 at Gettysburg and imprisoned at Fort Delaware until sent to Point Lookout in October 1863, exchanged 18 February 1865, no further record.

Stephens, Leonard F. Enlisted 11 June 1861, age 23, shown as 5th sgt. on May/June 1862 roll, d. 17 November 1862 at Staunton VA Hospital of chronic dysentery, death claim filed by father Dison Stephens, buried Thornrose Cemetery, Augusta County VA.

Sweatman, H. N. C. Enlisted 25 June 1861, age 17, deserted 10 August 1861 at Lynchburg, no further record.

Tatum, Floyd H. Enlisted 1 March 1862, d. 1 June 1862 at Camp Pritchard SC of disease, son of Solomon and Susannah Trotter Tatum, age 23 in 1860 Habersham County census.

Taylor, Isaac N. Enlisted 1 March 1862, WIA (knee) and captured 14 September 1862 at Fox's Gap MD, exchanged 6 October 1862, shown AWOL on roll dated 19 January 1864 and on all later rolls, no further military record, b. 1838 in Cobb County, applied for pension from Carroll County in 1898.

Taylor, Zachary F. "Zack." Enlisted 1 March 1862, shown hospitalized in Lynchburg 29 November 1862 suffering from debility, transferred to 3rd GA Sharpshooter battalion in May 1863, captured 16 August 1864 at Front Royal VA and imprisoned at Elmira NY until exchanged 14 March 1865. b. 14 February 1840 in Cobb County, Married Nanch E. Osborn 20 November 1865, d. 7 September 1911 in Dade County GA, Buried at Whitt Sitton Cemetery in Dade County.

Tennant, William A. Enlisted 1 August 1861, KIA 13 December 1862 at Fredericksburg, son of Gilbert and Caroline Tennant, born in SC, age 22 in 1860 Cobb census.

Thomas, N. Cleveland. Enlisted 12 July 1862, WIA 30 August 1862 at Second Manassas, sent home on sick furlough 29 July 1864 from Richmond's Jackson Hospital suffering from chronic dysentery, listed AWOL on all later rolls, captured/paroled 3 May 1865 at Anderson SC, son of Mary Thomas, born in SC, age 20 in 1860 Cobb census.

Thomas, Thomas Benton. Enlisted 1 March 1862, WIA 30 August 1862 at Second Manassas, WIA (knee) 13 December 1862 at Fredericksburg, WIA (shoulders) 2 July 1863 at Gettysburg per casualty list in 20 July 1863 *Atlanta Southern Confederacy*, roll dated 19 January 1864 shows him home on wounded furlough, listed AWOL on all later rolls but Federal records indicate he took the Oath of Allegiance 5 April 1864 at Chattanooga, Oath shows him to be 5'6" tall with black hair and hazel eyes, no further record.

Thompson, Joseph W. Enlisted 25 June 1861, age 20, late 1864 roll shows him captured at Strasburg (Cedar Creek) but he does not appear in Federal POW records, 1906 Roster Commission roll states he was KIA at Strasburg (Cedar Creek), son of Wiley and Artemia Thompson.

Thompson, Willis Wylie. Enlisted 11 June 1861, age 19, shown as 1st cpl. on 1 December 1862 roll, WIA (arm amputated) and captured 29 November 1863 at Knoxville, sent to Fort Delaware for exchange 29 February 1864 but not exchanged until 18 September 1864, disabled remainder of war, b. 14 August 1842 to Willis and Mary Thompson, d. 12 March 1930, buried at Oakland Cemetery in Atlanta GA.

Tribble, Benjamin F. Enlisted 3 April 1862 in Co. L and transferred to Co. C 1 May 1862, d. 26 June 1863 in Forsyth County GA, cause not stated, death claim filed by father Thomas C. Tribble.

Trotter, Benjamin C. Enlisted 1 August 1861, d. 8 December 1862 at Richmond's GH #9 from pneumonia, buried at Richmond's Oakwood Cemetery as

Benjamin C. Trothers or D. C. Troters, son of Nathaniel and Nancy West
Trotters, brother of Elias, James, and William Trotters.

Trotter, Elias N. Enlisted 1 March 1862, WIA (head) 13 December 1862 at
Fredericksburg, present on all rolls until captured 6 April 1865 at Sailor's Creek,
imprisoned at Point Lookout until released 20 June 1865, Oath shows him to be
5'8 1/4" tall with black hair and hazel eyes, age 17 in 1860 Habersham census,
son of Nathaniel and Nancy West Trotters, brother of Benjamin, James, and
William Trotters.

Trotter. James R. Enlisted 11 June 1861 as 3rd sgt., age 25, captured 3 July 1863 at
Gettysburg, sent to Chester PA Hospital until exchanged 17 August 1863, roll
dated 5 October 1864 shows him home on wounded furlough, casualty list in 2
July 1864 *Richmond Enquirer* covering period from 6 May 1864 through 16 May
1864 lists him severely wounded as sgt. J. R. Foster, present on January 1865
roll, detailed for light duty 20 February 1865, surrendered 9 April 1865 at
Appomattox, filed for a pension in Alabama stating that he was wounded at the
Wilderness (explaining why he was on wounded furlough in 1864), son of
Nathaniel and Nancy West Trotters, brother of Benjamin, Elias, and William
Trotters, d. in Alabama 23 May 1906.

Trotter, William M. Enlisted 11 June 1861, age 26, WIA (left arm and right hand
amputated) 6 May 1864 at Wilderness, roll dated 5 October 1864 shows him
absent wounded at hospital retired 17 January 1865, discharge shows him to be
5'10" with dark hair and eyes, b. 28 March 1835 in Nacoochee Valley GA to
Nathaniel and Nancy West Trotters, brother of Benjamin, Elias, and James
Trotters, filed for pension in Alabama in 1907 stating age as 73.

Underwood, William Jasper. Enlisted 1 March 1862, d. 19 May 1862 at Camp Elzey
SC from disease, death claim filed by widow Minerva A. Underwood, age 28 in
1850 Habersham census.

VanDiver, Hunter. Enlisted 19 July 1861, age 19, KIA 14 September 1862 at Fox's
Gap MD, death claim filed by father Adam T. VanDiver.

Vaughn, George W. Enlisted 1 March 1862, d. 1 May 1862 at Camp Elzey SC of
disease, age 22.

Vaughn, M. R. Enlisted 1 February 1864, present on January 1865 roll, no further
record.

Ward, William W. Enlisted 25 June 1861, age 23, present on all rolls through war
until roll dated January 1865 where he is listed as home on furlough, no further
military record but postwar pension application states that he was furloughed
home at the end of January 1865 and could not return, application also states
that he was wounded in the head 14 September 1862 at Boonsboro (Fox's Gap
MD), b. 10 December 1837 in Union County to Jeremiah and Moriah Ward, d.
2 June 1923 at Jacksonville FL.

Watson, Robert Douglas. Enlisted 1 March 1862, age 20 in 1860 Cobb County
census. last shown on roll dated 14 January 1864 as present, casualty list in 2 July

1864 *Richmond Enquirer* for period between 6 May 1864 and 16 May 1864 shows R. D. Walker of Co. C as KIA, since there was no R. D. Walker in the Legion it is probable that R. D. Watson died at the Wilderness or Spotsylvania, son of Paris c. and Nancy Boon Watson.

Whitehead, William H. Enlisted 1 May 1862, WIA (face) 2 July 1863 at Gettysburg, roll dated 19 January 1864 shows him home on wounded furlough, retired to Invalid Corps 13 April 1864 and detailed to Richmond as a shoemaker, retirement document shows him to be 49, 5'6" tall with dark hair and gray eyes, documents in his record show that he obtained an appointment as a 4th lt. in the Georgia State Militia in April 1864 but clearly Confederate authorities retained him in Richmond since he was still there in December 1864, no further military record but a postwar pension application filed in Alabama indicates that he survived the war.

Wyly, Camillus P. Enlisted 25 June 1861, age 16, KIA 13 December 1862 at Fredericksburg, death claim filed by father John H. Wyly, b. February 1845 to John H. and Mary Parks Wyly, brother of Levi Wyly. Buried at Old Clarkesville Cemetery.

Wyly, Levi W. Enlisted 11 June 1861 as 4th sgt., age 18, roll dated 1 July 1862 lists him as an ordnance sgt., promoted to 2nd lt. 27 July 1863, roll dated 19 January 1864 shows him sick at hospital and later rolls show him home on sick furlough, Officer roster dated 3 December 1864 states sick one year, Inspection report dated 27 February 1865 states absent sick medical examining board approved, son of John H. and Mary Parks Wyly, brother of Camillus Wyly.

Young, John C. Enlisted 11 June 1861 as 4h cpl., age 27, d. 1 June 1862 at Camp Elzey SC of disease, death claim filed by father Levi F. Young.

Zachary, William D. Enlisted 11 June 1861, age 18, KIA 17 September 1862 at Sharpsburg MD, death claim filed by father James Zachary, son of James and Eliza Russell Zachary, buried at Townville Baptist Church Cemetery in Townville SC.

Casualties, Other Losses for Phillips Legion infantry battalion, from available records. Company D was formed from Polk County.

Company D

Total Enrollment	175
Death/Disease/Accident	22
Retired to Invalid Corps	3
Executed as Spy	1
Discharged/Disability	18
Resigned	2
Discharged/Furnished Substitute	1
Detailed as Shoemaker	1
KIA	16
MWIA	3
WIA	52
Surrendered/Paroled	20
Exchanged	11
Deserted	12
AWOL	6
Imprisoned/Rock Island IL	6
Imprisoned/Point Lookout MD	20
Imprisoned/Elmira NY	1
Imprisoned/Johnson's Island OH	3
Imprisoned/Camp Douglas IL	2
Imprisoned/Fort Delaware DE	4
Imprisoned/Newport News VA	1
Imprisoned/Camp Chase OH	1
Galvanized Yankees	3
Transferred Out	16
Transferred In	1
Sent North to Ohio	1
Sent North to Des Moines IA	2
Sent North to Boston MA	1
Sent North to Philadelphia PA	2
Enlisted/no other information available	4
Enlisted as Substitute	1

Note: Any one individual may appear in several categories; e.g., he may have been captured, sent to prison and exchanged. "Galvanized Yankees" are imprisoned

Confederate soldiers who enlisted in a branch of the US Army or Navy during the
war.

PHILLIPS GEORGIA LEGION
INFANTRY BATTALION

Company D
The Polk Rifles

Adkins, Edward. Enlisted 14 September 1861, died from injury received on railroad
near Augusta GA, (en route from South Carolina to Richmond VA) 20 July
1862, A. J. Reese letter dated 21 July 1862 tells of the accident "I am sorry to say
that we happen to have had a very unfortunate accident resulting in the death of
one of the Polk Rifles. He was sitting in the door of one of the car boxes just
before me. By some means (I did not see him as the post struck him) he was
knocked out and killed. I have thought of the poor fellow several times since
then," son of Bryant and Parthena Adkins, age 14 in 1860 Polk census.

Atwood, Samuel J. Enlisted 14 June 1861, age 31, discharged 5 July 1861.

Baldwin, James M. Enlisted 20 June 1861, court-martialed for violation of AIG SO
#3 (see ANV GO #55 dated 9 April 1863, fined one month's pay), shown as 5th
sgt. on roll dated 14 January 1864, WIA (left thigh) at Wilderness, 6 May 1864,
furloughed home 28 May 1864, still shown absent wounded on roll dated 30
January 1865, paroled 23 May 1865 at Talladega, Alabama, b. 1846 in SC to
Thomas and Elizabeth Davis Baldwin, brother of J. T. L. Baldwin, d. 28 April
1913.

Baldwin, John Thomas LaFayette. Enlisted 21 June 1861, age 23, WIA (fingers off)
in Maryland campaign (either 14 September 1862 or 17 September 1862), home
disabled rest of war, 1906 Roster Commission rolls lists him as A. J. Baldwin and
states wounded at South Mountain MD 14 September 1862, b. 26 August 1838
at Greenville SC to Thomas and Elizabeth Davis Baldwin, brother of James
Baldwin, d. 2 May 1902 at Cedartown GA, buried Bethlehem Church cemetery
in Polk County.

Barrett, Arthur J. Enlisted 14 May 1862, transferred to 3rd GA Sharpshooter
battalion May 1863, captured at Cedar Creek 19 October 1864, imprisoned at
Point Lookout until exchanged 17 March 1865, b. 10 June 1844 in GA to David
and Margaret Barrett, brother of Joseph Barrett, d. 17 October 1906, buried at
Blackwood Springs Baptist Church, Calhoun GA.

Barrett, Joseph W. Enlisted 14 June 1861, age 21, 2nd sgt. on 31 October 1861 roll,
shown as pvt. on later rolls, transferred to 3rd GA Sharpshooter battalion as 2nd
lt. 1 May 1863, WIA (arm) at Chancellorsville, resigned in late 1864, son of
David and Margaret Barrett, brother of Arthur Barrett.

Barton, Andrew O. Enlisted 14 June 1861, age 28, died of pneumonia at Meadow
    Bluff in western VA 31 October 1861, 1860 census shows him living at
    Draketown in Paulding County.

Barton, David Humphrey Posey. Enlisted 24 April 1861, WIA (left leg and shoulder)
    and captured at Fox's Gap MD 14 September 1862, exchanged at City Point VA
    18 December 1862, captured 6 April 1865 at Sailor's Creek, released from Point
    Lookout prison 24 June 1865, age 25 in 1860 Cobb County census, son of James
    Lewis and Louella Johnson Barton, half brother of James and William Barton.

Barton, James Louis. Enlisted 14 June 1861, age 18, WIA (thigh) 2 July 1863 at
    Gettysburg per casualty list in 20 July 1863 *Atlanta Southern Confederacy*, shown
    as 3rd cpl. on roll dated 14 January 1864, captured 6 April 1865 at Sailor's
    Creek, released from Point Lookout Prison 24 June 1865, 1906 Roster
    commission roll also shows WIA at the Wilderness 6 May 1864, b. 23 April
    1843 in Cass (Bartow) County, son of James Lewis and Sarah Ellis Barton,
    married Sarah A. Powell 18 September 1866, moved to Bentonville AR after the
    war and was mayor of Winthrop AR, d. 13 February 1929 at Winthrop and is
    buried there.

Barton, John. KIA at Gettysburg PA 2 July 1863, not shown in surviving muster rolls
    but is listed in 1906 Roster Commission roll and is shown on a newspaper
    casualty list in the 20 July 1863 *Atlanta Southern Confederacy*, he was probably a
    new recruit who joined Co. D in the spring of 1863 after the last surviving
    muster roll prior to Gettysburg was filled out in February.

Barton, William Stephen. Enlisted 14 June 1861, age 20, shown home sick on all
    rolls after January/February 1863, hospital records showed him in Virginia
    hospitals as late as September 1863, a roll dated 5 October 1864 stated POW
    captured at home, but no Federal POW records list his name, b. 20 June 1841 in
    Cass County to James Lewis and Sarah Ellis Barton, brother of James Barton
    and half brother of David Barton.

Berry, Andrew J. Enlisted 14 May 1862, shown sick from enlistment and at home
    until detailed as a hospital attendant at Lumpkin Hospital in Rome GA, roll
    dated 14 January 1864 showed him absent sick, roll dated 5 October 1864 stated
    POW captured 1 June 1864 (Cold Harbor), d. 6 August 1864 from typhoid at
    Point Lookout, buried at Point Lookout Confederate Cemetery, Scotland MD,
    b. 1835 in AL to Edmund and Elizabeth Hales Berry, brother of Daniel, John,
    Marshall, and W. Travis Berry.

Berry, Daniel Sylvester. Enlisted 28 November 1862, surrendered at Appomattox 9
    April 1865, b. 7 June 1825 in Newton County to Edmund and Elizabeth H.
    Berry, brother of Andrew, John, Marshall, and W. Travis Berry, d. 6 January
    1889, buried at Shiloh Baptist Church Cemetery, Esom Hill GA.

Berry, John D. Enlisted 28 November 1862, shown as absent sick at home' on all
    rolls after September/October 1863, b. 1827 in GA to Edmund and Elizabeth
    H. Berry, brother of Andrew, Daniel, Marshall, and W. Travis Berry.

Berry, Marhsall A. Enlisted 11 April 1863 in Virginia, WIA at Cold Harbor 1 June 1864, d. of wounds 29 August 1864 at Stuart Hospital in Richmond, b. 1838 in AL to Edmund and Elizabeth H. Berry, brother of Andrew, John, Daniel, and W. Travis Berry.

Berry, Wilson Travis. Enlisted 14 June 1861, age 29, d. of small pox at Howards Grove Hospital in Richmond, 25 December 1862, b. 1832 in AL to Edmund and Elizabeth H. Berry, brother of Andrew, Daniel, John, and Marshall Berry.

Best, Hezekiah S. Enlisted as 2nd Sgt, transferred to cavalry company H/B 18 September 1861.

Bishop, Solomon J. Enlisted 26 June 1861, age 30, 1st cpl. on roll dated 2 December 1862, deserted at Bermuda Hundred 26 January 1865, took Oath and sent to Des Moines IA, 1896 Alabama pension application stated that he was wounded in the left knee at Spotsylvania, casualty list in 18 June 1864 *Athens Southern Banner* showed him wounded in knee, d. in Alabama 15 May 1900, his widow's pension was discontinued in 1914 when an informer told the state that he was a deserter.

Blaylock, George R. Enlisted 14 June 1861, age 23, furloughed home sick 16 January 1865, no further record.

Bramblett (Bramlett), L. O. Enlisted 14 June 1861, age 19, wounded in thigh and right foot during Gettysburg campaign, admitted to hospital 21 July 1863, captured at Sailor's Creek 6 April 1865, imprisoned at Point Lookout until released 24 June 1865, applied for pension in Alabama in 1906.

Brockman, W. D. Enlisted 14 June 1861, age 22, discharged 5 July 1861.

Brooks, Carter. Enlisted 21 June 1862, d. 21 December 1862 from pneumonia at Richmond GH #26, buried at Oakwood Confederate Cemetery, Richmond, b. 1843 to Micajah and Margaret Brooks, brother of Green Brooks.

Brooks, Francis Marion. Enlisted 21 June 1862, d. 12 February 1863 from catarrhus at Richmond GH #19, buried at Oakwood Confederate Cemetery, Richmond, as F. M. Brinks.

Brooks, Green Lee. Not shown in service records but is listed in 1906 Roster Commission rolls with notation of "died in service," he is shown in the 1860 Polk County census in the household of H. H. Brooks and would appear to be the younger brother of Carter Brooks, he was 14 in 1860 so it seems likely that he joined Co. D during the spring of either 1863 or 1864 and died before ever being recorded on a muster roll.

Brooks, John A. Enlisted 14 May 1862, transferred to 3rd GA Sharpshooter battalion, May 1863, WIA (severe) at Wilderness 6 May 1864, no further record, widow applied for pension in Alabama noting that he d. 25 August 1881, 1906 Roster Commission roll also notes a wound received at South Mountain MD, 14 September 1862.

Brooks, James. Enlisted 14 May 1862, shown as wounded on roll dated 5 October 1864, admitted to Richmond Hospital 2 June 1864 so wound occurred at Cold

Harbor, postwar pension application confirms that he was wounded in the arm at Cold Harbor and was at home on wounded furlough at the end of the war, b. in 1834 in Henry County GA.

Brooks, William. Enlisted 28 November 1862, shown sick in Richmond Hospital in November 1863 then shown home sick on all later rolls, 1899 Alabama pension application notes age as 73 and states that he lost a testicle to disease in 1864, d. in Alabama 19 March 1903.

Brown, James M. Enlisted 20 February 1864 in Tennessee, present on roll dated 30 January 1865, no further military record, pension application states he was b. 1845 in Habersham County GA, also says he was captured 8 April 1865.

Brown, Virgil V. Enlisted 14 June 1861, age 25, WIA at Gettysburg (thigh), WIA at Cold Harbor (leg), furloughed home 7 June 1864, captured at home in Georgia and executed as a spy, b. 4 July 1842 in Cass County GA to Vincent and Leannah Henderson Brown.

Brown, William B. Enlisted 14 June 1861, age 25, roll dated 5 October 1864 shows him home sick, December 1864 roll states captured at home, Federal records show that he took the Oath 24 November 1864 at Chattanooga, an additional Federal record shows him admitted to a Chattanooga Hospital 14 December 1864, released 4 January 1865.

Byers, James D. Enlisted 14 June 1861, age 16, casualty list in 8 June 1864 *Athens Southern Banner* lists him as wounded in the arm (Wilderness), captured at Sailor's Creek 6 April 1865, imprisoned at Point Lookout until released 10 June 1865.

Byrd, Samuel Masters Hankins. Enlisted 11 June 1861 as a pvt., appointed cpt. and asst. QM 19 July 1861, promoted to maj. and brigade QM 19 February 1864, surrendered at Appomattox 9 April 1865, b. 11 March 1830, d. 26 March 1895, buried Greenwood Cemetery in Cedartown GA.

Campmire, Marion W. Enlisted 14 June 1861, age 18, captured at Knoxville 29 November 1863 and imprisoned at Rock Island until released 18 June 1865, Alabama pension application makes note of a wound at Sharpsburg 17 September 1862 and also states that he was born 15 December 1841 in SC.

Cason, Levi C. Enlisted 14 June 1861, age 23, died of measles 14 December 1861 in western Virginia per pension application of widow Sarah J. (Whisett) Lankford (witnessed by J. M. Scott), 1906 Roster Commission roll states that he died in 1861.

Carter, R. H. Enlisted 14 June 1861 as 1st cpl., age 34, 1906 Roster Commission roll states accidentally shot in foot in 1862, transferred to Blaylock's Co., 1st Georgia Cavalry per SO #215/8 dated 13 September 1862.

Carter, Thomas J. Enlisted 14 June 1861, age 23, shown as 4th cpl. on May/June 1862 roll, KIA at Knoxville 29 November 1863.

Clark, W. J. Enlisted 14 June 1861, age 23, shown sick at Beckley VA on October roll, discharged 20 December 1861.

Cox, Lewis Skidmore. Enlisted 1 March 1862, WIA and captured at Knoxville 29 November 1863 requiring amputation of arm, sent to Fort Delaware 4 March 1864, exchanged 18 September 1864, furloughed home 26 September 1864, roll dated 30 January 1865 shows at home disabled, b. 21 October 1835, buried at Marietta Citizens Cemetery.

Crow, Aaron C. Enlisted 14 June 1861, age 29, extensive record of illness, detailed as hospital attendant at Richmond in 1863, captured 3 April 1865 at Richmond's Jackson Hospital, paroled 3 May 1865, d. at Watkinsville GA in 1885, widow's pension application shows his name as C. Aaron Crow.

Crowell, Watson Witherspoon. Enlisted 14 June 1861, age 21, discharged 28 December 1861, b. 23 February 1840 in SC to Rev. Churchwell Anderson and Linna Ramsour Crowell, d. 26 February 1929 in Buncombe County NC, buried at Montgomery United Methodist Church, Buncombe County NC.

Crutchfield, Daniel C. Enlisted 25 November 1862 as a substitute for L. C. Peek, served as a teamster, surrendered at Appomattox 9 April 1865, widow's Alabama pension application notes that he d. 29 May 1893.

Dennis, James H. Enlisted 14 June 1861 as 4th cpl., age 21, shown as a pvt. on May/June 1862 roll, captured at Knoxville 29 November 1863, imprisoned at Rock Island until exchanged 2 March 1865, no further record, son of Jacob and Elizabeth Dennis.

Dodds, John Luther. Enlisted 14 June 1861 as 2nd lt., age 33, promoted to cpt. 4 October 1862, WIA (head) at Wilderness 6 May 1864, captured 6 April 1865 at Sailor's Creek, imprisoned at Johnson's Island until released 17 June 1865.

Echols, R. H. Enlisted 14 June 1861, age 19, WIA (arm) in 1862 Maryland campaign, (either Fox's Gap or Sharpsburg), all later rolls show either wounded furlough or AWOL since December 1862, no further record.

Everett, L. Peter. Enlisted 14 June 1861, age 19, 1906 Roster Commission roll states that he transferred to Co. C of the 23rd GA Infantry 31 August 1861, he shows up on the rolls of the 23rd in 1863.

Ezzell, James Mason. Enlisted 14 June 1861, age 22, captured 6 April 1865 at Sailor's Creek, imprisoned at Point Lookout until released 11 June 1865, son of Thomas and Elizabeth Thompson Ezzell, brother of Jesse Ezzell.

Ezzell, Jesse A. Enlisted 14 June 1861, age 23, d. at Martinsburg VA from disease 29 September 1862, son of Thomas and Elizabeth Thompson Ezzell, brother of James Ezzell.

Fincher, Henry J. Enlisted 14 May 1862, WIA at 2nd Manassas, transferred to 3rd GA Sharpshooter battalion 1 May 1863, WIA at Chancellorsville 2 May 1863 (hand amputated), sent home from Richmond Hospital July 1863 disabled.

Gardner, Joshua B. Enlisted 14 June 1861, age 20, WIA (thigh) 2 July 1863 at Gettysburg per casualty list in 20 July 1863 *Atlanta Southern Confederacy*, admitted to Richmond Hospital 2 August 1863, captured 6 April 1865 at Sailor's Creek, imprisoned at Point Lookout until released 27 June 1865.

Gardner, William E. Enlisted 14 June 1861, age 24, surrendered 9 April 1865 at Appomattox (listed as W. E. Geordon).

George, Greenville N. Enlisted 14 June 1861, shown as 3rd sgt. on September/October 1863 roll, KIA at Knoxville 29 November 1863.

Gibson, William T. Enlisted 14 June 1861, age 17, WIA (lung) 17 September 1862 at Sharpsburg, admitted to Richmond Hospital 30 July 1863 with gunshot wound right arm, recommended for transfer to cavalry by surgeon's certificate, transferred to 1st GA Cavalry by SO #198/7 dated 20 August 1863, b. 6 May 1844, d. 5 May 1912, buried Greenwood Cemetery at Cedartown GA.

Gladden, Green. Enlisted 14 June 1861, age 17, discharged 20 December 1861.

Gladden, J. M. Enlisted 14 June 1861, age 19, 2nd cpl. on roll dated December 1864, deserted 24 January 1865 at Bermuda Hundred, sent to Philadelphia 25 January 1865.

Godwin, Henry Kinchen. Enlisted 25 October 1863 at Chattanooga TN, captured at Cedar Creek 19 October 1864, imprisoned at Point Lookout until exchanged 17 January 1865, no further military record, b. 26 May 1820 in Hancock County GA to Barnabus and Francis Pope Godwin, d. 10 February 1893, buried at Friendship Baptist Church Cemetery in Polk County GA, father of Moses A. Godwin.

Godwin, Moses Andrew. Enlisted 1 August 1862, surrendered at Appomattox 9 April 1865 (listed as M. A. Goodwin), b. 2 December 1844 to Henry K. and Eliza Hamilton Godwin in Fayette County GA, d. 25 February 1907, buried at Rose Hill Cemetery, Rockmart GA.

Graham, Thomas A. Enlisted 14 June 1861, age 17, February 1863 rolls states he deserted from camp February 1863, no further record.

Green, Joseph B. Enlisted 14 June 1861, age 20, transferred to 3rd GA Sharpshooter battalion May 1863, August 1863 roll shows at hospital Marietta, rolls through August 1864 show at hospital, no further military record, 1899 Alabama pension application states he is 58 years old and also claims he was discharged from the army 11 April 1865, a later application from his widow notes that he d. 13 January 1904, b. in SC to Henry W. and Musa Green, brother of James Green.

Green, James R. Enlisted 14 June 1861, age 22, discharged 1 November 1861, b. in NC to Henry W. and Musa Green, brother of Joseph Green.

Hamilton, Joel F. Enlisted 11 March 1862, d. 28 November 1862 of small pox at Richmond, b. 2 March 1837 in GA to Moses and Nancy Fain Hamilton, brother of James W. and Moses P. Hamilton.

Hamilton, James L. M. Enlisted 24 February 1862, list shows present on roll dated 14 January 1864, 1906 Roster Commission roll states that he was killed at Wilderness 6 May 1864.

Hamilton, James W. Enlisted 14 June 1861, discharged 2 July 1861, reenlisted 25 October 1863 in Tennessee, listed as home sick on all rolls after 5 October

1864, no further record, b. 12 September 1834 in GA to Moses and Nancy Fain
Hamilton, brother of Joel F. and Moses P. Hamilton.

Hamilton, Moses Parks. Enlisted 4 March 1862, surrendered at Appomattox 9 April
1865, b. 6 March 1832 in Meriwether County GA to Moses and Nancy Fain
Hamilton, brother of Joel F. and James W. Hamilton, d. 8 September 1904 in
Lee County TX.

Hammack, James W. Not shown on rolls but service record does contain a hospital
record showing him assigned (as hospital attendant?) to Richmond General
Hospital #9, probably enlisted during spring of 1863, may have rejoined Phillips
Legion as they pulled out of Richmond at war's end as he was captured at
Amelia Court House on 6 April 1865, imprisoned at Point Lookout until
released 28 June 1865.

Hargis, Richard O. Enlisted 14 June 1861, age 26, disability discharge 22 May 1862.

Harper, Jesse. Enlisted 14 September 1861 in Virginia, captured at Russellville TN
10 March 1864 and imprisoned at Rock Island 30 May 1864, last on Rock Island
roll 24 June 1864 with a notation indicating that he has taken the Oath and
joined the U. S. Navy, U. S. Navy records show that he enlisted 10 June 1864 at
Chicago and served on the ships *Potomac*, *W. G. Anderson*, *Sciota*, and was then
assigned to the *Trefoil* but never reported for duty, his enlistment shows him to
be 21 years old, 5'9" tall with blue eyes and light hair, listed as a deserter on
postwar records until applying to the government in 1890 to have his desertion
record removed, in his application he states that the *Sciota* was blown up on 14
April 1865 while he was detailed to the gig crew, that he then became seriously
ill and, when recovered, served on the *Trefoil* until departing for home on 5 July
1865, at the time this was submitted Jesse was living at Corsicana in Navarre
County TX, the Navy agreed to remove the desertion charge from his record in
March 1891.

Harrell, John C. Enlisted 14 June 1861, age 24, last shown on 14 October 1861 as
sick Green Sulphur Springs, 1906 Roster Commission roll states that he died in
service so appears likely he died of disease in western Virginia in 1861.

Harrell, L. R. Enlisted 14 June 1861, age 22, last shown present on roll dated 14
January 1864, 1906 Roster Commission roll states he was killed at Wilderness 6
May 1864, casualty list in 8 June 1864 *Athens Southern Banner* states "wounded
in head and since died."

Harrell, W. G. Enlisted 24 February 1862, present on roll dated 30 January 1865, no
further record.

Haynes, Wilson. Enlisted 14 June 1861, age 26, appears as "deserted 26 January
1863" on roll dated 14 January 1864, later rolls show same until roll dated 30
January 1865 states he was discharged at Russellville TN on 27 December 1863.

Hazelwood, John C. Enlisted 14 June 1861, age 19, furloughed home to Alabama 19
January 1865, no further military record, buried at Holly Springs Methodist
Church Cemetery in Martins Mill TX.

Heaton, James Madison. Enlisted 14 May 1862, captured 6 April 1865 at Sailor's
Creek, imprisoned at Point Lookout until released 28 June 1865, Alabama
pension application states he was WIA at Chancellorsville, later widow's
application states he d. 26 May 1911.

Hedrick, W. Tobe Enlisted 14 June 1861, age 17, WIA (leg) 13 December 1862 at
Fredericksburg, last shown on 14 January 1864 roll as home wounded, 1906
Roster Commission roll states he was killed at Wilderness 6 May 1864, casualty
list in 8 June 1864 *Athens Southern Banner* states "wounded in breast and since
died."

Hobbs, Harold R. Enlisted 14 June 1861, deserted 21 June 1861, son of James H.
and Dorcas Weisenhut Hobbs.

Hobbs, William A. Enlisted 14 June 1861, age 16, discharged 20 December 1861,
son of Andrew and Elizabeth Hobbs.

Howard, S. A. Enlisted 14 May 1862, furloughed home 22 January 1865, no further
record.

Hughes, William. Enlisted 14 June 1861, age 23, last shown as present on 31
October 1861 roll, no further record.

Jenkins, Almon (or Allen). Enlisted 1 March 1862, WIA 29 November 1863 per
casualty list in 3 February 1864 *Athens Watchman*, present on roll dated 30
January 1865, no further military record but 1901 Arkansas pension application
indicates he was born about 1828 and was living in Franklin County, Arkansas, it
also states that he was discharged 9 April 1865 but his name is not listed in the
Appomattox surrender records, a later application from his widow Mrs. M. E.
Jenkins stated that he died 15 November 1907, b. February 1828 to John and
Margaret Jenkins.

Jenkins, Henry Clay. Enlisted 20 September 1863, captured 6 April 1865 at Sailor's
Creek, imprisoned at Point Lookout until released 28 June 1865, Alabama
pension application states he was WIA at the Wilderness (head), casualty list in 8
June 1864 *Athens Southern Banner* confirms this wound, a later widow's
application states that he died 3 March 1904.

Johnson, Isaac. Enlisted 14 June 1861, age 25, teamster, captured at Sailor's Creek 6
April 1865 and imprisoned at Point Lookout until released 28 June 1865, son of
Elija and Casandra Johnson.

Jones, Abraham "Ham." Enlisted 14 June 1861 a 1st lt., age 33, KIA at Fox's Gap
MD 14 September 1862, younger brother of Lt. Col. Seaborn Jones.

Jones, Seaborn. Enlisted 14 June 1861 as cpt., promoted to lt. col. of infantry
battalion of legion soon thereafter, resigned because of poor health 3 July 1862.
Older brother of Lt. Abraham Jones, son of John A. and Martha Jenkins Jones,
b. 5 October 1825, d. 13 February 1891, buried Rose Hill Cemetery at
Rockmart GA.

Jones, William E. Enlisted 14 June 1861, age 21, captured at Frederick MD 12
September 1862, exchanged 2 October 1862, last shown on February 1863 roll

in Richmond hospital, not on later rolls but did make it back to Georgia as he surrenders at Kingston 12 May 1865.

Jones, William H. Enlisted 3 March 1862, WIA at 2nd Manassas (left ankle), in Lynchburg Hospital February 1865, retired to Invalid Corps 24 March 1865, b. 10 January 1842, d. 4 March 1909.

Kelly, Lacey W. Enlisted 14 June 1861, age 21, appointed to regimental band, present on roll dated 30 January 1865, took Oath at Chattanooga 25 May 1865.

Kelly, William. Enlisted 14 June 1861, age 20, last shown on roll dated 31 October 1861 as sick at White Sulphur Springs, 1906 Roster Commission roll states he died in 1861.

Kilgore, Henry S. Enlisted 14 May 1862, transferred to 3rd GA Sharpshooter Battalion May 1863, shown as deserted at Bull's Gap, TN 5 September 1864, sent to Camp Douglas prison in Chicago, took Oath November 1864 and joined Co. G, 5th US Volunteers for frontier service, enlistment shows him to be 35 years old, 5'11" tall with gray eyes and dark hair, deserted 19 July 1865 at Cottonwood Crossing KS, not heard from again, age 30 in 1860 Polk County census.

King, Jonathon F. Enlisted 14 June 1861, age 28, transferred to 3rd GA Sharpshooter battalion 1 May 1863, WIA (abdomen) at Chancellorsville 2 May 1863, shows sick on August 1863 roll then furloughed home, joined 6th GA cavalry, son of Noah and Rebecca Lynch King, brother of Samuel King, age given at enlistment appears to be incorrect as other records show him born NC in 1837.

King, Samuel. Enlisted 14 June 1861, age 20, d. in Georgia 23 October 1861 of disease, son of Noah and Rebecca Lynch King, brother of Jonathon King.

Knight, William Clarence. Enlisted 14 June 1861, appointed QM sgt. 2 August 1861, surrendered at Appomattox 9 April 1865 (listed as QM sgt. Co. E), b. 27 January 1824, d. 17 November 1905, buried Greenwood Cemetery Cedartown GA.

Lang, Robert G. Enlisted 14 June 1861, age 21, casualty list in 8 June 1864 *Athens Southern Banner* lists him as wounded in the arm (Wilderness), deserted 24 January 1865 at Bermuda Hundred, took Oath and sent to Des Moines IA, son of John C. and Nancy Estes Lang, brother of J. T. Lang.

Lang, J. Thomas. Enlisted 11 April 1863 in Virginia, left hand accidentally shot off near Chattanooga 9 October 1863, retired to Invalid Corps 11 February 1865, age 19, son of John C. and Nancy Estes Lang, brother of Robert G. Lang.

Ledbetter, Dennis Hankins W. Enlisted 18 July 1864 in Virginia, last shown present on roll dated 30 January 1865, no further military record. 1920 Florida pension application states he moved to Marion County FL in 1910 and says he was discharged from service at Warsaw VA 10 May 1865, b. 11 December 1846 in Henry County to Lewis L. and Cornelia Byrd Ledbetter, d. 1934 at Tampa FL.

Lewis, John L. Enlisted 14 June 1861, age 29, last shown on 31 October 1861 roll as present, no further record.

Lockwood, George W. Enlisted 14 June 1861, age 26, WIA (hand) at Wilderness 6 May 1864, retired to Invalid Corps 6 February 1865.

Long, James. Enlisted 2 August 1862 in Virginia, surrendered at Appomattox 9 April 1865, b. about 1845, son of Jonathon Long, brother of John W. Long.

Long, John Bayliss. Enlisted 14 May 1862, shown as missing 1 June 1864, later rolls show captured but no Federal POW records, 1906 Roster Commission roll states he was captured at Cold Harbor 1 June 1864 and died at Point Lookout, not listed as a known burial at Point Lookout, age 23 in 1850 Paulding census, son of Margaret Long.

Long, John W. Enlisted 1 March 1862, KIA at Knoxville 29 November 1863, b. about 1843, son of Jonathon Long, brother of James Long.

Lovell, Jefferson. Enlisted 14 May 1862, d. from pneumonia at Richmond GH #16 8 January 1863, b. 29 April 1832 in GA to John and Malinda McAdams Lovell, brother of William Lovell.

Lovell, William Wiley. Enlisted 28 November 1862, shown as AWOL on October 1863 roll and all rolls thereafter, b. 1 February 1840 to John and Malinada McAdams Lovell, brother of Jefferson Lovell, d. 2 September 1928, buried at Pleasant Valley Cemetery in Floyd County GA.

Luke, Frank B. Enlisted 14 June 1861, age 18, WIA in 1862 Maryland campaign (shoulder), captured 6 April 1865 at Sailor's Creek, imprisoned at Point Lookout until released 29 June 1865.

Madden, A. R. Enlisted 14 May 1862, d. 20 June 1862 at Camp Elzey SC from disease.

Madden, Austin. Enlisted 21 April 1862, captured 7 April 1865 at Amelia Court House VA, shown on POW record as sgt., imprisoned at Point Lookout until released 29 June 1865.

Madden, John W. Transferred into Co. D 4 January 1863 (old unit unknown), records indicate he served as a teamster, captured at Farmville VA, 13 April 1865, paroled and released.

Mathias, John A. Enlisted 14 June 1861, promoted to sgt. maj. 2 August 1861, WIA 14 September 1862 at Fox's Gap MD (foot), promoted to 1st lt. and adjutant 12 May 1863, captured 6 April 1865 at Sailor's Creek and imprisoned at Johnson's Island until released 19 June 1865, age 26 at release.

McDowell, J. M. Enlisted 14 June 1861, age 27, KIA 19 October 1864 at Cedar Creek.

McElroy, Johnson J. Enlisted 14 June 1861, age 20, shown sick at private house on late 1861 roll, no further record, 1906 Roster Commission rolls states he died in service, probable death from disease in 1861 in western Virginia.

McElroy, Thomas H. Enlisted 14 June 1861, age 18, roll dated 2 December 1862 states he went home to Alabama wounded (head) 1 November 1862, no further record, 1906 Roster Commission roll states that he died in service.

McGinnis, J. M. Enlisted 1 March 1862, discharged 27 October 1864, over age.

McGregor, Hugh Brewster. Enlisted 14 June 1861, age 21, captured 6 April 1865 at Sailor's Creek and imprisoned at Point Lookout until released 29 June 1865, b. 11 June 1840 to Reese and Charotte Brewster McGregor, d. 17 November 1928, buried at Greenwood Cemetery, Cedartown GA.

Moore, T. H. Enlisted 1 March 1862, roll dated 2 December 1862 shows furloughed home sick, no further record.

Morris, G. H. R. Enlisted 14 June 1861, age 22, transferred to Co. D 20th GA 8 February 1865, captured at Richmond 3 April 1865, released at Newport News VA 3 July 1865.

Mountain, Thomas B. Enlisted 14 June 1861, age 18, court martialed for violation of AIG SO #3 (see ANV GO #55 dated 9 April 1863, fined one month's pay), MWIA (shot through pelvis) and captured at Knoxville 29 November 1863, d. 10 December 1863, "Buried in woods near shops 4 miles from Knoxville."; b. in Alabama 22 April 1844 to William E. and Mary Stevens Mountain.

Murphy, J. M. Enlisted 3 September 1862, WIA (back) and captured at Sharpsburg MD, 17 September 1862, exchanged at Fort Monroe 13 October 1862, furloughed home 10 November 1862, no further record.

Murphy, John F. Enlisted 24 April 1862, WIA and captured 14 September 1862 at Fox's Gap MD, d. at Baltimore in late October per 1863 death claim filed by wife Phebe Murphy.

Nix, Thomas Enlisted 14 June 1861, age 47, discharged 14 October 1862, overage.

Partain, James M. Enlisted 29 March 1864, WIA at Wilderness 6 May 1864, right arm and leg amputated, furloughed from Charlottesville Hospital 14 February 1865 then at Richmond hospitals, captured at war's end, sent to US Small Pox Hospital at Richmond 23 May 1865, discharged and released 10 June 1865, age 18 at release, son of B.W. and Nancy Partain, age 14 in 1860 Polk County Census.

Peek, Julius Algernon. Enlisted 14 June 1861 as 3rd lt., age 23, shown as 2nd lt. on roll dated 31 August 1861, promoted 1st lt. 4 October 1862, WIA at Fredericksburg 13 December 1862 (neck), shown as acting asst. QM on 5 October 1864 roll, surrendered at Appomattox 9 April 1865, b. 4 April 1838 to William W. and Elizabeth Reid Peek, brother of Luthur Peek, d. 12 July 1924, buried Greenwood Cemetery, Cedartown GA.

Peek, Luther C. Enlisted 24 February 1862 as a musician, discharged by furnishing a substitute (Daniel Crutchfield) 25 November 1862, son of William W. and Elizabeth Reid Peek, brother of J.A. Peek.

Poor, L. M. Enlisted 14 June 1861, discharged 2 July 1861.

Rentz, George S. Enlisted 14 June 1861 as 3rd sgt., age 18, WIA (neck) 2 July 1863 at Gettysburg per casualty report in 20 July 1863 *Atlanta Southern Confederacy*, shown as a pvt. on roll dated 14 January 1864 and all rolls thereafter, shown present on roll dated 30 January 1865, no further record, b. 11 June 1843 in

Houston County GA to John A. and Josephine Moore Rentz, d. 5 May 1919 in
McLennon County TX, buried at Bosqueville Cemetery, McLennon County.

Riddlesperger, William H. Enlisted 21 June 1862, last shown on January/February
1863 roll as sick, this entry for him was later lined out, 1906 Roster Commission
roll states Died January 1863, probably d. in the hospital January 1863 from
disease, possibly buried at Fredericksburg Confederate Cemetery under a
tombstone marked "W. R. — Ga." b. February 1843 in Pickens County to
Thomas and Mary Brooks Riddlesperger.

Robertson, D. J. Enlisted 14 June 1861, only shown on one roll dated 14 January
1864, 2 July 1864 *Richmond Enquirer* casualty list for period 6 May 1864 to 16
May 1864 lists him as being mortally wounded—since died, it is probable that
he had transferred into the Legion from another unit in late 1863 which would
explain his absence on earlier Legion muster rolls.

Robertson, D. Jasper. Enlisted 25 October 1863 in Tennessee, shows furloughed
home sick on roll dated 5 October 1864, hospital record shows furloughed to
Macon GA on 23 August 1864, still listed as absent sick on roll dated 30 January
1865 no further military record but known that he survived the war and
returned to Georgia since he witnessed James Brown's and N W Robertson's
pension applications, son of James and Malinda Robertson, brother of Newton
Robertson, age 6 in 1850 Paulding census.

Robertson, Newton W. Enlisted 20 September 1863, paroled at Burkeville, VA 14
April 1865, son of James and Malinda Robertson, brother of D Jasper
Robertson, age 8 in 1850 Paulding County census

Robinson, Jasper. Enlisted 14 June 1861, age 17, last shown on roll for
January/February 1863, Federal records indicate that he deserted at Atlanta and
took the Oath of Allegiance on 2 September 1864, sent north of the Ohio River
for duration of the war on 26 September 1864, oath shows him to be 5'6" tall
with dark eyes and light hair, b. 4 July 1840, d. 28 December 1925, buried Hills
Creek Cemetery in Polk County

Rogers, Minor M. Enlisted 14 June 1861, age 21, discharged due to disability 17
December 1861.

Rosser, James T. Enlisted 5 May 1862, Sick on June 1862 roll, no further record,
1906 Roster Comrnission roll states he was discharged due to disability.

Sanders, Samuel H. Enlisted 14 June 1861, age 33, roll dated 2 December 1862
shows him detailed as a shoemaker at Richmond VA, later rolls show him
detailed as a shoemaker in Atlanta GA, still shown on this detail on final roll
dated 30 January 1865, no further record, b. Habersham County GA 24
September 1826.

Scott, Asa C. Enlisted 14 June 1861, age 20, WIA and captured 29 November 1863
at Knoxville, sent to Fort Delaware 4 March 1864, paroled and released
February 1865, no further military record, b. 12 January 1837, d. 25 February
1907, buried at Hills Creek Church Cemetery in Polk County.

Scott, B. F. Enlisted 14 June 1861, age 18, roll dated 14 January 1864 shows home wounded, shown present on all later rolls until 30 January 1865, no further record.

Scott, John Matthew. Enlisted 14 June 1861, age 19, shown present on all rolls throughout the war, paroled and released at Burkeville VA, 14 April 1865.

Scott, John A. Enlisted 14 June 1861, age 24, KIA at Fox's Gap MD, 14 September 1862.

Scott, T. R. Enlisted 19 November 1863, furloughed home sick 6 August 1864, still listed as home on sick furlough on roll dated 30 January 1865, no further record.

Scott, William Jackson. Enlisted 19 March 1862, present on 30 January 1865 roll, no further military record, 1906 Roster Commission roll states he was wounded at 2nd Manassas 28 August 1862, Alabama pension application states that he was wounded at both Second Manassas and Fredericksburg (hand and head) and also states that he was captured while on picket duty the Friday before the surrender, b. 1842, d. in Cleburne County, Alabama 26 January 1914.

Searcey, David T. Enlisted 14 June 1861, age 26, present on roll dated 30 January 1865, no further record, 1906 Roster Commission roll states he was wounded at Sharpsburg MD 17 September 1862."

Sherrel, H. Bruce. Enlisted 14 June 1861, KIA at Knoxville 29 November 1863.

Shular, A.J. Enlisted 14 June 1861, age 18, transferred to 3rd GA Sharpshooter Battalion on 1 May 1863, WIA (heel) May 1863 at Chancellorsville per casualty list in 19 May 1863 *Atlanta Southern Confederacy*, roll dated February 1864 states he was in the 3rd GA Calvary, roll dated June 1864 states he was in 6th GA Calvary, no further record.

Sims, Todger J. Enlisted 14 June 1861, age 23, last shown on 31 October 1861 roll as sick at Meadow Bluff, no further record.

Sims, M. Young. Enlisted 21 January 1862, KIA at Fredericksburg 13 December 1862.

Sims, Nathan G. Enlisted 14 May 1862, captured at Sailor's Creek 6 April 1865 and imprisoned at Point Lookout until released 19 June 1865, son of A. B. and Silla Sims, b. 1845 in Abbeville SC, d. 1925, buried at Rose Hill Cemetery in Rockmart GA.

Sims, William Jasper. Enlisted 14 June 1861, age 22, WIA (finger) 13 December 1862 at Fredericksburg, roll for December 1862 shows he was in a hospital in Richmond for a wound in hand, deserted 23 February 1865 at Bermuda Hundred, took Oath 27 February 1865 and sent to Boston.

Smith, John. Enlisted 14 June 1861 as 5th sgt., age 39, became a teamster in June 1863, shown as a pvt. on rolls after this date, surrendered 9 April 1865 at Appomattox.

Spence, R. D. Enlisted 14 June 1861 as 3rd cpl., age 22, 31 October 1861 roll shows him sick at Beckley, no further record.

Spratling, James W. Enlisted 14 June 1861, age 29, KIA at Fox's Gap MD, 14
  September 1862.
Stanford, Thomas. Enlisted 8 March 1862, captured 29 November 1863 at Knoxville
  and imprisoned at Rock Island until released 21 May 1865, age 26, widow
  Elizabeth Gant Stanford filed for a pension in Alabama noting that he d. 8
  March 1901 in Lineville AL.
Steward (Stewart), John M. Enlisted 14 May 1862, transferred to 3rd GA
  Sharpshooter battalion May 1863, in Virginia hospitals with ulcerated foot June
  to November 1863 then furloughed home 24 November 1863, deserted 5 July
  1864, captured 5 September 1864 in Tennessee, imprisoned at Camp Douglas
  IL until released 12 May 1865, b. 3 August 1838, d. 18 December 1896, buried
  at Greenwood Cemetery in Cedartown GA.
Stidham, George H. Enlisted 14 June 1861, age 25, appointed color cpl. 2 August
  1861, shown as color sgt. on May/June 1862 roll, elected Jr. 2nd lt. 17 October
  1862, captured 6 April 1865 at Sailor's Creek and imprisoned at Johnson's
  Island until released 20 June 1865.
Stidham, W. P. Enlisted 14 June 1861, age 22, last shown present on roll dated 30
  January 1865, no further military record, b. 14 January 1839 in Cass County, d.
  1911 in Paulding County.
Stone, Thomas Jefferson. Enlisted 14 June 1861, age 25, transferred to 3rd GA
  Sharpshooter battalion as 3rd sgt. in May 1863, d. from disease at Rome GA
  Hospital 1 December 1863, b. 1836 in SC to Abner and Rebecca Starnes Stone.
Sumner, W. J. Enlisted 14 June 1861, age 22, captured at Fox's Gap MD 14
  September 1862, exchanged 15 December 1862, deserted 24 January 1865 at
  Bermuda Hundred, took Oath and sent to Philadelphia.
Terrell, Hezekiah M. Enlisted 1 March 1862, age 24 in 1860 census,
  January/February 1863 roll states he was sent to a hospital at Staunton VA and
  not heard from since, no further record.
Thompson, Ivy F. Enlisted 14 June 1861, age 23, shown as 2nd sgt. on May/June
  1862 roll, captured at Knoxville 29 November 1863 and imprisoned at Rock
  Island until released 21 June 1865, d. 27 November 1894 at Cedartown GA.
Thompson, William H. Enlisted 14 May 1862, captured at Knoxville 29 November
  1863 and imprisoned at Rock Island until exchanged 15 February 1865, no
  further military record, b. in Gwinnett County GA 14 August 1832, d. at
  Soldiers Home Hospital, Atlanta 13 June 1903, buried at West View Cemetery,
  Atlanta, grave #81.
Thurmond, Warren Troupe. Enlisted 14 May 1862, absent sick throughout the war,
  shown as AWOL on roll dated 30 January 1865, no further record, b. in
  Georgia 1833, d. in 1894.
Tomlinson, Augustus Jackson. Enlisted 14 June 1861 as 4th sgt., age 21. elected 2nd
  lt. 17 October 1862, captured 29 November 1863 at Knoxville and sent to Camp
  Chase, Ohio, transferred to Fort Delaware 27 March 1864, released 12 June

1865, b. 26 January 1840 in Walton County GA to Eleven Summers and Olivia Jackson Tomlinson, married to Sarah A. McIver 22 August 1867 at Cedartown GA, d. 19 November 1908, buried at Greenwood Cemetery, Cedartown GA.

Turner, Samuel M. Enlisted 1 August 1862, WIA and captured at Fox's Gap MD 14 September 1862, at Camden Hospital Baltimore until exchanged 5 November 1862, shown sick at hospital on roll dated 14 January 1864, in Richmond hospitals March/April/May 1863 then transferred to Danville 14 May 1863, furloughed from Danville for 30 days 15 May 1863 citing chronic dysentery, AWOL on all further rolls, no further record.

Vaughn, W. P. Enlisted 14 June 1861, age 22, January/February 1863 rolls shows under arrest for being AWOL, sick at Richmond Hospital in July/August 1863, no further record.

Waters, Thomas Willoughby. Enlisted 14 June 1861, age 22, WIA at Sharpsburg MD 17 September 1862, transferred to 3rd GA Sharpshooter battalion in May 1863 as 1st sgt., captured at Front Royal 16 August 1864, d. at Elmira Prison 17 April 1865 of pneumonia, buried Woodlawn National Cemetery grave #1364, b. in Spartanburg SC to Thomas Willoughby and Hannah Musgrove Waters.

White, George W. Enlisted 14 June 1861, age 19, last shown on 31 October 1861 roll as a nurse at Green Sulphur Springs, VA hospital, 1906 Roster Commission roll states he died in WV 1861.

Wilcoxon, John B. Enlisted 11 June 1861 as cpt., elected maj. commanding Phillips Legion cavalry battalion 14 June 1861, resigned 4 July 1862.

Williams, E. Cannon. Enlisted 1 March 1862, captured at Fox's Gap MD, 14 September 1862, exchanged 2 October 1862, WIA (finger) at Fredericksburg 13 December 1862, WIA near Chattanooga 24 September 1863, final entry in service record states he was wounded leg amputated in hospital, 1906 Roster Commission roll states "died of wounds September 1863 near Chattanooga."

Williams, Ellis E. Enlisted 14 June 1861, age 26, KIA at Fox's Gap MD 14 September 1862.

Wilson, John H. Enlisted 14 June 1861, age 24, shown as 4th sgt. on roll dated 2 December 1862, captured 6 April 1865 at Sailor's Creek and imprisoned at Point Lookout until released 22 June 1865.

Wimberly, August P. Enlisted 14 June 1861 as 2nd sgt., age 21, admitted to Richmond Hospital 12 May 1864 with wound (WIA at Wilderness in thigh per casualty list in 8 June 1864 *Athens Southern Banner*), roll dated 5 October 1864 shows at home on wounded furlough, roll dated December 1864 states he was promoted cpt. Co. G Murchison's Cavalry Battalion 6 September 1864 but is then shown as captured with the legion 6 April 1865 at Sailor's Creek, imprisoned at Point Lookout until released 21 June 1865, son of Henry F. and Ann Wimberly, brother of John Wimberly.

Wimberly, Henry F. Enlisted 14 June 1861 as cpt., age 48, resigned 3 October 1862 because of poor health.

Wimberly, John R. Enlisted 5 May 1862, promoted to 3rd sgt. October 1864, last
shown present on roll dated 30 January 1865, pension application states he was
furloughed home 1865 and unable to return, son of Henry F. and Ann
Wimberly, brother of Augustus Wimberly, age 16 in 1860 Polk County census.

Wimpee, Henry E. Enlisted 14 May 1862, shown as present on roll dated 30 January
1865, no further record, age 21 in 1860 Polk County census.

Wimpee, Robert F. Enlisted 1 March 1862, WIA at Fredericksburg 13 December
1862 (head), transferred to 3rd GA Sharpshooter battalion in May 1863,
captured at Gettysburg 3 July 1863, sent to Fort Delaware, deserted and joined
Federal artillery unit in August 1863, son of David and Emily Wimpee, age 18
in 1860 Polk County census.

Wimpee (Wimpey), Mark J. Enlisted 14 June 1861, age given as 22, furloughed
home 1 January 1865, paroled and released at Augusta GA 23 May 1865, b. 11
September 1842, d. 7 January 1907, buried at Wax Community Cemetery in
Floyd County GA.

Winn (Wynn), Joseph Fletcher. Enlisted 14 June 1861, age 17, surrendered at
Appomattox 9 April 1865, 1906 Roster Commission roll states he was appointed
mail carrier for brigade.

Wood, James Springer. Enlisted 14 June 1861, age 22, captured at Fox's Gap MD,
14 September 1862, exchanged 6 October 1862, surrendered at Appomattox 9
April 1865, b. 4 December 1838, died 8 August 1902, buried at Greenwood
Cemetery in Cedartown GA.

Wood, William H. Enlisted 14 June 1861, age 21, d. 24 October 1861 at New River
in western VA from typhoid.

Woody, John. Enlisted 14 June 1861, age 18, WIA Sharpsburg MD 17 September
1862, furloughed home from Richmond Hospital 26 October 1862,
January/February 1863 roll states he was not heard from, no further record.

Woorley, J. W. Enlisted 29 April 1862, shown on June 1862 roll but no status
indicated, no further record.

York, Jr., Josiah Cowan. Enlisted 14 June 1861, age 19, WIA (eye) 2 July 1863 at
Gettysburg per casualty list in 20 July 1863 *Atlanta Southern Confederacy*,
admitted to Richmond Hospital 18 July 1863, 2nd cpl. on roll dated 14 January
1864, same roll shows him home wounded, further research shows that he
joined Co. A of the 1st GA Cavalry in February 1864, a roll for
November/December 1864 lists him as AWOL, no further military record, b. in
1841 to Josiah Cowan and Sarah Blake York, married to Lucie Virginia Mason
of Henry County after the war, d. in 1922, buried in Rosehill Cemetery,
Rockmart GA.

Casualties, Other Losses for Phillips Legion infantry battalion, from available records. Company E was formed predominantly from Lumpkin County.

Company E

Total Enrollment	116
Death/Disease/Accident	21
Discharge/Disability	9
Resigned	1
Captured	23
KIA	11
MWIA	6
WIA	37
Detailed as Shoemaker	1
Surrendered/Paroled	17
Exchanged	6
AWOL	27
Deserted	22
Court Martialed	9
Imprisoned/Point Lookout MD	10
Imprisoned/Elmira NY	5
Imprisoned/Johnson's Island OH	1
Imprisoned/Camp Chase OH	3
Imprisoned/Camp Douglas IL	2
Imprisoned/ Fort Delaware DE	1
Galvanized Yankees	7
Transferred Out	9
Sent North (Destination Unknown)	2
Enlisted/no other information available	6

Note: Any one individual may appear in several categories; e.g., he may have been captured, sent to prison and exchanged. "Galvanized Yankees" are imprisoned Confederate soldiers who enlisted in the US Army or Navy during the war. Company E had the second lowest number of men compared to all other companies of the Phillips Legion infantry battalion. Comparative high levels of desertion, AWOLs, and court martials suggest morale problems among the men and, perhaps, a cultural factor. Company E was composed of men from the mountain country in and around Dahlonega GA. These men were often "Unionist" in their sympathies and opposed to secession in the early days. Also six of these men enlisted later in Federal units. Many of the Company E men mutinied against their company commander, Cpt. Joseph Hamilton in early 1862 because of his efforts to withhold money from their pay in order to buy better uniforms. The literate and ubiquitous Lt. A. J. "Jack" Reese commented about frequent complaining among the troops in several of his letters.

PHILLIPS GEORGIA LEGION
Infantry Battalion

Company E
The Blue Ridge Rifles

Anderson, Abraham. Enlisted 9 July 1861, age 14 in 1860 Lumpkin County census, honorably discharged 9 August 1861, son of William and Margaret Anderson.

Austin, John P. Enlisted 9 July 1861, honorably discharged 9 August 1861, buried at Old Concord Cemetery in Henry County GA.

Barber, William H. Enlisted 9 July 1861 as 2nd lt., age 31, promoted 1st lt. 13 December 1862, promoted cpt. 26 January 1863, resigned 29 June 1864, buried at Mt. Hope Cemetery, Dahlonega GA.

Bates, James K. Enlisted 12 April 1864, captured at Gaines Farm (Cold Harbor) 1 June 1864, imprisoned Point Lookout until transferred to Elmira NY 12 July 1864, released 7 July 1865, age 62 in 1911 per Georgia pension application.

Bates, Jasper M. T. Enlisted 7 August 1861, age 19, WIA at Fredericksburg VA 13 December 1862, arm amputated and sent home disabled 25 January 1863, d. 12 September 1914 in Cobb County.

Bates, Newton L. Enlisted 9 July 1861, age 20, captured at Gaines Farm (Cold Harbor) 1 June 1864, imprisoned at Point Lookout prison until transferred to Elmira NY 12 July 1864, released 7 July 1865, applied for a veteran's pension in Alabama, married in 1885 to Laura Catherine Herring, d. 14 August 1914.

Blackwell, Andrew Jackson. Enlisted 12 March 1863, b. 22 February 1844, shows present on August 1864 roll dated 30 January 1865, no further military record however a descendant provided the information that he survived the war and died in Texas 25 December 1919, brother of James and Jesse Blackwell, son of Jeddiah and Nancy Blackwell.

Blackwell, James Madison. Enlisted 9 July 1861, b. 22 October 1840, captured at Fox's Gap MD 14 September 1862, exchanged 2 October 1862, WIA at Fredericksburg 13 December 1862, October 1863 roll states he deserted 8 November 1863 near Cleveland, TN but is back on the March/April 1864 roll (dated 5 October 1864) with the notation of WIA at Hanover Junction VA 27 May 1864, received clothing 5 November 1864, no further military record but a descendant provided the information that he survived the war and died in Oklahoma 11 April 1908, brother of Jesse and Andrew Blackwell, son of Jeddiah and Nancy Blackwell.

Blackwell, Jesse Green. Enlisted 9 July 1861, b. 2 October 1842, captured at Fox's Gap MD 14 September 1862, exchanged 2 October 1862, shows as 3rd cpl. on January/February 1863 roll and as 5th sgt. on September/October 1863 roll, shows furloughed home on March/April 1864 roll dated 5 October 1864 then AWOL on later rolls, a descendant provided the information that he survived the war and died in Texas 21 April 1910, brother of James and Andrew Blackwell, son of Jeddiah and Nancy Blackwell.

Boyd, Augustus Franklin. Enlisted 9 July 1861 as 1st cpl., age 17, transferred March 1862 as sgt. maj. of the 52nd GA commanded by his father, Col. Weir Boyd, elected cpt. of Co. B in December 1862, KIA at Bakers Creek MS 16 June 1863, has a memorial marker at Mt. Hope Cemetery, Dahlonega GA, but was buried on the battlefield.

Boyd, John M. Enlisted 15 August 1861, age 44, discharged 4 March 1862 as overage.

Boyt, John D. Enlisted 9 July 1861, age 31, shown as deserted 16 September 1862 on rolls from September 1862 through February 1863, court martial record ANV GO #66 dated 25 May 1863 finds him innocent of desertion but guilty of lesser charge of being AWOL, sentenced to one month at hard labor, September/October 1863 roll dated 14 January 1864 shows he deserted at Chattanooga 4 October 1863 and was carried AWOL on all further rolls, no Federal desertion or POW records.

Brown, Martin. Enlisted 4 March 1862, d. at Charlottesville VA 7 January 1863 of pneumonia, his mother Elizabeth Brown filed a death claim in June 1863 stating that previous death claim filed 12 March 1863 by purported wife Rebecca Brown is false and that her son was not married.

Brown, Merida (Meridith). Enlisted 4 March 1862, present throughout the war, WIA (left side and back) by shell at Sailor's Creek VA 6 April 1865 and captured, d. Lincoln General Hospital, Washington DC 25 April 1865, buried in Arlington National Cemetery.

Brown, Terrell. Enlisted 9 July 1861, age 20, 2nd cpl. on October 1863 roll, WIA at Gaines Farm (Cold Harbor) 1 June 1864 and on wounded furlough 22 July 1864, 1906 Roster Commission states that he was wounded at Cold Harbor and died from these wounds, the 1906 Roster Commission was in error because he is shown on South Carolina's 1901 roll of pensioners living in Greenville County where he was listed as a Class C pensioner or veteran disabled by wounds, his disabling wound is listed as being to the right thigh.

Burt, James C. Enlisted 9 July 1861 as 5th sgt., age 18, WIA at Sharpsburg 17 September 1862, promoted to 2nd lt. 26 January 1863, surrendered at Appomattox 9 April 1865, age 17 on 1860 Dawson County census, son of Reuben and Caroline Burt, brother of Reuben E. Burt.

Burt, Reuben Elisha. Enlisted 10 May 1864, surrendered at Appomattox 9 April 1865, age 14 in 1860 Dawson County census, son of Reuben and Caroline Burt, brother of James Burt.

Cain, Jesse. Enlisted 23 September 1861 at Lynchburg VA, 1906 Roster Commission roll states he died in WV 9 November 1861, pension application filed by his widow Mary in the 1890's states that he died between 9 November 1861 and 20

December 1861 in WV or Dublin VA of measles, three Co. E veterans attested
to his death from disease as stated in 1861.

Campbell, Martin V. Enlisted 3 July 1861, age 21, WIA (hand) 2 July 1863 at
Gettysburg per casualty list in 20 July 1863 *Atlanta Southern Confederacy*,
captured at Cold Harbor 1 June 1864, imprisoned at Point Lookout until
transferred to Elmira NY 9 July 1864, Federal POW records show him
forwarded to James River for exchange on 14 March 1865, but a later record
shows he d. on 20 March 1865, age 9 in 1850 Lumpkin County census, son of
Robert and Catherine Campbell, brother of William M. Campbell.

Campbell, William M. Enlisted 9 July 1861, age 17, d. 19 November 1861 on retreat
from Cotton Hill in western Virginia, cause not stated but almost certainly
disease, age 6 in 1850 Lumpkin County census, son of Robert and Catherine
Campbell, brother of Martin V. Campbell.

Cavender, David. Enlisted 4 March 1862, d. at Camp Winder Hospital. Richmond
15 March 1863 of pneumonia, age 7 in 1850 Lumpkin County census, son of
Joseph and Eliza Cavender, brother of William Cavender.

Cavender, William P. Enlisted 8 August 1861, age 21, captured at Knoxville 29
November 1863, service record shows sent to Camp Chase in Ohio 15
December 1863 but d. in US Military Hospital at Knoxville of pneumonia,
buried Knoxville City Cemetery, age 9 in 1850 Lumpkin County census, son of
Joseph and Eliza Cavender, brother of David Cavender.

Cimmermon, Daniel J. (See Daniel J. Simmermon.)

Clements (Clemens), James M. Enlisted 9 July 1861, age 20, served reliably through
entire war, surrendered at Appomattox as Sgt. J. M. Clemmons although this
rank is not shown in his service record, age 8 in 1850 Lumpkin County census,
son of Benjamin and Esther Clemens, d. 14 August 1903 in Shelby County,
Alabama.

Collins, Nathaniel V. Enlisted 9 July 1861, age 21, WIA (shell concussion) at
Chancellorsville May 1863, WIA (hand) at Spotsylvania 12 May 1864, shows as
AWOL on all rolls thereafter, age 10 in 1850 Lumpkin County census, son of
Edley and Jane Collins.

Croft, Benjamin Franklin. Enlisted 5 August 1861, age 22, WIA (lungs and left
thigh) at Knoxville 29 November 1863, captured and d. at Middlebrook General
Hospital 18 December 1863, buried "in woods near shops 4 miles from
Knoxville."

Croft, George Washington. Enlisted 16 May 1862, b. April 1828 in SC, issued
clothing 26 November 1864, no further military record but known that he
survived the war as he applied for a pension, on the application he stated that he
was furloughed home in January 1865 but could not return to Virginia as
Sherman's Federals had blocked the route back, d. 11 January 1908.

Davis, Henry. Enlisted 9 July 1861, age 23, deserted at Fredericksburg 23 January
1863, arrested 12 February 1863, court martial record ANV GO #41 dated 17

March 1863 finds him guilty of desertion and sentenced to branding with a "D" on left hand and hard labor for remainder of war, shows as AWOL on September/October 1863 and March/April 1864 rolls, May/June/July/August, 1864 rolls state he deserted at Petersburg 14 July 1864," A. J. Reese letter dated 20 July 1864 notes this desertion and describes Davis as a "very poor soldier," he then shows as captured at Harrisonburg (in the Shenandoah Valley) on 25 September 1864, imprisoned at Point Lookout until released 13 May 1865, age 13 in 1850 Lumpkin County census, son of Thomas and Jemima Davis.

Davis, J. Fountain. Enlisted 9 July 1861, age 21, d. at Ladies Relief Hospital, Lynchburg 7 September 1861 of disease, buried Lynchburg City Cemetery #6 in 2nd line, lot 159.

Davis, John Newton. Enlisted 9 July 1861 as 4th cpl., age 23, 5th sgt. on November 1862 roll, WIA (forehead) at Fredericksburg 13 December 1862, 1st sgt. on October 1863 roll, WIA at Chattanooga (hip) 24 September 1863, WIA at Petersburg 30 June 1864, furloughed home 16 July 1864, carried on later rolls as AWOL, pension application stated that he joined Johnson's regiment of Georgia Militia and surrendered at Kingston GA 12 May 1865, buried Auraria Cemetery, Lumpkin County GA.

Davis, William. Enlisted 9 July 1861, age 25, deserted at Fredericksburg 8 February 1863, arrested 19 February 1863, court martial record ANV GO #55 dated 9 April 1863 found him innocent of desertion but guilty of lesser charge of AWOL, sentenced to twelve months at hard labor and forfeiture of pay, KIA at Chattanooga 24 September 1863.

Dempsey, James M. Enlisted 19 July 1861, age 15, WIA (back) at Fox's Gap MD 14 September 1862, furloughed home 13 October 1862, February 1863 roll noted he was still absent wounded, no further military record but 1888 pension application stated that half of his right shoulder blade was shot away rendering his right arm virtually useless, a doctor's certification confirms this, he further stated that he was discharged from the army because of the wound, the fact that he was not shown as AWOL on rolls after February 1863 suggests the truth of this allegation, d. in 1917 at Atlanta Confederate Soldier's Home, buried at Westview Cemetery, grave #320, Fulton County GA.

Dempsey, John M. Enlisted 19 July 1861, age 25, deserted at Fredericksburg 8 February 1863, arrested 19 February 1863, court martial record ANV GO #55 dated 9 April 1863 found him innocent of desertion but guilty of lesser charge of AWOL, sentenced to 12 months of hard labor and forfeiture of pay, deserted at Cleveland TN 7 November 1863, no further record.

Dowdy, John H. Enlisted 8 August 1861, age 22, last on November 1861 roll, card for manuscript #1966 dated 6 December 1863 stated he died, actual record in National Archives is a small scrap of paper requisitioning two coffins for the remains of J. H. Dowdy of Co. E and G. White of Co. D Phillips Legion, requisition appears to be signed by "G. C. Thresher - Surgeon in Charge - Sue

(or Lue) Springs Hospital," a letter written 6 December 1861 by Jesse R. Duke
to Dowdy's father, John M. Dowdy, related that he died on 2 December 1861 at
Red Sulphur Springs VA from consumption and pneumonia fever.

Duke, Jesse Rowland. Enlisted 9 July 1861, age 33, discharged for disability 5 May
1862, b. 9 September 1828, d. 25 March 1920.

Dyer, William M. Enlisted 9 July 1861, age 19, deserted at Cleveland TN 18
November 1863 but later records show him captured at Elgin Creek TN 21
June 1864, imprisoned at Camp Douglas prison in Chicago until he took the
Oath of Allegiance and joined Co. I of the 5th U. S. Infantry 15 April 1865,
enlistment showed him to be 22, 5'6 " tall with brown eyes and brown hair, d. 6
August 1865 at Fort Dodge, Kansas Post Hospital from inflammation of the
bladder, age 8 on 1850 Lumpkin County census, son of Daniel and Jane Dyer.

Fields, James. Enlisted 19 July 1861, age 17, MWIA (thigh) at Fredericksburg 13
December 1862, d. 30 or 31 December 1862 at Richmond GH #14, buried at
Oakwood Confederate Cemetery in Richmond.

Fields, Maleath H. Enlisted 19 July 1861, age 24, b. 1837 in North Carolina,
captured near Knoxville 5 December 1863, October 1864 roll stated AWOL,
later roll stated paroled not exchanged, January 1865 roll stated absent, no
Federal POW records, postwar pension application stated that he escaped from
the Federals and went home.

Fields, R. J. Enlisted 9 July 1861, age 19, WIA at Fredericksburg 13 December 1862,
deserted near Cleveland TN November 1863, captured at Gaines Farm (Cold
Harbor) 1 June 1864, imprisoned at Point Lookout MD until transferred to
Elmira NY 17 July 1864, d. at Elmira of variola (smallpox) 5 March 1865, buried
at Woodlawn Cemetery, Elmira NY, grave #1969.

Forest, Champion. Enlisted 9 July 1861, age 28, 1906 Roster Commission roll stated
he died in Dublin VA, the legion was in this location only toward the end of
1861 and he is not carried on rolls after 1861 so it is probable that he was one of
many who died of disease during the 1861 campaign in western Virginia, age 16
in 1850 Lumpkin County census, born in SC, son of Berry and Matilda
Forrester.

Forest, Hardy D. Enlisted 9 July 1861 as cpl., age 21, promoted to sgt. January, 1863,
WIA (both thighs) at Hanover Junction VA 27 May 1864, furloughed home in
July 1864, joined Findley's regiment of the Home Guard and served out the war
in Georgia.

Gaddis, A. W. Enlisted 9 July 1861, honorably discharged 5 August 1861.

Gearing (Gerrin), William M. Enlisted 9 July 1861, age 30, WIA at Fredericksburg
VA 13 December 1862, admitted to Farmville VA Hospital 12 June 1863 with
gunshot wound to left eye (he had been at home in Georgia recuperating),
received clothing 20 November 1864, no further military record but he applied
for a pension in 1887, his application stated that he was hit in the corner of the
left eye with a minie ball which ranged around inside his skull and lodged

behind his left ear, this wound received 13 December 1862 at Fredericksburg, a doctor certified the bullet was still in his head, that he was blind in his left eye and unable to work, application also stated that he surrendered at Appomattox, but he is not on the parole list, d. 19 June 1917.

Glass, William F. Enlisted 25 February 1863, casualty list in 2 July 1864 *Richmond Enquirer* showed him as WIA between 6 May 1864 and 16 May 1864 indicating that he was wounded at Wilderness or Spotsylvania, surrendered at Appomattox 9 April 1865, b. in 1828, d. 1 February 1897, buried at New Harmony Church Cemetery on Cherokee/Forsyth County line.

Grizzle, Eli J. Enlisted 9 July 1861, age 22, cpl. in late 1862, sgt. in 1863, WIA at Knoxville 29 November 1863, captured and sent to Camp Chase OH, paroled/exchanged February 1865, d. 10 March 1865 at Richmond GH #9 of chronic dysentery, buried at Oakwood Confederate Cemetery as E. J. Grezzetway.

Grizzle, James A. Enlisted 4 March 1862, WIA at Fredericksburg VA 13 December 1862 (right thigh), AWOL thereafter, pension application stated that he was hospitalized at Lynchburg for three months after being wounded and was then furloughed home, further stated that the wound never properly healed rendering him incapable of returning to his company during the war, b. 18 July 1844, d. 1926, buried in Yahoola Cemetery, Lumpkin County GA.

Grizzle, Marvin (Marvel) M. Enlisted 8 August 1861, age 23, teamster, deserted at Petersburg VA, 16 July 1864, A. J. Reese letter dated 20 July 1864 noted this desertion and describes Grizzle as "a very poor soldier," no Federal deserter or POW records, applied for a Georgia veterans pension, application stated that he was furloughed by the QM in August of 1864, joined another unit while home in Georgia and surrendered at Kingston GA in May 1865, age 12 in 1850 Lumpkin County census, son of John and Sally Grizzle, brother of William Grizzle.

Grizzle, William. Enlisted 9 July 1861, b. 5 April 1831, teamster, AWOL on roll dated 5 October 1864, and all rolls thereafter, he stated in his pension application that he was furloughed home in February 1864 while in Tennessee, also stated that he was cut off and joined Finley's regiment Co. E and surrendered at Kingston GA in May 1865, age 21 in 1850 Lumpkin County census, son of John and Sally Grizzle, brother of Marvin (Marvel) Grizzle.

Hamilton, Coatsworth C. Served as volunteer aide to his older brother Cpt. Joseph Hamilton when the legion went north to Lynchburg in August 1861, a November 1861 letter from A. F. Boyd of Co. E mentioned that Cpt. Hamilton had gone home with the body of his brother "Coates" Hamilton, in an ironic twist of fate, fifteen year-old Coatesworth Hamilton, a cadet at Georgia Military Institute who had been drilling troops at Camp McDonald, was, at the request of his father, assigned to older brother Joe as a volunteer aide, Dr. Hamilton hoped that the youngster would quickly tire of the rigors of the field and return to his studies at GMI, unfortunately, the firestorm of disease (typhoid, measles and mumps) that swept through Phillips Legion that fall claimed the youngster in November.

Hamilton, Joseph E. Enlisted 9 July 1861, elected cpt., stated age as 22 but may have been only 19, WIA (left arm) at Fox's Gap MD 14 September 1862, promoted to maj. 18 December 1862, WIA (right arm) at Knoxville 29 November 1863 per A. J. Reese letter and January 1864 roll, promoted to lt. col. commanding Phillips Legion infantry battalion 31 December 1863, WIA (neck) at Cold Harbor 3 June 1864, absent on wounded furlough until January 1865, captured 6 April 1865 at Sailor's Creek and sent to Johnson's Island OH, released 25 July 1865, Oath of Allegiance showed his residence as Social Circle GA, described as being 5'8" tall with light hair and blue eyes, married Julia Stokes 13 January 1864, became a teacher and moved to Los Angeles in 1875, d. 12 June 1907, there is a VA marker for him at the Marietta Confederate Cemetery in Cobb County GA but he is actually buried at Rosedale Cemetery in Los Angeles CA.

Helton, Martin. Enlisted 9 July 1861, age 16, present on rolls until sent to a hospital in Richmond 17 May 1863 with fever, Transferred to Danville VA Hospital 12 June 1863, furloughed home from Danville 20 August 1863, shown on September/October 1863 roll dated 14 January 1864 as AWOL and on all rolls thereafter, Federal records show that he took the Oath of Allegiance 16 April 1864 at Chattanooga but it is not clear whether he deserted or was captured.

Hendrix, William H. Enlisted 8 May 1862, MWIA (lung) at Sharpsburg, MD 17 September 1862, d. at Richmond GH #9 20 November 1862, buried in Oakwood Confederate Cemetery in Richmond as M. H. Henrich.

Holyfield, John H. Enlisted 19 July 1861, age 23, deserted near Chancellorsville 2 May 1863, AWOL on later rolls, took Oath of Allegiance at Chattanooga 20 February 1864, age 13 in 1850 Lumpkin County census, b. in NC, son of Jacob and Manimmia Holyfield.

Howell, James E. Enlisted 1 February 1864, captured at Burkeville VA 6 April 1865, imprisoned at Point Lookout until released 13 June 1865.

Hulsey, Andrew Jackson. Enlisted 5 August 1861 as a cpl., age 17, WIA at the Wilderness 6 May 1864, admitted to Chimborazo Hospital Richmond 8 May 1864, no record of furlough from hospital, AWOL on rolls thereafter, Oklahoma state pension office asked Washington DC for records in 1915 which would indicate that either he or his widow was requesting a pension, b. 3 September 1844 in Dawson County GA to James M and Martha Hulsey, d. 18 October 1932 at Old Soldiers Home in Norman Oklahoma, buried at Collins Cemetery, Pottawatomie County OK.

Hulsey, Rice Ross. Enlisted 9 July 1861, age 28, d. 5 February 1862 at Hardeeville SC from disease, b. 1833 in Hall County to Burrell and Lauriette Bates Hulsey, married 27 January 1854 to Mary Hamilton.

Hutcheson, William John Turner. Enlisted 9 July 1861, age 21, promoted to 3rd cpl. in early 1862, WIA (leg) 29 August 1862 at Second Manassas, promoted to sgt. January 1863, WIA (thigh) at Chancellorsville May 1863, WIA (lost finger on left hand) at Spotsylvania 12 May 1864, furloughed home 23 May 1864, shown as AWOL on all further rolls, b. 18 December 1839, d. 8 April 1922, buried Antioch Baptist Church Cemetery at Auroria GA.

Johnson, J. W. Enlisted 3 September 1862, WIA (shell fractured left tibia) and captured at Sailors Creek 6 April 1865, no further record.

Johnson, Lewis W. Enlisted 9 July 1861, age 20, d. 20 January 1863 at Chimborazo Hospital in Richmond of pneumonia, buried at Oakwood Confederate Cemetery in Richmond.

Johnson, Willis. Enlisted 6 September 1862, last entry in service record is August 1864 muster roll that showed him present, 1906 Roster Commission roll stated he was killed near Appomattox VA April, 1865, age 5 in 1850 Lumpkin County census, born in NC, son of Jacob and Crisa Johnson.

Jones, Anson. Enlisted 1 March 1863, roll dated 14 January 1864 showed desertion near Cleveland TN 7 November 1863, carried as AWOL on rolls thereafter, took Oath of Allegiance at Chattanooga and joined Co. I of 12th Tennessee Federal Cavalry 29 February 1864, enlistment showed him to be 18 years old, discharged from U. S. Service on 7 October 1865 at Fort Leavenworth KS, b. 1844, moved to California in 1866, married Catherine Agnes Daugherty 3 July 1875, d. at Colfax CA 26 July 1898, brother of Barnabus and Samuel Jones.

Jones, Barnabus. Enlisted 24 June 1861 in Co. G 18th GA, WIA (eye) at Second Manassas, A. J. Reese letter dated May 1863 stated that Jones had been transferred into Co. E in exchange for William A Spencer, Deserted around 20 September 1863, AWOL on rolls thereafter, took Oath of Allegiance at Chattanooga 13 April 1864 and joined Co. I of 12th Tennessee Federal Cavalry, died at sea shortly after war en route to California, brother of Anson and Samuel Jones.

Jones, Samuel. Enlisted 9 July 1861, age 21, AWOL on roll dated 14 January 1864 and on all rolls thereafter, took Oath of Allegiance at Chattanooga 30 March 1864 and joined Co. I of 12th Tennessee Federal Cavalry at Nashville TN, enlistment showed him 22 years old, 6'1 1/2" tall with blue eyes and light hair, paid a $100.00 bounty, mustered out at Fort Leavenworth KS 7 October 1865, d. 1918, buried at Damascus Baptist Church Cemetery, Lumpkin County GA, brother of Anson and Barnabus Jones.

Land, William D. Enlisted 15 August 1861, age 25, captured 9 July 1864 while home on furlough, d. 25 December 1864 at Camp Douglas IL of small pox, buried at Oak Woods Cemetery, Chicago IL.

Lannier, Harrison M. No enlistment data, not shown on any muster rolls, only records are Federal POW records which may indicate he was using an assumed name, captured at Cleveland TN 14 February 1865 and sent to Camp Chase

OH 24 March 1865, entry dated 22 April 1865 stated that he had enlisted in the U S Army.

Lee, Andrew. H. Enlisted 13 August 1861, age 38, AWOL on roll dated 14 January 1864 and all rolls thereafter, no further military records but known that he survived the war because he applied for a veteran's pension in Georgia, application stated that he went home sick in 1863 and remained too ill to return, b. 31 July 1823 in SC.

Loggins, E. Thomas. Enlisted 4 March 1862, MWIA at Spotsylvania 14 May 1864, d. at Winder Hospital, Richmond 26 June 1864, father of Thomas Loggins.

Loggins, Thomas. Enlisted 4 March 1862, captured at Sailor's Creek 6 April 1865 and imprisoned at Point Lookout until released 29 June 1865, b. 7 October 1839, son of Thomas E. Loggins.

London, Joseph Newton. Enlisted 9 July 1861, age 18, WIA (hand) at the Wilderness 6 May 1864, furloughed from Danville Hospital 5 July 1864, shown as AWOL on all rolls thereafter, applied for a veteran's pension in Alabama, stated that he joined Ed Monson's cavalry when furloughed home in 1864 and surrendered in May 1865 at Kingston GA, brother of Samuel London.

London, Samuel. Enlisted 9 July 1861, age 21, d. 4 October 1861 at Ladies Relief Hospital Lynchburg VA of disease, buried in Lynchburg City Cemetery #2 in 5th line lot 159, brother of Joseph N. London.

Lowery (Lowry), Samuel. Enlisted 9 July 1861, age 22, KIA at Fredericksburg VA 13 December 1862.

Mayes, E. Frank (or Frank E.). Enlisted 9 July 1861, age 17, 2nd cpl. on February 1863 roll, WIA 24 September 1863 near Chattanooga, A. J. Reese letter 26 September 1863 noted that Frank Mayes was wounded "in the right thigh pretty bad" and stated "they started him off yesterday to the hospital in Atlanta," Nancy Wimpy letter to A. J. Reese dated 5 October 1863 stated that "Dr. Howard had seen Frank and thought it doubtful about his recovery," UDC burial lists showed a Cpl. E. Mayes, Co. E, Phillips Legion buried in the Whelchel Family Cemetery in Lumpkin County, probable that he died in Atlanta and was sent home for burial.

McAfee, Franklin Alexander. Enlisted 9 July 1861, age 21, KIA at Beverlys Ford VA on the Rappahannock 23 August 1862, "Both legs torn off by shell" (chaplain George Smith's account), b. 10 April 1840, brother of William McAfee, age 9 in 1850 Lumpkin County census, son of Thomas and Eliza McAfee.

McAfee, William Hamilton. Enlisted 9 July 1861, age 28, transferred to 22nd GA as 3rd lt. 20 October 1862, age 16 in 1850 Lumpkin County census, son of Thomas and Eliza McAfee, brother of Franklin McAfee.

McDonald, Jesse M. Enlisted 9 July 1861, age 21, 2nd lt. 13 December 1862, promoted to 1st lt. 26 January 1863, WIA (left thigh) near Chattanooga 24 September 1863, promoted to cpt. 29 June 1864, furloughed home 20 January 1865, AWOL 20 February 1865, never returned to his company, reputed to

have murdered one or two Federal soldiers at Dahlonega Post sometime after
the war. Dahlonega Post returns for 11 July 1868 showed that a Pvt. James
Wiseman of Co. F, U. S. 33rd Infantry Regiment, was murdered one half mile
from camp, Wiseman was from Boston MA 22 years old, 5'5 1/2" tall, light
complexion and was a hatter before his enlistment. Supposedly McDonald was
angered when a soldier/soldiers kicked his dog and he murdered him/them.

McManus, Alvis. Enlisted 12 April 1864, captured at Burkeville VA 6 April 1865,
imprisoned at Point Lookout until released 29 June 1865.

Morgan, W. C. Enlisted 9 July 1861, honorably discharged 9 August 1861.

Morris, Hezekiah. Enlisted 9 July 1861, age 20, shown as sick at hospital on February
1863 roll, at Liberty VA Hospital March 1863, at Lynchburg VA Hospital 8 July
1863, shown as AWOL on all rolls after February 1863, captured in Cherokee
County GA August 1864, took Oath at Louisville KY 27 August 1864 and sent
north, age 8 in 1850 Lumpkin County census, son of John and Rebecca Morris.

Morrison, E. P. Enlisted 9 July 1861 as 2nd cpl., age 26, 2nd sgt. on December 1862
roll, MWIA (abdomen) at Fredericksburg 13 December 1862, d. at Chimborazo
Hospital #2, Richmond VA 18 December 1862.

Moss, A.J. Enlisted 9 July 1861, age 22, deserted near Petersburg VA 14 July 1864, a
letter written by Lt. A. J. Reese on 20 July 1864 stated "I am sorry to say that
five of the boys deserted a few nights ago. Two of them were very poor soldiers;
H. Davis and M. M. Grizzle, but Moss and the two Norrises were very good
soldiers," no Federal POW or deserter records, descendants relate that he was
killed by Home Guards at Silver City, Forsyth County while trying to return to
the legion and was buried in an unmarked grave.

Myers, Andrew. Enlisted 9 July 1861, age 27, captured at Gettysburg 2 July 1863,
sent to Fort McHenry 6 July 1863, sent to Fort Delaware July 1863, in prison
hospital 1 January 1864 to 10 March 1864 and again 24 May 1864 to 15 June
1864, no further military records but known that he survived the war because he
applied for a veterans pension in Alabama in 1899, this application stated that he
was wounded in the right arm at Fredericksburg and in the right side at
Gettysburg.

Norris, Alford. Enlisted 9 July 1861, age 22, cited for gallantry at Gettysburg 2 July
1863, deserted near Petersburg VA 14 July 1864, a letter written by Lt. A. J.
Reese on 20 July 1864 stated: "I am sorry to say that five of the boys deserted a
few nights ago. Two of them were very poor soldiers; H. Davis and M. M.
Grizzle, but Moss and the two Norrises were very good soldiers," no Federal
POW or deserter records, a descendant provided information stating that he
applied for a pension in Virginia after the war so it is known that he survived.

Norris, Wesley. Enlisted 9 July 1861, age 20, WIA (thigh) at Gettysburg 2 July 1863,
deserted near Petersburg VA 14 July 1864, a letter written by lt. A. J. Reese on
20 July 1864 stated: "I am sorry to say that five of the boys deserted a few nights
ago. Two of them were very poor soldiers; H. Davis and M. M. Grizzle. But

Moss and the two Norrises were very good soldiers." No Federal POW or deserter records, a descendant provided information that he lived in Louisville KY after the war so known that he survived.

Parker, Gilbert F. Enlisted 9 July 1861, age 17, drummer, d. 18 October 1861 at Richmond Ferry VA (now WV) on New River of brain congestion.

Price, Hardy D. Enlisted 9 July 1861, as 1st lt., age 40, MWIA (left side and hip) at Fredericksburg VA, 13 December 1862, d. 26 January 1863 at Richmond GH #4, posthumously promoted to company cpt. effective 13 December 1862.

Pruitt, E. B. Conscript enlisted 2 September 1862, captured at Gaines Farm (Cold Harbor) 1 June 1864, imprisoned at Point Lookout until transferred to Elmira NY 12 July 1864, released from Elmira 7 July 1865.

Quillian, Robert A. Enlisted 9 July 1861 as color cpl., age 19, transferred to 52nd GA 17 June 1862, age 8 in 1850 Lumpkin County census, son of George F. and Elizabeth Quillian.

Ray, John. Enlisted 9 July 1861, age 23, deserted near Fredericksburg VA 8 February 1863, arrested and returned for court martial 19 February 1863, court martial record ANV GO #55 showed him as found innocent of desertion but guilty of a lesser charge of going AWOL, sentenced to 12 months at hard labor and forfeiture of 12 months' pay, deserted again near Chattanooga 23 September 1863, carried AWOL on rolls until a roll dated 30 January 1865 stated, "John Ray was killed by Wheeler's scouts at home, exact time not known."

Reese, Andrew Jackson. Enlisted 9 July 1861 as 1st sgt., age 20, promoted to 2nd lt. 26 January 1863 upon death of Lt. Price, promoted 1st lt. 29 June 1864, surrendered at Appomattox 9 April 1865 as commanding officer of Co. E, d. in 1884 and buried at Mt. Hope Cemetery, Dahlonega GA.

Reese, Thomas Benton. Enlisted 1 February 1864, younger brother of Lt. A. J. Reese, WIA (left leg amputated) at Gaines Farm (Cold Harbor) 30 May 1864, furloughed home 5 August 1864, at Charlottesville VA Hospital 4 December 1864, transferred to Richmond Hospital 28 March 1865, age 4 in 1850 Lumpkin County census.

Riley, Jr., H. W. Enlisted 9 July 1861, age 14, WIA (left hip) at Hanover Jct. VA 27 May 1864, furloughed from Richmond Hospital 11 July 1864, shown as AWOL on roll dated 30 January 1865, no further record.

Roberts, James. Enlisted 9 July 1861, age 15, surrendered at Appomattox 9 April 1865.

Rumney, Benjamin F. Enlisted 9 July 1861, age 16, discharged from service 9 February 1862.

Satterfield, William. Enlisted 9 July 1861, age 22, d. 5 October 1861 at Lewisburg VA (now WV) of disease.

Simmermon (Simmenson), Daniel J. Enlisted 9 July 1861, age 18, KIA 29 August 1862 at Second Manasses by artillery fire, age 17 in 1860 Dawson County census, son of Jacob and Loucinda Simmenson.

Sitton, Benjamin Franklin. Enlisted 9 July 1861 as sgt., age 46, discharged 14 October 1862.

Smith, Edward Jasper. Enlisted 15 September 1861, captured a Federal color at Gettysburg, WIA (lost finger) 6 May 1864 at the Wilderness, received clothing 16 May 1864 at Liberty VA hospital, no further record.

Smith, T. R. Enlisted 9 July 1861, age 30, discharged 4 March 1862.

Sparks, Archibald Wimpy. Enlisted 4 March 1862, KIA 23 August 1862 at Beverlys Ford VA on Rappahannock River by artillery fire.

Spencer, William A. Enlisted 19 July 1861, age 19, WIA at Fredericksburg 13 December 1862, admitted Chimborazo #2 Hospital in Richmond 15 December 1862 with shell wound in hip, furloughed for 30 days 31 December 1862, AWOL on February 1863 roll, elected cpt. of Co. G, 8th GA Cavalry while at home and did not return to the legion. May and June 1863 letters from J. M. McDonald and A J. Reese stated that Spencer had stolen money from the mails and had been reduced to the ranks and transferred to the 18th GA Infantry in exchange for Barnabus Jones, Spencer is not listed on the rolls of the 18th GA after February 1863.

Spriggs, A.J. Enlisted 9 July 1861, age 47, discharged for disability 6 April 1862.

Stancel, David. Enlisted 9 July 1861, age 17, deserted near Cleveland TN 8 November 1863, must have returned because he deserted again near Winchester VA 7 September 1864, no Federal POW or deserter records, no further record.

Stancel, John W. Enlisted 9 July 1861, age 21, 21 October 1863 court martial sentences him to death but Jefferson Davis commuted sentence (see A and IG SO #75/18 dated 30 March 1864) to spending remainder of war at hard labor on the Richmond fortifications, apparently rejoined legion near war's end as he surrendered at Appomattox 9 April 1865, pension application stated birth date as 14 February 1829 which conflicts with age given at enlistment.

Stevens (shown as Stearns in service records), Martin. Enlisted 9 July 1861, age 23, KIA 29 November 1863 at Knoxville TN per lt. A. J. Reese letter dated 1 /1863.

Stephenson, R. F. Enlisted 9 July 1861, captured at Gettysburg 2 July 1863 and imprisoned at Point Lookout until exchanged 18 February 1865, no further record.

Stone, James A. Enlisted 9 July 1861, age 19 MWIA (through knee) and captured at Knoxville 29 November 1863, d. at Middle Brook US GH 14 February 1864, buried "at brick house near Knoxville."

Tippen, G. W. Enlisted 9 July 1861, age 19, discharged 13 December 1861.

Vaughn, George William Asbury. Enlisted 4 March 1862, deserted near Fredericksburg 23 January 1863, returned under arrest 12 February 1863, court martial record ANV GO #40 dated 16 March 1863 noted that he was found guilty of desertion and sentenced to spend the rest of the war at hard labor, forfeit all pay and be branded with a "D" on his left hand, sentence must have been remanded or shortened because he was captured at Gettysburg 5 July 1863

and sent to Fort McHenry, he was transferred to Point Lookout 15 September
1863 and d. 14 November 1863 of chronic dysentery, buried at Point Lookout
Confederate Cemetery at Scotland MD.

Wade, Stephen G. Enlisted 9 July 1861, age 18, deserted near Fredericksburg 23
January 1863, returned under arrest 12 February 1863, ANV GO court martial
O #40 dated 16 March 1863 showed him guilty of desertion and sentenced to
the same as George W. Vaughn (see above), sentence must have been remanded
or shortened because he returned to his company, last shown on roll dated 30
January 1865, no further military records although he stated in a postwar
pension application that he surrendered at Appomattox, records do not confirm
this, d. in Bartow County September 1920, age 7 in 1850 Lumpkin County
census, son of Tyler and Winnie Wade.

Walker, George Washington. Enlisted 8 August 1861, b. 4 April 1845 to West and
Fatima Bryan Walker, AWOL on a roll dated 5 October 1864 and all rolls
thereafter, 1906 Roster Commission roll and his pension application stated that
he was furloughed home in March 1864 because of loss of use of his right hand,
younger brother of James Berry Walker, d. 29 August 1915, buried at Yahoola
Baptist Church Cemetery, Lumpkin County.

Walker, James Berry. Enlisted 8 August 1861, age 26, AWOL on rolls from 10
August 1862 through February 1863, February 1863 entry states he deserted,
WIA (head) May 1863 at Chancellorsville, roll dated 14 January 1864 states that
he deserted near Chattanooga 20 September 1863 implying that he had
returned to the company in 1863, deserted again near Winchester VA 7
September 1864, no further record however a postwar listing show that he was
living in Warrenton, Ohio indicating that he may have taken the Oath of
Allegiance and gone north, age 14 in 1850 Lumpkin County census, son of
West and Fatima Walker.

Ward, Henry W. Enlisted 9 July 1861 as 2nd sgt., age 41 (b. in Tennessee 16
December 1820), detailed as a shoemaker at Richmond until February 1864,
furloughed home 12 February 1864 and does not return, pension application
stated that he joined another (unspecified) unit, d. in 1897

White, Francis M. "Frank." He appeared on the 1906 Roster Commission roll for
Co. E with the notation that he was killed at the Wilderness VA May 1864 but
he was not listed in the compiled service records for Phillips Legion, likely that
he had just joined Co. E shortly before his death and had not been recorded on a
muster roll, he was listed in the January 1864 "Joe Brown Militia Census"
(which delineated all Georgia men age 16 to 60 not in service) in Lumpkin
County as F. M. White, age 16 yrs., 5 mos., a 31 May 1864 letter from Lt.
Andrew Jackson Reese of Co. E stated that Frank was killed 31 May 1864 which
would place his death in the actions around Cold Harbor VA, younger brother
of Noah White, son of Joabert and Sally White.

White, Noah. Enlisted 8 August 1861, age 20, WIA at Fox's Gap MD, 14 September 1862, promoted cpl. during 1863, roll dated 5 October 1864 showed him sick at home, AWOL thereafter, pension application stated that he was recruiting at home at war's end, d. in 1910, buried Corinth Church Cemetery in Lumpkin County, older brother of F. M. "Frank" White, son of Joabert and Sally White.

Wilson, H. Lee. Enlisted 9 July 1861, age 26, KIA at Gettysburg 2 July 1863.

Woody, Aaron W. Enlisted 9 July 1861, age 14, honorably discharged 5 August 1861, he and his father John Woody later joined Co. G, 10th Tennessee (USA) Cavalry, Woody enlisted 15 February 1864 at Nashville and was promoted to cpl. 23 February 1864, he was reduced to private 1 April 1864 and court-martialed (offense unknown) at New Orleans in early 1865 and his pay was reduced by $5.00/month, mustered out 1 August 1865 at Nashville, age 18.

Casualties, Other Losses for the Phillips Legion infantry battalion
from available records. Company F was formed solely from Irish
immigrants living mostly in Bibb County.

Company F

Total Enrollment	85
Death/Disease/Accident	3
Resigned	3
Discharged/Disability	19
Captured	32
KIA	4
MWIA	3
WIA	15
MIA	1
Surrendered/Paroled	6
Exchanged	7
AWOL	9
Deserted	5
Imprisoned/Rock Island IL	11
Imprisoned/Fort Monroe VA	1
Imprisoned/Point Lookout MD	1
Imprisoned/Old Capitol, DC	1
Imprisoned/Johnson's Island OH	1
Imprisoned/Fort Delaware, DE	5
Imprisoned/Camp Chase OH	1
Galvanized Yankees	7
Transferred to Band	2
Detailed as Boilermaker	1
Detailed as Shoemaker	1
Sent North (Destination Unknown)	1
Enlisted/no other information available	4

Note: Any one individual may appear in several categories; e.g., he may have been
captured, sent to prison and exchanged. "Galvanized Yankees" are imprisoned
Confederate soldiers who enlisted in the US Army or Navy during the war.

An article that appeared in the 31 August 1861 edition of the *Macon Daily Telegraph*
hailed the departure for war of Company F, The Lochrane Guards. The company's
founder and benefactor, Col. (Judge) O. A. Lochrane, was there to see them off.

> This noble band of patriots, all natives of the "Emerald Isle",
> under their worthy captain, Jackson Barnes, full 80 strong,

departed on yesterday morning by the Macon and Western
Railroad for Virginia. A large concourse of our citizens assembled
at the depot to bid them farewell and wish them a safe return
when the war is ended and peace declared; and as the train moved
off, cheer after cheer went up for the gallant and the brave.
"There were sad hearts in many a home
When the brave left their bower;
But the strength of prayer and sacrifice
Was there with them in that hour."
Col. Lochrane accompanied them. They expect to receive recruits
at Atlanta, Calhoun, Dalton and other cities sufficient to increase
their numbers to one hundred men, exclusive of officers. We are
confident the warm hearted and generous sons of "Green Erin"
will acquit themselves like men. They are adopted citizens it is
true, but yield to none in devotion and love to the south—the
sunny home of their choice. Irishmen naturally spurn wrong and
oppression, and he who is found fighting against the South does
grave injustice to the Celtic race. The members of the Lochrane
Guards are:
"No hirelings trained to the fight
But men, firm as the mountains who will
Pour out their life blood like rain,
And come back in triumph and honor, or come not again."

The Lochrane Guards were a star-crossed band of warriors. Their losses in
combat were not remarkable. Nor were those to disease and disability above the
average for other legion infantry companies. However, all of the company officers
had resigned, died, or been captured by the end of 1863. Thirteen men were
captured in the fiasco at Knoxville in November 1863 and were sent to prison at
Rock Island IL. Six of these soldiers joined the U.S Army or Navy. Seven men
deserted, but many more are classifed as AWOL and never returned. There were
only four pvts. and one sgt. remaining when the legion's infantry battalion left
Richmond in early April 1865 and headed west with the Army of Northern Virginia.
Only 1st Sgt. R. P. O'Neill and Pvts. James O'Neill and John Sweeney surrendered
at Appomattox 9 April 1865 as part of Company A.

PHILLIPS GEORGIA LEGIONS
Infantry Battalion

Company F
The Lochrane Guards

A'Hern, Daniel. Enlisted 1 January 1863, captured at Falling Waters MD 14 July 1863, no Federal POW records, no further record, strong possibility he may be the man listed as Daniel Hearn.

Barnes, Jackson. Enlisted 1 August 1861 as cpt., resigned 12 September 1862 because of poor health, age 49 in 1860 Bibb County censs, born in Ireland.

Barry, Michael N. Enlisted 1 August 1861 as 2nd sgt., discharged because of disability 1 September 1862, age 34.

Barry, Patrick. Enlisted 1 August 1861, discharged because of hernia 25 September 1862, age 35.

Blake, Thomas. Enlisted 1 August 1861, captured 5 December 1863 near Knoxville and imprisoned at Rock Island until released 23 May 1865.

Bonner, John. Enlisted 1 August 1861, discharged because of respiratory problems 10 November 1862, age 29.

Brady, Francis. Enlisted 1 August 1861, discharged because of poor health 23 September 1864.

Brown, Robert. Enlisted 1 August 1861, AWOL 20 July 1862, never returned.

Bryce, Robert. Enlisted 1 August 1861, discharged 30 October 1862, postwar pension application from widow Alathea stated that he d. in the spring of 1884 from the effects of rheumatism contracted in the service, also stated that he was so deformed from this ailment that his body could not be straightened out and a special coffin had to be built to accommodate his corpse.

Carey, William. Enlisted 1 August 1861, 2 December 1862 roll stated "deserted at battle of Sharpsburg 17 September 1862 and not heard from since," no Federal POW or deserter records.

Carroll, William. Enlisted 1 August 1861, WIA (thigh) and captured 14 September 1862 at Fox's Gap MD, Federal hospital record (Washington, DC) stated sent to Provost Marshall (for exchange) 16 October 1862, no further record.

Caughlin, Daniel. Enlisted 1 August 1861, present on all rolls, paroled at Farmville VA between 11 April 1865 and 21 April 1865.

Caughlin, Hugh. Enlisted 1 August 1861, captured at Knoxville 29 November 1863 and imprisoned at Rock Island, released 17 October 1864 with the notation he joined the USA (Army), Federal records showed that he enlisted 17 October 1864 for one year as a pvt. in Co. E 3rd US Volunteer Infantry, shown as b. Roscommon, Ireland, age 39, 5'8" tall with blue eyes and red hair, his enlistment credited to quota of Venango County PA and he was paid $100.00 bounty, served in the west, mustered out at Fort Leavenworth, KS 29 November 1865.

Caughlin, Terrence. Enlisted 1 August 1861, discharged 30 October 1862 because of disability, age 47.

Caughlin, Timothy. Enlisted 1 August 1861, drew clothes 27 November 1864, no further record.

Conway, Bernard. Enlisted 1 August 1861, captured 14 September 1862 at Fox's Gap MD, exchanged 2 October 1862, d. 24 January 1863 at Richmond GH #2 from pneumonia.

Corcoran, Patrick. Enlisted 1 August 1861, discharged 25 November 1863, age 30.

Deignan, Patrick. Enlisted 1 August 1861, captured at Knoxville 3 December 1862 and imprisoned at Rock Island until released 17 June 1865, age 27, d. at Columbus GA in 1896, buried there at Linwood Cemetery.

Deignan, Richard. Enlisted 1 August 1861 as 2nd cpl., shown as 4th sgt. on roll dated 2 December 1862, captured 14 September 1862 at Fox's Gap MD, exchanged 2 October 1862, elected 2nd lt. 18 December 1862, captured at Knoxville 29 November 1863 and imprisoned at Camp Chase OH until transferred to Fort Delaware 27 March 1864, released 12 June 1865, buried at Columbus, Georgia's Linwood Cemetery.

Dever, Francis. Enlisted 1 August 1861, shown as 5th sgt. on 2 December 1862 roll, shown as 1st sgt. on January/February 1863 roll, captured at Knoxville 29 November 1863 and imprisoned at Rock Island, enlisted in US Army for frontier service, Federal records showed that he enlisted 6 October 1864 for one year in Co. E of the 2nd US Volunteer Infantry, shown as b. Ireland, age 27, 5'6" tall with blue eyes and brown hair, his enlistment credited to quota of Warren County PA and he was paid $100.00 bounty, promoted to cpl. 17 September 1865, served in the west, mustered out at Fort Leavenworth, KS, 7 November 1865.

Dowd, Andrew. Enlisted 1 August 1861, present on roll dated 5 October 1864, no further record.

Dowd, James. Enlisted 1 August 1861, captured at Knoxville 29 November 1863 and imprisoned at Rock Island until released 17 June 1865, age 33.

Dowd, James A. Enlisted 1 August 1861, shown absent sick on roll dated 14 January 1864, casualty list in 2 July 1864 *Richmond Enquirer* for period 6 May 1864 through 16 May 1864 listed Dowd as KIA indicating that he d. at Wilderness or Spotsylvania.

Downing, Thomas F. Enlisted 1 August 1861, captured 2 July 1863 at Gettysburg and imprisoned at Fort Delaware, took Oath of Allegiance and released 31 March 1865.

Doyle, John. Enlisted 1 August 1861 as 3rd sgt., MWIA (leg amputated) and captured at Knoxville 29 November 1863, d. at Middle Brook Hospital near Knoxville 10 December 1863.

Doyle, Miles. Enlisted 1 August 1861, AWOL on 1 August 1862 roll, discharged on surgeon's certificate at Richmond 25 September 1862, age 18.

Drew, Dennis. Enlisted 1 August 1862, WIA 30 August 1862 at Second Manassas
(left leg amputated), disabled remainder of war, age 30.

Driscoll, Dennis. Enlisted 1 August 1861, WIA and captured at Sailor's Creek 6
April 1865 (left thigh and hip), released from Lincoln Hospital, Washington DC
12 June 1865.

Duggan, Cornelius. Enlisted 24 August 1861, present on 1 November 1861 roll, no
further record but high probability that this is the same man as Neill Duggan.

Duggan, John W. Enlisted 1 August 1861 as 2nd lt., KIA at Fox's Gap MD 14
September 1862.

Duggan, Neill S. Enlisted 1 August 1861, WIA at Fredericksburg 13 December
1862, newspaper casualty list showed severe wound to ankle, all further rolls
showed disabled or at hospital, listed on 31 October 1864 roll at Columbus,
Georgia Confederate Hospital.

Fahey, William. Enlisted 1 August 1861, June 1862 roll showed under arrest,
captured at Frederick MD 12 September 1862, exchanged 2 October 1862,
AWOL on rolls from 1 November 1862 through February, 1863, captured at
Knoxville, 29 November 1863 and imprisoned at Rock Island, took Oath and
joined US Army for frontier service, Federal records showed that he enlisted 13
October 1864 for one year as a pvt. in Co. II US Volunteer Infantry, shown as b.
Cork, Ireland age 28, 5'8" tall with hazel eyes and dark hair, paid $100.00
bounty, served in the west, mustered out at Fort Leavenworth, KS 17
November 1865.

Flanagan, John. Enlisted 1 August 1861, WIA at Fredericksburg 13 December 1862
(shoulder), all further rolls showed him absent at hospitals, last shown on a roll
at Liberty VA Confederate Hospital 21 April 1864, no further record, b. in
Ireland 1825.

Flynn, James C. Enlisted 1 August 1861 as 1st sgt., discharged 15 April 1862 because
of disability.

Foley, Matthew. Enlisted 1 August 1861, shown as 2nd cpl. on January/February
1863 roll, 1st cpl. on September/October 1863 roll, last shown on roll dated 5
October 1864 as sick at hospital but there are no hospital records for him, no
further record, b. in Ireland in 1838, filed for pension so known to have survived
the war.

Fullam, James H. Enlisted 1 August 1861, joined legion band May 1862, present on
roll dated 30 January 1865, no further record.

Furlong, Patrick. Enlisted 1 August 1861, WIA at Fredericksburg 13 December 1862
(wrist), shown as 3rd cpl. on January/February 1863 roll and 2nd cpl. on
September/October 1863 roll, all further rolls showed sick at hospital, last
shown on roll at Liberty VA Confederate Hospital 4 August 1864, no further
record.

Furlong, Richard. Enlisted 1 August 1861, roll dated 2 December 1862 stated
"Captured 14 September 1862 at South Mountain and not heard from since,

deserted" but no Federal POW or deserter records were located. No further record.

Garey, Francis P. Enlisted 1 August 1861 as 2nd lt., resigned 20 July 1862 claiming paralysis of side.

Garey, Patrick G. Enlisted 1 August 1861, WIA and captured at Fox's Gap MD 14 September 1862, sent to Fort Monroe for exchange 18 December 1862, discharged for disability 24 July 1863, age 47.

Gillespie, Richard G. Enlisted 1 August 1861, WIA (arm and side) at Sharpsburg 17 September 1862, WIA (neck) at Fredericksburg 13 December 1862, MWIA (leg amputated) and captured at Gettysburg, d. 8 July 1863 in Federal II Corps Hospital four miles southeast of Gettysburg, body disinterred in 1872 and reburied at Hollywood Cemetery in Richmond VA.

Gleason, Patrick. Enlisted 1 August 1861, captured at Knoxville 29 November 1863 and imprisoned at Rock Island, took Oath and joined US Army for frontier service, Federal records showed that he enlisted 13 October 1864 for one year as pvt. in Co. H 2nd US Volunteer Infantry, shown as b. Limerick, Ireland, age 25, 5'9" tall with gray eyes and dark hair, his enlistment credited to quota of Mercer County PA and he was paid $100.00 bounty, served in the west, mustered out at Fort Leavenworth, KS 7 November 1865.

Glenn, Andrew. Enlisted 1 August 1861 as 5th sgt., demoted to pvt. and detailed to service as a boilermaker at Savannah GA 22 March 1862 to 5 October 1864, late 1864 rolls showed him AWOL, no further record.

Graham, Dennis. Enlisted 1 August 1861, shown AWOL on roll dated 20 July 1862 and on all rolls through 14 January 1864, later rolls showed at hospital, no further record.

Haffey, James. Enlisted 1 August 1861, captured 20 October 1864, at Harrisonburg VA and imprisoned at Point Lookout until released 13 May 1865.

Halligan, Anthony. Enlisted 1 August 1861, shown as 2nd cpl. on roll dated 2 December 1862, then as 2nd sgt. on January/February 1863 roll, 14 January 1864 rolls showed at hospital, no hospital records, AWOL on all further rolls.

Harrigan, Timothy. Enlisted 1 August 1861, shown as 1st cpl. on January/February 1863 roll, captured at Gettysburg 3 July 1863 and imprisoned at Fort Delaware, took Oath of Allegiance and joined the 1st Connecticut Cavalry.

Harvey, James. Enlisted 1 August 1861, deserted 1 May 1862, not clear when he returned but is not shown on 1862/1863 rolls, declared unfit for service in 1864 and detailed as a shoemaker at Macon GA.

Hearn, Daniel. (Some possibility that this may be the man listed earlier as Daniel A'Hern.) Enlisted 1 August 1861, roll dated 5 October 1864 stated he was missing since 8 July 1863, no further record.

Huban, Thomas. Enlisted 1 August 1861, sick at hospital 12 August 1862, all later rolls showed same status, one hospital record showed him at Danville Confederate Hospital 20 May 1863, no further record.

Hughes, John. Enlisted 1 August 1861, captured at Knoxville 29 November 1863 and imprisoned at Rock Island until released 20 June 1865, age 32.

Kavanaugh, John. Enlisted 1 December 1862, May/June 1864 rolls showed MIA 3 June 1864, July/August 1864 roll showed him at the hospital, roll dated 5 October 1864 showed him at hospital wounded, no further record, postwar pension application from widow M. A. Kavanaugh states that he was shot in the hip at Cold Harbor and then burned to death when the woods caught fire.

Keating, Patrick. Enlisted 1 August 1861, WIA at Fredericksburg (left leg amputated), d. 6 March 1863 at Richmond GH #16 from after-effects of amputation.

Kelly, John. Enlisted 1 August 1861, MWIA and captured at Sharpsburg MD 17 September 1862, d. 23 September 1862.

Kennelly, Joseph. Enlisted 24 August 1861, discharged because of hernia 21 September 1861.

Lawler, James. Enlisted 1 August 1861, captured 15 September 1862 in Maryland, exchanged 6 October 1862, discharged 18 November 1862.

Lynch, Walter. Enlisted 1 August 1861, age 51, discharged 31 October 1862 but later rejoined company, WIA (per casualty list in 12 August 1863 *Athens Southern Banner*) and captured 5 July 1863 at Gettysburg, exchanged 23 August 1863, shown AWOL on all later rolls, paroled at Augusta GA 2 June 1865.

McCabe, John. Enlisted 1 August 1861, roll dated 14 January 1864 showed absent sick, AWOL on all later rolls, no further record.

McCullough, William. Enlisted 1 August 1861 as 4h sgt., deserted at Dublin VA, 20 January 1862, no further record.

McDowell, Stephen. Enlisted 24 August 1861, absent at home sick 1 October 1861, deserted at Macon 1 June 1862, no further record.

McEvoy, Bernard. Enlisted 24 August 1861, discharged because of disability 30 April 1862.

McGinley, Cornelius. Enlisted 1 August 1861, KIA at Sharpsburg MD 17 September 1862.

McGovern, Dennis. Enlisted 1 August 1861, discharged 26 December 1862 but rejoined company later, captured at Falling Waters MD 14 July 1863, imprisoned at Old Capitol Prison in Washington, took Oath 20 December 1863 and sent north, no further record.

McGovern, Michael. Enlisted 1 August 1861, shown absent sick since battle of Second Manassas, then AWOL on all further rolls, he is listed on the Roll of Honor for conspicuous gallantry on 2 July 1863 at the battle of Gettysburg, this indicated that he returned to his company after the February 1863 muster roll was completed, fought with it at Gettysburg and then disappeared before the next roll was completed in October 1863, no further record.

McGovern, Patrick. Enlisted 1 August 1862, promoted to 1st lt. 30 January 1862, captured at Fox's Gap MD 14 September 1862, exchanged 6 October 1862, promoted to cpt. 4 December 1862, dropped from rolls for prolonged absence 24 February 1864, buried at Columbus, Georgia's Linwood Cemetery 18 September 1895.

McGovern, William. Enlisted 1 August 1861, 5th sgt. on January/February 1863 roll, 4th sgt. on September/October 1863 roll, WIA and captured at Knoxville 29 November 1863 (right arm amputated), at Louisville Federal Hospital until sent to Fort Delaware 7 March 1864, paroled from Fort Delaware 14 September 1864, in Richmond Hospital 22 September 1864, furloughed home disabled 26 September 1864, b. 15 September 1839, arrived Columbus GA from Ireland in 1853, d. 12 November 1893 from pneumonia, buried at Columbus, Georgia's Linwood Cemetery.

McGuire, Patrick. Enlisted 1 August 1861 WIA (head) at Fredericksburg 13 December 1862, furloughed home 15 December 1862, in hospitals thereafter until retired by Medical Examining Board 13 April 1864.

McIntyre, Charles. Enlisted 1 August 1861, present on rolls throughout war, paroled and released at Farmville VA between 11 and 21 April 1865.

McLane, Patrick. Enlisted 1 August 1861, WIA (left side) 2 July 1863 at Gettysburg, age 30 in 1863, WIA (right arm) at Spotsylvania and admitted to Richmond Hospital 17 May 1864, furloughed for 60 days on 19 July 1864, no further record.

Meara, James. Enlisted 1 August 1861 as 1st lt., disabled by accidental gunshot wound to knee October 1861, resigned 13 January 1862.

Mitchell, Joseph. Enlisted 1 August 1861, WIA at Second Manassas 30 August 1862, d. 25 September 1862 in Danville Hospital from pyemia (blood poisoning).

Moore, John A. Enlisted 1 August 1861, promoted to 2nd lt. 18 December 1862, WIA and captured at Knoxville 29 November 1863, at Louisville Federal Hospital until sent to Fort Delaware 27 March 1864, released 12 June 1865.

Murphy, Michael. Enlisted 1 August 1861, AWOL 30 June 1862, no further record.

Murphy, John. Enlisted 1 August 1861, deserted at Bermuda Hundred 8 March 1865, took Oath and sent to Oil City PA.

Nolan, Thomas. Enlisted 1 August 1861, d. 5 November 1862 at Charlottesville VA Hospital from typhoid, buried University of Virginia Confederate Cemetery, Charlottesville VA.

O'Brien, James. Enlisted 24 August 1861, joined legion band in 1862, last shown present on roll dated 30 January 1865, no further record.

O'Byrne, Dominick. Enlisted 24 August 1861, d. 8 September 1861 at Claytor's Tobacco Factory Hospital in Lynchburg VA of typhoid, buried Lynchburg City Cemetery #7 in 5th line of lot 178, name shown in cemetery record as D. O. Byne, age 28, b. in Ireland.

O'Connel, Michael. Enlisted 24 August 1861, captured at Knoxville 29 November 1863 and imprisoned at Rock Island, took Oath and joined US Army for frontier service 4 October 1864.

O'Neill, James. Enlisted 1 August 1861, last shown present on 1 January 1863 Co. F
roll, no further Co. F. record but it is likely this is the same man as James
O'Neill who was a member of the legion band, surrendered at Appomattox 9
April 1865 as J. Oneal of Co. A.

O'Neill, Robert P. Originally enlisted in Co. B 11 June 1861 as 4th sgt., transferred
to Co. F 20 April 1862 as 1st sgt., surrendered at Appomattox 9 April 1865 as a
member of Co. A.

Rush, Felix. Enlisted 24 August 1861, captured at Knoxville 29 November 1863 and
imprisoned at Rock Island, took Oath and joined US Navy 25 January 1864.

Shanahan, Cornelius. Enlisted 24 August 1861, captured 29 November 1863 at
Knoxville and imprisoned at Rock Island until released 20 May 1865.

Sweeney, John. Enlisted 24 August 1861, surrendered at Appomattox 9 April 1865 as
a member of Co. A.

Walsh, Michael. Enlisted 4 August 1861, roll dated 5 October 1864 showed at home
on sick furlough, all later rolls showed same status, captured at Macon GA 30
April 1865

Walsh, Michael S. Enlisted 21 August 1861 as 1st cpl., elected 2nd lt. 31 November
1862, promoted to 1st lt. 4 December 1862, captured at Gettysburg 3 July 1863
and imprisoned at Johnson's Island until released 12 May 1865, age 26,
interesting document in his record showed that he applied to take the Oath of
Allegiance for release in December 1864, this statement reads "Was born in
Ireland and went to Savannah, Ga. in 1858 and was employed as a printer in the
Savannah Morning News office at the commencement of the war. Voluntarily
joined the C S Army in July 1862 [sic] as a pvt. in which capacity he served
about five months when the company elected him 2nd lt. Served as such until
December 1862 when he was promoted 1st lt. Says that when the army fell back
from the field of Gettysburg he concealed himself among some rocks for the
purpose of giving himself up to the first Federals which he done to the first ones
he saw; that he wishes to take the Oath of Amnesty because he is tired of C S
service and does not wish to fight for the South any longer; that all his relatives
reside in Ireland and he wishes to go there. Says he has one brother who is
under British protection; that he could have had the same protection had he
waited longer before entering the Army. Is twenty-five years of age." Obviously
his request was not acted upon as he was not released until after the war had
ended.

Casualties, Other Losses for Phillips Legion Infantry battalion from available records, Company L was formed predominantly with men from Cobb County.

Company L

Total Enrollment	107
Death/disease/accident/unknown	14
Discharged/disability	16
Retired	1
Captured	43
KIA	3
MWIA	3
WIA	33
Surrendered/paroled	8
Exchanged	22
AWOL	12
Deserted	10
Imprisoned/Rock Island IL	7
Imprisoned/Point Lookout MD	6
Imprisoned/Elmira NY	1
Imprisoned/Camp Douglas, Chicago IL	1
Imprisoned/Fort Delaware DE	5
Transferred out	7
Transferred in	12
Transferred to cavalry	1
Detailed as nurse	1
Detailed Provost Guard Militia	1
Detailed Brigade Commissary Clerk	1
Detailed as Teamster	1
Detailed as Shoemaker	1
Court Martialed	1
Sent North of Ohio River (Destination unknown)	2
Sent to Illinois (Destination unknown)	2
Sent to Richmond OH	2
Enlisted/no other information available	6

Note: Any one individual may appear in several categories; e.g., he may have been captured, sent to prison and exchanged. Company L was one of three companies added to the infantry battalion in early 1862. Company L was mustered in to the Phillips
Georgia Legion Infantry battalion on 15 March 1862.

PHILLIPS GEORGIA LEGION
Infantry Battalion

Company L
The Blackwell Volunteers

Alexander, Andrew J. Enlisted 15 March 1862, captured at Fox's Gap MD 14
  September 1862, exchanged November 1862, present throughout the war,
  deserted near Richmond 19 March 1865, took Oath of Allegiance and sent to
  Illinois, age 25 in 1860 Cobb County Census.

Alexander, Robert G. Enlisted 15 March 1862, in and out of hospitals throughout
  1862, 1863 and 1864, showed as AWOL on August 1864 roll, no further
  military record but known he survived the war because he was shown in the
  1870 census for Cobb County GA, age 30 in 1860 Cobb County census.

Algood, Nathan Y. Enlisted 3 April 1862, medical discharge 28 January 1863, age 41.

Ardis, Payson L. Enlisted 9 May 1861 in Co. I, 2nd SC Infantry, age 20, transferred
  to Co. L, Phillips Legion 8 August 1862 per ANV SO 177/8, promoted to 1st lt.
  Co. E, 3rd Georgia Sharpshooter battalion 5 June 1863, captured at Front Royal
  16 August 1864, released from Fort Delaware 17 June 1865, Oath showed him
  to be 5'11" tall with dark hair and blue eyes, son of David and E. C. Ardis.

Austin, Marcus D. Enlisted 15 March 1862, cited for gallantry at Gettysburg on 2
  July 1863, WIA (lost finger) at Funkstown MD 26 July 1863, another record
  stated that he accidentally wounded 11 August 1863, furloughed home, detailed
  as nurse in Richmond Hospital June 1864, reassigned to Danville VA hospital,
  January, 1865, age 34, no further record.

Baber, J. G. W. Transferred in from 1st Arkansas November 1863, court martialed
  23 December 1864 for being AWOL and sentenced to company punishment,
  deserted near Petersburg 19 March 1865, took Oath of Allegiance, no further
  record, age 22 in 1860 Cobb County census.

Baswell, Alexander H. Enlisted 15 March 1862, b. 1839, WIA (hip, though
  newspaper casualty list indicates finger shot off) at Chancellorsville 2 May 1863,
  WIA (left foot) 1 June 1864 at Gaines Farm (Cold Harbor) and furloughed
  home, showed AWOL on August 1864 roll, no further military record (although
  Alabama pension application showed that he was captured and held until the end
  of the war).

Baswell, Jefferson A. Enlisted 15 March 1862, accidentally wounded January, 1863
  (hip) detailed to Provost Guard Atlanta, in Farmville VA Hospital June and July
  1864, furloughed home, captured in Cobb County 18 August 1864, took Oath
  of Allegiance and sent north of Ohio River, b. 23 September 1841 in
  Spartanburg SC.

Baswell, John T. Enlisted 31 March 1862, present on August 1864 roll, in Richmond
  Hospital 8 August 1864, discharged from hospital 30 November 1864, no
  further military record, b. September 1845, survived the war and applied for

pension, stated that he surrendered at Appomattox 9 April 1865 although surrender/parole records do not support his claim.

Biggerstaff, Aaron. Enlisted 5 April 1862, present on August 1864 roll dated 28 January 1865, no further record, b. in NC, age 30 in 1860 Cobb County census.

Bowie, John Middleton. Enlisted 15 March 1864, August 1864 roll showed he was detailed as brigade commissary clerk, no further military record although an Alabama pension application stated that he was in Atlanta at war's end on the staff of Gen. W. T. Wofford, d. 19 March 1921, age 14 in 1860 Cobb County census, son of J. E. and Almedia Bowie, born in Alabama.

Briant, Henry C. Enlisted 15 March 1862, captured at Fox's Gap MD 14 September 1862, exchanged October 1862, promoted to 1st sgt. 1 April 1864, WIA (toe amputated) 6 May 1864 at Wilderness per casualty list in 8 June 1864 *Athens Southern Banner*, WIA (right arm) at Cedar Creek 19 October 1864, no further record, age 18 in 1860 Cobb County census.

Burton, James. Enlisted 15 March 1862, in Staunton VA Hospital 29 October 1864, still there in January 1865, no further military record, b. July 1835 in SC, survived war and applied for pension, d. 19 October 1909.

Burton, William Crow R. Enlisted 15 March 1862, present on March 1863 roll, transferred to 3rd GA Sharpshooter Battalion May 1863, captured 6 April 1865 at Sailor's Creek and imprisoned at Point Lookout until released on 24 June 1865, b. in SC 5 November 1840, Alabama pension application stated that typhoid fever crippled his legs in 1862, son of Benjamin and Mary Burton, d. 4 February 1922 in Cullman County AL, buried Cullman City Cemetery.

Campbell, Isaac. Enlisted 8 April 1862, captured at Fox's Gap MD 14 September 1862, exchanged October 1862, WIA (lost index finger, right hand) at Chancellorsville 2 May 1863, furloughed home 6 June 1863, furloughed home again 11 July 1864, captured August 1864 in GA, took Oath of Allegiance and sent north of Ohio River.

Carpenter, Thomas A. Enlisted 26 March 1862, detached duty as a brigade teamster until August 1864 roll showed him AWOL, no further record.

Cheek, James H. Enlisted 15 March 1862, transferred to 3rd GA Sharpshooter Battalion May 1863, WIA (leg) in May 1864, no further record.

Christian, William. P. Enlisted 8 April 1862, sent to hospital November 1862, no further record.

Cler, Charles Frank. Enlisted 19 May 1862, age 19, served in legion band in 1862, captured 5 December 1863 near Knoxville and imprisoned at Rock Island until released 18 June 1865, b. 22 September 1842, d. at Savannah 25 November 1929, son of Elizabeth Cler.

Conger, Asa F. Enlisted 29 March 1862 as 3rd cpl., present on December 1862 roll, deserted December 1863, took Oath at Knoxville TN, January 1864, age 21 in 1860 Cobb County census.

Davis, Eli Madison. Enlisted 4 April 1862, in hospitals with small pox December 1862–May 1863, March 1863 roll stated he was detailed as a shoemaker in Richmond, showed as shoemaker in Atlanta in 1864, present on August 1864 roll, no further military record, b. 14 August 1826, d. 3 September 1880, buried Davis Cemetery, Mableton, Cobb County.

Dickerson, Allen. Enlisted 5 April 1862, captured 3 December 1863 near Knoxville, POW at Rock Island until released 21 June 1865 at age 27.

Donehoo, Aaron C. Enlisted 28 April 1862 in Co. M, transferred to Co. L 1 June 1862, captured at Strasburg (Cedar Creek) 19 October 1864, POW at Point Lookout until released 26 June 1865, d. 1 February 1903.

Donehoo, Barnett W. Enlisted 5 April 1862, transferred to Legion Co. C 1 May 1862, disability discharge 1 September 1862 due to poor eyesight, age 54.

Dunn, John. Enlisted 28 April 1862, transferred to Co. M 1 June 1862, transferred back to Co. L 1 November 1862, WIA (hip) and captured at Gettysburg 2 July 1863, exchanged in 1863, casualty list in 9 November 1864 *Athens Southern Banner* lists him as wounded in the back 19 October 1864 at Cedar Creek, shows surrendered at Appomattox 9 April 1865 as part of Co. M but roll dated January 1865 shows him disabled at home, age 26 in 1860 Cobb County census, b. in SC, Pension application states that he is disabled due to having the upper left part of his hip bone shot away by a shell fragment at Gettysburg.

Dunn, Joseph. Enlisted 28 April 1862, transferred to Legion Co. M, June 1862, age 32 in 1860 Cobb County census, b. in SC.

Esler, William J. Enlisted 19 May 1862, captured at Fox's Gap MD 15 September 1862, exchanged October 1862, often hospitalized during 1862 and 1863, AWOL after 28 September 1863, hospital records showed him hospitalized July/August 1864, a January 1865 note also showed him in hospital, age 22 in 1860 Cobb County census, born in Ireland.

Eubank, George W. Enlisted 10 April 1862, KIA at Knoxville TN 29 November 1863, age 14 in 1860 Cobb County census.

Frey, Daniel Washington. Enlisted 15 March 1862, present through war, deserted 23 March 1865, took Oath of Allegiance and sent to Richmond Ohio, b. 15 February 1838 in SC, d. 18 March 1909, buried Camp Ground Cemetery, Cobb County GA, son of M A Frey, brother of James and Samuel Frey, pension application states that he was captured on the skirmish line near Richmond in March 1864 (1865?) and imprisoned at Rock Island until war's end but records do not support this claim.

Frey, James Leopard. Enlisted 15 March 1862, captured 5 December 1863 near Knoxville TN, POW at Rock Island, exchanged at New Orleans, LA May 1865, b. 27 March 1846 near Columbia SC, d. 26 June 1914, buried Barlow Cemetery, Barlow KY, son of M. A. Frey, brother of Daniel and Samuel Frey.

Frey, Samuel George. Enlisted 15 March 1862, present through war, captured at Burkville VA 6 April 1865, released 27 June 1865, b. 13 May 1836 in Lexington

District South Carolina, d. 17 March 1911, buried New Hope Methodist Cemetery, Cobb County GA, son of M A Frey, brother of Daniel and James Frey, pension application states he was hit in the shoulder by a shell fragment at Gettysburg and a doctor's statement confirms a problem with this shoulder.

Fridell, John William. Enlisted 1 June 1862, captured at Gaines Farm (Cold Harbor) 1 June 1864, POW at Point Lookout until released 14 May 1865, b. 30 May 1845 in SC, moved to Texas after war, killed in a knife fight 12 September 1912 in Jacksonville FL.

Gasaway, James G. Enlisted 15 March 1862, age 37 in 1860 Cobb County census, present on June 1862 roll, transferred to Co. H 7th GA infantry in 1862, no further military record, d. 24 December 1900, buried Powder Springs GA.

Gober, Newton Napoleon. Enlisted 15 March 1862 as 1st lt., promoted to cpt. of Co. F, 3rd Georgia Sharpshooter battalion in June 1863, b. 1 December 1836 in Nashville TN, d. 25 May 1912, buried Citizens Cemetery, Marietta GA, was a physician before war.

Green, Byron B. Enlisted 23 August 1861 in Co. I 7th GA infantry, transferred to legion Co. L 11 February 1862, WIA (leg) at Second Manassas, promoted 4th sgt., mid-1863, WIA (arm) at Wilderness per casualty list in 8 June 1864 *Athens Southern Banner*, surrendered and paroled at Appomattox 9 April 1865 (listed as D. D. Green.)

Hamby, David M. Enlisted 15 March 1862, d. Winchester VA 10 September 1862 of disease, buried Stonewall Cemetery, Winchester VA, b. 28 January 1846 in Marietta GA.

Hamby, Micajah Leonard. Enlisted 15 March 1862 as 2nd sgt., WIA (arm) at Second Manassas 30 August 1862, returned to company by June 1863, present on rosters through June 1864, surrendered and paroled at Appomattox 9 April 1865, b. 21 July 1839 in Walton County GA, d. 1910, buried Maloney Springs Church Cemetery, Fair Oaks GA.

Haney, Friend. Enlisted 8 April 1862, sick much of 1862/1863, shown as present on August 1864 roll, in Richmond Hospital 2 April 1865, d. 9 February 1897, buried Mt. Bethel Church, Cobb County, age 40 in 1860 Cobb County census.

Haney, William. Enlisted 2 February 1863, in Petersburg Hospital September 1863, 13 June 1864 note stated died at home, d. 7 December 1863, buried Newnan GA, age 34 in 1860 Cobb County census.

Harper, Thomas. Enlisted 15 March 1862, MWIA (thigh) at Chancellorsville 2 May 1863, d. 8 May 1863 in Richmond, buried at Hollywood Cemetery, Richmond VA.

Hayes, Isaac N. Enlisted 15 March 1862, detailed as shoemaker in Atlanta GA March 1863, August 1864 roll showed same status, no further record, age 21 in 1860 Cobb County census, b. 20 April 1839, d. 29 December 1901.

Hayes, John Wesly. Enlisted in Co. C 25 June 1861, age 17, transferred from Co. C June 1862, in hospitals much of 1862 and early 1863, detailed as shoemaker in

Atlanta mid 1863, showed as AWOL on August 1864 roll, no further military
record, postwar pension application stated he was captured and sent to Cairo IL
in September 1864, b. 24 September 1844 in SC, d. 27 August 1919 in Cobb
County.

Hill, Hilliard J. Enlisted 15 March 1862, WIA 30 August 1862 at Second Manassas,
captured 29 September 1862 at Warrenton VA and immediately exchanged,
transferred to Co. H 7th GA infantry 8 June 1863, discharged from service in
August 1863, discharge showed him as 46 years old, 5'10" tall with blue eyes and
dark hair.

Hill, John. Enlisted 1 1862, Discharged overage with bad eyesight October 1862, age
56.

Hogan, James. Enlisted 7 April 1862, discharged 22 December 1862, age 40 in 1860
Cobb County census, born in SC.

Hughes, Toliver Y. Enlisted 16 March 1862, in hospital September 1862 then
furloughed home, deserted to join Co. I Bonaud's Battery near Charleston SC,
August 1864 roll still showed him AWOL, surrendered with legion 9 April 1865
at Appomattox as T L Huse, d. 5 September 1937, buried DeKalb County, age
16 in 1860 Cobb County census, son of W. And M. Hughes.

Hunt, Clement J. Enlisted 15 March 1862, captured at Fox's Gap MD 14 September
1862, exchanged October 1862, WIA and captured at Gettysburg July 1863,
exchanged August 1863 and furloughed home to GA, showed AWOL on August
1864 roll, no further record.

Hunt, John James. Enlisted 15 March 1862 as 4h sgt., discharged underage 6 August
1862, served in Phillips State cavalry regiment in 1863, age 14 in 1860 Cobb
County census, b. 3 March 1847 in Marietta to W. H. and M. J. Hunt, became a
legislator and judge postwar, d. October 1932 in Atlanta, buried at Oak Hill
Cemetery Griffin GA.

Ivey, John A. Enlisted 18 July 1862, WIA at Chancellorsville 2 May 1863, WIA (left
hand) at Spotsylvania May 1864, furloughed home then captured in Cobb
County GA July 1864, imprisoned at Camp Douglas IL, d. 21 November 1864
from smallpox, buried Oak Woods Cemetery, Chicago IL.

Ivey, Newton J. Enlisted 18 July 1862, MWIA at Fox's Gap MD 14 September 1862,
d. Boonsboro MD 15 September 1862, death claim filed by Charlotte Ivey.

Johnson, American Ford. Transferred into Co. L Phillips Legion during late 1862
from Co. G 10th Alabama as 5th sgt., WIA (foot) 2 July 1863 at Gettysburg per
casualty list in 20 July 1863 *Atlanta Southern Confederacy*, elected 2nd lt. 27 July
1863, WIA (left thigh and right shoulder) and captured 29 November 1863 at
Knoxville TN, returned through lines same day, retired 14 October 1864, b. in
Cherokee County GA 10 August 1840 to Bennett S. and Ella P. Johnson, filed
for an invalid pension from Haralson County GA in 1897, younger brother of
Cpt. James M. Johnson.

Johnson, James M. Enlisted 15 March 1862 in Marietta GA as cpt., WIA (thigh) and
    captured at Fox's Gap MD 14 September 1862, exchanged October 1862, WIA
    (foot) at Fredericksburg 13 December 1862, KIA at Knoxville TN 29
    November 1863, (shot through body, died at Federal Hospital #5 at 2:30 P.M.),
    buried Knoxville City Cemetery, Federal GH #5 report dated 18 January 1864
    stated that he was "buried in the public burying ground of the City, his grave is
    not numbered. The rebel sympathizers of the city will be able to identify his
    grave," born in NC in 1836 to Bennett S. and Ella P. Johnson, older brother of
    Lt. American F. Johnson.

Johnson, John R. Enlisted 15 March 1862, d. 8 May 1862 of disease at Camp
    Pritchard SC.

Johnson, Richard. Enlisted 11 June 1861 in Co. A 18th Georgia Infantry, transferred
    into Phillips Legion Co. L during July or August 1862 in exchange for Benjamin
    R. Whitfield, captured at Sharpsburg MD September 1862, exchanged October
    1862, descriptive list dated 12 November 1862 showed him as age 17, 5'5" tall
    with blue eyes and dark hair, cpl. 1 April 1864, furloughed 23 January 1865, no
    further record, born in Cherokee County GA.

Lord, Nimrod N. Enlisted 15 March 1862 as 1st cpl., sent to hospital at Marietta GA
    May 1863, AWOL thereafter, demoted to pvt., no further military record, age
    20 in 1860 Cobb County census, son of A. L. and Veodica Lord, listed in 1870
    and 1880 censuses for Attala County MS.

Lowrey, James Fletcher. Enlisted 15 March 1862 as 2nd lt. in Marietta GA age 22 or
    23, promoted 1st lt. June 1862, promoted cpt. 29 November 1863, WIA (hit in
    leg by shell) and captured at Sailor's Creek 6 April 1865, d. 7 or 8 April 1865 at
    Federal General Hospital, Burkeville VA during operation to amputate leg, son
    of Basil and Emily Yarbrough Lowrey, older brother of Joseph Lowrey.

Lowrey, Joseph Tarpley. Enlisted 7th GA Infantry in May 1861, age 17, transferred
    into Co. L Phillips Legion August 1862, deserted 11 March 1865, took Oath of
    Allegiance 18 March 1865 and sent to Richmond OH, returned to Marietta
    after the war and married Charlotte A. Northrup 12 April 1866, younger
    brother of Cpt. J. Fletcher Lowrey, son of Basil and Emily Yarbrough Lowry.

Loyd, James. Enlisted 22 March 1862, deserted 14 December 1863 near Knoxville
    TN, took Oath of Allegiance 3 January 1864, no further record.

Malone, Doctor L. Enlisted 1 April 1862 as 2nd cpl., WIA (neck) and captured at
    Fox's Gap MD 14 September 1862, imprisoned at Fort Delaware until
    exchanged 15 December 1862, promoted to 5th sgt. between September and
    December 1863, surrendered and paroled at Appomattox 9 April 1865, age 27 in
    1860 Cobb County census.

Massey, John Andrew. Enlisted 15 March 1862, WIA (hand) at Chancellorsville 2
    May 1863, captured at Burkeville VA 6 April 1865, imprisoned at Point Lookout
    MD until released 29 June 1865, b. 30 March 1843, d. 20 December 1919,
    buried Citizens Cemetery, Marietta GA.

Mauldin, Alfred (Albert) W. Enlisted 15 March 1862, WIA (groin) 6 May 1864 at Wilderness per casualty list in 8 June 1864 *Athens Southern Banner*, deserted 22 March 1865, took Oath of Allegiance and sent to Illinois.

Mauldin, Fleming P. Enlisted 15 March 1862 as 3rd cpl., discharged overage, 15 October 1862, age 54.

McCown, Robert W. Enlisted 15 March 1862 as 2nd lt. at Marietta GA, promoted 1st lt. 11 June 1863, WIA (neck) at Knoxville TN 29 November 1863, WIA (ankle) and captured at Sailor's Creek 6 April 1865, released 19 June 1865.

McGinty, Manasseh Benjamin. Enlisted 8 April 1862, promoted 4th sgt. December 1862, promoted to 2nd lt. 21 March 1864, captured at Sailor's Creek 6 April 1865, released 19 May 1865, b. 13 April 1840, d. 23 February 1899, buried Oconee Hills Cemetery, Athens GA.

McClellan, Ira F. Enlisted 15 March 1862, captured at Fox's Gap MD 14 September 1862, POW at Fort Delaware until exchanged in October 1862, AWOL 22 July 1863, still shown AWOL as of August 1864, b. 30 May 1845, Alabama pension application stated he was in a convalescent camp in Macon GA at war's end, also stated that he was wounded in the leg and shoulder at Fredericksburg, and wounded and captured at Cold Harbor in June 1864, no Federal POW records substantiate this claim.

Megarity, Kindred. Enlisted 15 March 1862, age 53 in 1860 Cobb County census, admitted to Richmond General Hospital #14 12 August 1862, transferred 31 August 1862 to Mayo Island, no further record.

Montgomery, William Rhadamanthus. Enlisted 9 May 1861 in 2nd SC Infantry for one year, reenlisted in Legion Co. L as 1st sgt., April 1862, transferred to 3rd GA Sharpshooter battalion as 1st lt., in May 1863, furloughed home February 18, 1865, returned to VA on foot but arrived after surrender.

Moon, Edwin R. Enlisted 15 March 1862, WIA (thigh) 6 May 1864 at Wilderness per casualty list in 8 June 1864 *Athens Southern Banner*, surrendered and paroled at Appomattox 9 April 1865.

Morris, Patrick J. Present on June 1862 roll, no further military record but known he survived the war because he was listed in the 1870 Cobb County census, age 31.

Moore, William T. Enlisted 15 March 1862, captured at Gaines Farm (Cold Harbor) 1 June 1864, POW at Elmira NY, d. of smallpox 4 February 1865, buried Woodlawn Cemetery #1738 (or #1832), Elmira NY.

Moore, Thomas A. Enlisted 4 April 1862, captured 5 December 1863 in TN, POW at Rock Island until exchanged 23 May 1865 at New Orleans, LA.

Oglesby, William W. Enlisted 15 March 1862, present on 31 December 1862 roll., transferred to 3rd GA Infantry per ANV SO #177 dated 27 April 1863.

Owens, William C. Enlisted 15 March 1862, d. of disease 12 November 1862 at Washington VA.

Pilgrim, William B. Enlisted 15 March 1862, WIA (shoulder) at Fox's Gap MD 14
September 1862, present on August 1864 roll, hospitalized October 1864,
paroled 19 April 1865 at Newton NC.

Ray, John E. Enlisted 15 March 1862 in legion Co. M, transferred to Legion Co. L
spring of 1863, captured at Gettysburg 2 July 1863, POW at Fort Delaware
until exchanged 20 November 1864, furloughed from Richmond Hospital in
November 1864, no further record.

Rice, George D. "Duff." Enlisted 7 September 1863, WIA (big toe, left foot) and
captured at Knoxville 29 November 1863, returned across the lines that same
day, wounded 1 July 1864, d. 3 July 1864, 3 July 1864 entry in W. R.
Montgomery diary states "Duff Rice was wounded night before last while asleep
in camp and died this morning at 3 o'clock." The Legion was in the Petersburg
trenches at this time and would pull back to camps behind the line when not on
duty in the trenches, it appears that a stray round from the front lines must have
mortally wounded Rice as he slept.

Richardson, Joseph B. Enlisted 23 August 1861 in Co. I 7th GA infantry, discharged
16 July 1862, reenlisted in legion Co. L 17 August 1862, WIA (lost arm) at Fox's
Gap MD 14 September 1862, furloughed from Richmond Hospital, February
1863, still being paid at home in 1863/1864.

Roberts, Hezekiah N. Enlisted 10 July 1861 in Co. H 7th GA Infantry, WIA (hand)
at First Manassas, discharged 1 March 1862 due to wound, discharge shows him
to be age 21 5'2" with blue eyes and black hair, reenlisted 10 March 1863 in Co.
L, furloughed 27 December 1864, no further record.

Ruede, William E. Present on March 1863 roll as 4th cpl., transferred to 3rd GA
Sharpshooter Battalion 1 May 1863 (KIA at Chancellorsville per W. R.
Montgomery letter dated 7 May 1863 and casualty list in 15 May 1863 *Atlanta
Southern Confederacy*), age 15 in 1860 Cobb County census, son of A. D. and E.
B. Ruede.

Sanders, Solomon H. Captured at Fox's Gap MD 14 September 1862, exchanged 10
November 1862, d. 17 February 1863 of pneumonia at Danville VA.

Sauls, James H. Enlisted 15 March 1862, WIA (lost leg) at Sharpsburg MD 17
September 1862, at home disabled for remainder of war.

Self, Henry. Enlisted 15 March 1862, present until captured 6 April 1865 at Sailor's
Creek, POW at Point Lookout until released 8 June 1865.

Self, James T. Enlisted 15 March 1862, discharged 15 October 1862, overage, age
52.

Shaw, Albert R. Enlisted 9 June 1862, discharged 29 September 1862, underage.

Sherman, Sr., Hiram. Enlisted 15 March 1862, discharged, 15 October 1862,
overage, age 70.

Sherman, Jr., Hiram. Enlisted 15 March 1862, MWIA (hit in back with shell) at
Fredericksburg 13 December 1862, d. 21 December 1862. Note: not found in
census, so relationship to Hiram Sherman, Sr., unknown.

Smith, Theophilus A. Enlisted 4 March 1862 as 2nd Cpl., WIA (arm) 2 July 1863 at
    Gettysburg per casualty list in 20 July 1863 *Atlanta Southern Confederacy*,
    captured 29 November 1863 at Knoxville, POW at Rock Island until exchanged
    early 1865, d. Jackson Hospital, Richmond, 31 March 1865 of ascites, age 26 in
    1860 Cobb County census, b. in SC.
Stephens, William Pitchford. Enlisted 5 April 1862, elected lt. Co. M April 1862.
Taylor, H. M. Enlisted 15 August 1862, sick most of 1862/1863, captured in
    Richmond Hospital 3 April 1865, d. of chronic diarrhea 7 August 1865 in
    Savannah Hospital, buried Laurel Grove Cemetery, Savannah GA.
Taylor, Simeon J. Enlisted 26 March 1862, last shown present on August 1864 roll,
    death claim filed 1864, no further record.
Tribble, Benjamin J. Enlisted 3 April 1862, transferred to Cavalry Co. C, of Legion 2
    May 1862, death claim filed by father 23 February 1864, date of death shown as
    26 June 1863.
Walraven, Mitchell. Enlisted 5 April 1862, captured at Fox's Gap MD 14 September
    1862, considered exchanged 10 November 1862, WIA (foot) at Gettysburg 2
    July 1863, accidentally wounded in foot 13 June 1864, deserted 11 March 1865.
Waters, William O. Enlisted 15 March 1862, WIA (head) at Second Manassas 30
    August 1862, captured 2 July 1863 at Gettysburg and POW at Fort Delaware
    until exchanged 18 February 1865, no further record.
Weems, Ira J. Enlisted 15 March 1862, present on roll dated 28 January 1865, no
    further record.
White, Henry C. Enlisted as 1st sgt. 15 March 1862, medical discharge 14
    September 1862, age 21 in 1860 Cobb County census.
Whitfield, Benjamin R. Enlisted 5 April 1862, transferred to Co. A 18th GA Infantry
    in July or August 1862 in exchange for Richard Johnson, WIA 30 August 1862
    at Second Manassas, medical discharge 17 October 1863, b. in GA 25 June
    1836.
Willingham, Green B. Enlisted 8 April 1862, d. 25 December 1862 at Richmond of
    smallpox.
Wilmoth, Harrison. Enlisted 8 April 1862, captured at Fox's Gap MD 14 September
    1862, exchanged 10 November 1862, captured at Knoxville TN 29 November
    1863, POW at Rock Island until exchanged 15 February 1865, no further
    military record, b. in NC 28 February 1829, d. 15 April 1902 in Marietta GA,
    brother of Light and William Wilmoth.
Wilmoth, Light Heckleman. Enlisted 28 April 1862, present until final record
    January 1865 showed furloughed, b. 1844 in GA, d. 11 April 1886, buried
    Marietta Citizens Cemetery, brother of Harrison and William Wilmoth.
Wilmoth, William J. Enlisted 8 April 1862, captured at Gettysburg 2 July 1863, d. 18
    November 1863 of smallpox at Point Lookout, buried Point Lookout
    Confederate Cemetery, Scotland MD, b. about 1841 in GA, brother of Harrison
    and Light Wilmoth.

Wooten, Franklin M. Enlisted 5 April 1862, deserted from Richmond Hospital 18 October 1862, showed deceased on 25 June 1863 report but 1911 pension application showed him very much alive, in it he stated that he was discharged because of poor health in November 1862.

Wooten, J. G. Enlisted 15 March 1862, furloughed 30 May 1864, last entry August 1864, showed him AWOL.

Wooten, William J. Enlisted 16 May 1862, AWOL May 1862, "forged discharge papers and deserted," captured and confined in Atlanta December 1862, back with unit March 1863, roll dated December 1864 stated discharged from hospital June 1864 and not heard from since, no further military record but known he survived the war as he was listed in the 1870 Cobb County census, age 29.

Wylie, James L. Enlisted 15 March 1862 as 3d sgt., WIA (shell fragment chest and shoulder) at Chancellorsville May 1863, present until captured at Farmville VA 6 April 1865, imprisoned at Point Lookout until released 22 June 1865.

Wylie, Richard C. Enlisted 28 April 1862, died of pneumonia at Lynchburg VA 15 February 1864, buried Lynchburg City Cemetery.

Young, James B. Enlisted 15 March 1862 as 5th sgt., WIA at Sharpsburg MD 17 September 1862, A and IG SO #212 dated 10 September 1862 had already discharged him for being underage, 14 years old in 1860 census.

Zibemy, (Zibenne) Joseph B. Enlisted March 1862, discharged, overage 30 October 1862, age 54.

Casualties, Other Losses for Phillips Legion Infantry battalion from available records; Company M was formed predominantly with men from Cobb County.

Company M

Total Enrollment	125
Death/disease/accident/unknown	23
Retired to Invalid Corps	1
Discharged/disability	15
Resigned	2
Captured	46
KIA	3
MWIA	3
WIA	32
Surrendered/paroled	24
Exchanged	15
AWOL	5
Deserted	7
Imprisoned/Rock Island IL	4
Imprisoned/Point Lookout MD	12
Imprisoned/Elmira NY	5
Imprisoned/Johnson's Island OH	1
Imprisoned/Fort Delaware DE	5
Imprisoned/Newport News VA	5
Imprisoned/Louisville KY	1
Imprisoned/Camp Chase OH	3
Imprisoned/David's Island, New York Harbor NY	1
Imprisoned/Fort McHenry MD	1
Galvanized Yankees	1
Transferred out	8
Transferred in	8
Transferred to cavalry	5
Detailed as division blacksmith	1
Detailed as brigade HQ guard	1
Detailed as Pioneer (construction worker)	1
Detailed as brigade provost guard	1
Court Martialed	1
Sent to Columbus OH	1
Sent to Jeffersonville, IN	1
Sent north of Ohio River (destination unknown)	2

Sent north (destination unknown)   1
Enlisted/no other information available   9

Note: Any one individual may appear in several categories; e.g, he may have been captured, sent to prison and exchanged. Company M was one of three companies added to the infantry battalion in early 1862. Company M was mustered in to Phillips Legion on 28 April 1862.

PHILLIPS GEORGIA LEGION
Infantry Battalion

Company M
The Denmead Volunteers

Anderson, J. M. P. Enlisted 28 April 1862 as 3rd sgt., discharged 25 August 1862, age 23.

Anderson, William D. Enlisted 22 May 1861 in 2nd SC infantry, reenlisted in Co. M Phillips Legion 28 April 1862, promoted to 2nd lt. 26 February 1863, declined appointment to cpt. Co. F, 3 GA Sharpshooter battalion 9 June 1863, seriously WIA at Cold Harbor, retired to Invalid Corps 20 January 1865, b. 24 June 1833, d. 19 February 1894, buried in Marietta Citizens Cemetery.

Arrowood, Toliver J. Enlisted 28 April 1862, WIA (face) 2 July 1863 at Gettysburg per casualty list in 20 July 1863 *Atlanta Southern Confederacy*, captured at Knoxville 29 November 1863 and imprisoned at Rock Island, took Oath and joined US Army for Frontier service enlisting in Co. I 3rd US Infantry 31 October 1864, enlistment showed him to be 32 years old, 5'9" tall with blue eyes and dark hair, mustered out at Fort Leavenworth, KS 29 November 1865, b. April 1833 in NC, d. 11 September 1913 in Cobb County, physician's statement with pension application noted that he lost the top part of three fingers on his left hand during the war.

Ballenger, Albert C. Enlisted 28 April 1862, discharged 20 October 1862, age 15 in 1860 census.

Bannister, William. Enlisted 28 April 1862, WIA (left arm) at Fox's Gap MD 14 September 1862 and disabled for remainder of war, b. 1826 Pendleton District SC, d. 19 June 1900, buried at Sandy Plains Cemetery in Cobb County GA, uncle of William M. Bannister.

Bannister, William M. Enlisted 28 April 1862, shown as 1st cpl. on September/October 1862 roll, KIA at Fox's Gap MD 14 September 1862, nephew of William Bannister, death claim filed by father John Bannister, b. in 1843 in Abbeville District SC.

Barber, William M. "Billy." Enlisted 28 April 1862, WIA at Spotsylvania (hand), interesting story in Paulding County Heritage book tells how Barber went to hospital after his mangled finger became infected, but after listening to the screams of soldiers inside who were having limbs amputated he decided to handle the problem himself, he did so by shooting the remains of his infected finger off with his rifle to cauterize the wound, furloughed home and captured at Macon GA 20 April 1865, b. 8 March 1824 in Clarke County, d. 25 May 1926, buried at Mount Zion Baptist Church Cemetery, Paulding County GA.

Bell, William S. Enlisted 28 April 1862 as 2nd sgt., captured 12 September 1862 at Frederick MD, exchanged 2 October 1862, promoted to 1st sgt. 28 January 1863, surrendered at Appomattox 9 April 1865.

Bentley, Green B. Enlisted 28 April 1862, discharged 18 November 1862, captured later in Georgia and sent north, took Oath 26 September 1864 at Louisville KY, b. 29 November 1832, d. 25 December 1905, buried at Gresham Cemetery in Cobb County.

Bishop, Henry H. Enlisted 28 April 1862, WIA at Gettysburg (leg), all further rolls show him hospitalized, postwar pension application of his widow states that he d. 18 June 1866 from consumption and chronic diarrhea, age 28 in 1860 census.

Bishop, J. A. Enlisted 28 April 1862, captured at Sailor's Creek 6 April 1865 and imprisoned at Newport News until released 25 June 1865, age 33 in 1860 census.

Blackwell, Dempsey Smith. Enlisted 28 April 1862, WIA (head) May 1863 at Chancellorsville per casualty list in 19 May 1863 *Atlanta Southern Confederacy*, WIA at the Wilderness 6 May 1864 (hand), captured at Sailor's Creek 6 April 1865 and imprisoned at Newport News until released 25 June 1865, b. 19 April 1829 in SC, d. 29 November 1888, buried at New Providence Baptist Church Cemetery, Cobb County, cousin of Jasper L. and Marion C. Blackwell.

Blackwell, Jasper L. Enlisted 28 April 1862 as 2nd lt., d. at Hardeville SC of typhoid 12 June 1862, b. 17 March 1842, brother of Marion C. Blackwell, buried at Blackwell family cemetery on Piedmont Road in Cobb County.

Blackwell, Marion C. Enlisted 28 April 1862, WIA at Sharpsburg MD 17 September 1862, surrendered at Appomattox 9 April 1865 (listed as W. C. Blackwell), b. 20 December 1843, d. Cobb County GA 25 August 1867, brother of Jasper L. Blackwell, buried at Blackwell family cemetery on Piedmont Road in Cobb County.

Boatner, John. Enlisted 28 April 1862, all rolls showed him sick at hospital until discharged for chronic ascites 6 March 1863, d. in Henry County GA 28 December 1925, postwar pension application stated that he was WIA December 1862 and his right leg was disabled, age 20 in 1860 census.

Booker, Silas W. Reenlisted 28 April 1862 (previously in Co. C. 22nd GA Infantry until discharged for disability 10 March 1862), WIA 29 November 1863 at Knoxville per casualty list in 3 February 1864 *Athens Watchman*, roll dated 14 January 1864 shows him wounded in hospital, surrendered at Appomattox 9 April 1865, b. 2 June 1832, d. 5 August 1905.

Brasselton, Robert W. Enlisted 28 April 1862, transferred to Phillips Legion cavalry battalion Co. C 16 October 1862, age 26 in 1860 census.

Brown, John M. Reenlisted 28 April 1862 (previously in Co. A 3rd GA State Troops until mustered out in April 1862), surrendered at Appomattox 9 April 1865, b. Cobb County GA 21 September 1841.

Bryan, John Pleasant. Reenlisted 28 April 1862 (was previously in Co. I, 7th GA Infantry, WIA at First Manassas and discharged in December 1861), captured at Fox's Gap MD 14 September 1862, exchanged 2 October 1862, captured at Knoxville TN 29 November 1863 and imprisoned at Camp Chase OH until he took the Oath, turned up in Richmond Hospital 16 March 1865, furloughed home 30 March 1865, b. 2 May 1841 in Franklin County GA, d. 17 May 1925, buried at Pleasant Grove Cemetery, Hulaco, Alabama.

Cleveland, Henry C. Enlisted 28 April 1862, transferred to 3rd GA Sharpshooter Battalion in May 1863, captured at Front Royal VA 16 August 1864 and POW at Elmira until exchanged 2 March 1865, age 16 in 1860 census.

Coker, A. Sherwood. Enlisted 28 April 1862, surrendered at Appomattox 9 April 1865 (listed as A. S. Coke), b. 1833 in Franklin County.

Coker, John V. Enlisted 28 April 1862, last entry in service record showed him furloughed home from a Richmond Hospital 3 March 1863, Coker family bible showed that he d. in April 1863 but did not indicate cause or location (information provided by Martha W. Mangum of Marietta GA), age 32 in 1860 census.

Coker, L. H. Not shown on muster rolls so enlistment date not known, only entry on service record is an Appomattox surrender/parole entry.

Collins, Charles B. Enlisted 28 April 1862, captured 14 September 1862 at Fox's Gap MD, exchanged 2 October 1862, shown sick on rolls in 1863, sent to Atlanta Hospital 17 July 1863, WIA 29 November 1863 at Knoxville per casualty list in 3 February 1864 *Athens Watchman*, deserted 14 December 1863, took Oath of Allegiance 16 January 1864, b. 1840 in Cobb County.

Dawson, William Pinckney. Enlisted 28 April 1862, sick in 1862 and early 1863, last shown on roll dated 30 January 1865, no further record, b. 18 June 1842, d. 20 May 1905, buried at Dawson Cemetery in Cobb County.

DeVore, William. Enlisted 28 April 1862, sick in 1862 and early 1863, d. 1863 at Richmond GH #26 of cancum oris, death claim filed by wife Mary DeVore, buried Oakwood Cemetery in Richmond as W. Devan.

Dobbs, James P. Enlisted 28 April 1862, d. 14 November 1862 at Farmville VA Hospital of typhoid pneumonia, death claim filed by father Selcer Dobbs, age 16 in 1860 census.

Dobbs, Sr., J. P. Enlisted 28 April 1862, a card in his record showed him dying 13 November 1862 at Winder Hospital from typhoid but his was almost certainly a misplaced entry for James P. Dobbs because J. P. Dobbs, Sr., is not reflected on rolls after 1 July 1862, he d. 6 November 1864 and is buried in the Marietta Citizens Cemetery so it is likely that he was discharged in 1862, b. 10 January 1833.

Dobbs, William B. Enlisted 28 April 1862, WIA (hand) 17 September 1862 at Sharpsburg MD, January/February 1863 roll stated "discharged on account of wound received in battle of Antietam," d. 28 December 1887, widow's pension application stated that he died from chronic diarrhea contracted in the war, age 23 in 1860 census.

Donehoo, Aaron C. Enlisted 28 April 1862, transferred to Legion Co. L, 1 June 1862.

Drake, Samuel. Enlisted 28 April 1862, MWIA (left shoulder and face) 13 December 1862 at Fredericksburg, d. 24 December 1862 at Richmond GH #4, buried at Hollywood Cemetery in Richmond under the name of S. Drink, age 26 in 1860 census, article in 1901 Marietta newspaper claims that Drake shot General T.R.R. Cobb at the battle of Fredericksburg in retaliation for an earlier disciplinary incident.

Dukes, William P. Enlisted 15 June 1862, d. 25 September 1862 at Martinsburg VA, cause of death not known, death claim filed by widow Anna Dukes.

Dunn, Hastings (Haston). Enlisted 28 April 1862, present through war, roll dated 30 January 1865 stated Absent on furlough of indulgence, no further military record, age 25 on 1870 Cobb County census, b. in SC to Allen and Elizabeth Dunn, brother of Hosea Dunn, d. 4 December 1905 in Calhoun County MS.

Dunn, Hosea. Enlisted 28 April 1862, present on roll dated 14 January 1864, no further record, b. in SC to Allen and Elizabeth Dunn, brother of Hastings Dunn.

Dunn, John. Enlisted 28 April 1862, transferred to Co. L, Phillips Legion, 1 June 1862.

Dunn, Joseph. Enlisted in Co. L, Phillips Legion, transferred into Co. M 1 June 1862, present on roll dated 30 January 1865, no further military record but known he survived the war because he was shown in the 1870 Cobb County census, age 44.

Edwards, Enoch R. Enlisted 28 April 1862, shown as 3rd sgt. on roll dated 14 January 1864, AWOL on 1 October 1864 roll, 12 December 1864 roll stated he resigned as sgt. 1 October 1864, captured at Sailor's Creek 6 April 1865 and imprisoned at Newport News VA until released 25 June 1865, b. 23 August 1829 at Spartanburg SC, d. 11 April 1913.

Fickett, A.W. R. Enlisted 28 April 1862, discharged for disability 12 June 1862.

Folds, Hiram W. Enlisted 28 April 1862, KIA 14 September 1862 at Fox's Gap MD, death claim filed by father Eli Folds.

Frey, William Martin. Enlisted 28 April 1862, WIA (side) and captured at Gettysburg 2 July 1863 and imprisoned at Point Lookout until paroled 3 May 1864, received at Aikens Landing for exchange 8 May 1864, present on roll dated 30 January 1865, no further military record, b. 2 June 1831, d. 9 July 1909, buried at New Hope United Methodist Church Cemetery in Cobb County.

Galtol, William. No enlistment date shown, discharged at Richmond 1 November 1862.

Gantt, John D. Enlisted 28 April 1862, shown as 5th sgt. on roll dated 14 January 1864, furloughed to Hamburg SC 18 December 1864 from Jackson Hospital Richmond after bout of pneumonia, no further military record, b. 14 June 1834, d. 2 June 1903, buried at Sardis Baptist Church Cemetery, brother of Reuben Gantt.

Gantt, Reuben D. Enlisted 28 April 1862, d. 25 December 1862 at Howards Grove Hospital of smallpox, death claim filed by brother John D. Gantt.

Gilham, W. D. Enlisted 28 April 1862, detailed as Division blacksmith on roll dated 14 January 1864 with notation left in Virginia which indicates that he did not go west with McLaws' division in September 1863, surrendered at Appomattox 9 April 1865.

Gray, William Frank. Enlisted 28 April 1862, d. in camp near Fredericksburg VA 16 February 1863 (cause unknown), death claim filed by wife Mary M. Gray.

Grimes, Travis. Enlisted 28 April 1862, AWOL 20 October 1862 and on all rolls thereafter.

Grist, W. W. Enlisted 28 April 1862, casualty list in 9 November 1864 *Athens Southern Banner* showed as severely wounded in the arm 19 October 1864 at Cedar Creek, admitted to Charlottesville Hospital 24 October 1864 with gunshot wound to left arm, shown as 4th sgt. on roll dated 3 December 1864, sent home on wounded furlough 13 December 1864, captured 6 April 1865 at Sailor's Creek and imprisoned at Newport News VA until released 25 June 1865.

Hamby, Benjamin Judson. Enlisted 28 April 1862 as 1st sgt., elected brevet 2nd lt. 27 January 1863, WIA (left wrist) 29 November 1863 at Knoxville, surrendered at Appomattox 9 April 1865, b. 11 October 1836, d. 5 July 1917, buried at Maloney Springs Cemetery, Fair Oaks (now part of Marietta) GA.

Hardman, Francis Marion. Enlisted 28 April 1862, captured at Gettysburg, 2 July 1863, d. at Point Lookout 13 March 1864 from pneumonia, buried at Point Lookout Confederate Cemetery, Scotland MD, b. in GA 20 May 1828, older brother of James N. Hardman.

Hardman, James Newton. Enlisted 28 April 1862, WIA (left heel) 2 July 1863 at Gettysburg, surrendered at Appomattox 9 April 1865, b. 6 June 1837 in GA, d. 1 August 1913 in Cullman County AL, buried at Valley Springs Cemetery, younger brother of Francis M. Hardman.

Harris, Samuel Young. Enlisted 28 April 1862 as 4th sgt., promoted to 1st lt. 12 August 1862, promoted to cpt. 1 February 1863, Harris was furloughed in February 1865 and went to South Carolina where his family had refugeed, he married Miss Mary Catherine Elizabeth Latimer there and then returned to Virginia in late March, he was wounded (flesh, scalp and left index finger) and captured at Sailor's Creek 6 April 1865 and d. in Burkeville VA 9 April 1865, there is a comment in a reminiscence penned by his younger sister Mattie Harris Lyon that her "Bro Sam was killed by a stray round the day after the surrender," in view of the apparent minor nature of his wounds this may well have been an accurate description of his death, records indicate that he was buried in the small Confederate Cemetery there, b. in 1838 in Abbeville SC to Ezekiel Calhoun and Rebecca Young Harris.

Hembree, David H. Enlisted 28 April 1862, d. 17 June 1862 at Camp Pritchard SC of measles, death claim filed by widow Sarah Hembree.

Herring, E. R. Enlisted 28 April 1862, transferred to 3rd GA Sharpshooter battalion in May 1863, last shown on roll for August 1863, no further record.

Hodge(s), John W. Enlisted 18 April 1862, captured 14 September 1862 at Fox's Gap MD, exchanged 2 October 1862, casualty list in 2 July 1864 *Richmond Enquirer* showed him slightly wounded between 6 May 1864 and 16 May 1864, deserted near Petersburg VA 25 March 1865, took Oath of Allegiance and sent to Jeffersonville, IN.

Hudson, W. H. Enlisted 8 January 1864, detailed as a Brigade HQ guard, surrendered at Appomattox 9 April 1865, b. 14 March 1845, d. 28 February 1914, buried at Greenwood Cemetery, Cedartown, Polk County GA.

Hunton, John Thomas. Enlisted 28 April 1862, captured at Sailor's Creek 6 April 1865 and imprisoned at Point Lookout until released 28 June 1865, b. 10 May 1833 in Campbell County GA, d. 6 October 1910, buried at Marietta Campground Cemetery in Cobb County.

Inzer, Andrew J. Enlisted 28 April 1862, WIA 14 September 1862 at Fox's Gap MD, MWIA (bladder) 29 November 1863 at Knoxville TN, d. 13 December 1863 at Middlebrook GH, buried "in woods near shops four miles from Knoxville."

Johns, Eliph E. Enlisted 28 April 1862, present on all rolls throughout the war, casualty list dated 2 July 1864 in *Richmond Enquirer* lists him as slightly wounded during the period 6 May 1864 and 16 May 1864, surrendered at Appomattox 9 April 1865.

Jolly, John A. Enlisted 28 April 1862, furloughed home 8 December 1863, suffering from chronic dysentery, d. at home 26 January 1864, death claim filed by father Jesse Jolly.

Kemp, John M. Enlisted 28 April 1862, roll dated 5 October 1864 showed wounded in hospital, casualty list in 2 July 1864, *Richmond Enquirer* showed him wounded (leg amputated) between 6 May 1864 and 16 May 1864 1906 Roster Commission roll showed him "wounded in left leg necessitating amputation above the knee at Wilderness 6 May 1864," roll dated 13 December 1864 showed him disabled and at home in Georgia.

Kemp, Solomon M. Enlisted 28 April 1862, d. at Camp Pritchard SC 15 June 1862 from measles.

Kemp, William M. Enlisted 28 April 1862, WIA (chest) 2 July 1863 at Gettysburg per casualty list in 20 July 1863 *Atlanta Southern Confederacy*, captured at Deep Bottom 28 July 1864 and imprisoned at Elmira NY 8 August 1864, shown on a prison list dated 20 February 1865 of men to be sent to James River for exchange with the notation "unable to travel," he died at Elmira 26 February 1865 from pneumonia and is buried at Woodlawn Cemetery grave 2117.

Knight, Elisha N. Enlisted 28 April 1862, shown as a teamster 1862/1863, WIA (hip) 2 July 1863 at Gettysburg per casualty list in 20 July 1863 *Atlanta Southern*

Confederacy, listed as Brigade blacksmith on roll dated 5 October 1864, roll dated 30 January 1865 showed. him absent on furlough of indulgence, no further record.

Knight, Ephraim M. E. Enlisted 28 April 1862 as 5th sgt., captured 2 July 1863 at Gettysburg and sent to DeCamp Hospital, David's Island, New York harbor with fever, exchanged during August 1863, shown as a pvt. on roll dated 14 January 1864,captured again at Cedar Creek 19 October 1864 and imprisoned at Point Lookout until released 28 June 1865.

Lamaster, Robert M. Enlisted 28 April 1862, shown detailed as a pioneer (construction worker) on 1862 rolls, listed sick at hospital on rolls dated 14 January 1864, 5 October 1864 and 30 January 1865 but there are no hospital records in his file to indicate the nature of his wounds or illnesses, surrendered at Appomattox 9 April 1865.

Land, William H. Enlisted 28 April 1862, elected 2nd lt. 12 August 1862, found incompetent by an examining board 29 January 1863 and returned to the ranks as a pvt., transferred to Phillips Legion cavalry Co. C 12 February 1863.

Lemaster, Thomas. Enlisted 23 November 1863, shown sick on all rolls, final entry at Lynchburg Hospital 21 December 1864 showed him transferred to Brigadier General Colston.

Martin, John. Enlisted 28 April 1862 as 4th cpl., discharged for disability 8 October 1862, age 29, b. 11 March 1833, d. 18 June 1909.

Martin, W. B. Enlisted 28 April 1862, shown absent sick at hospital on all 1862 rolls and roll for January/February 1863, shown AWOL since 11 November 1863 on roll dated 14 January 1864 but returned as he is shown present on later 1864 rolls, deserted 23 February 1865 near Petersburg, took Oath of Allegiance and sent to Columbus OH.

Mason, Ezekial L. Enlisted 28 April 1862, captured 26 July 1864 at Deep Bottom and imprisoned at Point Lookout until transferred to Elmira 8 August 1864, released from Elmira 7 July 1865, b. 1835, d. 1920, buried at Marietta Citizens Cemetery.

Mason, William T. Enlisted 28 April 1862, captured 2 July 1863 at Gettysburg and imprisoned at Fort Delaware until exchanged 7 March 1865, no further military record, b. 14 July 1842, d. 1913, buried at Marietta Citizens Cemetery.

McCleskey, James Franklin. Enlisted 28 April 1862 as cpt., resigned 1 February 1863 to return to former job as sheriff of Cobb County, resignation of Lt. John T. Robertson stated that McCleskey was actually the deputy sheriff.

McCleskey, Milton Turk. Enlisted 28 April 1862, promoted to 3rd sgt. 28 June 1862, demoted to pvt. in 1863 (see ANV GO 55 9 April 1863, court martialed for violation of AIG SO #3), WIA 2 July 1863 at Gettysburg per casualty list in 12 August 1863 *Athens Southern Banner*, present on roll dated 30 January 1865, no further military record, b. 15 April 1842, d. 7 November 1922, pension application stated he surrendered at Appomattox but he is not shown on the parole list, buried at Marietta Citizens Cemetery.

McGarity (Megarity), Francis Marion. Enlisted 28 April 1862, transferred to legion Co. C in January 1863, WIA (right leg) 6 April 1865 at Sailor's Creek, paroled at Farmville VA 9 April 1865, b. 15 March 1831, d. 8 March 1901, buried at Holly Springs Memorial Cemetery in Cobb County.

McKee, Harvey E. Enlisted 28 April 1862, WIA 14 September 1862 at Fox's Gap MD, d. 6 June 1864 at Liberty VA Hospital from pneumonia, originally buried on Piedmont Hill but moved to Longwood Cemetery at Bedford VA in 1921, b. in 1831.

Meek, Thomas J. Enlisted 28 April 1862, WIA (right arm) and captured at Knoxville 29 November 1863, imprisoned at Louisville KY until transferred to Camp Chase OH 25 February 1864, paroled at Fort Delaware 14 September 1864, age 24, admitted to Jackson Hospital Richmond 22 September 1864 with wound to arm (original Knoxville wound), furloughed 26 September 1864 for 60 days, no further military record, 1906 Roster Commission roll noted that wound left him permanently disabled, b. 28 July 1843, d. 3 December 1898, buried at Midway Presbyterian Church Cemetery in Cobb County.

Moore, Jesse H. Enlisted 28 April 1862, transferred to 3rd GA Sharpshooter battalion in May 1863, captured 6 April 1865 at Sailor's Creek and imprisoned at Point Lookout until released 29 June 1865.

Murdock, Cornelius T. Enlisted 28 April 1862, shown as 4th cpl. on September/October 1862 roll, promoted to 1st cpl. in early 1863, captured 2 July 1863 at Gettysburg and imprisoned at Fort Delaware until transferred to Point Lookout in October 1863, exchanged 13 February 1865, no further military record, postwar pension application stated he was at home on furlough when the war ended, b. 25 February 1840, d. 12 May 1918, buried at Holly Springs Memorial Cemetery.

Murdock, James R. Enlisted 28 April 1862, WIA (right arm) at Spotsylvania, captured 6 April 1865 at Sailor's Creek and imprisoned at Newport News VA until released 25 June 1865, b. 16 March 1832 in South Carolina, d. 30 September 1899, buried at Holly Springs Memorial Cemetery.

Murdock, Willis R. Enlisted 28 April 1862, promoted 4th cpl. 1 December 1862, last shown on roll dated 30 January 1865 as being on furlough of indulgence, no further military record, pension application stated he was home on furlough at war's end and noted he was shot in left temple at Fredericksburg in 1862 causing loss of sight in left eye, b. 13 November 1841, d. 21 February 1920, buried at New Providence Baptist Church Cemetery.

Pitts, Joseph P. Enlisted 28 April 1862, service record indicates he died 27 January 1863 at Howards Grove Hospital from measles and typhoid but hospital/burial records at Lynchburg make it clear that he died 28 January 1863 at Knight's Factory Hospital, Lynchburg VA of smallpox, buried at Lynchburg City

Cemetery #9 in 3rd line, lot 101, b. 1839, death claim filed by widow Molly Ann Pitts.

Pitts, Malachi W. Enlisted 28 April 1862, captured in Maryland September 1862, paroled at Keedysville MD 20 September 1862, roll dated 14 January 1864 showed him detailed to the Brigade Provost Guard as did later rolls, last shown on roll dated 30 January 1865, no further military record, b. 20 December 1836 in SC, murdered 15 June 1895 in Cobb County by neighbor J. W. Eaton over a land boundary line dispute, buried at Sardis Baptist Church Cemetery.

Ponder, Daniel Hollingsworth. Enlisted 28 April 1862, captured 14 September 1862 at Fox's Gap MD, exchanged 2 October 1862, surrendered at Appomattox 9 April 1865, b. 13 March 1837 in Forsyth County, d. 24 March 1914 in Grady County, buried Trinity Primitive Baptist Church Cemetery, brother of James Ponder.

Ponder, James Tillman. Enlisted 28 April 1862, roll dated 14 January 1864 listed him wounded at hospital, captured 1 June 1864 at Cold Harbor, imprisoned at Point Lookout until transferred to Elmira NY 12 July 1864, released 7 July 1865, b. 1839 in Forsyth County, d. 1918 in Grady County, buried at Elpino Baptist Church Cemetery, brother of Daniel Ponder.

Price, John W. Enlisted 28 April 1862, d. 19 June 1862 from measles at Camp Pritchard, Hardeeville SC, death claim filed by father Calvin Price, brother of Robert J. Price.

Price, Robert J. Enlisted 28 April 1862, d. 6 August 1862 at home in Cobb County GA from measles relapse and scarlet fever, death claim filed by father Calvin Price, brother of John W. Price.

Quinn, David M. Enlisted 28 April 1862, shown at Richmond's Chimborazo Hospital 1 August 1862, returned to duty 3 August 1862, no further record.

Ray, John E. Enlisted 28 April 1862, captured 2 July 1863 at Gettysburg and imprisoned at Fort Delaware until transferred to Point Lookout 22 October 1863, paroled for exchange 11 October 1864, furloughed (30 days) from Jackson Hospital Richmond VA 20 October 1864, AWOL On 28 January 1865 roll, no further record.

Reid, Joel Posey. Transferred in from Phillips Legion infantry Co. C 20 January 1863, transferred from Co. M. to legion cavalry Co. C. 11 February 1863.

Reid, Thompson H. Enlisted 28 April 1862, teamster, often sick in 1862/1863, captured at Cedar Creek 19 October 1864 and imprisoned at Point Lookout until released 17 June 1865.

Reeves, Mark. Enlisted 28 April 1862, present on rolls throughout war, shown present on roll dated 30 January 1865, no further military record, postwar pension application stated he surrendered at Appomattox but his name was not listed on the parole list, b. 9 November 1834, d. 1918.

Robertson, Isaac K. Enlisted 28 April 1862, captured 3 July 1863 at Gettysburg and imprisoned at Fort Delaware until transferred to Point Lookout 20 October

1863, d. 4 November 1863 from typhoid, buried at Point Lookout Confederate Cemetery, Scotland MD.

Robertson, J. P. Enlisted 28 April 1862, WIA 17 September 1862 (hand) at Sharpsburg MD, furloughed from Richmond GH #8 13 October 1862, discharged 7 April 1863, 1906 Roster Commission roll listed him as I. P. Robertson.

Robertson, John T. Enlisted 28 April 1862 as 2nd lt., resigned 6 August 1862 to return to duty as Sheriff of Cobb County GA.

Robertson, Nathaniel Pinkney. Enlisted 28 April 1862 as 2nd cpl., AWOL on roll dated 28 January 1864 and all later rolls, deserted and took Oath of Allegiance at Camp Nelson KY 8 February 1864, sent orth of the Ohio River, no further record.

Sanders, Richard. Enlisted 28 April 1862, d. 26 November 1862 at Charlottesville VA from pneumonia, buried at University of Virginia Confederate Cemetery at Charlottesville VA, death claim filed by widow Martha.

Sauls, William H. Enlisted 28 April 1862, WIA (arm amputated) and captured 14 September 1862 at Fox's Gap MD, exchanged 17 October 1862, at home disabled for remainder of war, b. 23 August 1844, d. 17 June 1908, buried at Holly Springs Memorial Cemetery in Cobb County.

Sewell, Columbus T. Enlisted 28 April 1862, transferred to cavalry battalion, Phillips Legion 1 November 1862 as blacksmith, b. 24 January 1833, d. 11 June 1919, buried at Mayes-Sewell Family Cemetery in Cobb County.

Sewell, Isaac A. Enlisted 28 April 1862, transferred to Phillips Legion cavalry Co. B 1 November 1862, b. 9 August 1832, d. 5 July 1907, buried at Mayes-Sewell Family Cemetery in Cobb County.

Sewell, John W. Enlisted 28 April 1862, WIA (head) 14 September 1862 at Fox's Gap MD, last shown present on roll dated 30 January 1865, no further record.

Sewell, John W. A. Enlisted 28 April 1862, teamster, last shown present on roll dated 30 January 1865, no further record.

Simpson, M. Fletcher. Enlisted 28 April 1862, teamster, captured 6 April 1865 at Sailor's Creek and imprisoned at Newport News VA until released 25 June 1865.

Sizemore, William M. Enlisted 28 April 1862, no further record.

Smith, James E. No enlistment date, captured 14 September 1862 at Fox's Gap MD, exchanged 2 October 1862, captured 17 January 1864 at Dandridge TN, imprisoned at Rock Island until exchanged 2 March 1865, no further record.

Smith, Joseph. Enlisted 28 April 1862, rolls showed he deserted 4 December 1863 but Federal records showed him captured in TN 20 December 1863 and sent to Camp Chase OH 4 February 1864 (or 4 January 1864), no further record.

Stallings, Irvin. Enlisted 28 April 1862, captured 29 November 1863 at Knoxville TN, imprisoned at Rock Island until death 31 March 1864 from smallpox, buried Rock Island prison cemetery grave #960.

Stancell, Joel C. Enlisted 28 April 1862, captured 14 September 1862 at Fox's Gap
MD, exchanged 2 October 1862, rolls showed he deserted 4 December 1863
near Knoxville TN but Federal records showed him captured in TN 18
December 1863, imprisoned at Rock Island until escaping 26 September 1864,
entry stated "escaped by placing a board against and scaling fence," no further
record, age 17 in 1860 census, brother of John H. and William R. Stancell.

Stancell, John H. Enlisted 28 April 1862, d. 7 April 1863 at Lynchburg GH #4 of
fever, buried at Lynchburg City Cemetery #2 in 4th line, lot 199, death claim
filed by widow Hulda, age 29 in 1860 census, brother of Joel C. and William R.
Stancell.

Stancell, William R. Enlisted 28 April 1862, roll stated he deserted 4 December 1863
at Knoxville but Federal records showed him captured there 5 December 1863,
imprisoned at Rock Island until released 18 June 1865, age 20, brother of Joel C.
and John H. Stancell.

Stephens, John. No enlistment date, shown as 2nd lt. on November 1862 roll, no
further record, strong possibility that this is an erroneous entry for Lt. William
P. Stephens.

Stephens, William Pinckney. Enlisted 28 April 1862 as 2nd lt., promoted to 1st lt. 1
February 1863, captured 6 April 1865 at Sailor's Creek and held at Johnson's
Island OH until released 20 June 1865, b. 18 January 1837, d. 28 February 1892.

Stewart, Noah H. Enlisted 28 April 1862, transferred to 3rd GA Sharpshooter
battalion in May 1863, KIA at Knoxville TN 24 November 1863.

Talbert, William. Enlisted 28 April 1862, discharged 17 October 1862 at request of
father Clinton C. Talbert who stated his son was only 16 at enlistment and
suffered from heart disease.

Tapp, Patillo F. Enlisted 15 June 1862, promoted to 2nd sgt. 28 January 1863,
admitted to Jackson Hospital Richmond 15 May 1864 with shell wound to left
foot, shown present on roll dated 30 January 1865, no further military record, d.
14 September 1893.

Thomas, William Jasper. Enlisted 28 April 1862, surrendered 9 April 1865 at
Appomattox, b. 17 August 1830, d. 13 April 1887, buried at New Hope
Methodist Church Cemetery in Cobb County.

Trout, Gideon. Enlisted 1 July 1862, shown sick at hospital through February 1863
then shown as AWOL on all further rolls, no hospital records.

Vaughn, Memory C. Enlisted 28 April 1862, d. 1 September 1862 at Old College
Hospital at Lynchburg VA of typhoid, buried Lynchburg City Cemetery #7 in
3rd line lot 177.

Vawter, Raleigh A. Enlisted 26 March 1862, transferred to 3rd GA Sharpshooter
battalion in May 1863, deserted 14 December 1863 in TN, took Oath 10
January 1864 and sent north of the Ohio River.

Whelan, Peter Duane. Enlisted 28 April 1862 as company secretary, admitted
Jackson Hospital Richmond 28 July 1864 with head wound, captured 6 April

1865 at Sailor's Creek and held at Newport News VA until released 25 June
1865.

Whitehead, Simeon. Enlisted 28 April 1862, transferred to 3rd GA Sharpshooter
battalion in May 1863, shown present on January 1865 roll, no further military
record, survived war, buried in unmarked grave at Oak Hill Cemetery in
Cartersville GA.

Winn, Dewitt Clinton. Enlisted 28 April 1862, surrendered 9 April 1865 at
Appomattox.

Wise, Henry Lee. Enlisted 28 April 1862, surrendered 9 April 1865 at Appomattox,
b. 7 October 1832, d. 9 August 1914, buried in Queen City TX.

Wood, Robert M. Enlisted 28 April 1862, transferred to 3rd GA Sharpshooter
battalion in May 1863, WIA (foot) 12 May 1864 at Spotsylvania, captured 16
August 1864 at Front Royal VA and Imprisoned at Elmira NY until released 19
July 1865.

Wylie, David Stephen. Enlisted 28 April 1862 as 2nd cpl., captured at Cedar Creek
19 October 1864 and imprisoned at Fort McHenry until exchanged 20 February
1865, no further military record, pension application filed in TX in 1913 stated
he was b. 15 July 1833 and moved to TX in 1872, d. 24 December 1913, buried
at Cahill Methodist Church Cemetery in Johnson County, TX

Wylie, John. Enlisted 28 April 1862 as 1st cpl., shown as pvt. on roll dated 3
December 1862 and thereafter, captured 2 July 1863 at Gettysburg and
imprisoned at Fort Delaware until transferred to Point Lookout MD in October
1863, d. from smallpox 27 November 1863, buried at Point Lookout
Confederate Cemetery, Scotland MD.

Casualties, Other Losses for Phillips Legion Infantry battalion from available records, Company O was formed predominantly with men from Cobb and Bartow Counties.

Company O

Total Enrollment	104
Death/disease/accident/unknown	24
Discharge/disability	3
Resigned	1
Captured	39
KIA	10
MWIA	3
WIA	19
Surrendered/paroled	13
Exchanged	7
AWOL	14
Deserted	5
Retired	1
Imprisoned/Rock Island IL	3
Imprisoned/Point Lookout MD	17
Imprisoned/Elmira NY	3
Imprisoned/Johnson's Island OH	1
Imprisoned/Camp Douglas, Chicago IL	1
Imprisoned/Camp Chase OH	2
Imprisoned/Fort Delaware DE	1
Transferred out	12
Transferred in	9
Transferred to cavalry	1
Detailed to service at Macon GA	1
Detailed as nurse at Winder Hospital, Richmond VA	1
Detailed to service in Atlanta GA	1
Detailed as aide to General W. T. Wofford	1
Detailed as wardmaster at Wayside Hospital, Bristol TN	1
Detailed as hospital nurse/guard Richmond VA	1
Sent to Washington DC	1
Sent north of Ohio River (destination unknown)	2
Sent to New Orleans LA for release	1
Enlisted/no other information available	3

Note: Any one individual may appear in several categories; e.g., he may have been captured, sent to prison and exchanged. Company O was one of three companies added to the infantry battalion in early 1862, Company O was mustered in to Phillips Legion on 16 May 1862.

PHILLIPS GEORGIA LEGION
Infantry Battalion

Company O
The Marietta Guards

Adams, David R. Enlisted 6 May 1862, absent sick on 30 November 1862 roll and thereafter, furloughed home from Richmond Hospital 15 November 1862, absent at home sick on February 1863 roll, transferred to Co. A, 40th GA in exchange for A. C. Brake, captured July 1863 at Vicksburg and paroled same month, shown present on a December 1863 roll, no further record.

Argo, Andrew Jackson "Jack." Enlisted 6 May 1862, MWIA (left arm) 19 October 1864 at Cedar Creek, d. 27 October 1864 at Charlottesville VA hospital, buried at University of VA Confederate Cemetery, Charlottesville VA.

Arwood, Alfred G. Enlisted 6 May 1862, KIA at Sharpsburg MD 17 September 1862, death claim filed by widow, Lucinda Arwood.

Austin, Thomas C. Enlisted 6 May 1862, captured at Fox's Gap MD 14 September 1862, exchanged 2 October 1862, casualty list in 9 November 1864 *Athens Southern Banner* listed him as slightly wounded in the head 19 October 1864 at Cedar Creek, roll dated October 1864 stated absent wounded in hospital, shown at Lynchburg VA Hospital 31 December 1864, no further military record but known that he survived the war because Arkansas pension records showed he died 12 March 1916.

Barfield, David D. Enlisted 6 May 1862, sick from June/September 1863, listed sick at Liberty VA Hospital 26 November 1864, roll dated 30 January 1865 showed him sick at Piedmont VA Hospital, no further record.

Benedict, Thomas. Enlisted 6 May 1862, d. at Winchester VA Hospital 5 October 1862, cause of death not stated, buried at Stonewall Cemetery, Winchester VA.

Bowie, Theophilus G. Enlisted 6 May 1862 as 3rd lt., promoted 2nd lt. 17 October 1862, promoted 1st lt. 25 April 1863, KIA at the Wilderness 6 May 1864.

Bradley, J. M. Enlisted 1 February 1864, deserted 31 March 1864 at Jonesboro TN, no further record.

Brake, A. C. Enlisted 4 March 1862 as 1st sgt., d. at home in Sumter County GA 1 July 1864, cause of death not stated, likely that this is Alva C. Brake from Co. B 41st GA Infantry, Alva shown as having enlisted in Co. B of the 41st GA on 4 March 1862, his record with this unit ended without explanation in November 1862 but records for David R. Adams of Co. O indicated that he and Brake swapped units.

Brake, John H. Enlisted in Co. D 7th GA Infantry 23 August 1861 and served until 5 February 1862 when given a disability discharge, reenlisted in Co. O Phillips Legion 6 May 1862 as 2nd cpl., promoted 5th sgt. 16 October 1862, WIA (left shoulder) 13 December 1862 at Fredericksburg, WIA (hand) 6 May 1864 at the Wilderness, captured 6 April 1865 at Sailor's Creek and imprisoned at Point

Lookout until released 24 June 1865, Oath showed him to be 5'10" tall with brown hair and hazel eyes, b. 2 January 1840, he married and became a policeman in Americus GA after the war and was murdered 28 December 1880 in a dispute with a man named Stovall, buried at Oak Grove Cemetery, Americus GA.

Bruce, J. Harrison. Enlisted 15 May 1862, medical discharge 15 July 1862.

Brumbaloe, Cicero L. Enlisted 6 May 1862, deserted near Petersburg VA 19 March 1865, took Oath of Allegiance and sent to Springfield IL, 1907 pension application filed in Alabama states his age as 65.

Camp, G. A. No muster roll entries, possible late war recruit or conscript, a G. H. Camp was listed in the 1860 Cobb census which may be the same man, captured 6 April 1865 at Sailor's Creek and imprisoned at Point Lookout until released 9 June 1865.

Camp, Thomas L. Enlisted 6 May 1862, transferred to Co. A 40th GA Infantry 1 January 1863, elected 2nd lt. 4 April 1863, resigned 13 April 1865.

Carlisle, James H. Enlisted 6 May 1862, furloughed home sick from Richmond GH #13 16 October 1862, absent sick on 1863 rolls and on roll dated 19 January 1864, detailed as nurse to Winder Hospital Richmond 6 May 1864, furloughed to Griffin GA 20 August 1864, paid at Atlanta 16 October 1864, AWOL on 31 December 1864 roll, no further military record but filed pension application stating he was WIA (left leg) 17 September 1862 at Sharpsburg, b. 20 October 1837, d. 7 April 1891 in Cobb County.

Channel, George W. Enlisted 6 May 1862, KIA 29 November 1863 in Knoxville, "shot through lung and fractured radius," brother of Henry and Thomas Cannell.

Channel, Henry M. Enlisted 6 May 1862, last shown sick at Charlottesville Hospital on February 1863 roll, no further record, Lt. Marcus Green's diary entry for 2 May 1863 at Chancellorsville mentions what appears to be a Herin Cammel as wounded (letter is faded and handwriting is poor), since Henry Channel is the only name in the company close to Herin Cammel it is possible that he may have been wounded at Chancellorsville and died from the effects of his wound, born 6 August 1840 to John and Elizabeth Greer Channell, brother of George and Thomas Channell.

Channel, Thomas J. Enlisted 6 May 1862, AWOL 15 January 1864 until 1 July 1864, deserted 20 February 1865 near Petersburg, sent to Washington DC 22 February 1865, no further record but we know he survived the war since he applied for a pension in 1897, application stated that he was captured near Richmond in February 1865 and held at Washington for the rest of the war, b. 6 August 1840 in Cobb County to John and Elizabeth Greer Channell, brother of George and Henry Channell, d. 25 February 1897, buried at Greer Family Cemetery in Cobb County.

Childers, Emsley J. Enlisted 6 May 1862, KIA at Fox's Gap MD 14 September 1862, age 14 in 1850 Cass County census, brother of Lewis Childers, son of Martin and Elizabeth Childers.

Childers, Lewis G. Enlisted 6 May 1862, WIA 13 December 1862 at Fredericksburg, captured 6 April 1865 at Sailor's Creek and imprisoned at Point Lookout until released 26 June 1865, Oath showed him to be 5'7 1/4" tall with auburn hair and blue eyes, age 12 in 1850 Cass County census, son of Martin and Elizabeth Childers, brother of Emsley Childers.

Colbert, Thompson. Enlisted 6 May 1862, shown absent sick on all rolls through 30 January 1865, no further military record but GA pension application stated that he left his unit because of illness November 1862 and never returned, b. 16 December 1828 in Hancock County, d. in 1906, buried in Greenwood Cemetery, Cedartown, Polk County GA, age 21 in 1850 Cass County census.

Conger, William R. Enlisted 6 May 1862, WIA (side) 2 July 1863 at Gettysburg, captured 6 April 1865 at Sailor's Creek and imprisoned at Point Lookout until released 26 June 1865, Oath showed him to 5'7" tall with light brown hair and blue eyes, born in GA 1837.

Conger, Zachariah M. Enlisted 6 May 1862, captured 19 October 1864 at Cedar Creek and imprisoned at Point Lookout until exchanged 17 March 1865, no further military record but GA pension application stated he was home on furlough at the end of the war, b. 16 January 1830.

Culver, William Rufus. Enlisted 6 May 1862, captured at Jackson Hospital Richmond 3 April 1865, d. 3 May 1865 at Jackson Hospital Richmond of chronic dysentery, buried at Hollywood cemetery Richmond grave #95, age 9 in 1850 Cass County census, son of Gabriel and Lavinia Culver.

Davis, Andrew J. Enlisted 6 May 1862, WIA (compound fracture of humerus) and captured 14 September 1862 at Fox's Gap MD, exchanged 17 October 1862, disabled at home remainder of war, roll dated 30 January 1865 showed him sick at hospital, no further record.

Dunton, James C. Enlisted 6 May 1862, shown absent sick on rolls dated 30 November 1862 and February 1863, a roll dated 19 January 1864 showed him on detached service in Atlanta, a roll dated 5 October 1864 indicated he was at a Richmond Hospital with heart/lung disease, last shown at Richmond barracks 3 March 1865, 1906 Roster Commission roll listed him as J. D. Denton and stated that he died in hospital, can't be found in postwar census records so possible that he died in Richmond in March or April 1865, age 21 in 1860 Cobb County census.

Earp, George Perryman. Enlisted 6 May 1862, designated to transfer to 3rd GA Sharpshooter battalion in May 1863 but all muster roll entries for him in that unit stated absent sick or absent in Phillips Legion, AWOL 19 September 1863 (when Phillips Legion passed through Cobb County on their way north to Ringgold) through roll dated 5 October 1864, present on roll dated 30 January

1865, Appomattox surrender record for G. P. Carp was likely for him since there was no one named Carp in the Legion, postwar pension application indicated he was b. in NC in 1827, d. 10 December 1910.

Earp, Grey. Enlisted 6 May 1862, d. 18 June 1864 at Howards Grove Hospital in Richmond of measles, buried at Oakwood Confederate Cemetery Richmond as G. Eppes.

Edwards, Allen C. Enlisted 16 May 1862, shown absent sick furlough on all rolls through 19 January 1864 and Present on roll dated 5 October 1864, captured 6 April 1865 at Sailor's Creek and imprisoned at Point Lookout until released 11 June 1865, Oath showed 5'7" tall with dark brown hair and blue eyes.

Edwards, Reuben J. Enlisted 22 September 1863, d. 19 October 1863 of dysentery at Chattanooga (per Lt. Marcus Green's diary).

Eubanks, William J. Enlisted 6 May 1862 as 3rd sgt., detached as aide to General W. T. Wofford in 1864, returned to GA with General Wofford in January, 1865, surrendered Kingston GA in May 1865, b. 30 May 1834 in Lumpkin County, d. 22 August 1907 in Cobb County, buried at New Salem Baptist Church Cemetery.

Fenn, George Washington. Enlisted 6 May 1862, transferred 1 July 1862 to Legion Co. C, age 15 in 1850 Cass County census, son of Thomas A. and Lydia Fenn.

Fields, Samuel E. Enlisted 6 May 1862, KIA at Fox's Gap MD 14 September 1862.

Finch, John T. Enlisted 4 April 1863, AWOL 19 September 1863 (when Legion passed through Cobb County on way to Ringgold), captured 6 October 1864 Cobb County, POW at Camp Douglas until released 17 June 1865, his Oath showed him to be 5'10" tall with black hair and gray eyes.

Free, Elisha. Enlisted 15 April 1863, furloughed 15 December 1863 suffering from debility, at Danville Hospital with a gunshot wound to the hand 4 June 1864 (probably wounded Cold Harbor), present on roll dated 30 January 1865, b. 1845 in Habersham County to Elisha and Mary Crow Free.

Greene, James Newton. Enlisted 6 May 1862, KIA 30 August 1862 at Second Manassas, uncle to Lt. M. L. Greene, death claim filed by mother Elizabeth Greene.

Greene, Marcus Lafayette. Enlisted 6 May 1862, promoted 3rd lt. 16 October 1862, promoted 2nd lt. 25 April 1863, furloughed home 28 March 1864, sent resignation letter to 1st Lt. T. Bowie in late April but Bowie was KIA at Wilderness 6 May 1864 before he turned the letter in, resulted in Greene declared AWOL, dropped from company roll 6 December 1864, Greene joined cavalry in Georgia, served out the war and was on detached service at Macon at war's end, nephew of James N. Greene, b. 24 May 1841, d. 17 December 1914.

Greer, James C. Enlisted 6 May 1862, present on all rolls through the war, surrendered 9 April 1865 at Appomattox (listed as J. C. Green).

Guess, Benjamin F. Enlisted 6 May 1862 as 3rd sgt., reduced to pvt. 17 October 1862 at his own request, d. 20 January 1864 at Emory and Henry College VA of disease, death claim filed by father Henry Guess, b. 25 December 1837, buried at Emory Cemetery.

Hardage, Alexander Roberson. Enlisted 6 May 1862, d. 9 November 1862 at Staunton VA from typhoid, buried at Thornrose Cemetery, Augusta County VA, death claim filed by father John T. Hardage.

Hardage, Jesse N. Enlisted 6 May 1862, transferred to Co. D 7th GA Infantry 20 June 1863 (his brother Thomas J. Hardage was the 1st lt. of this company), served with this unit until furloughed home 20 January 1865, shown AWOL as of 16 February 1865, a January 1865 descriptive list showed him to be 20 years old, 5'6" tall with light hair and blue eyes.

Hardage, William N. Enlisted 6 May 1862, promoted to 3rd cpl. 16 October 1862, shown as 2nd cpl. on roll dated 19 January 1864, captured 6 April 1865 at Sailor's Creek and imprisoned at Point Lookout until released 28 June 1865, Oath showed him to be 5'7" tall with dark hair and blue eyes, b. 29 November 1829 in Hall County, d. 3 September 1910, buried at Shiloh Baptist Church Cemetery in Cobb County.

Hardy, Thomas J. Enlisted 6 May 1862, transferred to 3rd GA Sharpshooter Battalion in May 1863, captured 16 August 1864 at Front Royal VA and imprisoned at Elmira until released 16 June 1865.

Harris, C. Wesley. Enlisted 6 May 1862, WIA (foot) between 6 May and 16 May 1864 per casualty list in 2 July 1864 *Richmond Enquirer*, surrendered 9 April 1865 at Appomattox, age 8 in 1850 Cass County census, son of C. F. and Rachel Harris, brother of Jesse Harris.

Harris, Jesse B. Enlisted for 12 months as a pvt. 1st Confederate Infantry 18 March 1861, discharged in March 1862, reenlisted 6 May 1862 as 2nd sgt, in Phillips Legion, promoted 1st sgt. 16 October 1862, promoted 3rd lt. 29 June 1863, d. 25 February 1864 at Dandridge, TN (Lt. Marcus Green's diary stated he died at Jonesborough TN on this date), cause of death not stated, age 12 in 1850 Cass County census, son of C. F. and Rachel Harris, brother of C. Wesley Harris.

Harrison, Hiram A. Enlisted 6 May 1862, WIA 29 November 1863 at Knoxville per casualty list in 1864 *Athens Watchman*, shown absent wounded on 19 January 1864 roll then listed as AWOL on 1864 rolls, Lt. Marcus Green diary states that Harrison was severely wounded in the head at Knoxville 29 November 1863, captured at Greenville SC 24 May 1865, b. 20 March 1833, postwar pension application stated that his skull was fractured by a grapeshot at Knoxville.

Hawkins, John Ransom. Enlisted for 12 months as pvt. 1st Confederate Infantry 18 March 1861, discharged March 1862, reenlisted in Phillips Legion 6 May 1862, KIA 14 September 1862 at Fox's Gap MD.

Hayes, Newton T. Enlisted for 12 months as pvt. 1st Confederate Infantry, discharged Mar, 1862, reenlisted in Phillips Legion 6 May 1862, transferred to 18th GA Infantry between March and August 1863, captured 1 June 1864 at Cold Harbor, imprisoned at Elmira NY until released 11 July 1865.

Henderson, Charles Pinckney. Enlisted 6 May 1862, WIA (right leg) 14 September 1862 at Fox's Gap MD, Subsequent rolls show him absent on wounded furlough then absent sick through 30 January 1865, No further military record but Alabama pension application (from Winston County) indicates he survived the war, b. in SC 14 February 1840 to Sterling and Anna Brenks Henderson, married Eugenia Rice at Powder Springs, GA 5 October 1865, moved to Winston County Alabama in 1880, d. 10 April 1924 at Leoma TN and buried there.

Henderson, John F. Enlisted 6 May 1862, d. 13 March 1863 at Richmond GH #9 from chronic dysentery, buried at Richmond's Oakwood Confederate Cemetery as J. S. Henderson.

Henderson, John M. Enlisted 20 September 1862, transferred to 3rd GA Sharpshooter battalion in May 1863, WIA (shoulder) during May 1864, furloughed home then captured in Cobb County in August 1864, took Oath of Allegiance and sent north of the Ohio River, no further military record but Alabama pension application (from Calhoun County) indicates that he survived the war, application stated he was wounded through both shoulders at the battle of Spotsylvania in May 1864, age 59 in 1900.

Henderson, William H. Enlisted 20 September 1862, transferred to Co. F 22nd GA Infantry in early 1863, September/October 1864 roll stated that he d. 18 October 1864 at Richmond's Jackson Hospital from wounds received 8 October 1864.

Henderson, Willis H. Enlisted 6 May 1862, WIA (leg) between 6 May 1864 and 16 May 1864 per casualty list in 2 July 1864 *Richmond Enquirer*, surrendered 9 April 1865 at Appomattox.

Hill, William P. Does not appear on muster rolls, d. 28 March 1863 at Gordonsville from typhoid, death claim filed by widow Martha Hill, probable that he was a March conscript or enlistee who died before ever being recorded on a muster roll, b. 1829 in Habersham County.

Houze, Darius N. Enlisted 6 May 1862, transferred to 3rd GA Sharpshooter battalion May 1863, last shown on January 1865 roll on furlough, no further record.

Houze, John H. Enlisted 6 May 1862, WIA (shoulder) 13 December 1862 at Fredericksburg, d. at home in GA 10 January 1863 from effects of wound (and smallpox per Lt. Marcus Green diary), death claim filed by Stephen Jackson guardian of Houze's orphaned brothers and sisters (Sarah E., Nancy Ann, James S., Harris (or Jarvis) N. and William Y.)

Jackson, Jesse M. Enlisted 6 May 1862, KIA 14 September 1862 at Fox's Gap MD.

Johnson, William T. Enlisted for 12 months as a pvt. 1st Confederate Infantry 18 March 1861, discharged March 1862, reenlisted Phillips Legion 6 May 1862, surrendered 9 April 1865 at Appomattox.

Lane, Marcus A. Enlisted 6 May 1862, captured and paroled by Federal cavalry at Warrenton VA Hospital 29 September 1862, d. 5 November 1862 at Warrenton, buried at Warrenton Confederate Cemetery.

Lindsey, Augustus. Enlisted 6 May 1862, captured 1 June 1864 at Cold Harbor, d. 30 October 1864 at Elmira NY prison from chronic dysentery, buried Woodlawn Cemetery, Elmira NY grave #745.

Lindsey, James E. Enlisted 6 May 1862, WIA (head) 12 May 1864 at Spotsylvania, captured 6 April 1865 at Sailor's Creek and imprisoned at Point Lookout until released 29 June 1865, Oath showed him to be 5'10 1/4" tall with light brown hair and dark blue eyes.

Lovell, M. C. Enlisted 6 May 1862, deserted 24 December 1862 at Fredericksburg, no Federal desertion or POW records so must have headed south, no further record.

Mann, R. No enlistment record, Appomattox surrender record only, may have been late war recruit or conscript.

Manning, William Jeter. Enlisted 6 May 1862, shown AWOL on all rolls through roll dated 19 January 1864, present on roll dated 5 October 1864, captured 6 April 1865 at Sailor's Creek and imprisoned at Point Lookout until released 29 June 1865, Oath showed him to be 5'10 1/2" tall with light hair and blue eyes.

McCormack, Henry Johnson. Enlisted for 12 months as a pvt. in 1st Confederate Infantry 18 March 1861, discharged in March 1862, reenlisted 6 May 1862 in Phillips Legion as 2nd lt., accidentally wounded (foot amputated) near Pocataligo SC 31 May 1862, detailed to serve as enrolling officer in Bartow County GA (and later in Macon GA), promoted 1st lt. 17 October 1862, promoted cpt. 25 April 1863, retired 24 February 1865, b. in SC 10 February 1838, d. 17 November 1930 in Bartow County and buried at McCormick/Hawkins Cemetery at Taylorsville GA.

McGinnis, Stephen Thompson. Enlisted 6 May 1862, Marcus Greene diary indicates McGinnis was WIA at Chancellorsville, present on all rolls through war, captured 6 April 1865 at Sailor's Creek and imprisoned at Point Lookout until released 29 June 1865, Oath showed him to 5'9" tall with light hair and blue eyes, b. in 1836, nephew of Cpt. T. K. Sproull, age 15 in 1850 Cass County census, son of Hames and Leah McGinnis.

Meadows, John C. Enlisted 6 May 1862, captured 2 December 1863 at Knoxville and imprisoned at Rock Island until released 19 June 1865, Oath showed him to be 24, 5'6 1/2" tall with dark brown hair and light blue eyes, b. 24 March 1837 in SC.

Miles, Joseph A. Enlisted 6 May 1862, d. 25 August 1862 at Augusta GA from disease.

Miles, William O. Enlisted 6 May 1862, shown sick at Hospital on rolls from September 1862 through February 1863, shown hospitalized June 1863 and again in August and September 1863 with typhoid, roll dated 19 January 1864 listed him AWOL, present on rolls dated 5 October 1864 though 30 January 1865, captured 6 April 1865 at Sailor's Creek and imprisoned at Point Lookout until released 29 June 1865, his Oath showed him to be 5'9" tall with light hair and blue eyes, b. 17 May 1840.

Mize, Martin Van Buren. Enlisted 6 May 1862, present on rolls throughout war until roll dated 30 January 1865 showed him absent on furlough, no further military record but postwar pension application stated that he was unable to return to Virginia at the conclusion of his furlough due to Federal troops in the Carolinas so he joined General Wofford's State troops.

Moore, Robert. Enlisted 6 May 1862, WIA (hip) and captured 14 September 1862 at Fox's Gap MD, exchanged 17 October 1862, WIA (hand) between 6 May 1864 and 16 May 1864 per casualty list in 2 July 1864 *Richmond Enquirer*, captured 6 April 1865 at Sailor's Creek and imprisoned at Point Lookout until released 29 June 1865, Oath showed him to be 5'6" tall with dark brown hair and hazel eyes, b. 1840 in Henry County GA to John and Hannah Ewing Moore, d. Polk County GA 12 September 1908.

Mote, Drury. Enlisted 22 September 1863, roll dated 19 January 1864 listed him AWOL, rolls date October and December 1864 showed him hospitalized in Richmond VA and Macon GA suffering from chronic dysentery, present on 30 January 1865 roll, captured 6 April 1865 at Sailor's Creek and imprisoned at Point Lookout until released 29 June 1865, Oath showed him to be 5'7" tall with auburn hair and blue eyes.

Nowell, Reuben. Enlisted 4 March 1862 in Cavalry Co. B, transferred to legion Co. O 21 August 1862, present on roll dated 30 January 1865, no further military record, b. 1835 in Johnson County NC to William and Martha Earp Nowell, d. McCulloch County TX 11 March 1898.

Pace, John Theodore. Enlisted 6 May 1862, promoted 4th cpl. 26 January 1863, shown as 3rd cpl. on roll dated 19 January 1864, WIA (lung) 6 May 1864 at Wilderness, captured at home in Cobb County 11 August 1864, took Oath of Allegiance 16 August 1864 and sent north of the Ohio River, Oath showed him to be 5'6" tall with brown hair and gray eyes.

Parker, Jason E. Enlisted 6 February 1863, d. 2 November 1863, at Atlanta GA Fairground Hospital #2, no cause stated, buried in Atlanta's Oakland Cemetery Row 19 #4.

Parker, Milford C. Enlisted 6 May 1862, captured 29 November 1863 at Knoxville and imprisoned at Rock Island until released 19 June 1865, his Oath showed him to 24, 5'10" tall with black hair and hazel eyes.

Pendley, William. Enlisted 6 May 1862, present on all rolls until captured 6 April 1865 at Sailor's Creek, imprisoned at Point Lookout until released 17 June 1865, Oath showed him to be 5'11" tall with brown hair and gray eyes.

Pritchett, W. George. Enlisted 6 May 1862, listed as AWOL on roll dated 5 October 1864 and all rolls thereafter, no further record.

Randall, Henry J. Enlisted 6 May 1862, surrendered 9 April 1865 at Appomattox (listed as W. J. Randle), age 15 in 1850 Cass County census, son of Charles and Sally Randall.

Rutledge, William P. Enlisted 6 May 1862 as 4th cpl., promoted to 2nd cpl. 16 October 1862, final entry on February 1863 roll stated that he was sent to Winchester Hospital and not heard from since, d. 22 October 1862 at Winchester VA from disease and is buried at Stonewall Cemetery as W. J. Ruddleday.

Saggus, Stephen S. Enlisted 6 May 1862, shown absent sick on rolls through 19 January 1864 then detailed as a ward master at Wayside Hospital in Bristol TN, because of serious effects of variola, captured there 14 December 1864 and imprisoned at Camp Chase, sent to Point Lookout for exchange 26 March 1865 but not released until 6 June 1865.

Scott, F. Calaway. Enlisted 6 May 1862 as 1st cpl., promoted 4th sgt. 16 October 1862, captured at Gettysburg 2 July 1863, imprisoned at Fort Delaware until transferred to Point Lookout in October 1863, d. 23 December 1863 of pneumonia, buried at Point Lookout Confederate Cemetery, Scotland MD.

Scott, Samuel Hunter. Enlisted 6 May 1862, left legion in September 1863 while it was in Georgia and joined Co. A 1st GA Cavalry in the Army of Tennessee, he was carried on legion rolls for the remainder of the war as AWOL but with the notation that he had joined the 1st GA Cavalry, he became a 2nd lt., and surrendered in NC in late April 1865, paroled at Charlotte NC 3 May 1865, b. 12 March 1837 in Gwinnett County GA, d. 12 April 1910 in Travis TX and buried there in Phillips Cemetery.

Shuffield (Sheffield), Jasper. Enlisted 6 May 1862, served reliably through war until deserting near Petersburg VA 11 March 1865, took Oath of Allegiance and sent to Chicago IL.

Smith, James M. Enlisted 6 May 1862 as 4th sgt., shown as 2nd sgt. on 30 November 1862 roll, WIA (side) May 1863 at Chancellorsville per casualty list in 19 May 1863 *Atlanta Southern Confederacy*, promoted 2nd lt. 21 March 1864, promoted 1st lt. 6 December 1864, captured 6 April 1865 at Sailor's Creek and imprisoned at Johnson's Island OH until released 20 June 1865, Oath showed him to be 24, 5'4" tall with dark hair and hazel eyes.

Smith, Jasper. Enlisted 6 May 1862, d. 4 September 1862 at Richmond GH #13, one entry stated he died from mumps while another stated that the cause of death was erysipelas following typhoid.

Smith, Newton. Enlisted 6 May 1862, d. 20 November 1862 at Richmond GH #9 from colitis, buried at Richmond's Oakwood Confederate Cemetery.

Sproull, George McDuffie. Enlisted 6 May 1862, absent sick on rolls from September 1862 through February 1863, present on roll dated 19 January 1864, WIA (side) between 6 May 1864 and 16 May 1864 per casualty list in 2 July

1864 *Richmond Enquirer*, d. 9 August 1864 at Danville VA Hospital of chronic dysentery, brother of Cpt. T. K. Sproull.

Sproull, Thomas Kary. Enlisted 6 May 1862 as cpt., resigned 25 April 1863 citing failed health, later joined Co. E 10th Battalion GA State Guards 1 August 1863 as a 4th cpl. and served for six months until the unit was discharged in February 1864, brother of G. M. Sproull, uncle of S. T. McGinnis, d. 11 September 1885 at Grand Island FL and buried at Old Fort Mason Cemetery, Eustis FL.

Spurlock, Newton. Enlisted 6 May 1862, KIA 12 May 1864 at Spotsylvania.

Stidham, Benjamin F. Enlisted 6 May 1862 as 3rd cpl., promoted to 1st cpl. 16 October 1862, WIA (thigh) between 6 May 1864 and 16 May 1864 per casualty list in 2 July 1864 *Richmond Enquirer*, present on all rolls through war, deserted 18 March 1865 near Petersburg VA, no further record.

Summers, Alvan H. Enlisted 6 May 1862 as 1st sgt., voluntarily became a pvt. 16 October 1862 and became a teamster, captured 14 September 1862 at Fox's Gap MD, exchanged 6 October 1862, present on all rolls, surrendered 9 April 1865 at Appomattox (listed as A. Sommers), b. 13 July 1838 in Cobb County, d. 16 May 1910 at Clarkesville GA.

Taylor, William G. Enlisted 6 May 1862, WIA 14 September 1862 at Fox's Gap MD, promoted to 2nd sgt. 21 March 1864, present on all rolls until captured 19 October 1864 at Cedar Creek, imprisoned at Point Lookout until released 20 June 1865, Oath showed him to 6'1/4" tall with black hair and hazel eyes.

Walraven, Christopher C. Enlisted 6 May 1862, promoted 4th cpl. 16 October 1862, reduced to pvt. 25 January 1863, shown absent sick on roll dated 19 January 1864 and AWOL on all later rolls, no further military record, b. 3 April 1836 at Buckhead in DeKalb County GA to Archibald and Mary Walraven, d. from typhoid 11 May 1881 at Marietta, buried in Marietta Citizens Cemetery.

Watson, William O. Enlisted 6 May 1862, as 1st lt., KIA at Fox's Gap MD 14 September 1862.

Weesner, Benjamin F. Enlisted 6 May 1862, WIA 6 May 1864 at Wilderness, admitted to Williamsburg VA Hospital 12 June 1864 with gunshot wound left forearm, transferred to Richmond's Jackson Hospital 19 June 1864, furloughed home 13 July 1864, at Jackson Hospital in Richmond 14 October 1864 with "fibris int," returned to duty 1 November 1864, back at Jackson Hospital, Richmond 23 November 1864 for resection of arm wound, furloughed 18 December 1864, all late war rolls showed home on furlough, age 9 in 1850 Cass County census, son of John and Nancy Wesner, b. in North Carolina, d. 4 November 1909.

West, Rufus M. Enlisted 6 May 1862, KIA 14 September 1862 at Fox's Gap MD.

White, Henry H. Enlisted 3 September 1861 in Co. F, 22nd GA Infantry, transferred to Phillips Legion in exchange for William H. Henderson in early 1863, first appeared in legion records in March 1863, shown as absent sick on roll dated 19 January 1864 and listed AWOL on all later rolls, no further record.

White, Thomas J. Enlisted 6 May 1862, WIA (left leg disabled) and captured 29 November 1863 at Knoxville, at Louisville KY until transferred to Camp Chase OH 22 October 1864, sent to New Orleans for release 2 May 1865, b. 14 December 1838.

Williams, Jesse N. Enlisted 6 May 1862, d. 2 January 1863 at Richmond GH #14 of pneumonia, death claim filed by widow Sarah Williams.

Wilson, William Nicholas. Enlisted 6 May 1862, transferred to Co. I 7th GA Infantry 11 August 1862, surrendered 9 April 1865 at Appomattox.

Womack, John W. Enlisted 6 May 1862, listed sick on rolls through February 1863, detailed as a hospital nurse/guard in Richmond 8 March 1863, still detailed as of September 1863, shown present on legion rolls dated 19 January 1864 through 30 January 1865, no further military record but a pension application filed in AL indicates that he survived the war, b. in Cartersville GA in 1829, d. Etowah County AL 3 April 1911, son of Thomas J. and Esther Womack, brother of Matthew Womack.

Womack, Matthew Marion. Enlisted 6 May 1862, captured 2 July 1863 at Gettysburg and imprisoned at Point Lookout until exchanged in February 1865, listed on a roll for Camp Lee (a prisoner exchange camp near Richmond) 21 February 1865, no further military record, b. 26 January 1839 in Cass County to Thomas J. and Esther Womack, brother of John Womack, d. 16 May 1919, buried Pleasant Hope Cemetery in Floyd County.

Young, John. Enlisted 6 May 1862, captured 29 November 1863 at Knoxville and imprisoned at Rock Island, d. 6 February 1864 of smallpox, buried at Rock Island Cemetery grave #390.

APPENDIX A

THE MACON LIGHT ARTILLERY

The Legion Orphan

Thomas Leroy Napier, Jr., must have been proud of his creation: a fully-equipped, intensively trained and well staffed artillery battery. At first designated Napier's Artillery in honor of its financial benefactor, Leroy Napier, Sr., Thomas Leroy must have regarded the new unit as his proudest possession. Scion of a prominent Macon family and an 1858 graduate of West Point, his community must have felt certain that no better officer could have been found to organize and lead what came to be known later as The Macon Light Artillery. The Napier family's contribution to Thomas Leroy Napier, Jr.'s (called "Lee" by friends and family members) unit and to the Confederacy itself was well documented in the 24 January 1924 *Confederate Veteran*:

> Leroy Napier's name occupies a very prominent place in Confederate history. It was he who equipped the Napier Artillery, the cannons costing in excess of $60,000.00. When the cause of the Confederacy was facing a very severe crisis. Leroy Napier, Sr., father of the famous commander, sold his entire cotton holdings in Liverpool and diverted the proceeds to the cause of State Rights. To him belongs the honor of buying the first Confederate bond to finance the war.[1]

Thomas Leroy Napier, Jr., and Lt. Henry N. Ells, completed the equipping and organization of the battery by 31 October 1861. Ells wrote to the secretary of war, Judah Benjamin, on this date to discuss plans for the unit.

> We have engaged a full battery for field service, consisting of four (4) brass sixpounders, two (2) brass twelve pounder Howitzers, six (6) caissons, battery wagon and forge, all complete for nine thousand and five hundred dollars, deliverable at New Orleans, Louisiana when battery is ready for shipment, say 19th proximo. This being the time agreed for its full and final completion. We have also furnished the company with tents and uniforms-for all of which (including battery, etc.) are of course expected to be reimbursed by the government after being accepted into service.[2]

The Napier Artillery was in Georgia state service by 29 January 1862 when Napier, his second-in-command, Henry N. Ells and their artillery soldiers departed for Savannah. After the Napier Artillery got underway one of the artillerymen

---

[1] "H. Napier to Blackman," *Confederate Veteran* 32/1 (3 July 1904): 5.
[2] H. Ells to J. Benjamin, secretary of war, CSA. October 1861.

discovered that a Negro woman disguised as a soldier had accompanied them. She found herself in jail in Augusta later.[3] In Savannah the Napier Artillery served under Brigadier General William Henry Talbot Walker's division, Brigadier General States Rights Gist's brigade. They were assigned at the behest of Governor Joseph Emerson Brown to defend the Georgia coast from an expected Yankee invasion. The *Savannah Daily Morning News* of 26 February 1862 read:

> The NAPIER ARTILLERY OF MACON-This fine Artillery Corps are in camp about two miles from the city, on the farm of Dr. Cuyler [Dr. William H. Cuyler, whose farm is also known as Camp Shorter]. They are attached to General Walker's brigade and number ninety-six men, rank and file. They are commanded by Capt. Leroy Napier, Jr., of Macon, a graduate of West Point, an old Army Officer. As an officer, it is said he has few equals. Since the arrival of the Corps, Lieut. Findlay has been appointed on Gen Harrison's staff with the rank of cpt., (James N. Findley, later Pvt. Findley of the Macon Light Artillery) and Lieut. B. H. Napier (Briggs Hopson Napier, younger brother of Thomas Leroy Napier, Jr.) has been elected in his place … this company had 82 horses and 8 mules. When the Corps passed through our city last Thursday, Generals Jackson and Harrison both complimented them on the appearance of their pieces and the fine condition of their horses (General Jackson was Brigadier General Henry Rootes Jackson, a Mexican War veteran, and Brigadier General George Paul Harrison, Sr., of the Georgia militia.[4]

The cannons for Napier's Artillery had been shipped by train to Camp Shorter so the Macon artillerymen were probably assigned to that location to shore up local defenses since they were fully armed and equipped on arrival.

Cpt. Napier's duties included assignments to the Savannah River batteries on 13 November 1862 as well as acting inspector general under Maj. General John Horace Forney and Maj. General Dabney Herndon Maury later in 1862 in Mobile, Alabama.

Surviving documentation confirms the fact that plans to attach Napier's Artillery to the Phillips Legion were well established although the exact order of events is far from clear. The political maneuvering between Governor Joseph E. Brown and President Jefferson Davis was joined by William Monroe Phillips. Phillips and Brown had tried to assign at least one battery from the artillery units that had trained at Camp McDonald in July of 1861 to the Phillips Legion. President Davis disapproved of these plans. Internecine squabbling among these leaders continued. Phillips must have been determined to get the same treatment that his sister unit, Cobb's Legion, received; i.e., the logic being that since Cobb's Legion had an artillery battery assigned (The Troup Artillery) then Phillips Legion should have

---

[3] M. McInvale, "Macon, Georgia: The War Years, 1861–1865" (MA thesis, Florida State University, 1973) 54.

[4] *The Daily Morning News*, 26 February 1862, p. 2, col. 2.

one. Since Davis had disapproved of any assignment of artillery from Camp McDonald to the Phillips Legion, it is likely that Brown and Phillips began maneuvering to have the available Napier's Artillery attached to Phillips during the spring of 1862. By the time the Phillips Legion arrived in Richmond in late July, it appears that Davis and the War Department had gotten wind of these behind-the-scene activities and brought a halt to it all by keeping the Napier Artillery independent from any larger unit.[5]

As discussed in chapter 1, Brown had intended that Phillips be granted the rank of Brigadier General and commander of the Fourth State Brigade when it was accepted into Confederate Service. Davis denied Phillips's promotion, and the Fourth State Brigade was dismantled by August 1861, at the close of training at Camp McDonald in Marietta, Georgia. One can only speculate about the course of this bickering but the result is clear: the Napier Artillery (later The Macon Light Artillery) was assigned to the Phillips Legion only on paper. Success in this effort by Brown and Phillips would have made the Phillips Legion a true legion in that it would have been composed of three sub-units: an infantry battalion, a cavalry battalion, and an artillery battalion or battery. (The precursor for future combined arms units.) In the end, all of this was an exercise in futility: Army of Northern Virginia Special Order #104 eventually separated the infantry and cavalry battalions but these two sub-units of the Phillips Legion kept the name designation even though each was assigned to brigades within the Army of Northern Virginia's infantry and cavalry corps.

The artillery battalion that trained at Camp McDonald in 1861 under the command of Lt. Col. Marcellus A. Stovall met a similar fate. The Cherokee Light Artillery under Cpt. James G. Yeiser became Co. A of the 3rd Georgia Infantry Battalion. This unit was then converted to artillery in May 1863 and became Van Den Corput's battery of the Army of Tennessee. Wilson's battery under Cpt. R. E. Wilson became Co. B of the 3rd Georgia Infantry Battalion. In May 1863, the 3rd Battalion was combined with the 9th Battalion to form the 37th Georgia Infantry Regiment of the Army of Tennessee. The County Line Volunteers that comprised the Lewis and Phillips Guards under Cpt. M. Kendrick became Co. C of the 3rd Georgia Infantry Battalion. In May 1863, they became Co. B of the 4th Georgia Sharpshooter Battalion of the Army of Tennessee. The Barnesville Blues under Cpt. G. M. McDowell became Co. D of the 3rd Georgia Infantry Battalion. In May 1863 they became Co. B of the 4th Sharpshooter Battalion of the Army of Tennessee. No artillery soldiers from Bibb or surrounding counties were included in any of these units.[6]

Napier's unit returned to Macon in early 1862 for reorganization. Most of the re-enlistments plus new enlistments took place by 3 May 1862. By 20 May 1862,

---

[5] See chapter 2 of part 1 of the Phillips Legion infantry battalion and endnotes for chapter 2.

[6] Ibid.

the battery had been mustered into Confederate service. The artillerymen trained intensively, recruited and prepared to elect officers. Charles Atwater Ells, brother of Cpt. Henry N. Ells, noted in his diary dated Monday, 12 March 1862, that the Napier Battery was "fast filling up." The intensive training would have made loading and firing second nature. At the command to load, one soldier would have stepped to the muzzle with a stick-like tool called a rammer, held it parallel to the bore of the cannon. Another soldier would have been handed a round of ammunition by two other soldiers who would have inserted the round into the bore, then the soldier with the rammer would have rammed it home. A crew member positioned by the vent in back would have covered the vent with his thumb which would have been covered by a leather thumbstall. Next, the gunner would have sighted the piece by operating the elevating screw to set the range, and directed his partner with the handspike in setting the aim. After sighting and loading, the command to ready the cannons would have been shouted, the charge would have been pricked by a vent pick, the lanyard would have been hooked to a friction primer that was then inserted into the vent. At the command to fire the lanyard would have been pulled and the cannon discharged, forcing it to roll backward. The men would then have pushed the cannon back into position, sponged the bore to rid the piece of hot residue and the process started all over again. This well-trained crew could have fired two to three rounds a minute...assuming that the enemy was not firing on the cannoneers.[7]

The Macon artillerists organized elections for officer positions. They elected four of their men to fill these positions.

Charles A. Ells described the electioneering:

Clear fine day-stayed in store all day-attended the Election of Officers at the Academy of the Macon Light Artillery which was changed from Napier [artillery]

H. N. Ells was elected cpt.—49 [votes]
W. H. Anderson 1st lt. —49
Troutman 2nd lt. —49
Slating [Slaten] 3rd lt. —48.[8]

Apparently Thomas Leroy Napier had decided to pursue his career in the Infantry—perhaps to find greater opportunities for career advancement and glory in a more elite unit. His second-in-command, Lt. Henry N. Ells, was now the commander of the re-named Macon Light Artillery.

By Wednesday, 21 April 1862, the Phillips Legion had been stationed in South Carolina so that the infantry and cavalrymen could recover from their grueling experience in the western Virginia campaign. C. A. Ells' diary entry of Wednesday, 21 April 1862, stated that "Henry gone to S.C. to see General Phillips."[9] Cpt. Henry

---

[7] M. Switlik *The More Complete Cannoneer*, 3rd ed. (Mowroe MI: Museum & Collector Specialties Company, 1990) 1–63.

[8] C. Ells Diary, 15 May 1862, 18.

[9] Ibid. 19.

Ells was probably discussing plans to attach the Macon Light Artillery to the Phillips
Legion. A Confederate form 19, Subsistence Statement for $1,796.00 dated 3 May
1862 confirmed these plans:

> That my company was accepted by the Secretary of War and allowed to fill
> up at Macon, GA and towards the last of May attached to Phillips Legion
> stationed on coast of South Carolina in General Drayton's brigade there
> being at the time no QM or Commissary Dept. at Macon I had instructions
> to purchase all my supplies and Col. Phillips said he would have it
> refunded. I have never been able to get with my command and [they] are
> now stationed near Richmond.[10]

The preponderance of evidence suggests that the Macon Light Artillery was
caught in the crossfire and confusion among Confederate and state authorities but
was clearly intended to complete the "true Legion" organization by assignment to
the Phillips Legion. The Macon boys did not return to Savannah after
reorganization, recruiting and refitting, but went directly to Richmond from Macon
shortly after the Legion headed north to Richmond from South Carolina on 19 July
1862.

Perhaps Phillips and Brown were of the "short war" mentality. By the time
General Robert E. Lee issued Army of Northern Virginia Special Order #104,
officially separating the infantry and cavalry battalions in early 1863, all three sub-
units were independent but still thought of themselves as members of the same
military family. They all contributed their firepower and soldierly skills to the needs
of the Confederacy in the eastern theater.

By mid-May 1862, the Macon Light Artillery, now under the command of Cpt.
Henry N. Ells, was fully equipped and prepared for combat. In a letter from Ells to
the Honorable A. W. Randolph dated 12 May 1862, Ells assured Randolph of his
combat preparedness.[11] Unfortunately, Ells, unable to withstand the rigors of camp
life and in failing health, resigned on 25 May 1862. He was succeeded by Cpt.
Charles William Slaten. (From this point on, the Macon Light Artillery appears in
the Official Records as Ells Battery/Artillery or Slaten's Battery/Artillery.) Slaten
remained in command until the end of the war.[12]

The Macon Light Artillery was on its way to war. They arrived in Augusta,
Georgia on 29 July for an overnight stay before reloading the train and proceeding to
Columbia, South Carolina. Surrounded by an adoring crowd the artillerymen were
cheered by all:

> At every station, at every crossing along the road, at every farm, cheering
> was heard and handkerchiefs seen waving. A perfect hail of peaches and
> apples was showered upon us, and not infrequently did this acceptable fruit,

---

[10] H. Ells, Confederate States to H. N. Ells, Capt.-Macon Light Artillery (form 19), H. N.
Ells, subsistence statement, 3 May 1862.

[11] H. Ells to Honorable A. W. Randolph, 12 May 1862.

[12] H. Ells to Adjutant General C. S. Cooper, 25 May 1862.

kindly tossed from the hand of some gentle maid, miss its destined aim and fall less harmlessly than was the intention of the fair donor. One companion near me received a blow upon his cranium that detracted his attention for the day from catching at apples, and another, while holding out his hands with eager expectancy, had his left eye so besmeared and completely plastered over, as never again to catch at peaches.[13]

They arrived in Columbia the next day, stayed six days, and went on to Charlotte, North Carolina, where, again, they were royally treated. After five days in Charlotte, they finally arrived in Richmond on 11 August. "Rebther" (Sgt. Carnes), writing to the *Macon Daily Telegraph*, noted in the same issue: "Col. Phillips' Legion, to which we are attached, started for Stonewall (Jackson at Fredericksburg) this morning. We will follow as soon as our horses arrive."[14]

They had left for Richmond on 28 July 1862. While in Richmond they exchanged their obsolete four 6-pound brass and two 12-pound brass guns for two 20-pound and two 30-pound Parrott rifled guns. On the following day, the Macon Light Artillery arrived near Richmond. Their two thirty-pound Parrotts, often referred to as "Long Toms" would turn out to be fragile instruments.[15]

The puppy, chasing the mother dog, never quite reached her. By 2 September 1862, the Macon artillerymen, located at camps near Richmond, experienced but one exciting event: minor surgery to remove a musket ball from the hand of one of the Macon soldiers. This work was done by Dr. Fleming G. Castlen, the unit surgeon, after one of the men accidentally discharged his musket and the ball lodged in his hand.[16]

By 1 October 1862, their camps had been removed to Randolph's Grove then to an undesignated camp near Richmond by 22 October, where a small party of the Macon boys took the time to visit the battleground at Malvern Hill where they received a firsthand look at the war's horrors. They were assigned to Lt. Col. C.E. Lightfoot at battalion level at this time. Fresh graves with rude headboards, pine trees drilled with bullets. cannonballs and grapeshot must have had a sobering effect on the Macon Cannoneers.[17]

The fat was in the fire. On 28 November 1862 late in the evening, Cpt. Ells was ordered by General Robert E. Lee at Fredericksburg, to send his two thirty-pound rifled Parrott Long Toms, mounted upon field carriages and drawn by twelve horses each and four ammunition wagons drawn by six horses each, with two lts. and fifty men. This group departed the next morning. some by train, others on horseback, arriving shortly at Fredericksburg.

---

[13] *Macon Daily Telegraph*, 19 August 1862, 2.

[14] Ibid.

[15] *Macon Daily Telegraph*, 2 September 1862, 2.

[16] Ibid., 22 October 1862, 2.

[17] Ibid.

12–13 December 1862 found the Macon boys camped near Fredericksburg, anticipating a fight around the city. Pits had been constructed for the Long Toms near the Howison house group under Col. Cabell and his assistant, Maj. S. P. Hamilton. [18] The official records are revealing: "What the probabilities of a fight around Fredericksburg are, it is impossible to conjecture successfully. Yet the wall may be opened at any moment. The Yankees can be plainly seen on the opposite side of the river, making haste with their formidable batteries, under the cover of which they calculate to cross the Troops [*sic*]."[19]

They found their army on the south bank and the Yanks on the north of the Rappahannock River, both armies watching each other's movements. On the night of the tenth of December, the Yankees tried to cross the river to get into Fredericksburg but were thrown back by Confederate defenders. Early the following day the Macon gunners harnessed their horses, cooked breakfast and waited for orders. By 7 A.M. they were instructed to take up a position on a hill about one mile from the city and six miles from their camp. From their new position they could see the Yankee encampments and pontoon bridges, and had panoramic view of Fredericksburg. In the portion of the Official Records describing the Battle of Fredericksburg, the Macon Light Artillery appears as Ells' Georgia Battery, one of two miscellaneous batteries, under the artillery chief, Capt. J. B. Brockenbrough.[20]

By the time they were settled into their positions the Yankees were pouring fire into the city in order to dislodge Brigadier General William Barksdale's Mississippians. Barksdale's troops were fired on throughout the day, finally falling back out of town permitting the Yankees to cross the river. Lee intended to lure them into attacking him in his well-fortified position south of the town. Col. Henry Coalter Cabell, Chief of Artillery for Maj. General McLaws's division described the location of the Macon Light Artillery:

> The Telegraph road passes on the right of the hill [Marye's Hill] and
> then turns almost directly at right angles at the foot and in front of the
> hill. The railroad cut and embankment would have enabled the enemy
> to come in almost perfect security within a short distance of the right
> flank of our troops drawn up behind the stone wall on the Telegraph
> road and by a rabid charge to have our troops at the most serious
> disadvantage. Their advance could not have been effectively checked
> by the artillery of Marye's Hill, owing to the conformation of the
> ground. It is due to the skillful officers and cannoneers to say that their
> cool, well-directed, and most efficient fire not only aided materially in
> repulsing the direct attack on Marye's Hill, but in preventing the right
> flank of this position being turned by the enemy. Forty-eight guns
> were placed under my charge during the engagement. Captain Read's

---

[18] Ibid.

[19] *OR*, vol. 30, chap. 33. p. 544, 1888.

[20] *OR*, vol. 30, chap. 33, p. 586, 1888.

battery [three guns] occupied the position immediately to the right of the Telegraph Road. Next to his battery one of the 30–pounder guns [Richmond manufactory] was placed. It was replaced by a Whitworth gun of Captain Lane's battery. Next on the right and on the hill back of Howison's house, and in the following order were placed two 6–pounder smooth bore guns and two 10–pounder Parrotts under the command of Cpt. Macon, of the Richmond [Fayett] Artillery. The smooth-bore guns fired only round shot. Next three pieces of (Parrotts) of Capt. R. L. Cooper's battery [three "Parrott" cannons]. This battery was withdrawn to another position and replaced by three pieces (one "Parrott" and two 3–inch rifles) of Captain [J. R.] Branch's battery. Next two Parrotts of Captain Carleton's battery and one 30–pounder Parrott [Richmond manufactory]. This gun was commanded by Lt. W. F. Anderson of Cpt. Ells' battery. Both of the Richmond guns did good service, but exploded during the engagement.[21]

By 11 A.M. on 12 December, the northern enemy had opened up his batteries directly at the Macon boys who responded with cannonading of their own. The cannons on both sides blasted away at each other throughout the day resulting in only a few casualties. Skirmishing continued until Saturday, 13 December, when the Federals began a terrific cannonading, shaking the earth:

Onward moved the columns of the enemy against our right, their pace considerably accelerated by out shell…the lead of their column has encountered Stonewall Jackson and Stewart's forces…our right gives way…our men rally-they charge…the enemy gives way, Stuart's cavalry charge, and with a yell, penetrate their lines. They wheel their steeds and charge again- Fresh troops come to the assistance of the enemy. Their line of battle is again formed and the fight becomes general again on the right…onward they move at a brisk pace. They near the railroad—they descend into the cut. Now it is our time. Bang! A thirty pound shell has torn through their midst, dealing death and destruction. Another and another is sent on its mission of death to the same place.[22]

General Lee, standing on the parapet of the Macon artillerymen, studying the situation with field glasses, and watching the progress of the fight, praised the Macon men, saying, "Well done. Give them another."[23]

The battle of Fredericksburg continued at the same pace throughout the day, resulting in the deaths of thousands of northern troops. On the southern side, casualties were comparatively light. The only real damage done on this fateful day to

---

[21] Ibid.

[22] *Macon Daily Telegraph*, 29 December 1862, 2.

[23] Ibid.

the Macon cannoneers was the explosion of the thirty pounder Parrotts. By the
following Monday, the enemy was in full retreat.

In a letter to Reverend J. William. Jones, Maj. N. M. Hodgkins, former
fourth sgt. and adjutant of the Macon Light Artillery, described the performance of
the Macon boys by quoting E. Porter Alexander's words:

> General E. P. Alexander says: Their advance [the Federals] exposed their
> left flank to a raking fire from the artillery of Lee's Hill [the position held
> by the Macon Light Artillery] which with good ammunition ought to have
> routed them without the aid of infantry. As it was some single shots were
> made which were even terrible to look at. Gaps were cut in their ranks
> visible at the distance of a mile and a long cut of the unfinished Orange
> Railroad was several times raked through with troops...the gun exploded
> during the afternoon at the thirty-ninth discharge, but fortunately did no
> harm, though Generals Lee, Longstreet, and others were standing very
> near it. Now, what I have to state is, this gun was one of a section of the
> Macon Light Artillery, of Macon, Georgia, referred to in General A's first
> paper wherein he says, 'Among the guns on Lee's Hill were two thirty-
> pound Parrotts, under Lieutenant Anderson, which had just been sent from
> Richmond, and which did beautiful practice until they burst, one at the
> thirty-ninth round, and the other at the fifty-fourth.[24]

From Fredericksburg, the Macon gunners under Maj. John C. Haskell, and now
equipped with four 20-pound Parrott rifles, were ordered to North Carolina. By 8
March 1863, they were bivouacked at Falling Creek, twenty-six miles fiom
Goldsborough, eight from Kinston. On the same day, they were ordered to Kinston
where just two days later, their four 20-pounder caused them no end of grief; the first
gun of their 20-pound battery smashed through a wooden bridge and had to
extracted by hand. The caused Haskill much delay as the bridge also had to be
repaired.

Haskell then organized his artillery to fire on an earthwork and gunboats at
Barrington's Ferry. Slaten's 20-pounders and their crew did their best but had little
effect. They fired at a gunboat which was almost two miles away. Although they
struck the gunboat several times, the ammunition was so poor that no actual damage
was done. Worse, after firing for an hour one of Slaten's 20-pounders exploded,
mortally wounded one man and severely wounding two others. The guns were all
withdrawn. Haskell's unit remained in position at its earlier encampment. On 15
March 1863, they moved on to Swift Creek and set up to repel and expected attack.
On the way to Swift Creek, the Macon boys discovered a cracked axle in another one
of their 20.-pounders. They decided to abandon the piece. Haskell described his
feelings about the Macon artillerymen's misfortune to his superior: "I would most

---

[24] N. Hodgkins to W. Jones in *Southern Historical Papers*, vol. 2, 1883, 138–39; *OR*, vol. 30,
chaps. 10–12, p. 567.

respectively recommend that the 20-pounders be taken from the Macon Light Artillery, as it is a good company and deserves better than to have its members wounded and killed by a defective gun." [25]

By year's end, the Macon cannoneers were located near Weldon, North Carolina where Brigadier General Matt Whitaker Ransom, in a letter dated 30 December 1863 to Maj. General George E. Pickett, was planning the formation of a new regiment of cavalry and artillery which included the attachment of the Macon Light Artillery under Cpt. Slaten. Ransom wished to shore up defenses in the local area. [26]

The fourth sgt. and uncle of the southern poet Sidney Lanier, Melville Anderson, was in poor physical condition a few weeks later. Sidney Lanier's brother Clifford A. Lanier met his Uncle Melville near Kinston:

I met Uncle Melville this morning. His battery is here, just arrived from Weldon. He is up but by no means well, has a huge sty on his eye and suffers with headache in consequence. I found him squatting around a little fire near the railroad, and would never have recognized him, had I seen him casually, without knowledge of his proximity...his tents were all hung in icicles. I brought him around to my comfortable room at Hdqrs. and talked with him some time. He is now acting as Surgeon to the battery, never did a man have such a number of titles-in the course of half an hour I heard him addressed as doctor, maj., sgt., Mell, etc. Shall go to see him this evening. [27]

Approaching spring, in March 1864, while in camp near Franklin, Virginia, the Macon Light Artillery was involved in a fight with the Yankees that included the execution of a Negro soldier. In an article in the *Macon Daily Telegraph*, "Rebther" stated:

We have just returned from the neighborhood of Norfolk, where our forces met and repulsed a Yankee force, consisting of Negro troops commanded by white officers. You have been informed by telegraph of the success of our expedition into the enemy's lines but as a short account of the incidents connected with the fight, etc., may prove interesting to the friends of the company, I propose to give a description of this our first encounter with the Negro soldiers of the Yankee army. We marched from Weldon ten days ago-come to Franklin where we remained four or five days, and then took up our line of march for Suffolk, Virginia. At Bethlehem Church, three miles from the city, we were met by the troops of Brig. M. W. Ransom, who commanded the expedition, and preparations were commenced for dislodging the enemy from their camps in the rear of Suffolk, bordering the

---

[25] *OR*, vol. 17, ch. 30, 1887, p. 191.

[26] *OR*, vol. 39, ch. 40, p. 895.

[27] C. Anderson and A. Starke, *Centennial Edition, Sidney Lanier Letters, 1878–1881*, (Johns Hopkins Press, 1945) 134.

river. General Ransom...advanced down the road for the purpose of reconnoitering.[28]

All of the artillery, including Slaten's battery, entered the city, and fired en masse at the Federal enemy, "charging them eight different times." The Federal forces were defeated, losing not only the fight but much of their guns and provisions. A black cavalry soldier was captured after the fighting ended:

> Some of our troops, while scouring the field beyond the town where the greatest slaughter was committed, chanced upon a Negro skulking in the grass, armed with saber, pistols and a carbine. He did not ask for quarter, nor did he offer resistance, although opposed by only one man...but, rising upon his feet and casting a woeful look upon his antagonist, he placed both hands on the back of his head, leaned forward and received a pistol shot from his enemy, who did not fire until the muzzle of his weapon touched the Negro's head-deluded Negro, he felt he deserved his fate and dared not beg for mercy.[29]

During February and March of 1864, the Macon men had the honor of serving with the Washington Light Artillery of New Orleans during the skirmishing at New Bern, North Carolina.[30] The Macon cannoneers provided some of the artillery support for this operation which resulted in the capture and burning of the U. S. gunboat *Underwriter*, with four guns, ninety men and officers, with a minimal Confederate loss of twenty killed and wounded and four missing. (The Official Records have differing accounts for both sides.) On 14 March 1864, Pvt. J. D. Chadwick of the Macon Light Artillery, was severely wounded requiring amputation of his leg below the knee.[31]

The next maj. engagement for the Macon gunners was at Drewry's Bluff in Virginia in late May of 1864. Drewry's bluff was a series of fortifications on the south side of the James River. Early on the morning of 16 May 1864, the Confederate artillery, including the Macon cannoneers and the Washington Light Artillery, opened fire on the Yankee defenders while the Confederate attackers under General Hoke jumped over the works and charged the enemy. At the same time, Confederate Maj. General Robert Ransom's infantry had advanced onto the James River and struck the enemy's right. A company of the Washington Light Artillery under Cpt. Owen then engaged a heavy battery of enemy artillery in front of them and directly on the river road turnpike. Yankee guns were destroyed and some captured. Both Cpt. Owen and his Lt. Galbraith, were wounded and some captured. Slaten's battery was sent to relieve Cpt. Owen, and Slaten himself was severely wounded while

---

[28] *Macon Daily Telegraph*, 29 December 1862, 1.

[29] Ibid.

[30] E. Young, J. Gholson, C. Hargrave, *History of Macon. Georgia*, (Lyon: Marshall & Brooks, 1950) 249; *OR*, vol. 33, ch. 45, 1890, pp. 59–60.

[31] Anonymous, "Role of the Macon Light Artillery," 19 August 1940, p. 7, Georgia Department of Archives and History, Morrow GA.

getting into position. With this fighting the battle ended and the Confederate units proceeded toward Petersburg on the morning of 17 May 1864.[32]

18 June 1864 was a bad day for the Macon Light Artillery gunners. They had established themselves with skill in a position to support the infantry in the Petersburg area when Federal troops overran the battery. The Macon boys lost four 12–pounder Napoleons. A soldier from the Macon Light Artillery remarked: "The men of this battery fought with unsurpassed bravery and only abandoned their guns after losing 21 horses, which rendered the saving of their guns simply an impossibility."[33] Also, another source stated: "In the fight at Petersburg, seven men (from the Macon Light Artillery) were captured and six wounded with one gun; 200 rounds and fired from one gun in five hours."[34]

The Macon Light Artillery played a supportive role in the struggles at Bermuda Hundred where Yankee General Benjamin "Beast" Butler had been bottled up and at the Battle of the Crater at Petersburg (30 July 1864). After final preparation of the mine, General Burnside's staff and superiors fumbled around trying to decide who would lead the assault after the explosion. For political reasons Grant had decided not to allow black troops in the van but ordered them in later. William Miller Owen of the Washington Light Artillery of New Orleans recounted one of the major events: "It appears the explosion occurred on General Bushrod Johnson's front, blowing up Pegram's battery of four guns, and the Eighteenth South Carolina regiment. An assaulting column then advanced, with the Negro troops in front and occupied our lines; thousands crowded into the crater formed by the explosion, and lost all organization." [35]

The battle see-sawed back and forth in the vicinity of the crater. The Official Records described the contributions of the Macon boys under the command of Lt. Col. Edgar F. Moseley at battalion level:

> The assailing force of the enemy, consisting of the Ninth and parts of two other Army corps, was directed upon the breach of Pegram's salient and was held in check by little more than three regiments of Elliot's, two regiments of Ransom's and two regiments of Wise's brigades, with the efficient aid of artillery, especially of Wright's battery and four mortars, under Captain Lamkin, on the Jerusalem plank road. The enemy also made considerable demonstration in front of Wise's brigade, and appeared in front of their works occupied by Ransom's brigade. It came forward in irregular order and took shelter at the foot of a steep hill which descends to Taylor's Creek, in front of that portion of our line. This force was engaged without any important results by Ransom's brigade and the right Howitzer

---

[32] W. Owen, *In Camp with the Washington Artillery of New Orleans* (Baton Rouge: Louisiana State University Press, 1885) 316; Slaten is shown to be on furlough at this time.

[33] McInvale, "Macon, Georgia: The War Years, 1861–1865," 60.

[34] Young, Gholson, and Hargrave, *History of Macon, Georgia*, 249.

[35] W. Owen, *In Camp with the Washington Artillery of New Orleans*, 342.

of Slaten's battery. Our whole line, from the front of Colquitt's to the left of Gracie's brigade, suffered from artillery fire.[36]

After the Battle of the Crater, the Macon cannoneers settled down into the siege of Petersburg. Apparently the Napoleons they had lost earlier had been replaced or recovered. As events unfolded, two of them were surrendered at Appomattox and two destroyed near Lynchburg, Virginia.

One hundred and four officers and enlisted troops left for Virginia from Macon on 20 July 1862. This figure expanded to a total of 190. Two officers surrendered at Appomattox: Cpt. Charles William Slaten and 1st Lt. H. M. Varner. 1st Lt. W. F. Anderson had resigned earlier on 3 April 1863, preferring to serve in the ranks.[37] 1st Lt. H. A. Troutman was last shown on a roll for 8 August 1862 and disappeared from all records by October 1863. 1st Lt. Marion Folds was listed as under arrest on the November/December 1864 rolls and absent without leave by 12 February 1865. F. G. Castlen was shown as the unit surgeon. He enlisted as a private and was appointed surgeon. In later records he appears as surgeon for the Third Georgia Reserves and at Andersonville. Sgt. Maj. J. W. Weddon was elected 2nd lt. on 24 July 1863 and last appears on a roll for January/February 1865.[38] (See table for full disposition of all Macon Light Artillery soldiers at the end of this appendix.)

The Macon Light Artillery took part in over thirty engagements and demonstrations under four battalion commanders: Maj. Charles E. Lightfoot, Maj. John C. Haskell; Maj. Edgar F. Moseley and Maj. Joseph G. Blount.[39]

The demise of their flawed cannons occurred at war's end when a portion of the command under Maj. Joseph G. Blount crossed overland, reached Lynchburg, destroyed their guns and disbanded.[40] This even occurred after the artillery along with the wagon train, turned off on the Jamestown Road on 6 April 1865. They were headed north just prior to the final battle of Sailor's Creek where the Phillips Legion Infantry was badly battered. The Macon Light Artillery gunners deployed on a ridge and helped General John Brown Gordon's rear guard push the Federals back.[41] The two guns with Maj. Blount's detachment then headed for Lynchburg. The remaining Macon men surrendered at Appomattox with their commander Cpt. Charles William Slaten and the battery's last two guns.

In a letter to "Dear Maggie" dated 10 April 1865, Maj. Blount described the destruction of his cannons and his sadness at the Confederacy's loss: "I would have written you a note before but have not had the heart. Before you receive this you will know all the particulars of our defeat. All the infty and a large part of the Cavl were

---

[36] OR, vol. 40, chap. 50, 1892, p. 791.

[37] W. Anderson to S. Cooper, 3 April 1862 from Richmond VA.

[38] Compiled Service Records.

[39] J. Walter, Institute for Civil War Research, Macon Light Artillery, August, 1893, rev. May, 1966, 1.

[40] C. Calkins, "Confederates on Jamestown Road" in *Thirty Six Hours before Appomatox*, n.p.

[41] Ibid.

captured. My little Artillery. We had to disable and abandon our guns and let the men take care of themselves the best they could. I escaped with the men of my Batt. I sent them all home and shall try and join Genl. Jos. Johnson if I can."[42] And what of their original leader, Thomas Leroy Napier, Jr.? He served throughout the war, was promoted to maj. and lieutenant colonel. A letter from General Bryan Morel Thomas, an 1838 West Point classmate of Napier, dated 11 March 1879, addressed to Brevet Maj. General George Washington Cullum, who was doing research for a book of biographical sketches of West Point graduates, described Thomas Leroy's death at his mother's farm in Union Springs, Alabama on 5 September 1867, in a postscript: "P. S. Entre Nous — too much whisky caused Napier's death—but don't put that in your book. B. M. T."[43]

Perhaps the real reason for Thomas Leroy Napier's death had mostly to do with financial loss, southern devastation and a broken heart. His condition may have been the modern diagnosis known as post-traumatic stress disorder. The Macon unit's benefactor and namesake, Leroy Napier, Sr., died just a few years after his son on 16 August 1870. Thomas Leroy's younger brother and companion at Savannah, Briggs Hopson Napier, died of throat cancer on 11 April 1895.[44]

Born in confusion and tried by fire, the men of the Macon Light Artillery followed the Confederate flag from their home in Macon, Georgia, to Savannah, then to North Carolina and Virginia. The closest they ever came to actually serving with their distant parent, the Phillips Legion, was at Fredericksburg in December of 1862. The rounds they fired in support of the men behind the stone wall at the foot of Marye's Heights may have helped to win the battle as well as saved lives of Legion infantrymen. The Macon gunners had done all they could do for Georgia and the Confederacy. They had given it all. Their service was finished and it was time to go home and rebuild.

---

[42] J. Blount to Dear Maggie, 10 April 1865.
[43] B. Thomas to G. Cullum, 11 March 1897 from Millidgeville GA.
[44] "Family History of Charles Culver Corbin III and Natalie Corbin."

FIELD AND STAFF ROSTER/OFFICERS AND
NON-COMMISSIONED OFFICERS

Cpt. Napier, Thomas Leroy. Resigned, transferred to 2nd Battalion, Georgia
   Infantry, Later 8th Battalion and 10th Battalion Georgia Infantry and Bibb
   County Calvary

Napier, Briggs Hopson. Elected 2nd lt., Cpt. T.L. Napier's Battery, 20 January
   1862; 2nd lt. Co. A, 66th Regiment, Georgia Infantry, 1 August 1863; cpt., 1
   November 1863, wounded Peachtree Creek, 20 July 1864, leg amputated

Ells, Henry N. Resigned for reasons of poor health

Slaten, Charles William. Promoted cpt., commanded until end of war

1st lt. Anderson, William Francis 1st lt., 3 May 1862; resigned 3 April 1863,
   preferred the ranks

Junior 1st lt. Troutman, H. A. Resigned, appointed QM

Junior 2nd lt. Folds, F. M. Elected lt.

Sgt. maj.	Weddon, J. E.
QM sgt.	Cooper, W. C. H.
First sgt.	Vamer, H. M.
Second sgt.	Vardell, H. T.
Third sgt.	Reese, George W.
Fourth sgt.	Anderson, Melville
Fifth sgt.	Cames, C. E.
Sixth sgt.	Hodgkins, N. M. Later detailed as acting adjutant at Col. Moseley's HQ
Seventh Sgt.	Gray, W. J.
First cpl.	King, Jacob
Second cpl.	Hines, Richard H.
Third cpl.	Ells, E. M.
Fourth cpl.	Shepherd, George
Fifth cpl.	Strong, E. P.
Sixth cpl.	Rutherford, E. H.
Seventh cpl.	Corbin, H. C.
Eighth cpl.	Blue, William Fletcher
Ninth cpl.	Moffitt, Alexander
Tenth cpl.	Minard, L. R.
Eleventh cpl.	Waitz, A.
Twelfth cpl.	McKinney, Michael
Surgeon	Castlen, F. G.
Secretary	Strong, F. W.
Cpt.'s Orderly	Stewart, H. J.

THE MACON LIGHT ARTILLERY

Aldrich, C. (Clarence). Enlisted at 17 on 3 May 1862 at Macon GA.

Aldrich, W. D. Enlisted on 26 November 1862 at Macon GA, d. of wounds May 1864.

Anderson, C. C. Enlisted on 11 July 1862 at Yorktown VA.

Anderson, Melville. Enlisted at 34 on 3 May 1862 at Macon GA.

Anderson, W. F. (William Francis). Enlisted at 28 on 3 May 1862 at Macon GA, resigned 10 May 1863.

Angle, (Angel) James. Enlisted at 16 on 3 May 1862 at Macon GA, POW Elmira—exchanged 1865.

Bacon, B. A. Enlisted on 17 December 1862 at Macon GA, surrendered at Appomattox 9 April 1865.

Bacon, J. R. B. Enlisted on 31 March 1864 at Laurens County GA, February 1865, AWOL since August 1864.

Baird, (Beard) F. J. Enlisted on 16 February 1863 at Macon GA, surrendered Appomattox and Albany GA.

Baird, J. P. Enlisted on 18 December 1862 at Macon GA, surrendered Appomattox.

Bankston, J. R. Enlisted on 20 September 1863 at Jackson GA.

Barnett, J. Enlisted on 16 December 1862 at Macon GA as blacksmith.

Barton, J. H. Enlisted on 30 July 1862 at Calhoun GA.

Bates, S. S. (L. S.). Enlisted at 22 on 3 May 1862 at Macon GA, February 1865, sick-absent since last muster.

Belgen, (Belyne) T. C. Enlisted on 3 May 1862 at Macon GA, paroled Farmville VA 11 April 1865.

Berryhill, A. Enlisted on 6 December 1862 at Macon GA, transferred to Wise Guards Siege Artillery June 1864.

Blue, W. F. (William Fletcher). Enlisted at 24 on 3 May 1862 at Macon GA.

Boone, A. H. (Alfred). Enlisted on 14 February 1863 at Cobb County, paroled Newton County NC, transferred from Co. A, Phillips Legion infantry battalion.

Boone, J. D. Enlisted on 16 August 1862 at Calhoun GA, paroled Farmville VA 11 April, 21 April 1865.

Bracewell, M. B. W. Enlisted on 17 December 1862 at Macon GA, surrendered Appomattox.

Brannen, J. L. Enlisted at 23 on 3 May 1862 at Macon GA.

Broadway, Robert. Enlisted on 15 May 1863, captured Petersburg, POW, Point Lookout, released June 1865.

Brooks, T. Enlisted on 17 December 1862 at Macon GA.

Bryce, J. Y. Enlisted 31 May 1864, surrendered Appomattox.

Burgamy, Elisha. Enlisted at 33 on 3 May 1862 at Macon GA, d. of smallpox in North Carolina 9 February 1863.

Burns (Burnes), J. (James). Enlisted at 16 on 3 May 1862 at Macon GA, captured Richmond Hospital, POW at Point Lookout, released.

Carnes (Caines), C, E. Enlisted at 23 on 3 May 1862 at Macon GA.

Carroll, Thomas. Enlisted at 36 on 3 May 1862 at Macon GA, captured Petersburg, POW Elmira, released 8 May 1865.

Castlen, F. G. Enlisted at 29 on 3 May 1862 at Macon GA, discharged September 1863 by order of Secretary of War, no additional information.

Clarcy, S. J. Enlisted on 15 July 1862 at Macon GA, captured Petersburg, no additional information.

Chadwick, J. D. Enlisted on 1862 at Calhoun, Geprgia, (December 1864), Sick since 20 March 1864 (wounded 15 March 1864)

Clark, S,. Enlisted on 24 December 1864 at Macon GA, in hospital with pneumonia 30 March 1864 (wounded 15 March 1864.)

Cleek, W. S. Enlisted on 1 September 1862 at Macon GA, discharged 1863, diabetes.

Cordey, William. Enlisted on 7 September 1862 at Richmond, Virginia.

Collins, J, A. Enlisted on 21 July 1862 at Macon GA, paroled Farmville, Virginia, 11 April 1865.

Collins, S. Enlisted on 20 September 1863 at Jackson GA, hospitalized sick at Richmond VA 4 April 1865, no additional information.

Cooper, W. C. H. Enlisted at 28 on 3 May 1862 at Macon GA.

Corbin, H. C. Enlisted on 3 May 1862 at Macon GA.

Corbin, Jake (asst. cook), One card 31 August 1862, 31 October 1862 (no additional information.)

Craddock, Dormick. Enlisted at 48 on 3 May 1863 at Macon GA.

Craft, C. H. Enlisted on 3 May 1862 at Macon GA, d. at Leeksville NC on 1 February 1865 (no additional information.)

Crosby, John. Enlisted on 25 July 1862 at Calhoun GA, dropped 1864, sick at Farmville.

Crow, (Crown) Abel M. Enlisted 10 August 1862 at Calhoun GA, February 1865, AWOL since 20 February 1865.

Crow, (Crown) M. S. Enlisted 30 July 1862 at Macon GA.

Daniels, T. S. (Thomas L.). Enlisted on 26 November 1862 at Macon GA, transferred to Co. B, 2nd GA Battalion 30 December 1864.

Deas, (Dease/Dees) C. Enlisted on 18 December 1862 at Macon GA.

Deas, W. B. Enlisted 26 August 1864 at Petersburg, Virginia.

Denton, M. Enlisted on 18 December 1862 at Macon GA, discharged January 1863, surgeon's certificate (no additional information.)

Dickenson, L., enlisted 14 February 1863 at Macon GA, February 1865, AWOL.

Dixon, J. K. Enlisted 15 June 1862 at Macon GA.

Dixon, P. Enlisted 15 June 1862 at Macon GA, Gunshot wound 1864, on extended furlough as of 4 April 1865.

Donahoo, B. F., Enlisted on 30 June 1862 at Calhoun GA, February 1865 AWOL.

Dunavent, W. W. (Richard). Enlisted 8 September 1862 at Richmond, Virginia, February 1865 roll states sick since 10 September 1864.

Durden, W. J. Enlisted at 23 on 3 May 1862 at Macon GA, captured Petersburg,
   POW Point Lookout, released 23 June 1865.

Eckridge, E. R. Enlisted on 1 November 1864 at Petersburg, transferred to 2nd GA
   Battalion 19 January 1865.

Edge, William. Enlisted at 28 on 3 May 1862 at Macon GA, February 1865, detailed
   to Fayetteville NC 8 February 1865.

Ellis, R. J. Enlisted at 16 on 3 May 1862 at Macon GA.

Ellis, T. J. Enlisted on 26 August 1862 at Macon GA, one card 31 August 1862, 31
   October 1862 (no additional information.)

Ellison, William. H. Enlisted at 23 on 3 May 1862 at Macon GA, captured Macon,
   paroled at Farmville.

Ells, C. W. Enlisted on 1 August 1862 at Macon GA, captured Macon 20 April 1865
   (no additional information.)

Ells, E. M. Enlisted at 21 on 3 May 1862 at Macon GA, detailed to Salisbury NC
   March 1864, paroled Salisbury NC.

Ells, H. N. Enlisted at 35 on 3 May 1862 at Macon GA, resigned May 1863, poor
   health.

Evans, W. A. Enlisted on 25 July 1862 at Macon GA, captured Petersburg, POW
   Hart's Island, released 14 June 1865.

Feeley, D. P. Enlisted on 14 July 1862 at Macon GA, deserted 2 December 1863,
   dropped from rolls 28 December 1863.

Findley, G. W. Enlisted on 25 May 1864 at Petersburg, Virginia, paroled at
   Farmville VA 11–04 April 1865.

Findley, James W. Enlisted on 11 June 1862 at Macon GA, paroled at Farmville VA
   11 April 1865.

Fleming, P. Enlisted at 37 on 3 May 1862, captured Petersburg 4 April 1865, POW
   Point Lookout, Released.

Flemming, George W., Co. F, 3rd Regiment, State Guards Cavalry.

Flynn, J. W. Enlisted on 13 December 1862 at Macon GA, February 1865 AWOL

Folds, F. M. Enlisted at 28 on 3 May 1862 at Macon GA, February 1865 AWOL.

Freeman, E. Enlisted on 1862 at Calhoun GA, February 1865 AWOL.

Gallagher, J. Q. Enlisted on 5 June 1862 at Macon GA, discharged at Goldsboro NC
   1 February 1863, Surgeon Cert. Hernia.

Gibson, Joel W. T. Enlisted on 24 September 1862 at Richmond, Virginia.

Gibson, John T. Enlisted 24 September 1862 at Richmond, Virginia.

Gray, W. J. Enlisted 3 May 1862 at Macon GA, February 1865, AWOL 5 October
   1864.

Green, H. W. Enlisted 19 September 1862 at Calhoun GA.

Green, J. R. Enlisted 1 August 1862 at Calhoun GA.

Groover, J. N. Enlisted 30 July 1862 at Calhoun GA, December 1864, sick since
   September 1862, dropped 1864.

Gunn, Andrew. Enlisted 10 July 1862 at Macon GA, d. 4 September 1862 of diarrhea.

Hancock, J. C. Enlisted at 17 on 3 May 1862 at Macon GA, d. 27 June 1862, no further information.

Harden, George (Musician). Enlisted 3 May 1862 at Macon GA, discharged by Special Order 5 June 1863, no further information.

Harge, G. Enlisted 30 July 1862 at Calhoun GA, Dropped 2 December 1864, sick since 1862.

Harrison, K. Enlisted 30 June 1862 at Calhoun GA, February 1865, AWOL since 6 February 1865.

Haynes, W. G. Enlisted 11 December 1862 at Macon GA, d. 20 December 1864 at Jackson hospital from dysentery.

Hines, James. Enlisted at 23 on 31 May 1862 at Macon GA, transferred to Maryland Line 29 April 1864 by special order.

Hines, R. H. (Richard H.). Enlisted at 21 on 3 May 1862 at Macon GA, captured Petersburg 1865, POW Point Lookout, released.

Hodgkins, N. M. Enlisted at 20 on 3 May 1862 at Macon GA, August 1864), detailed as acting adjutant at Col. Edgar Moseley's HDQ.

Holland, W. F. Enlisted at 19 on 3 May 1862 at Macon GA, d. 9 December 1862 in Richmond Hospital, pneumonia.

Holloway, M. C. Enlisted at 36 on 3 May 1862 at Macon GA, October 1865, transferred to Co. B., 2nd GA Battalion 22 August 1864.

Humphries, J. T. (James/Farrier). Enlisted at 31 on 3 May 1862 at Macon GA.

Jacoba, Julius (asst. cook). One card 31 August 1862, 31 October 1862, no additional information.

Johnston, R. A. Enlisted 28 February 1863 at Macon GA.

Judson, John C. Enlisted at 24 on 3 May 1862 at Macon GA, wounded June 1864, shell in right arm, retired 17 December 1864.

Kennedy, T. Enlisted 18 December 1862 at Macon GA, surrendered Appomattox.

Killingsworth, J. A. (H.). Enlisted at 17 on 3 May 1862 at Macon GA, captured Petersburg, POW Point Lookout, oath and released 28 June 1865.

King, Jacob. Enlisted at 25 on 3 May 1862 at Macon GA, captured Petersburg 17 June 1864, no further information.

Lamb, George W.- Enlisted at 27 on 3 May 1862 at Macon GA, d. 19 March 1863 at Wilson NC, no additional information.

Lawson, D. W. Enlisted 10 December 1862 at Macon GA, paroled Newton NC 19 April 1865.

Lawson, Hugh. Enlisted at 18 on 3 May 1862 at Macon GA.

Lawson, J. W. Enlisted 10 December 1862 at Macon GA, captured Petersburg, POW Elmira NY, d. of smallpox 13 March 1865.

Leachman (Lehman), Charles W. Enlisted at 31 on 3 May 1862 at Macon GA, appeared on Register of Refugees and Deserters, DC 12 April 1865.

Lewis, E. J. Enlisted at 22 on 3 May 1862 at Macon GA, 8 August 1862, deserted.

Lightfoot, R. J. Enlisted 1 May 1862 at Macon GA, transferred from 2nd GA Battalion, captured Richmond 3 April 1865, deserted 3 June 1865.

Lingold, R. J. Enlisted 15 July 1862 at Macon GA, wounded and d. at Petersburg 16 June 1864.

Lingold, W. J. Enlisted 16 September 1863 at Macon GA.

Lockett, S. H. Enlisted 29 May 1862 at Macon GA, 31 October 1862 one card, no further information.

Lundy, A. Enlisted 18 December 1862 at Macon GA, April 1863, no further information.

Lundy, R. A., captured Petersburg, POW, paroled March 1864, Surrender Albany 18 May 1865.

Macarthy, Bill (chief cook). 31 October 1862 one card, no further information.

Maddox, William. Enlisted 16 December 1862 at Macon GA, transferred to Co. I, 6th GA 8 August 1864.

Mapp, R. H. Enlisted 16 August 1862 at Greensboro, North Carolina, discharged for disability 16 October 1862.

Mason, W. F. Enlisted 17 December 1862 at Richmond, Virginia, 31 August 1863, Commissioned as 2nd lt., Dept. Middle FL by special order

Matthews, J. M. (blacksmith). Enlisted 1 March 1862 at Wilmington, North Carolina, detailed from 21 NC Infantry, returned to his regiment 31 March 1864.

McCracken, J. Enlisted 16 December 1862 at Macon GA.

McDonald, J. W. Enlisted at 24 on 3 May 1862 at Macon GA.

McGinty, P. A. Enlisted at 19 on 3 May 1862 at Macon GA.

McGlown (McGowan) P. Enlisted 20 June 1862 at Macon GA.

McKenna (McKinney), Michael. Enlisted at 36 on 3 May 1862 at Macon GA, captured Petersburg, POW Elmira NY, released 17 May 1865.

McKenny, J. Enlisted at 30 on 3 May 1862 at Macon GA, February 1865 AWOL, dropped as deserted 1865.

McQueen, A. Enlisted on 9 July 1864 at Petersburg, Virginia, paroled Farmville, 11 April 1865.

Menard (Mindard), L. R. Enlisted at 30 on 3 May 1862 at Macon GA, wounded at Petersburg, February 1865, absent sick since 31 October 1864.

Mixon, John. Enlisted at 24 on 3 May 1862 at Macon GA, surrendered Appomattox.

Moffett, Alex. Enlisted at 29 on 3 May 1862 at Macon GA, transferred to 23rd SC Regiment 1 March 1863.

Moran, P. Enlisted 10 January 1862 at Camp, deserted 11 November 1862.

Morton, C. G. Enlisted at 23 on 3 May 1862 at Macon GA, detailed Chalk Laurel Home Guard 20 November 1864.

Murphy, J. Enlisted 17 January 1862 at Goldsboro, North Carolina, d. 16 November 1862 at Wilson, North Carolina, sick, Haematemesa (sic.)

Murphy, T. J. Enlisted 6 June 1862 at Macon GA.

Murry (Murray), Silas. Enlisted 21 December 1862 at Grahamsville, South Carolina, captured Petersburg, POW Elmira, oath and released 19 May 1865.

Musselwhite, G. Enlisted 16 December 1862 at Macon GA.

Napier, Thomas Leroy, first commander as "Napier Artillery", see text.

Napier, Briggs Hopson, Thomas Leroy's younger brother and second in command, see text.

Norris, J. L. Enlisted at 25 at Macon GA on 3 May 1862, One card, 16 May 1862, no further information.

Norris, L. G. Enlisted 17 June 1862 at Macon GA, one card, 31 August 1862, deserted.

Olmstead, W. E. (Willis E.). Enlisted 22 July 1862 at Calhoun GA, February 1865 muster showed sick (wounded) since 17 June 1864 but later card showed oath at Chattanooga 27 September 1864.

Oppenhamer, D. Enlisted 18 August 1862 at Calhoun GA, admitted to Richmond Hospital 1862, furloughed 1862, no additional information.

Parham, (Parhoom), J. M. Enlisted 20 August 1862 at Calhoun GA, February 1865, AWOL since 23 February 1865.

Powers, E. C. (Eugene). Enlisted age 19 on 3 May 1862 at Macon GA, captured Petersburg, POW Elmira, oath and release 14 June 1865.

Pugh, D. P. Enlisted at 21 on 3 May 1862 at Macon GA, captured Petersburg, POW Hart's Island, Released 14 June 1865.

Purvis, W. H. Enlisted 6 December 1862 at Macon GA.

Reese, George W. Enlisted at 35 on 3 May 1862 at Macon GA.

Richert, F. Enlisted at 30 on 3 May 1862 at Macon GA, dropped from rolls, medical 28 December 1863.

Robertson, A. Enlisted at 25 on 3 May 1862 at Macon GA.

Rogers, A. Enlisted 16 December 1862 at Macon GA, February 1865, AWOL.

Ross, A. Enlisted at 24 on 3 May 1862 at Macon GA, transferred to Maryland Line 29 April 1864.

Ross, H. G. Enlisted 10 July 1862 at Macon GA.

Ruckert (see F. Richert), F. Transferred to the employ of Mr. S. G. Gustin 16 August 1863.

Rutherford, E. H. Enlisted at 25 on 3 May 1862 at Macon GA, February 1865 AWOL.

Rutherford, R. W. Enlisted 4 May 1864 at Augusta GA.

Sanders (Saunders), J. M. Enlisted 25 July 1862 at Macon GA, d. 23 January 1865 of wounds received 28 December 1864.

Scarborough, William, Enlisted. 17 December 1862 at Macon GA, surrendered Appomattox.

Schell (Shell, Sheer), William. Enlisted 10 July 1862 at Macon GA, captured Petersburg, POW Point Lookout, Oath and Released 19 June 1865.

Searcy, William J. Enlisted 15 July 1862 at Macon GA, captured Petersburg, POW

Point Lookout, released 4 May 1865.

Shepherd, G. Enlisted at 22 on 3 May 1862 at Macon GA, absent sick since 31 January 1865.

Shepherd, W. G. Enlisted 24 May 1862, captured at Petersburg, POW Elmira, oath and released 29 May 1865.

Siles, Alex. Enlisted 16 June 1862 at Macon GA, one card (8 August 1862) deserted.

Slaten, C. W. Enlisted at 27 on 3 May 1862 at Macon GA, surrendered Appomattox.

Slaughter, George. Enlisted 25 June 1862 at Macon GA, appeared on list of prisoners captured by the 1st brigade, 2nd cavalry division during month of April 1865, no further information.

Smith, A. Enlisted 31 December 1862 at Macon GA.

Smith, James. Enlisted 11 December 1862 at Macon GA, surrendered Appomattox.

Snipes. L. G. Enlisted at 32 on 3 May 1862 at Macon GA.

Snipes, W. W. Enlisted at 26 on 3 May 1862 at Macon GA, discharged 1862 with chronic rheumatism.

Solomon, J. L., Enlisted age 32 on 3 May 1862 at Macon GA, surrendered Appomattox.

Stapleton, E. Enlisted 24 May 1862 at Macon GA, d. 21 January 1863 of smallpox, Goldsboro NC.

Stewart, H. J. Enlisted 29 May 1862 at Macon GA, paroled at Newton NC 19 April 1865.

Strong, E. P. Enlisted at 26 on 3 May 1862 at Macon GA, no further information.

Stubbs, Joseph. Enlisted 31 October 1862, no further information.

Sutton, J. Y. Enlisted 15 December 1862 at Macon GA, d. 1865 from gunshot wound to cheek.

Swinson, T. E. Enlisted 17 December 1862 at Macon GA, d. in hospital 31 August 1863, Raleigh NC, no cause listed.

Taylor, William J. (Machinist). Enlisted at 18 on 3 May 1862 at Macon GA, February 1865, detailed to Macon.

Timmons, L. Enlisted 30 July 1862 at Calhoun GA, February 1865 AWOL since 31 January 1865.

Tripod, A. P. (bugler). Enlisted at 23 on 3 May 1862 at Macon GA, February 1865 AWOL since 22 February 1865.

Troutman, H. A. Enlisted at 30 on 3 May 1862 at Macon GA, no further information.

Vardell, H. T. Enlisted at 26 on 3 May 1862 at Macon GA, Admitted to hospital at Petersburg 8 April 1865, gunshot wound.

Varner, H. M. Enlisted at 20 on 3 May 1862 at Macon GA, surrendered Appomattox.

Varner, J. A, surrendered Appomattox (transferred from 2nd GA Battalion 1865.)

Virgin, W. H. (William). Enlisted 1 March 1863 at Macon GA, captured Salisbury 21 April 1865–POW Camp Chase, released 13 June 1865.

Waitz (Waidze), A., Enlisted at 24 on 3 May 1862 at Macon GA, killed 16 June 1864
    in front of Petersburg.
Warren, W. Enlisted 17 December 1862 at Macon GA.
Washington, L. H. Enlisted 21 July 1862 at Macon GA, February 1865 AWOL since
    6 September 1864, dropped as deserter 9 January 1865.
Weaver, W. J. Enlisted 27 May 1862 at Macon GA, February 1865 AWOL since 30
    June 1864, dropped as deserter 9 June 1865.
Weddon, J. E. Enlisted at 33 on 3 May 1862 at Macon GA, last appeared on roll for
    January-February 1865.
Westor, John (Teamster). Enlisted at 28 on 3 May 1862 at Macon GA, captured
    Richmond hospital, POW Point Lookout, released 7 July 1865.
White, Donavon B.— (No information.)
Williams, B. Enlisted on 16 December 1862 at Macon GA, captured Petersburg,
    POW Elmira, d. 7 July 1865, smallpox.
Woodard (Woodward), J. Enlisted 6 December 1862 at Macon GA.
Wynne, C. N. (A.). Enlisted at 19 on 3 May 1862 at Macon GA, captured
    Petersburg, POW Hart's Island Released 15 June 1865.
Wynne, R. C. Enlisted 9 August 1862 at Calhoun GA, February 1865, AWOL since
    3 February 1865.
Young, Thomas. One card, amnesty oath 5 October 1865.
Youngblood, J. Enlisted 26 July 1862 at Macon GA, paroled Farmville, 11 April
    1865.
Youngblood, T. K. Enlisted at 19 on 3 May 1862 at Macon GA, captured
    Petersburg, POW Point Lookout, oath and released 22 June 1865.
Note: See parentheses, final muster was on January/February 1865.

Total Enrolled and Status at End of War

Death, Disease or Accident	16
Discharged / Physical Disability	6
Desertion	9
Captured / POW	28
Promoted /Transferred Out	7
Wounded	7
AWOL	18
Killed or Died of Wounds	5
Resigned	2
Hospitalized (at least once)	7
Surrendered	15
Paroled	11
Unknown	59
Total Enlistments	190

Appendix B

Order of Battle: Phillips Legion, 10 August 1861–1 May 1865

10 August 1861–4 January 1862
Army of the Kanawha: Brigadier General John Buchanan Floyd
Phillips Legion: Col. William Monroe Phillips

Field and Staff Officers
Col. William Monroe Phillips, Commander
Maj. John Butler Willcoxon, Cavalry
Lt. Col. Seaborn Jones, Infantry
Cpt. Samuel Masters Hankins Byrd, QM
Cpt. Robert Walton, Jr., Commissary
1st Lt. James H. Lawrence, Adjutant of Legion
Reverend George Gilman Smith, Chaplain of Infantry
Doctor Levi J. Willcoxon, Surgeon of Cavalry
Doctor Iverson Lewis Harris, Asst. Surgeon of Cavalry
Doctor Alva Connel, Surgeon of Infantry

Infantry Companies—Lt. Col. Seaborn Jones, Jr.

A. Green Rifles	Cpt. Oliver P. Daniel
B. Dalton Guards	Cpt. Robert Thomas Cook
C Habersham Volunteers	Cpt. Elihu Stuart (Sandy) Barclay
D. Polk Rifles	Cpt. Henry S. Wimberly
E. Blue Ridge Rifles	Cpt. Joseph Hamilton
F. Lochrane Guards	Cpt. Jackson Barnes

Cavalry Companies—Maj. John Butler Willcoxon

G. DuBignon Cavalry (Governor's Horse Guards)	Cpt. Charles DuBignon
H. Johnson Rangers	Cpt. William Wofford Rich
I. Cherokee Dragoons	Cpt. William B. C. Puckett
K. Coweta Rangers (Physician)	Cpt. Robert Leeper Young Long

Artillery Battery—Cpt. Henry N. Ells[45]

4 January 1862–25 August 1862
Department of South Carolina, Georgia, and Eastern Florida: General Robert Edward Lee
Department of South Carolina, Georgia, and Florida: Lt. General John Clifford Pemberton
Fourth Military District: Brigadier General Thomas Fenwick Drayton
Phillips Legion: Col. William Monroe Phillips

Field and Staff Officers
Lt. Col. William Wofford Rich, Cavalry
Maj. John Butler Willcoxon, Cavalry (resigned 6 July 1862)
Cpt. William B. C. Puckett (promoted to maj. 1 September 1862), Cavalry
Lt. Col. Seaborn Jones, Infantry (resigned 6 July 1862)
Maj. Elihu (Sandy) Stuart Barclay, Infantry (promoted 6 July 1862)
Cpt. Samuel Masters Hankin Byrd, QM
Cpt. Robert Walton, Commissary
1st Lt. James H. Lawrence, Adjutant (resigned 12 June 1862)
Reverend George Gilman Smith, Chaplain
Doctor Alva Connel, Surgeon of Infantry
Doctor Isaac D. Moore, Asst. Surgeon of Infantry (effective 30 June 1862)
Doctor Iverson Lewis Harris, Asst. Surgeon of Cavalry (transferred to Holcombe Legion August 1862)

Infantry Companies—Lt. Col. Seaborn Jones (resigned 6 July 1862, replaced by Lt. Col. Robert Thomas Cook)

A. Green Rifles	Cpt. Oliver P. Daniel
B. Dalton Guards	Cpt. Robert Thomas Cook (see above)
	Cpt. Thomas Hamilton (promoted cpt. 6 July 1862)
C. Habersham Volunteers	Cpt. Elihu (Sandy) Stuart Barclay (promoted to maj. 6 July 1862; see above)
	Cpt. John S. Norris (replaced Barclay, promoted cpt. 8 July 1862)

---

[45] As noted in chapter 1, the artillery battalion/battery was never officially assigned to the Phillips Legion. There being no brigade or division organization at this phase of the conflict, the Phillips Legion (infantry and cavalry battalions) were loosely assigned as one discrete component of the Army of the Kanawhla under Brigadier John Buchanan Floyd.

D. Polk Rifles	Cpt. Henry S. Wimberly
E. Blue Ridge Rifles	Cpt. Joseph Hamilton
F. Lochrane Guards	Cpt. Jackson Barnes

Cavalry Companies, Maj. John Butler Willcoxon (resigned 6 July 1862, replace by Capt. William Wofford Rich)

A. DuBignon Cavalry	Cpt. Charles DuBignon (resigned 9 August 1862)
(Governor's Horse Guards)	Cpt. Charles Nichols (replaced DuBignon)
B. Johnson Rangers	Cpt. William Wofford Rich (promoted to lt. col. 6 July 1862) 1st Lt. John Fielding Milhollin (promoted to cpt. 26 September 1862; replaced Rich)
C. Cherokee Dragoons	Cpt. William B. C. Puckett (promoted to maj. 1 September 1862) Cpt. Eli C. Hardin (Replaced Puckett)
D. Coweta Rangers (Physician before war)	Cpt. Robert Leeper Young Long

Three companies of infantry and two of cavalry were added to the Phillips Legion in spring 1862:

Infantry

L. Blackwell Volunteers mustered in 15 March 1862	Cpt. James M. Johnson
M. Denmead Volunteers mustered in 28 April 1862	Cpt. James F. McClesky
O. Marietta Guards mustered in 16 May 1862	Cpt. Thomas K. Sproull

Cavalry

| N. Bibb Cavalry mustered in 12 May 1862 | Cpt. Samuel S. Dunlap |
| P. (Unknown) mustered in 16 May 1862 | Cpt. Wesley W. Thomas |

25 August 1862–1 September 1862, Second Manassas (Second Bull Run)

Army of Northern Virginia: General Robert E. Lee
Right Wing: Lt. General James Longstreet
Infantry Division: Maj. General David Rumph Jones
Infantry Brigade: Brigadier General Thomas Fenwick Drayton
Phillips Legion: Col. William Monroe Phillips (absent sick)

Field and Staff Officers
Lt. Col. Robert Thomas Cook, Infantry
Maj. Elihu S. Barclay, Infantry
Cpt. Samuel Samuel Masters Hankin Byrd, QM
Cpt. Robert Walton, Commissary
Reverend George Gilman Smith, Chaplain of Infantry
Doctor Alva Connel, Surgeon
Doctor Isaac D. Moore, Asst. Surgeon

Infantry Companies: Lt. Col. Robert Thomas Cook

A. Green Rifles	Cpt. Oliver P. Daniel
B. Dalton Guards	Cpt. Thomas Hamilton
C. Habersham Volunteers	Cpt. John S. Norris
D. Polk Rifles	Cpt. Henry S. Wimberly
E. Blue Ridge Rifles	Cpt. Joseph Hamilton
F. Lochrane Guards	Cpt. Jackson Barnes
L. Blackwell Volunteers	Cpt. James M. Johnson
M. Denmead Volunteers	Cpt. James F. McCleskey
O. Marietta Guards	Cpt. Thomas K. Sproull

Cavalry Companies: Lt. Col. William Wofford Rich

A. DuBignon Cavalry (Governor's Horse Guards)	Cpt. James H. Nichols
B. Johnson Rangers	1st Lt. John Fielding Milhollin
C. Cherokee Dragoons	Cpt. Eli C. Hardin
D. Coweta Rangers	Cpt. Robert Leeper Young Long
N. Bibb Cavalry	Cpt. Samuel S. Dunlap
P. (Name Unknown)	Cpt. Wesley W. Thomas

The cavalry battalion was officially assigned to Maj. General James Ewell Brown Stuart at this time. They were engaged in scouting/reconnaissance/training activities and were not engaged at Second Manassas. The Phillips Legion's cavalry battalion would be officially detached from the infantry battalion and assigned to the Army of Northern Virginia's Cavalry Corps via Special Order #104 dated 14 April 1863.

4 September 1862–20 September 1862, South Mountain/Sharpsburg (Antietam)

Army of Northern Virginia: General Robert E. Lee
First Corps: Maj. General James Longstreet
Division: Maj. General David Rumph Jones
Brigade: Brigadier General Thomas Fenwick Drayton
Phillips Legion: Col. William Monroe Phillips (absent sick)

Field and Staff Officers
Lt. Col. Robert Thomas Cook
Maj. Elihu (Sandy) Stuart Barclay
Cpt. Samuel Masters Hankins Byrd, QM
Cpt. Robert Walton, Jr., Commissary (resigned 4 October 1862)
Reverend George Gilman Smith, Chaplain (WIA 14 September 1862, disabled, resigned 13 February 1863)
Doctor Alva Connel, Surgeon (resigned 4 October 1860)
Doctor Isaac D. Moore, Asst. Surgeon and Surgeon

Infantry Companies: Lt. Col. Robert Thomas Cook

A. Green Rifles	Cpt. Oliver P. Daniel (WIA Fox's Gap, 14 September 1862)
B. Dalton Guards	Cpt. Thomas Hamilton
C. Habersham Volunteers	Cpt. John S. Norris
D. Polk Rifles	Cpt. Henry S. Wimberly
E. Blue Ridge Rifles	Cpt. Joseph Hamilton (WIA Fox's Gap, 14 September 1862)
F. Lochrane Guards	Cpt. Jackson Barnes (resigned 12 September 1862)
L. Blackwell Volunteers	Cpt. James M. Johnson (WIA Fox's Gap, 14 September 1862)
M. Denmead Volunteers	Cpt. James Franklin McCleskey
O. Marietta Guards	Cpt. Thomas Kary Sproull

11 December 1862–13 December 1862, Fredericksburg

Army of Northern Virginia: General Robert E. Lee
First Corps: Lt. General James Longstreet
Division: Maj. General Lafayette Mclaws
Brigade: Brigadier General Thomas Reade Roots Cobb (KIA Fredericksburg 13 December 1862)
Phillips Legion: Col. William Monroe Phillips (absent sick, resigned 13 February 1863)

Field and Staff Officers
Lt. Col. Robert Thomas Cook (KIA Fredericksburg 13 December 1862)
Maj. Elihu (Sandy) Stuart Barclay (absent, wounded, promoted lt. col. 13 December
    1862)
Cpt. Samuel Masters Hankins Byrd, QM
Cpt. Andrew M. Norris, Commissary (replaced Walton 10 October 1862)
1st Lt. Frederick C. Fuller, Adjutant (replaced J. H. Lawrence November 1862)
Doctor Isaac D. Moore, Surgeon (acting surgeon replacing Connel until made
    surgeon in January 1863)

Infantry Companies: Lt. Col. Robert Thomas Cook (KIA Fredericksburg 13
December 1862)
Lt. Col. Elihu (Sandy) Stuart Barclay (replaced Cook effective 13 December 1862)
Maj. Joseph Hamilton (absent, wounded, promoted maj. 13 December 1862)

A. Green Rifles	Cpt. Oliver P. Daniel
B. Dalton Guards	Cpt. Thomas Hamilton (promoted cpt. 6 July 1862)
C. Habersham Volunteers	Cpt. John S. Norris
D. Polk Rifles	Cpt. Henry S. Wimberly (resigned because of poor health 3 October 1862)
	Cpt. John L. Dodds (promoted cpt. 4 October 1862, replaced Wimberly)
E. Blue Ridge Rifles	Cpt. Joseph Hamilton (promoted maj. 13 December 1862)
	1st Lt. Hardy Price (MWIA at Fredericksburg 13 December 1862, promoted cpt. effective 13 December 1862, but died 26 January 1863 before assuming command)
F. Lochrane Guards	Cpt. Jackson Barnes (resigned 12 September 1862 because of ill health)

(promoted cpt. 4

L. Blackwell Volunteers
M. Denmead Volunteers

O. Marietta Guards

Cpt. Patrick McGovern[46]
December 1862, replaced
    Barnes)
Cpt. James M. Johnson
Cpt. James Franklin
    McCleskey
Cpt. Thomas Kary Sproull

2 May 1863–4 May 1863, Chancellorsville

Army of Northern Virginia: General Robert E. Lee
First Corps: Lt. General James Longstreet
Infantry Division: Maj. General Lafayette Mclaws
Infantry Brigade: Brigadier General William Tatum Wofford
Phillips Legion

Field and Staff Officers
Lt. Col. Elihu (Sandy) Barclay (absent due to 1862 wounds)
Maj. Joseph Hamilton (commanded battalion at Chancellorsville)
Cpt. Samuel Masters Hankins Byrd, QM
Cpt. Andrew M. Norris, Commissary
1st Lt. Frederick Fuller, Adjutant (promoted to Cpt. of Co. A, infantry battalion, 1
    May 1863)
Cpt. John A. Matthias, Adjutant (replaced Fuller 12 May 1863)
Doctor Isaac D. Moore, Surgeon
Doctor George M. Willis, Asst. Surgeon

Infantry Companies: Lt. Col. Elihu "Sandy" Barclay (absent wounded)
Maj. Joseph Hamilton (commanded battalion at Chancellorsville)

A. Green Rifles

B. Dalton Guards

Cpt. Oliver P. Daniel
(resigned 27 April 1863
because of ill health)
Cpt. Frederick Fuller
(promoted 1 May 1863,
succeeded Cpt. Daniel)
Cpt. Thomas Hamilton

---

[46] Although 1st Lt. Patrick McGovern is shown as having replaced Capt. Jackson Barnes, he was absent more than present for duty. Actual combat leadership was likely in the hands of other junior officers and sgts. Maj. Elihu (Sandy) Stuart Barclay is listed as maj. of infantry but did not participate in the battle of Fredericksburg because of wounds received in Maryland at Fox's Gap.

C. Habersham Volunteers
D. Polk Rifles
E. Blue Ridge Rifles

Cpt. John S. Norris
Cpt. John L. Dodds
1st Lt. Hardy Price (died at
Richmond Hospital 26
January 1863)
Cpt. William H. Barber
(Promoted cpt. 26 January
1863, replaced Price)

F. Lochrane Guards
L. Blackwell Volunteers
M. Denmead Volunteers

Cpt. Patrick McGovern
Cpt. James M. Johnson
Cpt. James Franklin
McCleskey (resigned 31
January 1863)
Cpt. Samuel Young Harris
(promoted cpt. 1   February

1863, replaced McCleskey)
O. Marietta Guards Cpt.

Thomas Kary Sproull
(resigned 25 April 1863
because of ill health)
Cpt. Henry Johnson
McCormick (promoted cpt.
25 April 1863, replaced
Sproull, Mccormick was
absent disabled and
company was commanded
by 1st Lt. T. G. Bowie)

The implementation of Army of Northern Virginia Special Order #104, March 1863, was a key event for the Phillips Legion in that the infantry and cavalry battalions were officially separated and each one integrated into larger dedicated units. The infantry battalion at this stage of the war was assigned to Maj. General Lafayette McLaws's division. The cavalry battalion was assigned to Maj. General James Ewell Brown Stewart's cavalry division, Brigadier General Wade Hampton's brigade. Col. William M. Phillips resigned 13 February 1863 because of chronic illness (effects of typhoid fever.) Brigadier General William T. Wofford established a specialized unit in April 1863 known unofficially as the 1st Georgia Sharpshooters. The unit was officially designated the 3rd Georgia Sharpshooters in June 1863.[47] At the battle of Chancellorsville, the unit was commanded by Cpt. R. H. Patton of Co. E, 18th Georgia. Patton was killed leading the unit in a charge and was succeeded by

---

[47] See Appendix F for a description of the Third Georgia Sharpshooters. Included is an annotated roster of Co. F.

Lt. Col. Nathan Louis Hutchins of the 16th Georgia. Of the six companies comprising the 3rd Georgia Sharpshooters, Co. F was made up of men from the Phillips Legion.

9 June 1863–14 July 1863, Gettysburg

Army of Northern Virginia: General Robert Edward Lee
First Corps: Lt. General James Longstreet
Infantry Division: Maj. General Lafayette Mclaws
Infantry Brigade: Brigadier General William Tatum Wofford
Phillips Legion

Field and Staff Officers
Lt. Col. Elihu (Sandy) Barclay (absent due to 1862 wounds)
Maj. Joseph Hamilton (commanded battalion at Gettysburg)
Cpt. Samuel Masters Hankins Byrd, QM
Cpt. Andrew M. Norris, Commissary
Cpt. John A. Matthias, Adjutant
Doctor Isaac D. Moore, Surgeon
Doctor George M. Willis, Asst. Surgeon

Infantry Companies: Lt. Col. Elihu (Sandy) Barclay (absent due to effects of 1862 wounds)
Maj. Joseph Hamilton (commanded battalion at Gettysburg)

A. Green Rifles	Cpt. Frederick Fuller
B. Dalton Guards	Cpt. Thomas Hamilton
(absent, disabled)	
	1st Lt. James Byers
C. Habersham Volunteers	Cpt. John S. Norris
D. Polk Rifles	Cpt. John L. Dodds
E. Blue Ridge Rifles	Cpt. William H. Barber
F. Lochrane Guards	Cpt. Patrick McGovern
L. Blackwell Volunteers	Cpt. James M. Johnson
M. Denmead Volunteers	Cpt. Samuel Young Harris
O. Marietta Guards	Cpt. Henry Johnson McCormick (absent, disabled)
	1st Lt. T. G. Bowie

21 September 1863–4 November 1863, Chattanooga

First Corps (two divisions, independent command): Lt. General James Longstreet

Infantry Division: Maj. General Lafayette McLaws
Infantry Brigade: Brigadier General William Tatum Wofford
Phillips Legion

Field and Staff Officers
Lt. Col. Elihu (Sandy) Stuart Barclay (absent due to effects of 1862 wounds)
Maj. Joseph Hamilton (commanded battalion at Chattanooga)
Cpt. Samuel Masters Hankins Byrd, QM
Cpt. John A. Matthias, Adjutant
Doctor William F. Shine, Surgeon
Doctor George M. Willis, Asst. Surgeon and Surgeon

Infantry Companies Lt. Col. Elihu (Sandy) Barclay (absent due to effects of 1862 wounds)
Maj. Joseph Hamilton (commanded battalion at Chattanooga)

A. Green Rifles	Cpt. Frederick Fuller
B. Dalton Guards	Cpt. Thomas Hamilton (absent, disabled)
	2nd Lt. William Hamilton
C. Habersham Volunteers	Cpt. John S. Norris
D. Polk Rifles	Cpt. John Luther Dodds
E. Blue Ridge Rifles	Cpt. William H. Barber
F. Lochrane Guards	Cpt. Patrick McGovern
L. Blackwell Volunteers	Cpt. James H. Johnson
M. Denmead Volunteers	Cpt. Samuel Young Harris
O. Marietta Guards	Cpt. Henry Johnson McCormick (absent, disabled)
	1st Lt. T. G. Bowie

21 October 1863–29 November 1863, Knoxville/Tennessee/Fort Loudon (Sanders)

First Corps (two divisions, independent command): Lt. General James Longstreet
Infantry Division: Maj. General Lafayette McLaws
Infantry Brigade: Brigadier General William Tatum Wofford (absent on leave)
Phillips Legion
Infantry Battalion

Field and Staff Officers
Lt. Col. Elihu (Sandy) Stuart Barclay (absent due to effects of 1862 wounds, resigned 31 December 1863)

Maj. Joseph Hamilton, Infantry (commanded battalion at Knoxville, WIA 29 November 1863)
Cpt. Samuel Masters Hankins Byrd, QM
Cpt. John A. Matthias, Adjutant of Infantry
Doctor William F. Shine, Surgeon
Doctor George M. Willis, Asst. Surgeon

Infantry Companies, Lt. Col. Elihu (Sandy) Stuart Barclay (absent due to effects of 1862 wounds)
Maj. Joseph Hamilton

A. Green Rifles	Cpt. Frederick Fuller
B. Dalton Guards	Cpt. Thomas Hamilton (absent, disabled) 2nd Lt. William Hamilton
C. Habersham Volunteers	Cpt. John S. Norris
D. Polk Rifles	Cpt. John Luther Dodds
E. Blue Ridge Rifles	Cpt. William H. Barber
F. Lochrane Guards	Cpt. Patrick McGovern
L. Blackwell Volunteers	Cpt. James M. Johnson (MWIA, captured at Knoxville 29 November 1863, d. in hospital of wounds same date a few hours after being captured)
M. Denmead Volunteers	Cpt. Samuel Young Harris
O. Marietta Guards	Cpt. Henry Johnson McCormick (absent, disabled) 1st Lt. T. G. Bowie

1 May 1864–7 May 1864, Battle of the Wilderness

Army of Northern Virginia: General Robert Edward Lee
First Corps: Lt. General James Longstreet (WIA Wilderness 6 May 1864)
Lt. General Richard Heron Anderson (replaced Longstreet temporarily 6 May 1864)
Infantry Division: Brigadier General Joseph Brevard Kershaw
Infantry Brigade: Brigadier General William Tatum Wofford
Phillips Legion
Infantry Battalion

Field and Staff Officers

Lt. Col. Joseph Hamilton (promoted lt. col. 31 December 1863)
Maj. John S. Norris (promoted maj. 31 December 1863)
Cpt. Samuel Masters Hankins Byrd, QM (promoted maj. and brigade QM 19 February 1863)
Cpt. John A. Matthias, Adjutant
Doctor William F. Shine, Surgeon
Doctor George M. Willis, Asst. Surgeon
Doctor Samuel W. Field, Asst. Surgeon

Infantry Companies, Lt. Col. Joseph Hamilton
Maj. John S. Norris

A. Green Rifles	Cpt. Frederick Fuller
B. Dalton Guards	Cpt. Thomas Hamilton (absent, disabled)
	2nd Lt. William Hamilton
C. Habersham Volunteers	Cpt. Alexander Smith Erwin (promoted to cpt. 31 December 1863; absent, wounded)
D. Polk Rifles	Cpt. John Luther Dodds (WIA)
E. Blue Ridge Rifles	Cpt. William H. Barber
F. Lochrane Guards	(All remaining officers captured and held in prison until war's end, company probably commanded by a capable NCO)
L. Blackwell Volunteers	Cpt. James Fletcher Lowery (promoted cpt. 29 November 1863, replaced Johnson)
M Denmead Volunteers	Cpt. Samuel Young Harris
O. Marietta Guards	Cpt. Henry Johnson McCormick (absent, disabled)
	1st Lt. T. G. Bowie (KIA 6 May 1864)

8 May 1864, 19 May 1864, Battle of Spotsylvania

Army of Northern Virginia: General Robert Edward Lee

First Corps: Lt. General Richard Heron Anderson
Infantry Division: Maj. General Joseph Brevard Kershaw
Infantry Brigade: Brigadier General William Tatum Wofford
Phillips Legion
Infantry Battalion

Field and Staff Officers
Lt. Col. Joseph Hamilton
Maj. John S. Norris
Cpt. John A. Matthias, Adjutant
Doctor William F. Shine, Surgeon
Doctor Georgia M. Willis, Asst. Surgeon
Doctor Samuel W. Field, Asst. Surgeon

Infantry Companies, Lt. Col. Joseph Hamilton
Maj. John S. Norris

A. Green Rifles	Cpt. Frederick Fuller (KIA Spotsylvania 10 May 1864) Cpt. Daniel Benjamin Sanford (promoted cpt. 10 May 1864, replaced Fuller)
B. Dalton Guards	Cpt. Thomas Hamilton (absent, disabled) 2nd Lt. William Hamilton
C. Habersham Volunteers	2nd Lt. Levi W. Wyly (absent, sick) Commanding officer/NCO unknown
D. Polk Rifles	Cpt. John Luther Dodds (absent, wounded) 2nd Lt. George H. Stidham
E. Blue Ridge Rifles	Cpt. William H. Barber
F. Lochrane Guards	All remaining officers captured and held in prison until war's end, company probablycommanded by a capable NCO.
L. Blackwell Volunteers	Cpt. James Fletcher Lowery
M. Denmead Volunteers	Cpt. Samuel Young Harris
O. Marietta Guards	2nd Lt. James M. Smith (replaced Bowie)

21 May 1864, 3 June 1864, North Anna and Cold Harbor

Army of Northern Virginia: General Robert Edward Lee
First Corps: Lt. General Richard Heron Anderson
Infantry Division: Maj. General Joseph Brevard Kershaw
Infantry Brigade: Brigadier General William Tatum Wofford
Phillips Legion
Infantry Battalion

Field and Staff Officers
Lt. Col. Joseph Hamilton (WIA Cold Harbor, 3 June 1864)
Maj. John S. Norris
Cpt. John A. Matthias, Adjutant
Doctor William F. Shine, Surgeon
Doctor George M. Willis, Asst. Surgeon
Doctor Samuel W. Field, Asst. Surgeon

Infantry Companies: Lt. Col. Joseph Hamilton
Maj. John S. Norris

A. Green Rifles	Cpt. Daniel Benjamin Sanford
B. Dalton Guards	Cpt. Thomas Hamilton (absent, disabled)
	2nd Lt. William Hamilton
C. Habersham Volunteers	2nd Lt. Levi W. Wyly (home on sick leave until end of war)
	Commanding officer/NCO unknown
D. Polk Rifles	Cpt. John Luther Dodds (absent, wounded)
	2nd Lt. George H. Stidham
E. Blue Ridge Rifles	Cpt. William H. Barber
F. Lochrane Guards	All remaining officers captured and held in prison until war's end, company probably commanded by a capable NCO.
L. Blackwell Volunteers	Cpt. James Fletcher Lowery
M. Denmead Volunteers	Cpt. Samuel Young Harris
O. Marietta Guards	2nd Lt. James M. Smith

9 October 1864, 2 March 1865, Battle of Cedar Creek/Shenandoah Valley, and Siege of Petersburg

Army of Northern Virginia: General Robert Edward Lee
First Corps: Lt. General Richard Heron Anderson (Lt. General Longstreet resumed Corps command in late October 1864))
Infantry Division: Maj. General Joseph Brevard Kershaw
Infantry Brigade: Brigadier General William Tatum Wofford (Remained in command of his brigade when his horse fell on him at Front Royal in the Valley 16 August 1864 and was still in command until 26 September 1864 when he had to remain at Gordonsville while Kershaw's division was returned to Early in the Valley. Wofford then received medical furlough on 18 October 1864 and went home to Georgia.)
Brigadier General Dudley McIver Dubose (replaced Wofford officially January 1865 actual replacement occurred in November 1864)

Phillips Legion
Infantry Battalion

Field and Staff Officers
Lt. Col. Joseph Hamilton (returned from wounded furlough January 1865)
Maj. John S. Norris
Cpt. John A. Matthias, Adjutant
Doctor William McClung Piggott, Surgeon
Doctor George M. Willis, Asst. Surgeon
Doctor Samuel W. Field, Asst. Surgeon (sick furlough November 1864, returned in early 1865)

Infantry Companies: Lt. Col. Joseph Hamilton
Maj. John S. Norris

A. Green Rifles	Cpt. Daniel Benjamin Sanford
B. Dalton Guards	Cpt. Thomas Hamilton (absent, disabled)
	2nd Lt. William Hamilton
C. Habersham Volunteers	2nd Lt. Levi W. Wyly (absent, sick)
	Commanding officer/NCO unknown
D. Polk Rifles	Cpt. John Luther Dodds

E. Blue Ridge Rifles	Cpt. William H. Barber (resigned 29 June 1864) Cpt. Jesse M. McDonald (replaced Barber 29 June 1864)
F. Lochrane Guards	Unknown
L. Blackwell Volunteers	Cpt. James Fletcher Lowery
M. Denmead Volunteers	Cpt. Samuel Young Harris
O. Marietta Guards	1st Lt. James M. Smith

2 March 1865, 9 April 1865, Petersburg to Sailor's Creek and Surrender at Appomattox

Army of Northern Virginia: General Robert Edward Lee (surrendered at Appomattox Court House on 9 April 1865)
First Corps: Lt. General James Longstreet (surrendered at Appomattox Court House on 9 April 1865)
Infantry Division: Maj. General Joseph Brevard Kershaw (captured at Sailor's Creek on 6 April 1865, not released from Fort Warren until July 1865)
Infantry Brigade: Brigadier General Dudley McIver Dubose (captured at Sailor's Creek on 6 April 1865, not released from Fort Warren until July 1865)

Phillips Legion
Infantry Battalion

Field and Staff Officers
Lt. Col. Joseph Hamilton (captured 6 April 1865 at Sailor's Creek, released from Johnson's Island 25 July 1865)
Maj. John S. Norris (captured 6 April 1865 at Sailor's Creek, released from Johnson's Island 25 July 1865)
Cpt. John A. Matthias, Adjutant (captured at Sailor's Creek 5 April 1865, released from Johnson's Island 19 July 1865)
Doctor William M. Piggott, Surgeon (surrendered at Appomattox 9 April 1865)
Doctor George M. Willis, Asst. Surgeon (surrendered at Appomattox 9 April 1865)
Doctor Samuel W. Field, Asst. Surgeon (surrendered at Appomattox 9 April 1865)

Infantry Companies: Lt. Col. Joseph Hamilton
Maj. John S. Norris

| A. Green Rifles | Cpt. Daniel Benjamin Sanford (WIA and captured at Sailor's Creek 6 April 1865) |
| B. Dalton Guards | Cpt. Thomas Hamilton |

(Retired for health reasons, necrosis 27 February 1865) 2nd Lt. William Hamilton (replaced Thomas Hamilton, captured Sailor's Creek 6 April 1865, released from Johnson's Island 18 June 1865, age 24)

C. Habersham Volunteers 2nd Lt. Levi W. Wyly (home on sick leave from January 1864 to end of war)

D. Polk Rifles Cpt. John Luther Dodds (captured 6 April 1865 at Sailor's Creek, released from Johnson's Island 18 June 1865)

E. Blue Ridge Rifles Cpt. Jesse M. McDonald (Furloughed home 20 January 1865, never returned to duty) 1st Lt. Andrew Jackson Reese (promoted 1st lt. 29 June 1864, surrendered at Appomattox Courthouse 9 April 1865, replaced McDonald)

F. Lochrane Guards Unknown (Co. F not listed in surrender)

L. Blackwell Volunteers Cpt. James Fletcher Lowery (MWIA and captured at Sailor's Creek, d. 8 April 1865)

N. Denmead Volunteers Cpt. Samuel Young Harris (MWIA and captured at Sailor's Creek 6 April 1865)

O. Marietta Guards 1st Lt. James M. Smith (captured 6 April 1865 at Sailor's Creek, released from Johnson's Island 20 June 1865, age 24)

Appendix C

Higher Echelon Officials and Officers
Who Commanded the Phillips Legion

Joseph Emerson Brown[48]

Governor of Georgia 1857, 1861 and 1863, Brown was an extremely controversial figure who was sometimes believed to have fought more with the Confederate Chief Executive Jefferson Davis that against his Yankee foes. Born in 1821 in South Carolina he graduated from Yale where he studied law. He entered the Georgia legislature and was named Superior Court Judge before being elected to Governor in 1857. He is remembered for seizing Federal Forts Jackson and Pulaski in January 1861. He put two regiments in the field before the Confederacy was organized and personally seized the government arsenal at Augusta. Allied with Robert Toombs and Alexander Stephens, he opposed Davis's administration of the government and his conduct of the war, and after the surrender, advised acquiescence to the Reconstruction program. His unique political career ranged from precipitate secessionism to Radical Republicanism and back to the established Democratic party of the south. In 1868 he was named Chief Justice of the State Supreme Court. He engaged in railroading in the same year and in 1880 went to the United States Senate. During the war he quarreled relentlessly with Jefferson Davis over the state control and promotions of officers and fought for promotion of William Monroe Phillips to brigadier general. He lost this last clash with the president. Phillips became Col. William Monroe Phillips in command of Phillips Legion.

Lt. General Richard Heron Anderson[49]

Born 7 October 1821 at "Hill Crest," Sumter County, South Carolina, Anderson graduated from West Point with the class of 1842. Out of the thirty-seven graduates in this class, twenty-two general officers were supplied to the Union and Confederate armies in 1861. Anderson won honors and was brevetted 1st lt. in the Mexican War. He resigned his commission on 3 March 1861 and was commissioned maj. of infantry in the regular Confederate service to rank from 16 March 1861. He was present at the reduction of Fort Sumter. On 18 July 1861 he was promoted to brigadier general and was placed in command of Charleston. There he was assigned the command of D. R. Jones's South Carolina brigade in February 1862. He led them competently through the battles around Richmond in May and June 1862. On

---

[48] Mark M. Boatner III, *The Civil War Dictionary* (David McKay Co., Inc., 1987) 91–92.

[49] Ezra J. Warner, *Generals in Gray* (Baton Rouge and London: Louisiana State Press, 1959) 8, 9.

14 July 1862, he was appointed maj. general and assigned command of Benjamin Huger's division. He commanded his division in the I Corps and after Chancellorsville, in the III Corps. After Longstreet was wounded at the battle of the Wilderness, Anderson was promoted to lt. general commanding the I Corps with temporary rank from 31 May 1864. On Longstreet's return to the army after being wounded in the Wilderness, Anderson was placed in charge of a segment of the Richmond defenses. His troops were shattered and dispersed after the battle of Sailor's Creek on 6 April 1865. He was reduced to poverty after the war and died on 26 June 1879 in Beaufort, South Carolina. The Phillips Legion was assigned to Wofford's brigade, Kershaw's division, and Anderson's I Corps during 1864 when Longstreet was absent and recovering from his wounds.

Brigadier General Thomas Fenwick Drayton[50]

Born in 1808, Drayton attended the United States Military Academy where he graduated in 1828 in the same class as Jefferson Davis. After serving in garrison and on topographical duty, he resigned from the army in 1836 to run his South Carolina plantation and engage in railroad surveying. He was active in the militia, sat in the state legislature and was also a railroad director. He was appointed a brigadier general in the Confederate army on 25 September 1861. He was commanding the military district around Port Royal where, his brother, cpt. Percival Drayton, led the attacking Union fleet. Later he was assigned a brigade in Virginia in July 1862 under Longstreet which fought at Thoroughfare Gap, Second Manasses, South Mountain and Sharpsburg. Widely regarded as an incompetent officer after his performance at Second Manassas and South Mountain/Sharpsburg, the brigade was restructured and he was assigned court martial and other non-combat duties in Arkansas and Texas. He was president of the court of inquiry convened for Price's Missouri expedition. After the war, he returned to farming and was also involved with a life insurance company. He died 18 February 1891 in Florence, South Carolina and was buried in Charlotte, North Carolina. Drayton was the Legion's brigade commander from June to November 1862.

Brigadier General John Buchanan Floyd[51]

Born 1 June 1806 in Montgomery City, Virginia, General Floyd was a talented politician whose earlier accomplishments were dimmed by his later poor command performance. As a result, both his military reputation and personal credibility suffered. He attended South Carolina College, pursuing careers as a lawyer and planter until elected to the House of Delegates in 1847. In 1857 President Buchanan appointed Floyd Secretary of War. Floyd resigned his post on 29 December 1860 when then-president Buchanan's harsh policy over Charleston Harbor caused great

---

[50] Mark M. Boatner III, *The Civil War Dictionary* (David McKay Co., Inc., 1987) 246–47.

[51] Patricia L. Faust, ed., *Times Illustrated Encyclopedia of the Civil War* (New York City: Harper Perennial, 1986); *Confederate Military History*, vol. 2.

resentment throughout the south. Floyd was accused by rabid Northerners of transferring arms to southern arsenals in preparation for war. Floyd returned to western Virginia to raise a brigade of mountaineers and on 23 May 1861, was appointed a brigadier general in the Confederate Army. He participated in battles at Cross Lanes, Carnifix Ferry and Gauley Bridge in western Virginia and, later at Fort Donelson. At Fort Donelson, Floyd, the ranking commander, found his troops completely surrounded on the land side of the Cumberland River. After a failed attack to attempt a breakout, Floyd relinquished command to Brigadier General Simon B. Buckner and fled to Nashville leaving Buckner to surrender his army. Because of his poor judgment in deserting his command, Floyd was relieved on 11 March 1862.

In spite of his dismal performance, Floyd continued in an active position in southwestern Virginia. He was commissioned a maj. general in the militia and used his influence to raise a band of partisans to terrorize unionists in his area and succeeded only in annoying Confederate authorities with his efforts to recruit troops. His constant campaigning ruined his health and Floyd died near Abingdon, Virginia on 25 August 1863. Floyd was commander of the Army of the Kanawha while the Legion served in this command from September through December 1861.

Brigadier General States Rights Gist[52]

Born in South Carolina in 1831, Gist attended South Carolina College and Harvard Law School. Named the adjutant and inspector general of the South Carolina state army early in 1861, he served during the Fort Sumter crisis and was General Bernard Bee's volunteer aide de camp at First Manassas. He succeeded him in command of his brigade and returned to South Carolina as adjutant general. Appointed brigadier general, Confederate States of America on 29 March 1862, he served under General Pemberton on the South Carolina coast and was sent to Vicksburg on 10 May 1863. He commanded Walker's division at Chickamauga and Missionary Ridge and led his own brigade in the Atlanta campaign. He was killed at Franklin, Tennessee on 30 November 1864 while leading his brigade on foot after his horse had been shot. He was buried near Franklin but was later reinterred at Trinity Episcopal Church in Columbia, South Carolina. The Napier Artillery (which later became the Macon Light Artillery nominally assigned to the Phillips Legion in May 1862) served in Gist's Brigade near Savannah in early 1862.

Major General David Rumph Jones[53]

Born to Donald B. and Mary Elvera Rumph Jones on 5 April 1825 in South Carolina's Orangeburg District, David Rumph Jones became a cadet at the United States Military Academy in 1842. He graduated in 1846 forty-first in a class of fifty-

---

[52] Mark M. Boatner III, *The Civil War Dictionary* (David McKay Co., Inc., 1987) 344–45.

[53] Ibid., 442; *The Confederate General*, vol. 3.

nine which included Georgia B. McClellan, Thomas J. Jackson and George E. Pickett. Jones served with honor in the Mexican War where he took part in many of the maj. campaigns. When the Civil War broke out, Jones resigned from the Old Army on 15 February 1861 and was commissioned maj. in the Confederate States Army on 16 March 1861. He is known for having offered Maj. Robert Anderson terms of surrender at Fort Sumter and is said to have lowered the Stars and Stripes. He was promoted to brigadier general on 17 June 1861. His brigade fought at First Manassas and after assignment to Maj. General James Longstreet's division relieved Brigadier General Samuel Jones as commander of a brigade that included the 7th, 8th, 9th, and 11th Georgia infantry regiments. By late March 1862, Jones was in command of a two-brigade division in Maj. General Magruder's corps and on 5 April, was promoted to maj. general. His troops engaged the enemy throughout the Seven Days campaign. Shortly thereafter, Jones regained command of one more brigade and was assigned to the army wing led then by Maj. General James Longstreet. Jones's troops participated in the campaign that resulted in the Second Battle of Manassas where his unit hammered the Union left on Chinn Ridge until it crumbled. Jones harshly criticized Brigadier General Thomas Fenwick Drayton at Second Manassas for his failure to move his troops quickly enough. Jones's division fought bravely in the Maryland campaign. He was commended by Longstreet for his leadership at Thoroughfare Gap, Manassas Plains, Boonsboro and Sharpsburg. In mid-October 1863, Maj. General David Rumph Jones was stricken by a heart attack. He died in Richmond, Virginia on 15 January 1863 and was buried in Hollywood Cemetery. The Phillips Legion served in Jones's Division from August through October 1862.

Major General Joseph Brevard Kershaw[54]

Born on 5 January 1822 in Camden, South Carolina, Kershaw became a lawyer and legislator and fought in the Mexican War. He was commissioned col. of the Second South Carolina in April of 1861, serving at Morris Island and in Bonham's brigade at First Manassas. He was appointed brigadier general on 13 February 1862 and commanded his brigade under Longstreet on the Peninsula, Second Manassas, South Mountain, Fredericksburg, Chancellorsville and Gettysburg. Kershaw fought in the west with Longstreet at Chickamauga and Knoxville, and returned to the Army of Northern Virginia where he was appointed to maj. general on 15 February 1864. After taking command of McLaws' division, he fought at the Wilderness, Spotsylvania, Cold Harbor, with Early's army in the Shenandoah Valley, the battles around Petersburg and Sailor's Creek where he surrendered with Ewell. Kershaw spent several months in a Boston prison then returned to South Carolina and became a legislator and a jurist. He died on 19 April 1894 and was buried at Camden's

---

[54] Mark M. Boatner III, *The Civil War Dictionary* (David McKay Co., Inc., 1987) 457.

Quaker Cemetery. The Phillips Legion infantry battalion served in Kershaw's division from February 1864 until war's end.

Lt. General James Longstreet[55]

Born in South Carolina on 8 January 1821, Longstreet attended the United States Military Academy and graduated in 1842. He served in Florida, the Mexican War where he was wounded and brevetted twice, and on the frontier against Indians before resigning on 1 June 1861. Seeking the post of paymaster which he had held in the Old Army, he was instead appointed to brigadier general in the Confederate Army on 17 June 1861. He led the fourth brigade at First Manassas then was promoted to maj. general on 7 October 1861. He then led a division at Yorktown and Williamsburg and the Right Wing at Fair Oaks and Seven Pines where his mistakes caused the operation to fail. Nevertheless, he retained Lee's confidence and was later given command of a wing containing over half of Lee's infantry. He delivered a crushing counterattack at Second Manassas and performed with distinction at Fredericksburg. He was sent with Pickett's and Hood's divisions to Suffolk, Virginia where, as commander of the Confederate Department of North Carolina and Southern Virginia, he displayed minimal talent for independent command. He disagreed with Lee at Gettysburg in that he felt that the campaign should be strategic in offense but tactically defensive. Years after the war he was criticized for his delay in attacking on the second day and his poor performance in organizing Pickett's Charge on the third day. A recent scholar has described Longstreet as the only Confederate Corps commander at Gettysburg who functioned competently. In September of 1863, he was sent with two of his divisions (McLaws' and Hood's) to support Bragg in the west. He again displayed ineptitude for independent command in the Knoxville campaign. He was severely wounded in the Wilderness campaign and put out of action until he resumed command of the I Corps in the Richmond defenses. He served as president of an insurance company after the war and joined the Republican Party holding a number of government appointments. Longstreet has been widely regarded by southerners after the war as being responsible for the Confederate defeat because of his actions at Gettysburg. This was largely due to a group of Confederate officers who wrote numerous inaccurate statements to "punish" him for becoming a Republican and for committing the unpardonable sin of criticizing General Lee. Longstreet died on 2 January 1904 in Georgia and was buried at Alta Vista Cemetery in Gainesville. The Phillips Legion infantry battalion served in Longstreet's I Corps from August 1862 until the end of the war.

Major General Lafayette Mclaws[56]

---

[55] Ibid., 490–91.
[56] Ibid., 586.

Born 15 January 1821 in Augusta GA, McLaws attended the United States
Military Academy and graduated in the class of 1842. He served in garrison on the
frontier, in the Mexican War, on the Utah expedition and in Indian fighting before
resigning on 10 May 1861 as a cpt. He was then commissioned a maj. in the
Confederate States Army and was elected col. of the 16th Georgia on 17 June 1861.
Shortly thereafter he was appointed to brigadier general on 25 September 1861. He
fought at Yorktown before being promoted to maj. general on 23 May 1862 and
given command of a division in Longstreet' s wing of the Army of Northern
Virginia. His division was assigned to Jackson at Harpers Ferry, fought at
Sharpsburg, defended Marye's Heights at Fredericksburg and was heavily engaged at
Chancellorsville. His troops fought in the Peach Orchard, the Wheatfield and
Devil's Den at Gettysburg. After participating in the Knoxville campaign he was
relieved for general lack of cooperation. McLaws pressed the system for a court
martial. This resulted in charges being reduced to improper preparations for the
attack on Fort Sanders where the Phillips Legion suffered heavy losses. President
Davis disapproved of the court martial findings and McLaws was vindicated while
Longstreet was humiliated. His last assignment involved the defense of Savannah.
After the Carolinas campaign he surrendered with Lee's army. Returning home to an
impoverished existence, his old friend Ulysses S, Grant helped him with
appointments in the Internal Revenue Service and post office departments in
Savannah. He died in Savannah on 24 July 1897 and was buried there in Laurel
Grove Cemetery. The Phillips Legion infantry battalion served in McLaws's division
from November 1862 until McLaws was relieved from command in February 1864.

Lt. General John Clifford Pemberton[57]
Born in Philadelphia, Pennsylvania on 10 August 1814. Attended and graduated
from the United States Military Academy, class of 1837. Pemberton won two brevets
for gallantry in the Mexican War. He married Martha Thompson of Norfolk,
Virginia, which was likely one of the maj. reasons for his resignation from the Old
Army on 24 April 1861. In November, he was ordered to report to General Robert
E. Lee at Charleston, South Carolina, after having been promoted to maj. general on
14 January 1862. When Lee was ordered to Richmond on 2 March 1861 Pemberton
succeeded him as commander of the Department of South Carolina, Georgia and
Florida. On 10 October 1862 he was promoted to lt. general and assigned command
of the Department of Mississippi and Eastern Louisiana. He is best known for his
command and tenacious defense of Vicksburg and the subsequent surrender.
Pemberton was vilified because of his northern birth and resigned his commission in
May 1864. Jefferson Davis immediately appointed him a lt. col. of artillery and he
served out the war in the Richmond defenses and as an ordnance inspector. He lived

[57] Michael B. Ballard, *Pemberton, A Biography* (Jackson MS, 1991); Ezra J. Warner, *Generals in Gray* (Baton Rouge and London: Louisiana State Press, 1959).

on a farm near Warrrenton, Virginia from 1866 until 1875 when he returned to his native Pennsylvania where he died on 31 July 1881. He was buried in Philadelphia's Laurel Hill Cemetery. The Phillips Legion served on the Carolina coast in Pemberton's department from January through 19 July 1862.

Brigadier General William Tatum Wofford[58]
 Born 28 June 1824 in Habersham County to William Hollingsworth Wofford and Nancy M. Tatum, William Tatum Wofford and his family drew a lot in western Georgia in the Land Lottery of 1827. The family then moved to Cass County, settling near the town of Cassville. Wofford became a lawyer and distinguished military officer. He fought in the Mexican War, ran a plantation, published a newspaper and sat in the state legislature. When Georgia left the union Wofford became col. of the 18th Georgia then the only non-Texas regiment of Hood's Texas brigade. When Hood became a division commander in September 1862 Wofford assumed command of the brigade. He led the Texas brigade at Second Manassas, South Mountain and Antietam. After having been promoted to brigadier general on 23 April to rank from 7 January 1863, he was appointed to command the former brigade of T. R. R. Cobb who had been killed at the battle of Fredericksburg. His brigade consisted of the 16th Georgia, 18th Georgia, 24th Georgia, Phillips's Legion and Cobb's Legion infantry battalions. Just prior to the battle of Chancellorsville, Wofford received orders to establish a special battalion or corps of sharpshooters which was designed for skirmish duty and sniper harassment of the enemy. This unit would be designated the 3rd Georgia Sharpshooter battalion and became part of Wofford's brigade. Wofford followed Longstreet to the west, fought under Kershaw around Richmond and Petersburg and the Shenandoah and was injured at Front Royal in August 1864. Returning from sick leave he was placed in command of the Department of Northern Georgia in January 1865 and surrendered at Kingston on 12 May 1865. Following the Civil War, Wofford was elected to Congress in 1865 but was refused a seat by the Radical Republicans. Until his death in 1884, he was active in politics, law and public education. He is buried in Cassville, Georgia. Wofford commanded the brigade containing the Phillips Legion infantry battalion from January 1863 until September 1864.

---

[58] Ibid., 944–45; Gerald J. Smith, *"One of the Most Daring of Men"* (Murfreesboro TN: Southern Heritage Press, 1997) 65–66.

Appendix D

The Legion Band

After listening to a brass serenade in 1864, General Robert: E. Lee remarked: "I don't believe we can have an army without music."[59]

Carl Franz August Rauschenberg, one of four brothers, organized the Phillips Legion band on 1 May 1862. He and his brothers were all first-generation German immigrants from a medieval town bearing the family name "Rauschenberg." Like his brothers, August was an accomplished man. He was a talented musician, excelling as a cornetist, and an expert mechanical draftsman, pattern designer and maker. Residing in Dalton, Georgia at the outbreak of the Civil War in the spring of 1861, August enlisted in the Confederate army in Company B of the Infantry Battalion of Phillips Legion. Thirty years old at this time, he appears on the Company B muster roll as a pvt. from 2 August 1861 to 31 December 1862. His officers must have recognized his unusual musical talent and leadership potential. He first appears as a musician on the Legion's Field, Staff and Band Muster Roll for the period from 30 June to 1 December 1862 then as a Principal Musician from 31 November 1862 to 31 December 1862 and as Chief Musician for September and October 1863 to the end of the war. His official title became "Cornetist and Master of the Band" somewhere within this period. [60] August and his band served with the Legion throughout the war. Family records indicate that his band was shot to pieces at the Battle of Gettysburg although official records do not support this assertion. Faulty memory confusion as to particular combat incidents may account for this discrepancy. In fact, service records of band members indicate only one combat casualty during the war with Pvt. James W. Spratling killed in the 14 September 1862 fight on South Mountain in Maryland. In a letter dated 12 April 1864, August stated: "Yesterday I had a painful duty to perform. A Pvt. of our Brigade, 24h Georgia Regiment, was shot for desertion and I had to play a Dead March from the guardhouse to the place of execution. It was a very solemn and affecting scene. The prisoner seemed willing to die; he was firm and resigned and received the fatal bullets fired by his countrymen like a man. God grant I may never witness another such spectacle."[61] Court martial records reveal this unfortunate individual to be "W.H. Tanner" of Company K of the 24th Georgia Infantry Regiment.[62] August was

---

[59] Walter Clark, *North Carolina Regiments*, II, 397–400.

[60] Reverend Fritz Rauschenberg, "The Rauschenbergs," 1951, rev. 1961, n.p.

[61] Ibid.

[62] Jack A. Bunch, *Roster of the Courts Martial in the Confederate States Armies* (Shippensburg PA: White Mane, 2001.)

captured with much of the Legion at Sailors Creek VA on 6 April 1865. He was held in prison at Newport News VA until taking the Oath of Allegiance and being released on 24 June 1865. After his release from prison in 1865 at the age of 34, August married Annie Elizabeth Kanerian and spent the remainder of his life in Georgia, the majority of it in Atlanta.[63]

Bandmaster Rauschenberg's band must have been equipped much the same as most Confederate bands at the time. The men were probably equipped with brass and percussion instruments—possibly a few woodwinds. A letter from W. O. Milton dated 27 October 1863 directs the respondent to send his letter to him at "Phillips Legion Brass Band," Wofford's Brigade, McLaw's Division.[64] This suggests that brass instruments probably made up most of the band's instruments. The band probably played three types of music: martial (marches, quicksteps, patriotic airs), dance (polkas, waltzes, schottisches, gallops) and popular (sentimental ballads, operatic airs). The music was emotional, expressing sadness at being away from home and loved ones. Much of the actual music played by Confederate bands has survived and is now in private and public collections.[65]

The Phillips Legion Band would have provided the drumbeats needed to keep the men in step and to tighten up their formations on parade as well as on the march. They would have played reveille in the morning and tattoo at night as well as numerous calls at other times during the day such as advance and retreat. Their presence was indispensable for entertainment, organization, and in the actual fighting. The band members also served other vital roles such as stretcher-bearers, burying the dead and at times as regular soldiers. They were far more than mere musicians.

Calvin, Charles. Enlisted 24 March 1864, transferred to legion from 13th Mississippi Infantry Regt., transferred to FS&I (Field, Staff, and Inspection) Band 5 June 1864, captured at Sailors Creek 6 April 1865, held at Point Lookout, released 5 June 1864, 26 June 1865 Oath of Allegiance shows home as Richmond County GA.

Cler, Charles F. (Frank). Enlisted at age 19 on 19 May 1862 pvt., Infantry Co. L, transferred to FS&I Band shortly thereafter, served in band during 1862, returned to Co. L in 1863, captured near Knoxville 3 December 1863, held at Rock Island, released 18 June 1865, b. 22 September 1842.

Edwards, William R. Enlisted 11 June 1861 as pvt., Infantry Co. B, transferred FS&I Band 1863, last shown on roll dated 30 January 1865.

---

[63] Ibid.

[64] Http:users.erols/kfraser/music/bands.html; also see Robert and Mark Elrod, *A Pictorial History of Civil War Era Musical Instruments and Military Bands* (Missoula MT: Pictorial Histories Publishing Company, n.d.).

[65] Robert Garofalo and Mark Elrod, *A Pictorial History of Civil War Musical Instruments and Military Bands* (Missoula MT: Pictorial Publishing Company, n.d.).

Fink, George. Joined FS&I Band late in the war, captured Sailor's Creek 6 April 1865, held at Newport News until released June 1865.

Fullham, James H. Enlisted 27 August 1861 as pvt., Infantry Co. F, transferred FS&I Band 1 May 1862, last shown on roll dated 30 January 1865.

Hargrove, John T. Enlisted at age 21 on 26 June 1861 as pvt., Infantry Co. A, transferred FS&I Band 1 May 1862, last shown on roll dated 30 January 1865.

Higgins, Oliver Sanford. Enlisted 19 June 1861 in Infantry Co. B, transferred to FS&I Band 1 May 1862, surrendered Appomattox 9 April 1865.

Kelly, Lacey W. Enlisted at age 21 on 14 June 1861 as pvt. Infantry Co. D transferred to FS&I Band 1 May 1862, last shown present on roll 30 January 1865, took oath and released at Chattanooga 25 May 1865.

King, Albert S. Enlisted age 22 on 26 June 1861 as 5th sgt., Infantry Co. A, transferred to FS&I Band 1 May 1862, often sick and absent, shown present on roll dated December 1864, surrendered at Appomattox 9 April 1865

Miller, John R. Enlisted April 1864 in FS&I Band, often sick, furloughed back to Georgia September 1864, shown at Macon Ocmulgee Hospital in November, returned to duty 18 November 1864, last shown on roll dated 30 January 1865.

Milton, William Oliver. Enlisted age 20 on 8 August 1861 as pvt., Cobb Legion Infantry Co. E, transferred into FS&I Band during 1863, surrendered at Appomattox 9 April 1865.

Moore, Robert G. Enlisted age 17 on 26 June 1861 as pvt., Infantry Co. A, transferred FS&I Band 1 May 1862, shown home on sick furlough 14 January 1864, no further record.

O'Brien, James. Enlisted 4 August 1861 as pvt., Infantry Co. F, transferred FS&I Band 1 May 1862, last shown on roll dated 30 January 1865.

O'Neill, James. Enlisted 27 August 1861 as pvt., Infantry Co. F, transferred FS&I Band 1 May 1862, surrendered at Appomattox 9 April 1865 as a member of Co. A.

Peek, L. C. Enlisted 24 February 1862, Infantry Co. D, discharged by furnishing substitute 25 November 1862.

Pritchard, David W. Enlisted 1861 as pvt., 2nd SC Infantry, transferred FS&I Band during 1863, Surrendered at Appomattox 9 April 1865.

Spratling, James W. Enlisted age 29 on 14 June 1861 as pvt., Infantry Co. D, transferred FS&I Band 1 May 1862, KIA Fox's Gap MD 14 September 1862.

Yarborough, Samuel S. Enlisted age 16 on 1 August 1861 as pvt., Cobb Legion Infantry Co. A, Transferred to FS&I Band January 1863, Surrendered at Appomattox 9 April 1865

Appendix E

Assistant Surgeons, Surgeons, and Physicians Serving in the Line with the Phillips Legion

"He was a large man in physique and, in his later years, considerably overweight." [66]

Ten physicians are known to have served as asst. surgeons and surgeons with the Phillips Legion during the Civil War years: three as surgeons; i.e., Drs. Moore, Piggott, and Sams began their service as asst. surgeons and were later promoted to surgeons. Four, Drs. Willis, Field, Willcoxon, and Harris began their service as asst. surgeons and remained in this rank until the end of their service. Three were designated surgeons without the intervening asst. position; i.e., Drs. Connel, Shine, and Castlen. One, Dr. Shine, was also promoted to brigade surgeon from his position as the Legion's surgeon. Five of these physicians served with the infantry battalion, two cavalry and one with the artillery; i.e., the Macon Light Artillery that was never officially assigned to the Legion. Records do not specify whether Dr. Willcoxon served the infantry or cavalry battalion. None of them served for the entire war. All of them were involved with the hellish experience of battlefield medicine. Drs. Connel, Field, Piggott, Sams and Castlen all served in Confederate general hospitals at one time or another. Dr. Castlen later served as medical officer at Andersonville, Georgia. All are known to have continued their medical practices after the war. Three, Drs. Connel, Sams and Field, went west to Texas after the war to start a new life away from the decimated south. Dr. Castlen went to California.

The law establishing the medical department of the regular army of the Confederate States of America was passed by the Confederate Congress on 26 February 1861. The surgeon general was to be ranked as col., surgeons and asst. surgeons as maj.s. Two more laws were passed on 16 March 1861, one allowing the president to appoint one surgeon and one asst. surgeon for each regiment when volunteers or militia were called into the military service in such numbers that the medical officers of the regular army could not furnish them proper attention. They would remain on active duty only so long as their services were needed for the militia or volunteers. The second law set annual salaries for the Surgeon General at $3,000.00, a surgeon at $162.00 to $200.00 per month and asst. surgeons at $110.00

---

[66] Webster Merritt, *A Century of Medicine in Jacksonville and Duval County* (Gainesville: University of Florida Press, 1949) 558 (Refers to Dr. William Francis Shine.)

to $150.00 per month.[67] Becase the Phillips Legion was a volunteer organization, the physicians were subject to these laws.

As the war progressed, the need for physicians increased. On occasion, contract surgeons were hired. Their competency varied from satisfactory to awful as reports indicate. [68] These men served at the pleasure of the Confederate authorities. No record of any such physicians for the Phillips Legion has survived.

One infantry line officer, Dr. Gober, and two cavalry line officers, Drs. Clinkscales and Long, were trained physicians who actually served as company grade line officers and participated in combat. Perhaps they were motivated by the search for battlefield glory, or enhanced political and community leadership opportunities after the war. Doctor J. H. Coxe was shown on one card in the Compiled Service Records as having served with the Phillips Legion. No other information on Dr. Coxe could be located. All of these men, soldiers and medical personnel alike, provided vitally needed leadership and medical expertise for the Phillips Legion and the Confederacy.

Fleming G. Castlen, MD[69]

Born in Bibb County, Macon, Georgia around 1834 or 1835, to John Castlen and wife Eliza, Dr. Castlen's medical training is unclear. He appears as a druggist in the 1860 Georgia census and as a physician in the Macon, Georgia 1866 and 1869–70 city directories with an office location in Macon, Georgia. His name does not appear in the *Directory of Deceased American Physicians, Volume I, 1804–1929*. Perhaps his training involved apprenticeship with a local physician or records have been lost. He served as a pvt. in the Macon Light Artillery from 16 May 1862 to 31 August 1862 at which date he was appointed surgeon and served in this capacity until April 1863 when he appears once more as a pvt. from 30 April to 31 August 1863. Finally, Dr. Castlen appears as a surgeon for the 3rd Georgia Reserves from 17 May, to 1 September 1864, first at Camp Sumter, Georgia and then on 26 October 1864 as medical officer at Andersonville, Georgia. He married Eppie Bowdre on 25 April 1860 and produced three children. Dr. Castlen died on 2 January 1874.

---

[67] H. H. Cunningham, *Doctors in Gray, The Confederate Medical Service* (1958; Baton Rouge: Louisiana State University Press, 1986) 21–22.

[68] Ibid., pp. 254–55.

[69] Compiled Service Records; Georgia Census for 1850, 1860, 1870, and 1880; Macon, Georgia City Directories for 1860, 1866, 1867, 1869–1870, 1872, 1877 and 1878; Marriage Records, Macon, Georgia; *The Macon Telegraph and Messinger*, 3 January 1874.

Alva Connel, MD[70]

Born of Irish parentage about 1817 in Greene or Hancock County, Georgia to Dr. Alva Connel, Sr. and his wife, Dr. Connel was first educated at the military school in Marietta, Georgia (Georgia Military Institute) and then attended the New Orleans Medical School (University of Louisiana) where he received his MD after his service in the Civil War. Another source states that Dr. Connel obtained his medical education in Pennsylvania and returned every other winter for lectures. He was married to Jane Richardson Baxter in 1845 and practiced medicine in Marietta, Georgia until 1861 when he entered Confederate service. Although some records state that Dr. Connel served for four years his compiled service records show that he enlisted in the Phillips Legion infantry battalion as a surgeon on 19 July 1861 and served until 4 October 1862 when he resigned. Records of the Freedman's Bureau show Dr. Connel serving as "Desp and Steward" in the Freedman's Hospital in Now Orleans, Louisiana on 3 February 1867. Later, Dr. Connel and his wife moved to Houston, Texas where he set up practice with Dr. D. F. Stuart. He fought the yellow fever scourge in Texas and came down with the disease himself. He was ill for two years and died in August 1871.

Samuel W. Field, MD[71]

Born in Atlanta, Georgia on 4 August 1839 to Samuel and Martha Bagwell Field, Dr. Field attended the University of Louisiana (Tulane University after 1884) where he received an M.D. degree in 1862. Following his graduation, he entered Confederate service as an asst. surgeon, his appointment effective 16 June 1862. He served as a medical officer in a number of hospitals in Virginia which included Warrenton in September 1862, Winchester in October and November 1862 and Staunton in December of 1862. He was then assigned to Danville in early 1863. Finally, Dr. Field was assigned to the Phillips Legion infantry battalion as an asst. surgeon in 1864 and served until he fell ill and was furloughed to his home in November 1864. He returned to his unit later in the war and surrendered at Appomattox on 9 April 1865. He moved to Dallas, Texas in 1866 after the war and married Vienna Johnson in 1871. His medical expertise was displayed in *The Dallas Herald* on 9 January 1879 where he advertised himself as a physician in general medicine, obstetrics and surgery. He also claimed to be competent in dealing with

---

[70] Dr. S. C. Red, *The Medicine Man in Texas*, 1930; Freedman's Bureau Rosters of Officers and Civilians on Duty in the Staff Offices of Louisiana; Transactions of the Texas State Medical Association, Sixth Annual Session, 1874; Compiled Service Records; *True Stories of Old Houston and Houstonians*.

[71] Compiled Service Record; M. Louise Giles, *The Early History of Medicine in Dallas, 1840–1900*, (Ph.D. diss. University of Texas, 1951); Robert E. Sherer, university archivist, Tulane University Library, New Orleans LA; The University of Texas, Southwestern Medical Center at Dallas (Texas); *A History of Greater Dallas and Vicinity* (Chicago: Lewis Publishing Co., 1909); *Medical and Surgical Directory of the United States* (Detroit, 1886).

chronic diseases of the eye. His first wife, Vienna Johnson, died in 1882. He married Margaret Parker shortly thereafter. He served two terms as City Health Officer during the 1880's and became surgeon of the Gould Railroad and State Inspector in Beaumont, Texas during the yellow fever epidemic. He fathered two children. Dr. Field died of pneumonia in Dallas, Texas on 6 May 1912.

Iverson Lewis Harris, MD[72]

Born in Milledgeville, Baldwin County GA, on 21 November 1835, to Judge Iverson Lewis Harris, Sr., and Mary Euphemia Davies, Dr. Harris received his medical training at the Medical College of Philadelphia, Pennsylvania. He married Ida Burnett and had two children. He served as 2nd sgt. in Cpt. DuBignon's Co. A of the Phillips Legion cavalry battalion from 11 September 1861 to 31 October 1861. He was appointed and served as asst. surgeon for the Legion cavalry battalion from April 1862 to 1 August 1862. His records show him as asst. surgeon for the Holcomb Legion from 17 August 1862 through 24 February 1862. This may be an error because of the overlapping dates or the dates may have been inaccurately recorded. Dr. Harris ended his tenure with the Confederacy by serving as surgeon for the 59th Georgia from December 1862 to 27 January 1865. He died in 1895 and is buried in the Milledgeville, Georgia cemetery.

Isaac D. Moore, MD[73]

Born in White Plains, Greene County GA on 14 November 1828, to William Jackson Moore and Sidney Connel, Dr. Moore attended Mercer University at Macon GA, graduating in 1858. He received medical training at the Georgia College of Medicine, Augusta GA, graduating with a medical degree in 1858. He served as asst. surgeon with the Phillips Legion infantry battalion from 30 June to 1 December 1862 and as acting surgeon as of November 1862. His records show that he passed his examination for surgeon on 31 January 1862. Dr. Moore served as surgeon until late 1863 when he was discharged. His pension application states, "I was dismissed from duty on account of Rheumatism of the heart in last of year 1863." Dr. Moore married Mary Jane Howell on 12 January 1852. She died in June 1869. Dr. Moore then married Mary Elizabeth Eley on December of 1869. The children of both marriages numbered at least ten (10). Dr. Moore d. on 10 June 1910.

---

[72] Compiled Service Records; Travis Hudson, "Soldier Boys in Gray, A History of the 59h Georgia Volunteer Infantry Regiment," *Atlanta Historical Society Journal* 23/1 (Spring 1979); Ancestry World Tree Project: Buckmaster, Holmes, Lanier and Thurber Family Tree.

[73] Compiled Service Records; Marriage Records of Georgia, Greene County; Cemeteries of Greene County GA, Section K; Indigent Pension 1903, Moore, Dr. I.D; Widow's Application, Greene County, Georgia; Personal Correspondence with Col. Carl Moore, US Army (ret.).

William McClung Piggott, MD[74]

Born in 1818 in Guilford County, Greensboro, North Carolina, Dr. Piggott was married to Amee and they had four children. Dr. Piggott's medical training is unknown. He is shown as serving with the 46th North Carolina, Co. F, in various hospitals such as Poplar Spring at Petersburg, Virginia, Phillips Legion infantry battalion and the 24th Georgia Infantry Regiment. He was promoted to surgeon on 9 March 1863. Dr. Piggott surrendered at Appomattox on 9 April 1865. His date of death is unknown.

Calhoun Sams, MD[75]

Born in Beaufort District, South Carolina on 12 January 1838 to Dr. Lewis Reeve Sams, Jr. and Sarah Givens Graham, Dr. Sams graduated from the South Carolina Medical College in 1861. He married Mary Ann Seabrook and two children were produced. He served as asst. surgeon at Camp Winder General Hospital, Richmond, Virginia in November 1862 and at Camp Winder itself in some unknown capacity from 15 May to 12 June 1862. He was promoted to surgeon on 16 April 1864. Dr. Sams served variously with the Phillips Legion cavalry battalion, Battery Dantztler, 1st South Carolina cavalry, 2nd North Carolina cavalry, and Stuart Hospital in Richmond, Virginia. He was relieved from duty with the Phillips Legion cavalry battalion on 18 July 1864 and served with Battery Dantzler to the end of the war. He left a diary describing his experiences with the 1st South Carolina cavalry which is dated from 19 October 1863 to 30 November 1863. Dr. Sams relocated to Texas after the war and died in November 1908 in Taylor, Texas.

William Francis Shine, MD[76]

Born in Tallahassee, Florida on 9 January 1835 to R. A. Shine, Sr. and wife, Dr. Shine studied at the Tallahassee Seminary before attending the University of Georgia where he received his medical degree. Dr. Shine married Maria Jefferson Eppes in 1868. She was a direct descendant of President Thomas Jefferson, Dr. Shine served with the 1st Florida Battalion from 17 February 1862 to 12 June 1862. He also served with the 7th South Carolina infantry from September 1862 until 19 April 1863 and then with the Phillips Legion Infantry Battalion as a surgeon from 10 July 1863 through 9 July 1864. He was promoted to brigade surgeon and served in

---

[74] North Carolina census for 1850 and 1860; Compiled Service Records.

[75] Compiled Service Records; *The Standard Blue Book*, Texas edition (1920); *History of Texas* (1893); South Carolina Genealogies, 1983; *South Carolina Historical Magazine*; Confederate abstract, South Carolina Archives and History Center.

[76] Compiled Service Records; Collected Papers of the Monticello Association of the Descendants of Thomas Jefferson; E. Ashby Hammond, *The Medical Profession in 19th Century Florida*; *Biographical Rosters of Florida's Confederate and Union soldiers, 1861–1865*, vol. 3, David W. Hartman, comp., and David Coles, assoc. comp.

that capacity from 10 July 1864 through 30 November 1864. Dr. Shine practiced in Saint Augustine, Florida after the war from 1867 to his death on 21 October 1910. He had one son, Dr. Frank E. Shine.

He was described in medical and historical records as a "large man in physique and, in his later years...considerably overweight." He is remembered as a pioneer in yellow fever research.

Levi J. Willcoxon, MD[77]

Born on 15 March 1835 in Coweta County, Georgia to Levi Willcoxon and wife Lennah, Dr. Willcoxon received his medical degree from the University of Pennsylvania in 1835. He was married to Fannie L. Turpin on 4 May 1858. They had seven children. Dr. Willcoxon served with the Phillips Legion beginning on 19 July 1861 and continuing through October of the same year. Records do not indicate whether he served with the infantry or cavalry battalion. He died in Alabama on 2 July 1891.

George Moore Willis, MD[78]

Born about 1829 in Greene County, Greensboro, Athens District GA, to Richard Willis and wife Sarah, the source of Dr. Willis's medical education is not known. He was appointed asst. surgeon 3 July 1863 to rank from 20 April 1863. Prior to this time he served as pvt., Co. I, 8th Georgia Regiment detailed to Hospital 14, Richmond, Virginia from 16 May 1861, the day of his enlistment, to 31 December 1862. He was then assigned to the Phillips Legion Infantry Battalion as asst. surgeon to the end of the war surrendering at Appomattox Courthouse on 9 April 1865. He married Mary V. and had three children. His date of death is unknown.

---

[77] Obituaries of unknown origin; Medical Degree (in Latin) from U. of Pennsylvania (courtesy of John Willcoxon, Memphis, Tennessee; Compiled Service Records; Family Tree (courtesy of John Willcoxon, Memphis TN).

[78] Compiled Service Records; 1870 Census, GA Calhoun Co., p. 593; 1850 Census, Clark Co., Athens Dist; Payment Voucher No. 128, 31 December to 20 April 1863; *Greene County History*; Lists of Medical Officers Recommended for Appointment or Promotion by the Surgeon General, Richmond VA 1863–1864.

PHYSICIANS SERVING IN THE LINE

Abner Lewis (Leonard) Clinkscales[79]

Born c. 1825–1830 in Macon, Georgia to Asa Franklin and Mary Kay Clinkscales, Dr. Clinkscales appears as a student at the Southern Botanico-Medical College, Macon, Georgia for the course of lectures for 1855–6. In later years, he graduated from the Eclectic Medical College of the City of New York, New York State in 1876. He served with the Phillips Legion cavalry battalion as 1st lt. of Co. N/E from May 1862 until his resignation for disability (typhoid fever, bilious fever) on 10 October 1862. He appears as a physician in census data in 1870 and is mentioned in an article in the Macon Telegraph for 30 August 1873 as a Professor of Anatomy for the College of Medicine and Surgery, Macon, Georgia. He died on 7 July 1880 and no records have been located that confirm or deny a marriage. His headstone shows him as 1st lt. of Co. A, cavalry (State Guard) and promoted to cpt. on 1 October 1863.

Milton Newton Napoleon Gober[80]

Born 1 December 1836 in Shelby County, Tennessee, names of parents unknown. Dr. Gober, as a child, was tutored by Professor Beman. After moving to Georgia, he attended high schools in Decatur and Smyrna. He studied medicine under Mr. N. H. Campbell and entered the Medical College of Macon., Georgia in 1858, graduating in March 1860. He practiced medicine until April 1862 when he enlisted as a 1st lt., Co. L, infantry battalion of the Phillips Legion. He was selected by General Wofford, the brigade commander, to become a company cpt. in the 3rd Georgia Sharpshooter Battalion and remained with this unique unit until captured at war's end in 1865. He was married, first, to Sicily Theresa Smith. One child was produced by this union. Later, he married Sarah Traylor White and produced two children. Dr. Gober d. in Atlanta, Fulton County GA, on 15 May 1912.

Robert Leeper Young Long[81]

Born 20 August 1818 in Marshall's Ferry, Tennessee, to a pioneer family whose names are unknown, Dr. Leeper moved with his parents to Carroll County, Carrollton, Georgia. He became Clerk of Court of Carroll County and was the judge in late years. He mother died when he was six months old. He served in the Creek Indian War and in he Seminole War. On 13 June 1839, he began his study of medicine with Dr. A. B. Calhoun for a year. He then attended the Medical College

---

[79] Compiled Service Records; *The Macon Telegraph*; Catalogue for Southern Botanico-Medical College, Macon, Georgia; Macon City Directories; *Directory of Deceased American Physicians, 1804–1929.*

[80] Compiled Service Records; Margaret Williams Taylor (descendants of Newton Napoleon Gober), Maryville TN; Paula Girouard to Kurt Graham, 29 April 1999.

[81] Compiled Service Records; *Coweta County Chronicles* (Jones and Reynolds, 1928).

of South Carolina in Charleston and, later, the University of Louisiana (now Tulane University.) He graduated from Transylvania College, Lexington, Kentucky, on 31 March 1841 and promptly relocated to Georgia. He practiced medicine until 11 June 1861 when he enlisted in the Phillips Legion Cavalry Battalion as a 1st lt. and was elected cpt. shortly thereafter. He married Martha Ann Powell on 23 October 1849. They produced eight children. He resigned his commission on 26 April 1864, citing his advancing age and the need to return to care for his sick wife. He died on 6 October 1898.

Author's Note: Asst. Surgeon John H. Cox and T. S. Stephenson appeared in the unassigned soldiers portion of the Field, Staff and Inspection Roster. No further information has been located for these two physicians. Dr. Stephenson surrendered at Greensboro with the legion cavalry battalion.

Appendix F

The 3rd Georgia Sharpshooters

"We are always in front of the brigade."[82]

Civil War sharpshooter battalions proved themselves not only useful to brigade commanders but, in many cases, indispensable. They incorporated the best and bravest marksmen in the infantry brigades into battalions whose mission was to provide intelligence via scouting details and skirmishing, as well as fixed position sniping on occasion. They were provided with the finest weapons available: northern troops under Col. Hiram Berdan are known to have used the Sharps rifle; southern soldiers used the awkward but effective Whitworth rifle, the Kerr rifle and British Enfields. Candidates were trained in intensive drills as well as target practice at ranges up to a half mile or more. They were selected not only for their marksmanship skills but also for overall military fitness. For the Third Georgia Sharpshooters, General Wofford specified clearly the qualifications for officer candidates in a letter to the division commander General McLaws dated 25 April 1863:

> I have laboured and taken great pains to select those who are best qualified and who are entitled to promotions for their gallantry upon the field of battle and general good conduct since entering the service. Opposite the name of each officer I have made a concise statement of the qualifications and where they have distinguished themselves in battle. All these officers without an exception, are young, healthy and athletic, and from the best evidence that I could procure are moral, intelligent gentlemen. In point of courage, intelligence and morality I feel justified in saying that they are equal if not superior to the officers of any Regiment or Battalion in this Brigade. As the time is no doubt near where active operations will commence I desire permission at the earliest moment to place this battalion in separate camp for the purpose of having them instructed in the battalion drill as skirmishers.[83]

Once the selection process for officers was complete the company grade officers selected the non-commissioned officers and enlisted troops. The same high standards were used. The result was the Third Georgia Sharpshooter Battalion of General Wofford's Georgia Brigade. General A. P. Hill is reputed as having said:

---

[82] George F. Montgomery, ed., *Georgia Sharpshooter, The Civil War Diary and Letters of William Rhadamanthus Montgomery* (Macon GA: Mercer University Press, 1997) 84

[83] Brigadier General William T. Wofford to Maj. W. H. Taylor, 25 April 1863.

"Sharpshooters, like fiddlers, are born and not made."[84] Whether this statement is true of not, the overall performance of the Third Georgia Sharpshooters was admirable by any standards. The unit was not officially formed until June of 1863 although they were engaged with the enemy at the battle of Chancellorsville in early May. The best evidence for their initial formation comes from the diary of William Rhadamanthus Montgomery who described the unit as having been formed in April under the leadership of Cpt. A. H. Patton of the 18th Georgia. Patton was killed on 2 May 1863 at the battle Chancellorsville and was succeeded by Lt. Col. Nathan L. Hutchins with rank effective 10 June 1863. Hutchins served as the 3rd Georgia Sharpshooters commander to war's end. Although not officially formed until June 1863, clearly the men of the 3rd Georgia Sharpshooters were operating informally as a discrete unit earlier during the battle of Chancellorsville as is attested by a casualty list for the "Battalion of Sharpshooters" published on 19 May 1863 in the Atlanta Confederacy where Patton is shown both as commanding and killed on 2 May [85] Montgomery notes that the unit was initially (informally) known as the 1st Georgia Sharpshooters at this time.[86]

General Wofford selected the Phillips Legion infantry soldiers for assignment to the new sharpshooter unit from those companies that had the most troops on hand. These were companies A (78), B (84), C (106), L (104), M (98), and O (99). Initially the majority of the men selected were placed into Co. B of the new unit under officers who had been nominated but not yet confirmed. These were Cpt. W. D. Anderson, 1st Lt. W. R. Montgomery, 2nd Lt. P. W. Fuller and 2nd Lt. J. W. Barrett. In addition P. L. Ardis was to be selected 1st lt. of Co. F which also contained several of the men who had been chosen from the Phillips Legion. Young Pvt. Fuller, not yet confirmed as a 1st lt., would perish at Chancellorsville just a few days after the unit's formation. Sgt. J. W. Barrett, also not yet confirmed as a 2nd lt., would also fall, severely wounded in this same battle.

After the Chancellorsville fight in which the Sharpshooters suffered 49 casualties, Lt. Anderson apparently reconsidered his decision to join the Sharpshooter unit and returned to the Legion infantry. He would be replaced by Cpt. (Milton) Newton Napoleon Gober from Phillips Legion Co. L. Co. B became Co. F in the final organization on 8 June 1863 with confirmation of officers' commissions and official designation of the unit as the 3rd Georgia Sharpshooter Battalion.

The original Co. F containing Lt. Ardis and a number of legion soldiers from Co. A would be redesignated Co. E of the 3rd Georgia Sharpshooter Battalion. The other companies were comprised of men from Wofford's other regiments; the 16th, 18th, 24th Georgia infantries and the Cobbs Legion's Infantry Battalion.

---

[84] "Sharpshooting in Lee's Army" in *Confederate Veteran* 3/1,3 (January, 1895): 3.

[85] *The Atlanta Southern Confederacy*, 19 May 1863.

[86] Montgomery, *Georgia Sharpshooter*.

From their initial organization the Sharpshooters served at Chancellorsville (described as a "big one" by Montgomery) May 1863; Salem Church, May 1863; the second and third days at Gettysburg (2 and 3 July 1863); skirmishing around Lookout Mountain, Chattanooga, Knoxville and Lenoir station; provided cover fire for the charge at Fort Sanders at Knoxville, November 1863; Bean Station near Tate Springs, Tennessee; the battle of the Wilderness, 6 May 1864; Spotsylvania (described as "the hardest of the war" by Montgomery), 10–12 May 1864; Cold Harbor (again a "big one" by Montgomery, 1–3 June 1864; several skirmishes around Petersburg, June and July; Front Royal, 16 August 1864; Cedar Creek, 19 October 1864; Sailor's Creek, 6 April 1865; and the surrender at Appomattox Courthouse, Virginia, on 9 April 1865.[87]

Whether or not the 3rd Georgia Sharpshooters were all born for the task or molded by intensive training, motivation and combat experience, they, like the cavalry, were the eyes and ears of General Robert E. Lee's army. They were more than brave soldiers—they were some of the finest troops the Confederacy had to offer as well as the ancestors of contemporary ranger and sniper units of the modern American army.

The following roster lists men from Phillips Legion who served in Cos. E and F of the Sharpshooter Battalion.

Ardis, 1st Lt. Payson L. Co. E. Captured at Front Royal 16 August 1865, released from prison 17 June 1865.

Bard, Henry H. Co. F. At Dalton Hospital August 1863, November 1863–March 1864 sick at hospital, died at home in 1864.

Barrett, Arthur J. Co. F. Captured at Cedar Creek 19 October 1864, POW at Point Lookout until exchanged 17 March 1865.

Barrett, J. R. Co. F. Furloughed from hospital 28 August 1863, March through August 1864 rolls show AWOL, no further record.

Barrett, Lt. Joseph W. Co. F. WIA at Chancellorsville in May 1863, in hospital and on detached duty Richmond in 1864, retired to Invalid Corps 11 January 1865.

Bellah, John H. Co. F. Rolls through 1864 state absent in Phillips Legion, KIA at Cedar Creek 19 October 1864.

Bellah, Richard W. Co. F. All rolls state absent in Phillips Legion, captured 6 April 1865, POW Point Lookout until released June 1865.

Brooks, John A. Co. F. WIA Wilderness 6 May 1864, no further record.

Burton, William Crow. Co. F. Captured 6 April 1865, POW Point Lookout until released 24 June 1865.

Calahan, John S. Co. F. Sick at Marietta 1863, AWOL thereafter, took Oath 1 March 1864 at Chattanooga.

---

[87] Ibid.

Carter, James A. Co. F. Captured 3 July 1863 at Gettysburg, POW Fort Delaware until released 16 June 1865.

Cheek, James H. Co. F. WIA May 1864 (leg), no further record.

Cleaveland, Henry C. Co. F. Captured at Front Royal 16 August 1864, POW Elmira until exchanged 2 March 1865.

Crawford, James Talbot. Co. E. WIA at Cold Harbor 1 June 1864, deserted March 1865, took Oath, sent to Knoxville.

Dawson, J. W. Co. F. Enlisted in late 1863, WIA Wilderness 6 May 1864, captured at home, took Oath October 1864.

Devenport, Josiah. Co. F. No record of him in Phillips Legion, died of disease October/November 1864 in Virginia.

Edwards, Sgt. A. M. V. B. Co. F. Captured 16 August 1864 at Front Royal, POW Elmira until released 27 June 1865.

Elliott, James W. Co. F. Captured 16 August 1864 at Front Royal, POW Elmira, d. 4 September 1864 of typhoid.

England, Joseph C. Co. F. WIA 12 May 1864 Spotsylvania (left arm), captured 6 April 1865, POW Point Lookout released 11 June 1865.

Erwin, Joseph Bryan. FS&I. QM Sgt, surrendered at Appomattox 9 April 1865.

Fincher, Henry J. Co. F. WIA 2 May 1863 Chancellorsville (lost hand), permanently disabled.

Fuller, 2nd Lt. Peyton W. Co. F. KIA Chancellorsville 2 May 1863.

George, P. Earp. Co. F. All rolls state absent sick or absent in Phillips Legion, surrendered with legion 9 April 1865 at Appomattox.

Gober, Cpt. Newton N. Co. F. Captured 6 April 1865, POW Johnson's Island until released 18 June 1865, also an MD.

Green, Joseph B. Co. F. Marietta Hospital August 1863, rolls through 1864 show at hospital, no further record.

Griffin, Thomas W. Co. F. WIA (hand) at Chancellorsville May 1863, rolls show sick until discharged during second half 1864.

Hardy, Cpl. Thomas J. Co. F. Captured 16 August 1864 at Front Royal, POW Elmira until released 16 June 1865.

Heaton, Zachariah. Co. F. Deserted at Caledonia PA 30 June 1863, joined 3rd MD (US) Cavalry September 1863, deserted from this unit December 1863, no further record.

Henderson, John M. Co. F. WIA May 1864 (shoulder), captured Cobb County August 1864, took Oath and sent north.

Herring, E. R. Co. F. Present on 1863 roll dated 12 October 1863, no further record

Houze, Darius N. Co. F. Present on roll dated 1864, Shows furloughed on 1865 roll, no further record.

Howard, John J. Co. F. Deserted or captured 3 July 1863 at Gettysburg, joined 3rd MD (US) Cavalry 22 September 1863.

Howell, James Franklin. Co. F. Captured at Fairfield, Pa 6 July 1863, POW Point
    Lookout until exchanged 18 February 1865.
Hughes, John J. Co. F. Captured 16 August 1864 Front Royal, POW Elmira,
    exchanged 1864, captured 6 April 1865, released 28 June 1865.
Kilgore, Henry S. Co. F. At Atlanta Hospital 1863, deserted September 1864 in
    Tennessee, joined 5th US Volunteers and served in the west.
King, Johnathon F. Co. F. Sick on 1863 roll, furloughed home, joins 6th GA Cavalry
    and does not return to VA.
Kistleburg, William Howard. Co. F. Captured 6 April 1865, POW Point Lookout
    until released 19 June 1865.
Maloy (Mallory), John H. Co. F. Captured 16 August 1864 at Front Royal, took
    Oath, sent to Indiana.
Manning, Sgt. John W. Co. F. WIA and captured at Gettysburg 3 July 1863,
    exchanged September 1863, present February 1864, retired to Invalid Corps 12
    July 1864.
Mills, Sgt. William H. Co. F. To hospital 11 October 1863, then AWOL, no further
    record.
Montgomery, 1st Lt. William R. Co. F. Furloughed February 1865, tried to return
    to VA but did not arrive until after surrender.
Moore, Jesse. Co. F. No record of him in Phillips Legion, captured 6 April 1865,
    POW Point Lookout until released 29 June 1865.
Owens, David. Co. F. Deserted 14 December 1863, took Oath 5 January 1864, sent
    north.
Pace, John T. Co. F. WIA 1864, All rolls state "in Phillips Legion."
Phillips, James Patton. FS&I. WIA 3 May 1863 at Chancellorsville, asst. QM 25 June
    1863, shown on duty at Anderson's Corps HQ 29 January 1865.
Porter, Sgt. William A. Co. E. Captured 6 April 1865, POW Point Lookout until
    released 17 June 1865.
Rich (Ritch), J. Newton. Co. F. WIA Chancellorsville 2 May 1863 and permanently
    disabled.
Richardson, David. Co. F. KIA near Chattanooga 22 September 1863.
Shoemaker, Thomas J. Co. F. WIA (right side) 3 May 1863 at Chancellorsville,
    deserted near Petersburg 22 March 1865.
Shular, A. J. Co. F. WIA (heel) May 1863 at Chancellorsville, February 1864 roll
    states AWOL in 3rd GA Cav, 1864 roll states AWOL in 6th GA Cav, no further
    record.
Stephens, Joshua P. Co. F. Transferred in from 7th GA infantry June 1863, age 25,
    captured at Gettysburg July 1863, POW Fort Delaware until released 15 June
    1865.
Steward(t), John M. Co. F. Deserted 5 July 1864, captured 5 September 1864 in TN,
    POW Camp Douglas until released 12 May 1865.

Stewart, L. A. Co. F. Enlisted Spring 1864, captured 6 April 1865, POW Point Lookout until released 30 June 1865.

Stewart, Noah H. Co. F. KIA at Knoxville 24 November 1863.

Stewart, Tapley H. Co. F. Captured 16 August 1864 at Front Royal, POW Elmira until exchanged 14 March 1865.

Stone, Sgt. Thomas J. Co. F. Died of typhoid pneumonia at Rome GA Hospital 1 December 1863.

Taylor, Zachary F. Co. F. Captured 16 August 1864 at Front Royal, POW Elmira until exchanged 14 March 1865.

Vaughn, William P. Co. F. Furloughed home wounded 8 September 1863, deserted, took Oath 23 December 1863, sent north.

Vawter, Rawley A. Co. F. Deserted 14 December 1863, took Oath 10 November 1864 and sent north.

Wagnon, Cpl. George H. Co. E. Captured at Front Royal 16 August 1864, POW Elmira until released 7 July 1865.

Wagnon, James D. Co. E. Enlisted 1 July 1863, captured 16 August 1864 at Front Royal, POW Elmira until exchanged 2 March 1865.

Wagnon, Pittman M. Co. E. WIA at Knoxville 29 November 1863, present 1864, AWOL after December 1864.

Waters, Sgt. Willoughby. Co. F. Captured at Front Royal 16 August 1864, POW Elmira, d. 17 April 1865 of pneumonia.

Watts, J. R. Co. F. Captured Gettysburg, POW Point Lookout, escaped 2 May 1864, captured Front Royal 16 August 1864, released 11 July 1865.

Whitehead, Simeon. Co. F. Present on roll dated 30 January 1865, no further record.

Wimpie, R. F. Co. F. Captured Gettysburg 3 July 1863, POW Fort Delaware until enlisting in Federal artillery August 1863.

Wood, Sgt. R. M. Co. F. WIA 12 May 1864 at Spotsylvania (foot), captured Front Royal 16 August 1864, POW Elmira released 19 July 1865.

Wright, Lorenzo Dow. Co. E. Surrendered at Appomattox 9 April 1865.

Appendix G

Their Name Was Legion

"Legion." A body of soldiers forming the principal army unit, varying from 3000 foot soldiers and 300 cavalrymen in early times, to 5000–6000 under the empire (Roman). A military force. An army. A great number, a multitude."[88]

"The entire military establishment was converted in 1792 into a legion, that is, into a field army in which the three combat branches, infantry, cavalry and artillery, were combined in the same organization. The legion consisted of four sub-legions. Each sub-legion contained infantry, riflemen, cavalry, and artillery, indeed it was the forerunner of the twentieth century regimental combat team."[89]

Few senior officers, both blue and gray, believed that the Civil War would last longer than a few months. Most felt certain that once the rebels confronted the might of the northern forces they would throw down their arms and surrender. Although these "short war" thinkers were disabused of this thinking after First Manassas many of these influential, wealthy men had organized and often themselves funded mini-field armies comprised of all three combat arms called legions. Many of these men were politically ambitious, ready to seek glory, fame and high office after the short rebellion was suppressed and they returned home to adoring supporters. Personal vanity probably played a role in most cases. Federal and Confederate Legions were quickly formed and rapidly dissected; the infantry battalions were reassigned to dedicated infantry brigades as were the cavalry battalions assigned to cavalry brigades. The artillery batteries were usually not assigned on a permanent basis or remained in an unassigned state to be used as needed in the future. Many numbered regiments were nominally called Legions but were not "true legions;" comprised of elements of all three of the combat arms-infantry, cavalry and artillery. (See attachment to this appendix for examples of all forms of Legions.)

Many Federal and Confederate officers were schooled in the classics. Union General Lewis Wallace's tour de force was "Ben Hur: A Tale of the Christ (1880)," written while living in the Governor's Palace in Santa Fe, New Mexico well after his Civil War service. Wallace was probably more erudite and scholarly than most of his contemporaries although he had received little formal education. He did study Law and the Classics. Wallace and others of his time had steeped themselves in the adventures of Julius Caesar and the famed "Roman Legions."

Civil War Legions had their origins in the earliest days of American history. They appeared in the Revolution in both the Loyalist and Patriot armies. Most

---

[88] *Webster's New Collegiate Dictionary* (Springfield MA: G. and C. Merriam, 1961) 480.

[89] J. K. Mahon and Romana Daynsh, *Army Lineage Series, Infantry, Part I. Regular Army*, (Washington: Office of the Chief of Military History, 1972) 12–13.

notably, the entire American Army was styled a Legion in 1792 under the leadership
of Washington appointee General "Mad Anthony" Wayne. Prior to Wayne's
appointment the army had been twice defeated by Northwest Indians in the early
1790's. Something had to be done. The result of these pressures was an experiment
in organization that resulted in the American military establishment's conversion
into a legion. Wayne combined the infantry and mounted soldiers as well as the
artillery into a unified field army. By 1794 his legion of 5,120 officers and men had
defeated the Northwest Indians and successfully deterred England. The need to
maintain a field army diminished after the threat from the Northwest evaporated.
The legion champion and Secretary of War, Henry Knox left office in 1794. By 1796
the Legion of the United States went out of existence by an act of congress effective
31 October 1796. Statesmen of the time believed an organization that could easily be
subdivided and organized to guard the frontiers and seacoast was needed. They were
also concerned that Wayne's Legion might evolve into a large and too influential
American army.[90]

Anthony Wayne's planning and creative imagination in military organization
did not go for naught. His legion concept foreshadowed the regimental combat
teams of the Second World War and the combined arms units in the Korean War
and the Vietnam War. For the American Civil War, the legion organization was
unworkable. The infantry and cavalry could only move as fast as the slowest artillery
soldier. The three combat arms were better served in larger, brigade-sized units.
Until the battle of Fredericksburg in December 1862, military tacticians did not fully
recognize the problem so, for a short time, the infantry and cavalry remained
together as integrated units.

A typical Confederate "true" legion consisted of six companies of infantry, four
of cavalry and a battery of artillery when first formed. Infantry and cavalry companies
were often added and troops were occasionally shifted between units and sub-units.
The organizational concept of a legion was used loosely in many cases. Regular
numbered infantry regiments or battalions of numbered units, or even Home Guard
units, were nominally designated legions.

Griffith's discussion of Civil War cavalry tactics touches on early planning that
involved early tactical ideas that included the legion concept.

These tactics were a mixture between true cavalry action in the 'mounted
charge' and 'mounted infantry action preparatory to fighting on foot. We
might perhaps suggest that it would have been possible to achieve a similar
effect in the maj. battles by attaching a mounted company to each infantry
regiment, creating an organic link between the two arms in order to draw
the best from each. *This had actually been tried in some of the early 'legions'
formed in 1861, but as with so many other tactical experiments in the Civil War*

---

[90] Richard H. Kohn, *Eagle and Sword* (New York: The Free Press, 1975) 126–27. Also see
D. J. Vetock, *Lessons Learned: A History of US. Army Lesson Learning*, (Carlisle Barracks: US
Army Military History Institute, 1972) 12–13.

it was not centrally directed or sustained The Cavalry and the Infantry remained
two separate and jealously independent services, and they did not normally
cooperate as closely as ideal low-level tactics might have demanded.[91]

The legion designation provided the same sense of pride that soldiers often have
in belonging to elite units. Soldiers in the Roman legions, the fabled French Foreign
Legion, the Condor Legion believed that they were a part of something special.
Grizzled veterans of the American Legion always ask the same question of
prospective members: "What unit did you belong to?" The term legion has become
synonymous with the fighting spirit of soldiers past and present.

Legions, North and South[92]

Hilliard's Legion (Alabama). This was a designation for four battalions of Gracie's
    Brigade.
Phillips Legion (Georgia). A true legion of six companies of infantry and four of
    cavalry and a battery of artillery (Macon Light Artillery which was never
    attached). Formed and commanded by Col. William M. Phillips. More infantry
    and cavalry companies were added later.
Cobb's Legion (Georgia). CS A true legion, commanded by Col. Thomas Rootes
    Reade Cobb. Eventually composed seven infantry and six cavalry companies and
    an artillery battery (the Troup Artillery). Cobb's and Phillips Legions often
    fought side-by-side. The exchanged individual soldiers and companies.
Wright's Legion (Georgia). An alternate designation for the 28th Georgia Infantry
    Regiment commanded by Augustus R. Wright.
CS Floyd's Georgia State Legion (Georgia). This was the Georgia State Guard
    commanded by Col. James G. Yeiser. It was formed for four months for local
    defense.
CS Cherokee Georgia State Legion (Georgia). A home guard unit commanded by
    Col. James E. Rusk. Composed of six infantry companies and four cavalry
    companies.
Indiana Legion (US). Unofficial designation of the emergency units called out by
    Indiana authorities during John Hunt Morgan's raid in 1863. Most Served for
    thirty days or less and all were Militia or home guard, commanded by Col. John
    A. Mann and composed of infantry, cavalry and artillery.

---

[91] P. Griffith, *Battle Tactics of the Civil War* (New Haven and London: Yale University
Press, 1987).

[92] *Official Records*; John F. Walter, Institute for Civil War Research, 79–13 67th Drive,
Middle Village NY; James Ripley Jacobs, *The Beginning of the U S. Army 1783–1812* (Princeton:
Princeton University Press, 1947) 130–35.

Kentucky Legion (Kentucky, US). A home guard unit formed by Brigadier General J. T. Boyle as a "Legion of Defense" composed of citizens consisting of seven regiments of infantry, a company of cavalry and a battery of artillery.

Louisville Legion (Kentucky, US). An alternate designation for the 3rd and 5th Kentucky Infantry regiments.

Morgan's Legion (Kentucky, CSA). An alternate name for John Hunt Morgan's cavalry brigade.

Militia Legion (Kentucky, US). Mentioned only once in the Official Records. Appears to be a home guard unit formed hastily to oppose the raid of John Hunt Morgan.

Mile's Legion (Louisiana CSA). Commanded by Col. William R. Miles. Composed of An infantry battalion that saw little combat and only in home state. Artillery seems to have been assigned but seldom operated with the infantry. Cavalry seems not to have been assigned. Referred to in the Official Records as "Louisiana" Legion.

Stewart's Louisiana Legion (Louisiana CSA). This Legion was composed of four infantry companies and two cavalry companies. Probably a home guard unit.

Purnell's Legion (Maryland US). Commanded by Col. Samuel A. Graham. Composed of eleven companies of infantry and four of artillery.

Pope Walker Legion (Mississippi CSA). Local designation of the 19th Mississippi infantry Regiment (named after the first Confederate secretary of war.)

Jeff Davis Legion (Mississippi CSA). A Mississippi cavalry unit with companies from three different states; Mississippi, Tennessee, and Georgia. Commanded by Lt. Col. J. F. Waring.

Lyon's Legion (Missouri US). Local designation for the 24th Missouri infantry.

Rosecran's Legion (Missouri US). Mentioned in official records as created for the purpose Of cooperating with commands of Cols. Forbes and Dyer to pursue Howard and Boone County bushwhackers. Was probably a local militia or posse Organized to chase local "bushwhackers" or outlaws.

Stanton Legion (New York US). Local designation for the 145th New York infantry regiment.

Irish (Corcoran's) Legion (New York US). Alternate designation of a brigade composed 155th, 164th, 170th and 175th infantry regiments.

Mountain Legion (New York US). Alternate designation for the 156th New York infantry. Commanded and organized by Col. Erastus Cooke.

Thomas North Carolina Legion (North Carolina CSA). Companies A and B cavalry composed of Cherokee Indians; companies C, D, E, F, G, I infantry companies non-Indians; Co. H was a mounted non-Indian company. The Thomas Legion of Southern Highlanders was one of the most unique units to participate in the battles and marches of the American Civil War. Organized by Col. William Holland Thomas, this legion was composed of mountain whites from western North Carolina and East Tennessee, and Cherokee Indians from the Qualla boundary. The Thomas Legion was composed of infantry, cavalry and artillery units in various proportions.

Love's Legion (North Carolina CSA). Mentioned vaguely in *Official Records*. Probably refers to Col. Love's cavalry battalion; probably never existed as a legion in any real sense.

Scott Legion (Pennsylvania US). Local designation of the 7th (3 months) and 20th (3 months) Pennsylvania infantry regiments and later used as local designation of the 68th Pennsylvania regiment.

Hampton's Legion (South Carolina CSA). Organized by legendary Wade Hampton. Composed of six infantry companies, three cavalry companies and one battery of artillery (Washington Artillery). A "true" legion.

Holcomb Legion (South Carolina CSA). Organized and commanded by Col. P. F. Stevens. A "true" legion composed of infantry, cavalry and artillery battalions.

Walker Legion (Tennessee CSA). Alternate designation for the 2nd Tennessee (Provisional Army) infantry Co. F; also the 28th Alabama infantry used this name.

Rucker's Legion (Tennessee CSA). A local designation of two or three Tennessee cavalry units.

Memphis Legion (Tennessee CSA). Alternate designation of an unidentified Tennessee infantry company.

First Texas Legion (Texas CSA). Also called "Whitfield's Legion"; alternate designation for the 27th Texas Cavalry Regiment. Commanded and organized by Col. Edwin R. Hawkins.

Waul's Legion (Texas CSA). Commanded by Col. T. N. Waul. Composed of infantry and cavalry units. Little else known.

Wise Legion (Virginia CSA). Alternate designation of the brigade commanded and Organized by Brigadier General Henry A. Wise.

Lee's Legion (Virginia CSA). Alternate designation of a Virginia cavalry battalion; more precise data not available.

Veteran Legion (Miscellaneous US). Mentioned in Official Records as a proposal from Provost-Marshall-General James B. Fray to Honorable Edwin M. Stanton, Secretary of War for a "Legion" to be formed and composed of officers and enlisted men who have been honorably discharged after two years' service and now exempt from the draft. Recommends Maj. General Hancock to command the organization, which was to be an army corps of the different arms of the service and call the "Veteran Legion," Veteran Corps d'Armee.

Legion Antecedents[93]

Revolutionary War

Armand's Legion. Formed on 11 June 1777. Commanded by Lt. Col. Charles Armand Tuffin, an officer in the French Army. Composed of a troop of Dragoons, three companies of Fusiliers and one company of Chasseurs.

Count Beniousky's American Legion. This legion was a collection of mercenaries of all nationalities commanded by Count Beniousky, a French Officer who had offered his services to the Americans on 24 May 1782. Beniousky and his services were accepted by Congress.

Lauzun's Legion. Formed in 1780, Lauzun's Legion derived its name from its *colonel-proprietaire*, *inspecteur* and commanding officer Armand Louis de gontaut. He had been born into a titled Family and pursued a military career. His legion was composed of infantry *(chasseurs orfusiliers)*, cavalry and artillery. This legion supported the American cause.

Lee's Legion. Also called Lee's Partisan Corps. Organized on 7 April 1778 and commanded by Cpt. Henry Lee (Lighthorse Harry Lee.) Lee was promoted to maj. The unit underwent several reorganizations and was eventually composed of three foot and three mounted troops as well as a band.

Pulaski's Legion. Formed on 28 March 1778 by Brigadier General Count Pulaski. The unit was composed of a staff, three troops of cavalry and one company of riflemen (Chasseurs) a grenadier company, two infantry companies and a supernumerary company. The unit also had a detachment of of artillery armed with a light brass field gun. Also referred to as the Maryland Legion.

Loyalist (Pro-British Legions, Revolutionary War.)

American Legion. Refers to Brigadier General Benedict Arnold's efforts to form a corps of cavalry and infantry from Loyalists faithful to the British cause.

---

[93] Fred A. Berg, *Encyclopedia of Continental Army Units, Battalions, Regiments and Independent Corps* (Stackpole Books) 9, 11, 15, 61, 75, 101; Trevor N. Dupuy, and Gay M. Hammerman, *People and Events of the American Revolution* (New York and London: R. R. Bowker Co., 1974) 282–83, 358–59, 390–91; Francis B. Heitman, *Historical Register of Officers of the Continental Army during the War of the Revolution April, 1775, to December, 1783* (Washington, DC: The Rare Book Publishing Company, Inc, 1914) 73, 74, 345, 454; Thomas H. Raddall, "Tarleton's Legion" (research paper),Nova Scotia Historical Society, 1949; Robert A. Selig, "The duc de Lauzun and his Legion, Rochambeau's Most Troublesome, Colorful Soldiers," americanrevolution.org. http://americanrevolution.org/lauzun.html; W. T. R. Saffell, *Records of the Revolutionary War: The Military and Financial Correspondence of Distinguished Officers* (New York: Pudney and Russell, Publishers, 1858) 32–37, 54–57, 218–21, 288, 289, 530–35; General Cadmus M. Wilcox, *History of the Mexican War* (Washington, DC: The Church News Publishing Company, 1892) 675; also the On-Line Institute for Advanced Loyalist Studies.

Tarleton's Legion. Also known as the British Legion, formed in 1778 and eventually commanded by Banastre Tarleton. Fought in at least seven engagements. Formed from the Philadelphia Light Dragoons, Caledonian Volunteers and Kinloch's Light Dragoons, all loyalists from the Pennsylvania and New Jersey area.[94]

Mexican War

Regiment of Missouri Volunteers: St. Louis Legion. Commanded by Col. Alton R. Easton. No other information available.

---

[94] Reference was also found for Lt. Col. Hezekiah Mayham's legion, but no other information has been located.

Index